SENTIENT FLESH

BLACK OUTDOORS INNOVATIONS IN THE POETICS OF STUDY

A series edited by J. Kameron Carter and Sarah Jane Cervenak

SENTIENT FLESH

THINKING IN DISORDER,

POIĒSIS IN BLACK

R.A. JUDY

DUKE UNIVERSITY PRESS · *Durham and London* · 2020

© 2020 DUKE UNIVERSITY PRESS
All rights reserved.

Designed by Matthew Tauch
Typeset in Garamond Premier Pro by Westchester Publishing Services

Library of Congress Cataloging-in-Publication Data
Names: Judy, R.A., [date] author.
Title: Sentient flesh : thinking in disorder, poiēsis in black / R. A. Judy.
Other titles: Black outdoors.
Description: Durham : Duke University Press, 2020. | Series: Black outdoors. | Includes bibliographical references and index.
Identifiers: LCCN 2020013671 (print)
LCCN 2020013672 (ebook)
ISBN 9781478009962 (hardcover)
ISBN 9781478011026 (paperback)
ISBN 9781478012559 (ebook)
Subjects: LCSH: Race—Psychological aspects. | African Americans—Race identity. | Mind and body. | Race. | Critical theory.
Classification: LCC E185.625 .J839 2020 (print)
LCC E185.625 (ebook)
DDC 155.8/496073—dc23
LC record available at https://lccn.loc.gov/2020013671
LC ebook record available at https://lccn.loc.gov/2020013672

Cover art: David Hammons, *Close Your Eyes and See Black*, 1970. Photo courtesy of Tilton Gallery, New York.

FOR SADIA ABBAS

The Gifts of the Body are Better than those

of the Mind, or of Fortune

—JOHN DONNE

CONTENTS

ix   LIST OF ILLUSTRATIONS
xi   NOTES ON TRANSLATION AND TRANSLITERATION
xiii   PREFACE: PRELIMINARY SIGNPOSTS
xxi   ACKNOWLEDGMENTS

459   NOTES
545   BIBLIOGRAPHY
573   INDEX

1	Introduction: Body and Flesh

[1ST SET]

25	On *Lohengrin's* Swan
25	A STYLE OF INTERIORITY AND THINKING
54	BY MODERNISM WITHOUT FLÂNERIE
86	ASYMPTOTIC THINKING
116	BY INTERIORITY FREE OF ESCHATOLOGY
150	Sentient Flesh
150	AN ONTOLOGICALLY DISCORDANT BEING
169	BY DISCREPANT TAXONOMY
179	A SEMIOSIS OF FLESH THINKING
200	BY FLESH SPEAKING SEMIOLOGICALLY

[2ND SET]

215	Sentient Flesh Dancing
215	JUBA AND THE BUZZARD LOPE PLAY
232	ETHNOGRAPHIC EPISTĒMĒ ABUTS PERFORMATIVE TECHNĒ POIĒTIKĒ
252	Poiēsis in Black
252	CONSCIOUSNESS ARTICULATED WITH SEMIOSIS
263	DOCTRINE OF SUBMISSION WITH "THE RENAISSANCE OF ETHICS"
319	Para-Semiosis
322	ALL THAT COMES WITH PARAONTOLOGY
376	IN PARA-SEMIOSIS, DIVISIBLE PERSON US BE
419	Coda: Gifting Blues Love-Improper

71	FIGURE 1.1	Arthur Dugmore, *Working by the Day in the Cotton Field*
72	FIGURE 1.2	Arthur Dugmore, *In the Cobbler's Shop*
73	FIGURE 1.3	Arthur Dugmore, *Her Week's Marketing*
74	FIGURE 1.4	Arthur Dugmore, *At Work Making Brooms*
75	FIGURE 1.5	Arthur Dugmore, *Learning to Shuffle Early, A Pickanny Cake Walk*
76	FIGURE 1.6	Arthur Dugmore, *"Big House" and Negro Quarters, Negro Cottages*
77	FIGURE 1.7	Arthur Dugmore, *A Negro School Near Albany, Georgia*
78	FIGURE 1.8	Arthur Dugmore, *A Typical Negro Store*
79	FIGURE 1.9	Arthur Dugmore, *Negro Woman Plowing in a Cotton Field*
80	FIGURE 1.10	Arthur Dugmore, *A Rest in the Furrow*
81	FIGURE 1.11	Arthur Dugmore, *Huts Near Albany, Georgia*
82	FIGURE 1.12	Arthur Dugmore, *Women from the Country, A Parson and Part of His Flock, On the Street*
83	FIGURE 1.13	Arthur Dugmore, *Log Cabin Home, Women "Sowing" Guano, A Friend of George Washington*
89	FIGURE 1.14	The Asymptotes of the Hyperbola
186	FIGURE 2.1	The Semiological Order of the Negro Problem
190	FIGURE 2.2	The Semiological Order of French Imperialism
270	FIGURE 4.1	Du Bois's Chart of the History of Thought in Western Christendom
273	FIGURE 4.2	Du Bois's "Lesson IV" Diagram

All translations in this work are mine, unless otherwise indicated. In keeping with the key concept of *para-semiosis* at play here, languages such as Greek, Hebrew, and Arabic are given in their native transcription, followed by an italicized Latin-script transliteration, then an English-language translation. Rather than following the established convention, which calls for all subsequent occurrences of such "foreign" terms to be Latin transliteration, the tripartite pattern shall be constant throughout with few exceptions. The exceptions are quotations, chiefly in German, where Greek is given in the original; in such cases, the Greek is transliterated, followed by an English translation. This accords with the postulate that cognition and consciousness are articulated *with* semiosis, the material expression of which is integral to effective signification, as well as the corollary postulate that *para-semiosis* is the nonsynthesizing confluence of multiplicious *semiosis*. The point in so persistently marking the material dynamics of transliteration is not to tediously and needlessly burden the reader, but rather to track iterations of *para-semiosis* entailed in the compositional form of *Sentient Flesh*—something that the established convention of having Latin-script transliteration displace the native obfuscates by muffling the phonetic and phonographic noise of the non-Latinate.

Preliminary Signposts

Sentient Flesh is a book about dynamic confluence that is composed in confluence. It exhibits what it exposits, and so is a working of *poiēsis*, a thinking-in-disorder, the enactment of which is called *para-semiosis*. The form it traces in chaos is arranged into two parts called "Sets." Each Set has its moments, and each moment has its *ostinato* riffs. While the play of *para-semiosis* is *to be* at the crossroads of confluence without any resolution or synthesis, each moment and riff can be attended to in itself, although the flow will always carry the reader to multiplicious crossroads, which will be encountered as interpolations of many discourses and knowledges: literary genre—short stories, novels, poetry—literary theory and philology; structuralism and semiotics; anthropology and ethnography; foundations of mathematics and number theory; philosophy, from classical Greek to twentieth-century phenomenology and existentialism, and the history of ideas; Arabic philosophy and scholasticism; music—spirituals, "folk music," blues and jazz—and ethnomusicology; political economy and legislative history. Such multiplicious interpolation has to do with the proposition that *Negro* is indicial of the circumstances of its genesis in North Atlantic commercial discourse as designator of a commodity asset—the casualness with which John Smith, writing from Jamestown colony in 1618, refers to the "Dutch man of warre that sold us twenty Negars" is indicative of how this denotation was already well established by the seventeenth century. Smith's "Negars" is an anglicized transcription of the Dutch term for the commodity sold to the Jamestown colony, *Neger*.[1] Then again, the English use of

Negro in reference to the same commodity asset long predates Smith's remark, as is evidenced by the numerous references in Richard Hakluyt's 1589 *The Principal Navigations, Voyages, Traffiques and Discoveries of the English Nation*, to the Spanish commerce in Negroes in the Americas, one of which—Richard Grenville's account of the governor of Isabela, Hispaniola, coming to his ship "accompanied with a lusty frier, & xx. Other Spaniards, with their servants, & Negroes"—the *Oxford English Dictionary* cites as the earliest use of the term to specifically connote "a slave of black African origin or descent."[2] Besides the Dutch *Neger*, there are other well-known cognates and reputed etymons, such as the French *nègre*, the Spanish *negro*, and the multilingual *nigger*. In this usage, the word *Negro*, along with all its cognates, entails an anthropological categorization, whereby those so designated belong to a physically distinct type of not fully human hominid, which is what makes them legitimately available as prospective commodity assets. While it is indeed the case that in every instance of its expression, *Negro* connotes the formations of political economy in the Atlantic World in modernity, it also has historical usage as an ethnographic designation for a specific population of people, "the Negro." In that designation, the term connotes not only the slave formed in capitalism but also the populations of people who may be enslaved, and who remain Negro after slavery's abolition. Yet even though that ethnographic sense of Negro contradicts the commercial *Negro* by recognizing the full humanity of the designated population, it is still within the ambit of the same anthropological categorization. There are moments in this work when I shall refer to the juridical designation in italics as *Negro*, and the ethnographic as Negro. There are also moments when the two connotations get confused. The confusion is unavoidable because both *Negro* and "the Negro" connote a type of human, whereby *human* denotes a type of being distinct from other extent life-forms. Thinking through how this anthropological categorization is underwritten by this metaphysics of being, by ontology, is part of the itinerary of *Sentient Flesh*; along the way, the historical practices of creative, dedicatedly emancipatory knowledges of those designated Negro are explored as entailing a radically different conceptualization of being from that implied by both the commercial and the ethnographic usages of the term. This work, then, is an involved generatively convoluted itinerary, for which a preliminary map might be useful.

1st Set in Two Moments

FIRST MOMENT: "On *Lohengrin*'s Swan" is an extended reading of W. E. B. Du Bois's short story "Of the Coming of John" as a poetic elaboration of his theory of the sociogenesis of human intelligence.

1ST RIFF: "A Style of Interiority and Thinking" explores Du Bois's narrative style, analyzing closely how he depicts a particular impressionistic consciousness in a manner akin to what Charles Baudelaire describes as modernist, which is compared to Edgar Allen Poe's depiction of consciousness in his short story "The Man of the Crowd."

2ND RIFF: "By Modernism without Flânerie" contrasts the nature of the interiority depicted through John Jones in "Of the Coming of John" to that of Baudelaire's *flâneur* and argues that Walter Benjamin's elaboration of *flânerie* as the emblematic figure of modernism cannot comprehend Jones. This is an extended critique of normative bourgeois accounts of interiority and consciousness, from Wilhelm Dilthey to Benjamin, elaborating how Du Bois's conceptual style reveals Negro consciousness as thoroughly modernist but not in accordance to the dominant paradigm of modernism.

3RD RIFF: "Asymptotic Thinking," which takes its title from Du Bois's own description to Herbert Aptheker in 1956 of his intellectual project, tracks the theoretical foundations of Du Bois's depiction of Jones's consciousness to his critical engagement with mathematics, specifically developments in analysis and number theory and its applications in statistical sociology. It establishes how Du Bois's asymptotic thinking relates to Richard Dedekind's work on number theory and Charles Sanders Peirce's theory of semiosis.

4TH RIFF: "By Interiority Free of Eschatology" deepens the critique of the Baudelaire/Benjamin *flâneur* as emblematic of modernity by elaborating how Jones's consciousness, here taken as exemplifying what Du Bois calls "double consciousness," is free of the redemptive eschatological anticapitalism Benjamin discerns in the *flâneur*. Jones's perception of the Swan Song in Wagner's *Lohengrin* is explored as Du Bois's depiction of a subjectivity, the expression of which is necessarily in relation to the world of things and others' thinking—a subjectivity that is wholly semiotic, and in that way ethical.

SECOND MOMENT: "Sentient Flesh" takes up the question of sentient flesh through a consideration of the freedman Tom Windham's remark, "We should have our liberty cause . . . us is human flesh."

1ST RIFF: "An Ontologically Discordant Being" discusses the conflict between the subjectivity of negrophilic ethnography—exemplified by John Lomax's domination of the Works Progress Administration (WPA) interview process in which Windham's remark was recorded—and that which is both exposited and exhibited by Windham himself. This other subjectivity is indicative of a taxonomy of being different from the one being utilized by the ethnographer; it is one in which flesh is paramount.

2ND RIFF: "By Discrepant Taxonomy" expounds on the taxonomy of flesh evoked by Windham's remark encompassing a range of animal life. Situating

Windham's remark in relation to Frederick Douglass's complaint of taxonomic confusion expressed throughout his published work, this riff establishes that Windham's "us is human flesh" challenges the Aristotelian distinction between free rational humans and animality, proffering an understanding of being flesh as entitlement enough to liberty.

3RD RIFF: "A Semiosis of Flesh Thinking" presents a careful reading of Hortense Spillers's exploration of the relationship between fleshliness and persona. Focusing on Spillers's concept of the hieroglyphics of flesh, this riff extrapolates a theory of vestibularity according to which the contestation between the enslaved from Africa and the capitalist system of slavery is accounted for as that of distinct semiological systems.

4TH RIFF: "By Flesh Speaking Semiologically" is where the nonontological nature of that semiology, exemplified by Windham's "us is human flesh," is first explored by showing how Spillers's hieroglyphics of flesh, while deploying elements of Roland Barthes's semiology, does not rely upon or embrace its underlying phenomenology. Rather than giving temporal primacy to flesh as the stolen sign, Windham's statement presumes that meaning and form are expressed contemporaneously: flesh is *with* and not *before* the body and person, and the body and person are *with* and not *before* or even *after* the flesh.

2nd Set in Three Moments

FIRST MOMENT: "Sentient Flesh Dancing" explores two forms of song and dance, Juba and the Buzzard Lope, which were performed by both slaves and their postemancipation descendants, as a signifying system that is contradictory and appositional to capitalism's commodification of the body.

1ST RIFF: "Juba and the Buzzard Lope Play" takes up Frederick Douglass's account of Juba beating as a carnivalesque ritual deployed by the slaveholders to suppress insurrection by "authorizing" regular symbolic actions of resistance. Arguing against that construal of the dance, it reads Juba as an enjoyment of the flesh in and of itself in communion. The performance of beating the flesh in complex polyrhythms contradicts the violence enacted on the flesh by slavery in order to yield the disciplined body. Along these lines, the riff explores another dance that is reported by the amateur ethnologist Lydia Parrish and recorded by the ethnomusicologist Alan Lomax, called the Buzzard Lope, which also expresses and enhances sentience without denying animality.

2ND RIFF: "Ethnographic Epistēmē Abuts Performative Technē Poiētikē" recounts how Lomax's collection of "authentic" African American music, chiefly from the Georgia Sea Islands, constitutes an official archive at the expense of the living transmission of performative *poiēsis in black*. Here is where the theory of *para-semiosis* is developed as the dynamic constitution of the world in the recombinant fluidity of multiple enactments of referentiality, whereby being human is enunciated in the flow. It is also where *poiēsis in black* is discussed as an instantiation of that *para-semiosis*.

SECOND MOMENT: "Poiēsis in Black" revisits Windham's assertion of basic freedom as flesh to elaborate how Du Bois's insistence on using the term *Negro* entails a theory of semiosis and human being that is nonontological.

1ST RIFF: "Consciousness Articulated with Semiosis" explores how the connotative history of *Negro* indexes the problematic of the capacity of the flesh to embody values of *person* in accord with the semiological system of emergent Enlightenment Europe—self-awareness, full self-possession of motive will and desire, liberty—while also, in accord with that same order, embodying values of property—real estate, personal, and chattel property.

2ND RIFF: "Doctrine of Submission with 'The Renaissance of Ethics'" carefully interrogates Du Bois's unpublished 1890 essay, "The Renaissance of Ethics," to show the extent to which such performance forms as Juba and Buzzard Lope are related to a radical critique of the tradition of philosophical ontology. This is then related to Du Bois's 1890 Harvard commencement speech, "Jefferson Davis as a Representative of Civilization," in which he postulates a doctrine of Submissive Man as the basis for a theory of human civilization contra the dominant historiography of individual virtue through might or strength, thereby construing the Negro in terms other than victim, or subjugated pariah.

THIRD MOMENT: "Para-Semiosis" is the elaboration of the theoretical concept *para-semiosis* as the dynamic of differentiation operating in multiple multiplicities of semiosis that converge without synthesis. This is what is referred to in the blues, but also in numerous instantiations of "Africanisms" across the New World, as *being-at-the-crossroads*.

1ST RIFF: "All That Comes with Paraontology" is an extensive engagement with Nahum Chandler's and Fred Moten's use of the term *paraontology*. After tracing Chandler's use to Oscar Becker and Martin Heidegger through Jacques Lacan's concept of *parêtre*, it underscores that lineage's investment in the historical project of philosophical ontology, and then takes up the problem posed by the Negro qua primitive to that project. It has four gestures:

1. *Worldliness*, which is an analysis of Heidegger's effort to discover fundamental ontology.
2. *Historicity*, which relates Heidegger's project to that of his colleague and friend, Oskar Becker, who developed the concept of paraontology as a corrective augmentation of Heidegger's phenomenological analysis.

3. *Primitive Thingliness*, which considers how both Heidegger and Becker expressly flounder in their respective projects with regard to the semiosis of black people.
4. *The They of Primitive We*, which accounts for that falling as a function of their primitivism and raciology. The argument is that Heidegger's admitted failure to be able to account for the signification of blacks, while acknowledging that they are indeed signifying human beings, speaks to the severe limits of the ontological project, its inability to say anything truly meaningful about anything not subsumable to the philosophical project. At issue in that inability is the limitation of personhood only to those entities that adhere to the philosophical concept of individuation, which is the indivisible integrity of subjective consciousness.

2ND RIFF: "In Para-Semiosis, Divisible Person Us Be" presents an account of personhood that is documented among various populations in Africa, as well as among those in the New World who were taken from Africa and enslaved as Negro. It begins by contrasting Heidegger's account of primitive semiosis to those of Maurice Leenhardt, Roger Bastide, and Geneviève Calame-Griaule, showing that the absence of an indivisible subject is not a flaw or failure, but rather a viable way of being. It also entails four gestures:

1. *Us Ain't Paraontological* relates the ethnographic reports of divisible personhood to the previously described performances of Juba and Buzzard Lope, as well as the practitioners' exegeses of what they are doing, and postulates that this is an aspect of *para-semiosis* as a widespread mode of human being. *Poiēsis in black*, as an instantiation of such *para-semiosis*, is characterized as thinking-in-disorder, which is not *para* or *contra* ontology; it simply has nothing to do with ontology.
2. *Para-Semiosis of Being in-Flight-with-One-Another* takes up the question of nowhere to consider what is blackness as an aspect of a life in common. In the aftermath of working our way through the project of philosophical ontology so as to leave it behind us, this gesture takes up Moten's question: What is blackness as an aspect of a life in common? Along these lines, the thinking-in-action concomitant with the advent of Negro as an embodiment of sentient flesh—that is to say, *poiēsis in black*—is considered as thinking-in-disorder. The moment at which the ontological project, by means of its derived juridico-legislative discourse of polity, decrees *Negro* indexes that project's failure at achieving a necessary universal account of existence qua existence, and hence a universal definition of the human. Saying, *Negro*, is indicial of a perennial crisis of ontology is not to say that *poiēsis in black*, although emergent in that crisis, is circumscribed by ontology. Rather, it is *in dynamis*, in active flight, moving according to un-ontological *para-semiosis*.

3 *Love Ain't Sacrificial* returns to "Of the Coming of John" in order to elaborate on Du Bois's "Doctrine of Sacrifice," showing how it is not a form of quietist submission, but rather a rejection of *caritas*, Christian love, in favor of a non-sacrificial, nonproprietary care for fellow beings. Following this reasoning, Du Bois maintains that community founded on the Pauline and Johannine gospel of love cannot bring about a viable ethical community on earth precisely because its prerequisite is fulfillment in the afterlife.

4 *Para-Semiosis, Poiēsis in Black, and Love-Improper* considers how, in rejecting the Pauline and Johannine gospel of love that hopes for the end-of-days and after-life, Du Bois's "Gospel of Sacrifice" calls us to embrace the very love Nietzsche attributes to aristocratic virtue, the love of living, of fulfillment in community of the living, but *without* the proprietary force Nietzsche gives it. The sacrifice Du Bois advocates does not stem from a love of that which is mine through force of arm or will, or which I can assimilate to myself in mimicry. It is what we might call *improper-love*, love that does not seek to comprehend the other; it does not bring the object of love into grasp, into the fold of a proper self, but encounters and opens the self up to its incomprehensibility. We may well think of it as the love of *poiēsis in black*. Insofar as that *poiēsis* is a function of *para-semiosis*, it is a potentiality-of-being that might attend multiple, multiplicious embodiments of flesh. While indissolubly associated with Negro embodiment, *poiēsis in black* as semiosis is not identical with black people, even though it indisputably belongs with them. Once we have left the line of philosophical ontology, the more generative question may be broached: What does the *para-semiosis* of *poiēsis in black* have in common with other embodiments of flesh? Can *para-semiosis* be a commonplace whereby a planetary worldliness of vestibularity enables multiplicious possibilities? Considering the multiplicious possibilities of *para-semiosis* as commonplace entails radically reimagining what is human.

Coda: "Gifting Blues Love-Improper"

This is a preliminary exploration of two such instantiations of *para-semiosis* that, while in resonant engagement with the love-improper of *poiēsis in black*, is neither derivative of nor identical with it. One instantiation is the Algerian writer, Nabile Farès's encounter with James Baldwin presented in his novel, *Un passager de l'occident*. The other is the writing of the Algerian Arabic writer aṭ-Ṭāhir Waṭṭār, which demonstrates an Arabic-expressed *para-semiosis*. This resonant conversation without the necessity of identity bespeaks the possibility of a human love that is non-agapeic and so not sacrificial, but also not egocentric.

The genesis of "On *Lohengrin*'s Swan" was a talked entitled "Sur la question du nègre: *Ames noires: essais et nouvelles* par W. E. B. Du Bois et la figure de récit," which I was invited to give by Didier Coste in 2002 for his conference *Récit émergent, récit renaissant: 1859–1939*, at the Centre de Recherche sur les Modernités Littéraires, Université de Bordeaux 3. An abridged version of "On *Lohengrin*'s Swan" was published in 2015 under the title "*Lohengrin*'s Swan and the Style of Interiority in 'Of the Coming of John'" in "Philology and the Future of Thinking," a special issue of the *New Centennial Review*, thanks to its editor, Nahum Dimitri Chandler. Portions of "Sentient Flesh" were presented at the Futures of America Summer Institute at Dartmouth College in 2016 and 2018, each occasion for which I am deeply thankful to Donald Pease. Another portion was presented at the Orientale American Studies Summer Institute at Università degli Studi di Napoli "L'Orientale" in 2018, thanks to the generous invitation of Donatella Izzo. Many colleagues, close friends, and loved ones have contributed to and encouraged this endeavor, as well as patiently awaited its outcome. To list all of them would take quite a few pages. But without meaning to slight any, I single out a few. Fred Moten has been a most invaluable interlocutor, as have Hortense Spillers, Donald Pease, Roy Kay, Richard Purcell, and Joe Razza. Thanks to J. Kameron Carter and Sarah Jane Cervenak, editors of the Black Outdoors: Innovations in the Poetics of Study series, for having seen something worthwhile in this endeavor. While the writing of a book is truly a solitary affair, its production is a collective endeavor involving many crafts, or as I am wont to say, technē poiētikē. This work would not have seen the light of day without the efforts of Kenneth Wissoker, Joshua Tranen, Jessica Ryan, and the entire production team at Duke. Among those who have cast glances at portions of this work and generously engaged its promise are Wlad Godzich, Didier Coste, Jim Merod, Kevin Bell, and Nahum Chandler. Among those who have patiently waited are my good friends Tony Bogues, Donald Pease, and Paul Bové. Not least of those who wait have been my children, Ashnfara, Alejandra, Javier Sidi Mansour, and Lucia Mari-Hilda. They have suffered innumerable days and nights of abandonment as I wrote and wrote and wrote . . . what my sister, Dyann, came to call "the book without end." Finally, there are more reasons than I can enumerate for why this work is dedicated to Sadia Abbas, whose imagination, astuteness, tenacity, and care convinced me it needed to be done, and who waited most of all.

> καὶ τοῦτ᾽ ἦν ὁ καλούμενος ὑπ᾽ αὐτῶν 'συγκρητισμός.
> (And that is their so-called *Syncretism*.)
> **PLUTARCH** · *Moralia*

> We knew that something was Jes Grewing just like the 1890s flair up.... Don't you understand, if this Jes Grew becomes pandemic it will mean the end of civilization As We Know It.
> **ISHMAEL REED** · *Mumbo Jumbo*

> I think we should have our liberty cause us ain't hogs or horses—us is human flesh.
> **THOMAS WINDHAM**

Body and Flesh

The last epigraphic remark is taken from the three-page typewritten transcript of an interview with the ninety-two-year-old freedman Tom Windham conducted by Bernice Bowden at Pine Bluff, Arkansas, sometime in 1937. This was one of the 696 done in the state over a two-year period under the aegis of the Works Progress Administration (WPA) Federal Writers' Project, 677 of which were submitted to the WPA Writers Unit of the Library of Congress to be eventually compiled for archiving, along with those of sixteen other participating states, into the seventeen-volume *Slave Narratives: A Folk History of Slavery in the United States from Interviews with Former Slaves*. Claiming the human entitlement of freedom is not at all extraordinary in the context of the WPA project mandate, which was to record the experiences and memories of those who had endured enslavement before they passed away. What's more, throughout the period during which these interviews were conducted, from April 1937 to August 1939, there was a sharp recession precipitated by Federal Reserve monetary policy that prolonged the worst effects of the Great Depression, which for black folk like Windham resulted in amplified peonage and forced labor under incarceration. So, claims of deserving freedom attended by comparisons with the conditions of antebellum slavery were par for the course throughout the entire interview qua narrative collection. Even so, asserting humanity as a predicate of the flesh rather than a condition of being beyond the flesh was remarkable. In stating "us is human flesh," Windham evokes a taxonomy of flesh encompassing a range of animal life; more precisely hogs, horses, and humans, all of which, in strictly zoological terms, belong to the class of vertebrate, neocortical, eutherian mammals. His privative "ain't" introduces a subdivision within that zoological class along the lines of a punctuated continuum of sentience moving from the basic to complex. On the one hand, there is the vital biological commonality of animal flesh, which may be sentient in a rudimentary sense of having the capacity to perceive and respond to the environment sufficiently enough to live actively without any signs of self-awareness or having psychological states, something we ascribe to hogs and horses. On the other hand, there is the manifest self-aware possession of psychological states and of being in relation to others and other things, which is associated with *Homo sapiens*. In this sense, Windham's "ain't" articulates a taxonomy of sentient flesh, which interpolates zoology and anthropology. Of course, the full force of his privative is directed at another, albeit related, taxonomy: the political economy of modern capitalist slavery, within which Windham, as a slave, belonged to the class of chattel property, along with the hogs and horses. In that political economic taxonomy, the flesh is valued for what it can produce in assets. This is a matter of speculation as much as it is of consumption in use. And, in that regard, asserting "us is human flesh" acknowledges the vital biological commonality—the form of life—while rejecting evaluation as chattel. Focusing on the rejection in her glossing of Windham's remark alongside those of another freedman named Charlie Moses, Saidiya Hartman understands him to be saying "the flesh, existence defined at its most elemental level, alone entitled one to liberty."[1] She then takes this to be his invocation of universal rights and entitlements based on humanism, well aware this same "discourse of humanism . . . was double-edged since [in accordance with Enlightenment anthropology] the life and liberty they [the slaves] held in esteem were racial entitlements denied them. . . . Thus, in taking up the language of humanism," she concludes, "they seized upon that which had been used against and denied them."[2] Yet the so-called discourse of humanism is vexed on the question of the flesh.

On the face of it, Windham's claim of entitlement to liberty seems to imply the distinction between the human as animal and the person as a social being with inalienable natural rights. Were it doing just that, however, it would not be all that remarkable, but simply a fair summary paraphrasing of Frederick Douglass's well-publicized arguments against slavery as a violation of the natural law expressed in the Declaration of Independence because, while its criminal codes offer "acknowledgment that the slave is a moral, intellectual, and responsible being," it denies that same slave full personhood.[3] Douglass's objection was well grounded in Enlightenment natural rights theory, particularly the liberalist concept of individual freedom found in Locke's political philosophy, as articulated in *The Two Treatises of Government*, but also the concept of personal identity given in his epistemology laid out in *An Essay Concerning Human Understanding*. The latter work, being conceptually foundational for the first, makes a hard distinction between the identity of biological man, which as an animal is a life-form consisting of constantly fleeting particles of matter in succession, vitally united to the same organized body—that fleshly thing—and the person as a social entity with inalienable rights, as well as moral and political responsibilities. Locke defined person as "a thinking intelligent being, that has reason and reflection, and can consider itself as itself, the same thinking thing, in different times and places."[4] In the Lockean sense, the person is attached to a body, or stands in a principal proprietary relationship to the flesh, disciplining it to embody a specific consciousness. By that same account, the idea in our minds signified by *man* is not merely any rational animal, let alone any sentient one, but rather a rational animal of a specific bodily form. "For I presume it is not the idea of a thinking or rational being alone that makes the idea of man in most people's sense," Locke states, "but of a body, so and so shaped, joined to it."[5] Locke's liberalism is problematized around the question of slavery, however. According to his epistemology, anthropologically, an individual human cannot be alienated from himself in body but is consistently and continually himself throughout the material existence, the life span of the body. His political theory of government, on the other hand, argues that an individual can be legitimately alienated from his rights *as a person* due to war—more precisely, by becoming the defeated aggressor in war, which implies an ethical judgment. What makes this even more vexed a matter is that during the time he was writing *The Two Treatises of Government*, Locke had a substantial hand in drafting the 1669 *Fundamental Constitution of the Carolinas*, clause 110 of which states: "Every Freedman of the Carolinas has absolute power and authority over his negro slaves, of what opinion or religion whatsoever."[6] The pertinent point here is that the Carolina Constitution's stipulating absolute proprietary power and authority over what it designates as "negro slaves" exceeds the limited paternal power Locke defines in the *Second Treatise* and is more in line with the Roman Law postulate *vitae necisque potestas* (power of life and death), making it akin to the illegitimate despotic political power of monarchy against which he contrasts the parental. The specificity of this stipulation indicates a relationship of person and body unique to the so-designated negro slave, who, not having been taken in war but purchased as property, is made an exception to natural rights. The basis for that distinction is in the capitalist process of enslavement—which clearly violates Locke's precept of legitimate alienation from rights—whereby the term *negro* designates a commodity asset that, while hominid, is not fully human. As far as this type of hominid is concerned, personhood is diminished or otherwise alienated in relation to the body, and the body has no rights.

Douglass, in his argument against slavery, while adhering to the Lockean proposition of the inherent freedom in natural personhood, asserts, contra the proposition implicit in the *Fundamental Constitution of the Carolinas*, that full personhood is a universal property in every instance of bodies with generally the same form; that is to say, it belongs to all *Homo sapiens*, irrespective of superficial physiognomic variation. The *person* has rights irrespective of the body. Windham's "we should have our liberty cause . . . us is human flesh" strikes an altogether more strident note of discord with Lockean natural rights theory, however, postulating it is the person *of* not *in* the flesh who has inviolable rights. An additionally noteworthy detail of Windham's assertion in this regard is the complete absence of any theological reference. Entitlement to liberty is not based on divine endowment or any other claim of transcendent purpose, nor even on providential or evolutionary teleology. It simply is a fact of the very nature of human flesh. And so, his privative rebuts the market evaluation without appealing to transcendence. Lacking as it does even a residual trace of the transcendent postulate, Windham's "us is human flesh" moves us away from the theological, as well as the metaphysical tendency of thought, the tendency to think the *I* that falls into the world of things, having its reality beyond them. We may well ask: What does it mean, however, to say flesh alone as existence defined at its most elemental level entitles one to liberty? What is the relationship between flesh and *one*? Is *one* predicable of flesh, or is flesh a predicate of the *one*?

Addressing this question, it is useful to distinguish between *person* in the quasi-biological Lockean sense to which Douglass adheres, and person as a social role. Better still, we gain a better sense of what is in play with Windham's declamation, when we take into account that the etymon of *person* is the Latin term *persona*, which connotes the performative assumption of character—what the *Oxford English Dictionary* defines as "the aspect of a person's character that is displayed to or perceived by others." While this initially denoted a theatrical mask akin to, and possibly derived from, the Greek term πρόσωπον (*próspon*), by the time of Justinian's *Corpus juris civilis*, it denoted a legal disposition that, contrary to the modern Lockean construal, was not affixed to a natural body. The thing to bear in mind here is that in each of those usages, *persona* connotes a determinate discursive sociality, rather than a state of nature. Bearing this in mind, according to the order of knowledge subtending modern capitalist slavery, to which Windham's testimonial remark refers, the crucial rift is between sentient animality and fully entitled humanity. This particular rift is enacted and sustained through systemic techniques of severing the captive enslaved body from its motive will and active desire, the latter being markers of personhood. The purpose of the system is not to completely eradicate motive will and desire, but rather to circumscribe them within it, seizing their efficacy in the service of economic value. We can say, then, that motive-will and desire are distorted, not erased, by the rift, a distortion that has been given the name of civilization. On one side of the divide is the captured individual, the particular process of whose individuation as a social being is in relation to, but not based on physically embodied presence. Whatever the particularities of that process of sociality, whatever its relational terms of identification and individuation, the *persona* articulated is its signifier. Simply put, the phenomenal body *purports* an order of signification, a semiological system, which is heterogeneous to that of capitalist slavery. In keeping with received representational practice, we can refer to this system and its sign as *African*. The rift demarcates civilization's interdicting the fluidity of this semiological system. Interdiction is not total eradication, however, and, *pace* Orlando Patterson's postulate of social death, elements of the African semiological system are subsequently iterated, albeit modified and adjusted on account of slavery—to wit, the barbaric elements of supposedly purely African origin in the "Negro song" that John Lomax, and later his son Alan, sought to collect and archive. What falls on the other side of the rift, then, is the *African* transformed in the interdiction of the semiological system for which the *persona* is a signifier into *enslaved captive body*, which is a signifier of particular value in the economy of slavery as an altogether alien order of meaningful sociopolitical living.

We can express this relationship as *African/enslaved captive body*. The dividing line is both conjunctive and transitive, symbolizing the activity of interdictory transformation. It presents the *African* as such; which is to say, as both the residual sign of a prior order of signification and a signifier of value in slavery's order. Yet, even though the supposedly indigenous meaningfulness is rendered inoperative, the efficacy of motive and desire implicated in it is not, becoming instead "liberated" from the first-order semiological system and made available to the economy of slavery in the form of the *enslaved captive body*. This semiological activity is the theft of the body, which can be read in the double sense of the physical capture of bodies from West Africa but also the *enslaved captive body*'s robbing the *persona* of its referentiality. We can, thus, just as easily recast the rift as being between *body* and *flesh*, with *flesh* functioning in place of *persona* as the synecdoche of the semiological system from which the *enslaved captive body* steals. "In that sense," as Hortense Spillers has said, "before the 'body' there is the 'flesh,' that zero degree of social conceptualization that does not escape concealment under the brush of discourse, or the reflexes of iconography."[7] What does it mean, however, to state that before the body there is the flesh? An even more probative question is: How does the flesh, formally expressed as the enslaved captive body, become Negro?

The articulated flesh become Negro, of course, is not tabula rasa. Human flesh, by definition, or at least by the definition taken from Windham's remark, is always already marked as interpolated in some signifying system, some thinking on the cosmic arrangement of things. Any discernable, not easily placed residuum of the dynamics—δύναμις (*dunamis*) in the Aristotelian sense of potentiality as a thing's capacity to be in a different more complete state—of those systems at play in the flesh prior to its entering modernity's cultural vestibularity gets assigned as *African*. We might well take this assignment as synonymous with Rousseau's hypothetical *savage*, the archaic human passing on the way to civilized society. Only, whereas Rousseau's savage is compelled by the interaction of exchange to make the passage in order to become a proprietary social subject, in this instance, the interaction *civilizes* the African *as* capital *of* the exchange system. The procedures of racialized capitalist modernity seek the energy—in the sense of "is-at-work-ness" denoted by another Aristotelian term, ἐνέργεια (*enérgeia*), which is in relation to the just-mentioned sense of *dunamis*—of motive-will and desire bound up with the flesh and body associated with the person of the prior African semiological system. The implication being that the modern capitalist semiological order acquires, or as we say, steals the potential of the prior system *in actuality* as the Negro body. The fruit of this theft is *le nègre* codified by the Marquis de Seignelay in Louis XIV's 1685 *Code Noir* as fungible property—"les esclaves être meubles, & comme tels entrent en la communauté [the slave is fungible property and enters the community as such]." *Le nègre* (Negro), thus, connotes in law racialized human capital, which is an alienable asset used but not consumed in the production of goods and services. And that asset's appreciation and depreciation is calculated relative to real as well as prospective use. What gets destroyed in this process, or rather what is supposed to be destroyed but is more aptly speaking parenthesized, is any semiological order that negates or otherwise compromises the Negro's capital value. In other words, any articulation of person, including gender, that contradicts capital value is supposed to be deracinated. Accordingly, the rift between flesh and body demarcates the distance between culture and, let us say for argument's sake, nature. The rift is not a singular event or action, but is rather an ongoing processual activity through and in which individual consciousness has actual presence in the order of things. We can say, then, that individual consciousness is a cognitive articulation of some process of sociality wherein biological, cultural, linguistic, ritualistic, and psychological fortunes converge—which is what is meant by the historicity of consciousness, its quality of being historically situated with and in the world.

Windham's assertion, "us is human flesh," instantiates this historicity; which is to say, it evokes the processual nature of the entire order of things. In a remarkably straightforward way, he is simply stating in respect to flesh: "us *is* it." The copula here functions as a sign of equality rather than attribution, situating person in some relational schema *with* things. In Windham's assertion of liberty, us is not *in this flesh*. By that same token, the actual living person is not predicable of the thingness of flesh; us is not *a piece of flesh*, but rather us *is flesh*. To the extent that Windham's "us is human flesh" implicitly postulates an irreducible elemental level of existence, it is *flesh/person*. This bifurcation is not to be confused with the one backing Western ontological tradition's underlying presumption (inclusive of the entire range of the humanities as well as natural sciences) that the world and consciousness are distinct orders of being, which the full force of philosophical/scientific thought, ἐπιστήμη (*epistēmē*) must contrive to reunite in recollection; a way of thinking Merleau-Ponty once aptly characterized as *pensées de survol*, "fly-over surveying thought."[8] Along this line of thinking, it is only within the purview of a particular subject-of-knowledge capable of seeing things that meaning is affixed to them, that their significance as things is determined *in being seen*.

Windham's "us is human flesh" troubles this orientation in a way that cannot be easily dismissed. Rather than giving temporal primacy to flesh as the stolen sign, his statement presumes that meaning and form are expressed spontaneously: the flesh is *with* and not *before* the body and person, and the body and person are *with* and not *before* or even *after* the flesh. Windham's person *is* in relation to his generally perceived fleshly thingness. It is not a representation of substance *for* some mind that, extricating it from the vagueness of things (the noumenality of being) through the transcendental activity of cogitation, might claim to *see* it. Neither is Windham's personal consciousness the expression of such transcendentality, parenthesizing the flesh so that the body can be experienced as the bridge connecting agential intellectuality and the world of physical things. The point being that Windham's person is inextricably of the flesh, lives life as flesh. The flesh Windham speaks of is material, but it is not embodied, in the sense of corpuscles that combine to form a discrete entity. This flesh is not a fact or sum of facts. This flesh is not consecrated, nor could it ever have been consecrated. The long history of its consumption is not sacrificial, nor is it purely capitalistic. Douglass's distinction between devouring hard earnings and feeding on flesh catches the issue quite rightly. Returning, for a moment, to the earlier-mentioned legal definition of Negro as an alienable capital asset (*le nègre être meubles*), when this definition is embodied, that body, that Negro body, with all its inherent mental and physical capacities, is owned fully by its proprietor. Said proprietor also owns any use-value engendered or produced therewith, the commodification of which results in revenue—or as Douglass says, "earnings"—that is consumable by definition, leaving the body, a capital assert, to continue producing more over an extended time: a lifetime. The flesh of that same body, however, as a legal property of unfettered access, is the object of unbounded desire—the flesh of the slave belongs to one as much as one's own flesh does, there being no personal other associated with it, no sovereign subject who is necessarily recognized as having superior prerogative. *This is the gist of Husserl's objection to the juridical treatment of human beings as things: it undermines the person of intersubjectivity; which is to say, it ultimately interferes with the actuality of human community.*

Feeding on the flesh has no capital use-value. Whether done through sexual violence, wherein the flesh feeds carnal desire as elemental, or through physical torture, when pieces of flesh are cut away and discarded, cooked, or branded, or when such flesh is fed to dogs, worms, or even other human beings, the act of consumption belongs to a condition of pleasure that is fueled by and sustains structures of desire and imagination epiphenomenal to the capitalist economics of slavery. "Whipping darkies was the joy of the white man back in those days," an ex-slave told Ophelia Settle Egypt of Fisk University in a 1929 interview.[9] Such enjoyment was inseparable from the expenditure and ravishment of the flesh, to paraphrase Hartman.[10] There is no redemption or salvation derived from this consumption of flesh; just sheer delight in the consumption, which abolitionists such as Lydia Maria Child and Theodore Dwight Weld abhorred and denounced as non-Christian and corrosive to the moral and social fabric of the republic. What was less apprehensible to them was how the scale of the quotidian enactments of violence against the Negro body was a practical actualization of the underlying speculative epistemology of modernity, which operates on the basis of its presumptive capacity to assimilate everything, all existence, to its structures: the theory of everything. Again, the flesh of Windham's statement is not consecrated, nor could it ever have been consecrated. It reverberates with the sense of the indissoluble animality of the human. "Us" connotes the actuality of human flesh thinking in the world and expresses that thinking in a communicative system of meaningful signification of the world. "Us" is performing subjectivity, which, in contradistinction to the transcendental ego-subject of theology and modern metaphysics, does not ground sociality but is articulated by and in relation to it—the myriad actualizations of which are in accord with the myriad possibilities of the actualized world, within its horizons, so to speak; and so speaking is to speak of a *nonegocentric* world. This not to say that there is no ego-subject, but that it does not exist a priori, or prior to the world, and is, in fact, given by the world in the continuous dynamic process of the meaningful signification of reality as *semiosis*, construing this to be the sort of mimetic activity Aristotle sought to describe. "Us" is fully cosmological, exscribing being-in-the-world while simultaneously being elemental to the world. The word need not become flesh; it was already flesh. Nor need flesh become parenthesized in order that the word, the transcendental ego-subject, can be seen in an attitude of mystical discovery. The issue is not about seeing, or even touching the flesh. It is about being flesh. To restate this for the sake of a certain clarity, "Us" *represents* nothing but *signifies* everything. It can be said that in his taxonomy of sentient flesh, Windham's anthropological distinction demarcates a profoundly semiotic *form of life*. Going one step further, it can also be said that cognition and consciousness are articulated *with* semiosis, in which our concepts and ideas are signs. Cognition as semiosis is neither an a priori—as in divinely revealed, or providential—nor merely an epiphenomenon of the flesh; it is actualized in the process of semiosis. Human flesh is sentient *in semiosis*—or to use a more familiar, although no less daunting expression, in its language-games.

Sentient Flesh: Thinking in Disorder, Poiēsis in Black is an interrogation of the relationship between the terms *Negro*, *poiēsis*, and *humanism*. The focus of that attention is the indicial force of the nominative. Names do more than designate things; they indicate an orientation in life, not in some abstract nominalist sense, but in the sense of a grammar that emerges out of a set of human practices in life that work in the creation of the world. In this sense, they are material indices of a particular semiosis. And, as shall be argued throughout this work, they may well be indices of multiplicious semiosis, a dynamics referred to here as *para-semiosis*. Giving a full account of what *para-semiosis* means is the work of *Sentient Flesh*. The thing to keep in mind at this moment is the issue of what the usages of *Negro* and *poiēsis* have to do with each other and *humanism* as designators. The focus here is on the relationship between *poiēsis* and *humanism*; or rather, it is on a certain history of knowledge that presumptively identifies itself with humanism, with *the* humanism, as if there were such a thing, and claims *poiēsis* as its unique definitive property.

Returning to Spillers's saying flesh comes before the body, the statement, which stems from her extended exploration of the relationship between fleshliness and persona, suggests the physiological basis of consciousness and intelligence. But if intelligence is always embodied, regardless of the morphology—so that intelligence is everywhere—then does that mean human flesh necessarily entails human intelligence, and if so, what is the character of that intelligence? Furthermore, to the extent that there are variations in the human morphology, however slight, does that suggest variations of intelligence? These questions are at least as old as Kant's anthropology, beginning with his precritical essays *Of the Different Races of Human Beings* (1775) and *Determination of the Concept of Race* (1785), reaching a critical crescendo with *On the Use of Teleological Principles in Philosophy*, published the same year as his *Critique of Practical Reason*, 1788. Kant's theoretical engagement with these questions yields a theory of race that is physiological not moral; that is to say, it seemingly has little to nothing to do with his universalist moral theory, set out in *Toward Perpetual Peace* (1795). His postulating a natural hierarchy of races—delineated according to physiognomic distinctions held to be indicative of cognitive capacities, with darker races, particularly the Negro and Amerind at the bottom and so most cognitively deficient—while also postulating that the realization of universal morality is grounded in the sovereignty of reason, yields an antinomy. It is an antinomy precisely because both Kant's theory of race and his theory of universal morals are *grounded* in reason. Yet, how can those who are existentially deficient in reason have access to the universal morals based on reason? Kant's answer, expressed in *On the Use of Teleological Principles in Philosophy*, is that those races with deficient capacity of reason, particularly the Negro, fit within the imagined cosmopolitan order as a permanent labor force directed by Europeans.[11] Regarding Spillers's meditations on human flesh in light of Kant, the crucial question becomes: Is human flesh sentient flesh, and if it is, what makes it human?

That is the keynote question of *Sentient Flesh: Thinking in Disorder, Poiēsis in Black*, and it launches an exploration of what Du Bois refers to as "the thousand and one little actions which go to make up the group life taken as a whole" of those portions of humanity designated Negro. We might well term these *practices-of-living* to indicate their dynamic aspect as a doing of being in the world in relation to its conceptualization, but also their conventionality; that is, they entail transmissible traditions of knowing-how, comprising lineages of thinking about the human condition in the midst of the existential disorder attending the political economy of capitalism's advent as a global order, with its concomitant system of racialized slavery and colonialism. While that economy itself has been rigorously organized and predicated on a rigidly bifurcated order of being—*humans* and those *things* humans create, possess, and appropriate—its becoming a planet-wide system entailed the disarticulation of *practices-of-living-in-common* from their cosmogonies. In other words, interpolation into capitalism's terms of order, to paraphrase Cedric Robinson,[12] results in the dissolution of long-enduring formations of human community, engendering cosmic disorder by throwing disparate cosmogonies together under the anthropological rubric *primitive*. This term has a rather broad connotation, comprehending both an original inhabitant, an aboriginal, and a person belonging to a preliterate nonindustrial society, but also ancestral early man, or anything else that is archaic. It has been inclusively applied to a wide array of types of *natives*—also a conceptual category—engendered along the way in capitalism's global expansion and colonial rule. Not all colonial natives are designated primitive, however; there are those who belong to age-old civilizations, the effects of which, according to the narrative of *translatio*, transferred westward to feed the foundations of capitalism—outstanding examples of which are China, India, and most of the Muslim world. The distinction of having been civilizationally long-in-the-tooth does not mitigate the disordering effects of capitalist expansion, however. On the contrary, being construed as archaic civilizational formations surpassed by Western capitalist modernity is another sense of primitive and tends to exacerbate the disordering effects with an aura of civilizational degradation and loss of authenticity. Terminologically, *primitive* and *Negro* share the same semantic space to the point of synonymy. Those populations designated Negro, however, are seemingly always primitive, this attributed state playing a role, almost as a neo-Aristotelian afterthought, in legitimating their designation: the absurdly Hegelian argument that the primitive, enslaved and made Negro, enters into civilization and thus benefits from the transformation. Be that as it may, whether as Negro, primitive, or native, all are subsumed by the logic of capitalist production and propriety, and so compelled to think in disorder.

This *thinking-in-disorder* is akin to what Alejo Carpentier sought to depict in the style he termed *lo real maravilloso*, "the marvelous real," as that modality of being that truly eschews the *Entzauberung* (disenchantment) Max Weber claimed characterized capitalist modernity.[13] During his eleven-year exile in Paris, Carpentier became a member of André Breton's surrealist movement writing for the journal *La Révolution surréaliste*. He came subsequently to disavow the beautiful marvelous celebrated in Breton's *Surrealist Manifesto* as "produced by means of conjuring tricks, bringing together objects that would never normally meet: . . . the umbrella or lobster or sewing machine, or whatever it may be, on an operating table, in the interior of a desolate, in a desert of rocks."[14] The fault Carpentier finds with surrealism is not its pursuit of the strange as marvelous, but rather that its representations of the marvelous are all manufactured outside of reality. In his judgment, the surrealists forget that the marvelous "arises from an unaccustomed or singularly favorable illumination of unnoticed riches of reality, . . . perceived with peculiar intensity by virtue of an exaltation of the spirit that leads to a kind of limit state."[15] Even as a matter of aesthetics, or, rather especially as a matter of aesthetics, the marvelous must stem from a thinking investment—Carpentier calls it *faith*, which can be taken to mean what we might call *a-epistemic* knowledge and thinking—in a reality in which spirits, malevolent and beneficial, as well as saints and their miracles, actually exist. The surrealists' marvelous "invoked in disbelief is never more than a literary trick [*artimaña*] that, over time, becomes as tedious as certain 'fixed' oneiric literature, certain eulogies of madness, with which we are all very familiar."[16] But neither should Carpentier's critique of surrealism's marvelous be taken as an argument for realism, which, in his view, is gregariously charged with political significance, merely substituting the surrealist bag of literary tricks for "the commonplaces of the committed literati and the perverse eschatological pleasure of certain existentialists."[17] No, the marvelous as an aesthetic mode must be of the real world. It is not a trivial fact that Carpentier's principal experience of *lo real maravilloso* was during his 1943 visit to Haiti, where he found himself "in daily contact with *lo real maravilloso*," as he puts it, "treading on a land where thousands of men longing for freedom believed in the lycanthropic powers of Mackandal, to the point that this collective faith produced a miracle on the day of his execution"; this provides the motif of his second novel, *El reino de este mundo* (*The Kingdom of This World*).[18] Nor is it at all surprising that he would extrapolate a general theory of the Americas (*América entera*) out of his encounter with Afro-Haitian practices and thinking. That is concordant with Carpentier's ethnographic investment, along with that of Fernando Ortiz, Lydia Cabrera, Rómulo Lachatañeré, Juan Marinello, and Nicolás Guillén, in *Afrocubanísimo*. His first novel, *¡Ecué-Yamba-O: Historia afro-cubana!*, which arguably sets the grounds for what will be his theory of *lo real maravilloso*, extrapolates from his ethnographic research on the secret Afro-Cuban men's society, *Abakuá*.[19]

What is most germane about Carpentier's *real maravilloso* here is his understanding that the something he encountered in Haiti was expressly beyond the pale of modern *epistēmē*. His sense of the Americas being constituted in the confluence of three heterogeneous cosmogonies, African, European, and Amerind—polyphorous lines that, like asymptotes of the hyperbola, ever approach one another without converging into one synthesizing line—which Carpentier proclaims to be a baroque reality without clean geometrical symmetry or uncluttered space, is resonant with the thinking-in-disorder being exposited here. Granting the resonance, however, there is a problematic aspect to Carpentier's negrophilic elaboration of *real maravilloso*, which is the central fissure (*grieta central*) Juan Marinello discerned in *¡Ecué-Yamba-O: Historia afro-cubana!*: "the scuffle [*pelea*] between the desire to touch the black interior [*entraña negro*] while retaining the [neutral] European vantage point."[20] This same problematic is at play in *El reino de este mundo*, where the narrative *allows* the blacks to believe in Mackandal's magical transformation into a bird and escape from his execution by burning, only to explain, as an aside, how he was in fact thrust back into the fire by his executioners. Taking into account the problematic nature of Carpentier's negrophilia, the asymptotic aspect of the confluent cosmogonies he describes raises some questions about the severe limitations of the category *human* as it has been elaborated in relation to the centuries-long tradition of philosophical ontology. Postulating the asymptotic confluence of disparate cosmogonies made to share common material historical grounds, but working that materiality in distinct ways, suggests that the arc of the world is not teleological, neither is it eschatological; it does not portend a synthesis that redeems the terrible violence of struggle as meaningful at the end. The struggle for the world, nevertheless, is a struggle of historical formation, of distinct sets of practices-of-living that may share comparable, even identical, values but have arrived at them following different courses, and those courses matter.

Along these lines, the phrase *poiēsis in black* designates a set of practices-of-living, which articulate conceptions of humanity that are appositional to the epistemology of raciology and the concomitant anthropology predominant in capitalist modernity. *Poiēsis* is hacked here—to use Denise Ferreira da Silva's term for a mode of critical engagement that "highjacks a concept in order to release its radical possibilities"[21]—from Aristotle's *Poetics*, where it is a particular calibration of μίμησις (*mimesis*); remembering that for Aristotle, mimesis was a dynamic process of engaging reality—entailing some material media that expressed an object in a particular modality. Precisely because *poiēsis* formally exhibits what it exposits, change in action in a duration of time, we can understand it to connote human creating in semiosis, in saying possibility. That is to say, it is the species-activity of actualizing in discrete material forms any given conceptualization of being-in-the-world, in accordance with a specifiable set of practices-of-living. With respect to *poiēsis in black*, these practices-of-living, while concurrent with the Enlightenment semiosis of *Man*—which is capitalized and italicized here per Sylvia Wynter's description of it as an abstraction predicated on the bio-economic taxonomy of life—articulate grammatically in apposition. Regarding the grammatical, or grammaticality, I have in mind the enacted conventional practices whereby a person is recognized as knowing *how* to act. In other words, what Cyril Lemieux's defines as "that which enables the members of a community to judge correctly; that is to say, to correctly link the discontinuities occurring in the world (bodies, objects, material, gestures, discourses) to descriptions, and to relate experience to certain of those descriptions as a feeling of fact."[22] Even more precisely, I mean something along the lines proposed by the eighth-century Arabic grammarian Sībawayhi, who thought of grammar as a technology of imagination through which a set of relations to things in reality and each other is articulated as constituting the human world. Again, this is a question of conventionality, or what Aristotle lists among the three constitutive elements of mimesis as *modality*: that which issues in the indissoluble relationship between mimetic media and modality—the τέχνη (*technē*) that works the mimetic media in relationship with its object. For, as Frantz Fanon says in this vein, "The talk [*parole*] of the nation, the verb of the nation prescribes the world by renewing it"; which is to say that with transformations of grammar—and grammars are always ultimately local—we encounter a transformative "dissonance [*bouleversement*] in basic perception, in the very world of perception."[23]

Turning to this question of the relationship between language, perception, and imagination as a technology of life, which is where the poetic and sociality meet, Albert Murray provides guiding insight. Taking up Susanne Langer's postulate that "what all art represents or expresses is human feeling, how human beings feel about what they are aware of," Murray understands this to "mean that local circumstances and predicaments and the idiomatic procedures evolved to cope with them may have worldwide implication and application. Indeed, such is the function of fiction, which is also to say poetry, which is to say metaphor."[24] On another occasion, when talking with Don Noble about this relationship between fiction, metaphor, and thinking in the world as humans, Murray remarks that he thinks of fiction in terms of entropy, as "an attempt to order chaos" by creating conceptual form. "Everything is fiction," he says. "It's a matter of finding an adequate metaphor that would be commensurate with the complexities and possibilities of our surroundings . . . it means documenting concepts." What serious fiction—such as poetry—"tries to do is bring the deepest, the most comprehensive insights to bear upon" that documentation."[25]

Speaking of documenting concepts, that which Murray calls fiction, Ibn Rushd (aka Averroes, in the West), along with ibn Sīnā (Avicenna), and before them al-Fārābī, proceeded by al-Jāḥiẓ along with al-Kindī, called this المُحاكاة (*al-muḥākāh*), which is the philosophical Arabic translation of *mimesis*. Following Aristotle, they held *poiēsis* as the most superior mode of *mimesis*. What Murray calls documentation they referred to as الأمة الشعرية (*al-umma aš-šiʿriya*, the poetic or aesthetic community), by which they indicated the living community of humans articulated and sustained with the poetic expression of profound, serious imagination. By ibn Sīnā's account, the performance of poetic expression animates the imaginative faculty, called التخيل (*takhyîl*), engendering affective excitement (انفعال, *infaʿāl*), from awe, sublime grandeur, and delight to belittlement, grief, and agony; without the purpose of what is said being to establish any ideological or chauvinistic conviction or belief (اعتقاد, *iʿtiqāḍ*) at all.[26] This precognitive mental activity—in the sense that the conscious mind, or psyche, is aroused to delight or dejection about a condition without conception or experiencing it perceptually—arranges the schemata of human behavior and activity in general, and is itself engendered by poetic expression. The imaginative representation generates assent through its use of mimesis, which involves generating a faithful image of some original, or thinking in images. The image is both a function of poetic statements, which are conventional as in historical and material—they have particular media and modality—as well as the imaging capacity of the mind, suggesting an isomorphic relationship between poetic representation (expression) and the mental activity of image creation, or imagination. In contrast to the apophantic syllogism, poetic expression does not achieve demonstrative knowledge about the physical world as objective reality, but exhibits the workings, the capacities of the type of mind capable of achieving such knowledge. The emphasis here is on the person as meaningfully discovered in the sheer pleasure of المُحاكاة (*al-muḥākāh*), of *mimesis*—that is, the pleasure of the resonance between the expression and the world, and then discovering to be so in common with others. This conception of الأمة الشعرية (*al-umma aš-ši'irīya*, the poetic or aesthetic community) is akin to Murray's understanding that all poetic expressions represent or express human feeling, how humans are constituted affectively; whereby there is no rigid bifurcation between feeling and conception. In fact, as Murray says, the poetic expression of feeling deepens conception. There is also a resonance here with Spillers's sense of performative persona. Holding the subject as the focus of poetic expression's activation of التخيل (*takhyîl*, imaginative faculty) engenders the aforementioned aesthetic community, which ibn Sīnā postulates is imbued with الاغراض المدنية (*al-aḡrāḍ al-madanīya*, civic tendency), explicitly meaning the identification of character and sociality, or more precisely, the individual person's ethical action living in community. Further riffing on the Arabic line of thinking, this can be termed *poetic socialities*, holding such to be resonant with what Fred Moten and Stefano Harney call *undercommons*, and Tony Bogues, *common association*. Because we are talking about documentation of discrete forms of human intelligence in relation to practices-of-living *as such*, these resonances matter.

A set of propositions form the confluence of Murray's fiction, the Arabic الأمة الشعرية (*al-umma aš-ši'irīya*), and Spillers's performative persona. Practices-of-living, we may say, articulate specific ways of thinking and knowing-how—those being necessary to those practices. By that same token, ways of thinking articulate the possibilities for infinite modalities of living. One's way of living either facilitates one's openness to certain intelligences or not, and one's openness to certain intelligences enables certain ways of living. That certain ways of thinking have been expressed in terms of eschatology is beyond dispute. Arguably, such is the thinking of the already dead, the thinking that can have no hope or aspiration, but rushes toward the end of everything in order to find true justice and freedom. Simply put, there are known ways of thinking that seek to achieve a tightly regulated homeostasis between thinking and living, that aim to so conserve a specific balance of energy within the system that no free energy is allowable. All known eschatologies aim at such arresting of thinking into a rigid habit of thought and tightly policed way of life. This is so for the most rigorous *Entzauberung*-inflected positivism as much as it is for the most Pauline millenarianism. In truth, however, such ways of thinking are irrefutably dedicated to curtailing, even the ultimate ending of life—*eschaton*, the general theory of everything—and not its repair in the world.

Gramsci remarks in his *Notebooks* that the beginning of critical elaboration is "consciousness of what one really is, namely to 'know yourself' as a product of the historical process that has taken place so far and left in you an infinity of traces without the benefit of an inventory. What is needed is to initiate such an inventory," he states. A different cord is struck, if we quietly change *process* into *processes* and, taking a cue from Edward Said, *inventory* into *itinerary*. So now we are going somewhere having been *somewheres* else, and the task is to come up with a plan of travel on the spot with no true bearing other than where we are now—which is with Fanon when he declares, and I will quote him from the original French, followed by an English shadow so as not to lose the affect altogether:

> Je demande qu'on me considère à partir de mon Désir. Je ne suis pas seulement ici-maintenant, enfermé dans la choséité... Je réclame qu'on tienne compte de mon activité négatrice ~~en tant que je poursuis autre chose que la vie~~; en tant que je lutte pour la naissance d'un monde humain, c'est-à-dire d'un monde de reconnaissances réciproques.
>
> From the moment I desire, I demand to be considered. I am not merely here-now circumscribed by this thingness... I insist that my negative activity be taken into account, ~~to the extent that I am in pursuit of something other than life~~, that I am struggling for the birth of a humane world; that is to say, a world of reciprocal recognitions.[27]

The struck clause could just as well have been paraphrastically qualified to read, "in pursuit of something other than [mere] life." But that would be tantamount to reinstating the taxonomic division *Sentient Flesh* plays no part in: the ontological division between what Aristotle refers to as ζωή (*zōē*, mere physical biological existence) and ἄνθρωπος (*anthrōpos*, human). Striking the clause through puts it under erasure, thereby marking the struggle in Fanon's own thinking to slip the tentacle-grasp of ontology. In that struggle, his recognizing the importance of poetic invention in the formation of popular imagining about our collective reality calls us to ponder whether *poiēsis* as mimesis can foster a social formation analogous to the intellectual class so essential to the historical formation of the bourgeoisie in modernity as a transformative force. It may very well be the case that *poiēsis* fosters the formation of certain ways of thinking and conceiving, indeed perceiving the world—let us say imagining the world. The question is whether those ways are, or can ever be arranged into community, capable of articulating and sustaining a tradition of thinking, a historiography of intelligence in relation to polity or social formation. We would need to call this something other than "ideology." A viable candidate in this context may simply be "poetry," but poetry in relation to consciousness as an issue of love and understanding—"hantée par le problème de l'amour et de la compréhension [haunted by the problem of love and understanding]," Fanon says—which brings to the fore the question of how desire functions or is articulated as an element of techniques of thinking.[28] Alternatively, staying with Fanon, we might refer to this as rhythmic attitude (*attitude rythmique*), in the sense of timely or eventful thinking; and as he says, the adjective should be given its full weight, for its expression as well as its source is a poetic practice that is a living style of spontaneous creation. But what can be meant by spontaneous creation except that the poetic image is a material form of imagination as the technique of living essential to thinking *in the world as humans*. The question still remains: What is the human, according to whom?

The human condition is perennially transitional, or to use an older language, metabolic. Indeed, we cannot speak here in any way that is generatively meaningful or enabling, of "the part of no part," or the propertyless—the *Eigentumslosen*—as either being the subjects *of* politics or subjects *in* politics. It bears noting that what Etienne Balibar, in keeping with Jacques Rancière, designates as the propertyless and de-propertied the poet Claude McKay aptly called *vagabondage*, referring to what he took as a constitutive element of radical humanism. A personification of this vagabondage is found in his novel *Banjo*, where the dissolution of aesthetic distinction is not indicative of a desire for return to proper corporeal integrity in relation to things; rather, it indicates the desire to be free among things. As the Haitian exile, Ray, thinks to himself reflecting on Banjo's vagabondage: "Man loves individuals. Man loves things. Man loves places. And the vagabond lover of life finds individuals and things in many places and not in any one nation."[29] In this sense, yes, the vagabond is poetic but not as Benjamin understood the *flâneur* to be so.

W. E. B. Du Bois, whose work looms large in the lineage of thinking in disorder, designated this desire to be free among things "intellect-in-action," a dynamic process of becoming, occurring, in his account, "between chance and law . . . possibility and necessity." All of these terms were his descriptors for an existential attitude, the most apt figuration of which cannot be the *flâneur*, but rather Ellison's rhythmical Zoot-suited boys, who are "men outside of historical time, who were untouched and did not believe in [political] Brotherhood, no doubt had never heard of it; . . . men of transition whose faces were immobile."[30] These rhythmical elaborately stylized beings are ontologically incomprehensible and uncomprehending, which means that they cannot be persuaded of their inequality. It is not that they make sounds that have no voice and do not signify. Their voice is soundless. It is not a cacophonous noise transformed into reasonable speech through the action of civil discourse. Their jive-talk is not the force of a new deal. It does not articulate a conflict over the terms of order and distribution. This is why Du Bois's intellect-in-action is aptly paraphrased as "thinking-in-action" distinguishing it from a vitalist *Lebensphilosophie* (philosophy of life), or even the sense of thinking as merely the mediating agency between experience and knowledge—which is to say, it is a *thinking-in-disorder*. The question of sentient flesh is a paramount aspect of Du Bois's extended investigations of the Negro, precisely because the general problem guiding those investigations is the relation of consciousness to the world. Consciousness is more than merely grounded in its historical occasion, in the milieu, but is primarily a function of milieu. It is a socially extended consciousness. Not in the sense that the individual mind extends into the world, but rather in the sense that the mind is constituted in the world. The world, in Du Bois's account, is the complexity of material environmental forces, including the activity of humanity that constitutes and sustains society and its various institutional practices of what he calls interchangeably "culture" and "civilization." This sense of human society as a function of material, natural—as opposed to supernatural—forces is central to his phylogenetic account of civilizational diversity in "The Conservation of Races." Yet, in *The Souls of Black Folk*, as well as the preponderance of his writings expressly concerned with the constitution of consciousness, Du Bois emphasizes the societal, across the full range of its institutions, over the physiological. In this, he departs from the neutral monism of his avowed mentor in psychology, William James—according to which reality is *neither* mental nor physical but has a distinct, and seemingly intrinsically mysterious, basic character that can be regarded as either mental or physical from certain viewpoints. It is certainly not a trivial fact that Du Bois already saw an indissoluble connection between the novel as a form and modern psychology—both in the sense of the formation of individual personality types and the nascent scientific study of them—in his Harvard school days. He expressly makes that connection in a paper titled "The Renaissance of Ethics," which was written for the philosophy course he took with James during the 1888–1889 academic year. Already in that essay, there is a discernable move in Du Bois's thinking contra the Kantian formulation of the transcendental *I* out of time in favor of the person in time who is fully situational, in Spillers's sense. Time is not something the *I* imposes; rather, the *I* is given with time and so is an affect, one could even say a function, of the world as horizon. And the latter is historical and actualized in the cumulative species activity of mimesis: we make the world as one of the elements and forces on earth in *community* in time. And it is important to remember the beat, as Rufus Scott's father tells him in Baldwin's novel *Another Country*: "*A nigger ... lives his whole life, lives and dies according to the beat. Shit, he humps to that beat and the baby he throws up in there, well, he jumps to it and comes out nine months later like a goddamn tambourine.*"[31] This, in some measure, is what Ignace Meyerson was aiming to account for with historical psychology and what Gilbert Simondon subsequently elaborates as the problem of animality and humanity.[32] Yet, the resonance between their thinking and thinking-in-disorder is only up to a point. Even those efforts are a writing over the flesh, whereas the persona in-and-of-the beat that Scott's father declaims is written *with* the flesh. The intellect-in-action Du Bois remarks, which is to say, *thinking-in-disorder*, is in itself not a condition of sociality, but an inevitable affect, as in disposition, of sociality—it does not ground sociality, but is articulated by and in relation to it—the myriad actualizations of which are in accord with the myriad possibilities of the actualized world, within its horizons, so to speak. We do not fall into the world, we exist in the world; which is to say, we exist in common. As a species, as a form of life, we will always be worldly, be worlding, but that need not be transcendent, transcendental, or even propositionally phenomenological, which is the same as transcendental. Rather, the existence of any given particular population as a collective actor in history, and supposedly therefore an agent of change, is a function of known and discernable configurations and transformations of power. One might well add that these configurations and transformations of power are exclusively in the mode of human institutions that delineate ranges of possible activity, usually through directing our desires by capturing or managing our imagination, and so spawning certain types, certain ways of living a life. Given that Kant's project of practical moral society and community is predicated on the priority and hyper-importance (hypostatization) of the transcendental *I* as the instantiation of self-consciousness, to displace it from its perch calls for a different ethics, one not grounded in the subject/object distinction. We should bear in mind while taking up the *quaestio* of sentient flesh that "fleshliness" has a long theological provenance, in which it is opposed to the active intelligence of the divine. It is the antithesis of thinking and so is an earthly threat to the being, to salvation of the immortal soul. Perhaps a way forward is something like "fleshlily thinking" in contrast to the personal embodiment—to think with world and earth both in view, and not situate thinking somewhere outside the flesh.

The principal proposition of *Sentient Flesh: Thinking in Disorder, Poiēsis in Black* is that those populations designated and constituted within the political economy of capitalist modernity as Negro enact practices-of-living, *poiēsis in black*, which are not fully comprehensible by the semiosis of that economy, particularly its grammar of ontology. More importantly, however, those practices articulate appositionally, opening up infinities of other ways of being human in community becoming, ever becoming. Invoking Fanon once more, he is often quoted as saying, "the black has no ontological resistance in the eyes of the White." But, let us give this in its full context freeing it from the shadow cast by Charles Lam Markmann's and Richard Philcox's respective translations:

> Ontology, once we have admitted once and for all that it leaves aside existence [*laisse de côté l'existence*], does not enable us to understand the existence of the black [*l'être du Noir*]. For the black no longer has to be black [*n'a plus à être noir*], except in front of [*en face du*] the White. Some will take it into their head to remind us that the situation is two-way [*est à double sens*]. We respond, that is false. The black [*le Noir*] has no ontological

resistance in the eyes of the White. The Negro [*Les nègre*], suddenly [*jour au lendemain*], had two systems of reference in relation to which they had to situate themselves [*leur a fallu se situer*]. Their metaphysics, or less pretentiously their customs and the instances to which they referred, were abolished because they were found to be in contradiction with a civilization they did not know and which was imposed on them.[33]

Taken in its full context, this is seemingly an engagement with Heidegger's critique of the project that began with Plato and Aristotle, but was truly elaborated by the Latin Scholastics, which skips over (*überspringen*) the question of existence qua existence by concentrating on the systematic study of existent entities. Admitting that skip is a preliminary move in Heidegger's effort to retrieve the pre-Socratic Greek investigation of being, what he calls "fundamental ontology." Then again, carefully attending to Fanon's remark reveals that it is also stating the epistemic defaillance of even that fundamental ontology regarding the black way of talking about existence. There is the notable casually abrupt shift of grammatical subject from "the black [*le Noir*]" to "the Negro [*les nègres*]"—which Markmann carries over into his translation by rendering "le Noir" as "the black man" and "les nègres" as "the Negro," but which Philcox elides altogether by following suit with "le Noir" but rendering "les nègres" as "the Blacks." Two points of reference are at issue with this shift. The one is that of what Fanon refers to as the "black existence [*l'être du Noir*]," about which he says, "Ontology, when we have admitted once and for all that it leaves existence aside, does not allow us to understand." The other, that of the Negro, is situated in a definite relationship to ontology's system of reference, along with some other referential systems—the Negro's metaphysics. The incomprehensibility of the black refers to the dynamic practices-of-living and conceptualizing being that articulate the existence *of* the black, which ontology cannot explain because, even as manifest things that plainly indicate some system of referentiality is at play, that referentiality is so discordant with ontology's it cannot be analyzed or explained. As we shall see later on when further elaborating the notion of *poiēsis in black*, Heidegger himself admits this epistemic defaillance of ontology regarding the black. By using the term *nègre* in a way that clearly evokes its juridical political-economic genealogy—the 1685 Code Noir—Fanon is marking its indicating a crossroad, a nexus of distinct semiosis, of systems of referentiality. There are multiple systems of referentiality that traverse the crossroad, including those metaphysics Fanon proclaims to have been abolished. The historical decreeing of Negro as some *thing*, a fungible commodity, is indisputably indicative of the semiosis of capitalist modernity in precisely the sense Du Bois accounts for the "color-line" as worldwide. Fanon hinders his own prospective account of the multiple semiosis confluent at the crossroads by erroneously proclaiming that the Negro's metaphysics have been abolished. Correcting for that error, we can follow how the black and the Negro are also confluent at the crossroads, that what he calls the ontologically unfathomable "black existence," but also "the black lived experience [*l'expérience vécue du Noir*],"[34] is the perpetually recombinant flow of *para-semiosis*. This *para-semiosis* of *poiēsis in black* is not only incomprehensible to ontology; it also articulates a way of being human that is nonontological. Elaborating the theory of *para-semiosis* as poetic sociality is not indicative of a desire for the return to proper corporeal integrity in relation to things, but rather the desire to be free among things. The charge, then, is to take seriously what Michel Foucault called "practices of freedom,"[35] to carefully explore and engage their potentialities, ever mindful of their limitations. This is not a search for a way out, or even forward; rather, it is an effort to keep on flying, to take heed of the call to "fly right."

[**1ST SET**]

> The impressions and sense perceptions of humans
> actually belong in the category of surprises; they are
> evidence of an insufficiency in humans.
>
> VALÉRY · *Analectica*

On *Lohengrin*'s Swan

A Style of Interiority and Thinking

Readers of W. E. B. Du Bois's famous 1903 work, *The Souls of Black Folk*, will recollect the pivotal scene of raising action in the thirteenth chapter of the book, "Of the Coming of John." John Jones. A young man named John Jones, having recently graduated from the Wells Institute, is on a postgraduate summer tour singing with its quartet, which takes him to New York City, where he finds himself standing in Times Square watching the bustling human activity of the streets. While at Wells, he had "wondered . . . how it must have felt to think all things in Greek," and grappled with the contradictory profundities of modern German thought, which aimed at achieving that state of enlightenment when the electrified intellect cuts through the dimming veil of superstition and surpasses its quotidian state. So, it is with a clarity of mind not unlike Leibniz's that Jones sits there in Times Square astutely attentive to the world of motion and men, which remind him of the sea, changelessly changing, bright and dark, grave and gay, invitingly tumultuous. Appreciating the details of clothing fabric and style in the hustle bustle of the crowd as indices of wealth, he recognizes the scene he is observing to be the world. And since many of the richer and brighter of the world seem to be hurrying all in one way, he concludes that the street they take is leading somewhere of significance. Jones is so spellbound by the moving crowd that when a tall light-haired young man in the company of a talkative young lady come by, he unhesitatingly and rather incautiously follows them through the crush of the crowd. They lead him on a short walk up from Times Square to the ticket office of the Metropolitan Opera House, which was then in Midtown at 1411 Broadway, where he unwittingly pays five dollars to enter he knew not what.

This New York scene is narrated from a third-person omniscient perspective, focused on Jones's impressions of things in a style that depicts the temporal immediacy of his perceptions as they occur and his impressions, without any reflection on their meaning. It is meticulously internalized, narrating Jones's thinking, and even then only minimally depicting his thinking *about* what is happening around him, presenting instead impressions that are more like thought-images than anything else. It is a pivotal scene on three counts. The first has to do with how the internalized impressionism marks a shift in what had been the narrative perspective for the first five pages, which is to say more than a third of the entire fourteen-page story. For those pages, the narration is in the third-person perspective of a character in the story, who recounts events in Jones's career at the Wells Institute. There are a number of explicit narrative markers indicating this portion of the story is being told by a teacher at the institute, who is not only personally acquainted with those events, but is also fond of Jones. Beginning with its opening description of the location of the Wells Institute at the end of Carlisle Street on the west side of Johnstown and moving on to its account of Jones's graduation, the opening five pages function as a lengthy exposition telling what we need to know about where Jones came from—"He came to us from Altamaha"—who or what he is, and what he had to contend with to get an education, all of which is as meticulously externalized as the New York scene is internalized.

The second reason for the New York scene being pivotal is that the shift from external to internalized narration marks the beginning of the raising action, which reaches its climax at the Metropolitan Opera where Jones achieves two moments of recognition. These are, in order of occurrence, his recognizing his full freedom and humanity while listening to the prelude to act 1 of Wagner's *Lohengrin*, followed by his recognizing the young man he followed to the opera as his white childhood playmate from Altamaha, John Henderson. The first moment is Jones's initiation into the conscientious struggle for freedom, when he decides his vocation is to return home to Altamaha and help his people. The second moment of recognition is in direct contradiction to that calling. It is the moment at which Henderson demands the enforcement of Jim Crow and has Jones expelled from the opera for inadvertently sitting next to the young woman accompanying Henderson. The convergence of these two moments of recognition and their contradiction is the third reason for the New York scene's importance. Whereas the first two reasons have to do with issues of narrative style and details of form, this third reason has to do with the significant role the style and form of Du Bois's fiction play in his concept of what he elsewhere called "intellect-in-action," referring to the dynamic activity of self-conscious human intelligence in the world, taking *Negro* to be a metonym for such.

Du Bois's using the term *Negro* in this way was not at all casual or incidental, but reflected a controversial investment in the relationship between language and socioeconomic structures. That controversy was neatly outlined in the well-known correspondence he had with the South Bend, Indiana, high school sophomore, Roland Barton, who initiated the exchange by writing on January 26, 1928: "the word 'Negro' is a white man's word to make us feel inferior."[1] At the time, *Negro* was a radical designation for those descended from African peoples who were enslaved in the Americas. Du Bois was a forceful proponent of the term, finding it "etymologically and phonetically much better and more logical than . . . 'colored' or any of the various hyphenated circumlocutions" in designating the "group of people."[2] While conceding that *Negro* "is not 'historically' accurate," he thought that, more than merely skin color or phenotype, it denoted a historical collective consciousness, a willful and transformative intelligence. As he wrote in reply to Barton:

> Suppose that we slip out of the whole thing by calling ourselves "Americans." But in that case, what word shall we use when we want to talk about those descendants of dark slaves who are largely excluded still from full American citizenship and from complete social privilege with white folk? Here is something that we want to talk about; that we do talk about; that we Negroes could not live without talking about. In that case, we need a name for it, do we not? In order to talk logically and easily and be understood . . .
>
> And then too, without the word that means us, where are all those spiritual ideals, those inner bonds, those group ideals and forward strivings of this mighty army of 12 millions? Shall we abolish these with the abolition of a name? Do we want to abolish them? Of course we do not. They are our most precious heritage.[3]

Du Bois's decision to publish his full exchange with Barton over the term *Negro* in the March 1928 issue of *Crisis* had everything to do with the NAACP campaign he was leading for its capitalization, which resulted in the *New York Times* announcing in an editorial published exactly two years later that it would capitalize the word as "an act in recognition of racial self-respect for those who have been for generations in the 'lower case.'"[4] For the most part, Du Bois uses the term to designate a specific type of human intelligence actualized in a specific people under specific historical circumstances, what he refers to as "the Negro." But in that usage, there is constantly at play a set of conceptual issues related to the prospects of the species as a whole, for which this specific type of intelligence and people are a heuristic. As for those conceptual issues, Du Bois's attention was on how the existence of any given particular population as a collective actor in history, and supposedly therefore an agent of change, is a function of known and discernable configurations and transformations of power. One might well add that these configurations and transformations are exclusively in the mode of human institutions, which delineate ranges of possible activity, usually through directing our desires by capturing or managing our imagination, spawning certain types of subjects and certain practices-of-living. Conceptually, *Negro* designates practical humanistic ways of life, as well as the ways of thinking concomitant with those practices and the modes of knowing they in turn facilitate. It connotes a historical process with determinate inception and multiplicious vectors. Those practices-of-living, thinking, and knowledge thrived at the interstices of an American political economy that was itself undergoing profound transformations in its configuration as it shifted from the European-centered national market system of imperialist colonialism into the U.S.-centered anti-imperialist international financial system emerging in the period coincidental with the end of Reconstruction in 1868. Positing *Negro* as designating a distinctive manifestation of human intelligence and agency in-community, as it were, Du Bois is confronted, however, with two fundamental problems of representation. On the one hand, there is the formal challenge of giving an adequate representation of *Negro* as the figuration of an intelligence that is not epistemological or ontological but literary, or more precisely poetic. On the other hand, there is the challenge of representing and studying the Negro as a socioeconomic and political fact that indicates the limits of American power as the vanguard of international finance capitalism. The Negro seems destined to be exterminated under that system as a life-form ill-suited for it—this is the gist of what those in power, such as Nathaniel Shaler, meant by "the Negro problem." But then again, *Negro* denotes the extent to which that power suffers a strange forgetfulness of its humanistic ideals. "Of the Coming of John" was the first and, given the wide international circulation of *The Souls of Black Folk*, best-known instance of Du Bois's attempt to tackle both the formal and political problems of representation. What makes the short story stand out from the other essays in the book is the political engagement's being a function of the formal experiment. It is the formal performance that achieves its political significance.

Without rehearsing the already familiar context of the attempt to move beyond the distinctions of naturalism and realism, the formal challenge was, as Du Bois states in the postscript to his novel *The Ordeal of Mansart* (the first volume of *The Black Flame Trilogy*), "to interpret historical truth by use of creative imagination. . . . It is possible for the creative artist to imagine something of . . . what men thought, the actual words they used, the feelings and motives which impelled them."⁵ This requires a narrative form that can engage the historical without historicism and can take up the question of the conditions of thinking without falling into the metaphysical habit of the traditions of philosophy and psychology. In other words, a style that immediately expresses the full affective force of the thinking coincidental with the events of social formation, depicting what used to be called the human condition in a strikingly dynamic historical way. At stake, above all, in this style of narration is the possibility of thinking change.⁶ This has no small consequence, I think, for how we situate his bricolage experiments in relation to the development of modernism in English-language literature as an aspect of an international style of expression and thought. My point is that his experiments in narrative style are germane to how the problematic of representing *Negro* intelligence is engaged by Du Bois. However unmasterful they may be in literary craft, his formal experiments, beginning with "Of the Coming of John" as the first published example, strive to do more than merely display a poetic capacity; they aim at narrating a thinking-in-action that, being in the world, works to transform it. Grappling with the narration, the style of Jones's thinking brings us closer to finding a way of thinking that is eventful and moves us that much farther away from the necessity to think categorically.

There is some controversy among scholarly readers of Du Bois over how to read "Of the Coming of John" in relation to Du Bois's overall project, which turns on the significance of its evocations of Wagner's *Lohengrin* opera, mostly at the conclusion of the story. In light of that controversy, the Metropolitan Opera scene warrants careful reading, giving thoughtful attention to its style, which will entail marking and following its filiations with the other essays in *The Souls of Black Folk*, as well as elements in Du Bois's overall monumental corpus.⁷ Having the fullest sense of what is at play in that scene, however, requires knowing what Jones is doing in New York, who he is, and where he came from, all of which is provided by the lengthy five-page opening exposition, justifiably called the teacher's tale.

The opening paragraph of the story offers little more than a brief description of the situation and isolated location of the Wells Institute, reporting on its two large buildings at the outskirts of Johnstown, removed from any regular dealings with the city's whites. What follows is a sense of Jones as a student: never on time, bedraggled, awkward, and ill-kempt, yet so good natured and forthright that "one glance at his face made one forgive him much." He is a person of "bubbling good-nature and genuine satisfaction with the world."⁸ It isn't until the third paragraph that some of his background is provided: "He came to us from Altamaha, away down there beneath the gnarled oaks of Southeastern Georgia, where the sea croons to the sands and the sands listen till they sink half drowned beneath the waters, rising only here and there in long, low islands." This picturesque description of Jones's hometown in the South sets up an analepsis or flashback to a time before he came to the institute that begins with the second sentence of the paragraph: "The white folk of Altamaha voted John a good boy,—fine plough-hand, good in the rice-fields, handy everywhere, and always good-natured and respectful." That analepsis is a lengthy interlude of four and a half paragraphs, amounting to a fifth of the entire exposition. Still recounting events from the familiar limited omniscient third-person perspective of the teacher's tale, its function is twofold. Utilizing direct discourse, it presents the background events most crucial to the subsequent action of the story, recounting the white folk of Altamaha's trepidation over Jones mother's decision to send him off to school: "'It'll spoil him,—ruin him,' they said." In contrast, is the black folk's sending him off to Wells Institute in Johnstown with high hopes, taking up the refrain "When John comes," which is reported to have been said so often it becomes a lingering quasi-messianic legend: "And they that stood behind that morning in Altamaha . . . had thereafter one ever-recurring word,—'When John comes.' Then what parties were to be, and what speakings in the churches; what new furniture in the front room,—perhaps even a new front room; and there would be a new schoolhouse, with John as teacher . . . all this and more—when John comes."[9] This refrain is much appreciated by Judge Henderson, reigning patriarch of the planter family that had owned Jones's father. Not in reference to Jones, but rather to his own son, John, the close childhood playmate Jones encounters in New York, who was then away at Princeton. The account of how the refrain comes to acquire the force of an oracular motto goes to the second aspect of the interlude's function, which is to foreshadow the story's denouement when both Johns come back to Altamaha; this is clearly given in its concluding paragraph:

> Thus in the far-away Southern village the world lay waiting, half consciously, the coming of two young men, and dreamed in an inarticulate way of new things that would be done and new thoughts that all would think. And yet it was singular that few thought of two Johns,—for the black folk thought of one John, and he was black; and the white folk thought of another John, and he was white. And neither world thought the other world's thought, save with a vague unrest.[10]

In recounting how these two aspects of this world share the refrain created by the blacks, the interlude portrays what Du Bois earlier on in the ninth chapter, "Of the Sons of Master and Man," calls the "essential part to a proper description of the South . . . in fine, the atmosphere of the land, the thought and feeling, the thousand and one little actions which go to make up life . . . and [are] yet most essential to any clear conception of the group life taken as a whole."[11] Whereas, as he states in that chapter, these little actions elude the comprehension of statistics and sociological analysis of the social reality of "neo-slavery"—to deploy Arnold Rampersad's term for what Du Bois describes in the second chapter, "Of the Dawn of Freedom," as the peonage of the post-Reconstruction South—they can be portrayed in the short story.[12] And what gets portrayed is a Southern town where "as deep a storm and stress of human souls, as intense a ferment of feeling, as intricate a writhing of spirit, as ever a people experienced"; where "within and without the somber veil of color vast social forces have been at work."[13] This story of the refrain presents a world in which both the black and white aspects of the world share the exact same language, more precisely the exact same expressions, but with radically different references and meanings. Showing thereby how "despite much physical contact and daily intermingling, there is almost no community of intellectual life or point of transference where thoughts and feelings of one race can come into direct contact and sympathy with the thoughts and feelings of the other."[14] Yet, even this statement taken from "Of the Sons of Master and Man" intimates what the Altamaha interlude demonstrates, which is that the veil is more porous in one direction than it is in another, so that thoughts and feelings from "without" do come across "within." It's just not so in the other direction, which is why the white world cannot see "the Negro as he really is," to evoke an earlier essay of Du Bois's that finds its way in *The Souls of Black Folk* revised as two chapters, "Of the Black Belt" and "Of the Quest for the Golden Fleece."[15] This portrayal of the veil precluding reciprocal recognition of one world's thoughts—and in the story it is only thoughts, attended by vague unrest—by the other also foreshadows the story's climax in New York City.

Foreshadowing Altamaha interlude aside, in the main, the teacher's tale recounts the Wells Institute faculty's concern about Jones's initial difficulty adjusting to scholarly life and his troublesome behavior, resulting in his expulsion from Wells for a term by the dean, who agrees not to inform Jones's mother of the fact and to readmit him after a year of his working in Johnstown. Eliding the one-year period Jones spends in the city away from the Wells Institute, the last two paragraphs of the exposition focus on his dedicated struggle to acquire a solid liberal arts education and how that education changed him "in body and soul." A progressive shift in perspective begins midway through the last paragraph, however, with the last passage that is clearly from the teacher's limited external perspective, which consists of two sentences beginning with: "And we who saw daily a new thoughtfulness growing in his eyes began to expect something of this plodding boy."[16] This marks a correspondence between the externally discernable changes engendered by Jones's acquiring a liberal arts education and the change in how the faculty perceive him. That correspondence is emphasized in the next sentence with its conjunctive adverbial clause: "Thus he passed out of the preparatory school into college, and we who watched him felt four more years of change, which almost transformed the tall, grave man who bowed to us commencement morning."[17]

But just what is transformative about that education? The answer is suggested in the penultimate, tenth paragraph of the exposition, which begins the account of Jones's struggle to acquire a solid liberal arts education. His earlier formation in the atmosphere of Altamaha proves a hindrance. As the Altamaha interlude shows, its social structures articulate an order of thought that enables the members of the community to correctly link the events occurring in the world (bodies, objects, material, gestures, discourses: the thousand and one little actions Du Bois refers to as making life) to descriptions and expressions in a way that reinforces, or simply enforces how each member thinks and feels as someone living in the world. We might call the articulation of such structures a "grammar of sociality," indexing its function as articulating and enforcing communal intersubjectivity. Corollarily, we might regard its linkages as an assemblage of conceptual, perceptual schemata, an architectonic that achieves a type of subject and mind properly integrated into the social order. Given how the grammar of Altamaha is geared almost exclusively toward the practical economic problems of neo-slavery capitalism, the type of subject and mind it fosters, the "always good-natured and respectful darkie," is unsuitable to the grammar articulated in the humanist education of Wells Institute, which enables a radically different type of subject, the grounding subject of knowledge. The teacher reports on Jones's unsuitability in this way: "It was a hard struggle, for things did not come easily to him,—few crowding memories of early life and teaching came to help him on his new way; but all the world toward which he strove was of his own building, and he builded slow and hard."[18]

This should not be taken as an account of a failure of translation—the absolute unfungiblity of the neo-slave subject into the economy of Enlightenment knowledge; rather, it is an account of what happens with the confluence of two incommensurable grammars, what happens in the break. There is no total deracination of the neo-slave subject; the memories of his formation and its grammar crowd Jones, some of them, albeit few, being of use. There is a key point in our earlier discussion of the Altamaha's bifurcated thought-world sharing a single language and expression that must be emphasized here. The shared refrain, "When John comes," was *created* by the blacks, who, under the pressure of being constituted as a separate community in accordance with the socially and legally enforced grammar of segregation, have achieved their own grammar, articulating the thousand and one little actions that make up life into a particular order of conceptual schemata, a distinctive pattern of thought and feeling.

Du Bois refers to this pattern in the opening chapter of *The Souls of Black Folk*, "Of Our Spiritual Strivings," as black folk being "gifted with second-sight in this American world, ... which yields him no true self-consciousness, but only lets him see himself through the revelation of the other world."[19] Further elaborating on "this sense of always looking at one's self through the eyes of others, of measuring one's soul by the tape of a world that looks on in amused contempt and pity," he labels it the "peculiar sensation [of] double consciousness," which he then describes in language approaching diagnosis of some sort of personality disorder: "It is a peculiar sensation, this double consciousness, this sense of always looking at one's self through the eyes of others, of measuring one's soul by the tape of a world that looks on in amused contempt and pity. One ever feels his twoness—an American, a Negro; two thoughts, two unreconciled strivings; two warring ideals in one dark body, whose dogged strength alone keeps it from being torn asunder."[20]

This is the only occurrence of the term "double consciousness" in the entire volume, and Du Bois never subsequently expounded or elaborated on it, having, as Ernest Allen once remarked, almost immediately put it up for adoption. Nevertheless, these two sentences have been among the most frequently invoked, studied, and belabored from *The Souls of Black Folk*. And they have been so across a wide variety of fields of scholarly research, from sociology and African American literary studies, to multiculturalism and postcolonial studies, the general consensus being that Du Bois's usage of "double consciousness" refers to some sort of dual or multiple consciousness as a psychic state.[21] This considerable, wide-ranging investment in Du Bois's usage of double consciousness has fostered a preponderance of speculation and research into its provenance, with two lineages being primary areas of interest. One is the prior nineteenth-century literary expressions of duality or conflict in consciousness, particularly in the work of American Transcendentalists and European Romantics, with Emerson's 1841 essay, "The Transcendentalist," being the frequently cited example of the former, and Goethe's tragic play, *Faust*, which is held to be an inspiration for it, the latter.[22] The other is the clinical and experimental psychology of William James and Alfred Binet.

Pursuit of the literary lineage has been wholly speculative and circumstantial, whereas that of experimental psychology has direct evidentiary support in the corpus of Du Bois's work and intellectual biography. We can reasonably assume the likelihood of James's *The Principles of Psychology* providing at least some inspiration for Du Bois's usage of "double consciousness," given that during the time he studied experimental psychology under James at Harvard, much of the material of James's lectures came from that book.[23] Through his engagement with James, Du Bois encountered Binet's work, as well as that of Wilhelm Wundt. On this assumption, reading with the consensus, the clearest resonance of Du Bois's description of the psychosomatic effect of looking at one's self through the eyes of disdainful others is with James's account of what he labeled "pathological cases known as those of double or alternate personality." That account, which occurs well into the tenth chapter of *The Principles of Psychology*, "The Consciousness of Self," is a consideration of what James took to be "mutations of the self" and is more precisely focused on, in his language, "alternating personality"—called in current clinical vocabulary "dissociative identity disorder"—as an effect of lapses of memory. At the time James was writing, the chief method for diagnosing this disorder was hypnosis, and the primary, most famous case study, with which he begins his account, was that of Félida X, reported in Dr. Étienne Eugène Azam's *Hypnotisme, double conscience et altérations de la personnalité*.[24] When Du Bois's usage of the term "double consciousness" is held to be in relation to, or somehow informed by this aspect of James's work, then it does indeed reference a psychic disturbance or disorder.

An even older preoccupation in the long history of engaging and invoking Du Bois's usage of "double consciousness" than its provenance, however, has been determining the etiology of this psychic dualism. Informed as it was by James's *Psychology*, Du Bois's description of consciousness seriously challenged the then-prevailing phylogenetic biological account of racial diversity and hierarchical difference, espoused by prominent scientists such as Francis Galton, Louis Agassiz, and Nathaniel Shaler. Indeed, there is ample material in Du Bois's paradigmatic 1899 empirical study of an urban social group, *The Philadelphia Negro*, to support Daryl Scott's assessment that he was one of the first social scientists to engage in psychological sociology, postulating the sociogenesis of personality.[25] The etiological question arose in the earliest scholarly engagement with Du Bois's reference to "double consciousness" as an analytic concept in the study of race relations among his fellow sociologists. Two lines of thought occur here as well. On the one hand, there was the prevailing phylogenetic biological account, identifying miscegenation as the cause of Du Bois's double consciousness, both as an analytical concept and as a biographical "fact." A prime example of this line is found in John Moffatt Mecklin's 1914 book, *Democracy and Race Friction; A Study in Social Ethics*, which appears to be the earliest published scholarly engagement with the etiological question that expressly cites Du Bois.[26] Relying rather heavily on Gabriel Tarde's theories of group mind and imitation, along with Herbert Spencer's theory of social evolution, Mecklin adduces the passage from "Of Our Spiritual Strivings" in support of the proposition that double consciousness was the inherent psychic state of the mulatto personality precisely because he is a biological hybrid. On this account, it is a personality disorder with pathological consequence for both the individual and the society.[27] This line would persist, gaining momentum in, for instance, Alexander Johnson's behavioralist reduction of social problems to ontogenetic pathologies.

The other etiological theory is a structuralist, sociogenetic one, according to which double consciousness is the subjective manifestation of transformative social forces. This was the line taken up by Robert Ezra Park, one of the central figures in the Chicago School of Sociology, who in his 1923 essay, "Negro Race Consciousness as Reflected in Race Literature," invoked the same "Of Our Spiritual Strivings" passage as a credible account of "an experience that comes sometime in life to every Negro," and not merely the mulatto.[28] As such, it is an introspective recognition of conflict that is "itself the manifestation of a new race-consciousness," although one whose motivating desire is, in Park's terms, "amalgamation."[29] Five years later in "Human Migration and the Marginal Man," Park developed this identification of becoming mulatto with a type of consciousness into his well-known and influential theory of the marginal man: "Ordinarily the marginal man is a mixed blood, like the Mulatto in the United States or the Eurasian in Asia, but that is apparently because the man of mixed blood is one who lives in two worlds, in both of which he is more or less of a stranger."[30] Even though Park's account of the etiology of double consciousness suggests structural social causality, contrary to Mecklin's biological phylogenetic one, it still presumes a correlation, if not a simple isomorphic relation, between the sociological and the biological. He remarks elsewhere: "What I have called the mentality of racial hybrid—that is to say, his peculiar mental bias, the character of the intelligence which he displays, and the general level of the intellectual life he has achieved—is very largely due to the social situation in which his mixed origin inevitably puts him. He is biologically the product of divergent racial stocks, but just because of that fact he is, at the same time, the cultural product of two distinct traditions. He is, so to speak, a cultural as well as a racial hybrid."[31]

Park's interpretation of Du Bois's usage of the term "double consciousness" became ascendant, and very much remains so.[32] Such a reading finds some support in Du Bois's own description of the psychosomatic effects of having to constantly struggle against nonrecognition as well as his subsequently remarking, "The history of the American Negro is the history of this strife,—this longing to attain self-conscious manhood, to merge his double self into a better and truer self . . . to be a co-worker in the kingdom of culture." Construing in this way Du Bois's usage "of double consciousness" to mean psychic dualism requires giving disproportionate weight to those remarks, along with reading the description of psychosomatic effect as resonant with the already mentioned account of alternating personality near the end of the tenth chapter in James's *Psychology*.

We construe things differently, however, if we read that description as resonant instead with the theory of self-consciousness set out at the beginning of that same chapter of James's book, in the section on "The Empirical Self or Me."

Having set out the four constituent elements of self-consciousness—the material Self, the social Self, the spiritual Self, and the pure Ego[33]—James states: "*A man's Social Self* is the recognition which he gets from his mates." Elaborating this social recognition is essential to our psychic well-being, he concludes that total nonrecognition would engender "a kind of rage and impotent despair . . . from which the cruellest [*sic*] bodily tortures would be a relief."[34] James goes on to account for the sociodynamic character of this self-consciousness; it is, for the most part, a function of collective interaction in relation to social institutions and activity, within which he includes love, from the erotic to the collective. James's elaboration in this section moves toward providing a functionalist account of self-consciousness, according to which even the constituent "Spiritual Self . . . so far as it belongs to the Empirical Me . . . means . . . psychic faculties or dispositions, taken concretely; not the bare principle of personal Unity, or 'pure' Ego."[35] This account of the constituent elements of empirical self-consciousness sets James well on the course to what will become his radical empiricism and his postulating consciousness has no existence as an entity, as a primary substance of being in contrast to material things, out of which our thoughts of them are made. The point is not that thoughts don't exist; undoubtedly they do, but there is "a function in experience that thoughts perform and for the performance of which 'consciousness' as a quality of being is invoked. The function is knowing, and 'consciousness' is supposed necessary to explain the fact that things not only are, but get reported, are known."[36] James is alluding to Kant's Transcendental Deduction of the *Critique of Pure Reason*, which, pursuant to its agenda of discovering the requisite faculties thinking beings need to have cognizance of the world, distinguishes between thinking something and having even phenomenal knowledge of it. And by his account, if the fruit of Kant's endeavor, "the transcendental ego," undermined the soul and put the Cartesian body/soul bipolarity off balance, it then established as fact that experience is indefeasibly dualistic in structure, so that the fundamental Kantian proposition is epistemic dualism.[37] Consciousness in the Kantian system is the logical correlative of content in an experience, the peculiarity of which is "that *fact comes to light* in it, that *awareness of content* takes place," even though we cannot have any direct phenomenal (experiential) evidence of its being there; hence its epistemological necessity as a first principle.[38] To be self-conscious, or conscious of having will, in the Kantian way "means only that certain contents, for which 'self' and 'effort of will' are the names, are not without witness as they occur."[39]

Contra the Kantian thesis of epistemic dualism, James's radical empiricist thesis is that there is only one primal stuff or material in the world that constitutes everything, which he called "pure experience." On this thesis—which aligns with the neutral monism James came to expose, holding that both conscious mental properties and physical properties are derived from a primal reality that is itself neither mental nor physical—knowing as a function of mind can easily be explained as a particular sort of relation toward one another into which portions of pure experience may enter. The relation itself is a part of pure experience; one of its terms becoming the subject or bearer of the knowledge, the knower, the other becomes the object known.[40] A key task of *Principles of Psychology* is to demonstrate that there is no need for any knower other than the stream of thought itself, identified with continuous self-consciousness. As for the individualized self, it is part of the content of the world experienced, which James also called the "field of consciousness," maintaining that it "comes at all times with our body as its centre, centre of vision, centre of action, centre of interest."[41] There lies in the body a systematization of things, of everything with reference to focused action and interest. As for the activity of thoughts and feelings, these also terminate in the activity of the body, "only through first arousing its activities can they begin to change those of the rest of the world."[42] On this basis, James then offers the formulation that will be so crucial for Edmund Husserl in his own phenomenology and subsequently for Maurice Merleau-Ponty as well: "The body is the storm centre, the origin of co-ordinates, the constant place of stress in all that experience-train."[43] This means that "I" is primarily a noun of position, just like "this" and "here," but not in the Kantian sense of merely a necessary logical, purely propositional and hence conceptual correlate for knowledge. The positioning of the self indexes a complexity—James's term is "plurality"—of relations in experience that articulate the field of consciousness in their dynamic interactivity.

A central concept, some might say *the* central concept of James's thought, is the reflex action theory, which he took to be a "fundamental and well established . . . doctrine" of scientific physiology, according to which "the acts we perform are always the result of outward discharges from the nervous centres, and these outward discharges are themselves the result of impressions from the external world, carried along one or another of our sensory nerves."[44] The physiological study of reflex action attended to neural functioning and structure in relation to external stimuli.[45] Proclaiming the speculative consequences of physiology's explorations into the function of reflex action in the constitution and integrity of the physical organism "dominates all the new work done in psychology,"[46] James offers a classical Cartesian division of the structural unit of the nervous system into the "departments" of sensation or perception; the central process of reflection is akin to Aristotelian imagination, but James calls it "synonymously thinking"; and reaction or behavioral response. In terms of physiological function, sensory impression exists only for the sake of "awaking the central process of reflection," which is to say thinking.[47] The latter exists only for the sake of calling forth the final act: the behavioral response to the external stimuli. "All action is thus re-action upon the outer world," James concludes; "and the middle stage of consideration or contemplation or thinking is only a place of transit, the bottom of a loop, both whose ends have their point of application in the outer world . . . In plainer English, perception and thinking are only there for behavior's sake."[48] We can state this summarily as the proposition governing all James's theorizing about consciousness: *Access to phenomena lies in experience and the basis of the phenomena lies in the body.* Admittedly, there is a pronounced, unresolved inner tension in James's psychology between the phenomenological analysis entailed in his doctrine of pure experience, and the causal-explanatory account of experience in his physiological realism.[49] While this methodological admixture may very well rescue James from Husserl's transcendental turn to subjectivism, it does not disentangle him from the psychophysical problem plaguing psychology since Descartes.[50] When it comes to the foundations of the social self, James's psychology falls into methodological individualism, the doctrine introduced into sociology by Max Weber, which explains social phenomena as resulting from individual actions determined by the motivating intentional states of individual actors.[51]

Du Bois avoids such entanglement, not by disregarding or trivializing the physiological, but by recognizing the experience of the body centering the "field of consciousness" is itself gained in accord with the symbolic order of the social. This is akin to what Paul Schilder designates as "body-image" in his 1934 essay, "The Somato-Psyche in Psychiatry and Social Psychology," which he maintains is partially based on sensations and partially on representations and thoughts and is in many respects different from the actual body. "The body-image belongs to the community," Schilder states. "Whatever we may do the body images are never isolated. There is a continual interchange between our own body image and the body images of others."[52] Even though Du Bois does not explicitly refer to body image, or to the concept of the body for that matter, his adhering to James's theory of the material self, along with its investment in reflex action theory, leads one way or another to a critique of the social articulation of what the body-image signifies about the persona assumed in association with it. To the extent body-image involves not only conscious perception of the body (body-awareness) but also beliefs and affective attitudes that can be made conscious, then the specifics of those beliefs and attitudes, their organization into a distinctive order of things, are of paramount significance.[53]

Along these lines, we can now read Du Bois's asserting that the Negro self-consciousness consists of two warring ideals in one dark body to mean little more than an individual's entailing two social selves. Leaving aside for now the pressing question of embodiment implied here, to which we will attend in some detail later on, to the extent consciousness is taken to be a set or series of representations in interrelation with phenomenal events (neural change or activity as well as external nonpsychic phenomena), the duality is of two different parallel series of representations. Insofar as that activity of interrelation is material, a function of societal structures and forces interacting in the experienced world (the field of consciousness), then Du Bois's usage of "double consciousness" refers to an extreme breakdown in the normative processes of socialization internalized by the Negro, resulting in a psychic disturbance of a different type than dissociative identity disorder. The Negro's psychic disturbance at non- or misrecognition is aligned with a general societal turmoil. In some sense, this is the rhetorical thrust of Du Bois's usage, highlighting a general social anxiety about cultural miscegenation—defiling admixture—in order to diffuse it. Accordingly, the striving of the two souls can be construed as two orders of psychic personification, reflecting social formations and functions. As psychic states, they are different orders of thinking (ways of cognizance), two modes of personification. One of these is autonomous or free, in the practical sense of a spontaneously motivated will: consciousness determining itself for itself independent of its physical impulses and necessities, including fear for its survival. The other is heteronomous, again in the practical sense of a will governed by some external force or authority—this is the Negro personality construed as natural or primitive man, ruled by his physical desires and inclinations, so needing the moral tutelage of civilization.

At stake is the distinction between nature, or rather the physical laws of nature, and freedom in Kant's account of it as a transcendental idea. The transcendental idea of freedom is the faculty of beginning a state from itself, without any other cause determining it in time in accordance with the law of nature. Du Bois's common cause with James in rejecting the Kantian transcendental ego is expressly stated in the unpublished 1889 essay, "The Renaissance of Ethics," written for the course he took with James at Harvard during the 1888–1889 academic year called "Philosophy IV," in which he equates Kant's deontological ethics—particularly its predicating duty (the ought) on the order of transcendental reason—with Scholastic metaphysics, then dismisses both as "fake theories."[54] The problem is, the transcendental ego's being a logical correlate of the functioning of cognition implies that its integrity is isomorphic with the integrity of reasoning knowledge. More precisely, the apophantic judgment of the transcendental logic as set out in the Deduction is defined as the field of truth or error not only of propositions but also knowledge of the phenomenal world. All sensorial perception, down to the most elementary intuitions, as well as all associated discrete images, whether of empirical phenomena or imagination, with their attendant concepts, are necessarily in relation to the "I think," a relationship Kant describes as "an act of spontaneity." And he means by this that thinking as the activity of synthesis in representation of things is free from—as in not at all determined by in any causal way—its representations. It works completely independent of those representations, in the sense that "it cannot be regarded as belonging to sensibility." Such an analysis, which Kant termed in the first edition of *Critique of Pure Reason* "Transcendental Psychology," may aim to give an account of self-consciousness—consciousness of myself in thought in general—but it cannot provide any knowledge about what sort of thing a thinking being is. Du Bois's concern with consciousness is not transcendental in that sense, and expressly so; nor is it epistemological, at least not in the sense of treating thinking as isomorphic with discursive structures that are fundamentally propositional and apodictic.

Put another way more in keeping with current phenomenological theories of consciousness, Du Bois's usage of the phrase "double consciousness" describes a socially extended consciousness, not in the sense that the individual mind, the integrity of its self-consciousness already established, extends itself into the world, but rather in the sense that the mind is constituted with and in the world. While even the most minimal form of pre-reflective self-consciousness—as a constant feature, whether structural or functional, of conscious experience—may be present, whenever I am living through an experience, whenever I am consciously perceiving the world, it is never an event alone, never a moment reduced in isolation and fully disengaged from, or unaware of other perceiving minds.[55] Even though experience always has a subjective feel to it, it has this in relation to others feeling so too. Of course there is subjective experience, but it is always already social—social, not intersubjective, because none of these subjects, not even at the pre-reflective level, have come into being alone. It is in this way that self-consciousness is embodied and embedded in the world—meaning in the complexity of material environmental forces, that chaotic spontaneity of aggregation and disaggregation of physical phenomena, including the neural network of the brain, but also including the activity of humanity that constitutes and sustains society and its various institutional practices. So, paraphrasing John Tyndall, the passage from the physics of the brain to the corresponding facts of consciousness is unthinkable without the social.[56] This is not to imply consciousness is heterogeneous from physical matter, or even that it is an epiphenomenon of the matter. Rather, working from the postulate of the causal efficacy of consciousness put forward by James, Du Bois presumes the "fact" of spontaneity as intelligence: he is a self-activating being, both formally and phenomenally, and so he is not at all concerned in any explicit way with the question of how he knows he is such. What concerns him is *how* he *is* such in relation to his generally perceived thingness. As he states in "Of Alexander Crummell":

> The nineteenth was the first century of human sympathy,—the age when half wonderingly we began to descry in others that transfigured spark of divinity which we call Myself; when clodhoppers and peasants, and tramps and thieves, and millionaires and—sometimes—Negroes, became throbbing souls whose warm pulsing life touched us so nearly that we half gasped with surprise, crying, "Thou too! Hast Thou seen Sorrow and the dull waters of Hopelessness? Hast Thou known Life?"[57]

But if this is so, then what account can there be of the distinction Du Bois makes between being Negro and American that does not revert to an idealism, according to which the two different orders of representation lose their distinction, their putative heterogeneity, in an overarching absolute order: the transcendental ego? A question warranted by Du Bois's characterizing the Negro struggle of two unreconciled souls as "longing to attain self-conscious manhood, to merge his double self into a better and truer self. In this merging he wishes neither of the older selves to be lost." What follows this seems to underscore some investment in salvation through the synthetic unity of admixture: "He would not Africanize America, for America has too much to teach the world and Africa. He would not bleach his Negro soul in a flood of white Americanism, for he knows that Negro blood has a message for the world. He simply wishes to make it possible for a man to be both a Negro and an American, without being cursed and spit upon by his fellows, without having the doors of Opportunity closed roughly in his face."[58]

Casting this longing in terms of social justice raises a different, pertinently related question: What do the terms *Negro* and *American* denote in Du Bois's usage of them? Part of the answer to the question can be found by attending to the differences between the "Of Our Spiritual Striving" passage and the earlier 1897 *Atlantic Monthly* essay, "Strivings of the Negro People," italicizing the relevant segments: "*He does not wish to* Africanize America, for America has too much to teach the world and Africa; *he does not wish to* bleach his Negro soul in a flood of white Americanism, *for he believes—foolishly, perhaps, but fervently*—that Negro blood has *yet* a message for the world. He simply wishes to make it possible for a man to be both a Negro and an American, without being cursed and spit upon by his fellows, *without losing the opportunity of self development.*"[59] The substitution of the repeated "He does not wish" with "He would not" and breaking the one sentence into two does more than slow down the rhythmic flow; it diminishes the volitional force that carriers through to, "He simply wishes." Even put privatively, the expression of the Negro wishing signals an autonomous structure of desire. It foregrounds what the Negro wants, while "would" suggests the more passive position of not being a threat. In contrast, the substitution of "for he believes—foolishly, perhaps, but fervently—" with "for he knows," along with the removal of "yet," is a more forceful expression of the conviction the Negro is a creative force of world significance, not as a matter of opinion, but of fact. That more forceful expression in the revision, however, further diminishes what was already a very forceful expression of self-conscious will in the earlier version. Stating the simple fact that the Negro has a message is not the same as reporting the Negro's willful (fervent) determination to have a message still. There is a shift in perspective from what the Negro wants to what the Negro is perceived by whites to be. This shift is firmly set with the revision of "without losing the opportunity of self development" as "without having the doors of Opportunity closed roughly in his face." In both versions, it is all about adjusting what the white world perceives the Negro to signify. In the 1897 *Atlantic Monthly* essay, however, the adjustment is sought through assertion of Negro desire, showing that not only does the Negro not desire the dissolution of the putative cultural grounds of the republic, but the Negro positively wants the actualization of the highest ideal of the republic: individual freedom and development.[60] This gets reinforced two paragraphs later in the *Atlantic Monthly* essay where Du Bois writes: "In the days of bondage they thought to see in one divine event the end of all doubt and disappointment; eighteenth-century Rousseauism never worshipped Freedom with half the unquestioning faith that the American Negro did for two centuries. To him, slavery was indeed the sum of all villainies, the cause of all sorrow, the root of all prejudice; emancipation was the key to a promised land of sweeter beauty than ever stretched before the eyes of wearied Israelites. In song and exhortation swelled one refrain—Liberty."[61] In keeping with the perspectival shift, the invocation of Rousseauian freedom is erased in "Of Our Spiritual Strivings," its valence being assimilated to a more qualifying appositive added to the second sentence so it reads: "To him, so far as he thought and dreamed, slavery was indeed the sum of all villainies." These changes, along with the capitalized "Emancipation," are significant. They cast the Negro investment in freedom as a psychological disposition fully in keeping with the revision's title, whereas, in "Strivings of the Negro People," the Negro investment in freedom is not only expressly political, it is more radical than eighteenth-century Rousseauism. This raises the question of where in freedom that investment lay.

Rousseau's theory of freedom is a definitive element of his philosophical treatise, *The Social Contract*, which itself belongs to the lineage of European political philosophy traceable from Hobbes's effort to address the crisis of state after the English Civil War. At issue was determining under what conditions people form a political society constituting a commonwealth by entering a covenant of mutual obligation. The contract Rousseau describes is not meant to depict a historical event, but rather to serve as a normative ideal, in light of which the nature and justification, or want thereof, of existing institutions of political society are better comprehended. In that mode, what is described is the political system people would assent to without coercion. The beginning is in anthropology—a hypothetical general state of nature, "natural freedom," according to which man is physically free because he is not constrained by a repressive state apparatus or dominated by his fellow men. This hypothetical anthropology functions to provide a basis for understanding the justification for existing institutions of political society in order to gain an ideal of freedom that, in turn, grounds a viable theory of political transformation. The result is a speculative mapping of how to arrive at a political society that *changes* humanity from being creatures of nature like the rest of the animal species on the planet into moral beings who preserve their natural freedom through internally driven restraint based on reason. In the state of natural freedom, individuals' self-preservation is predicated on their perceived right to take possession of whatever they want, when and however they can. This freedom to take possession is not to be confused with property rights, which, as will be seen in a moment, Rousseau thought to be a consequence of the contract. It is rather, a state of nature in which there are no effective external restraints on an individual's desires or effort to realize those desires, except the presence of other such individuals. Although no external forces can absolutely curtail this "possessive individualism," there is a natural morality grounded in reason that is the seat of empathy as well as primitive forms of sociality, such as the family. Because such relatively unbridled individualism as a general state of nature threatens species extinction, those same individuals, being rational creatures and fearing extinction, form what Rousseau terms "an aggregation of force [*agrégation une somme de forces*]" in order to achieve greater security in common for the primary instruments of self-preservation than they can as independent individuals. In so doing, however, they confront the dilemma that in forfeiting their natural freedom, they risk losing those very instruments. The nature of things being what they are, the only viable social contract is one based on the stipulation of "the total alienation of each [individual] associate, together with all his rights to [possession], to the whole community."[62] The most important aspect of this total alienation is that in taking over the goods of individuals, the community, far from despoiling them, simply assures them as legitimate possession, changing usurpation—which is possession through simple seizure in the state of nature—into a true right and enjoyment as proprietorship. Thus those with possessions, who are now constituted in the contract as "depositaries of the public good, with their rights respected by all members of the State and maintained against foreign aggression by all its forces, have, by a cession that is advantageous both for the public and even more themselves, acquired, so to speak, all that they gave up."[63] Developing that line of thought, the viable political system unreservedly based on total alienation should offer its associates three forms of freedom: civil freedom, democratic freedom, and moral freedom. Bear in mind, the associates do not enter into the social contract to *become* free. They already *are* free, motivated to become mutually obligated through total alienation by the desire to preserve themselves and their possessions. Yet, the fullest realization of their freedom, in all its forms, is a direct consequence of the political system. Total alienation of possessive individualism to community possession guarantees the individual's "right to property." That is the ironic gist of the opening line to the first chapter of book 1 in *The Social Contract*: "Man is born free, and everywhere he is in chains."[64]

Regarded in relation to the Negro's situation in the American political system, Rousseau's theory of total alienation to the community was too radical. Although in principle an argument for republicanism—and one that, even though it became closely associated with revolutionary Jacobinism, was not quite as radical as Spinoza's—its attendant proposition that property begins with and is a consequence of political society contradicts a fundamental principle of the U.S. republic. What Rousseau takes as anarchic usurpation of things, "possession," Locke construed as property resulting from individual labor, which precedes political society as a natural right the state cannot arbitrarily dispose. In Locke's theory, the immediate preservation of "possessive individualism" in itself, without any alienation, is the basis and purpose of the social contract. That principle does more than inform the Constitution drafted in 1787; it defines the terms of its language and purpose, stated rather plainly in the preamble:

> We the People of the United States, in Order to form a more perfect Union, establish Justice, insure domestic Tranquility, provide for the common defense, promote the general Welfare, and secure the Blessings of Liberty to ourselves and our Posterity, do ordain and establish this Constitution for the United States of America.

On the premise that the right of property derives from labor, there is an assumed differential rationality between capitalists and wage laborers, and the division of society into distinct classes. Accordingly, only property owners can be fully enfranchised members of the political society.[65]

No matter the contradiction between Rousseau's theory of freedom and the U.S. Constitution's investment in property rights, the resonances between his theory and the 1776 Declaration of Independence's proposition, "all men are created equal," as well as between its concept of the "general welfare" and his "general will," are very much the focus of Du Bois's invocation of "eighteenth-century Rousseauism" in the 1897 *Atlantic Monthly* version of the "Strivings" essay. The extent to which this is the freedom in the thoughts and dreams of the Negro is emphatically stated near the end of the revised "Of Our Spiritual Strivings": "There are to-day no truer exponents of the pure human spirit of the Declaration of Independence than the American Negroes." The fact that this eighteenth-century Rousseauian ideal of individual freedom was enshrined in the Declaration of Independence and Locke's theory of property in the Constitution—these two documents together forming the foundation of the republic—indicates the extent to which American political society at the time presented what C. L. R. James described as "the *ideal* conditions for bourgeois *individualism*."[66] James offers that description in the course of his analysis of economic and social developments in the United States from 1776 to 1876—the same period covered by Du Bois's two "Strivings" essays—underscoring how the specific way in which economic and social opportunity was manifested in America made actual living conditions unlike anything existing in Europe, including Rousseau's favorite examples of economic independence, Switzerland and Corsica. To conclude, as James does, that "it is the peculiar historical development of the U.S. that allows the *ideals* of eighteenth-century Europe to be expressed in a manner so close (approximately) to reality" is to identify America as the material instantiation of Enlightenment philosophy's theoretical ideal political society and the American as the actual embodiment of naturalized bourgeois individualism.[67] Commending the drafters of the 1787 Constitution for their "sober disciplined adjustment of political ideas and economic forces" and realizing for government to be effective in actuality, it must represent certain substantial citizens and classes, James finds that the ideal of democracy as combined universal individual will and the principles of market-oriented authority face each other in the two foundational documents.[68]

The summary history of the Negro struggle Du Bois presents in both versions of the "Strivings" essays tracks how the Negro problem is at the center of the conflict between these two ideals. In a profoundly pronounced way, the Negro problem punctuates the conflict, drawing sharp focus on the indissoluble relation between individualism and the capitalist market. A relation that is made clear in the language of the Constitution, which, in order to achieve political compromise, casts the matter entirely in terms of property rights and commerce, thus eliding the underlying question of human rights and citizenship. In other words, putting aside the question: "Are they human and so have rights as citizens according to our first principles?" This also meant not raising the question: "What defines citizenship?" The Negro problem, then, indexes a fundamental constitutional crisis. And this crisis does not get resolved in the Civil War, or even properly recognized as such until the postbellum Reconstruction Amendments, beginning with the Thirteenth Amendment, legally abolishing and prohibiting slavery, "except as punishment for a crime whereof the party has been duly convicted," and empowering Congress to legislatively enforce that prohibition, which was ratified in 1865.[69] As already noted, the capitalization of "Emancipation" in the version of history presented in "Of Our Spiritual Strivings" is in specific reference to this Amendment, signaling the political, legislative realization of the ideal of natural freedom. More to the point, it marks the failure of that legislative realization to effect the full inclusion of the Negro into the social contract as citizen. Freedom in nature may be a precondition for the need of the social contract, or the grounds on which it is even possible, but it does not necessarily result in full citizenship, which rests on certain presumptions of maturity encapsulated in the Kantian ethics Du Bois was so critical of by the phrase *Sapere Aude*.

Stating that eighteenth-century Rousseauism never worshipped Freedom with half the unquestioning faith as the American Negro demarcates Emancipation as a point of transformation, if not a radical departure from the tradition of liberal political philosophy to which both Rousseau and Locke belong. Another way of putting it is, one cannot be given what one is supposed to be in nature. It is a question, instead, of whether what one is can possibly be recognized in the political society; and, in the case of the Negro, this meant being recognized as a natural man who in freedom is capable of entering into a viable social contract. Whether the Negro was constitutively capable of being a viable member of modern civilization is how the issue was posed among serious academics and intellectuals well into the third decade of the twentieth-century. In that regard, emancipation, especially as a legislative act of prohibition, has nothing to do with freedom. By the same token, neither it nor natural freedom as an ideal guarantees viable political or civil rights *in society*. "The old cry of freedom," as Du Bois calls it in his summary, has no civil or political force. The Fourteenth Amendment, ratified in 1868, attempts to redress this, most pointedly in the first and second clauses of Section 1. The first clause, known as the Citizenship Clause or Naturalization Clause, introduces into the Constitution language specifically defining citizenship as a *jus soli* ("right of the territory") birthright aimed at securing the freedmen's rights as citizens. The implicit refutation of the Negro's purported ontological distinction is reinforced by the second clause, the Privileges and Immunities Clause, which itself was an elaboration on Clause 1, Section 2, of Article IV in the Constitution. Just as the Thirteenth Amendment did little to establish the Negro's rights as citizen, so too the Fourteenth Amendment effort fails to secure full enfranchisement for the Negro and thus required the Fifteenth Amendment, ratified in 1870, prohibiting the federal or any state government from denying citizens the right to vote "on account of race, color, or previous condition of servitude." Still, the legislation of full political enfranchisement *fails* to effect the Negro's inclusion into the life of society as an equal, which meant that without any true civil or moral standing, the law could not be enforced. Hence the Civil Rights Acts of 1870, 1871, and 1875, settling nothing in the end, except to establish that freedom cannot be a consequence of the instrumentalities of political society.

This is where the Negro exceeds Rousseauism in his persistent striving. With the failure of the Fifteenth Amendment, a shift in relation to the old cry of freedom occurs. Instead of freedom being a consequence of political enfranchisement, the struggle for freedom becomes a political project aimed at transforming the freedmen through new structures of knowledge and life-practices—"of life, of business, of the humanities"—into a population that would compel reconstruction of the polity so that the establishment of "freedom of life and limb, . . . freedom to work and think, . . . freedom to love and aspire" becomes its purpose, and not just a consequence of its arrangement. Du Bois's account of the Negro's perpetual striving to realize the "ideal of liberty" as a matter of sociality as well as polity—and it is the same account in both versions of the "Strivings" essays—strengthens the identification of the Negro with that ideal. More than merely a "concrete test" of the republic's underlying principles, the Negro is, in a very material sense, their embodiment as a distinctive type of self-conscious intelligence.[70]

This last point is central to Du Bois's effort at thinking Negro consciousness, according to which consciousness is more than merely grounded in its historical occasion, in the milieu, but is primarily a function of milieu. Consciousness as a function of material, natural—as opposed to supernatural—forces is the keynote to Du Bois's phylogenetic account of civilizational diversity in his "Conservation of Races" address given in 1897 at the inaugural meeting of the American Negro Academy. In both the *Atlantic Monthly* "Strivings" essay published that same year and the opening chapter of *The Souls of Black Folk*, where he is expressly concerned with the constitution of consciousness, he gives considerable emphasis to the societal. In that vein, the version of Du Bois's account of Negro double consciousness in *The Souls of Black Folk* had considerable influence on subsequent developments in mainstream theories of social psychology, anticipating William Isaac Thomas's 1904 "The Psychology of Race Prejudice." Du Bois's usage of double consciousness being a principle inspiration for Park's marginal man theory having already been noted, it is worth pointing out that Park's theory was instrumental in the study of the psychological effects of urbanization on immigrants carried out by his Chicago School colleagues, Gustave Le Bon, E. A. Ross, and William McDougall.

Significantly, the Chicago School work would come to play a fundamental role in Richard Wright's investment in relating literary representation to social psychology and psychoanalysis in his effort to shift the cultural perspective on the social problem of race prejudice from a question of the inherent suitability or unsuitability of a given group to those of personality formation in social dynamics. As he says in his introduction to *Black Metropolis*: "It was from the scientific findings of men like Robert Park, Robert Redfield, and Louis Wirth that I drew the meanings for my documentary book, *12,000,000 Black Voices*; for my novel *Native, Son*; it was from their scientific facts that I absorbed some of the quota of inspiration necessary for me to write *Uncle Tom's Children* and *Black Boy*."[71] Wright's formulation of this relationship of literature, social psychology, and psychoanalysis in regard to an antiracist activism establishes a viable dynamic between the aesthetic and political, which, as he says apropos *Black Metropolis*, opens up generally unimagined tangents of thought. Among the examples of these Wright ponders are:

> What peculiar personality formations result when millions of people are forced to live lives of outward submissiveness while trying to keep intact in their hearts a sense of the worth of their humanity? . . . Why do the personalities of American Negroes show more psychological damage than the personalities of the Negroes of the West Indies? And is this psychological differential between British and American Negroes in any way derived from their different relationships to the two Anglo-Saxon imperialisms?[72]

This truly is Wright channeling Du Bois through Park, indicating the extent to which Park's reading of Du Bois's double consciousness and his assimilating it to the Chicago School social psychology, facilitated its influence on mid-twentieth-century black literature. It is certainly not a trivial fact, therefore, that in "The Renaissance of Ethics," Du Bois discovers the intimate connection between the novel as a form and modern psychology—both in the sense of the formation of individual personality types and the nascent scientific study of them. Noting in the course of the argument he sets out against Kant's deontological ethics as metaphysics that one of the main hindrances to achieving a proper science of ethics is want of a positive phenomenological science of mind distinct from the "new physiological psychology," which he takes to be "no more than a science of the brain" inadequate to presenting a deep analysis of actual human psychology, he writes: "The world demands such a [phenomenological] science [of mind]; nothing so well attests this fact as the phenomenal rise and development of the modern novel, synchronous with empirical science—it has in some measure balanced our rapid tendency towards the Huxelian automaton."[73]

Construing the modern novel to be a harbinger, or at least a signal, of the need for the phenomenological science of mind is profoundly insightful. The novel is a sibling institution of science; both emerge with the unfolding of European modernity and the advent of bourgeois consciousness. They complement one another in enabling increasing knowledge of the mind, the instrument of collaboration and correction being William James's theory of stream of consciousness, the priority of some thinking going on in experience. Just as scientific psychology enables formal innovation in the novel, the novel gives a corrective for the scientific reductivism resulting from an absolutist conviction that inductive (deductive) scientific method, elaboration on hypotheses, is the only way to the truth of humanity. It is not so much that Du Bois equates the novel with myth, but rather it performs the function myth played in the world of gods and blood sacrifice in a way that complements science. On this it is useful to recall his argument in the 1957 preface to the first volume of his *Black Flame Trilogy, Mansart*, about the novel depicting what science cannot yet, and that is "the dynamic interaction between the anonymous forces of social formation and individual desire and thought." The *Mansart* preface clearly reiterates what Du Bois had already stated about the novel in "The Renaissance of Ethics." That this was a matter of some importance to him is further indicated by his also reiterating it in his 1905 essay, "Sociology Hesitant," where, arguing the need for a more cogent and rigorous sociology, he asserts: "Three things at the birth of the New Age bear weighty testimony to an increased and increasing interest in human deeds: the Novel, the Trust, and the Expansion of Europe."[74] There is intimated here an admittedly inchoate theory of the modern novel as the aesthetic form capable of entailing expressions of the myriad societal and civilizational institutions of the species writ large, thereby supplanting the historiography of development underwriting racialized European imperialism.

What all this brings us to is a clear sense of how Du Bois's usage of double consciousness, and its literary instantiation with John Jones, lest we lose sight altogether of the particular passage we are still engaged in reading, suggests a theory of human sociality. The history of positive striving after a self that would be "truer" in its conscious representation of itself—which is to say, recognizes its distinctive actual capacities and expressions free from the white gaze—Du Bois recounts in the "Striving" essays is what yields the Negro patterns of thinking and behaving that develop to not merely endure the violence of slavery and neo-slavery, but to sustain a concomitantly long sense of a dignified human self, a tradition of self-consciousness transmittable in certain forms of expression—sorrow songs, for instance. Once again quoting Wright in eloquent and forceful echo of Du Bois on this: "There is, however, a culture of the Negro which is his and has been addressed to him; a culture which has, for good or ill, helped to clarify his consciousness and created emotional attitudes which are conducive to action."[75] If "The Conservation of Races" can be taken as postulating a theory of the historical formation of human sociality, then this culture—the "subtle forces . . . of common history, traditions and impulses," determining the manner in which human beings are brought into "striving together for the accomplishment of certain more or less vividly conceived ideals of life"[76]—can be construed along the lines of what Du Bois's associate in sociology, Max Weber, called *Vergemeinschaftung* (communitization), denoting a sociality rooted in a subjective feeling that may be affectual or traditional.[77] This is resonant with what was earlier designated as a "grammar of sociality," foregrounding the dynamic psychological aspect of this tradition, which, in light of Du Bois's analysis of sorrow songs in the closing chapter of *The Souls of Black Folk*, can arguably be recognized as the "tradition of Negro humanism": a distinctive institution of the meaning of black being, not just at the dawning of the twentieth century but concomitant with the unfolding of our modernity. Du Bois identifies Negro consciousness with the Enlightenment ideal of reciprocal recognition of each and every individual as the ethical foundation of a viable social contract. Achieving this entails struggling to overcome the racial conceptual schemata of "this American world," making it realize the ethical ideal without transforming it fundamentally, except to bring about a better alignment of its legal and social institutions with its founding political project—the project of Reconstruction as the second revolution.

That struggle is what the black community of Altamaha is expressing in a language of hope and anticipation with the refrain: "'When John comes.' Then what parties were to be, and what speakings in the churches; what new furniture in the front room,—perhaps even a new front room; and there would be a new schoolhouse, with John as teacher . . . all this and more—when John comes." Due weight needs to be given to the semicolon in this passage. The clause to its left calls on the black community's institutional home of hope, the church, and that to its right expresses aspiration for a new institution, the particularities of which can only be imagined. These are the memories of early life and teachings crowding Jones as he struggles to learn the history of thought from which the ideal of reciprocal recognition of each individual as human comes. Notwithstanding the fact that the conditions of their nascence are in the pathological institutions of racialized capitalist society, these are not traumatic memories. So, coming from that Altamaha community, Jones's persona is something other than the "always good-natured and respectful" Negro laborer the teacher perceives; even though that account of the two aspects of the town is what brings attention to there being a Negro grammar. In pondering Jones as an objective problem of knowledge, the teacher's tale brings us to the point where nascence and nescience co-articulate, where two incommensurable grammars collide; and that point is the semicolon connecting the clause of crowding memories and the clause of Jones world building. The semicolon marks the extreme limit of how far the black grammar of Altamaha can take him, and so the break. What follows—"but all the world toward which he strove was of his own building"—emphatically describes the autopoetic quasi-autodidactic nature of Jones learning; it is idiopathic in relation to the institute's established paideia, as is announced in the next sentence: "As the light dawned lingeringly on his new creations, he sat rapt and silent before the vision, or wandered alone over the green campus peering through and beyond the world of men into a world of thought." The faculty have no clear idea of what is being generated or how; they merely detect, perhaps imagined, the teacher says, a change. But if the transformation is self-generated outside the track of predictable study, and if the neo-slave subject is constitutively unsuitable for such study, then what is bringing it about, what is its agency? The answer is found there in the break, in the co-articulation of two incommensurable grammars with two radically different types of subjects. In the space marked by the semicolon, the fact of the subject's grammaticality, its being a function of a set of relations describing the reality of lived experience, is discovered. In the collision of two incommensurable grammars is revealed the conventionality of the subject, that subjecthood is a function of discursive grammatical relations and arrangement. While the subject is a discursive, and so social, function, it is not to be misconstrued as something akin to the social persona Paul Laurence Dunbar evokes when he writes those famous lines:

> *We wear the mask that grins and lies,*
> *It hides our cheeks and shades our eyes,—*
> *This debt we pay to human guile;*
> *With torn and bleeding hearts we smile,*
> *And mouth with myriad subtleties.*
> *Why should the world be over-wise,*
> *In counting all our tears and sighs?*
> *Nay, let them only see us, while*
> *We wear the mask.*[78]

The subject is not so readily jettisoned, but is intricately bound with the psyche in a way that determines, or at least indicates, the nature of one's interiority. Belonging to two incommensurable grammars is the war of "two unreconciled strivings" Du Bois designates as the Negro's peculiar sensation of double consciousness. Simply put, Jones is struggling to find himself, not so much in thought, but in thinking.

> And the thoughts at times puzzled him sorely; he could not see just why the circle was not square, and carried it out fifty-six decimal places one midnight,—would have gone further, indeed, had not the matron rapped for lights out. He caught terrible colds lying on his back in the meadows of nights, trying to think out the solar system; he had grave doubts as to the ethics of the Fall of Rome, and strongly suspected the Germans of being

thieves and rascals, despite his textbooks; he pondered long over every new Greek word, and wondered why this meant that and why it couldn't mean something else, and how it must have felt to think all things in Greek. So he thought and puzzled along for himself,—pausing perplexed where others skipped merrily, and walking steadily through the difficulties where the rest stopped and surrendered.[79]

Bricolage, rather than synthesis, is unleashed in the collision of grammars. Jones's search for himself is not introspective but, as was fitting for a subject formed in neo-slavery, outward, working to make sense of languages and discourses that are totally alien to his way of thinking. Doing the work in the interstices between what he knows and wants to know, between how he has been formed to think and the thinking he struggles to engage on its terms, he discovers the poetic capacity to create and fashion structures of the self. The self discovered at the semicolon has no prior transcendent, or even transcendental origin, in the sense that it has no origins outside of the lived experiences of space and time. It is not descendant from a metaphysical legislating order in the Platonic or Neo-Platonic sense of ideal. Neither is it a necessary function of conceptual, perceptual schemata of the phenomenal world in the Kantian and Neo-Kantian, or even Hegelian sense of psychology and epistemology. In contrast to these theories, it is the function of an intersubjectivity of poetic sociality. Jones's interiority, his self-consciousness, is articulated between necessity—the grammatical imperatives of a violently enforced dominant world order: the law of segregation and white supremacy—and chance—the opportunities emergent in the interstices, the gaps in the law's dominion: the possibility of creating a grammar for thinking and feeling beyond the law. Both law and possibility are expressly immanently made up along the way in their interaction, and so expressly poetic. This self is articulated in and with the work of living and thinking.

The teacher's tale has recounted events in a way that reports things said and done with the most minimal signs of introspection up until a third of the way into the fifth page, when, having described Jones's matriculation from preparatory school to college, where "we who watched him felt four more years of change, which almost transformed the tall, grave man who bowed to us commencement morning," there is an abrupt shift to the narration of introspection and affect attributed to Jones. This happens in the text, with the teacher's expression of how they "felt" watching Jones, which is followed by the narration of Jones's own feelings: "He had left his queer thought-world and come back to the world of motion and of men. He looked now for the first time sharply about him, and wondered he had seen so little before. He grew slowly to feel almost for the first time the Veil that lay between him and the white world."

It is as though the teacher's tale proper ends with the fulfillment of Jones's institutional instruction. From here on, instead of an exposition of what was done to John and what he did, we now have the narration of him perceiving the world in which he exists in an enhanced way—"He first noticed now the oppression that had not seemed oppression before, differences that erstwhile seemed natural restraints and slights that in his boyhood days had gone unnoticed or been greeted with a laugh"—and articulating how he feels about it, so that "he felt angry now when men did not call him 'Mister,' he clinched his hands at the 'Jim Crow' cars, and chafed at the color-line that hemmed him in and his." At this first moment in the story when Jones's feelings are presented, the schemata that has been articulated, elaborated, and disciplined by the rich tapestry of knowledge and learning of humanism—what Du Bois calls the kingdom of culture[80]—begins to deconstruct. Incongruences start to appear between concepts and perception, revealing a failure to actualize fundamental ideas, principally the earlier-mentioned ideal of reciprocal recognition of each and every individual as the ethical foundation of society. Jones feels denied the very normative status of a full human member of society his education has formed him to hold as a natural right. Because he is fully interpolated into that conceptualization of the human condition, having learned the history of thought behind the ideal, and so knowing its providential scope, he feels the denial is a betrayal.

It is crucial to the story that what Jones is depicted as coming to understand is the incongruence between the ethical ideal and the juridically enforced daily preemption of the ideal as an *external social conflict*, and the veil is an instrumentality of epistemic enforcement: it enforces what can be perceived primarily by whites. If there is a "conflictual-twoness," or strife, a false self-consciousness, it is in the world on the side of the veil that cannot admit the possibility of another conceptualization. Jones's feeling angry at the quotidian manifestations of the incongruence indicates his not having internalized this strife. Sharing the same conceptual schemata as the white world about what it means to be human may enable Jones to see what they see when looking at him; but that same schemata means he does not identify with what they see. It is not what he knows himself to be. Although his self-consciousness entails a keen awareness of the white perception and its incongruence with the underlying conceptual schemata of America writ large, that does not negate or preempt his awareness of himself as a full human being in accord with that very schemata. The first after-effect of this condition is an intense withdrawal into his self. "A tinge of sarcasm crept into his speech, and a vague bitterness into his life; and . . . daily he found himself shrinking from the chocked and narrow life of his native town," where he knows he is destined to return, while still dreading the thought. Yet, the most powerful after-effect is neither sarcasm nor dread, but Jones's acquiring voice. The eagerness with which he accepts being selected to sing with the institute's quartette in a postgraduate summer tour of the North is given voice, if even only to himself: "A breath of air before the plunge, he said to himself in half apology." These are the last words of the opening five-page exposition, and they are Jones's. With them, a break occurs in the narrative, marked by a caesura, after which the opening passage of the New York City scene exhibits a living-moment in Jones's life as he has it, the duration of which is identical to that of narration. Story and narrative now share the same present, but from a far less limited omniscient third-person perspective than the teacher's tale. Just at the point Jones is narrated as feeling and thinking in his own right, with a greater awareness of the doings and goings-on of the world around him, those feelings and thoughts, and those goings-on, as well as the feelings and thoughts of others besides Jones, become fully accessible to the narrative.

By Modernism without Flânerie

With regard to the overall compositional style of *The Souls of Black Folk*, the sudden transition from the teacher's tale to the New York scene is not fundamentally different from what occurs in many of the other essays Du Bois gathered together in the volume. In fact, anachronicity and formal bricolage are distinctive characteristics of the book overall, which Du Bois once described as "bits of history and biography, some description of scenes and persons, something of controversy and criticism, some statistics and a bit of storytelling. All this leads to rather abrupt transitions of style, tone and view-point and, too, with doubt, to a distinct sense of incompleteness and sketchiness."[81] This bricolage demands of the literary form something it cannot give according to the conventions of literary composition. As Du Bois says, "Through all the book runs a personal and intimate tone of self-revelation. In each essay I sought to speak from within—to depict a world as we see it who dwell therein. In thus giving up the usual impersonal and juridical attitude of the traditional author I have lost in authority but gained in vividness."[82] Du Bois is aiming for *ekphrasis*, to achieve a narrative style that so energizes the readers' imagination that they can approximate that feeling for the world out of which emerges the lived experience of the Negro.

John Jones is so unmoored from his "ethnic roots" by an education—the institutional formations of which infuse him with an ardor for universal ideals it is their very function to assure he will never embody—that the most basic quotidian perception is infused with the reverberations of affect and historical experience-lived-in-the moment, what Wilhelm Dilthey called *Er-*

lebnis. A remark from Dilthey's important essay on aesthetics, "Die Einbildungskraft des Dichters: Bausteine für eine Poetik," is germane here: "Perception enlivened and saturated by an affect of life shining through in the clarity of an image: that is the essential characteristic of the content of all poetry."[83] "Poetik" belongs to the second phase of Dilthey's philosophical theory of descriptive psychology, during which he focused on aesthetics, particularly poetic imagination, as a model of *Geisteswissenschaften* (the human sciences) and stressed the reality of lived experience. Its principal task is to determine the way "poetic effect," which is Dilthey's designation for the psychological functions attending all mimetic modes, but most emphatically with literature, enables and intensifies the natural process of reflecting on the meaning of our existence, which is a part of life itself. All of this was an effort to eliminate the transcendent standard at play in historicism since Hegel, which subordinates the individual self-experience to the patterns and motifs of large historical features. Dilthey seeks to correct Hegel by insisting on the direct accessibility of inner-experience, in contradiction to Kant's postulating it was merely phenomenal. Kant's "I-think," which grounds the natural sciences' conceptual cognition, is preceded by a direct knowing that combines feeling, knowing, and will, and so is more inclusive of the entirety of human cognitive faculties, thereby making it the true transcendental condition of lived human reality. Dilthey uses the term *Innewerden* (reflexive awareness) to designate this principal form of consciousness that "does not place a content over against the subject of consciousness (it does not re-present it)."[84] More than a theoretical representation, *Erlebnis*, the world of lived experience is immediately present to the individual self as embodying all the values pertinent to its will, desires, and purposes. It is the transcendental condition of intersubjective understanding in contradistinction to Hegel's dialectic. In other words, it entails a direct knowing of reality as "present-for-me" prior to any subject-object distinction or reflective act of contemplation characteristic of conceptual phenomenal representations. For Dilthey, the individual is the ultimate element of a historical society, and, in being conscious, is already an embodiment of that society. As such, individuals are important for understanding history, not as monadic elements, but as points of intersection. Reflexive awareness is a microcosm of the confluences of a psychophysical complex.[85] This notion of the individual as microcosm of the historical *Weltanschauung* is key to Dilthey's development of descriptive psychology as the most basic *Geisteswissenschaft*, and so is crucial to the understanding of individuality as a radical element of human existence. Precisely the relationship of microcosmos and macrocosmos is at stake in his claiming the core content of poetry is the intensity of lived experience; poetic expression intensifies lived experience by embodying it in symbols and language.[86]

Although Du Bois did not study philosophy while a doctoral student at the University of Berlin in 1892–1893, opting instead to work most closely with Gustav Schmoller in the then-emergent fields of political economy and sociology, he had enough interest in Dilthey's work to include his seminar as the only course in philosophy listed among those he elected to attend. No matter that it cannot be determined with certainty whether he actually did attend those lectures—which some argue is doubtful on the basis of his neglecting to mention Dilthey in his autobiographical writings as one of his German influences—it is extremely hard to imagine him not having already encountered Dilthey's philosophy during his studies at Harvard with William James, whose intense engagement with Dilthey's theory of descriptive psychology as consonant with his own psychology is beyond any doubt. The question of direct lines of influence preoccupied with placing Du Bois—in a manner analogous to the history of philosophy's placement of Arabic philosophy—as a point of transmission for ideas originating with others, is the wrong one to ask here. As Maurice Lee once remarked concerning the diverse literary influences on Du Bois's first novel, *The Quest of the Silver Fleece*, "Transmission points will remain, for skeptics, speculative, though no more speculative than the cultural contexts we assume by fiat of 'discourse.'"[87] On that note, the question here is the pertinence of conceptual resonances to style. And if every impressionism is a transitional form, refusing contemplation and putting all form to the service of life, what is striking about "Of the Coming of John"—and what may make it the most stylistically ambitious of the writings in *The Souls of Black Folk*—is its vivid depiction of the transient fleeting impressions of this present as all there is and so as the past for a future, but not the future of a past, which is resonant with Dilthey's struggle to define the relationship among the functions of experience, expression, and understanding as where the historical world gets constructed with poetic expression—so much so that Du Bois's depiction of John Jones is arguably a poetic test of the proposition that the core content of poetry is the intensity of lived experience.

Whether or not Dilthey's effort to reorient psychological theory away from Hegelian schematic abstraction to "immediate data of consciousness" was a capitulation to positivism, as Georg Lukács claimed, is a question to be taken up a bit later.[88] The point to make at this juncture in our engagement with "Of the Coming of John" is the way Dilthey's struggle to define the relationship of experience, expression, and understanding as where the historical world gets constructed with poetic expression is resonant with Du Bois's depiction of John Jones. With that depiction, in contradistinction to Dilthey's notion, Du Bois achieves a poetic representation of an intelligence full of historical immanence and force, without an authenticating tradition. This does not mean without any orientation of convention; but, rather than there being a privileged prioritized authenticating canonical one, there is the dynamic of the myriad, not as data, but as the confluences of poetic practice and conceptualization.

All this may at first seem precipitous and maybe somewhat speculative, based on the résumé of the New York scene offered so far, where Jones's immanence of consciousness and his agitation about it is no more than intimated. It becomes more pronounced, however, when slightly more careful consideration is given to the moment of his first encounter with his childhood playmate, John Henderson, on that New York street.

Caught up as he is with his impressions of the crowd, Jones does not recognize that the tall light-haired young man with the talkative young lady whom he follows heedlessly to the Metropolitan Opera is Henderson. His attention is completely absorbed with the ambient stimuli of the crowd and not really focused on the particulars of individual identity or even details of place and time. Following the couple in a half daze, he is pushed toward the ticket office with all the others and pays his admission as a semi-reflex. Only after he had thoughtlessly given up the five dollars does Jones realize what he has done and stops dead in his tracks, forcing the still unrecognized Henderson to stumble over him. Henderson too fails to recognize that the Negro who has vexed him by stopping so abruptly in his way is Jones. In response to his companion's chiding him for being annoyed at the colored gentleman for being in his way, he proclaims she will never understand that there is greater intimacy and cordiality between blacks and whites in the South than in the North, offering as evidence the fact that his closest childhood playmate was a little Negro named after him. This obvious parody of southern sentimentality turns comedic with Henderson's becoming enraged at his instructing his companion on the finer details of Southern familiarity with Negroes being interrupted by finding the Negro whom he had just stumbled over in the hallway sitting next to her in the reserved orchestra seats. Still not recognizing Jones, he angrily instructs the usher to remove the offending Negro. Jones is absolutely oblivious to all of this because he is enraptured by the thematic and orchestral majesty of the prelude to act 1 of *Lohengrin*. Not until the prelude has finished does he become fully cognizant of what is taking place in the immediate social world around him. Getting up from his seat in response to the usher's request, he is finally recognized by and recognizes Henderson, but they now both know too much about the world to acknowledge each other. No sooner has Henderson recognized his childhood playmate than, in his consternation over the Negro's social forwardness, he lets him be led off. And, no sooner has Jones registered the significance of his childhood playmate's disavowal of him than he sees, with a clarity of mind equally as intense as his recent reverie, what Henderson has seen all the time—merely a foolishly presumptuous Negro. All these things transpire in just three paragraphs, spanning nearly two pages, which, nevertheless, cover considerable stylistic ground.

As has already been noted, nearly the entire New York scene is focused on Jones's impressions of things and narrated in terms of his thinking. There are, however, three events that are exceptions, where the third-person narration depicts occurrences involving Jones's physical person, without his perceiving them and so having any impressions. All three detail the two Johns' physical encounter at the Metropolitan Opera, and in all but one instance it is Henderson's perception that is on display, the one being a simple description of physical touching and reaction. The other two begin as speech acts appearing in tandem with Jones's thought, one of which he is unaware. The simple description is of the dialogue between Henderson and his companion, narrated as direct discourse initiated by the young lady. It is also the first of the three events to occur and immediately follows the narrating of Jones's stopping in amazement at his own thoughtlessness in buying a ticket. This amazement, the first sign of Jones's reflecting on what is happening, is narrated as purely introspective as well as internalized. There is no indication of perspective shift in the narrative movement from Jones's introspection to the young lady's speaking beyond quotation marks and the starkest of narrative mediation or tag, indicating only that something has been said in a low voice behind Jones. What follows is the rather sharp verbal response from Henderson to his companion's remark. We can better appreciate how all of this flows as a unit or one event when the paragraph is presented in full:

> He was pushed toward the ticket-office with the others, and felt in his pocket for the new five-dollar bill he had hoarded. There seemed really no time for hesitation, so he drew it bravely out, passed it to the busy clerk, and received simply a ticket but no change. When at last he realized that he has paid five dollars to enter he knew not what, he stood stick-still amazed. "Be careful," said a low voice behind him; "you must not lynch the colored gentleman simply because he's in your way," and a girl looked roguishly into the eyes of her fair-haired escort. A shade of annoyance passed over the escort's face. "You *will* not understand us in the South," he said half impatiently, as if continuing an argument. "With all your professions, one never sees in the North so cordial and intimate relations between white and black as are everyday occurrences with us. Why I remember my closest playfellow in boyhood was a little Negro named after me. And surely no two,—*well*!" The man stopped short and flushed to the roots of his hair, for there directly beside his reserved orchestra chairs sat the Negro he had stumbled over in the hallway. He hesitated and grew pale with anger, called the usher and gave him his card, with a few peremptory words, and slowly sat down. The lady deftly changed the subject.[89]

The physicality of all this, from Henderson's being upset at stumbling over Jones in the crowd as something in his way to his becoming enraged over the seating arrangement and his speaking to the usher, peremptorily puts in motion a set of actions predicated on Jones's physical presence, in which his thinking, his interior psychology is of no significance and has no proactive part. It should now be more apparent that Jones's absorption in the flood of things, of events, or rather the intensity of their impressions, drives him inside himself. But Jones does not experience this interiority as a transcendental perspective. He is not like the older cousin in E. T. A. Hoffman's last published story, "Des Vetters Eckfenster" ("The Cousin's Corner Window"), viewing the crowd clandestinely from a high perch at home, leisurely categorizing based exclusively on his "fancy."[90] Arguably, the most salient aspect of the New York scene is how Jones is not only in the crowd but *of* it. What he perceives, thinks, and feels, as well as *how* he perceives, thinks, and feels are fully contingent with the crowd. Consider, for example, the almost seamless continuity of Jones's stream of consciousness at the very beginning of the New York scene when he is contemplating the street up to his being expelled from the opera. He has a certain nondescript awareness of what is going on around him. The push and pull of the crowd, the transient impressions of its fashions, the unexplained attraction to its movement and the young couple, these things "reminded John of the sea." More to the point, his perception of these things is depicted as analogous to the awareness a swimmer might have of the sea as a complexity of surrounding indeterminate forces, "so changelessly changing, so bright and dark, so grave and gay."[91]

This depiction of Jones's perception bears resemblance to the lines from Edgar Allan Poe's influential story, "The Man of the Crowd," that run: "At this particular period of the evening I had never before been in a similar situation, and the tumultuous sea of human heads filled me, therefore, with a delicious novelty of emotion."[92] The resemblance is more than just coincidental. But if Du Bois is quoting Poe here, he sets out on a different course. Poe's convalescent is presented in a state of "inquisitive interest in everything." Like Jones, his observation of the urban scene initially takes an "abstract and generalized turn"; but, in remarkable contrast to Jones, the convalescent notes in sharp exquisite detail not only the attire of the passersby, but also its class significance. He attends to the crowd with the logical abstraction of taxonomy, carefully registering the forces of aggregation and differentiation constituting the crowd: "There are noblemen, merchants, attorneys, tradesmen, stock-jobbers—the Eupatrids and the common-places of society—men of leisure and men actively engaged in affairs of their own." He is revived by the occasion the crowd provides him to exercise his anthropometric and sociological knowledge and so reassert a robust sense of his healthy self. He is in a heightened state of awareness about the habitual order of things; or, rather, he sees clearly the working relationship between fashion and social identity.

The thinking of Poe's convalescent is consciously driven by an aporia of literacy. He watches the London crowd undetected from a safe perch in a café—admittedly not at home like Hoffman's cousin, but a safe perch nonetheless—until nightfall when the "more orderly portion of the people" retire and "its harsher ones [come] out into bolder relief features." Then his attention is excited, and he pursues his inquisitiveness into "darker and deeper themes for speculation," carefully examining individual faces, because they begin to pose a problem of categorization. Whereas earlier in the day "the rapidity with which the world of life flitted before" the convalescent prevented him "from casting more than a glance upon each visage," by dusk he remained in such a "peculiar mental state" that he could still solve the problem of category by reading "even in that brief interval . . . the history of long years." In this heightened state of awareness, in which he can discern the true place of each face, the convalescent is struck by a stranger, who is somehow unreadable, somehow a problem not readily solved. The text runs as follows: "With my brow to the glass, I was thus occupied in scrutinizing the mob, when suddenly there came into view a countenance (that of a decrepid [sic] old man, some sixty-five or seventy years of age)—a countenance which at once arrested and absorbed my whole attention, on account of the absolute idiosyncrasy of its expression. Anything even remotely resembling that expression I had never seen before."[93]

To be sure, this is an impression of a not fully comprehensible event, but its attraction is in its "incomprehensibleness," being a puzzle to solve, and not its eventfulness. The convalescent is not drawn to the unknown because he discerns in it any evidence of the poetry in life, any *poēsis*. He is drawn to it because it does not readily fit the categories. He is drawn to it to find its proper category, or invent one. In his effort to "form some analysis of the meaning conveyed" by the old man's countenance—note the narrative's language is not one of impressionism but of logic—the convalescent arrives at a confusing and paradoxical set of "ideas of vast mental power, of caution, of penuriousness, of avarice, of coolness, of malice, of blood-thirstiness, of triumph, of merriment, of excessive terror, of intense—of supreme despair." It is this "wild history," imagined by the convalescent perforce of his inability to read the old man that fascinates. After a thoroughly exhausting evening and night of following the old man about footstep for footstep in a wild circumnavigation of the city quarter, the convalescent does indeed discover his place in the order of things. He discovers him to be a drunkard. This discovery, however, does not really solve the problem; it does not make the old man any more legible. Recognizing that he has learned nothing more of him than that he is simply the man of the crowd, the convalescent ceases to follow the old man, although he remains absorbed in contemplation, concluding: "The worst heart of the world is a grosser book than the *Hortulus Animæ*, and perhaps it is but one of the great mercies of God that "er lasst sich nicht lesen."⁹⁴

With this closing sentence, "The Man of the Crowd" returns to where it began, repeating its opening line: "It was well said of a certain German book that 'er lasst sich nicht lesen,'—it does not permit itself to be read" and incorporating the gist of its epigraph from La Bruyère: "Ce grand Malheur, de ne pouvoir être seul." The story's closing identifies the German book cryptically announced at the beginning, where the phrase with which Poe frames his story, "*er* lasst sich nicht lesen," clearly refers to it. This reference translates into German the judgment Isaac D'Israeli passes in his *Curiosities of Literature* (1791–1823) on John Grunninger's *Hortulus Animæ, cum Oratiunculis aliquibus superadditis quæ in prioribus Libris non habentur* (1500), itself a German edition of the predominantly Latin prayer books filled with woodcuts from the emblemists Hans Springinklee and Erhard Schön, which was popular in the beginning of the sixteenth-century.⁹⁵ Poe famously "mistranslates" the German at the beginning of the story—referring to a certain German book, he correctly states in English "it does not permit itself to be read," keeping agreement between the neuter "book" and the pronoun "it"; but he incorrectly offers this English sentence as the translation of the German, which itself presents an ungrammaticality by offering the third person masculine pronoun *er* (he) in reference to the same German book, instead of the more grammatically correct neuter pronoun *es* (it). His refraining from translating the German at all in the closing lines of the story does not so much elide the error as exacerbate its effect. Clearly, *er* refers to the old man as "the worst heart of the world"; his identification with that certain German book underscores the fact that the initial mistranslation and ungrammaticality are deliberate, suggesting the principal theme of "The Man Of the Crowd" is the error of equating understanding a man (*er*) with deciphering a thing (*es*).⁹⁶

Poe's preoccupation with emblems and baroque emblem-books is well known and long a subject of scholarship. He signed the first published version of his most celebrated poem, "The Raven,"⁹⁷ with the pseudonym "Quarles," for the most celebrated English baroque emblematist, Francis Quarles, whose *Emblems Divine and Moral* he was rather familiar with. A familiarity put on display in his 1836 review for the *Southern Literary Messenger* of S. C. Hall's *The Book of Gems: From the Poets and Artist of Great Britain*, which included excerpts from Quarles's book. Emblems are crucial to Poe's aesthetic theory of the short story as a form dedicated to achieving a singular affect. Indeed, should we read the formal composition of "The Man of the Crowd" according to the tripartite structure of the baroque emblem-book, this short story from the *Tales of the Grotesque and Arabesque* is readily recognizable as one of his playful diddlings with the baroque emblem-book. The opening epigraph,

"Ce grand Malheur, de ne pouvoir être seul,"[98] gleaned from La Bruyère, stands in relation to the story as a motto or *inscriptio*. And the story, beginning as it does with "It was well said of a certain German book that '*er lasst sich nicht lesen*,'" is cast, then, as the icon or *pictura*. The closing paragraph, particularly the final sentence—"The worst heart of the world is a grosser book than the *Hortulus Animæ*, and perhaps it is but one of the great mercies of God that '*er lasst sich nicht lesen*'"—assumes the place of *subscriptio* or epigram.

Writing "his dreams as text to the image" is how Baudelaire construed "The Man of the Crowd," calling it "un tableau (en vérité, c'est un tableau!) écrit par la plus puissante plume de cette époque [a tableau—it truly is a tableau—written by the most powerful pen of this epoch]."[99] And, as Walter Benjamin has shown us, Baudelaire's emphasizing the importance of Poe's short story in the advent of modernism had to do with Baudelaire's weaving a connective tissue between the baroque emblem-book—the tableau/*pictura* of *Tableaux Parisienne*—and Poe's paradigmatic depiction of the modern-day urban crowd. Baudelaire's engagement of the tableau, the crowd, and allegory in his reading of Poe as emblematist is representative of urban capitalist modernity, or rather, of the sort of subjectivity at once enabled by and under siege from capitalist commodification.

Whether the old man of the crowd's deep crime is simply to refuse to be alone—that is, refusing to be invisible in his unreadableness—he is the object, and not the agent, of reading. The agency of reading, the act of equating particular individuals with organic totalities, is not just exclusively the convalescent's; it is emphatically grounded in the economy of rational knowledge—from the "vivid candid reason of Leibnitz," as Poe's convalescent would have it, to Dr. Cagliari's phrenology. Balzac's notion of *flânerie* as "the gastronomy of the eye" comes to bear here, about which Victor Fournel wrote: "It is by strolling about Paris [*en flânant dans Paris*] that Balzac made so many precious finds, heard so many words, dug-up so many types."[100] This "art of *flânerie*," which Fournel claimed is by definition rubbernecking (*du badaud*), when practiced by the "intelligent *flâneur* who conscientiously fulfills his duties, observing and remembering everything can play a leading role in the republic of art. It is," as he puts it, "a passionate and mobile daguerreotype that retains the slightest traces, which have reproduced, with their changing reflections, the course of things, the movement of the city, the multiple physiognomies of the public spirit, the beliefs, antipathies, and admirations of the crowd."[101]

We are well within the ambit of Baudelaire's construal of Poe's convalescent as a portrait ("en vérité, c'est un tableau!") of one who playfully contemplates the crowd ("contemplant la foule avec jouissance"), for whom "the crowd is his domain, as the air is that of the bird, as the water of the fish, whose passion and profession is to marry the crowd. For the perfect *flâneur*, for the passionate observer, it is an immense enjoyment to set up house [*d'élire domicile*] in the heart of the multitude, amid the ebb and flow of movement, in the midst of the fugitive and the infinite."[102] There is a remarkable resonance between this description of the crowd and the lines in "Of the Coming of John" depicting Jones's experience of the crowd in the New York scene, which we merely glossed before, but give in full now:

> It was a bright September afternoon, and the streets were brilliant with moving men. They reminded John of the sea, as he sat in the square and watched them, so changelessly changing, so bright and dark, so grave and gay. He scanned their rich and faultless clothes, the way they carried their hands, the shape of their hats; he peered into the hurrying carriages. Then, leaning back with a sigh, he said, "This is the World."

The resonance is so strong that it seems as though Du Bois is quoting Baudelaire besides Poe. Taking our cue from the introspectively expressed desire to catch a "breath of air before the plunge" at the end of the teacher's tale, it can even be said that Jones, like Baudelaire's *flâneur*, sets out "to be away from home and yet feels at home everywhere, seeing the world, being at the center of the world, . . . entering the crowd as into an immense reservoir of electricity, a kaleidoscope gifted with consciousness that, in every movement, represents the multiplicity of life and the flickering grace of all the elements of life."[103] Except, whereas the *flâneur* is one who strolling everywhere rejoices in his anonymity—as Baudelaire says of Constintin Guys, "a great lover of the crowd and the incognito [*de l'incognito*]"—Jones's unknowability is of a different, more un-rejoicing sort. He may indeed be a "lover of life [*L'amateur de la vie*]" who wishes "to make the whole world his family,"[104] but he cannot be admitted into the fold. Nor is he "an 'I' insatiably seeking the 'non-I'."[105] In stark contradistinction, Jones is the "non-I," and what he renders and expresses in increasingly vivid images is the lived-experience of being *it*, some *thing* fully caught up in the instability and restless of life itself.

Returning, for a moment, to the question of *flânerie* that arises with "The Man of the Crowd," Poe's story starts out in the mode of the physiologies then *en vogue* in France, combining eighteenth-century physiognomy with fanciful speculation to make out the profession, character, background, and lifestyle of passers-by; Balzac's *Physiologie du mariage* is a frequently cited example of this.[106] As Benjamin remarked, the physiologies helped fashion the phantasmagoria of modern urban life, particularly "the singular debasement of things by their price as commodities."[107] In the role of scout of the marketplace exploring the crowd, the *flâneur* is so driven to curiosity by the impressions on the senses passers-by make that he seeks to get beyond them at the "special singularity of each person."[108] But the very categorical imperative of the physiognomist, what Benjamin calls "the nightmare of illusory perspicacity," consists in seeing those distinctive traits peculiar to the person revealed to be nothing more than the elements of a new type. This points to, he maintains, "an agonizing phantasmagoria at the heart of *flânerie*," so that the crowd as the *flâneur*'s refuge "is the veil through which the familiar city is transformed for the *flâneur* into phantasmagoria, in which the city appears now as a landscape, now as a room, seems to have inspired the décor of department stores, which thus put *flânerie* to work for profit.[109] Having begun in that mode of *flânerie*, Poe's story turns to a radically different mode, the detective story of his invention—he called them "tales of ratiocination"—which presumes the urban space to be one of the potentially dangerous unknown. The *flâneur*'s rejoicing in the incognito is now of the order of forensic knowledge coupled with pleasant nonchalance, exemplified in Alexander Dumas's *Mohican de Paris*, whose hero goes in search of adventure by following a scrap of paper.[110] Benjamin instructs here as well that no matter what traces the *flâneur* follows, every one of them leads him to a crime, which shows that the detective story also participates in the phantasmagoria of modern urban life. In the dangerous space of the city where the crowd contains unknown danger, the *flâneur* is the savvy watcher who develops reactions in sync with the ever-changing tempo of the big city. Arguably, there is a direct line from the redoubtable C. Auguste Dupin of Poe's "The Murder in the Rue Morgue" to the equally redoubtable M. Jackal of Dumas's *Mohican de Paris*.

As the title of Dumas's book indicates, it is somehow inspired by James Fenimore Cooper's Leatherstocking tales, in which the frontiersman, Natty Bumppo, is the self-possessed away-from-home figure who deciphers the mysteries and dangers of the unknown primeval forest. What Cooper had done was make good on a foundational problematic of the American novel, in the wake of Charles Brockden Brown's earlier effort to state, if not settle things with *Wieland* (1798). Brown, echoing Ann Radcliffe's notion of the *explained supernatural* as a device of fiction, held that fiction, and novels in particular, are "verbal portraitures" of the "wonderful diseases or affections of the human nature."[111] The imperative for Brown was to elaborate on the local settings, local events, and color of America in a way that fulfilled the novel's function of relating "common things . . . in an uncommon way, [leading into] worlds of a new creation . . . under the dispensations of a romantic imagination." The presumption was that this would introduce a "new" American archetype, in Goethe's sense of *Urphaenomen*,[112] into the literary tradition in which, on the one hand, nature becomes the substitute for, or alternative to, history; on the other, the American Indian a tangible and recognizable ghost, the white man's foil or alter ego, if not the dark side of his conscience. An example of this is the unrecognizable scenery of *Wieland*, as well as the virtual absence of the social and political, and the grounding pedigree of Theodore Wieland, lover of God and builder of the temple in the garden, whose principle inheritance from his father is the weight of guilt and sin. Along similar lines, in *Edgar Huntly*, Brown employs "incidents of Indian hostility and perils of the Western wilderness" in lieu of the "puerile superstitions and exploded manners, and Gothic castles and chimeras" utilized in the European novels of his era.[113] It is in this way that we come to the naturalization of the Gothic romance in North America as the superimposition of Christian demonic supernatural onto the unknown present of the frontier, which Cooper perfects in his *Pioneers* and *Last of the Mohicans*, and Dumas transposes to the new modern urban scene. What Balzac described as "the poetry of terror that pervades the American woods" attaches to the smallest details of urban life.[114]

It is understandable, then, how Benjamin can see in Poe's story three urban types of modern subjectivity: the *flâneur*, the *badaud* (strolling gaper), and the detective. Poe's convalescent's interest, like that of all his detectives, is in logical structure, the determination to make sense of the mysterious, "to know more" of it. If the real *flâneur* of Poe's story is the convalescent, then the only thing he is observing is the textual economy of his knowledge: the old man's crime is to present an instance of human thinking that exposes the poetic failing of that knowledge.[115] But should we follow Benjamin in recognizing the old man as a dark version of the *flâneur*, then we are presented with another order of curiosity: How does the unreadable read?

If Du Bois gives Jones the aspect of the old man in Poe's story, it is from the perspective of the unreadable who is reading. Relating this to the crowd as multitude, then bearing in mind Baudelaire's obsession with the optical image—"Glorify the cult of the images (my great, my singular, my primal passion)"[116]—raises an even more challenging question: How does the invisible, thinking in the world, represent itself in any materially legible way as thinking, without assuming the trappings of conventionally established knowledge? This question has everything to do with Fournel's notion of *flânerie* as mobile daguerreotype, which involves a specific photographic iconography contested by Du Bois throughout *The Souls of Black Folk*. The field of contest is already set with Poe's reference to Grunninger's *Hortilus*, evoking the history of the image in printing and an involved dispute about the imagistic function of early typography that turns on the question: What media—iconographic imagery or typographic denotation—conveys the attitude essential in the formation of the modern persona? With respect to the formal experimentalism of *The Souls of Black Folk*, this question is a corollary to that of the invisible's material legibility; so that the question of iconographic imagery and typographic denotation is correlated to the book's critique of typology.

The relation between Du Bois's formal experimentalism and the question of representation has been duly remarked in passing by others.[117] But Robert Stepto, in his description of John Jones as one of Du Bois's three portraits of "weary travelers"—the other two being Du Bois's deceased infant son in "Of the Passing of the First Born" and Alexander Crummell in "Of Alexander Crummell"—provides the most direct access thus far into the question of the correlation between typology and typography. The key to that access is his distinguishing John Jones as "an archetypal figure."[118] Stepto predicates this distinction on his postulate of what he terms "pregeneric myths," which is extrapolated from Northrop Frye's concept of collectively shared canonical stories or myths shaping a people's collective consciousness. These pregeneric myths not only exist prior to all literary forms but also eventually shape those forms. Stepto discovers traces of that shaping through a historicist stylistic analysis of a particular selection of literary works by Afro-American writers that, beginning with English-language slave narratives, delineates a teleological literary generic genealogy, at the apex of which he places *The Souls of Black Folk* as an archetypal narrative form. By Stepto's reading of that narrative form, there is a language of horizontal binding, expressing a special unity between "we" and "I," "our" and "my," that is central to its narrative and rhetorical strategies. He finds this horizontal binding most emphatically at work in Du Bois's epigraphic placement of the sorrow songs, recognizing in them the expression of "the quintessential, atemporal Afro-American 'we.' The narrative that becomes one with that 'we' has indeed achieved an affirmative posture against the nightmare and travels, weary but not forlorn, above the Veil."[119] *The Souls*'s resulting narrative manifestations of personal history amounts to the fashioning of a self beyond history that "necessarily involves the assumption of a spiritual posture in a spiritual space," which is to be taken as "a cultural archetype within the Afro-American *temenos*, or cultural circle."[120] This is to presume—again, in alignment with Goethe's *Urphaenomen*—that the cultural circle is already there to be within, and accordingly, that literary style is a derivative isomorph. Not to suggest there is no profound poetic expression, no spontaneous utterance concomitant with events that exceed comprehension; but rather, greater emphasis is given to the conservative recapitulation of an idealized type of collective mind. Working from the premise that "the primary Afro-American pregeneric myth [is] the quest for freedom and literacy," Stepto construes Jones as archetypal because his portrait displays elements of all the previous narrative forms in the genealogy of that myth—most notably Olaudah Equiano's, Ukasaw Gonniosaw's, and Frederick Douglass's respective representations of arriving at a conception of freedom in tandem with gaining literacy—while at the same time inaugurating a new phase of generic literary form.[121] We have, then, the archetypal as both commemorative and revisionist, whereby Du

Bois's process of textual revision transforms a collection of preliminary texts—the "fugitive pieces," as he called them, from the *Atlantic Monthly* and three other journals initially commissioned by A. C. McClurg and Company to go into *The Souls of Black Folk*, as well as the antecedent narratives in the delineated mythological genealogy—into an integrated narrative. Arguably, this is what Stepto is describing as *The Souls*'s self-authenticating narrative style that "fashions the narrator as one of the narrative's archetypal 'weary travelers' and, finally, as a black man of vision and voice."[122]

As has already been indicated, with respect to the perspectival shift from the teacher's tale to the New York scene, the matter of the type of self, of the very articulation of self in "Of the Coming of John," is complicated by the way experience tends to flow into certain repetitive patterns of perception, the exchange of which in poetic expression reveals repetitions and coincidences tantamount to a common group experience. The crucial thing to focus on at this juncture is, in referring to the three portraits of "weary travelers," Stepto means they are emblematic *picturae* (icons) or tableaux; and "the weary traveler" functions as their caption or epigram. Epigrammatic function is crucial to his analysis of Du Bois's style as successfully struggling, through revisions to the preliminary texts of *The Souls of Black Folk*, for authorial control over the narrative of the book. That is to say, Stepto derives the epigram "the weary traveler" from the epigraphic force of the sorrow songs. This is clear when we recall the epigraph is a special kind of epigram. Regarding that epigrammatic function, it warrants noting the pertinence of the long-vexing issue of the relationship between narrative style and historical forms of the human self. So noted, the importance of epigrammatic function in the struggle for narrative control is most evidently at stake in Du Bois's substantial revision of the essay "The Negro as He Really Is" into two chapters.

"The Negro as He Really Is" originally appeared in 1901 in the *World's Work*, the monthly journal edited by Walter Hines Page and published by Doubleday, the publishing house he co-founded with Frank Nelson the year before.[123] Page, who had already published Du Bois's essay, "Strivings of the Negro People," in 1897 when he was editor of *Atlantic Monthly*, wanted to continue publishing him at Doubleday. Du Bois, however, declined to give any more of his writing to Doubleday after it published Tom Dixon's best-selling novel, *The Clansman: A Historical Romance of the Ku Klux Klan* (1905), on which D. W. Griffith would subsequently base his 1915 film, *Birth of the Nation*. What was for Du Bois an issue of the relationship between narrative representation and structures of knowledge in forming the popular imagination, Page took to be a simple matter of absolute freedom of expression, a position fully in keeping with the Wilsonian progressivism that inclined him to be an ardent opponent of virulent anti-Negro racism in his journalism, while simultaneously adhering to an attitude of liberal paternalism in his positivist sociological analysis of the so-called Negro problem. Opposed to the *politics* of white supremacy, Page nonetheless was certain of Negro inferiority. This has some bearing on the photographs he commissioned from Arthur Radclyffe Dugmore to be included along with the text of Du Bois's "The Negro as He Really Is." Dugmore was a pioneering American wildlife photographer, adventurer, and big-game hunter. Although he started out a portrait painter, his work consisted chiefly of wildlife studies, beginning with his first published book of images, the 1900 *Bird Homes*, a study of the nesting and breeding habits of land birds in the eastern United States that included instructions and advice on photographing young birds, entailing tips on rearing hatchlings to be more easily posed for photo shooting. Such commentary on the challenges posed to capturing the desired image of the photographic subject in its natural habitat, as well as solutions, always based on the photographer's vision and cunning, was a common feature of his later work, which included nine more wildlife studies, four of which were on African safari.[124] All of the Africa books contained images of native people, urban and rural scenes, and photos and paintings of wildlife. Ever the naturalist, Dugmore set out in his photographs of these scenes to capture documentary images of natives in their natural habitat, expressing concern about some of the same challenges he faced capturing images of wildlife in its habitat. He once remarked, "There are few subjects more difficult to make good film of than native street scenes," claiming that they are more difficult than "photographing charging rhino or elephant."[125] The primitivist ethnographic naturalism implied in this identification of natives with wildlife was the conceptual basis for his compositional iconography and was well aligned with Page's conception of the Negro as an inherently primitive and inferior subspecies of humanity.

There are nineteen Dugmore photographs included in the eighteen-and-a-quarter-page published article.[126] Without the photographs, the text of Du Bois's essay amounts to approximately ten pages, with one full page taken by a population distribution map and one quarter of another a chart of racial ratios in Dougherty County, Georgia, from 1820 to 1899, leaving eight or so pages of prose. All nineteen of the photos are given the same documentary aspect in their composition Dugmore gave to his African Safari images. Stepto draws attention to how Dugmore's photographs "wrestle with Du Bois's prose for authorial control," focusing on three as particularly offending in challenging that authority.[127] We see this challenge, however, from the very first page (figure 1.1), which opens, even before the title and byline, with a photo of a black woman in the field working a mule-drawn plow, preceded by the caption "Working by the Day in the Cotton Field," the syntax of which suggests local vernacular speech patterns. The overall effect is the preeminence of the documentary photograph, the emblematic aspect of which is established by the caption occupying the place of the motto, over the written one. Emblematic photographic preeminence is sustained in the very next page (figure 1.2), which is completely given over to a photo of two men engaged in cobbling, with the older man in the foreground staring directly at the camera, its caption, "In the Cobbler's Shop," now in the place of the epigram. That placement, which is maintained with all the captions throughout the remainder of the essay, brings Stepto to insightfully, and somewhat ironically, label them, "light-hearted epigrams."[128] With respect to photographic layout in relation to the prose text, in scale and placement on the page, Dugmore's photographs dominate all but six pages of "The Negro as He Really Is." The extent to which this interferes with the essay's tone is significant enough to warrant careful consideration.

Besides the photo of the cobbler's shop, there are two more single photo full-page spreads without any prose text (figures 1.3 and 1.4). There is one double-photo full-page spread (figure 1.5), also without any prose text; and one page (figure 1.6) is divided in half by two photos with their epigrams, one on top, the other the bottom, taking up three-quarters of the page, sandwiching Du Bois's prose in between them. There are a total of five half-page spreads. In two of these (figures 1.7 and 1.8), a single photo occupies the top half and the prose text the bottom. In the remaining three (figures 1.9, 1.10, and 1.11), the photo is placed off-center in the middle of the page with the prose text framing it. Two of these three photos are shots of the same single woman plowing: one taken from the front is on the verso page (figure 1.9), positioned off-center to the left; the other taken from the rear is on the recto page (figure 1.10), positioned off-center to the right. There are two more pages (figures 1.12 and 1.13) on which the remaining photos are spread three to a page, dividing it into segments of equal distribution between text and photos: three photos to three fragments of text.

All of these photos are accompanied by epigrams that interpret them exclusively, with little or no regard to the narrative of Du Bois's text. The photos themselves, even when they appear on pages with his text, also have no immediate connection to it, with one exception. The frontal photo of the woman plowing (figure 1.9) accompanies Du Bois account of the debt structure of share-cropping. Its epigram, "Negro Woman Plowing in a Cotton Field," interpreting the photographic image, has the subcaption "A field cultivated on the rent system," which is a direct reference to the topic of the Du Bois text surrounding it. Yet, even with this exception of direct reference, the uppercase formatting catches the eye and is consistent with the formatting for all nineteen photos, foregrounding it as the caption proper, while the lowercase subcaption functions as a filament connecting this particular photo to the prose text. There are three more such lowercase subcaptions connecting a photo to the Du Bois text. There are four other lowercase subcaptions, none of which connects the photos to the text it shares the page with, instead referring in paraphrase to passages of Du Bois's text occurring many pages before or after. This asynchronism between Du Bois's prose text and the captions (both main and sub-) further separates what the photos are showing from what his prose is doing. And guidance in how to "properly" interpret what they're showing is provided by the epigrammatic captions, not by Du Bois's prose text. Two of the subcaptions do, however, quote Du Bois's text directly. The caption and subcaption of the photo of children in school (figure 1.7) reads, "A NEGRO SCHOOL NEAR ALBANY, GEORGIA," with the subcaption "Where children go after 'crops are laid by.'" And the caption for one of the three photos of street scenes in Albany (figure 1.12) reads: "ON THE STREET," with the subcaption "'They meet and gossip with their friends.'" Even with these direct quotations and paraphrase, the asynchronism, combined with the iconicity of the photo/epigram, as well as the uppercase formatting of the epigrams that visually connects them as a series, establishes a tight emblematic narrative structure to the photographs and epigrams, which is superimposed onto Du Bois's text, overwhelming it in a way that is effectively palimpsestic.

This relationship between image and word, which is common in naturalist, ethnographic, and travelogue photography, enforces an authoritative hermeneutics, according to which the written word is invested with the authority to correctly interpret the image. The underlying assumption is that the photographer, with whom the reader identifies, was the one there, seeing in a way that is pertinent. Its resemblance to the classical Greek *theoria*—who functioned as legates for the polis at formal occasions of importance in other city-states, mediating between events and their entry into public space with an undeniable authority invested by the polity—is not inconsequential.[129] The authority to mediate between events and the public discourse about them is invested in the photographer not by an express act of political authorization, but by the structures of knowledge underwriting the privileged relationship between the camera and just who is taking the photo. More than the technical expertise of the cameraman, this has to do with what he is: an indubitable subject of knowledge, the white man who in the end, authorized by true legitimate knowledge and society, understands the meaning of all he sees. And that relationship is asserted in the epigram, which puts in proper context the elements of the photographic scene, reinforcing a particular order of imagistic motifs and composition that are supposed to authenticate the proper conception of things—in other words, an iconography.

Du Bois's struggle for authorial narrative control in revising "The Negro as He Really Is" for *The Souls of Black Folk* is, at bottom, against this iconography. What bears emphasizing is that this a struggle over the relationship

WORKING BY THE DAY IN THE COTTON FIELD

THE NEGRO AS HE REALLY IS

A DEFINITE STUDY OF ONE LOCALITY IN GEORGIA SHOWING THE EXACT CONDITIONS OF EVERY NEGRO FAMILY—THEIR ECONOMIC STATUS—THEIR OWNERSHIP OF LAND—THEIR MORALS—THEIR FAMILY LIFE—THE HOUSES THEY LIVE IN AND THE RESULTS OF THE MORTGAGE SYSTEM

BY

W. E. BURGHARDT DUBOIS

PROFESSOR OF ECONOMICS AND HISTORY IN ATLANTA UNIVERSITY

Photographically Illustrated by A. Radclyffe Dugmore

OUT of the North the train thundered, and we woke to see the crimson soil of Georgia stretching away bare and monotonous right and left. Here and there lay straggling unlovely villages; but we did not nod and weary of the scene for this is historic ground. Right across our track DeSoto wandered 360 years ago; here lies busy Atlanta, the City of the Poor White, and on to the southwest we passed into the land of Cherokees, the geographical centre of the Negro Problems—the centre of those 9,000,000 men who are the dark legacy of slavery. Georgia is not only thus in the middle of the black population of America, but in many other respects this race question has focused itself here. No other state can count as many as 850,000 Negroes in its population, and no other state fought so long and strenuously to gather this host of Africans.

On we rode. The bare red clay and pines of North Georgia began to disappear, and in their place came rich rolling soil, here and there well tilled. Then the land and the people grew darker, cotton fields and delapidated buildings appeared, and we entered the Black Belt.

Two hundred miles south of Atlanta, two hundred miles west of the Atlantic, and one

1.2 *In the Cobbler's Shop*

ARTHUR RADCLYFFE DUGMORE

1.3 *Her Week's Marketing*

ARTHUR RADCLYFFE DUGMORE

1.4 *At Work Making Brooms*
ARTHUR RADCLYFFE DUGMORE

LEARNING TO SHUFFLE EARLY

A PICKANINNY CAKE WALK

1.5 *Learning to Shuffle Early, A Pickanny Cake Walk*
ARTHUR RADCLYFFE DUGMORE

"BIG HOUSE" AND NEGRO QUARTERS
The house is no longer in use although the Negro quarters are

hundred miles north of the great Gulf lies Dougherty County. Its largest town, Albany, lies in the heart of the Black Belt, and is to-day a wide-stretched, placid, southern town, with a broad street of stores and saloons flanked by rows of homes—whites usually to the north, and blacks to the south. Six days in the week the town looks decidedly too small for itself, and takes frequent and prolonged naps; but on Saturday suddenly the whole country disgorges itself upon this one spot, and a flood of black peasantry passes through the streets, fills the stores, blocks the sidewalks, chokes the thoroughfares, and takes

NEGRO COTTAGES
Owned by the Negro who keeps the store pictured on page 858

1.6 *"Big House" and Negro Quarters, Negro Cottages*
ARTHUR RADCLYFFE DUGMORE

A NEGRO SCHOOL NEAR ALBANY, GEORGIA
Where children go after "crops are laid by"

full possession of the town. They are uncouth country folk, good-natured and simple, talkative to a degree, yet far more silent and brooding than the crowds of the Rhine-Pfalz, Naples, or Cracow. They drink a good deal of whiskey, but they do not get very drunk; they talk and laugh loudly at times, but they seldom quarrel or fight. They walk up and down the streets, meet and gossip with friends, stare at the shop-windows, buy coffee, cheap candy and clothes, and at dusk drive home happy.

Thus Albany is a real capital—a typical southern country town, the centre of the life of ten thousand souls; their point of contact with the outer world, their centre of news and gossip, their market for buying and selling, borrowing and lending, their fountain of justice and law.

We seldom study the condition of the Negro to-day honestly and carefully. It is so much easier to assume that we know it all. And yet, how little we know of these millions —of their daily lives and longings, of their homely joys and sorrows, of their real shortcomings and the meaning of their crimes.

Dougherty county, Georgia, had, in 1890, ten thousand black folks and two thousand whites. Its growth in population* may thus be pictured:

YEAR	NEGROES	WHITES	TOTALS
1820	225	551	776
1830	276	977	1,253
1840	1,779	2,447	4,226
1850	3,769	4,351	8,120
1860	6,088	2,207	8,295
1870	9,424	2,093	11,517
1880	10,670	1,952	12,622
1890	10,231	1,975	12,206
1899	9,000	.....	.....

* The boundaries of the county have frequently changed. It was a part of Early County first, then of Baker, and finally was laid out as Dougherty in 1853.

A TYPICAL NEGRO STORE

plantation, or if he took a notion to sell the slave, Sam's married life with Mary was usually unceremoniously broken, and then it was clearly to the master's interest to have both of them take new mates. This wide-spread custom of two centuries has not been eradicated in thirty years. Probably seventy-five per cent. of the marriages now are performed by the pastors. Nevertheless, the evil is still deep seated and only a general raising of the standard of living will finally cure it.

The ignorance of the ex-slaves is far deeper than crude estimates indicate. It is ignorance of the world and its meaning, of modern economic organization, of the function of government, of individual worth and possibility—indeed, of all those things as to which it was for the interest of the slave system to keep the laboring class in profound darkness. Those very things then which a white boy absorbs from his earliest social atmosphere— starts with, so to speak, are the puzzling problems of the black boy's maturer years. And this, too, not by reason of dullness but for lack of opportunity.

It is hard for an individual mind to grasp and comprehend the real social condition of a mass of human beings without losing itself in details and forgetting that after all each unit studied is a throbbing soul. Ignorant it may be, and poverty-stricken, black and curious in limb and ways and thought; and yet it loves and hates, it toils and tires, it laughs and weeps its bitter tears, and looks in vague and awful longing at the grim horizon of its life —all this, even as you and I. These black thousands are not lazy; they are improvident and careless, they insist on breaking the monotony of toil with a glimpse at the great town-world on Saturday, they have their loafers and ne'er-do-weels, but the great mass of them work continuously and faithfully for a return and under circumstances that would call forth equal voluntary effort from few, if any, other modern laboring class. Over 88 per cent. of them, men, women and children, are farmers.

1.8 *A Typical Negro Store*

ARTHUR RADCLYFFE DUGMORE

This is the Cotton Kingdom, the shadow of a dream of slave empire which for a generation intoxicated a people. Yonder is the heir of its ruins—a black renter, fighting a failing battle with debt. A feeling of silent depression falls on one as he gazes on this scarred and stricken land, with its silent mansions, deserted cabins and fallen fences. Here is a land rich in natural resources, yet poor; for despite the fact that few industries pay better dividends than cotton manufacture; despite the fact that the modern dry-goods store with its mass of cotton-fabrics represents the high-water mark of retail storekeeping; despite all this, the truth remains that half the cotton-growers of the south are nearly bankrupt and the black laborer in the cotton fields is a serf.

The key-note of the Black Belt is debt. Not credit, in the commercial sense of the term, but debt in the sense of continued inability to make income cover expense. This is the direct heritage of the south from the wasteful economics of the slave regime, but it was emphasized and brought to a crisis by the emancipation of the slaves. In 1860 Dougherty County had 6,079 slaves worth probably $2,500,000; its farms were estimated at $2,995,923. Here was $5,500,000 of property, the value of which depended largely on the slave system, and on the speculative demand for land once marvellously rich, but already devitalized by careless and exhaustive culture. The war then meant a financial crash; in place of the $5,500,000 of 1860, there remained in 1870 only farms valued at $1,739,470. With this came increased competition in cotton culture from the rich lands of Texas, a steady fall in the price of cotton followed from about fourteen cents a pound in 1860* until it reached four cents in 1893. Such a financial revolution was it that involved the owners of the cotton belt in debt. And if things went ill with the master, how fared it with the man?

The plantations of Dougherty in slavery days were not so imposing and aristocratic as those of Virginia. The Big House was smaller and usually one-storied, and set very near the slave cabins.

The form and disposition of the laborers' cabins throughout the Black Belt, is to-day,

* Omitting famine prices during the war.

NEGRO WOMAN PLOUGHING IN A COTTON FIELD
A field cultivated on the rent system

1.9 *Negro Woman Plowing in a Cotton Field*
ARTHUR RADCLYFFE DUGMORE

the same as in slavery days. All are sprinkled in little groups over the face of the land centering about some dilapidated Big House where the head tenant or agent lives. There were reported in the county outside the corporate town of Albany 1,424 Negro families in 1899. Out of all these only a single one occupied a house of seven rooms; only fourteen have five rooms or more. The mass live in one and two-room homes.

The size and arrangements of a people's homes are a fair index to their condition. All over the face of the land is the one-room cabin; now standing in the shadow of the Big House, now staring at the dusty road, now rising dark and sombre amid the green of the cotton fields. It is nearly always old and bare, built of rough boards and neither plastered nor sealed. Light and ventilation are supplied by the single door and the square hole in the wall with its wooden shutter. Within is a fire-place, black and smoky, and usually unsteady with age. A bed or two, a table, a wooden chest and a few chairs make up the furniture, while a stray show-bill or a newspaper decorate the walls.

We have come to associate crowding with homes in cities almost exclusively. Here in Dougherty county, in the open country, is crowding enough. The rooms in these cabins are seldom over twenty or twenty-five feet square, and frequently smaller; yet one family of eleven lives, eats and sleeps in one room, while thirty families of eight or more members live in such one-room dwellings.

To sum up, there are among these Negroes over twenty-five persons for every ten rooms of house accommodation. In the worst tenement abominations of New York and Boston there are in no case over twenty-two persons to each ten rooms, and usually not over ten.

A REST IN THE FURROW

Of course, one small, close room in a city, without a yard, is in many respects worse than the larger single country room.

The one decided advantage the Negro has is a place to live outside his home—that is the open fields, where most of his life is spent.

Ninety-four per cent. of these homes are rented and the question therefore arises, what in the industrial system of the Black Belt is responsible for these wretched tenements? There would seem to be four main causes. First, long custom, born in the time of many newly-married young couples, but comparatively few families with half-grown and grown children.

The families of one are interesting. Some of them—about a fifth—are old people. Away down at the edge of the woods will live some old grizzle-haired black man, digging wearily in the earth for his last bread. Or yonder, near some prosperous Negro farmer, will sit alone a swarthy auntie, fat and good-humored, supported half in charity and half by odd jobs.

Probably the size of Negro families is decreasing, and that, too, from postponement of marriage, rather than from immorality or loss of physical stamina. To-day in this county only two per cent. of the boys and sixteen per cent. of the girls under twenty are married. Most of the young men marry between the ages of twenty-five and thirty-five, and the girls between twenty and thirty—an advanced age for a rural people of low average culture.

The cause of this is without doubt economic stress—the difficulty of earning sufficient to rear a family. The result is the breaking of the marriage-tie and sexual looseness.

The number of separated persons is thirty-five per 1000—a very large number. It would of course be unfair to compare this number with divorce statistics for many of these separated are in reality widowed, were the truth known, and in other cases the separation is not permanent. Nevertheless here lies the seat of greatest moral danger; there is little or no prostitution among these Negroes, and over four-fifths of the families, after house to house investigation, deserve to be classed as decent people with considerable regard for female chastity. The plague-spot in sexual relations is easy marriage and easy separation. This is no sudden development,

HUTS NEAR ALBANY, GEORGIA
Showing old mud and wood chimney

nor the fruit of emancipation. It is a plain heritage from slavery. In those days Sam, with his master's consent, "took up" with Mary. No ceremony was necessary, and in the busy life of great plantations of the Black Belt it was usually dispensed with. If now the master needed Sam's work on another plantation or in another part of the same

1.11 *Huts Near Albany, Georgia*

ARTHUR RADCLYFFE DUGMORE

WOMEN FROM THE COUNTRY
A Saturday group in Albany, Ga.

slavery, has assigned this sort of a home to Negroes, until land owners seldom think of offering better houses. Should white labor be imported here, or the capital here invested be transferred to industries where whites are employed, the owners would not hesitate to erect cosy, decent homes, such as are often found near the new cotton factories. This explains why the substitution of white for black labor is often profitable—the laborer is far better paid and cared for. In the second place, the low standard of living among slaves is naturally inherited among freedmen and their sons; the mass of them do not demand better houses because they do not know what better houses are. Thirdly, the landlords as a class have not yet come to realize that it is a good business investment to raise the standard of living among laborers by slow and judicious methods; that a Negro laborer who demands three rooms and fifty cents a day would give far more efficient work and leave a larger profit than a discouraged toiler herding his family in one room and working for thirty cents. Lastly, among such conditions of life there are few incentives to make the laborer become a better farmer. If he is ambitious, he moves to town or tries other kinds of labor; as a

A PARSON AND PART OF HIS FLOCK

ON THE STREET
"They meet and gossip with their friends"

tenant farmer his outlook is almost hopeless, and following it as a makeshift he takes the house that is given him without protest.

That we may see more fully the working out of these social forces, let us turn from the home to the family that lives in it. The Negroes in this country are noticeable both for large and small families; nearly a tenth of all the families are families of one—that is, lone persons living by themselves. Then, too, there is an unusual number of families of ten or more. The average family is not large, however, owing to the system of labor and the size of the homes, which tends to the separation of family groups. Then the large and continuous migration of young people to town brings down the average. So that one finds many families with hosts of babies, and

THE NEGRO AS HE REALLY IS

LOG CABIN HOME

ignorance and stunting physical development.

Among this people there is no leisure class; ninety-six per cent of them are toiling—no one with leisure to turn the bare and cheerless cabin into a home, no old folks to sit beside the fire and hand down traditions of the past, little of careless, happy childhood and dreaming youth. The dull monotony of daily life is broken only by the Saturday trips to town.

The land is still fertile, despite long abuse. For nine and ten months in succession the crops will come if asked; garden vegetables in April, grain in May, melons in June and

The rest are laborers on railroads, in the turpentine forests and elsewhere, teamsters and porters, artisans and servants. There are ten merchants, four teachers, and twenty-one who preach and farm.

Most of the children get their schooling after the "crops are laid by" and very few there are that stay in school after the spring work has commenced. Child-labor is found here in some of its worst phases, as fostering

WOMEN "SOWING" GUANO.

A FRIEND OF GEORGE WASHINGTON

He believes that he was with Washington when the cherry tree was cut down and allowed his photograph to be taken only on condition that a copy would be sent to his old friend

July, hay in August, sweet potatoes in September, and cotton from then to Christmas. And yet over two-thirds of the land there is but one crop and that leaves the toilers in debt. Why is this?

The merchant of the Black Belt is a curious institution—part banker, part landlord, part contractor, and part despot. His store which used most frequently to stand at the crossroads and become the centre of a weekly village, has now moved to town and thither the Negro tenant follows him. The merchant keeps everything—clothes and shoes, coffee and sugar, pork and meal, canned and dried

1.13 *Log Cabin Home, Women "Sowing" Guano, A Friend of George Washington*

ARTHUR RADCLYFFE DUGMORE

between media and style of mimesis and the order of thinking and perceiving things—which is to say the matrix of conceptualization and perception of reality. It is not so much that these are distinct, heterogeneous conceptualizations of reality—the same order of things, in this case Negro life, is perceived; rather, it is that there is a conflict over what things are, what they mean. Du Bois's revisions mark the sort of cognitive, and so epistemological, limit he designates "the Veil." At stake is the epistemological institution of "scientific knowledge'—including Dilthey's *Geisteswissenschaft*—that authorizes the ethnographic gaze.[130] This is why it is important that the two chapters generated out of Du Bois's revisions of "The Negro as He Really Is" are situated, according to the partitioning demarcated in his "Forethought," in "the world of white men"—those first nine chapters where he deploys a mixture of statistically informed inductive method, as learned from Schmoller, historiographic documentary, sociological analysis, and nativist anecdotage to expose the severe limitations of positivistic methodology to understanding the human condition, and so shift the epistemological paradigm by reorienting it.

The extensive rewriting of "The Negro as He Really Is" may indeed purge Du Bois's preliminary text of the interference of the ethnographic epigrams; but it does more besides. To the extent they do achieve, as Stepto says, "the inculcation of a system of symbolic geography as well as of a new race-conscious and self-conscious tone,"[131] the resulting two chapters dispense absolutely with the necessity for the epigram, assuming the function of the photograph. Or rather, they achieve a compositional style that combines the conceptualizations of the object of study, which becomes thereby a subject instead, and the authenticating narrative. The reorientation is not iconoclastic, but rather a shift to a more inclusive in-this-world iconology, which is why Stepto can read *The Souls of Black Folk* as a fundamentally archetypal narrative, identifying the compositional style of John Jones's portrait with the overall compositional style of the book. From here, Du Bois's account of imagining Crummell in a tableau ("I sometimes fancy I can see that tableau: the frail black figure, nervously twitching his hat before the massive abdomen of Bishop Onderdonk . . ."), evoking John Foxe's *Lives of the Martyrs*, looks very much like a moment of narrative self-reference, announcing the compositional form of the short story to follow. John Jones is another fancied tableau. Hence Stepto's claiming "the weary traveler" is the epigram for both. That this epigram is taken from the sorrow song "Let Us Cheer the Weary Traveler," which concludes the last chapter of *The Souls of Black Folk*, reinforces its epigrammatic function for the book as a whole. The last chapter, "The Sorrow Songs," which is the only chapter in fourteen that does not begin with the preposition "Of," is where Du Bois explains the function of the bars of music he has placed in relation to quotations of poetry as epigraphs to each chapter—explaining, in other words, how to properly read the text of the whole book. A statement at the beginning of the chapter indicates the book's compositional resonance with the emblem-book: "They that walked in darkness sang songs in the olden days—Sorrow Songs—for they were weary at heart. And so before each thought that I have written in this book I have set a phrase, a haunting echo of these weird old songs in which the soul of the black slave spoke to men." Simply put, they function as mottos to the text that follows and in relation with it constitute the book's narrative.

So the prose text of *The Souls of Black Folk* composes its image in process, deploying an eclectic mixture of elements of style and material but in only one media—even the sorrow songs are given in score as notated bars of music without lyrics. The whole thing moves along until that final chapter, which having explained the compositional form and the meaning of the iterations of motto in relation to what can now be called the "picture in prose," combines them together into integrated tableaux by ending with a vocal score—throughout the last chapter Du Bois provides pieces of vocal scoring of sorrow songs as exempla—transcribing music *with* lyrics. Almost ends with, because the final lines of the chapter are in stand-alone prose: "And the traveller girds himself, and sets his face toward the Morning, and goes his way." It is still not quite over with; there is an "Afterthought," a prayer to "God the Reader," seeming to reassert the gap between image and word, which is meaningfully bridgeable only by the word. Except that, as Stepto correctly assess, the final chapter has already achieved the narrative syncretism of vertical and horizontal dimensions he characterizes as the special unity between "we" and "I" articulated by the narrative voice that is both temporally synchronic and diachronic, situating the thinking of the narrative in the same time as the thinking of the subjects described. This achieves not so much a unity of identity, however, as a contemporaneity that can be arguably construed as ethical in its avoiding the pitfalls of ethnographic authority and epistemological hierarchy by way of the narrative's self-conscious race-conscious identification with its subjects. "These are mine" and "I am one of them" are meant in the sense of being reflexive human beings thinking in and about the world together. Diachrony (the vertical dimension), in contrast, achieves a unity of identity that extends across time, which is performed in the last chapter with phrasings such as "the hope that sang in the songs of my fathers well sung . . . my little children are singing up to the sunshine."

If Stepto is right, and I think he is, that "the weary traveler" is the epigram for all of this and that the portrait of John Jones is its archetypal figure, then "Of the Coming of John" is a paradigmatic representation of a human intelligence fully conceived and formed in the world without any mythical or otherwise transcendent authority grounding or orienting it. For such an intelligence, its humanity is overwhelmingly imaginative, a poetic, hence historical, invention. Regarded in this way, Du Bois's tableau depicts a particular historical knowledge whose conceptual speculations and reflections—its thinking—begin where the matter they treat begin. In this way we can say it is a *Negro* tableau, a tableau of thinking-in-disorder. Put differently, John Jones is emblematic of a formation of the mechanized political economy of capitalist modernity that is distinct from both the bourgeoisie and proletariat.

Asymptotic Thinking

The problem of thinking presented in "Of the Coming of John" is posed in terms of the relation between forces that are materially immanent in the world, which Du Bois called *chance*, and historical human institutions of thought and practice, which he called *law*. For the sake of momentary clarity, the question could be understood in terms of a dynamism that attributes no purposeful necessity to the immanent forces of the world, so that human institutions are themselves nothing more or less than particular manifestations of force. Those institutions, whether practical or theoretical, have no basis outside of time. They are, in each and every instance, absolutely historical modes of force; and their material formality records a particular understanding, or, to more precisely stick with Du Bois's language, way of thinking reality. The formal aspects of law objectify a particular glimpse of the dynamic relationship between forces in reality. The formal, or, if you like, structural, aspects of human institutions objectify a particular glimpse of the dynamic relationship between forces in reality. To use the Aristotelian language implied in Du Bois's own description of his literary work, each and every human institution is a mimesis, "a representation," of reality, remembering that for Aristotle, mimesis was a species of thought. It was a dynamic process of engaging reality—entailing some material media that expressed an object in a particular modality—rather than a limited and limiting technique of copying it, which was Plato's sense of the term. We know, of course, that of the different types of mimesis Aristotle identified, *poiēsis* held the greatest fascination—the exemplary instance being tragedy. Aristotle's elaboration of the rules of tragic form emphasizes the way in which the object of poetic representation—changing men in action—is indissolubly connected to the process of representation; and that process is itself the action of thinking. It is precisely because *poiēsis* formally exhibits what it exposits—change in action in a duration of time—that Aristotle recognized it as an enduring material record of a historical moment of thought in reality. There is much more that can and will be said about this. Relating it now, however, to Du Bois's portrait of Jones as an archetypal figure of the Negro as thinking-in-action, we note once more the resonance with Dilthey's concept of *Erlebnis* as the concrete living present in process, whereby the consciousness one has of one's body as a center of action occupies a moment of duration heterogeneous from our abstract conception of chronological time. Let us add Bergson's elaboration of this into his conception of the *durée*, according to which being is a continually varying spatio-temporal rhythm, a flow of states that is the basis of matter, extended in space as a present that is always beginning anew. In Bergsonian *durée*, every perception occupies a specific *épaisseur de durée*, a "depth of duration," which carries the past into the present in order to prepare the future. Given that Du Bois was directly influenced by William James's theory of streams of consciousness, and that James thought Bergson's philosophy concordant with his own older investigations, it is not altogether surprising that the Bergsonian notion of "thinking-in-time" resonates with Du Bois's of "intellect-in-action," thus further warranting my paraphrase "thinking-in-action." That resonance is amplified in Benjamin's remark, referring to *Matière et mémoire* being overshadowed by Dilthey's *Das Erlebnis und die Dichtung* (*Poetry and Experience*), that Bergson's particular definition of experience in *durée* prompts one to conclude, "Only a poet can be the adequate subject of such an experience." The poet he expressly had in mind was Proust, whose *A la Recherche du temps perdu* tests and transforms through paraphrase Bergson's *mémoire pure*, or image-remembrance—that which stems from the *vita contemplativa* in the classical sense of this—into *mémoire involontaire* (involuntary memory), in a manner akin to how "Of the Coming of John" tests and transforms Dilthey's *Innewerden* (reflexive awareness). Except that, with the portrait of Jones, Du Bois transforms the reflexive awareness of the primal scene of thinking into the material dialectic image of law and chance, in which the image may indeed record historical moments of thought in transmittable form, thereby continuing a particular technology of thinking, but it cannot comprehend the infinite possibilities of thinking. Although in the texts where Du Bois explicitly employs the dyad chance and law he does so as part of an argument against determinism—the chief proponent of which he identifies as Herbert Spenser, whose methodology he considers pseudo-scientific—his principal concern is not with either conceptual possibility or physical possibility in the strict technical sense of these. In other words, there can be no worldly perch from which an absolute history of thought can be successfully achieved, let alone sustained, without disregarding the multiplicities of ways of thinking actualized in how human beings exist and live.

Even though the immediate exigencies of political action commanded the main of his attention and energies, Du Bois never completely abandoned his concern with how the ways in which the Negro developed and deployed not only practices of life but modes of thinking those practices as theories of being—let us call them ethical styles—presented an immediate instance of the dynamic interactive relationship between the phenomena of experience, the perception of things, and the conceptual conventions of thought. This is made abundantly clear in a letter he wrote to Herbert Aptheker at the beginning of 1956, in which he once again explains his turn from positivism:

> I gave up the search of "Absolute" Truth; not from doubt of the existence of reality, but because I believe that our limited knowledge and clumsy methods of research made it impossible now completely to apprehend Truth. I nevertheless firmly believed that gradually the human mind and absolute and provable truth would approach each other and like the "Asymptotes of the Hyperbola" (I learned the phrase in high school and was ever after fascinated by it) would approach each other nearer and nearer and yet never in all eternity meet. I therefore turned to Assumption—scientific Hypothesis. I assumed [read "postulated"] the existence of Truth, since to assume anything else or not to assume was unthinkable. I assumed that Truth was only partially known but that it was ultimately largely knowable, although perhaps in part forever Unknowable. Science adopted the hypothesis of a Knower and something Known. The Jamesian Pragmatism as I understood it from his lips was not based on the "usefulness" of a hypothesis ... but on its workable logic if its truth was assumed. Also of necessity I assumed Cause and Change. With these admittedly unprovable assumptions, I proposed to make a scientific study of human action, based on the hypothesis of the reality of such actions, of the causal connections and of their continued occurrence and change because of Law and Chance. I called sociology the measurement of the elements of Chance in Human action.

The asymptote is a straight line that approaches but never meets or crosses the curve. It is said naively in non-formal geometric expression that the curve meets the asymptote at infinity.[132] This can be diagrammatically expressed as shown in figure 1.14.

Given the extensive employment of mathematical statistics in his sociology research, Du Bois was undoubtedly familiar with asymptotic analysis as a method for studying the hypothetical distribution of a sequence where exact statistical result is difficult to get. The foundations of such analysis were laid by Henri Poincaré's theory of asymptotic expansion, also known as *asymptotic series* or *Poincaré expansion*, which is a formal series of functions that may not converge, but the terms of which decrease at a fast enough rate that the truncation of the series at any finite order provides an approximation to a given function as the argument of the function tends toward a particular, often infinite,

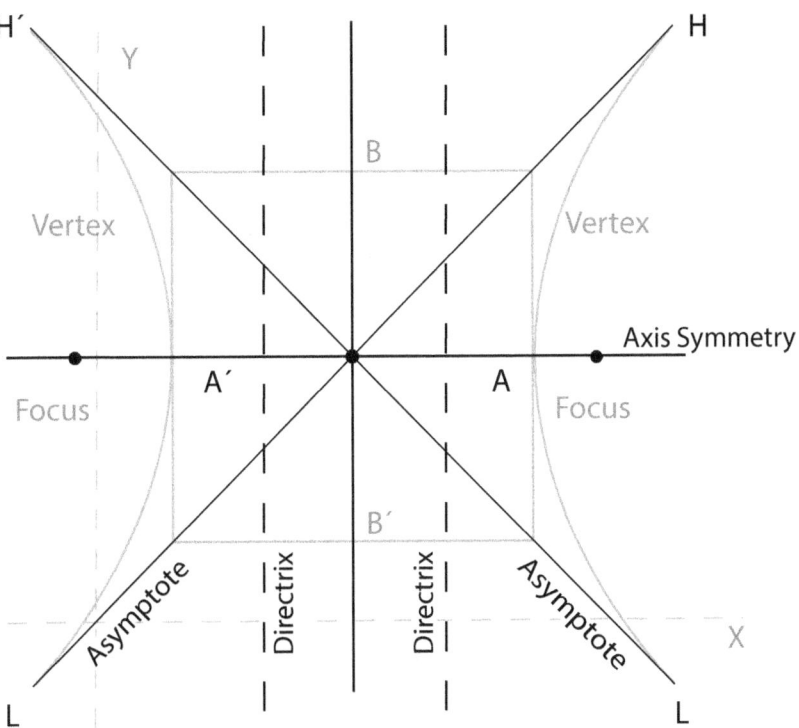

1.14 The Asymptotes of the Hyperbola

point. The typical situation in which a divergent infinite series may be used for the numerical calculation of a quantity that in many cases can be regarded as the "sum" of the series is that of a series of variable terms, the "sum" of which is a function. The approximation afforded by the first few terms in the series is better the closer the independent variable approaches a limiting value, which, again, more often than not is infinity (∞). Poincaré was the first to designate this an *asymptotic series*, an abridgement of the following definition:

I would say that a divergent series,

(1) $\quad A_0 + \dfrac{A_1}{x} + \dfrac{A_2}{x^2} + \cdots \dfrac{A_n}{x^n} + \cdots$

where the sum of the first $n+1$ terms is S_n, asymptotically represents a function $J(x)$ if the expression,

$x^n (J - S^n)$

tends toward 0 when x grows indefinitely. Indeed, if x is sufficiently large, we will have,

$$x^n(J-S^n) < \varepsilon$$
ε being very small....

Hence it follows that the series (1) will behave quite like the Stirling series—if x is very large, its terms will first decrease rapidly and then grow beyond all limits—and that, in spite of its divergence, it will be legitimate to use it in the calculation of J. I will also say sometimes in abridgement that the series (1) is an asymptotic series.[133]

This definition gives some sense of the analogy's pertinence to Du Bois's construing the work of sociology to be the measurement of chance as a variable in relation to law. But what is it doing in respect to his construal of thinking in relation to continuity?

Naively put, Du Bois's analogy suggests that thinking is analogous to the functions of the area of a determinate curve, expressed relative to the infinitesimal points of the tangential line. In one sense, Du Bois seems to be stating that we can have as clear an idea of truth as we have of, say, a triangle, but we cannot have as clear a mental image of truth as of a triangle. That is, we cannot imagine truth, but we can, indeed conceive it. Keeping to this paraphrase, however, this does not mean that we have no image of truth at all; rather, any such image is in asymptotic relation to the concept. To turn it around, the concept is an expression imagined along certain tangential lines of possibility, progressing toward but never reaching truth. In this respect, Du Bois's claim that studying the rate of change in societal functions leads to reevaluating the nature of knowledge as necessarily hypothetical touches on the problem of constructing functions in regard to general domains with general boundary conditions, otherwise called "Green's functions."[134] More to the point, construing thinking as analogous to functions along the tangential line suggests Gustav Dirichlet's solution to the problem, according to which a function is an arbitrary injective correspondence between numerical values.[135] In addition to this definition of *function*, Dirichlet defined the infinite series of positive integers, known as the *Dirichlet series*. Bernhard Riemann elaborated an analytic continuation of the Dirichlet series to define the *Riemann zeta function*, the asymptotic behavior of which remains a topic of interest in analytical number theory. Riemann also defined the conditions of a function to have an integral, what we now call the condition of Riemann integrability, or the *Riemann integral*.[136] That work, in turn, influenced Richard Dedekind, who took Riemann's integral as the starting point for his own analysis of discontinuous functions, leading to his defining *Dedekind cuts* in 1854, with which he proved the purely arithmetic construction of real numbers, significantly furthering the arithmetization of analysis.[137] Georg Cantor employed Dedekind's terminology in his own work; and in correspondence with him from November 29 to December 7, 1873, established that the real numbers are uncountable; this led to Cantor's 1874 publication, "Ueber eine Eigenschaft des Inbegriffes aller reellen algebraischen Zahlen" (On a property of the collection of all real algebraic numbers).[138]

It is not at all a far-fetched to suppose that this lineage of thinking in the foundations of mathematics is germane to Du Bois's drawing an analogy between hyperbola asymptotes and thinking in relation to continuity. Direct support can be found in his 1905 essay, "Sociology Hesitant," where Du Bois refers to "the New Humanism of the nineteenth-century" as calling for scientific knowledge of human activity.[139] The reference translates Friedrich Paulsen's designation *Neue Humanismus*, which he also conflated as *Neuhumanismus*, and so is usually rendered as *Neohumanism*. Paulsen coined the term in 1885 to designate the nineteenth-century German cultural movement, stemming from Wilhelm von Humboldt's and Friedrich August Wolf's ideas that classical Greek language and literature were to be studied because of their absolute value as "die exemplarische Darstellung der Idee des Menschen [the exemplary representation of the idea of man]."[140] Pedagogically, in accordance with the concept of *Bildung*—the integral education of the individual—the Neohumanists held that "nothing was more important than knowledge of Greek to [acquiring] self-knowledge [*Selbsterkenntnis*] and self-education [*Selbstbildung*]."[141] This Hellenophilia (*Griechensehnsucht*) was bolstered by the then emergent "scientific" philology Christian Gottlob Heyne was promulgating in his influential seminar at Göttingen, regularly attended by Carl Friedrich Gauss, whose *Disquisitiones Arithmeticae* was the point of departure for Dirichlet's and Dedekind's work on number theory.[142]

In the course of characterizing Neohumanism as calling for scientific knowledge of human activity, Du Bois commends Auguste Comte's having "crown[ed] his scheme of knowledge with Knowledge of Men."[143] Comte initially called this science *social physics*, before settling on *sociology* as the designation for the sixth and last science in the classificatory scheme of his positive philosophy of science, following mathematics, astronomy, physics, chemistry, and biology. The order of classification indicates the order of historical development of the sciences overall in accordance with the process Comte designates, *loi des trois états*, "the law of the three stages"; these are the theological, metaphysical, and scientific qua positive stages of civilization and its knowledge. It is at the final, positive stage, when sociology becomes possible and the relation between the diverse sciences—the encyclopedic scale from general and simple to the particular and complex—is comprehensible, that a philosophy of science establishes itself. At that stage, science, by definition, has completely abandoned typically metaphysical, indeed scholastic, notions of cause, constituting itself instead as a knowledge of relations and correlations between antecedents and consequents expressible in mathematical formulas. A fundamental dictum of positivism is that "there is no question whatsoever which cannot ultimately be conceived as consisting in determining certain quantities from others by means of certain relations, and consequently as reducible, in final analysis, to a simple question of numbers.... In all our researches, on whatever order of phenomena they relate to, our object is to arrive at numbers, at measurements."[144] In this regard, we should not lose sight of the fact that Comte's positivist sociology entails two orders of mathematical operation.[145] The first order, which he terms *concrete mathematics*, involves the quantification of observed phenomena; specifically, the frequency of one phenomenon's occurrence in relation to another determines its evaluation as a relevant variable of measurement. Thus transforming observed phenomena into enumerated data yields variables as objects of analysis, of calculus, which is the second-order operation Comte terms *abstract mathematics*. Every calculable variable is derived from the observed frequency in distribution of the related phenomena and defines a relevant category, so that a category of variable exists only if a certain observed frequency in the data sample corresponds to it. In this way, mathematical analysis is applied to social phenomena in order to abstract the axiomatic laws governing society.

Du Bois takes issue with Comtean sociology, but not with its abandonment of causality for relationality. As is suggested in his remarks to Aptheker in 1956 and made quite explicit in earlier writings, that is his own position. The problem with Comte is that, in his insistence on the invariance of axiomatic law and the absolute arithmetization of any and all phenomena, including humans and their actions, he is "strangely hesitant as to as the real elements of society— were they men or cells or atoms or something subtler than any of these."[146] Following Du Bois, we note that Comte's pronouncement of positivism's settling the long-standing dispute with the "theologico-metaphysical spirit" in favor of science signals his agenda to displace Kantian transcendental psychology with the methodological analysis of scientific procedures. Systematizing science as an encyclopedia of axiomatic laws, Comte abstracts methodological principles from their epistemological context, referring them directly to the process of historical development toward rationalization of social relations by way of scientific-technical progress. Positivist philosophy of science replaces Kantian transcendental philosophy as the grounds of scientific knowledge of the world on the argument that a philosophy restricting epistemology to methodology predicated solely on the verifiable operations of formal logic and mathematics can better determine true knowledge. Science, Comte insists, must abandon the concepts of human nature, of soul, even of Kant's transcendental ego because these concepts are categorical and substantial; accordingly, they are not manageable by the science of numbers. Such things as inner sense (*innerer sinn*) and the *I* of transcendental apperception are simply uncalculable; and positivism leaves aside the uncalculable in order to secure the efficacy of prediction (*la prévision scientifique*).[147] The integrity of method in defining relation has priority over the objects of analysis in guaranteeing reliable knowledge because the very certainty of knowledge of the object is gotten via sound method. In this sense, the precision of knowledge is attained only by systematic construction of theories that admit the axiomatic deduction of lawlike hypotheses. Comte remains indebted to Kantian epistemology, however, deriving his postulate that self-consciousness is an epiphenomenon of both biological and sociological functions from the epistemic dualism of the Transcendental Deduction—an indebtedness he acknowledges in *Cours* Lecture 50 when adducing Franz Joseph Gall's physiology of the brain in evidence. He thus effectively transvalues Kant's Transcendental *I* as Transcendental *system*—"Society as a whole"—taking it as a general principle of science and working from there to the elements, presupposing an order that is not in demonstration according to positivism's own principles. The result is what Du Bois characterizes as sociology's "vicious logical circle," in which the whole of reality is supposed to be rationalized in a hypostatizing formalism, the epistemological qua scientific ordering of things, including society, which is no more than a formal aggregate or class of individuals.[148] Hence his charge: "Comte and his followers noted the grouping of men, the changing of government, the agreement in thinking, and then, instead of a minute study of men grouping, changing and thinking, proposed to study the Group, the Change, and the Thought and call this new created Thing 'Society.'"[149] Comtean sociology thus confounds these "Thoughts of Things," with things existing beside thought.[150] Nor does Spencer's elaboration of Comte's positivism along the lines of Lamarckian evolution toward ever increasing individuation resolve the issue. Du Bois's critique of positivism's "confounding Things with Thoughts of Things" extends to Spencer's argument that the phenomenal is a mode of the noumenal—"all things known to us are manifestations of the Unknowable"[151]—and that the noumenal is only conceivable as a necessary correlative of our self-consciousness, so that we have the idea of force from the experience of our own power of volition, our willful ability to conceive things, the implication being that force of mind is the necessary condition of physical force, and not the other way around. Comtean materialism yields to Spencerian idealism, which carries us back into quasi-Scholastic "metaphysical wanderings."[152] Granted, Du Bois thinks Spencer's initial sociological project, *Descriptive Sociology, or Group of Sociological Facts*, achieved some good by attempting a systematic "description of the . . . Thoughts of Things, and Things that go to make human life [in] an effort to trace in the deeds and actions of men great underlying principles of harmony and development—a philosophy of history with modest mundane ends, rather than eternal, teleological purpose."[153] It is, nevertheless, a limited good because Spencer continues to regard society as an aggregate entity.[154] And those who follow him, those Du Bois call's "Spencer's imitators," predicate sociology on physics and chemistry, having established that the constant element of phenomena is force—Du Bois's term is *action*—which remains the same irrespective of its various manifest forms. Force is regarded as reality, such that the phenomena of nature and individual psychology are subject to the same "absolute unchanging physical laws of action, which are expressible in mathematical formula."[155] As a result, rather than seeking to obtain a verifiable account of the constitutive elements of existent social systems, the heirs of positivist and descriptive sociology sought "the genesis of our social ideas [making] society ... a mode of mental action, and its germ was—according to their ingenuity—'Consciousness of Kind,' 'Imitation,' the 'Social Imperative,' and the like."[156]

All these attempts to reduce human action to formalized axiomatic laws flounder on the problem of the uncalculable, or more precisely, on the problem of calculability with respect to human action, which Du Bois describes as the paradox stemming from the two irreconcilable epistemological assumptions: "A Categorical Imperative pushed all thought toward the Paradox: 1. The evident rhythm of human action; 2. The evident incalculability in human action."[157] On the one hand is the assumption that human beings exist in a world of physical forces operating according to universal axiomatic laws of nature—the mathematical realism epitomized in Galileo's dictum, "The book of nature is written in the language of mathematics," capturing the spirit of the scientific revolution presumed to have begun with his and Kepler's work.[158] On the other hand is the assumption that the same human beings are "capable in some degree of actions inexplicable and uncalculable according to these laws."[159] Those actions are manifest as seemingly random events of controlling energy that modify, restrain, and redirect the ordinary laws of nature, indicating an autonomous volitional intellect acting *by chance*, to paraphrase Du Bois.[160] Although he states that these chance activities of intellect "stalk" among the physical forces,[161] this is not to be construed in terms of Cartesian dualism—according to which the human body is a complex organized material field of causes and effects describable in the idioms of physics and biology, and the human mind is a counterpart complex of immaterial causes and effects that are not describable in those idioms but in a counterpart idiom of logic. Neither is he postulating a para-mechanical hypothesis by which human cognition, while an activity external to the causal process describe by physics and biology, functions in a parallel process of causality—such as Spencer's conception of the individual as indices of a transcendent psychological field of cause and effect, inhabiting the physical body like a ghost in the machine. By Du Bois's account, "The true students of Sociology ... frankly state the

Hypothesis of Law and the Assumption of Chance"; then, they apply statistical measurement and historical research to the minute study of every conceivable aspect of human social activity in the attempt "to determine as far as possible the limits of the Uncalculable—to measure, if you will, the Kantian Absolute and Undetermined Ego."[162]

The play on words here is pointed, underscoring the fundamental paradox of measuring the unmeasurable. And in that paradox is the situation whereby encountering the individual-acting-in-collective is possible.[163] That individual is not phenomenological, in Comte's sense, or transcendental, in Spencer's. Nor is it a representation indexing the point where the limits of transcendental psychological activity and the world of things in themselves, the noumena, meet. Du Bois's invocation of Kant's Transcendental *I* as a limit of calculation is ironic and subversive. He does not aim to reinstate the psychological idea of an integral persistent self that is a regulative principle, a logical function of pure reason, whereby the unfathomable is represented as given phenomena. On the contrary, the Du Boisian individual is grammatical or relational, somewhat in the sense Spencer speaks of the subject being a subject to the object and the object being an object to the subject, neither existing by itself as absolute. It is in the situation of communicative-spontaneity-in relation that individual possibility is and multiplies. Wanting to attend to that communicative-spontaneity-in-relation, looking back from 1905 at more than fifty years of work since Comte, Du Bois asks: "What then is the future path open before Sociology?" to which he answers: "It must seek a working hypothesis which will include Sociology and Physics." With that answer, what Du Bois proposes under the rubric "Sociology" is a long-range scientific exploration of how human intellect-in-action—which is spontaneously occurrent with the fluid multiplicative dynamics of physical existence, of necessity and contingency—constructs calculable completed orders of things—institutions of practice and thought, and individuals, namely, society.[164] On first glance, this is arguably recognizable as a call for a science in Dilthey's sense of *Geisteswissenschaft*—translating John Stuart Mill's "moral science"—in analytical relation to *Naturwissenschaft* ("natural science"). We should keep in mind, however, that while Dilthey disputed Mill's treatment of "moral sciences" as natural sciences with human objects of study, he shared his commitment to the proposition that while the "laws of the phenomena of society are, and can be, nothing but the laws of the actions and passions of human beings united together in the social state," as Mill put it, "men, however, in a state of society, are still men; their actions and passions are obedient to the laws of individual human nature. Men are not, when brought together, converted into another kind of substance with different properties."[165] This is akin to Weberian methodological individualism, which Du Bois, as has already been noted, avoids by attending to the somato-psyche, the body-image that belongs in community. His call, then, for "Sociology" as a long-range scientific exploration is for something besides *Geisteswissenschaft*. What that something is comes into sharper relief when his conception of sociology is considered in relation to his hyperbola asymptotes analogy.

Concerning thinking-in-action in that regard, there are punctuations along the asymptotic line of human knowledge, delimiting domains of well-ordered thought with axiomatic definitions determining how things are perceived, as well as conceptualized. These domains, which Comte termed *états* and we can call *orders of knowledge*, have two aspects. As orders of axiomatic definition, they generate laws, the force of which is determined by their general validity in relation to the things they define. These laws, then, become conversely the basis for the generalized definitions that, when satisfied, determine the situation of things as objects of thought. Put in the terms of the analogy, what we consider as *truth* is the generalizability of definitions deriving from the laws of any given order of knowledge *in relation to* eventful physical reality. The emphasis is because, for Du Bois, truth is not merely logical relation but is referential; which is to say, any given definition is a hypothetical probability expressed in a system of representation that is in relation to things. Truth is what can be known *by us* as truth in accord with the axiomatic laws. When a given order of knowledge encounters complex phenomena or events that cannot be comprehended by its calculations, generating dissonance, the limits of the axiomatic order are reached, and a new order of definition adequate to the emergent phenomena is created. This process by which achieving the limits of an established axiomatic order of knowledge generates a critical situation where a new order is created in the line dynamically extending thinking in time toward infinity is the activity Du Bois takes as indicative of will—meaning auto-dynamic, self-aware, intentional intelligence. Identifying such intelligence with immeasurable chance, as he does, means the activity of thinking is so constitutively dynamic that, even though a certain type of consciousness is probable according to the axiomatic definitions of any given order, the order remains vulnerable to an unpredictable moment of thinking that compels it to its limits and beyond, enabling the creation of a new, emergent intelligence. Immanently manifest in relation to the order of calculability, its activity defined as an uncalculable variable, thinking fostering emergent intelligence in relation to the system is the activity through which the system is constructed and extended as a plurality of relatives. We can say, then, that Du Boisean orders of knowledge are conventional axiomatic comprehensions of multiple multiplicities in the relation of belonging-together; and their laws, then, become conversely the basis for the generalized definitions that, when satisfied, determine the situation of things as objects of thought.

Having taken as our starting point in all this the pertinence of arithmetization of analysis to the analogy Du Bois draws between hyperbola asymptotes and thinking in relation to continuity, we can now discern in the analogy an indissoluble conceptual triplet: truth-knowledge-uncalculable. In this Du Boisian conceptualization, thinking-in-action does not strive for the truth of the uncalculable in univocity of knowledge. In other words, to the extent knowledge entails a love of wisdom (φιλοσοφία, *philosophía*), it is not predicated on the presumption of absolutely comprehending the uncalculable, of ultimately measuring every*thing*, construing truth (αλήθεια, *alétheia*) as equating the univocity of knowledge with that of being. Nor is the uncalculable a void or repository of transcendent value, escaping representation in numbers. Rather, numbers are indexes of thinking's topological relation with the uncalculable, whereof its representation there, in calculation, is not where it is. Thinking-in-action, thereby, perpetually foregrounds the situation in which encountering the individual-acting-in-collective is possible. Along these lines, we can say, paraphrasing Dedekind, that every object of thought by definition is some*thing*; and when a diversity of such things can be associated together in the mind, they form an aggregate, which Dedekind labels "system [*System*]," and Cantor "set [*Menge*]."[166] Put in Du Bois's terminology, assuming society to be such an aggregate system, it is calculable, up to a point. The issue is not just determining what that point is as a limit, but whether the calculation of those things constituting the aggregate—Du Bois's *individuals*—is to be one of cardinal measure, pure quantities of indistinct multiples, or of well-ordered series in distinction. Cardinal measure is a focal point in his critique of the statistical calculus sociologists deploy in studying the Negro to "gleefully count his bastards and his prostitutes, [while] the very soul of the toiling, sweating black man is darkened by the shadow of a vast despair."[167] In calculating ordinal series, whereby the individual is an element in an infinite serial progression, the paramount task is determining *how* the individual is an articulation of or exists in the aggregate dynamics—as already remarked, this is the individual-acting-in collective—not what it is as an iteration of a type. The point in noting this is not to argue whether Du Bois had set theory consciously in mind when critiquing the statistical sociology stemming from Comte's positivism or presenting Aptheker with his asymptotes of the hyperbola analogy. The point is that, in his critique and analogy, Du Bois's thinking is in alignment with these developments. Consider, for instance, Dedekind's remarks at the beginning of his 1854 *Habilitationsvortrag*, "Über die Einführung neuer Funktionen in der Mathematik," about the relationship between truth and knowledge, which are remarkably consonant with those Du Bois will make to Aptheker ninety-eight years later:

If, as one finds, the main task of every science is striving for the establishment of *truth*—that is, the truth which is either wholly external to us, or, if it refers to us, is not our arbitrarily willful creation [*willkürliche Schöpfung*], but a necessity independent of our activity—then the end results, the ultimate goal, which can usually only be approximated, however, are to be explained as being immutable, as invariable. Science itself, on the other hand, which represents [*repräsentiert*] the course of human knowledge approaching these results, is capable of an infinite manifold [*unendlichen Mannigfaltigkeit*], infinitely different representation [*unendlich verschiedener Darstellung*]. [This is] because [science] is subordinate to the arbitrariness of man's will [*Willkür unterworfen*] and to all the imperfections of his mental powers.... This diversity in the conception of the objects of science finds its expression in the diverse forms, the diverse systems, in which one seeks to embed those conceptions.[168]

These remarks also bear on Du Bois's ambivalence about positivism's systemic epistemology, specifically, Comte's postulating axiomatic sociology as the final science in the system that, having abolished the ancient distinction between *nómos* (νόμος) and *physis* (φύσις), between moral and natural philosophy, coordinates retrospectively the development of the entirety of human knowledge achieving the definitive science of man. Even if we grant the successful mathematization of nature carried out by the scientific revolution inaugurated by Kepler and Galileo, Comte's claim that *all* phenomena can be conceptualized mathematically and expressed arithmetically in numbers is exaggerated. Thinking about the human condition cannot be reduced to enumeration. In the course of insisting a viable sociology includes sociology and physics, Du Bois argues that to do so, it must be provisionally assumed "that this is a world of Law and Chance. That in time and space, Law covers the major part of the universe, but that, in significance, the area left in the world to Chance is of tremendous import."[169] Not to say that chance is inexplicable. On the contrary. "In the last analysis, Chance is as explicable as Law: just as the Voice of God may sound behind physical law, so behind Chance we place free human wills capable of undetermined choices, frankly acknowledging that in both these cases we [con]front the humanly Inexplicable."[170] The symmetry drawn between God and human free will parallels that between law and chance, but it does so without a mediating agency or event. God is not made man, nor man made God. Although, there is the implication that just as man makes God as a concept by which to explain teleologically the meaning in the order of things, so too man makes free will as a way to explain the meaning of the persistently random, as in nonteleologically explainable, human actions in relation to law. In other words, "The assumption of Chance ... does not in the least hinder the search for natural law, it merely suspends as unproven and improbable its wilder hypotheses."[171] In this respect, there is an additionally noteworthy consonance between Du Bois's conception of *autonomous will* in the construction of orders of knowledge and Dedekind's of science being subjected to the arbitrariness of man's will (*Willkür unterworfen*). Although their respective immediate objects of knowledge are different—society for Du Bois and number for Dedekind—both consider those objects in relation to the dynamics of thinking, and in that regard, in terms of the relation between language and existence. Yet, any consonance is offset by a difference in orientation about the jurisdiction of language over being, or to be more precise, over the subject. Understanding this difference in orientation is crucial to understanding just how the engagement with German Neohumanism Du Bois invokes in "Sociology Hesitant" bears on his asymptotes of the hyperbola analogy and how that bears on the portrait of John Jones as an archetypal figure of the Negro as thinking-in-action in "Of the Coming of John." What's more, the pedagogical project of that same Neohumanism is alluded to by Jones in a pivotal scene of the story, which we shall attend to closely in a bit. For now, having noted the iteration, there is call for some careful, albeit summarizing, consideration of Dedekind's project so as to gain a fuller sense of how Du Bois's *Negro* tableau depicts a particular historical knowledge whose conceptual speculations and reflections—its thinking—in relation to things open up a distinctly different construal of what it means to be human. We must skip across the foundations of mathematics, as it were, in order to understand what is mean by the statement, and here I am paraphrasing Du Bois, "The dynamic soul of black folk cannot be *properly* counted."[172]

THINKING BY NUMBER THEORY

Contradicting the assertion attributed to Leopold Kronecker that "Natural numbers [*ganzen Zahlen*] are made by God, all else is the work of man,"[173] Dedekind postulates that "numbers are free creations [*freie Schöpfungen*] of the human mind, serving as a means to comprehend more easily and sharply the diversity of things."[174] He takes arithmetic to be a part of logic, regarding what he calls "the number-concept [*Zahlbegriff*] entirely independent from the psychological ideas [*Vorstellungen*] or intuitions [*Anschauungen*] of space and time, considering it an immediate [*unmittelbaren*] outflow of the pure laws of thought [*reinen Denkgesetze*]." Disputing Kant's postulate that mathematical concepts are immediately exhibited *in concreto* in pure intuition as such psychological ideas, Dedekind argues: "It is only through the purely logical process of building up the science of numbers [*Zahlen-Wissenschaft*], thereby acquiring the continuous number-domain [*Zahlen-Reich*] that we can accurately investigate our notions of space and time by bringing them into relation with this number-domain created in our mind."¹⁷⁵ Under close scrutiny, the simple operation of counting an aggregate or number of things is revealed to be fundamentally the enactment of "the mind's capability [*Fähigkeit*] to relate things to things, to make one thing correspond to another, or to transform [*abzubilden*] one thing into another, a capability without which absolutely [*überhaupt*] no thinking is possible."¹⁷⁶ This indispensable cognitive capability, then, is to be the "foundation on which the whole science of numbers must be established."¹⁷⁷

Elaborating further on how the creation of numbers is occurrent with the inherently continual exercise of the human mind's faculty to relate things to things, Dedekind proclaims as his motto a "reworded well-known saying: ἀεὶ ὁ ἄνθρωπος ἀριθμητίζει [*aei o anthrōpos arithmetizeî*, "humanity always arithmetizes"]."¹⁷⁸ The saying he recasts is one attributed to Gauss: "ἀεὶ ὁ θεός ἀριθμητίζει [*Aei ho theos arithmetizeî*, "God continually arithmetizes"]," which itself paraphrases a statement Plutarch attributes to Plato: "ἀεὶ ὁ θεός γεωμετρεῖ [*Aei ho theos geōmetreî*, "God continually geometrizes"]." Both Gauss's motto and Dedekind's rewording fall well within the shadow of the closing couplet from Carl Gustav Jacob Jacobi's gloss of Schiller's poem, *Archimedes und der Schüler*, so loved and often cited by Gauss:

> *Was Du im Kosmos erblickst, ist nur der Göttlichen Abglanz,*
> *In der Olympier Schaar thronet die ewige Zahl.*
> *[What you see in the cosmos is only the reflection of the divine,*
> *In Olympian throng is enthroned the Number Eternal.]* ¹⁷⁹

From Jacobi to Gauss to Dedekind, we have a chain of paraphrasis that, as José Ferreirós notes, reflects the changing perception of mathematics and the corresponding rise of arithmetic as the paradigmatic mathematical discipline—per David Hilbert's assertion that nineteenth-century mathematics developed "under the sign of number."¹⁸⁰ Equally important, Gauss's paraphrase retains the theological aspect of the originary Platonic motto in accounting for the impressive applicability and effectiveness of mathematics, thus seeming to verify Comte's proposition that everything conceivable is enumerable. Dedekind's secularization of the Gaussian motto, displacing θεός (*theos*) with ἄνθρωπος (*anthrōpos*), may seemingly shed its theology, but not its investment in reflection on the foundations, or what Gauss called "the metaphysics of mathematics," meaning the foundations, or ontological postulates regarding the existence and nature of mathematical objects, such as numbers. The question of higher arithmetic foundation, of what number is, was foremost among Dedekind's generation of German mathematicians. This includes Gottlob Frege, who is credited with truly pioneering the detailed execution of logicism in his *Die Grundlagen der Arithmetik: Eine logisch mathematische Untersuchung über den Begriff der Zahlen* (The foundations of mathematics: A logico-mathematical enquiry into the concept of number).[181] Dedekind was aware of Frege's conception of number, having arrived at a somewhat similar logicism independently ten years earlier—keeping in mind that even though "Was sind und was sollen die Zahlen?" was not published until 1888, he had come to his views by 1874.[182] I say somewhat because, while Frege also held the number-concept to be the immediate outflow of the pure laws of thought, independent from ideas or intuitions of space and time, his conception of thought itself was decidedly Platonist in a way Dedekind's was not.[183]

For Frege, thoughts are conceptual (*der Begriff*), and not in the Kantian psychological sense, but in a decidedly Platonic sense: "Thoughts are neither things in the external world nor psychological ideas [*Vorstellungen*]."[184] They belong to what he terms a "third realm," the objects therein, "in accord with ideas, cannot be perceived by the senses, but, in accord with noumenal things [*Dingen*], do not require any [subjective] bearer [*Trägers*] to whose consciousness they belong."[185] These objects, the existence of which is completely non-spatiotemporal a priori, being neither psychological (ideas) nor material, include number. Number is what Frege calls, quoting Schröder, "a general concept-word [*allmeines Begriffswort*] or *notio communis*."[186] To put this in the context of Frege's overall system, there is a tripartition of concept, number-object, and number-sign, whereby it follows that "an ascription of number [*Zahlangabe*] contains [*enthält*] an assertion of a concept," in the sense that it is a predication of the concept.[187] For instance, in the proposition, "the number 0 belongs to the concept F," 0 is only an element in the predicate if we consider the concept F to be in fact the subject.[188] Precisely because number is an element in predication, it is revealed to be "a self-subsistent [*selbständiger*] objective object [*Gegenstand*]."[189] As such, number ascription is attached to concept, not as a property but as an extension (*Umfang*). By Frege's definition, "The number belonging to the concept F is the extension of the concept, is equinumerous [*gleichzahlig*] to the concept F."[190] Frege's investment is in the cardinality of number on the conviction that number consists—that is, has existence—in denoting the quantitative identity of concepts, for which he coined the term *gleichzahlig*, and which gets rendered accordingly in English as "equinumerous," denoting a one-to-one correspondence between two sets or classes that are said to have the same cardinality. And as he adds in the footnote to this definition, "For 'extension of the concept' we could simply say 'concept,'" reinforcing his postulate that all concepts have extensions, which are objects within the domain of all concepts: the a priori third realm. Having defined number in this way, he presents the proposition: "The extension of the concept 'equinumerous to the concept F'

is identical [*ist gleich*] with the extension of the concept 'equinumerous to the concept *G*.'" This proposition "is true if and only if the proposition, 'the same number belongs to the concept *F* as to the concept *G*,' is also true." Elaborating the argument, he states: "If all concepts that are equinumerous with *G* are also equinumerous with *F*, then conversely, all concepts equinumerous with *F* are also equinumerous with *G*." In other words, Frege's definition of number states that every concept *F* generates a number, the extension of the concept "equinumerous to *F*," which comprehends (*umfassender*) all of those concepts having the same quantity of extension as *F* and so is equinumerous to *F*. Number is what denotes this collection of concepts, thereby validating the statement: "is a concept equinumerous to *F*." This deduction of number as a consequence of the concept is achieved through the logical operation of equinumerosity. Accordingly, not only is number revealed to be an a priori objective object of the third realm, but the operations of logical expression, the propositional calculus (*Begriffsschrift*), are the most adequate means of denoting and proving number's objective existence.[191] Frege, thus, takes up of Leibniz's formula of substitutivity—"Eadem sunt, quorum unum potest substitui alteri salva veritate [Those things are the same of which one can be substituted for the other without violating truth]"—as a definition of identity.[192] Postulating from this, on "purely logical grounds," that "nothing falls under the concept 'not identical to itself [*sich selbst ungleich*],'" Frege arrives at his definition of zero (*Null*): "o is the number that belongs to the concept 'not identical with itself [*sich selbst ungleich*].'"[193] In other words, the extension of the concept "not identical with itself" is void, so that o is the number identical with the concept "not identical with itself" and is the number belonging to every concept whose extension is empty; thereby constituting a set of such concepts. As Bertrand Russell pointed out, this generates a disabling paradox.[194] Responding to Russell's discovery, Frege faults his "transformation of the generalization of an equality into an equality of value"—that is to say, of confusing "identical with itself," per Leibniz's principle, with equal to itself. This does not rescue the pure logic of his deduction. On the contrary, distinguishing identity from the logical predicate of equality casts doubt on the Leibnizian postulate that "every object is identical to itself" upon which Frege bases his definition of zero as an ontological statement, or what Cantor would call an unprovable axiom. Accordingly, Frege's Platonist logicism, which sets out to establish that thought itself is equinumerous with number—that is, it presupposes number—demonstrates in its operation of definition and deduction the anteriority of the thinking subject, which is the very psychologism he set out to dispel and attributed to Dedekind.

In contradistinction to Frege's Platonist construal of numbers as a priori *objects* presupposed in thought, Dedekind holds numbers to be merely possible objects *of* thought.¹⁹⁵ Whereas the context for Frege's work is the concept, and his construal of number cardinal, that for Dedekind is the multiplicity that counts for one, and his construal ordinal. The significance of the difference becomes clear when we reconsider his assertion about number as a free creation, which is where we earlier noted consonance with Du Bois. Free creation is a cognitive activity whereby numbers are generated as objects of thought in relation to things in aggregate, which Dedekind calls *System*, through a purely logical procedure. This is a key point where he and Frege deviate. For Frege, "concept" and "extension of concept" are logical notions, but *System*, or aggregate, is not.¹⁹⁶ To reiterate, Dedekind begins his account of number with a description of things in aggregate, or as he puts it, "Systeme von Elementen [Systems of Elements]." Let us take up what he states about the relationship between thinking and things:

> 1. I understand by *thing* [*Ding*] every object [*jeden Gegenstand*] of our thinking. In order to be able to conveniently speak of things, we designate them by signs [*Zeichen*], e.g., by letters; and we may, thus, speak in brevity of the thing *a*, or even simply of *a*, meaning the thing denoted by *a*, and not in any way the letter *a* itself. A thing is completely determined by all that can be predicated [*ausgesagt*] or thought [*gedacht*] concerning it. A thing *a* is the same as *b* (identical [*identisch*] to *b*), and *b* the same as *a*, if all that is thought concerning *b* can also be thought concerning *a*. That *a* and *b* are only signs or names for one and the same thing is indicated by the notation $a = b$, and also by $b = a$. If furthermore $b = c$, such that *c* like *a* is a sign for the thing denoted by *b*, then $a = c$. If the above correspondence [*Übereinstimmung*] of the thing denoted by *a* with the thing denoted by *b* is not present [*nicht vorhanden*], then these things *a*, *b* are different, *a* is another thing than *b*, *b* another thing than *a*; there is some property which comes to the one, does not belong to the other.¹⁹⁷

Having established that things, the objects of our thinking, are expressed in and identified with signs, Dedekind then describes the cognitive activity of aggregating them, forming a system of which they are the constituting elements, giving a naïve or nonformulaic definition of set, which Ernst Zermelo will subsequently formulate as the axiom of extension:

> 2. It often occurs that diverse things, *a, b, c,* ... for some reason can be considered from a common point of view [*gemeinsamen Gesichtspunkte*], can be associated [*zusammengestellt*] in the mind, and we then say that they form a *system* [*System*] *S*; we call the things *a, b, c,* ... *elements* of the system *S*, they are *contained* [*enthalten*] in *S*; conversely, *S* consists of these elements. Such a system *S* (an aggregate [*Inbegriff*], a manifold, a totality) as an object of

our thought is likewise a thing (1); S is completely determined when, for each and every thing, it is determined whether or not it is an element of S. The system S is hence the same as the system T, in signs $S = T$, when every element of S is also an element of T, and every element of T is also an element of S.[198]

The signs $S = T$ here do not only denote a logically necessary property of equality; they also express an assumption about membership, which Dedekind then presents in definition: "A system A is said to be *part* [*Teil*] of a system S when every element of A is also an element of S." Dedekind expresses this by "the sign $A \ni S$," corresponding to the more current $A \subseteq S$ denoting A is a subset of S, which he also states as "S is the whole of A," meaning "among the elements of S are found all the elements of A. Since further every element S of a system S by (2) can be itself considered a system, we can therefore employ the notation $s \ni S$."

It is pertinent to our concerns here, with regard to Du Bois's thinking, that not only is a system some *thing*, but so is its sign, about which can be predicated qualities such as form, color, magnitude, none of which has any pertinence for the thing the sign denotes, and so is "entirely neglected [*gänzlich absieht*]."[199] Only two qualities predicated of the sign are pertinent: its denoting system, which is the thing that is being-in-relation, community, with other things of its sort; and its being a function depicting this thing-in-relation with other things. Dedekind calls the latter of these two aspects *mapping (Abbildung)*, which is to be taken in the sense of mathematical morphism, or *function*, which he denotes by $\varnothing$, defining it as "a law according to which, for every determinate element s of [system] S there *belongs* [*gehört*] a determinate thing called the image [*Bild*] of s, which is denoted by $\varnothing(s)$."[200] His further elaboration that "we also say that $\varnothing(s)$ *corresponds* [*entspricht*] to the element s, that $\varnothing(s)$ *results* or is produced from s by the mapping $\varnothing$, that s is mapped into $\varnothing(s)$ by the mapping $\varnothing$," suggests one-to-one correspondence or bijective function.[201] The simplest mapping of a system is that by which each of its elements is mapped into itself; in Dedekind's notation, this is $\varnothing(S) \ni S$, which he also denotes as $\varnothing(s) = s'$, whereby s' is an element or part of S. By generalizing the conditions that a mapping into a system must satisfy in order to make proof by induction possible, Dedekind obtains his theory of *chain* [*Kette*],[202] by way of which he arrives at the definition of infinity: "A system S is said to be infinite when there is a proper part of S into which S can be distinctly (bijectively [*bijective*]) mapped."[203] What mapping determines is being-in-relation as an object of thought irrespective, as already noted, of any particularities or aspects (*der besonderen Beschaffenheit*) of the signs deployed in mapping that are not directly germane to the mapping relation.[204] This activity of freeing (*Befreiung*) the signs from those particularities, which Dedekind calls *Abstraktion* (abstraction), is a crucial operation in his paradigmatic definition of the simply infinite system, $\mathcal{N}$, the series of natural numbers:

> A system $\mathcal{N}$ is said to be simply infinite when there exists a bijective [*bijective*] mapping $\varnothing$ of $\mathcal{N}$ into itself such that $\mathcal{N}$ appears as the chain [*Kette*] of an element not contained in $\varnothing(\mathcal{N})$ We call this element, which we shall denote in what follows by the symbol 1, the *base-element* [*Grundelement*] of $\mathcal{N}$, and say the simple infinite system $\mathcal{N}$ is *well-ordered* [*geordnet*] by this mapping $\varnothing$.
>
> ... If in the consideration of a simply infinite system $\mathcal{N}$ ordered by a mapping $\varnothing$ we entirely neglect the special character of the elements, simply retaining their distinguishability and taking into account only the relations to one another in which they are placed by the ordering mapping $\varnothing$, then these elements are called *natural numbers* or *ordinal numbers* or simply *numbers*, and the base-element 1 is called the *base-number* of the *number-series* $\mathcal{N}$. With reference to this freeing [*Befreiung*] of the elements from every other content (abstraction) we are justified in calling the numbers a free creation of the human mind.[205]

We should take care to note that Dedekind does not mean by *Abstraktion* the erasure of the entire content, the quality of a thing; rather it acts to bring to consciousness the meaning of a certain relation *purely in itself*, independently of all particular cases of application. Number is meaningful as a concept/sign (*Zahlbegriff*) independently from the factual diversity of the things that can be enumerated. That diversity, therefore, is what must be disregarded in determining the character and existence of number; and it is in this sense number is free, or liberated. All said and done, abstraction means logical concentration on relational connection, paralleling the psychological circumstances of the subjective stream of presentations. Dedekind's aim is "to analyse the *structure* of the natural numbers, up to isomorphism"; so the paramount thing is the sequential relationship expressed between the elements constituting a system.[206] What is paramount for Dedekind is not the individuality, the peculiarities (*besonderen Beschaffenheit*), of each element, but the system they jointly exhibit. In other words, the elements of any given system at all, have no pertinent properties other than those relating them to other elements of the system, which is to say they exhibit the system in abstraction; or to put it in more contemporary terms, they characterize an *abstract structure*. Identifying abstract structure with a system of recursive progressing relations—whether in intension or in extension with the set of relations isomorphic to a given abstract structure—gets an arithmetic concerned with elaborating the properties of relation of all systems of objects (including concrete structures) exhibiting that abstract structure. Arithmetic is therefore the science that elaborates the abstract logical structure all progressions have in common merely by virtue of being progressions. And as is implied by the oft-cited proof for Theorem 66, "There exist infinite systems," only the self and the thought-world must exist a priori as a consequence of the pure laws of logic:

> Proof. My thought-world [*Gedankenwelt*]—that is, the totality S [*Gesamtheit S*] of all things [*aller Dinge*] that can be the objects of my thinking—is infinite. For if s denotes an element of S, then the thought s', that s can be object of my thought, is itself an element of S. If we picture this as an image $\emptyset(s)$ of the element s, then the result determined by this mapping $\emptyset$ of S has the property that the image S' is part of S; and S' is indeed a genuine part of S, because there are elements of S (e.g., my own ego) that are different from such a thought s' and therefore are not contained in S'. Finally, it is clear, if a, b are different elements of S, their images, a', b', are also different, so that the mapping $\emptyset$ is a distinct (bijective [*bijektive*]).... Hence S is infinite, which was to be proved.[207]

Dedekind's procedure in this proof is to explicate the one-to-one correspondence (bijection) between an "object of my thought," s, and the thought s', "that s is an object of my thought."[208] There is, in other words, a correspondence between a thought, and a thought of that thought such that a "possible object of my thought" is identical with *a* possible thought. There is, then, a bijection of two systems of thought: "thoughts in general," the object of which is anything at all, and thoughts that are "thought of a thought," the object of which is a thought. The second system, "thought of a thought," is a proper part (*Teil*) of the first, "all possible thoughts," given that there are thoughts that are not thoughts of thought. Consequently, in accord with the definition of infinity, the system of all my possible thoughts S is infinite because one of its proper parts can be distinctly bijectively mapped. Following the course of the proof: there exists a thought that is the thought of the thought, of the thought, of the thought, etcetera. The one thing assuring that this infinite recursive process of thought is properly reflexive is there being one thought that is not reflexive, not a thought of a thought, which Dedekind terms "my own ego." What does not allow itself to be thought as a distinct thought of a distinct thought is the act of thinking itself, or better put, the "I thinking," per Descartes's *ego cogito*, and contra Heidegger's paraphrasis "cogito me cogitare."[209] This pre-reflective thinking, *cogito*, cannot be counted but is what is revealed *in the counting*. For Dedekind, arithmetic is thinking; and to the extent number is an object of thought, there is an immanent identity, an ontological commensurability of thinking and its object, along the lines of Parmenides's poetic declaration: "Τό γάρ αυτο νοειν έστιν τε καί είναι, To gar auto noein estin te kai einai

(Thought and being are the same)]."²¹⁰ And, along those lines, arithmetic accesses the being qua being that subtends and enables all possible thought. Counting, the ordinal mapping of sequence, is supposed to *prove*, through sheer logical operation, pure thought, the existence of infinity.

Dedekind's conviction that notation follows notion notwithstanding,²¹¹ mapping obscures its conceptual foundation as a technique when it abstracts from deductive psychological procedures formal calculative operations and rules that are taken to be a logic rather than a technique. This allows for symbolic abstraction to be the only meaningful concept, the only pertinent *thing* for thinking, thereby displacing all other concepts. And per the exposition in paragraph one of section one, material sign denotes symbolic conception as the object of thought; so that the calculus can be rightly regarded as a "technique to manipulate signs [*eine Zeichentechnik*]."²¹² Clarity of knowledge about things is achieved through the operation with letters and various signs of relation according to postulated rules governing their arrangement, as in, for instance, the notation for the set of all even natural numbers: $\{n \in \mathbb{N} : (\exists k)[k \in \mathbb{N} \wedge n = 2k]\}$.²¹³ These letters and signs of arithmetical calculative operations map (*abzubilden*) objects of thoughts about thoughts. Again, this is not psychologism. Dedekind expressly does not, *pace* Michael Dummett, take subjective psychological ideas (*Vorstellungen*) as the reference of number.²¹⁴ Nor is his mapping (*Abbildung*) analogous to Frege's number as *extension* of concept. Rather the sign-designation (*Zeichen*) of number-concept (*Zahlbegriff*) is a creation that, contra Frege's existent abstract entity, is arrived at through the generative activity of disregarding (*abstraction*) otherwise cognizable qualities of the sign. It is of some pertinence, in this regard, that Dedekind's description of progression suggests a dynamics of signification, a semiosis in which the sign indicates the tripartite interrelationship: the sign *a* stands in relation to a thinking mind, for whom it denotes something. The formal calculative processes with signs, whereby the extension of the number field is validated on purely structural local grounds, in its very operations, manifests, as well as compensates for the finite temporal character of human knowledge. Indeed, whereas the surrounding world of concrete things is correlated with our perception as immediately present in experience, pure numbers and their laws—that is to say, infinite progression—are not present unless *we* adopt the arithmetical attitude by focusing thinking in abstraction. Even the contact between the world of concrete things carried out in the most elementary activity of counting aggregations of concrete objects exhibits what Paul Benacerraf terms the human being as "a decision procedure for nonrecursive sets."²¹⁵ We can take, then, the letter $\mathcal{N}$ of Dedekind's mapping as not merely designating but as constituting, that is, *being* an assemblage. Taken that way, the letter $\mathcal{N}$ reveals its laws in arithmetic operation—in the same way the grammar of a language is revealed in writing. Along these lines, Dedekind's metonymic chain (*Kette*) of letters, in which each individual is defined by the immediately preceding one through an act of transition (*Übergang*), in its bijective function—which is again another designation for mapping (*Abbildung*)—is deictic of the subject thinking.[216] As Russell's paradox points out, Dedekind does not fully achieve what he set out to do, which is to *deduce* the operative rule of number, as well as its existence, from pure logic or thought. Despite the structural deduction of the infinite, its existence is not determined by intuition or proof. Paraphrasing Alain Badiou, it is not gained by any *deduction*, but by a *decision*.[217] Continuing the paraphrasis, with regard to the infinite, there is nothing to say other than: it is. Number, then, not only indicates the necessity of the uncalculable subject thinking; it also indicates the ontological grounding of that subject.

Cantor, who is more explicit about the ontological commitment, was well aware of this when postulating the *absolute infinite* or *inconsistent multiplicity* as the relation (*Beziehungen*) in which the actual infinite is "realized in the highest perfection, in completely independent otherworldly Being [*außrweltlichen Sein*], *in Deo*."[218] Further emphasizing the nondeductibility and axiomatic status of the *inconsistent multiplicity*, he maintains: "the *Absolute* can only be recognized [*anerkannt*] not known [*erkannt*], not even approximately known."[219] Even for *consistent multiplicity* (*konsistente Vielheit*), what Cantor also calls a "set [*Menge*],"[220] including the *transfinite*, which because "it is manifestly limited to further augmentation [*Vermehrung*] and related to the finite ... is strictly the opposite [*strengstens entgegen*] of the absolute,"[221] a proof of consistency cannot be deduced but only postulated axiomatically as "an unprovable truth [*unbeweisbare Wahrheit*]."[222] Nevertheless, the transfinite with its abundance of transformations and forms necessarily points to an *Absolute*, to a "true infinity [*wahrhaft Unendliche*]," making it, Cantor claims, "a suitable symbol of the absolute."[223] To the extent it is possible to speak in any meaningfully immanent way of the *absolute infinite*, it is mathematically. And to the extent the *absolute infinite* indexes the transcendent Being *in Deo*, from which totality of existence derives, mathematics, particularly the higher mathematics of transfinites, is the best tool for gaining knowledge of being qua being. We can discern in this how Badiou discovers in Cantor's set theory the warrant for his postulate that mathematics is ontology. More to the point of our concerns, while Dedekind is not Platonic to the same degree as Cantor—the *simple infinite* indexes the human *ego* not God—his construing number concepts as free creations of the human mind and highlighting the true contingency of the number-domain (*Zahlenreihe*) still presume the operations of arithmetic to be indicating something that cannot be counted but enables counting. Putting this in terms of Dedekind's proof that infinite systems exist, with the thought of the *simple infinite*, thought therefore touches on and points beyond its own limits. Dedekind may call this *my own ego*, rather than Cantor's *in Deo*; nevertheless, it is through the technique of arithmetic thinking that being qua being has a meaningful appearance, εῖδος (*eidos*), in nature, φύσις (*physis*).²²⁴

Returning our focus back to Du Bois, we can discern in his asymptotes of the hyperbola analogy further indication of an alignment in his thinking about infinity with Poincaré, for whom, contra Cantor's theory of transfinite numbers, the actual infinite does not exist, but rather is an asymptotic postulate that enables progression in thinking. In fact, although Du Bois does not share Poincaré's Kantian view of mathematics as a priori synthetic—a view that Poincaré held also expressly contra set theory—his conception of the role chance qua free will plays in the discovery of the laws of physics echoes that set out by Poincaré in *Science et méthode*, where chance (*hasard*) is identified with the unconscious, which "plays an important role in mathematical creation."²²⁵ Du Bois is far more skeptical, however, about numbers, noting that arithmetic cannot expresses all orders of relation. A great deal happens besides birth and death rates, women's societies, the ethics of which are driven by something other than death, and whose principles of pleasure cannot even aspire to the eudaimonic. Even though society is a thing, the distinctiveness of its elements being a function of relation, and even though these elements are enumerable, there are prominent aspects of the relation—"the thousand and one little actions which go to make up life"—that are not. Regarding the Negro, to the extent arithmetic envelops a coordinated movement of thought coextensive with being, in which the distinction between a knowing subject and a known object is of no pertinence, exposing the decision-activity of the thinking subject—this is what Badiou means when he asserts "mathematics thinks"—that movement has little to do with the Negro except as a limit, the point at which calculation flounders. In other words, the distinction between a knowing subject and a known object is of the *greatest pertinence*; and the "Negro problem" instantiates the problem of infinity. As such, it exposes the activity of *decision* in human being, which, axiomatic as that may be, is conventional. At its core, the discourse of philosophical ontology is *doxa*, as is its corollary, anthropology; and their respective bijective mappings of things are fictive.

Du Bois's argument that statistical sociology cannot provide a definitive account of communicative intellect-in-action is not based on an objection to symbolic representation of the dynamic tripartite relationship between thinking, its objects, and its activity of signification. Numbers can and do signify something about the world. The objection is to the hypostatizing of the sign's technique at the cost of obscuring the conditions of its creation in thinking, whereby the sign's aspect as indicial of a dynamic tripartite semiosis—in which an individual sign's value is expressed in relation to adjacent existing things for some collectivity of thinking minds *in* communicative relation to one another—is diminished in favor of its being indicial of the correspondent identification between thought and things—what Du Bois characterizes as, "confounding Things with Thoughts of Things," or more precisely, taking the things that are thoughts and countable as the best, if not primary, way to truth. In Du Bois's corrective to that, the sign stands in relation to something for someone thinking, for whom the standing in relation is significant. It is irreducibly deictic, in the sense that it is indexical of the dynamic *standing-in-relation-to-for-which*. The *for-which* is not reducible to the sign; it is, however, articulated in the activity of signification. Any cardinality between the sign and thing is activated by the *for-which*, and that activity is determinate, or predicable, only within a defined system, without being confined to it. In contradistinction to the ontological tendency at play in Dedekind's incipient description of a tripartite semiosis, the sign or the letter is not approached as a mark of essence or existence that reveals the deep structure of being qua being, but rather of relational situation. The chance events of intentional will are occurrent with the creation of conceptual structures, taken to be instantiated in the order of things, not as the necessary reflective instantiation of the cosmic order, but as a contingent articulation of the forces of life. In this way, intellect-in-action is a thinking about things that *gets* reality *with* a particular order, in the strong phenomenological sense that thinking/willing is only one particular force among the forces of reality, acting in relation to them in constituting the world. To dissuade any inclination to detect Hegel here, I reiterate that things in nature are, in accordance with Dedekind's number theory, multiple multiplicities and not immediate singularities; so that any particular point of intellect-in-action, the specific actualization of dynamic placing-in-relation, is a multiplicity of multiplicities. This is in contrast to Hegel's conception of the individual identification with *Geist*. In this regard, we should pause for a moment and take note of the semantic range of this term in which Hegel invests so much. It is a Germanization of the Latin *spiritus*, in the sense of disembodied entities, called in English "ghost" or "spirits." *Spiritus* in the Latin Vulgate is the rendering of the Septuagint πνεῦμα (*pneuma*), traceable back to the Tanakhic רוּחַ (*rūakh*), meaning "breath." When used in phrases such as רוּחַ קָדְשׁוֹ (*rūaḥ qadshu*), "His holy spirit" (Isaiah 63:10), which is translated in the Septuagint and subsequently in the Gospels as τo πνεῦμα τo αγιον, (*pneuma to hagion*), becoming *spiritus sancti* in the Vulgate. In that scriptural discourse, *Geist* is an agential dynamic force that takes possession of and flows through the human, somewhat akin to the Stoic concept of φυχὴ κόσμου (*psyché kósmou*) *anima mundi* or "world soul." *Geist* acquires the sense of human intellect or mind in eighteenth-century German philosophical discourse under the influence of the Cartesian philosophical sense of *esprit*. Idiomatically, it still retains the Christian connotation of spiritual in the adjectival *geistlich* and the cognate adjective *geisterhaft* referring to the "ghostly" or "spectral," with *geistig* reserved for the "mental" or "intellectual." Hegel's concept of *Weltgeist*, set out in his *Phänomenologie des Geistes*, is resonant with the Stoic sense of *anima mundi*, insofar as it is a way of philosophizing history through the mediation of kinds of *Volkgeister* (specific collective types of mind) moving in space and time to ultimately arrive at the concrete universal history.[226] Because the semantic field of *Geist* is capacious in this way, it can be simply rendered in English as "spirit" or "mind," either of which loses the connotative range. To preclude that loss, it is sometimes rendered as "spirit/mind," which is rather awkward. An alternative, also well-traveled path, the one followed here, simply retains *Geist* as a German loanword. Taking this clarification in stride, according to Hegel's conception of individual identification with *Geist*, "The things of nature [*Naturdinge*] are only immediate and single, but man as *Geist* doubles [*verdoppelt*] himself, by being at first as things in nature are, but then he is just as much for himself; he sees himself, represents [*vorstellt*], thinks himself, and only by way of this active placing of himself before himself [*Fürsichsein*] is he *Geist*."[227] On this account, it is no small matter that Du Bois's exhibition of intellect-in-action is entitled *The **Souls** of Black Folk*, given that it is about multiple multiplicities.

The construal of intellect-in-action as the dynamic placing-in-relation of a multiplicity of multiplicities gets to the matter with the asymptotes of the hyperbola analogy. What begins as an account of possibility in knowledge turns out to be about the actuality of thinking in the world. Assuming the soundness of the preceding elaboration of his concept of law and chance as poetic, any sense of actuality Du Bois had regarding the relationship between thinking and knowledge—at least based on what he wrote, published and unpublished—was not of an essential regulating force of change that, while inherent in the process of change directs that process, a priori. Such an essentialist force would be by definition a sort of emanating energy whose origin transcends change, resembling Bergson's *élan vital*. Even if this force were held to inhere in the particular forms undergoing change as a property—say, Stepto's generic narrative forms—for it to be the regulating agency of change it would have to be continuous and so unchanging in itself—say, Stepto's "quintessential, atemporal Afro-American 'we,'" which assumes a disregarded ontological weight to be redeemed. Du Bois is not concerned with redeeming disregarded ontology, but rather with arresting the ongoing disregard for existent beings that is carried out in the service of enforcing ontological truth. Du Bois is not, in other words, proposing a vitalist notion of life, or even a Heideggerian notion of "Being" in the abstract. According to the sense of the 1956 letter to Aptheker, Du Bois's thinking about change lacks any such presumption of teleology, providence, or overarching deterministic progress. Any sense that Du Bois had of the energy or force of transformation was as capricious and eventful. It occurs with the coincidence of the complexities of force that make up our reality.

At stake is our understanding of the significance of events through time. Du Bois's thinking about the Negro brings us to ask: What is Time? This changes how we understand his argument for cultural continuity as the bulwark against capitalism's violent forces of commodification. On the one hand, Du Bois conceives the Negro as culture in the sense of ethnographic event (à la Edmund Tylor). On the other, he conceives the Negro as continuity of self-reflection (à la Arnold, Whitman, and Emerson). In both instances, his conception of Negro culture is derived from his understanding of temporal continuity being paralleled by the continuity of human consciousness, but not identified with it. So, it is not the case that thinking is merely the mediating agency between truth and knowledge, grounded in consciousness. On the contrary, it is always at the crux of infinity and finitude, where individual possibility multiplies and consciousness is always eventful, and so aleatory. Here is where Du Bois's paradox of equally evident uncalculability among the calculable is sharpest. What Du Bois proposes in insisting that sociology "flatly face the paradox" is reimagining the nature of necessity and contingency, as well as the dynamic relationship between them, in the course of which the human subject gets articulated. Without altogether abandoning the arithmetization of analysis, which has given us an exceedingly dynamic understanding of nature, physics, he leaves off the ontological commitment that still haunts arithmetic in such concepts as Dedekind's recognizably Schopenhauerian pre-logical *willful creation* (*willkürliche Schöpfung*). This has to do with Du Bois's seeking to ground sociology and social action in a "science of ethics" that has shed all trace of teleology, in the course of which he critically engages Josiah Royce's post-Hegelian idealism. Du Bois's flight from teleology will be taken up at some length in the 2nd Set. It will have to suffice here to point out that his critical engagement with Royce is not based on any investment in Royce's "'deflated' image of Hegel freed of ontological-metaphysical commitments, reduced to a general theory of discourse."228 The general theory of discourse, the semiotics Du Bois extrapolates from Royce, and by way of Royce, ultimately from Charles Sanders Peirce, is not a naturalism; it is not a cover-up for the idealist form of thought, any more than it is a neo-Kantian retrieval of the a priori transcendental of communication. Granted, such naturalism *can* be discerned lurking in the lines of Peirce's *synechism*—his neologism for continuity, community, and the evolutionary love of God (*agapism*) that resembles Spinoza's *deus sive natura*, whereby knowledge and acceptance of necessity is the true meaning of freedom. Peirce counterbalances this *synechism* with what he terms *tychism*, denoting the absolute contingency of the void of structure, which he construes as the material cause of semiosis. The extent to which Peirce's *synechism/*

tychism suggests the Hegelian relationship between necessity and contingency, whereby necessity (*agapē*) itself posits and mediates contingency (*tyche*) as the external field in which it expresses-actualizes itself, has to do with a persistent investment in teleology clearly evident in such statements as: "The agapistic development of thought should, if it exists, be distinguished by its purposive character, this purpose being the development of an idea.... The philosophy we draw from John's gospel is that this is the way mind develops; and as for the cosmos, only so far as it yet is mind, and so has life, is it capable of further evolution.... That is the sort of evolution which every careful student of my essay 'The Law of Mind' must see that synechism calls for."[229]

Du Bois expressly rejects such a teleological theory of mind, however, and also eschews the naturalism he finds haunting both Hume's and Kant's metaphysics.[230] When considered in relation to this critique of teleology, Du Bois's paradox of "Law" and "Chance" highlights how the vocabulary of modern ethics concerning necessity and contingency perpetuates the paradoxes of Western theology by reconfiguring them along the divide of natural and moral philosophy. Rather than naturalizing necessity and contingency as the double structure of providence in accordance with the mathematizing of nature, Du Bois problematized the traditional philosophical understanding of the relation between necessity and contingency, as inherited from the Greek world and mediated by Galilean science. Or to put it exactly in the terms of that tradition, he problematizes the necessity of θέσις (*thesis*), the necessity of conventions, as different from the necessity of φύση (*phusei*), or things that are "according to nature" and reducible to it. Bear in mind that θέσει (*thesei*) is the singular feminine dative of θέσις (*thesis*), which generally connotes placement or position; in the philosophical discourse, it refers to assumption requiring proof (Aristotle, *Topics*, 104b19), and in the legal, setting forth as convention. The object of Du Bois's "Law" is clearly φύση (*phusei*), which is subject to ὑπόθεσις (hypothesis)—the compound of ὑπο (*hypo*), "below" and θέσις (*thesis*)—and the "assumption of Chance" is a hypothesis about the efficacy of contingent human will in nature. Arguably, he is problematizing the traditional philosophical thinking about the relation between nature and conventions precisely in terms of making the paradox of the incalculability of human intellect-in-action available to what he called *science of mind*. What's more, he troubles the philosophical ontology's distinction between the mathematical abstraction of *dianoia* and that of mimetic poetry (ποιήσει [*poiēsei*]), whereby the former's de-anthropocentrizing of thinking is supposed to lead directly to truth, while the latter's toward illusion. Du Bois's argument is that both modalities of thinking are anthropocentric to the extent that both give expression to thinking in abstraction in relation to humans. Both are ways of thinking the dynamics of human intellect-in-action. By calling on sociology to be the combination of these, Du Bois seems to concur with Comte in imagining a unified field of thought, except whereas Comte's field is firmly based on the government of mathematics, on arithmetic as the purest expression of the idea, Du Bois recognizes, à la Dedekind, that numbers too are mimetic. And so the task is to achieve an assemblage of heteronomous *thinkings* capable of modeling the dynamic correlation of physical and intellectual energy in-action without slipping back into either a Platonic or a Scholastic metaphysics of being qua being. In this respect, the Negro cannot be counted. To be more precise, there is no bijection of Negro as a sign in the calculations of sociology and the intellect-in-action indicated by it. The intelligence it indexes is that of the signifying system engendering the sign. In this sense, Barton was on to something in complaint that, "the word 'Negro' is a white man's word to make us feel inferior." By that same token, so was Du Bois in his response: "And then too, without the word that means us, where are all those spiritual ideals, those inner bonds, those group ideals and forward strivings of this mighty army of 12 millions?" In this sense, *Negro* symbolizes the unmeasurable, the dynamic of intellect-in-action that cannot be counted as a thing but only encountered; and even then it cannot be properly formulated in terms of the discourse of being qua being. Simply put, "Ontology does not allow us to understand the being of black [*l'être du Noir*]."[231] We might well add in elucidation there is no proper ontological *eidos* or, paraphrasing Fanon, *il n'y pas paraître* (it does not appear)—a situation Ellison depicts as *invisibility*, which is not the same thing as nonexistence.[232] Black exists without the necessity of claiming absolute being, or even a privileged discursive access to absolute being. The reason Du Bois does not answer the question "How does it feel to be a problem?" has to do with the phrase, "feel to be," which indicates the semantic absurdity of what is really being asked: "How does it feel to be a problem for me?" In other words, how does it feel to be seen by me, who in asking the question, demonstrate manifestly my inability to see you, except as that which is seeing me? To ask the question in this way gives priority to the seer who is seen as the orientation of being, making the paradox of immanence/transcendence reflective: I have a thought of my thought of you thinking about my thought of you. We are firmly in the grip of Dedekind's proof of infinity, which secures itself in "my own ego." The only viable response to this egoist quaestio, and it must be a retort, is: one does not *feel to be* anything, one simply *is-in-action*, which does not appear but runs beside, indeed is *besides* appearing. Such is asymptotic thinking, which Du Bois sets out to illustrate, we could even say map (*abzubilden*), in "Of the Coming of John."

It might be asked at this point if all the discussion of the arithmetization of analysis was needed to bring us to this understanding of Du Bois's project. The plain answer is yes, and for two related reasons. First, it is germane to the problem of calculability and uncalculability central to Du Bois's critique and reformulation of sociology. Second, the statistical calculus Du Bois set out to revalue as a useful tool of analysis, but with severe limitations in describing the complex dynamics of intellect-in-action, is one of the fruits of the arithmetization of analysis. By carefully considering the developments in arithmetic theory attending the nineteenth-century German *neuhumanistischen Bildungsreform* (neohumanist education reform) Du Bois refers to in "Sociology Hesitant," we gain a better sense of the gist of his asymptotes of the hyperbola analogy, and an even fuller sense of its nonontological thrust. For Du Bois, it is not just that the souls of black folk present an ontological problem, or more precisely, punctuate a persistent crisis congenital to the ontological project: the necessity of ἀνθρωπος (*anthrōpos*, "the human") to thinking being. Rather, it is that ontology is a hindrance to black folks being. And, insofar as their way of being is one of the multiplicities of *Homo sapiens* in-action that are called "human," what ontology hinders is a more historically dynamic connotation of that term.

In illustration, we need merely recall the narrated spontaneity of John Jones's apperception of himself as free, concurrent with his intuition of the law directly controverting that freedom. Refocusing our attention on the text in this regard, Jones *knows* what he ought to do, what his duty is. Not only does he know he counts, he knows he *must* count. But it is not the voice of God that calls him to duty. Nor is it the processes of subjectification he experiences at the hands of the usher. What calls Jones to duty is precisely the contemporaneous spontaneity of autonomous self-awareness at the limits, the horizon against which it is. Yet, he gives expression to this existence not in terms of, or in relation to the world; rather he expresses it in relation to the community that has no place in the world, that is identified with the earth, literally, the Negro sharecroppers of Altamaha who belong to the soil, which is owned by the whites. Jones duty is not to free the Negro sharecroppers from their bondage, to sever their ties to the earth. It is to "help settle the Negro problem in Altamaha," which meant to transform their Negroness, their Negritude, to put it anachronistically, from a debased condition of being into an open-ended movement of intelligence. This means transforming the world of Altamaha even if, especially if, that means vandalizing the sacred something that keeps "this little world" going.

This depiction of the thinking-in-action so fully on displayed in "Of the Coming of John," foregrounds myth as an historical endeavor, a creative cut, in order to discover the material history of human thinking. While there may be ample literary evidence to support Robert Bone's appraisal of Du Bois's style as full of literary monstrosities, rather than taking this to be symptomatic of Du Bois's bad or weak literary ability, as he does, I think it indicates an experimental style aptly called hyperbolic—in the sense of the hyperbola analogy. Du Bois's deploying "the Negro" in this story as the tableau of a radically historical consciousness enables not only Pan Africanism as a political conceptualization of internationalism, but also has a role in fostering a distinctive style of literary expression that embodies that very consciousness. In this sense, it is the style of an internationalism that has no home in any logic of interiority: those discourses predicated on the organicistic presumption that any given expression's meaningfulness is derived from its originary relationship to a specific tradition, whose formal terms and conditions it either adheres to and reiterates or exceeds and overcomes, in accordance with an ultimately saving teleology. Du Bois's tableau of an intelligence irredeemably caught up with the immanent flow of things does not represent an integral consciousness cast out from a lost homeland whose memoria is carried like so much sustaining baggage—this is something Du Bois will invent later, after *The Souls of Black Folk*—grounding its self in the quest for redemption in a final return. What John Jones represents is a consciousness articulated in movement, driven by curiosity to assume equal access to the entirety of humanity's expressions and institutions. His interiority is one that is freed from eschatological redemption, defying any traditional grasp or apprehension. This a-traditional immanence describes a style the performance of which is not that of exile or homelessness, but rather freedom from eschatology.

By Interiority Free of Eschatology

To give as full as possible a sense of what I mean by this, and just what is at stake in attributing such a way of thinking and being to Du Bois's Negro, let us attend to how the narrative in "Of the Coming of John" stages the unreadableness of Jones's thinking to the world around him by representing the way his thinking is nearly self-contained. Even the teachers at Wells Institute, who apprehend Jones as a thinking entity, cannot fathom exactly what or how he is thinking. The only knowledge afforded them, by the fact that it was they who imparted to him a sizable body of knowledge, is the historicity of his thinking. As far as how Jones's thinking is represented in the narrative, it does not so much respond to externally presented or generated stimuli, but seems to feed on locally presented impressions. Jones is thinking about what he is thinking about with what is happening, and not thinking about what is happening. An even more apt way of putting it is that all that happens to him happens with his thinking, and it is what his thinking discerns or extracts from the impressions present to him that he is consciously aware of.

Obviously, this discrepancy could be read as little more than a narrative device with which Du Bois accentuates the sense of mental bifurcation. The faculties of perception and cognition are radically heterogeneous. This is a received, if not habitual reading of all that is contained in *The Souls of Black Folk*. But what is meant by it? Or rather, what does it mean here? The dominant school of thought suggests it to mean the duality of the Negro, the persistent tension between the perception of the Negro's body and its significance and the event of the Negro's consciousness. Put in terms of the postbellum political-economic transformation, the Negro slave had a precise commodity value (a price as a piece of requisitionable inventory in the plantation economy); because he had no socially recognizable self-possession—what Orlando Patterson describes as "the social death of slavery"—his commodity value was the dynamic energies of his body, including those of cogitation, which were also requisitionable as pieces of inventory. In contrast, the Negro freedman is in possession of himself, but because that self is not immediately available for requisitioning within the postbellum political-economic framework—now being interpolated into a mechanical technology of reproduction—it has no value, and indeed poses a danger in the form of indeterminate desire, or, as Du Bois would say, will. Within the postbellum economy, what remains is the devalued commodity of the Negro body's muscular energies, which are made requisitionable at a substantially cheaper price. This results in good measure from the Thirteenth Amendment's exception clause permitting slavery as punishment for the convicted criminal, which effectively legitimated continued requisitioning of Negro body energies through criminalization of the Negro person. While the majority of slave codes had recognized the Negro as person subject to punishment only when judged guilty of a crime, the exception clause arguably gave warrant to criminalization of the Negro person essentially *in toto*. A warrant that was rigorously exercised by nearly all the former slaveholding states through juridical devices such as Black Codes and the convict leasing system. The primary difference between the economies of slavery and neo-slavery is that in the latter, Negro muscular energy is a commodity devalued by freedom. That is to say, with emancipation, the cost of generating the energy, of producing and maintaining the bodies from which it is extracted, falls wholly on the Negro, who as a type of now free labor excluded by racism from the networks of social support available to white labor—philanthropic societies and trade unions as well as the juridical system—is cheap. Du Bois's great insight with respect to all this is recognizing that the changing evaluation of the commodity, concomitant with the transformation in the economy of requisitioning prompted by the prioritization of mechanical reproduction notwithstanding, the identification of the phenomenal Negro body and commodity remains constant. What also remains constant is the danger any sustained manifestation of Negro interiority poses to the integrity of that economic system by problematizing its anthropological framework. By definition,

Negro is an indefinable something that represents at a glance—*en un clin d'œil*, as Baudelaire would have it—the ongoing tension between body and soul.

This is precisely what "Of the Coming of John" is an emblematic tableau of *in its narrative style*. Nor is referencing Baudelaire here with regard to that style merely opportunistically coincidental. In defining modernism, Baudelaire equates the transient with the body, whose fashioning and costuming was the art of the present in which was contained—when well done as in the case of Guys's work—the eternal, which he equates with the soul of man. Modernist art is that which freezes instantaneously a moment in time while conferring on it the value of the eternal: "In short, for any form of modernity to be worthy of becoming antiquity, the mysterious beauty that human life unintentionally puts into it must have been extracted from it."[233] This magical operation, which Baudelaire also calls the heroism of modern life, is not a process of slavishly or truthfully—in the correspondence sense—copying reality. It is realized through the synthesis of imagination and memory in a nearly childlike manner. The implication, of course, is that Du Bois's portrait of John Jones is an instantiation of just such modernism, albeit one that problematizes the heroism of modern life by eschewing the nearly childlike manner. That is to say, the interiority exhibited with Jones's consciousness, taken as emblematic of double consciousness, is free of what Lukács discerns as the romantic anticapitalism shadowing Baudelaire's *flâneur*. This has everything to do with how the relation between commodity and artistic form central to Baudelaire's definition of modernism does not comprehend the interiority at play in Du Bois's emblematic Negro tableau. Not to suggest Du Bois is unconcerned with the relation between commodity and artistic form. Quite the contrary, he has it very much in mind when, at the beginning of his speech on the occasion of Garter Godwin Woodson's receiving the NAACP Spingran Medal in June 1926, he raises the question: "After all, what have we who are slaves and black to do with Art?" Addressing that question he famously says:

> Such is Beauty. Its variety is infinite, its possibility is endless. In normal life all may have it and have it yet again. The world is full of it; and yet today the mass of human beings are chocked away from it, and their lives distorted and made ugly. This is not only wrong, it is silly. Who shall right this wellnigh universal failing? . . . We black folk may help for we have within us as a race new stirrings; stirrings of the beginning of a new appreciation of joy, of a new desire to create, of a new will to be; as though in this morning group life we had awakened from some sleep that at once dimly mourns the past and dreams a splendid future . . . with new determination for all mankind. What has this Beauty to do with the world? . . . I am but a humble disciple of art and cannot presume to say. I am one who tells the truth and exposes

evil and seeks with Beauty and for Beauty to set the world right. That somehow, somewhere eternal and perfect Beauty sits above Truth and Right I can conceive, but here and now in the world in which I work they are for me unseparated and inseparable. . . . Thus all Art is propaganda and ever must be, despite the wailing of the purists. I stand in utter shamelessness and say that whatever art I have for writing has been used always for propaganda for gaining the right of black folk to love and enjoy. I do not care a damn for any art that is not used for propaganda. But I do care when propaganda is confined to one side while the other is stripped and silent.[234]

These remarks are often misconstrued to be little more than a rejection of the concept *l'art pour l'art*, usually attributed to Théophile Gautier, but, significantly for our concerns here, espoused by Poe in his 1850 essay, "The Poetic Principle." In fact, they express an understanding of art that, *avant la lettre*, is resonant with art historian T. J. Clark's exposition of the two constitutive features of modernism, which are contingency and desuetude. By *contingency*, Clark means the prevalence of immediate historical or situational reference—both thematically and formally—in the work of art, rather than transcendent rules of form, or fixed ideas of expression and significance. In other words, there is no other substance out of which art can now be made—no givens, no matters and subject-matters, no forms, no publicly universal usable pasts. The absence of a universal public agreement is symptomatic of a prevailing sense of disuse, the discontinuance from use or exercise, which is what Clark means by *desuetude*. This desuetude also indicates the openness or historicality of the public—that it is dynamically constituted in the course of events and material processes, rather than being given. Whether a work of art revels in contingency, mourns desuetude, or does both, it is properly modernist if it takes the one or other fact as determinant.[235] As for Du Bois claiming all art is propaganda, the two questions he poses at the start of his address, setting the stage for the one about what black folk have to do with art, makes it perfectly clear that he means art is political: "How is it that an organization like this, a group of radicals trying to bring new things into the world, a fighting organization which has come up out of the blood and dust of battle, struggling for the right of black men to be ordinary human beings—how is it that an organization of this kind can turn aside to talk about Art?" "Politics," according to Clark, "is the form par excellence of the contingency that makes modernism what it is."[236] This rebuts those who "resist to the death the idea that art, at many of its highest moments in the nineteenth and twentieth centuries, took the stuff of politics as its material and did not transmute it."[237] His paradigm example of this is Jacques-Louis David's painting *Marat à son dernier soupir*, with its public release on 25 Vendémiaire Year 2 (October 16, 1793) marking the beginning of modernism. Regarding "Of the Coming of John" along these lines reinforces situating it stylistically as well as thematically in relation to the modernism Baudelaire pulls from Poe's "The Man of the Crowd," while also marking its substantively significant divergence from it. Appreciating how, as well as why this is so requires a somewhat more careful engagement with the line on modernism developed from Baudelaire, and the way his aesthetics of *flânerie*, as mined by Sigfried Kracauer and Benjamin, cannot comprehend Jones's interiority, precisely because the *flâneur* is an emblematic figure of redemptive eschatological anticapitalism.

To begin with, Baudelaire's conceit of the "childlike" is based on the eighteenth- and nineteenth-century European (Enlightenment and Romantic) idea of children as creatures of nature in its purest form, who can be formed—in *Zucht* (the discipline of cultural breeding) Kant would say—into fully socialized subjects. Relating this to Jones, the analogue is primitivism, according to which the Negro—as well as the non-white "native," and even the European peasant—is childlike, needing civilization through culture. Because the child and the Negro as primitives are in a state of being prior to their interpolation into the constricting structures of commodification, they are both free to be naturally among things, reveling in the full splendor of the world in reality. And in the case of the modern artist such as Guys, this revelation is achieved by maintaining his childlike perspective through the synthesis of imagination and memory. Guys's heroism stems from his achieving this maintenance of childlike perspective against the overwhelming, increasingly ubiquitous order of the commodity, finding his way back to the magical displaced by what Weber designated capitalist modernity's *Entzauberung* (disenchantment) of the world. Baudelaire's childlike Guys is akin to Giambattista Vico's primitive gentile, who is closer to the sources of *poēsis*, and so the truth of being, than modern man, with the commodity functioning as the inspirational barbarism. Dilthey—who we've already determined is one of those Du Bois is playing with in *The Souls of Black Folk*—had some sense of this in his "Poetik," where he construes poetry as a cultural object giving particular material expression of *Weltanschauung* that, while historically conditioned, entails structures correlating to those of other *Weltanschauungen*, indicating a set of objective homologous structures. Alois Riegl elaborates on Dilthey's concept of poetic works as objective facts of life in given eras in his own influential concept of *Kunstwollen*. Dilthey's conception of *Geistesgeschichte* is very much at work in Riegl's theory of art, as is evident in his description of *Kunstwollen* as regulating the relationship of man to the sensible appearance of things, giving shape and color to things, interpreting them in accordance with a given set of desires, which change with respect to people, place, and time. "The character of these desires [*Wollens*]," Riegl says, "is decided by what may be termed the conception of the world [*Weltanschauung*] at a given time."²³⁸ Accordingly, *Kunstwollen* denotes that desire driving artistic production over time. As such, it is a fundamental human activity through which consciousness fashions self-understanding. Riegl notoriously never presented a cogent theory of *Kunstwollen*. Erwin Panofsky, however, embracing Heidegger in his reading of Kant, contra Ernst Cassirer's neo-Kantianism, elaborated a methodological definition of *Kunstwollen* in regard to artistic expression insofar as it is a possible object of the scientific investigation of art (*kunstwissenschaftlichen Erkenntnis*). Working from the assumption that artistic expression is neither merely indicative of a psychological reality or an abstracted generic concept, Panofsky maintains:

> *Kunstwollen* cannot be anything other than (and not for us, but objectively) what "lies" in the artistic phenomenon as its ultimate meaning.... For one thing presupposes the use and determination of the concept of *Kunstwollen*: that every artistic phenomenon can be ascertained as a unity for an interpretation aimed at its inner significance, such that "formal" and "imitative" elements ... need not be reduced to separable and irreducible concepts, but understood as distinct expressions [*Äußerungen*] of a common fundamental tendency, the comprehension of which as such is the task of the real "fundamental concepts of art."²³⁹

This definition of *Kunstwollen* as denoting a priori basic principles of organizing creative forces (*schöpferischen Kräfte*) provides a purchase for Kracauer's meditation on the work of art as providing a form that relates the phenomenal world to a meaningfulness beyond space and time. Kracauer, like Panofsky, was drawn to Riegl's concept of *Kunstwollen*, which he also engaged through a Heideggerian prism. Yet nine years before Heidegger's turn to "the riddle of the work of art," starting with his 1935 lecture, "Origin of the Work of Art"— which was part of a series of lectures at the Freiburg Kunstwissenschaftliche Gesellschaft, under the topic, "Origin and Beginnings of the Visual Arts"— Kracauer speaks of "*Dasein* disintegrating into a series of organizationally dictated activities in keeping with ... the forces of *mechanization* that do not aim beyond space and time."²⁴⁰ In an implicit critique of Positivism, he characterizes those forces as "the grace [*Gnaden*] of a merciless intellect that, convinced the world can be comprehended on mechanistic presuppositions, frees itself from all relations to the Beyond." This detached intellect aims at a rationalization of life accommodating it to an absolutely technologized reality extended across astronomical space and chronological time, so that human existence is totally circumscribed within it. There is, however, what Kracauer calls, "the *real* human, who leads a *double existence* [*Doppelexistenz*]."²⁴¹ Although thrust into technologized reality, "not having abdicated [*abgedankt*] to the figure of mechanized work and resisting dissolution [*Auflösung*] in space and time,"²⁴² he imagines a supra-spatial infinity (*überräumliche Unendlichkeit*) as well as an eternity (*Ewigkeit*) incomprehensible to either astrometric space or chronometric time respectively. The *real* human orients himself toward these coordinates of "the beyond [*Jenseitige*], in which everything in the here-and-now [*Hier*] finds meaning and completion."[243] Kracauer regards the work of art, including those mechanized media such as film, to manifest the here-and-now's dependence on this supplementation by "shaping phenomenal appearance, giving it a form connected with a non-inherent significance [*Bedeutung*] related to a supra-temporal meaning, which elevates the ephemeral into an objective pattern [*Gebilde*] . . . combining meaning with the extant into an aesthetic unity."[244] Kracauer construes modern travel (Reise) qua tourism as the way in which the common person actively seeks this *double existence*. Touristic travel is a commodified formal experience of space. Rather than traveling to someplace in search of one's soul, as Goethe did to Italy, the bourgeois traveler seeks the change of environment offered by travel, the experience of pure movement. There is no sought-after destination, only a new place, which is not altogether new but, as with the proliferation of Club Med–like resorts, is an extension of home in an exotic location. Travel, in this respect, like all commodities, is fashionable. And the adventure of movement as commodity is a function of the spatio-temporality of mechanization. By that same token, travel "has acquired a *theological* significance: it is the essential possibility by which those in the grip of mechanization can inauthentically live the *double existence* foundational to reality," Kracauer proclaims, further explaining that "*going* to foreign places demonstrates having outgrown the enslaving [*hörig*] regions of here-and-now. Experiencing supra-spatial infinity remains possible by traveling an endless geographic space, in a way that first and foremost has no particular destination."[245] The forces of mechanization extend their spatio-temporal circumscription around the globe, enabling the bourgeois travelers' movement in which they reconnect with the meaning formed from the beyond, "discovering in travel the surrogate for the sphere denied them."[246] The freedom of travel, then, is not aimless movement, but movement aimed at prehistorical experience of being human prior to mechanization.

Kracauer's notion of the traveler is related to Hessel's elaboration of Baudelairean *flânerie*, whereby the *flâneur* strolls about ungrounded, in transitory fashion or habitude, but responsive to the eternal possibilities of impression that are ever present in even the most mundane and fashionable.[247] There is also a slight resonance between Kracauer's concept of the real human's double existence and Du Bois's concept of Negro double consciousness, except Kracauer's notion turns on a dichotomy being drawn between a dreamlike fluid interiority oriented toward the infinity and eternity belonging to an older, premodern conceptions of the world and the rapidly progressing process of the mechanical technologization of every aspect of existence. On one side of the dichotomy, there is the *real* human who has not abdicated to mechanization, remaining committed to beyond the here-and-now of the technological world; on the other, is the fashionable bourgeois subject who is wholly determined by the vicissitudes of mechanical technological commodification.[248] Lukács places this dichotomy within the scope of "romantic anticapitalism" because of its being grounded in values supposed to be antecedent to the rise of urban commodity capitalism.[249]

Benjamin, like his friend Kracauer, was influenced by both Riegl's concept of *Kunstwollen* and Hessel's account of *flânerie* in his own effort to extend Marx's concept of the phantasmagorical form of the commodity fetish as the obfuscation of social relations to a consideration of the epistemological aspect of the commodity, how the everyday commodity objects make available critique of the very possibility of sensation and experience, by exposure. "The world dominated by its phantasmagoria—this is, to use Baudelaire's expression, 'modernity.'"[250] Benjamin's intense focus on the immediacy of sensual presence ran the risk of subjectifying the phantasmagoria, so it necessarily presumed an a-temporal Kantian transcendental subjectivity, the interiority of which was inherent. Benjamin sought to address this by attending to how the commodity economy, through pricing, reinforces the phantasmagoria of sameness, the ever-self-same appearance, suggesting that the interiority of the *flâneur* emulates the commodity economy: "He makes himself at home in purchasability."[251] But his own interest in the interiority of children and their transformation into social subjects through the commodity of illustrated children's books, which he surmised "have some connection with the emblem books of the Baroque period," leaned toward the same primitivist dichotomy Kracauer worked from. This is implied by the notion there is a pure childlike state of thinking that is natural and precedes subject-formation in the economy of commodity capitalism. Writing on a child's view of color, Benjamin states: "Productive adults derive no support from color; for them color can subsist only within law-given circumstances. Their task is to provide a world order, not to grasp innermost reasons and essences but to develop them. In a child's life, color is the pure expression of the child's pure receptivity, insofar as it is directed at the world."[252] From here, he maintains that "the concern of color with objects is not based on their form; without even touching on them empirically, it goes right to the spiritual heart of the object by isolating the sense of sight. It cancels out the intellectual cross-references of the soul and creates a pure mood, without thereby sacrificing the world."[253]

Elaborating on Lukács's characterization of this aspect of Benjamin's thought as romantic anticapitalism, we note there is a pronounced melancholic aspect to the investment in the childlike primitive, which is evident in Benjamin's obsessive collecting of the everyday inanimate objects of commodity production. From illustrated children's books to snow globes, he collected commodities as cultural artifacts carrying traces of a past life, the signs of which endure interpolation into the commodity, being made available by insightful critique. Theodor Adorno once said of his friend: "Petrified, frozen, or obsolete inventoried pieces [*Bestandstücke*] of culture, everything emptied of comforting vitality, appealed to him like the collector's petrifacts or plants in an herbarium.... The French word for still-life, *nature morte*, could be written above the portals to his philosophical dungeons.... He was engrossed not only in awakening the congealed-life in the petrified—as in the allegory—but also in contemplating the living in such a way it is presents itself as that which has long since passed away, 'prehistoric,' precipitously releasing its significance."[254]

Rendering the term *Bestandstücke* here as "inventoried pieces," rather than the more common "elements," is in keeping with Adorno's overall characterization of Benjamin as a taxonomizing collector. Moreover, it underscores the way his usage of the term accords with the "strict sense" Heidegger gave it to denote "exchangeable ready-to-order pieces of standing reserve" generated within the all-encompassing framing of mechanical technology.[255] Heidegger's turn to these matters of art and commodification was coincidental with Adorno's exchange with Benjamin over his construal of Baudelaire's *flâneur* in his *Arcades Project*, making his sense of *Bestandstücke* all the more germane to Adorno's critique of Benjamin's thinking about the commodity as insufficiently mediated, "appropriating to itself commodity fetishism [*Warenfetischismus*], whereby everything must be enchanted so as to disguise the terrible state [*Unwesen*] of thinghood [*Dinglichkeit*]."[256] This bears on Benjamin's reading of "The Man of the Crowd," where the masses are a code consisting of ciphers corresponding precisely to Balzac's types. Yet, Adorno observes, "Poe actually keeps his promise to decipher every code while Baudelaire, with his allegorical intention, does not."[257] Nevertheless, in the phantasmagoria of Poe's convalescent, as well as Baudelaire's *flâneur*, the people belonging to a particular type are actually the same. Benjamin's reply illuminates the underlying question of the commodity at issue here, pointing out that sameness [*Gleichheit*] has a very different appearance in Poe, as well as Baudelaire, from that in Balzac. Yet, there is a further distinction between the two of them having to do with the total disregard of the commodity question in Poe's "The Man of the Crowd," whereas Baudelaire "gives artificial assistance to the historical hallucination of sameness that had taken root with the commodity economy."[258] For Poe, the problem of indecipherability has to do with epistemological blockage—caused by illness with the convalescent in "The Man of the Crowd"—or the mystification of empirical facts caused by superstition or ancient irrational belief, as with his detective stories, and *The Narrative of Arthur Gordon Pym*. In either case, indecipherability is eventually exorcised through the sharpening of deductive faculties. For Baudelaire, the problem of indecipherability is an effect of historical hallucination congenital to the commodity economy, which he explores in his work through the tropes of hashish and intoxication. Along these lines, Benjamin says, "The commodity economy reinforces the phantasmagoria of sameness, which, as an attribute of intoxication, simultaneously reveals itself as the central figure of semblance." Then, taking Adorno's suggestions on type seriously, he explains this relationship in terms of price as the instrumentality of the commodity fetish: "Price makes the commodity identical to all other commodities that can be purchased for the same amount. The commodity insinuates itself not only and not so much with buyers as with its price. And it is precisely in that respect the *flâneur* is extremely well attuned to the commodity; in the absence of demand, that is to say, a market-price, he makes himself at home in purchasability [*Käuflichkeit*]."[259]

Giving due measure of Baudelaire's using "The Man of the Crowd" in his definition of modernism and conception of *flânerie*, as well as Benjamin's elaboration on that usage in formulating a theory of bourgeois interiority in the commodity economy of mechanical reproduction, whatever resonance there may be of all that in "Of the Coming Of John," we can draw no generative analogy between the dreamlike disposition of John Jones and the fluidity of the *flâneur* phantasmagoria. The images of Jones's impressions cannot be confused with the utopian wish-images (*Wunschbilder*) of the *flâneur* phantasmagoria. Those images involve tendencies that, as with Kracauer's *real* human, direct the imagination, which receives its impetus from the new, back to the primal past. "In the dream in which each epoch envisions images of its successor, the latter appears wedded to elements of prehistory," Benjamin says, paraphrasing the Jules Michelet aphorism—"Chaque époque rêve la suivante [Every era dreams the next]"—which he also makes the motto for his analysis of the phantasmagoria.[260] This interpenetration of the old with the new becomes deposited in the collective unconscious with the commodity economy, "engendering a utopia that has left its vestige in a thousand configurations of life, from long-lasting edifices to passing fashions. . . . Its innermost impetus is the advent of the machines."[261] Baudelaire describes the *flâneur* "releasing from fashion whatever element it may contain of the poetic within the historical, distilling the eternal from the transitory," defining modernism as "the transitory, the fugitive, the contingent, the half of art whose other half is the eternal and the immutable."[262] In that respect, Ernst Bloch's work functions for Benjamin as Guys's did for Baudelaire, "securing the not-yet future against the darkness of the lived moment."[263] One might well concur with Adorno: "This only requires the consistent insight, 'no difference is really worth anything,' and that the individual must keep before his eyes the concept of his own absolute interiority as a romantic Island where he undertakes to salvage his 'meaning' from the historical flood-tide."[264] Such an idealist conception of interiority raises two principal problematics. First is the relation of the present to the past, particularly the recent past. Second is the relation of the mind, primarily the imagination, to the material world in that first relation. This second problematic is the pivotal one, because of how it focuses attention on the question of the historical and situational nature of thinking. It is not just enough to state that thinking occurs in the world. We must ask how this is so: How is it that thinking is world? Do we mean by this that it is determined by the world, and so somehow a matter of experience? Or do we mean that it is the articulation of the world, such that the world is given to us only as an issue of our interiority?

These questions lie at the heart of Adorno's dispute with Benjamin over what he understood to be the "transposition of the dialectical image into consciousness as a dream" in Benjamin's account of phantasmagoria, specifically his assessment of the Paris arcades as a material articulation of the conjunction of technological production, capital expansion, empire as revolutionary terror, and artistic creativity. Equally dubious is Benjamin's investment in the revolutionary aspect of mechanical reproduction—the capacity of the commodity as art to negate the *aura* of so-called authentic high art, and in so doing raise the political consciousness of the masses—to which Adorno ardently objected, seeing in that investment an ability to think of culture as a natural object to the point of reifying instead of contradicting it in a constant dialectic. Benjamin's entire thinking, he says "could be called 'natural history [*naturgeschichtlich*].'"[265] Characterizing Baudelaire's *flâneur* as "the mythological ideal type" of modern subjectivity—the allegory of the agential subject in relation to commodification—Benjamin imagines his phantasmagoria of the everyday pieces of ready-to-order reserve inventory to be natural in a way that saves the *flâneur* from the terrible state of thinghood. The sore point for Adorno is the presumption of the immanence of consciousness as the basis for the dialectical image. For him, the immanence of consciousness as interiority is the dialectical image for the nineteenth-century as alienation; hence his recommending Benjamin remove the Michelet aphorism altogether as that in which all the motifs of the theory of the dialectical image crystallize as "undialectical."[266] The solipsist aspect—to use that very loaded philosophical term to characterize the epistemological and methodological orientation of *Geistesgeschichte*, as well as *Geisteswissenschaften* and its post-Dilthey permutations—of the interiority entailed in Benjamin's use of Bloch's principle of hope is little more than muted by his subsequently adopting Adorno's critical perversion of Michelet's aphorism: "The recent past always presents itself as if it were annihilated by catastrophes."[267] Adorno's reformulation aimed at externalizing the dream of the future through dialectical interpretation so that the immanence of consciousness itself—interiority—can be recognized as a constellation of reality. And in that effort, Adorno ever so resembles Johann Fichte, with transcendental idealism becoming transcendental critique; in which case, philosophy is the activity of articulating experience in concepts as a function of intellect.[268] Indeed, both Adorno and Fichte have recourse to will, which still leaves us caught up with consciousness. Or, more to the point, we are left with the identification of consciousness and the intelligence that enables its own conditions of possibility without presuming autonomy. That identification yields psychologism, as Kant teaches. It inclines toward understanding event as cause, the inclination being strongest in the account of agency as productive. On this score, the distinction between Fichte's benevolent will (creative imagination) and Adorno's contradiction of non-identity is minimal. We are, then, grappling with the problematic of definition (*Bestimmung*), which Adorno seeks to negotiate in recognition of the historicity of thought in mathematical understanding as a way to avoid both idealism and realism. He has much to say on this in *Aesthetic Theory*; and what he says there is not a departure from his previous thinking on dialectic, but exhibits his continued concern with the possibility of theoretically understanding it in relation to the same thousand configurations of life preoccupying Benjamin. Even Adorno, who attends to the danger of valuing the dignity of thinking over the body, cannot altogether give up on the ambition to somehow deliver thinking from the corruptive procedures and processes of mechanical technology.

Thinking as *poiēsis*, in Aristotle's sense, which Heidegger construes as involving the human mental disposition to disclose the truth of existence qua existence, "is the essential authentic human action, when action means, assisting the essence of existence [*Wesen des Seyns*] by preparing for it the place in which it brings itself and its essence to speaking language [*Sprache*]."[269] Vico names this in far fewer words, *Sapienza Poetica* ("poetic wisdom"), although his description of what he means takes nearly two-hundred pages.[270] Such an extremely abstract conception of thinking explicitly sets out to strip it of its historicity in modernity in order to save it from seeing that the danger of humans' transposition as pieces of inventory did not require a compromising or limiting of thinking's essence concomitant with the advent of mechanical reproduction. It is the historical precondition for the thinking of modernity; and in that respect, bear in mind that Locke expressly presumes the Negro's status as fungible property in 1669, based on eight-years of legal precedence. The particulars of this we shall take up presently. For now, as far as the modernist effort to guard the integrity of thinking from commodification is concerned, there is something palpably pernicious about Benjamin's remark that "in the *flâneur* is reborn the sort of idler Socrates picked out from the Athenian marketplace to be his interlocutor. Only, there is no longer a Socrates, so there is no one to address the idler. And the slave labor that guaranteed him his leisure has likewise ceased to exist."[271] His remark is pernicious not just because it disregards the long history and, at Baudelaire's time, present fact of slavery's enabling and sustaining the processes of commodity capitalism, but because that disregard performs a violence—in Benjamin's own sense of law-preserving violence—to the thinking of those who, having freed their selves from that enslavement, are engaged in something-else-thinking.[272] The essentialized thinking forgets the history of bodies doing and being done to as Negro bodies in its effort to restore and guard thinking; and what is to be restored and guarded is the innocence of thinking.

The point in relating Adorno's dispute with Benjamin over the dialectical image to Du Bois's portrait of Jones is to make it abundantly clear that Jones's thinking is not utopic, neither is it revisionist. Du Bois, too, it will be recalled, is concerned with "the thousand and one little actions which go to make up life" as constituting the collective consciousness, but not in wish-images directing imagination back to a childlike primitive awareness in the hopes of redeeming thinking from the catastrophe of its own making. To the extent Jones is at all hopeful, it is not in the Schopenhauer-derived Bloch sense of utopic futuristic hope. Perhaps it could be said that, like the Baudelaire/Benjamin *flâneur*, Jones's interiority is an articulation of being among things in the world; it is as robust as the social dynamics describing the moment. It is there, but always pronouncedly in relation to other things and other people, other personae. Even granting that, Jones's interiority is quite distinct from that of the *flâneur*, whose individuality is defined over and against the crowd, which is the emblem of the mass. If John Jones is an archetypal figure, he is not emblematic of a self-awareness seeking to ground itself in beyond the here-and-now spatial-temporal structures of society—that is the ambition of the churchmen of Altamaha, which he ardently critiques, as much as it is of Kracauer's *real* human. Nor is he emblematic of a thinking freeing itself by emulating the commodity economy. The sort of freedom entailed in Jones's interiority cannot be achieved by the *flâneur* precisely because of the difference in their respective relation to commodity. The *flâneur* is constitutively the spectator *for whom* the commodity circulates and who marks the alienation of commodification by *being able* to stand apart from it, to resist dissolution into the pieces of ready-to-order reserve inventory, *Bestandstücke*, by collecting them and subjecting them to aesthetic critique. Whereas John Jones's capacity to stand outside of commodification is precarious, at best. Within the ambit of juridically enforced neo-slavery, travel, rather than being a commodified experience of *double existence* in which freedom beyond is discovered, à la Kracauer's bourgeois traveler, is precarious movement. As with the Kracauer traveler, movement is the means to escape enslavement of one's humanity within the commodity economy. Unlike the Kracauer traveler, however, the freedom of movement is not in rediscovering prehistorical experience. This is no primitivist tourism, which is to say, it is not a modality of mechanized commodification imaginatively misconceived as a means of flight from commodification. Rather, it is perpetually being in flight perpetually open to the vicissitudes of commodification, without any point of reference or anchor outside its processes. This sense of freedom-in-flight is characteristic of the weary traveler Jones is supposed to emblemize.

We come again to the problem of the unreadable reader, of Jones, whose interiority may have a fluidity, it is even expressly marked as dreamlike, but it is not transcendental—there is no tendency to obfuscate the social relation of commodity capitalism, but rather to disrupt it; there is no urge to be at home in purchasability, but rather to be free from it. And here is the crux of it: Jones is not alienated from himself by the processes of commodity capitalism; his self is articulated *within* that economy, and not as a function of the superimposition of commodification onto an already self-conscious personhood. That tremendous terrible violence was already enacted centuries prior when humans from Africa were first transformed into the Negro as chattel slave commodity; the persistence of that trauma is constitutional, so its object is not the older forms of the human, but rather the persistent possibilities of the emergent human imagination set in play by the violence of capitalist slavery. The ongoing violence aims at policing the self it puts in play, but in spite of it, that emergent imagination works along lines never fully circumscribed by the technologies of police—read, the technologies for enforcing the authority of polity.

In our effort to elaborate more carefully how this intractable thinking is played out in "Of the Coming of John," we come at last to the climactic scene of what happens to Jones as he listens to the *Lohengrin* act 1 prelude. Recall for a moment our earlier account of the three objective events in the New York scene: the Prelude intervenes between Henderson's umbrage at Jones's presence and the usher's asking Jones to come with him. Jones is oblivious to everything except his own conception of things; the opera hall presents such a flood of indiscriminate stimuli of colors, odors, and sounds that he is disoriented and lost in a conceptual maze—"dreamland" we are told. Disorientation abruptly ends, and Jones is instantly brought to thoughtful reflection when the prelude begins. Even then, his reflection is introspective and extremely impressionistic. There is no depiction of the music in its performance. Instead, the intervention gets under way with an interpretation. The narrative runs: "After a hush, rode high and clear the music of Lohengrin's swan. The infinite beauty of the wail lingered and swept through every muscle of his frame, and put it all a-tune." As is well known, the sole subject of the prelude is the Holy Grail. It opens with muted reiterations of the cord of A major played by divisi violins, which is the motive of the Grail, in gradually increasing octave for some measures before being joined by flutes, clarinets, and oboes. This continues over the course of the prelude without any discernable cadence, achieving a sustained reiteration or continuity that increases in instrumental force with the gradual addition of full horns (bassoon, French-horn, trumpet, trombone, and bass-tuba) and timpani filling out the bottom register, moving to a triumphant climax only to then give way again to the divisi violins of the Grail motive.

Attending to the narrative of Jones's listening, rather than an account of his responding to the prelude's exposition of the Grail *motif*, we encounter the identification of another, "Lohengrin's swan." That identification at that moment is remarkable for a number of reasons. To begin with, there is no *motif* of "Lohengrin's swan," properly speaking, in the prelude or the opera; rather there are two distinct motives, one of the knight, Lohengrin, which occurs in scene 1 of act 1, and another of the swan, which occurs in scene 3 of act 1. This, then, is a conflation, the significance of which in the narration of Jones's listening is better appreciated by summarily rehearsing the reiterations of the prelude's Grail motive in association with the chief characters of Lohengrin and Elsa throughout the course of the three-act opera. The first reiteration occurs in act 1, scene 2, when Elsa makes her first appearance, before King Heinrich to be judged on the charge of fratricide. She is the sister of Godfrey, the legitimate heir to the Duchy of Brabant, and has been brought before the king by the banks of the river Scheldt near Antwerp, accused by Count Telramund of murdering her brother in order to secure her succession to the throne of Brabant. In her first appearance, the oboes take up sections of the prelude, accompanying Elsa's nonverbal responses to Heinrich's interrogation. The Grail motive of the prelude is then taken up with the orchestration of divisi violins in the cord of A major immediately before Elsa sings of the knight she dreamed would champion her cause against Telramund's charges in combat. The association of the Grail *motif* with Lohengrin and the swan is made explicit at the end of the scene, right after Elsa's handmaidens have prayed for divine intervention on her behalf, when the men on the river bank shout out:

> *Seht! Seht! Welch ein seltsam Wunder! Wie? Ein Schwan?*
> *Ein Schwan zieht ein Nachen dort heran!*
> *Ein Ritter drin hoch aufgerichtet steht!*
> *Wie glänzt sein Waffenschmuck! Das Aug vergeht*
> *vor solchem Glanz! - Seht, näher kommt er schon heran!*
> *An einer goldnen Kette zieht der Schwan!*
> [Behold! Behold! What strange and wondrous things is this? A swan?
> A swan is pulling a barge towards us!
> A knight is standing upright in it!

How his armor shines! The eye is dazzled
by such splendor! Behold, he is coming ever closer!
The swan is pulling on a golden chain!]

This is the first appearance of both swan and Lohengrin in the opera, and it continues into scene 3 when Lohengrin sends the swan back, singing:

Nun sei bedankt, mein lieber Schwan!
Zieh durch die weite Flut zurück,
dahin, woher mich trug dein Kahn,
kehr wieder nur zu unsrem Glück!
[I thank you, my dear swan!
Go back across the waters
to whence your boat brought me,
return again only to bring us happiness!]

After this, the Grail *motif* is consistently associated with Lohengrin and Elsa; there are instrumental allusions made to it in portions of the act 1 prelude and then are taken up by oboes and violins in the final scene (scene 5) of act 2, when the chorus of noble men and women sing: "Heil dir, Tugendreiche! Heil Elsa von Brabant! [Hail to you, virtuous one! Hail Elsa of Brabant!]," as Lohengrin leads Elsa past the nobles to the king and wedding altar. The Grail *motif* returns climatically with the orchestrated divisi violins of the act 1 prelude in the so-called Grail narration in act 3, scene 3, when Lohengrin reveals he is the son of Parsifal, who guards the Grail on Mont Monsalvat, and then again near the end when he removes the gold chain from the swan that first brought him and has returned for him, revealing it to be Godfrey.

With this summary, we can see the identification of the opening *motif* of the act 1 prelude with "Lohengrin's swan" in the narration of Jones's listening indicates a familiarity with the full opera orchestration; and the conflation of the motives of Lohengrin and the swan indicates not only a familiarity with the literary reference of the opera, but also with Wagner's style and conceptualization of music drama as a form. In other words, Jones is not narrated as listening to the music, but as thinking about what the music means to him. This is a function of knowledge rather than impressionistic thought; and it is not at all clear whether this knowledge is antecedent to the moment of Jones's hearing the music or spontaneous with it. Even the seeming depiction of a physical reaction to sound is a trick. It is the "beauty" of the wail that prompts Jones's muscular reaction, and not the wail. This is a matter of aesthetic judgment and not physics, a point that is articulated in the depicted participation of Jones's thinking and affect in Wagnerian form. A deep longing swells in his heart synchronously with the rise of what the narrative reports is "that clear music out of the dirt and dust of that low life that held him prisoned [*sic*] and befouled." The imagined movement of the swan is identical with the movement of Jones's feelings and thought. With it, he discovers and embraces the idea of freedom in creative work, becoming intensely conscious of his own free will as well as its absurdity. "If he could only live up in the free air where birds sang and setting suns had no touch of blood! Who had called him to be the slave and butt of all? And if he had called, what right had he to call when a world like this lay open before men?" Again, this interpretation of the swan is a function of knowledge rather than impression. Were we inclined to give a pedigree to Jones's interpretation, we might find in it the very same historicized redemption narrative—moving from debasement to transfiguration—Wagner himself claims in the program he wrote for the 1853 Zurich concert performance of the *Lohengrin* prelude. Such a pedigree is not at all evident at this or any other point in the narrative, however. Instead, at just this point, the narrative seems about to set aside any further allusions to interpretive knowledge and depict something of the musical performance itself. But this is momentary, and Jones is still engrossed in his impressions; only now they are somewhat more sharply focused on the people around him.

> Then the movement changed, and to a fuller, mightier harmony swelled away. He looked thoughtfully across the hall, and wondered why the beautiful gray-haired woman looked so listless, and what the little man could be whispering about. He would not like to be listless and idle, he thought, for he felt with the music the movement of power within him. If he but had some master-work, some life service, hard,—aye, bitter hard, but without the cringing and sickening servility, without the cruel hurt that hardened his heart and soul.

Because he "felt *with* the music" such a powerful movement within for grandeur and vocation, the goings-on of the people around him are registered as inconsequential and malapropos. Jones passes over these things as aesthetic failings, being driven to contemplate his own possibilities of action, of transforming into an agent of change. The intervening passage closes as impressionistically as it began with a decidedly parsimonious depiction of the crucial musical performance. There is an almost incidental reference to the violins in the closing measures of the prelude. Even then, however, the narrative remains impressionistic, depicting the effect of the music on Jones thinking. "When at last a soft sorrow crept across the violins, there came to him a vision of a far off-home,—the great eyes of his sister, and the dark drawn face of his mother. And his heart sank below the waters, even as the sea-sand sinks by the shores of Altamaha, only to be lifted aloft again with that last ethereal wail of the swan that quivered and faded away into the sky." It is the soft sorrow creeping across the violins that reminds Jones of Altamaha, which fills him with a sadness that is relieved by the closing wail of the swan, recalling the hope of free will expressed with the beginning of the prelude. All this comes to an impasse of sorts with the usher's taping him on the shoulder and saying politely, "Will you step this way, please sir?" The only gauge of how much time has passed between Henderson's rage and this speech of the usher that the narrative provides us with is the prelude. Yet, in that time of the prelude occurs Henderson's outrage at finding a Negro sitting next to him and his female companion, the usher's request, and the two John's mutual recognition, all of which serve to remind Jones of his place in the order of things. In other words, these are the moments in which Jones becomes aware of how his thinking is in the world. Significantly, the radical disjunction between the narration of Jones's thinking and the thinking around him that provides the Negro tableau with its perspectivism is most intense in the *Lohengrin* passage. What Jones thinks he hears in the prelude is not there in the performance. What is it that Jones thinks he is hearing, then?

He is aware of the impressions made by the things constitutive of the crowd. We might say he is acutely aware of those impressions to the extent that they are the most vivid things he perceives. He plainly perceives the habitude in which he is a participant, the faces, fashions, order of things; but these are pushed into the background by the profound newness of it all, a newness that has less definitive form than pure originality of affect, which is what attracts his full attention. Jones is a naïf, and as such is compelled by curiosity. What he hears, then, in the prelude to act 1 of *Lohengrin*, with its introductory Grail *motif*, is the eternal poetry of "the creative power within him." Here is the crux of it, for if this is so, then the music Jones hears is not the music being performed in the prelude. Jones's impressions are associated with a particular arrangement of sound but not representative of it. These impressions, discerned and extracted from the sound, are the composition of a *poēsis*—the power of creating, whereby "he could . . . live up in the free air where birds sang and setting suns had no touch of blood." Once extracted, they become the eternal truth of soul that is expressed in the transitory moment of musical play. At the very moment when John Jones becomes aware of his thinking in the world with the prelude, he thinks of "far-off home" and is then expelled from the Metropolitan Opera at the insistence of his now recognizing and recognized childhood playmate, John Henderson. It's as though the fluidity of impressions, culminating in a distinctive interiority of self-recognition freed in thinking, converging with the cumulative effects of the social constraints of Jim Crow directly controverting that freedom, compels Jones to go home with an expressed sense of his "duty to Altamaha . . . to help settle the Negro problems there." He has a duty, a calling to freedom. The dream is now reinforced by the desire and determination for its actuality.

As for the actuality of Altamaha, the narrative gives the black Altamaha's unmediated collective expectation and excitement that their quasi-messianic refrain was about to be realized:

> Down in Altamaha, after seven long years, all the world knew John was coming. The homes were scrubbed and scoured,—above all, one; the gardens and yards had an unwonted trimness, and Jennie bought a new gingham. With some finesse and negotiation, all the dark Methodists and Presbyterians were induced to join in a monster welcome at the Baptist Church; and as the day drew near, warm discussions arose on every corner as to the exact extent and nature of John's accomplishments. It was noontide on a gray and cloudy day when he came. The black town flocked to the depot, with a little of the white at the edges,—a happy throng, with "Good-mawnings" and "Howdys" and laughing and joking and jostling. Mother sat yonder in the window watching; but sister Jennie stood on the platform, nervously fingering her dress, tall and lithe, with soft brown skin and loving eyes peering from out a tangled wilderness of hair.

Just as Jones's earlier impressionistic sense of things was distinct from, indeed resistant to, the normative collective social meaningfulness of the things happening around him, so too his dream of what is actually possible is distinct from black Altamaha's normative collective sense of what is and is possible. Where they see "home," going to great lengths in preparation for his return to it, he sees narrow sordidness: "a little dingy station, a black crowd gaudy and dirty, a half-mile of dilapidated shanties along a straggling ditch of mud." The contrast in the two senses of things is such that the crowd is at first bewildered by Jones's comportment, with the Methodist preacher thinking him "down in the mouf," the Baptist sister complaining he seems "monstus stuck up," and the white postmaster of the opinion that the "damn Nigger . . . has gone North and got plum full o' fool notions; but they won't work in Altamaha."

Bewilderment gives way to outright confusion at the welcome home meeting at the Baptist Church where, again without uttering a word, Jones's demeanor has a profoundly disruptive effect on the discourse of the Methodist, Baptist, and Presbyterian preachers, the three standard bearers of the evangelicalism that was supposed to ground and sustain the community for its earthly, as well as its final salvation:

> When the speaking came at night, the house was crowded to overflowing. The three preachers had especially prepared themselves, but somehow John's manner seemed to throw a blanket over everything,—he seemed so cold and preoccupied, and had so strange an air of restraint that the Methodist brother could not warm up to his theme and elicited not a single "Amen";

the Presbyterian prayer was but feebly responded to, and even the Baptist preacher, though he wakened faint enthusiasm, got so mixed up in his favorite sentence that he had to close it by stopping fully fifteen minutes sooner than he meant.

The disruptive effect is precipitated by Jones's being illegible in precisely the same way the old man of the crowd is for Poe's convalescent. He is an aporia that does not permit itself to be read. Only, and this fact is key, Jones is a familiar; he is of them, the son of mother Jones, and brother of sister Jennie, the "always good-natured and respectful" Negro laborer. He should, accordingly, be quite legible. But Altamaha's expectation of his being readable is predicated on the same notion of translatability the convalescent worked with to finally sort out the old man's "wild history" and that was troubled in the teacher's tale of Jones's education. Just as in that tale, it is not a question of the unfungibility or untranslatability of one subjective meaning into another economy. It is the presentation of the self in the break where nascence and nescience co-articulate, where two incommensurable grammars collide, articulating an emergent intelligence, a not altogether predictable way of thinking. The fact that John Jones is one of them, is one of the crowd and not a transient, self-conserving spectator like the *flâneur*, exacerbates the disruptive affect. He does not conserve his self as the monadic salvation against the homogenizing forces of commodification, but rather he throws himself into the mix in a way that precipitates what Du Bois calls "anarchy" in "Of the Faith of the Fathers,"[273] functioning as a transformative catalyst initiating a process of change and thereby fulfilling the expectation of the refrain, "When John comes home." Yet, such transformative force is transgressive by definition, and unsettling to the fixed, supposedly transcendently grounded order of things. So, of course, "the people moved uneasily in their seats as John rose to reply" to the pastoral welcomes, both because of what he has to say and the form his saying takes, a form that calls them away from the "Church, white and black, . . . under the very shadow [of which] Home was ruined":

> He spoke slowly and methodically. The age, he said, demanded new ideas; we were far different from those men of the seventeenth and eighteenth centuries,—with broader ideas of human brotherhood and destiny. Then he spoke of the rise of charity and popular education, and particularly of the spread of wealth and work. The question was, then, he added reflectively, looking at the low discolored ceiling, what part the Negroes of this land would take in the striving of the new century. He sketched in vague outline the new Industrial School that might rise among these pines, he spoke in detail of the charitable and philanthropic work that might be organized, of money that might be saved for banks and business. Finally he

urged unity, and deprecated especially religious and denominational bickering. "To-day," he said, with a smile, "the world cares little whether a man be Baptist or Methodist, or indeed a churchman at all, so long as he is good and true. What difference does it make whether a man be baptized in river or wash-bowl, or not at all? Let's leave all that littleness, and look higher." Then, thinking of nothing else, he slowly sat down. A painful hush seized that crowded mass. Little had they understood of what he said, for he spoke an un-known tongue, save the last word about baptism; that they knew, and they sat very still while the clock ticked.[274]

The people's affective energy, gathered together for what was supposed to be a meeting of its revival with John's long-anticipated return, is defused and misdirected in an unanticipated way. As already stated, it is not a trivial fact that John Jones comes from and is of the neo-slave folk and is sent to the institute at their behest to fulfill *their* ambitions and expectations of social transformation. The shock prompted by his mode of expression, by his very bodily carriage stems from their fear that realizing those expectations means letting go of what they are, of what they know themselves to be, for something they do not know and cannot recognize as theirs. This is not a fear of death or collective extinction, or of losing what they have. Rather, it is a fear of realizing what they want. John has returned to them bearing the fruit of their dream, which is the plan to upend the only world they have known. And he offers that fruit to the combined Protestant congregations in the name of "charity"—a familiar term given to them as a principal tenet of faith in the King James Version, their source scripture, where I Corinthians 13 tells them:

> Charity suffereth long, *and is* kind; charity envieth not; charity vaunteth not itself, is not puffed up, Doth not behave itself unseemly, seeketh not her own, is not easily provoked, thinketh no evil; Rejoiceth not in iniquity, but rejoiceth in the truth, Beareth all things, believeth all things, hopeth all things, endureth all things. Charity never faileth; but whether *there be* prophecies, they shall fail, whether *there be* tongues, they shall cease; whether *there be* knowledge, it shall vanish away. For we know in part, and we prophesy in part. But when that which is perfect is come, then that which is in part shall be done away. When I was a child, I spake as a child, I understood as a child, I thought as a child; but when I became a man, I put away childish things. For now we see through a glass, darkly; but the face to face: now I know in part; but then shall I know even as also I am known. And now abideth faith, hope, charity, these three; but the greatest of this *is* charity.[275]

In claiming charity issues from contemporary earthly knowledge rather than from hope and faith in a divine future, John reverses, in paraphrase, the rhetorical thrust of I Corinthians 13. His further remarking on the edifying force of charity in terms of capitalist industrialization and philanthropy directly contradicts Paul's teaching in I Corinthians 8: 1: "Now as touching things offered unto idols, we know that we all have knowledge. Knowledge puffed up, but charity edifieth." Performing in effect a parodic paraphrase of Galatians 5:6—"For in Christ Jesus neither circumcision availeth any thing, nor uncircumcision; but faith working through love"—John intensifies the force of that contradiction by denouncing the value of baptism and confession, which is tantamount to refusing the meaningfulness of the Eucharist. In that refusal, he rejects the redemption of the passion, foreclosing on the hermeneutics that reads in Christ's suffering the supreme act of charity that redeems humanity. His deploying the familiar term "charity" of this central tenet of faith in a not fully recognizable form that reflects the ambitions of Altamaha's blacks but also something else they do not recognize, or recognize as antithetical to those ambitions, is disconcerting. That he does so expressly in the name of human brotherhood and destiny so threatens the idols of the tribe it warrants a fanatical response from the Amen corner, where an old bent man with "the intense rapt look of the religious fanatic" rose to denounce what he took to be a "trampling on the true Religion," with inarticulate gestures and "rude and awful eloquence."[276]

In staging this conflict over the nature of charity as the foundation of community, the narrative is tightly focused on John, who, although regretful that he has inadvertently vandalized "something this little world held sacred," is not at all deterred in his mission by the scathing diaconal denunciation.[277] Nor has the denunciation inoculated the community from his tendency. This is first indicated by his sister, Jennie, immediately after the denunciation, who, having asked him if learning makes everyone unhappy, responds to John's "yes" by telling him: "I wish I was unhappy,—and—and," putting both arms about his neck, "I think I am, a little, John." But the force of John's tendency is more evidenced in the factionalization of Altamaha's Negros over him and the gradual increase in attendance at his school.

Following the customary interpretation, we might read the homecoming scene and subsequent struggle over the school as emblematic of the tragic fate of the black man who, in striving to get beyond the debased heritage of slavery by seeking salvation through knowledge, has so internalized the normative perspective of the white world his interiority is one of "conflictual-twoness," or strife, and false self-consciousness.[278] When the scene is so interpreted, then the charity and philanthropy John invokes is condescending. And in accordance with to that same interpretation, Jones could be seen as a literary heuristic of why alienated double consciousness cannot be the basis of legitimate and authentic black leadership, or even the fictional depiction of Alexander Crummell.[279] There are indeed elements here that support reading Jones's remarks to the combined congregations as echoing Crummell's 1885 Harpers Ferry address, "The Need of New Ideas and New Aims for a New Era." For instance, Jones's opening two sentences paraphrase in summary the principal topic of Crummell's speech: the need for ideas commensurate with the "urgent needs of the present" and "the fast-crowding, momentous interests of the future." Distinguishing memory as the passive "unavoidable storage and recurrence of facts and ideas to the understanding and consciousness" from recollection as the active "seeking of the facts . . . the painstaking endeavor of the mind to bring them back again to consciousness," Crummell gives an extensive argument for the need to guard against not the memory of slavery, "but the constant *recollection* of it, as the commanding thought of a new people, who should be marching on to the broadest freedom of thought in a new and glorious present, and a still more magnificent future."[280] Then, on the basis of Anglican Archbishop and poet Richard Chenevix Trench's assertion that "language is as truly on one side the limit and restraint of thought, as on the other side that which feeds and unfolds it," he states his desire is that the Negro "escape 'the limit and restraint' of both the *word* and the *thought* of slavery. As a people," he continues, "we have been permitted by a gracious Providence to enter the new and exalted pathways of freedom. The thought, the routine, the usages, and calculations of that old system are dead things, absolutely alien from the conditions in which life presents itself to us in our disenthralled and uplifted state. We have new conditions of life and new relations in society."[281]

Considered in relation to Crummell's 1885 Harpers Ferry address, Jones's remarks become less cryptic. Each of Jones's topics, from popular education and wealth and work, to charity and philanthropy, can be found to be a summary paraphrase of Crummell's more detailed and elaborate presentation of the same. Moreover, the sense of providential progress intimated in Jones's remarks is in keeping with Crummell's view that what was needed was "the civilization of the Negro race in the United States, by the scientific processes of literature, art, and philosophy, through the agency of the cultured men of this same Negro race."[282] There is an important difference between them on the nature of civilization, however. For Crummell, civilization is "the *secondary* word of God, given in nourishment of humanity," which is to say that, when he then further defines it as "the action of exalted forces, both of God and man," he expressly means Christianity.[283] The need for civilization is, in this view, the need for a systematic cultivation of modern Christian minds that would both demonstrate the Negro's capacity and contribute to the formation of a viable culture, participating in the development of the human spirit. "The intellect is to be used . . . the intellect rightly discerning the conditions, and the gracious and godly heart stimulating to the performance of the noblest duties for a people," Crummell proclaims at the end of his 1885 Harpers Ferry address, adding: "Allow me, in conclusion, to express the hope that, mingled with the sweet melodies if poetry, the inspiring voices of eloquence and the mystic tones of science, you will have an open ear to the voice of God, which is the call to duty."[284] The value of civilization is its capacity to resist or transcend fluctuating political and economic structures, creating "a complete and rounded man" through "the force and application of the highest arts; not mere mechanism; not mere machinery; not mere handicraft; not the mere grasp on material things; not mere temporal ambitions."[285] Crummell designates this process of transformation "a grand *moral* revolution which will touch and vivify the inner life of a people," and declares, "The basis of this revolution must be character." Seeming to contradict all of this, Jones concludes his remarks at the church in the welcome-home meeting by challenging the continued value and usefulness of religiosity in determining a person's character, let alone achieving the Negro's contribution to furthering civilization.

Once again we encounter the issue of the historicity of interiority, of the type of self articulated in relation to a particular *Gemeinschaft*. And in the case of the Negro, as a human type emerging out of three hundred years of chattel slavery under capitalist modernity, "swept on by the current of the nineteenth century [into the twentieth] while yet struggling in eddies of the fifteenth century," it is a problem of the cart being before the horse.[286] The grammar still needs to be constituted before its types are articulable. The Negro as a type, for Du Bois, is an extraordinary instance in which the concurrent articulation of self-interiority and *Gemeinschaft* without any grounding mythical authority—in other words, the dynamic emergence of the *poēsis* of human institution with the reverberations of affect and historical experience-lived-in-the-moment—is fully on display in actuality. In this matter, Du Bois states in the tenth chapter, "Of the Faith of the Fathers," where he offers a cursory historical analysis of "Negro religion," that the Negro faces an unenviable dilemma: "Conscious of his impotence, and pessimistic, he often becomes bitter and vindictive; and his religion, instead of a worship, is a complaint and a curse, a wail rather than a hope, a sneer rather than a faith. On the other hand, another type of mind, shrewder and keener and more tortuous too, sees in the very strength of the anti-Negro movement its patent weaknesses, and with Jesuitic casuistry is deterred by no ethical considerations in the endeavor to turn this weakness to the black man's strength."[287] If this dilemma generates "two great and hardly reconcilable streams of thought and ethical strivings," with "one type of Negro almost ready to curse God and die [who] is wedded to ideals remote, whimsical, perhaps impossible of realization," and the other "too often found a traitor to right and a coward before force [who] forgets that life is more than meat and the body more than raiment," it is symptomatic of the then-emerging planet-wide economy of financial capitalism—Du Bois characterizes this in the *Black Flame Trilogy* as international capitalism—in which the forced dominance of a vapid commodification of existence proliferates a nihilistic reaction: "But, after all, is not this simply the writhing of the age translated into black,—the triumph of the Lie which to-day, with its false culture, faces the hideousness of the anarchist assassin?"[288] Anarchy or hypocrisy are the polar positions of the dilemma, which is cast in terms of the difference between the northern and southern Negro:

> To-day the young Negro of the South who would succeed cannot be frank and outspoken, honest and self-assertive, but rather he is daily tempted to be silent and wary, politic and sly; he must flatter and be pleasant, endure petty insults with a smile, shut his eyes to wrong; in too many cases he sees positive personal advantage in deception and lying. His real thoughts, his real aspirations, must be guarded in whispers; he must not criticise, he must not complain. Patience, humility, and adroitness must, in these growing black youth, replace impulse, manliness, and courage. With this sacrifice there is an economic opening, and perhaps peace and some prosperity. Without this there is riot, migration, or crime.[289]

This culture of practiced deception is to be condemned precisely because it is the ascendant mode among the oppressed for surviving the ascendant world order: "Nor is this situation peculiar to the Southern United States,—is it not rather the only method by which undeveloped races have gained the right to share modern culture? The price of culture is a Lie."[290] Yet, the opposite pole of the dilemma, for all its insistent adherence to self-expression and freedom, is susceptible to pessimistic and nihilistic tendencies:

> On the other hand, in the North the tendency is to emphasize the radicalism of the Negro. Driven from his birthright in the South by a situation at which every fiber of his more outspoken and assertive nature revolts, he finds himself in a land where he can scarcely earn a decent living amid the harsh competition and the color discrimination. At the same time, through schools and periodicals, discussions and lectures, he is intellectually quickened and awakened. The soul, long pent up and dwarfed, suddenly expands in new-found freedom. What wonder that every tendency is to excess,— radical complaint, radical remedies, bitter denunciation or angry silence. Some sink, some rise. The criminal and the sensualist leave the church for the gambling-hell and the brothel, and fill the slums of Chicago and Baltimore; the better classes segregate themselves from the group-life of both white and black, and form an aristocracy, cultured but pessimistic, whose bitter criticism stings while it points out no way of escape. They despise the submission and subserviency of the Southern Negroes, but offer no other means by which a poor and oppressed minority can exist side by side with

its masters. Feeling deeply and keenly the tendencies and opportunities of the age in which they live, their souls are bitter at the fate which drops the Veil between; and the very fact that this bitterness is natural and justifiable only serves to intensify it and make it more maddening.[291]

It is admittedly tempting to read the conflict between Jones and the preachers in the welcome meeting scene as a narration of this dilemma. What is described in "Of the Faith of the Fathers" in sociological terms as a type of Negro is narrated in "Of the Coming of John" as the articulation of Jones's self-awareness, only without the nihilistic or even pessimistic tendencies, yet unrelenting in the presumption of his full humanity and equality. Which is to say, Jones is something else than either anarchist or hypocrite. He is, the question of religiosity aside, the type of Negro Crummell claimed would be the basis of revolutionary transformation, answering what was a fundamental question: "And who are the agents to bring about this grand change in this race?" As such an answer, Jones is what Du Bois refers to in "Conservation of Races" as the "advance guard of the Negro people" and later famously called the "Talented Tenth," which he defined as "the Revolutionary group of distinguished Negroes," whose charge was to politicize the neo-slave black masses, transforming them into a viable collective capable of inclusion in the American republican experiment, while, at the same time, preserving the Negro's distinctive humanist patterns of living and thinking. "The Talented Tenth of the Negro race must be made leaders of thought and missionaries of culture among their people," Du Bois asserts; for him, the work of making them so can be done only by Negro colleges, such as Wells Institute.[292] Even if Du Bois does mean with such a statement to evoke Matthew Arnold's concept of culture as self-development to both describe the cultured individual who disseminates culture among the black masses and to represent the self-developing, the narration of Jones's self is still, per Dilthey, as a microcosm of the confluences of a psychophysical complex, and not in the narrow sense of psychology, but as the actualized global world, the *Weltanschauung*. Jones, accordingly, is the type of Negro intellectual who embodies the "truer self" referred to in "Of Our Spiritual Strivings," which, having rid itself of the contemptuous, falsifying picture of Negro life perpetrated by the white world, strives as "co-worker in the kingdom of culture" to interpolate the meaning of black being into the universal movement of civilization, achieving not only full inclusion into the American republican project, but for "the realization of that broader humanity which freely recognizes differences in men, but sternly deprecates inequality in their opportunities of development."[293]

So we find him several days after the welcome fiasco still determined to establish the school, and in a way that offends precisely because its agrammaticality entails familiar features. It is not, then, that the blacks or the whites altogether fail to understand how Jones expresses himself—they understand well enough; it is that, according to the grammar upholding their *Gemeinschaft*, ideally, he should not have any such sense of self, and if he does, it must not be expressed, either publicly or privately, under any circumstance whatsoever. A point Judge Henderson has occasion to make when, seeking permission to teach in the Negro school, Jones dares to present himself at the judge's front door. Assuming this blatant disregard of established social etiquette resulted from Jones's having become habituated during his stay up north to casually presume his equality with whites, Henderson brusquely tells him: "Go 'round to the kitchen door, John, and wait." Taking the point of the judge's rebuke, in those moments of waiting to be summoned, Jones reflects on his sense of *dis-emplacement*, that he no longer has any legitimately recognizable location in this world. Judge Henderson, nevertheless, is undaunted in his determination to relocate Jones in his proper place in the world, even if by force. So, after summoning and receiving him through the back door, he says straight away: "I want to speak to you plainly. . . . You and I both know, John, that in this country the Negro must remain subordinate, and can never expect to be the equal of white men. In their place, your people can be honest and respectful; and God knows, I'll do what I can to help them. But when they want to reverse nature, and rule white men, and marry white women, and sit in my parlor, then, by God! we'll hold them under if we have to lynch every Nigger in the land." The dilemma of the two types is presented when the judge demands of Jones, with his "education and Northern notions," not only that he must accept the status quo, but that he must reinforce it by teaching "the darkies to be faithful servants and laborers as your fathers were"—a reminder to Jones that his own father had been Henderson property and "was a good Nigger"—and not to "put fool ideas of rising and equality into these folks' heads." The "Lie" is performed when Jones replies: "I am going to accept the situation, Judge Henderson." It is not sustained, however, because Jones marks it publicly as a lie by breaking his promise and, in the words of the irate postmaster, proceeds to give "talks on the French Revolution, equality, and such like" to the blacks of Altamaha. This report, combined with the returned John Henderson's account of Jones as "the darky that tried to force himself into a seat beside the lady" he escorted to the opera, compels the judge to shut down the school; and that action, combined with the factionalism Jones has already been confronting from the Negroes of Altamaha, compels him to decide to leave Altamaha. "I'll go away," he says to himself right after his violent dismissal by Judge Henderson, "I'll go away and find work, and send for them. I cannot live here longer." Enraged by the situation, Jones heads home to inform his mother and sister of his decision, only to come upon John Henderson sexually assaulting his sister, Jennie, in the woods. After killing Henderson to stop the assault, Jones takes Jennie home, tells his mother he is "going—North," then returns to the scene of the crime, where, as the mounted lynch mob led by Judge Henderson races toward him, he unwaveringly faces them "softly humming the 'Song of the Bride,'—'Freudig geführt, ziehet dahin.' What does this German line mean here? Not in the sense of how might it be translated into English, which Du Bois pointedly does not do; but in the sense of what does it mean for John? Even when we do translate it, "Joyfully led, enter this place," we are still left with that question.

The line John softly hums is supposed to be from act 3 of *Lohengrin*. More precisely, it is the opening line of the song sung by the chorus in the bridal procession at the beginning of the first scene, which is more widely known as the Bridal Chorus. Yet, as always with Jones, there is something slightly askew. According to Wagner's libretto, the chorus begins singing, "Treulich geführt, ziehet dahin." In her interlineal translation of the libretto, Natalia Macfarren deconstructs the German adjective *geführt* as "*ge-führt*," then rather imaginatively mistranslates it as "and true," rendering the line as: "Faithful and true, we lead you forth."[294] The Oliver Ditson Company's Standard Edition of Opera Librettos and *The Authentic Librettos of the Wagner Operas* both follow Macfarren's suit.[295] Stewart Robb, in the Schirmer bilingual edition of the libretto, gives it as, "Faithfully led, enter this place."[296] More recently, the composer John Rutter translates it as, "Led here in faith draw near," adding the clause, "with joy," as if seeking to reconcile the libretto with Du Bois's misquotation.[297] Du Bois was not the first to modify the opening lines of the Bridal Chorus. We find in the pages of the May 12, 1860, issue of the prestigious *Dwight's Journal of Music* a generally unfavorable anonymous review of the excerpts from *Lohengrin* conducted by Wagner himself that year in Paris, where the critic says apropos the Bridal Chorus: "This march introduces the chorus: *Freudig geführt zieht dahin*, which one is surprised to find in this place, so small, I might almost say, so childlike in its style."[298] It is highly unlikely Du Bois is merely repeating this error, given that *Lohengrin* was one of his favorite Wagner operas, and he knew it quite well, having attended "six or eight" performances by his count, "under many circumstances, in different languages and Lands."[299] What's more, Du Bois gives clear indication that he knew the centrality of *Treulich* to the opera. In a short piece written for the *Pittsburgh Courier* from Berlin in October 1936 on the relevance of opera to the Negro problem, he says of *Lohengrin*: "It is a hymn of Faith. Something in this world man must trust. Not everything—but something. One cannot live and doubt everybody and everything. Somewhere in this world, and not beyond it, there is Trust, and somehow Trust leads to Joy."[300] There is no disputing, then, that he has deliberately modified the lines here, displacing an expression of trustful loyalty or faith-in (*Treulich*) with one of exuberant happiness (*Freudig*) because the latter flows from the former.³⁰¹ Our earlier question about the significance of the Bridal Chorus opening line is now further refined, becoming, What is meant by "Joy" here? What does it mean for John as the lynch mob approaches?

Considerable scholarly speculation has been offered about this, most of which remains committed to the customary interpretation of John as a tragic figure. There is also an uncustomary, somewhat more probative reading that interprets John's humming "Freudig geführt, ziehet dahin" to indicate his fantasizing about Elsa's enduring union with her champion, envisioning a joy not available to him in this world. In other words, it is an expression of Schopenhauerian resignation.³⁰² Read this way, "Of the Coming of John" is an allegory for the impossible marriage between thought and the world. This makes John's humming the modified opening line to the Bridal Chorus at the story's end tantamount to an aestheticizing of suffering, whereby, having somehow achieved through listening to Wagner an egocentric self-consciousness, John, the Schopenhauerian saint, identifies freedom with renunciation of the phenomenal world and discovers the real intelligible world articulated in the irrational will to live. By this account, humming *Freudig* is an expression of his renouncing the possibility of human agency being significant in the world. Consequently, the archetypical Negro intellectual is above and apart from the community—much like Baudelaire's *flâneur*'s relationship to the crowd—and so not fully engaged in sociality. There is ample reason to hesitate before such a reading of the story, however. Not only is there little to no support in the narration of the closing scene for identifying *Freudig* with renunciation, but Schopenhauer's conception of will and renunciation is pronouncedly contradictory to the overall depiction of John's consciousness in the story, particularly in relation to how he thinks about *Lohengrin*.

The impressionistic narrating of John's self-consciousness suggests a thinking concurrent with the world of things. His conscious perspective is articulated in the mess of the "struggle between the determination to see everything, to forget nothing, and the faculty of memory, which has acquired the habit of poignantly registering the general color and silhouette, the arabesque of contour."³⁰³ John's misconstruing the opening line to the Bridal Chorus is in keeping with his overall impressionistic thinking, which has already been understood to indicate the eventfulness of thinking in the world. The pivotal moment in which he knows the actuality of his auto-poetic capacity, his absolute freedom in *this* world, is that moment in the story when he first hears the act 1 prelude of Wagner's *Lohengrin* at the Metropolitan Opera House in New York. The type of thinking narrated in the New York scene patently does not suffer self-alienation, which troubles the Schopenhauerian reading of the end.

To see this, let's go back to the passage in the story where Judge Henderson closes the school and take up the narrative at the moment just prior to that. There is a tight series of shifts in narrative perspective and focus, three in all, which orchestrates the conclusion. The first of these is a shift in focus from a scene of conversation in Judge Henderson's parlor between him, his son, John, and the postmaster about Jones's "livenin' things up at the darky school," as the postmaster puts it. This scene comes at the end of extended narration of John Henderson's homecoming, which is itself an abrupt shift in perspective from the moment of dialogue in which John Jones has accepted Judge Henderson's conditions. This latter shift marks a specified passage of time, one month. In contrast, each of the three shifts orchestrating the story's end is within the same temporal duration, but from a parallel perspective. So, in the first, we move from the closing narration of the Judge taking his hat and cane in hand and walking "straight to the schoolhouse," to John:

> For John, it had been a long, hard pull to get things started in the rickety old shanty that sheltered his school. The Negroes were rent into factions for and against him, the parents were careless, the children irregular and dirty, and books, pencils, and slates largely missing. Nevertheless, he struggled hopefully on, and seemed to see at last some glimmering of dawn. The attendance was larger and the children were a shade cleaner this week. Even the booby class in reading showed a little comforting progress. So John settled himself with renewed patience this afternoon.
>
> "Now, Mandy," he said cheerfully, "that's better; but you mustn't chop your words up so: 'If—the—man—goes.' Why, your little brother even wouldn't tell a story that way, now would he?"
>
> "Naw, suh, he cain't talk."
>
> "All right; now let's try again: 'If the man—'

We have been returned to Jones's perspective and thinking, and as always that thinking and perspective is forward-looking and determined to be transformative, despite the perceived real obstacles. Jones's dialogue with his student, Mandy, presents a jocular moment of learning, in which "if—the man—goes" is a play on words, suggesting the euphemistic phrase then used in the South for the position of authority and power. The punning is confirmed by John's starting to repeat the phrase, only to be violently interrupted by Judge Henderson yelling "John!" and then proclaiming the closing of the school. Again, after that proclamation, there is a shift in perspective within the same temporal duration to focus on John Henderson. Disgruntled and bored by his prospects in Altamaha and self-indulgently bemoaning that "there isn't even a girl worth getting up a respectable flirtation with," he sees and sexually assaults Jones's sister, Jennie, in the pine woods. The third and final shift, still in the same duration, is back to Jones. It begins with his walking to the sea, and includes the already quoted statement: "'I'll go away,' he said slowly; 'I'll go away and find work, and send for them. I cannot live here longer.'" To which is added: "And then the fierce, buried anger surged up into his throat. He waved his arms and hurried wildly up the path." We are back firmly within the perspective with which the New York scene began, with Jones's impressionistic thinking colored in the affective tones of anger and giving us passages such as

> The great brown sea lay silent. The air scarce breathed. The dying day bathed the twisted oaks and mighty pines in black and gold. There came from the wind no warning, not a whisper from the cloudless sky. There was only a black man hurrying on with an ache in his heart, seeing neither sun nor sea, but starting as from a dream at the frightened cry that woke the pines, to see his dark sister struggling in the arms of a tall and fair-haired man.

Even the killing of Henderson is enacted in a dreamlike state. "He said not a word, but, seizing a fallen limb, struck him with all the pent-up hatred of his great black arm, and the body lay white and still beneath the pines, all bathed in sunshine and in blood. John looked at it dreamily, then walked back to the house briskly, and said in a soft voice, 'Mammy, I'm going away—I'm going to be free.'" The concluding three paragraphs of the story, beginning with his return to the scene of Henderson's murder, where he sits until nightfall, contemplating the blood stains left by Henderson's now removed body, remains in this mode and is totally in Jones's head. His thinking starts as a brief retrospection of how "he had played with that dead boy, romping together under the solemn trees," then turns to wondering about the boys at the institute and "what they would all say when they knew, in that great long dining-room with its hundreds of merry eyes," what he had done. Reminded by the stars of the Metropolitan Opera House's gilded ceiling, Jones somehow thinks he hears "stealing toward him the faint sweet music of the swan.... Clear and high the faint sweet melody rose and fluttered like a living thing, so that the very earth trembled as with the tramp of horses and murmur of angry men." The force of the impression was so strong, the music so clear it casts the noise of galloping horses and shouting men into the dark shadows, at which point Jones "roused himself, bent forward, and looked steadily down the pathway, softly humming the 'Song of the Bride,'—'Freudig geführt, ziehet dahin.'" It is at precisely this moment, having identified the music of Lohengrin's swan with the clamor of the lynch mob, that Jones recognizes Judge Henderson in their lead as "that haggard white-haired man, whose eyes flashed red with fury. Oh, how he pitied him,—pitied him,—and wondered if he had the coiling twisted rope. Then, as the storm burst round him, he rose slowly to his feet and turned his closed eyes toward the Sea. And the world whistled in his ears."

How do we account for the identification of Lohengrin's swan with both freedom and murderous oppression? It is clearly not the case that the music ultimately merges with the white oppressors and becomes, effectively, white.[304] Recall that in Jones's initial encounter with the *Lohengrin* prelude he is not narrated as listening to the music actually being performed, but as thinking about what the music means to him. At the story's conclusion, he is narrated listening to music that is not actually being performed, but he is certain he hears. This is indeed about recollection, and Jones is recalling the exuberant feeling of creative power and freedom he felt on hearing the prelude. As we have already noted, concurrent with Jones's being brought by the prelude to awareness of what we might well call "the joy of freedom," he also *knows* his duty, which is to be worthy of that joy by helping to "settle the Negro problem in Altamaha." This entails transforming the world of Altamaha even if, especially if, that necessitates vandalizing the sacred something that keeps "this little world" going; which ironically means, as his little sister Jennie remarks, hesitatingly, to "make ever one—unhappy." It must be borne in mind that Jones's desacralization of the world of Altamaha calls the blacks to give up the Pauline ethos of sacrifice. As is demonstrated in his homecoming speech at the church, Jones strives for a quality of person in whom the joy of freedom is identified with the duty to bring about, to the best of one's ability, an ethical future life in common, to *move* toward achieving a society worthy of happiness—"Freudig geführt, ziehet dahin." Humming that line as the lynch mob approaches, Jones recalls the sounds that gave him his self, that made him *know* he is free. And while being guided by such is somber determinate business, it should not be confused with resignation.

Rather than a tragic figure, or even a Schopenhauerian figure of renunciation and resignation, Jones represents the possibilities of thinking-in-action, of thinking freedom in the mist of contingency and disorder, occurring "between chance and law . . . possibility and necessity." It is by chance Jones comes to the Metropolitan Opera, where hearing the Prelude he knows his freedom as a human being, as well as his duty to transform the world of Altamaha; and it is by the same chance he recognizes at precisely that moment his white childhood playmate from Altamaha, who, functioning as the force of law, of Jim Crow, has him expelled. Thinking freedom is related to the aleatory as the event occurring in the break between chance and law, and the music of *Lohengrin* is its emblem. Jones's recognizing his freedom while listening to Wagner's *Lohengrin* is the crystallization of his becoming a self-conscious historical agent whose interiority is wholly a function of being in the world fully cognizant of the requisite conditions, as well as the price for achieving this. As for the conditions, they are a perpetually transformative sociality without any mythological ideal types. As for the price, it is the loss of blind faith in this world or any other—that is to say, the abandonment of eschatological salvation and redemption. The challenges of meaning, of justice, of ethical relations are always existential, not metaphysical. So eventful thinking's occurring in the break between chance and law is, paradoxically, a necessity of survival—the situation of the recently freed Negro masses *tout court* being denied normative membership status in American society through the juridically enforced (Jim Crow) sociopolitical betrayal of civic republicanism's ethical ideals—as well as the duty to choose to be free, to choose to *be*. This is reiterated at the story's conclusion with the two Johns' second chance encounter. The white John Henderson, in keeping with the law of the land, feels free to casually sexually assault the black John Jones's sister, Jennie, just because he chances upon her. He loses his life at the hands of Jones, who has chanced upon the assault right after Judge Henderson has closed his school. We might even say that for a brief moment, in that chance encounter when Jones kills Henderson with the fallen tree limb—and the analogy to lynching is strikingly apparent—he has taken the law into his hands, countering the proposition that all mediate violence is either lawmaking or law-preserving. Here, he simply, per chance, breaks the law. In this spontaneous act of violence, Jones does not establish new conditions in which a new revolutionary order can emerge, but he does establish the tenuousness of the law's grip on his self, that the "law is a white dog," and that to stay free he must keep on moving.[305] As he says to his mother: "I'm going away—I'm going to be free"; and in response to her asking if he means he is "gwine No'th agin," he offers: "Yes, mammy, I'm going—North." Getting under way North is both a geopolitical orientation and an allegory, taken from the sorrow songs, of absolute freedom. In Jones's case, however, there is no aspiration for final redemption in the next world, only dogged determination to be free in this world through his own agency, hence the recollection of how he felt on hearing the music from *Lohengrin*. Yet, whereas in the New York scene, Jones is narrated listening to and thinking with music being performed, in the conclusion, *he* is generating the music; first in his recollection, then with his voice. Here, Jones is articulating the sounds of his freedom; he is the poet, giving expression to his self, performing his humanity and freedom in the midst of violent barbarism.

It is not the world Jones renounces, but the unethical oppression of Jim Crow, to which he has never truly resigned himself. And if he is tranquil in his resistance, humming a song he associates with his freedom, rather than screaming in angst against his fate, that is the tranquility of self-possession. It is a direct retort to Judge Henderson's demand that the Negro not dream, not imagine any way of being beyond the grammar of capitalist neo-slavery, that he not think freely. Jones's retort, which so enrages, is to not only imagine and think freely, but to persistently express it publicly and clearly. His wondering in the end of how the boys at the institute will respond when they hear what he has done signals his purpose to be a pedagogic example of the ethical character in action, to indeed be an archetype of the *poiēsis* of human institution. John Jones, then, is an exhibition, a narration of thinking as generating complexities and complications in its density rather than resolving difference in its translucence. Jones's self is not the manifestation of an essential humanity deriving its legitimacy from a higher power or even a prior existence, but rather, it is the articulation of a subjectivity, a self-conscious agency, the expression of which is wholly in the set of relations established by the violence of neo-slavery. For the self articulated in such a narration, its humanity is overwhelmingly imaginative, a poetic, hence historical, invention, something that warrants being called the self-of-narrativity. Du Bois will return to this figure repeatedly, from Zora in *Quest of the Silver Fleece*, to Matthew Towns, in *Dark Princess*, and to Mansart in the *Black Flame Trilogy*. Because the narration of each of these is fundamentally an activity of collective elaboration, the self it articulates is necessarily in relation to the world of things and others thinking—in other words, ethical.

On that note, if "the weary traveler" is the epigram for *The Souls of Black Folk* as a whole, and John Jones is indeed the archetypal portrait of this, then the book's motto is to be found in the opening lines of its "Forethought"; not the often cited "for the problem of the Twentieth Century is the problem of the color-line," but the promissory proclamation that opens the text: "Herein lie buried many things which if read with patience may show the strange meaning of being black here in the dawning of the Twentieth Century." It is the *meaning of black being* that should be of interest to the "Gentle Reader." Du Bois strives in the book to provide a sketch of how those who have been compelled by historical circumstance to be black in the world have cognizance of the world—"the spiritual world in which ten thousand thousand . . . live and strive." Heeding his request to "study my words with me," we should give careful attention to the rhetorical question with which Du Bois concludes the Forethought: "And, finally, need I add that I who speak here am bone of the bone and flesh of the flesh of them that live within the Veil?" Attending to this question prompts a question of our own: What is entailed in being cognizant of the world in the flesh, and, in that knowing, loving the flesh?

Sentient Flesh

An Ontologically Discordant Being

I was twenty-one years old when the war was settled. My mother and grandmother kep' my age up and after the death of them I knowed how to handle it myself.

My old master's name was Butler and he was pretty fair to his darkies. He give em plenty to eat and wear.

I was born and raised in Indian Territory and emigrated from there to Atlanta, Georgia when I was about twelve or thirteen. We lived right in Atlanta. I cleaned up round the house. Yes ma'm, that's what I followed. When the Yankees came to Atlanta they just forced us into the army. After I got in the army and got used to it, it was fun—just like meat and bread. Yankees treated me good. I was sorry when it broke up. When the bugle blowed we knowed our business. Sometimes, the age I is now, I wish I was in it. Father Abraham Lincoln was our President. I knowed the war was to free the colored folks. I run away from my white folks is how come I was in the Yankee army. . . .

Before the war my white folks was good to us. I had a better time than I got now.

My father and mother was sold away from me, but old mistress couldn't rest without em and went and got em back. They stayed right there till they died. Us folks was treated well. I think we should have our liberty cause us ain't hogs or horses—us is human flesh.[1]

The most remarkable thing about this passage taken from the three-page typewritten transcript of an interview with the ninety-two-year-old freedman Tom Windham is his rather off-handed statement, "we should have our liberty cause . . . us is human flesh." Windham's interview, conducted by Bernice Bowden in Pine Bluff, Arkansas, sometime in 1937, is one of the 696 done in the state over a two-year period under the aegis of the Works Progress Administration (WPA) Federal Writers' Project, 677 of which were submitted to the WPA Writers Unit of the Library of Congress to be eventually compiled for archiving, along with those of sixteen other participating states, into the seventeen-volume *Slave Narratives: A Folk History of Slavery in the United States from Interviews with Former Slaves*. Claiming the human entitlement of freedom is not at all extraordinary in the context of the WPA project mandate, which was to record the experiences and memories of those who had endured enslavement before they passed away. It is noteworthy that throughout the period when these interviews were conducted, from April 1937 to August 1939, there was a sharp recession precipitated by Federal Reserve monetary policy prolonging the worse effects of the Great Depression, which for poor black folk like Windham resulted in amplified peonage and forced labor under incarceration. Given that immediate context, claims of deserving freedom attended by comparisons with the conditions of antebellum slavery were par for the course throughout the entire interview qua narrative collection. Be that as it may, the interview protocols made all the more remarkable Windham's asserting humanity as a predicate of the flesh rather than a condition of being beyond the flesh. Those protocols were set out in a twenty-item questionnaire prepared by John Avery Lomax as supplementary instructions to the *American Guide Manual*, which all WPA interviewers were to follow.

Composed in his capacity as national advisor on Folklore and Folkways for the Federal Writers' Project, Lomax's agenda with the questionnaire was to establish some uniformity of method across the project's seventeen state offices, where the majority of field interviewers not only were white and so often inclined to color the respondents' statements according to their own racial biases, but were also ignorant of interview techniques, or otherwise inattentive to the issues of distortion inherent in the interview process that those techniques were meant to correct. There was more to it than that, however. Uniformity in the method of collecting and recording the material was crucial to insuring the archival integrity of the final collection; and Lomax was an expert collector. His endeavors between 1907 and 1910, culminating in *Cowboy Songs and Other Frontier Ballads*, were instrumental in developing the methodology for collecting American folksong and establishing its study as a main constitutive element of the national heritage. A student of the renowned Harvard English literature scholar and American folklorist George Lyman Kittredge, from whom he acquired a philological attitude toward culture, Lomax defined folksong as the "intimate poetic and musical expression of unlettered people" not yet contaminated by the social transformations of industrial modernization such as rapid urbanization and commercialized popular culture. In accord with the tenets of earlier collectors of American folklore, such as Cecil Sharp and Franz Boas, he held that such folksongs were the artifice of communities isolated from mainstream American life. Lomax went further, however, maintaining that communities in which "the population was entirely black, [or] . . . plantations where in number the Negroes greatly exceeded the whites, as in the Mississippi Delta," yielded specimens of "Negro-songs that, in musical phrasing and in poetic content, are most unlike those of the white race, the least contaminated by white influence or by modern Negro jazz."[2] Southern penitentiaries and prison camps provided the most fertile field for collecting authentic specimens of Negro-songs, to stick with the designation of the moment, because of the extremity of their enforced isolation. As Lomax explained to Carl Engel, chief of the Library of Congress's Division of Music, under whose auspices, with funding from the Council of Learned Societies, he had embarked in 1933 on his first phonographic expedition through Texas prison farms:

> Negro songs in much of their primitive purity can be obtained probably as nowhere else from Negro prisoners in State and Federal penitentiaries. Here the Negroes are completely segregated and have no familiar contact with the whites. Thrown on their own resources for entertainment, they still sing, especially the long-term prisoners who have been confined for years and who have not yet been influenced by jazz and the radio, the distinctive old-time-Negro melodies.[3]

The main objective of this and subsequent expeditions to prisons and isolated rural communities throughout the South was to record the in situ performance of such authentic "Negro artifice"—and this is precisely what Lomax sough to collect—on acetate phonographic disk for categorization and preservation at the Library of Congress's Archive of American Folksong, where Lomax had been appointed honorary consultant and curator. Phonographic disk displaced field notebook as the recording media in those expeditions; being immediately archivable without needing decipherment or editing, it freed the collector from absolute reliance on musical notation and lyric transcription as the principal form of preservation. Even so, Lomax's in-field recordings, from musical performances to interviews, entailed transcribing observed events, the context of which he often set up in pursuit of a particular type of specimen for his collection in a way resonant with Adorno's characterization of Benjamin's *flânerie*. Indeed, his procedure was very much that of collector on the hunt, a particularly poignant illustration of which is provided by the 1940 recording session with Blind Willie McTell in Atlanta, Georgia. In the interview Lomax conducted during the session, he presses McTell to perform "Ain't It Hard to Be a Nigger, Nigger," as a specimen of what he calls "complaining songs." In requesting this particular song as a specimen of that typological designation, Lomax was directing the session to support the thesis of his 1917 *Nation* article, "Self-Pity in Negro Folk-Songs," in which he lays out a topical typology of Negro-singing, from spirituals to postbellum secular forms.[4] The article begins with a flat-out assertion, stated as a simple matter of fact: "A negro singing the folksongs of his race, might be termed a negro thinking out loud.... The negro readily drops into original composition, or, at any rate, original additions to the song he is singing."[5] Situating this thinking with music in the overall typology of American folksong, Lomax does not find it to be unique to the Negro. Yet, the way the Negro does it is quite distinctive:

> The negro minstrel is preeminent both in musical ability and in easy assimilation and imitation of any mood. Thus his song becomes a sort of soliloquy fitted to melody and rhythm.... The time and the tune seem to take care of themselves, adapting themselves easily to the words which the singer repeats one or perhaps many times until memory or, as often, some whim of his emotion supplies him another line or so to continue with. And working thus through a medium of which he is master, his unrestricted thought flows out through his singing; and fitting itself to the rhythmic motions of manual labor or to the unhurried pace of his progress along the street or to the relaxed mood of his little porch at twilight, he thus soliloquizes in song and reveals the emotion of his race with a unique ingenuousness.[6]

Lomax is picking up here a line of writing about Negro singing as the musical expression of thought first laid down by Frederick Douglass in his 1845 *Narrative*. In the rather well-known closing paragraphs of chapter 2, Douglass describes slaves' spontaneous singing in the course of doing a regular chore—going to the Great House Farm (their designation for the Lloyd plantation) to receive their monthly allowance:

> They would make the dense woods, for miles around, reverberate with their wild songs, revealing at once the highest joy and the deepest sadness. They would compose and sing as they went along, consulting neither time nor tune. The thought that came up, came out—if not in the word, in the sound;—and as frequently in the one as in the other.[7]

Let us give careful consideration to this line of Douglass's, attending to how it flows into Lomax's depiction of Negro-song. Having described the slaves' singing as spontaneous expression of thought in word and sound,

Douglass proceeds to give what is arguably the first published formal analysis of the oxymoronic character of the relation between lyric and music in Negro-song, challenging the then prevalent construal of their lyrics as fundamentally incomprehensible:

> They would sometimes sing the most pathetic sentiment in the most rapturous tone, and the most rapturous sentiment in the most pathetic tone. Into all of their songs they would weave something of the Great House Farm. Especially would they do this, when leaving home. They would then sing most exultingly the following words:
>
> > *I am going away to the Great House Farm!*
> > *O, yea! O, yea! O!*
>
> This they would sing, as a chorus, to words which to many would seem unmeaning jargon, but which, nevertheless, were full of meaning to themselves. I have sometimes thought that the mere hearing of those songs would do more to impress some minds with the horrible character of slavery, than reading of whole volumes of philosophy on the subject could do. . . . Every tone was a testimony against slavery, and a prayer to God for deliverance from chains.[8]

Nor is Douglass being sentimental when he then states:

> The hearing of those wild notes always depressed my spirit, and filled me with ineffable sadness, I have frequently found myself in tears while hearing them. The mere recurrence to those songs, even now, afflicts me; and while I am writing these lines, an expression of feeling has already found its way down my cheek.[9]

Rather, he is exhibiting how the thinking expressed in this singing is not so much nonconceptual, as it derives concept from affect, which is underscored by his immediately claiming: "To those songs I trace my first glimmering conception of the dehumanizing character of slavery. I can never get rid of that conception."[10] Presenting hearing this singing as one of the pivotal moments in his own awareness of the brutality of slavery, he then proclaims in what is rightly taken as a call to action:

> If any one wishes to be impressed with the soul-killing effects of slavery, let him go to Colonel Lloyd's plantation, and, on allowance-day, place himself in the deep pine woods, and there let him, in silence, analyze the sounds that shall pass through the chambers of his soul,—and if he is not thus impressed, it will be because "there is no flesh in his obdurate heart."[11]

Ten years later, in his autobiography, *My Bondage and My Freedom*, Douglass elaborates his formal description of the songs, adding that their notes "were not always merry because they were wild. On the contrary, they were mostly of a plaintive cast, and told a tale of grief and sorrow."[12] His description of the songs' oxymoronic character is abbreviated: "In the most boisterous outburst of rapturous sentiment, there is ever a tinge of deep melancholy."[13] Still, Douglass emphasizes the affective grounds of conception by changing the identity of those likely to be impressed at merely hearing the songs from "some minds" to "truly spiritual-minded men and women," with "reading of whole volumes of philosophy on the subject" becoming "reading of whole volumes of its mere physical cruelties," and adding, "They speak to the heart and to the soul of the thought."[14] Accordingly, the call on those who would wish to gain a full sense of the oppressive force of slavery to "in silence, analyze the sounds" the slaves at Colonel Lloyd's plantation make on allowance day is modified to "in silence, thoughtfully analyze the sounds."[15] It is the response to that call, albeit delayed, which carries Douglass's line further into what will become the field of American folklore where we encounter Lomax.

The response comes from Lucy McKim, the nineteen-year-old daughter of militant Philadelphia abolitionist, James Miller McKim. A correspondent of Douglass's and a Garrisonian, although not as stridently doctrinaire as William Lloyd Garrison, McKim was a leading agent for the Philadelphia-based Pennsylvania Anti-Slavery Society, editor of the *Pennsylvania Freeman*, and one of the three recipients of Henry Box Brown's famous crate. He was also instrumental in establishing the Philadelphia Port Royal Relief Committee in April 1862, which was formed in response to the request from Edward Lillie Pierce, who had recently been appointed supervising treasury agent at Port Royal and commissioner of Negro affairs by the secretary of the treasury, Salmon Chase. What Pierce requested was private-sector support to finance and provide the teachers, managers, and missionaries required to transform the approximately ten thousand Negro slaves abandoned on the South Carolina Sea Islands after their conquest by Union forces on November 7, 1861, into "freemen as industrious as any race of men are likely to be."[16] This was a rather controversial request given, that at the time Pierce made it, in January and February of 1862, the federal government policy was still to regard Negro slaves crossing into Union lines as property to be either returned or, following the practice established by General Benjamin Butler, confiscated as "contraband of war." Congress's enacting an article of war on March 13, 1862, prohibiting Union army command from returning slaves afforded Pierce the opportunity to promote the idea of an experiment in transforming the Negro as property into the Negro as freemen. In his office as secretary general of the Port Royal Relief Committee, McKim made a one-month tour of St. Helena Island in June 1862 to assess the conditions and educational needs of its freedmen, taking Lucy with him. Shortly after her return to Philadelphia from St. Helena, "being much struck by the songs of its people," Lucy published the sheet music, *Songs of the Freedmen of Port Royal*, comprising her notation and arrangement for piano of just one of six specimens she collected during her tour, the work song "Poor Rosy, Poor Gal." This was the second published musical notation of slave-singing, following Thomas Baker's *The Song of the Contrabands "O Let My People Go"* put out the year before. Baker's sheet brought the slaves' songs to the general public as a more authentic form than the parodic so-called Ethiopian Minstrelsy. But it was the letter Lucy McKim sent to *Dwight's Journal of Music* announcing the publication of her sheet music, which appeared in the November 8, 1862, issue under the headline "Songs of the Port Royal 'Contrabands'" that inaugurated the systematic study of spirituals. McKim's *Dwight's Journal* letter was groundbreaking. Presenting her transcription of the songs she'd heard as a fixed specimen that could be comparatively analyzed in relation to Western musical forms, she introduced what would become the two principal considerations among folklorists in the collection and analysis of not only the slaves' singing but also postbellum secular Negro folksong.[17] The first of these, with which she begins her analysis of "Poor Rosy," is the difficulty entailed in transcribing the sounds the slaves/Negroes made just as she heard them: "It is difficult to express the entire character of these negro ballads by mere musical notes and signs," she reports. "The odd turns made in the throat; and the curious rhythmic effect produced by single voices chiming in at different irregular intervals, seem almost as impossible to place on score, as the singing of birds, or the tones of Æolian Harp."[18] This difficulty of transcription, which extends as well to the peculiarities of the dialect of the song lyrics, underscores the inherent musicality of the slaves' expression. "The airs," as she calls them in the operatic sense, thereby differentiating them from recitatives and so emphasizing the unusual nature of their inflections and rhythms, "are too decided not to be easily understood, and their striking originality would catch the ear of any musician."[19] The challenge to transcription posed by the sounds the Negroes made, thus, demands an enhancement of the musicologist's hearing and expansion of categorical connotation so that those sounds could be appropriated as meaningful according to an established typological order, in which they "are valuable as an expression of the character and life of the race which is playing such a conspicuous part in our history."[20] McKim is brought, then, to describe the song form in a manner that is recognizably paraphrasing Douglass's description of the oxymoronic character of the singing, as well as what it signifies psychologically from *My Bondage and My Freedom*:

> The wild, sad strains tell, as the sufferers themselves never could, of crushed hopes, keen sorrow, and dull daily misery, which covered them as hopelessly as the fog from the rice-swamps. On the other hand, the words breathe a

trusting faith in rest in the future—in "Canaan's air and happy land," to which their eyes seem constantly turned.²¹

As with all paraphrasis, this is an interpretive commentary, a rewording aimed at clarifying concepts of the source text deemed particularly significant and worthy of elaboration as the basis for a further line of thinking. With it, McKim presents the second principal consideration of the folklorist analysis of Negro-song: it always entails a plaintive mood either in music or lyric. And this is fundamentally essential to the form.

The two considerations McKim presents in *her Dwight's Journal* letter became firmly established as foci in the scholarly folklorist study of Negro-song with the publication in 1867 of *Slave Songs of the United States*. The first work of its kind, this book was the largest published collection of Negro spirituals. Although the initial idea of publishing a compilation of the songs sung by the freedmen of Port Royal was McKim's, it was her husband, Wendell Garrison, who took the initiative to bring the book to light. William Lloyd Garrison's second-eldest surviving son, Wendell, with considerable fund-raising support from his father-in-law, James Miller McKim, had assisted Edward Lawrence Godkin in establishing the *Nation Magazine*. And it was from his perch as the magazine's literary editor that he began to actively promote the slave songs project, recruiting to it William Francis Allen. A number of things recommended Allen for the project. Not least of these was the fact that he too was a New England Unitarian from an abolitionist family who was also a veteran of the Port Royal Experiment, one of the so-called Gideonites, having served as a teacher of freedmen on St. Helena Island from November 1863 to July 1864.²² Moreover, he was an extremely well-trained classical philologist and proficient pianist and flutist who had become intensely interested in studying the Port Royal Negroes' way of life, focusing particularly on their language, as well as collecting and transcribing their songs. Allen brought on board his cousin Charles P. Ware, also a Gideonite, who, while working as a plantation superintendent at St. Helena a full year before Allen's arrival, had already amassed an impressive collection of songs. The general designation of McKim, Allen, and Ware as co-editors of *Slave Songs* is misleading; they were, more precisely, co-collectors, gathering songs they each heard directly, as well as songs recorded by thirteen other collectors. Allen, however, played the major role in transcribing and editing the songs, writing the introduction that delineates the provenance of each song, noting variations from state to state, plantation to plantation, and discussing the creative process of the singers. And it is his introduction to *Slave Songs*, with its description of the shout and delineation of European and African formal elements in the spirituals, which establishes the scholarly study of Negro-song, but chiefly spirituals. In the introduction, he credits McKim with the initial idea of collecting and transcribing the Port Royal songs for publication, citing her previously published arrangements of "Poor Rosy" and "Roll Jordan" as being "on all accounts the two best specimens," followed by the "well-chosen specimens" published by Henry G. Spaulding in the August 1863 issue of *Continental Monthly*.²³ He also credits Ware with having the "largest and most accurate single collection in existence," which was published in its entirety in *Slave Songs*, providing sixty-three of the 136 included in the book, a little more than 46 percent. Allen himself contributed twenty-one songs, augmenting McKim's nine. The three of them combined provided ninety-three specimens, just under 69 percent of the collection. The other contributing collectors are mentioned in the acknowledgments at the end of Allen's introduction, from Captain James Rogers and William A. Baker, who gave one song each, to Mrs. Charles Bowen and Lieutenant Colonel C. T. Trowbridge, who gave six and nine respectively. But Allen singles out Colonel Thomas Wentworth Higginson, "above all others," both for contributing from his own collection—his thirteen were the third largest contribution after Ware's and Allen's—as well as for his encouragement and direction without which "this *Lyra Africana* would have lacked . . . completeness and worth."²⁴

Like Allen, Higginson was a Unitarian and abolitionist, albeit a militant who was, alongside Theodore Parker, a member of the Secret Committee of Six that funded John Brown's failed raid on Harper's Ferry. During the Civil War, he commanded the Negro First Regiment South Carolina Volunteer Infantry and was so taken with the spirituals he heard sung by the men of his command he began collecting them. Just five month prior to the publication of *Slave Songs*, in the June 1867 issue of *Atlantic Monthly*, Higginson had presented his entire collection, thirty-six, under the title "Negro Spirituals."²⁵ Conceiving the Negro as belonging to a premodern order of life on the verge of being assimilated, Higginson construed spirituals as analogous to the Anglo-Scottish border ballads described by Sir Walter Scott: simple indigenous unwritten songs, although "more uniformly plaintive, almost always more quaint, and often as essentially poetic."²⁶ Higginson's *Atlantic Monthly* article is often thought to have been the first appearance in print of the term "spiritual" designating a particular style of Negro-song, even though he claims in it to have "for many years heard of this class of song under the name of 'Negro Spirituals.'"²⁷ What's more, two years prior, buried in a lengthy correspondence entitled "The Negro Dialect," published in the *Nation* on December 14, 1865, under the pseudonym "Marcel," Allen had already used the term in transcribing the Negroes' own designation for two types of songs they sang: *speritual*s, and *running speritual*s, referring to hymns and shouts respectively. "The Negro Dialect," the material of which gets incorporated into the introduction to *Slave Songs*, with its detailed information on the phonetic, lexemic, and morphological features of the

South Carolina Island's Negro dialect in analyzing the lyrical content of songs, is a prime example of the comparative philological work Allen did that was so admired by subsequent folklorists such as Lomax's mentor, Kittredge, who advocated and assimilated it into his own studies and teaching at Harvard. Allen ends the article's opening paragraph by stating what motivated him to publish his study of the Sea Island Negro dialect, even though his effort might not be as well informed as those of Colonel Higginson: "Fearing, however, that in the progress of civilization among these people these curious features will vanish." He then adds, in what is a succinct expression of the collector's fiduciary responsibility: "I wish to put them on record before they fade from my own memory."[28] The same motivation is expressed in the opening pages of his introduction to *Slave Songs*:

> Many other persons are interested in the collection of words and tunes, and it seems time at last that the partial collections in the possession of the editors, should not be forgotten and lost, but that these relics of a state of society which has passed away should be preserved while it is still possible.[29]

This urgency to publish for the record even an incomplete collection of a disappearing primitive expression was informed by and in the service of the Transcendentalist anti-modernism he acquired from Theodore Parker, who made an indelible impression on Allen in his youth. Informed as it was by that Transcendentalism, which was itself infused with the Rousseauian Romantic concept of primitive man, Allen's assessment of Negro musical and linguistic expression can be construed as anticipating twentieth-century French avant-garde primitivism.

The rapport becomes more evident when we consider Marcel Griaule's two-year long (1931–1933) ethnographic expedition, Mission Dakar-Djibouti, made famous by the Negrophile avant-gardist, Michel Leiris, who was its secretary-archivist, with the publication of his travel-journal *L'Afrique fantôme*.[30] Support for situating Allen's nineteenth-century Transcendentalist inflected proto-ethnomusicology and twentieth-century French avant-gardist ethnology in the same conceptual lineage of primitivism is provided by the striking resonance between their respective stated motivations. Indeed, the following passage from the *General Instruction for Collectors of Ethnographic Objects*, which was written jointly by key permanent Mission members and published in May 1931 as part of the fundraising, echoes Allen's sentiment about the reason for collecting Negro specimen, albeit somewhat more stridently:

> IT IS URGENT TO CREATE A COLLECTION OF OBJECTS.
> Because of the increasingly intimate quotidian contact between Europeans and indigenous [Africans], and the application of modern political and

economic methods, the institutions, languages, and indigenous crafts are being transformed or disappearing, so that it is already possible to predict a time near at hand when these practices and objects, so important to our knowledge of human history, will be irretrievably eliminated.[31]

We shall have cause momentarily to interrogate this resonance more carefully. What matters for now is that, taken in this way as a collected specimen, the Negro spiritual functioned as a bifurcated signifier. On the one hand, it was the expression of the inner world of the enslaved Negro in America. On the other hand, that inner world was a form of our collective human childhood, of an innocent way of being before the onslaught of modernity. Whereas for Allen, this was a matter of a somewhat disengaged scholarly recording of the imminently vanishing Negro culture, for Lomax, "The negro's songs . . . are by no means past history, but are living, growing organisms mirroring his mind as it is to-day."[32] Whether a specimen in Allen's collection of spirituals or one in Lomax's larger collection of American folklore, Negro-song is invested with the redeeming qualities of an aesthetics that purifies the collector from modern civilization's contamination. That purifying process is supposed to be the performance of Negro expression, which we have been designating thus far as *artifice* to signal its character as a mimetic practice engaging the imaginative working, the structures of desire and cognition at play in the so-called inner world it manifests. This designation is to underscore that what is being appropriated are the material expressions—in the case of folksong, the phonemes and phonemic patterns and forms (style), along with the music—of a dynamically fluid "life-form," captured on record in a particular moment, often choreographed for the recording, and collected in the archive, where they are placed in relation to other specimens according to the collector's typology. What the collector does in gathering and curating these expressions of Negro artifice is convert their significance from the elemental world in which they are *expressions* into another order of recollection and meaning: the transcribed sign of the collector's *experience of them*, which has its own propositions about the order of things and the essential elements of civilizing sociality. As a consequence of this conversion, only the collector's specimen signifies what the nature of Negro artifice is or has been, as well as its meaningfulness, which is the expression of primitive, natural, indeed innocent state of human being.[33]

There is a strong reverberation of Allen's assessment of the meaning of Negro artifice as a redemptive primitive aesthetic form throughout Lomax's work on Negro folksong. It is also very much at play in his work as national advisor on Folklore and Folkways for the Federal Writers' Project, where he effectively directed the WPA Slave Narrative project first through the questionnaire sent out to the field interviewers and then in his re-editing of the interviews. Significantly, in the course of doing so, Lomax disregarded the editorial input of the project's Office of Negro Affairs, which was headed by Sterling Brown and charged with ensuring that "the Negro was not neglected in any of the publications written by or sponsored by the Writers' Project."[34] As with phonographic recording of in situ performance, when it came to transcribing the interviews, Lomax held accuracy in capturing "authentic Negro culture" a paramount responsibility of the interviewer. This is evidenced in the introductory instructions he gives in the questionnaire:

> The main purpose of these detailed and homely questions is to get the Negro interested in talking about the days of slavery. If he will talk freely, he should be encouraged to say what he pleases without reference to the questions. It should be remembered that the Federal Writers' Project is not interested in taking sides on any question. The worker should not censor any material collected, regardless of its nature.
>
> It will not be necessary, indeed it will probably be a mistake, to ask every person all of the questions. Any incidents or facts he can recall should be written down as nearly as possible just as he says them, but do not use dialect spelling so complicated that it may confuse the reader.
>
> A second visit, a few days after the first one, is important, so that the worker may gather all the worthwhile recollections that the first talk has aroused.[35]

Insistence on transcribing accurately is already defined by the ethnographer's understanding of the relationship between what is heard and what is thought to have been heard. In correspondence from George Cronyn, associate director of the Federal Writers' Project, sent out to twelve of the state directors, including Arkansas, dated April 14, 1937, thirteen days before the questionnaire with its instructions, Lomax attached a memorandum "with suggestions for simplifying the spelling of certain recurring dialect words," aimed at producing a sufficiently stabilized transcription "more readable to those uninitiated in the broadest Negro speech."[36] Lomax's glossary of proper transcriptions of Negro vocalizations is predicated on a preconceived idea of what Negroes sound like and the need to translate this in a way that preserves the phenomenal integrity of the sound while rendering it in a way that is meaningful for a larger audience. Here we have another reverberation from Allen's work on spirituals; what he described as "the difficulty experienced in attaining absolute correctness," referring to the challenge of accurately transcribing the authentic sound, is the problem McKim first laid out as the principle difficulty in collecting viable specimen. The fullness of this reverberation warrants some consideration, however cursory, in order to better understand just how Lomax's instructions and questionnaire are a continuation of the lineage of scholarly collection and analysis of Negro artifice that is supposed to be taking up Douglass's call to thoughtfully analyze the sounds the Negro makes.

By both McKim's and Allen's accounts, they were presented with a problem of translating a complex ordering of sound in correlation with expressive, lyrical content and meaning—in other words, a semiotic process with intricate conventions of performance that is not altogether identifiable, in any facile way, with the dominant musicological system of ordering sound and lyric. Allen further notes that this problem was exacerbated by the prevalence of spontaneous variation within any given performance as well as across performances, making the absolute determination of an authentic specimen difficult. The solution was to vest the discipline of notation and transcription with the agency of authenticity, so that variations between notations of the same specimen, or even errors, are a reflection of the phenomenal event, as he reports:

> I have never felt quite sure of my notation without a fresh comparison with the singing, and have then often found that I had made some errors. I felt confident, however, that there are no mistakes of importance. What may appear to some to be an incorrect rendering is very likely to be a variation; for these variations are endless, and very entertaining and instructive.[37]

This applies as well to the transcribing of lyrics:

> The negroes keep exquisite time in singing, and do not suffer themselves to be daunted by any obstacle in the words. The most obstinate Scripture phrases or snatches from hymn the will force to do duty with any tune they please, and will dash heroically through a trochaic tune at the head of a column of iambs with wonderful skill. We have in all cases arranged one set of words carefully to each melody; for the rest, one must make them fit the best he can, as the negroes themselves do.[38]

Variations and irregularities in transcription and notation of any given specimen are mimicking what "the negroes themselves do," establishing the transcription's constant relationship to the performance. This is why Allen keeps comparing his notation with the performed signing, concluding that "the best that we can do, however, with paper and types, or even with voices, will convey but a faint shadow of the original. The voices of the colored people have a popular quality that nothing can imitate; and the intonations and delicate variations of even one singer cannot be reproduced."[39]

Note how, while remarking the impossibility of precisely mimicking the sound on paper, Allen still claims to perceive and accurately describe his perception of the performance, deconstructing it into its constitutive elements, but doing so according to the categorizations of musicology. What the notations transcribe is the collector's experience of proximity, which we can characterize as: "This is what I think is the sound I heard them make, measured by the familiar scale." References to the "familiar" as the point of navigational bearing in relation to the sonic of both music and voice abound in Allen's writing. It is the measure of proximate distance between the sound the slaves make and the aesthetic soundness of the white recorder's ear. For instance, describing the difficulty in fathoming the Sea Island dialect, he states: "The strange words and pronunciations, and frequent abbreviations, disguise the familiar features of one's native tongue, while the rhythmical modulations, so characteristic of certain European languages, give it an utterly un-English sound."[40] When it comes to the sound of music, however, the *familiar* is always identified with Christianity. Quoting at length McKim's remarks about how difficult it is to fully score Negro-singing because of the physical particularities of the sounds they make with their curious rhythmic effect, Allen is compelled to rejoin: "Still, the chief part of the negro music is *civilized* in its character—partly composed under the influence of association with the whites, partly actually imitated from their music. In the main it appears to be original in the best sense of the word, and the more we examine the subject, the more genuine it appears to us to be. In a very few songs . . . strains of familiar tunes are readily traced."[41] This is a matter of music for him, chiefly tempo and color, about which he notes, "There are very few songs which are of an intrinsically barbaric character, and where this character does appear, it is chiefly in short passages, intermingled with others of a different character."[42] And it is supposed that "such passages may very well be purely African in origin."[43] Their barbaric character is a cacophony that is remarked on but cannot be directly represented in notation. Bearing is regained with the familiar, however, mitigating the barbaric. Allen can claim: "The greater number of songs which have come into our possession seem to be the natural and original production of a race of remarkable musical capacity and very teachable, which has been long enough associated with the more cultivated race to have become imbued with the mode and spirit of European music—often, nevertheless, retaining a distinct tinge of their native Africa."[44]

Familiarity is enhanced in the songs' lyrics, the words of which "are, of course, in a large measure taken from Scripture, and from hymns heard at church; and for this reason these religious songs do not by any means illustrate the full extent of the debasement of the dialect."[45] That debasement is more fully evidenced in the nonreligious songs, as is testified to by a "gentleman from Delaware," whom Allen quotes: "'We must look among their nonreligious songs for the purest specimens of negro minstrelsy . . . Some of the best *pure negro* songs I have heard were those that used to be sung by the black stevedores, or perhaps the crews themselves, of the West India vessels, loading and unloading at the wharves in Philadelphia and Baltimore.'"[46]

Each song score in *Slave Songs* is annotated as consisting of signs that stand in relation to an unrepresentable *pure Negro* sonics, yet stand in relation to one another as a meaningful system of signification. These scores are more than translations of an affective experience that cannot be mimicked on paper; they are *conversions* of the elemental pure Negro sonics into the familiar body of "civilized," which, in this case, is expressly marked as Christian, music. And that conversion is enacted only through the semiotic mastery of the skilled collector, whose discourse of hominization places the Negro within the anthropology of "Man" as being archaic. So we see, then, that the specimen is a bifurcated signifier *only on the authority of the collector*, only to the extent we believe credible the claim that there was something there, marked, *in absentia*, by the sign. In this way, the transcription records a definitive relationship between two distinct economies of meaningful signification. There is, on the one hand, the economy of sounds the slaves make, which is ordered in a way meaningful to them but not fully comprehensible to the white auditor qua collector. On the other, is the notational and transcriptive economy of record, the order of which in itself is readily recognizable to the supposedly general public but can only point to an experience of encounter with the slave's system. Accuracy is determined by the *veracity* of the claim of the proximity of the auditor/collector's representation, which is also the determination of the specimen's authenticity. In other words, solving the problem of determining the authenticity of specimen by vesting the discipline of notation and transcription absolutely with the agency of authentication empties the reported experience of any phenomenality. We can once again characterize Allen's methodological account, this time as: "I experienced something that happened, which I cannot represent to you directly, but can approximate the experience of it with these transcribed signs. They are not a full representation of the affective force of the event, and little represent its intrinsic meaningfulness, but they are better than nothing." This is in keeping with Allen's motivation to preserve while still possible the relics, no matter how imperfectly, of a people on the verge of being absorbed presumably by the benevolence of a rapidly changing modernity. The distinction he makes between the civilized and barbaric character of the songs may very well be informed by his Transcendentalist primitivism, which holds the Negro as a pre-rational, affect-driven, and more innocent life form. This jibes with his speculation that if it had been possible for the collectors "to get at more of their secular music, we should have come to another conclusion as to the proportion of the barbaric element."[47]

Having recognized the barbaric, non-Christian character of certain songs as the most authentically Negro, Allen expresses the earnest desire "that some person, who has the opportunity, should make a collection of these . . . before it is too late."[48] Such worldly songs are hard to come by, however, and Allen claims to have "never fairly heard a secular song among the Port Royal freedmen, and never a musical instrument among them. The last violin, owned by a 'worldly man,' disappeared from Coffins Point, in November 1861, when Hilton Head was taken by Admiral Dupont."⁴⁹ For that matter, Higginson, whose testimony is invoked in support of rarity, claims to have heard but two songs among his men to which they did not give "this generic name [spirituals]."⁵⁰ Both of these are presented as supernumerary to the collection and designated "inscrutable myths," with only the first line of one song, which went "Rain fall and wet Becky Martin," being transcribed and the other song, "Hangman Johnny," transcribed in full but unnumbered.⁵¹ While Allen and Higginson identify the *pure Negro* character of the secular "worldly" songs, they both subsume it as one aspect—a "tinge" Allen called it—of the religious songs that constitute the canonical collection. Higginson, who was more emphatic in this, was inclined to postulate, based on what he could hear, that the culture forged by the enslaved Negro was a profoundly religious one. Accounts of the Negro's religious zeal are abundant throughout his Civil War memoir, *Army Life in a Black Regiment*, with Higginson going so far in one instance to attribute to them "the highest form of mysticism" and report the view that "they are all natural transcendentalists."⁵² But the identification of spirituals with deep religiosity is most succinctly stated in the concluding paragraph of "Negro Spirituals," giving the warrant for their preservation in transcription:

> These quaint religious songs were to the men more than a source of relaxation; they were a stimulus to courage and a tie to heaven. I never overheard in camp a profane or vulgar song. With the trifling exceptions given, all had a religious motive, while the most secular melody could not have been more exciting. A few youths from Savannah, who were comparatively men of the world, had learned some of the "Ethiopian Minstrel" ditties, imported from the North. These took no hold upon the mass; and, on the other hand, they sang reluctantly, even on Sunday, the long and short metres of the hymn-books, always gladly yielding to the more potent excitement of their own "spirituals." By these they could sing themselves, as had their fathers before them, out of the contemplation of their own low estate, into the sublime scenery of the Apocalypse. I remember that this minor-keyed pathos used to seem to me almost too sad to dwell upon, while slavery seemed destined to last for generations; but now that their patience has had its perfect work, history cannot afford to lose this portion of its record. There is no parallel instance of an oppressed race thus sustained by the religious sentiment alone. These songs are but the vocal expression of the simplicity of their faith and the sublimity of their long resignation.⁵³

The investment in spirituals as authentically Negro and worthy of record hinges on the familiar signs of Christianity, which Higginson held to be have "produced the highest results of all [religions], in manners, in arts, in energy."[54] Once the Negro is enfolded or otherwise included in the community of faith, then the Negro becomes an authentic being. For the most part, Higginson's, Allen's, and McKim's recognition of the Negro spiritual as indicative of a fully human spirit struggling for its dignity was predicated on *agapē*, Christian love. This holds as well for Douglass's assertion of natural rights. Hence the distinction he makes between American Christianity, which he thought sheer hypocrisy, and true Christianity, expressed in the epigraphic quotation of the line from Coleridge's *Dissertation*, attributing to Christianity the provenance of the proposition that personhood is a function of having a soul, along with the corollary that such souls have rights as creatures of God. The Negro is a member of the Beloved Community and so deserves the liberty and full rights of such a member. And so the plaintive tunes of the slaves' songs, giving voice to a resistant soul whose faith is with the future, are expressions of the dehumanizing cruelty of slavery. Allen states this in his introduction to *Slave Songs*, in explaining that the book's title was selected because it best described the provenance of the songs collected in it: " A few of those [songs] here given were, to be sure, composed since the proclamation of emancipation, but even these were inspired by slavery."[55] In support of this he quotes the passage from McKim's *Dwight's Journal* piece already given, in which she claims, paraphrasing Douglass, the value of these songs as an expression of the "daily misery, which covered then as hopelessly as the fog from the rice swamps."

As I say, this line of writing about Negro-singing, from Douglass and McKim, through to Higginson and Allen, is what Lomax plays out in the beginning of his 1917 *Nation* article, "Self-Pity in Negro Folk-Songs." Seeming to respond to Allen's call for a more extensive study of the Negro's nonreligious songs as specimens of pure Negro minstrelsy, he shifts the focus to these "worl'ly" tunes. In the course of that shift, he seemingly challenges Higginson as well as Allen when he expressly dismisses the "theory advanced by many writers on the subject" that Negro plaintive tunes are the natural outgrowth of the state of slavery.[56] Slavery, after all, had been a thing of the past for two generations that, according to Lomax, "formed but a brief interlude—an episode—between many generations of barbaric freedom and the present status of liberty in a civilized land. . . . The bulk of the negro's songs are not dead tradition of slavery, are by no means past history, but are living, growing organisms mirroring his mind today."[57] On that basis, he speculates, "the mood of self-pity may have characterized the negro mind of pre-slavery."[58] At the crux of his speculation is the distinction between "barbaric freedom" and "civilized liberty," which is to say, between humankind in its most primitive state of nature in Africa and in its most advanced state of society in America, the state at which all artifice reflects the long history of human socialization. The Negro "race may have suffered enslavement," Lomax observes, "but his music has never worn shackles"; in its "spontaneous outburst of intimate affections and impulses," it is the most primitive, most natural human song.[59] Although expressed in the context of modern Western civilization, there is a natural enduring primitiveness to Negro singing.[60] And this primitive naturalism makes it a more authentic specimen of pure uncontaminated-by-modernity folksong than that of white singers.[61] Even though Lomax dismisses the theory that the plaintive tunes, which he identifies with the mood of self-pity, pervading spirituals are the outgrowth of slavery, he does not reject the Higginson/Allen characterization of the Negro as an essentially religious being. In speculating that the mood is of archaic African origin, he suggests the spiritual's religiosity is somehow more African than Christian in its sentiment.[62] More to the point, whatever its provenance, the "phase of the negro's mind" supposed to be indicated by both the secular and religious songs is fundamentally eschatological. Notwithstanding the hard fact that in the "worl'ly" song "it is the present, not the mystic future, with which the individual negro is concerned each day," the Negro is by nature "care-free and joyous... looking forward as he does to another life of perfect satisfaction."[63]

When all this is taken into account and brought to bear on the twenty questions Lomax sets out in his questionnaire for the WPA interviewers to follow, a pattern emerges of how the ethnographically, culturally authentic Negro presents. Leaving aside the first five questions, which ask about the events of birth, domestic familial relations, work, culinary taste, seasonal attire, respectively, six of the remaining fifteen are phrased in a way that easily prompts some voicing of self-pity. Questions number 5, 6, 7, 11, and 20 inquire about the details of white privilege and class distinctions, the severity of labor and forms of punishment, imprisonment and separation through sales, rebellion and flight, the class and severity of overseers, respectively. Question 16 queries postbellum work and experiencing terror by the Ku Klux Klan and Nightriders. Of the other nine, four inquire about religion, one, question 10, exclusively so, and then about Christianity:

> 10. Did the slaves have a church on your plantation? Did they read the Bible? Who was your favorite preacher? Your favorite spirituals? Tell about the baptizing; baptizing songs. Funerals and funeral songs.

Two more questions, 13 and 14, ask about non-Christian practices, embedding them among other queries about worldly life:

> 13. What games did you play as a child? Can you give the words or sing any of the play songs or ring games of the children? Riddles? Charms? Stories

about "Taw Head and Bloody Bones" or other "hants" or ghosts? Stories about animals? What do you think of voodoo? Can you give the words or sing any lullabies? Work songs? Plantation hollers? Can you tell a funny story you have heard or something funny that happened to you? Tell about the ghost you have seen.

14. When slaves became sick who looked after them? What medicines did the doctors give them? What medicine (herbs, leaves, or roots) did the slaves use for sickness? What charms did they wear and to keep off what diseases?

The query in question 19 is once again exclusively about Christian practices, this time postbellum:

19. Now that slavery is ended what do you think of it? Tell why you joined a church and why you think all people should be religious?

The remaining five questions ask about holiday activities and commemorative practices on momentous occasions, the initial experience of freedom, marriage, and views of Abraham Lincoln, Jefferson Davis, and Booker T. Washington.

All these questions are rather leading and show strong signs of Lomax's investment in establishing the Negro as a particular American type in accordance with his conception of the distinctive "phases" of the Negro mind. Moreover, the distinction between the worldly and religious spiritual phases emphasized in "Self-Pity" is blurred in the questionnaire where there is a discernable interest in collecting specimen of faith even from the worldly material. Interest in specimen of Christianity—church, Bible, spirituals, and rites of baptism—is balanced with interest in specimen of non-Christian spirituality—charms, hants, ghost, and voodoo. The extent of the latter interest is exhibited in another letter from Cronyn to the state directors, dated May 3, 1937, just one week after the questionnaire was sent out, again quoting a Lomax memorandum that reports:

> Of the five states which have already sent in reminiscences of ex-slaves, Tennessee is the only one in which the workers are asking ex-slaves about their belief in signs, curses, hoodoo, etc. Also, the workers are requesting the ex-slaves to tell the stories that were current among the Negroes when they were growing up. Some of the best copy that has come in to the office is found in these stories.[64]

Cronyn received Lomax's enthusiasm for the type of stories as a suggestion and endorsed it to the state directors, believing such specimen "will add greatly to the value of the collection." According to Lomax's typology of specimen, which functioned as the hermeneutic frame for the interviewers' interpretive transcription, besides being naturally spontaneously creative, the authentic Negro specimen exhibits inherent a-rational belief, underscoring its primitive, and thus redemptive, nature.

With all this in mind, returning our focus at this point to the remarkable thing about the passage from Windham's interview, it is easy to see how closely Bowden was adhering to the Lomax questionnaire, with its underlying conceptualization of Negro artifice as valuable primitive specimen. Windham's account of being taught how to calculate his age by his mother and grandmother, the name of his master and how he treated his slaves, his place of birth, as well what work he did in slavery are direct responses to questions 2, 6, 1, and 3 respectively. Still, his remark "us is human flesh," even granting Lomax's admonition to allow the interview-subject to depart from the suggested line of questioning and to follow wherever he pleases to go, challenges not only the premises of the entire WPA interview project about what and how the Negro is; it also challenges the more general underlying premises about the nature of freedom and humanity. It does so by being discordant with the ontological grounds on which these things stand.

By Discrepant Taxonomy

In making his remark, Windham evokes a taxonomy of flesh encompassing a range of animal life; more precisely, hogs, horses, and humans, all of which, in strictly zoological terms, belong to the class of vertebrate, neocortical, eutherian mammals. His privative "ain't" introduces a subdivision within that zoological class along the lines of a punctuated continuum of sentience that moves from the basic to complex. On the one hand, there is the vital biological commonality of animal flesh, which may be sentient in a rudimentary sense of having the capacity to perceive and respond to the environment sufficiently enough to live actively—the reflex arc of perception, cognizance, and behavioral response—without any signs of self-awareness or having psychological states, something we ascribe to hogs and horses. On the other hand, there is the manifest self-aware possession of psychological states and of being in relation to others and other things that is associated with humans. In this sense, the "ain't" makes Windham's taxonomy one of sentient flesh, drawing a distinction between zoology and anthropology: "us ain't hogs or horses—us is human flesh." Of course, the full force of his privative is directed at another, albeit related, taxonomy: the political economy of modern capitalist slavery, within which Windham as a Negro slave belongs, along with the hogs and horses, to the class of chattel property. In that political economic taxonomy, the flesh is valued for what it can produce in asset. This is a matter of speculation as much as it is of consumption in use. And, in that regard, asserting "us is human flesh" acknowledges the vital biological commonality—the form of life—while rejecting evaluation as chattel. What distinguishes human flesh from other flesh is the inalienable entitlement to liberty, to be owned by no one, or to again be a bit more precise, the capacity to express that entitlement propositionally as communicative action: "We should have our liberty cause us ain't hogs or horses—us is human flesh."

On the face of it, Windham's claim of entitlement to liberty seems to imply the Aristotelian distinction between the human as animal and the person as a social being with inalienable natural rights. Were it doing just that, however, it would not be all that remarkable, but simply a fair summary paraphrasing of Frederick Douglass's well-publicized arguments against slavery as a violation of the natural law expressed in the Declaration of Independence because, while its criminal codes offer "acknowledgment that the slave is a moral, intellectual, and responsible being," it denies that same slave full personhood.[65] Douglass's objection was well grounded in Enlightenment natural rights theory, particularly the liberalist concept of individual freedom espoused in John Locke's political philosophy, *The Two Treatises of Government*, but also the concept of personal identity given in his epistemology, *An Essay Concerning Human Understanding*. The latter work, being conceptually foundational for the first, makes a hard distinction between biological "man" as an animal life-form consisting of constantly fleeting particles of matter in succession vitally united to the same organized body—that fleshly thing—and person as a social entity with inalienable rights as well as moral and political responsibilities. Locke defined person as "a thinking intelligent being, that has reason and reflection, and can consider itself as itself, the same thinking thing, in different times and places."[66] In that sense, the person is attached to a body or stands in a principal proprietary relationship to the flesh, disciplining it to embody a specific consciousness. So that the idea in our minds signified by the term *man* is not merely any rational animal, let alone any sentient one, but rather a rational animal of a specific bodily form. "For I presume it is not the idea of a thinking or rational being alone that makes the idea of man in most people's sense," Locke states, "but of a body, so and so shaped, joined to it."[67] Locke's liberalism is problematized around the question of slavery, however. According to his epistemology, anthropologically, an individual human cannot be alienated from himself in body but is consistently and continually himself throughout the material existence, the life span of the body. His political theory of government, on the other hand, argues that an individual can be legitimately alienated from his rights *as a person*, due to war—more precisely, by becoming the defeated aggressor in war, which implies an ethical judgment.[68] What makes this even more vexed a matter is that during the time he was writing *The Two Treatises of*

Government, Locke had a substantial hand in drafting the 1669 Fundamental Constitution of the Carolinas, clause 110 of which states: "Every Freedman of the Carolinas has absolute power and authority over his negro slaves, of what opinion or religion whatsoever."[69] There was precedence for this in the laws enacted by the Barbados House of Assembly in 1661 and the General Assembly of Virginia in 1662, the latter of which shall be attended to more closely momentarily apropos the history of the juridical definition of *Negro*. For now, the pertinent point is that the Carolina Constitution's stipulating absolute proprietary power and authority over "negro slaves" exceeds the limited paternal power Locke defines in the *Second Treatise* and is more in line with the Roman Law postulate *vitae necisque potestas* (power of life and death), making it akin to the illegitimate despotic political power of monarchy against which he contrasts the parental. The specificity of this stipulation indicates a relationship of person and body unique to the "negro slave," who, not having been taken in war but purchased as property, is made an exception to natural rights. The basis for that distinction is in the capitalist process of enslavement—which clearly violates even Locke's precept of legitimate alienation from rights—whereby the term *negro* designates a commodity asset that, while hominid, is not fully human. As far as this type of hominid is concerned, personhood is diminished or otherwise alienated in relation to the body, and the body has no rights. Adhering as he does to the Lockean proposition of the inherent freedom in natural personhood, Douglass's argument against slavery asserts that full personhood is a universal property in every instance of bodies with generally the same form; that is to say, it belongs to all *Homo sapiens*, irrespective of superficial physiognomic variation. A corollary proposition being that the universal is *real*; it exists independent of what some people may think about it. Indeed, the fact that they *need* to think about it goes to establish its reality. In Lockean terms, "that equal right every man has to his natural freedom, without being subjected to the will or authority of any other man."[70] By still adhering to the proposition of natural personhood, however, Douglass maintains the rights of the *person*, irrespective of the body, which may or may not be dismembered, tortured, and continually redistributed.

We find ourselves once again in conversation with Douglass, but not without warrant. The temptation to read Windham's remark, "we should have our liberty cause . . . us is human flesh," as following Douglass is amplified by the way his privative, "cause us ain't hogs or horses," seems to takes up and respond to the same complaint of taxonomic confusion expressed by Douglass throughout his published work, beginning with his 1845 *Narrative of the Life of Frederick Douglass*. If it is as it seems, then we have the playing out of another of the lines about the humanity of the Negro slave Douglass laid out. Let us play along Douglass's line a bit to determine where, if at all, we can place Windham's remark in relation to it. Recounting the death intestate of his *de jure* master, Captain Anthony, Douglass describes the scene where he and the other slaves were being assessed and divided along with the other property among Anthony's contending heirs:

> We were all ranked together at the valuation. Men and women, old and young, married and single, were ranked with horses, sheep, and swine. There were horses and men, cattle and women, pigs and children, all holding the same rank in the scale of being, and all were subjected to the same narrow examination.[71]

There is a discernable echo in the language Douglass uses of that found in the laws passed by the Virginia General Assembly, pertaining to the distribution of the estate of an orphan, in which it is determined that "Negroes may be appraised" in kind with sheep horse, and cattle.[72] The reverberation is sufficient enough to recognize in the language of this law something of the provenance of Douglass's "horses, sheep, and swine" and to further presume him to be making an ironic *riff* on it. Speaking in 1846 at Finsbury Chapel, in what became known as his "London Reception Speech," Douglass uses the same figure of humans equated with horses, sheep, and swine, only this time, it is in reference to the particular cruelty of the industry of slave-breeding as a legitimate practice, which he remarks the church does not condemn, in states such as "Maryland, where men, women, and children are reared for the market, just as horses, sheep, and swine are raised for the market."[73] He uses the figure again the next year, with slight variation, in his "Farewell Speech to the British People," which he delivered at London Tavern on the evening of March 30, prior to embarking on his return to the United Stated aboard the *Cambria*: "Why, sir, the Americans do not know that I am a man. They talk of me as a box of goods; they speak of me in connexion with sheep, horses, and cattle."[74] Having returned to the United States legally a free man, Douglass repeats the initial figure from his *Narrative* in his "Lecture on Slavery," delivered at Rochester in 1850: "The slave is a human being, divested of all rights—reduced to the level of a brute—a mere 'chattel' in the eye of the law—placed beyond the circle of human brotherhood—cut off from his kind—his name, which the 'recording angel' may have enrolled in heaven, among the blest, is impiously inserted in a master's ledger, with horses, sheep, and swine."[75] It occurs again in another Rochester oration, "What to the Slave Is the Fourth of July?," given nearly two years later on July 5, 1852: "I hear the doleful wail of fettered humanity, on the way to the slave markets, where the victims are to be sold like horses, sheep, and swine, knocked off to the highest bidder."[76] These oratory iterations are an elaboration of the first depiction of the scene of assessment, which Douglass presents as a defining moment—on par with that of hearing slaves singing—in his awareness of "the unnatural" power to which he was subjected as a slave. They reach a crescendo-like return to that first scene, with more elaborate and vivid depiction, in the thirteenth chapter, "The Vicissitudes of Slave Life," of his 1855 autobiography, *My Bondage and My Freedom*:

> What an assemblage! Men and women, young and old, married and single; moral and thinking human beings, in open contempt of their humanity, leveled at a low with horses, sheep, horned cattle and swine. Horses and men, cattle and women, pigs and children—all holding the same rank in the scale of social existence, and all subjected to the same narrow inspection, to ascertain their value in gold and silver.... Personality swallowed up in the sordid idea of property! Manhood lost in chattelhood!⁷⁷

Thus augmented by "horned cattle" and refined as the metonym for the cruelty of the entire system, Douglass deploys the figure to powerful effect in his "Dred Scott Decision" speech, delivered before the American Anti-Slavery Society on May 4, 1857. First chastising the Supreme Court for ruling "that slaves are within the contemplation of the Constitution of the United States, property... in the same sense that horses, sheep, and swine are property," he then declaimed:

> When great transactions are involved, where the fate of millions is concerned, where a long enslaved and suffering people are to be delivered, I am superstitious enough to believe that the finger of the Almighty may be seen bringing good out of evil, and making the wrath of man redound to his honor, hastening the triumph of righteousness.... The cries of the slave have gone forth to the world, and up to the throne of God.⁷⁸

A distinction is to be made, in Douglass's view, between what he considered "the pure, peaceable, and impartial Christianity of Christ," and the "Christianity of America," which either condoned outright the institution of slavery or adhered to the diminution of colored persons of African descent as unequal before the sacrament. The first year he was hired out to William Freeland, 1834, Douglass attempted to establish a Sabbath school at Saint Michaels on the insistence of his fellow slaves who wanted him to teach them "how to read the Will of God." He tells of how two white men, Messrs. Wright Fairbanks and Garrison West, attacked them with sticks and stones, breaking up the Sabbath school, all the while "calling themselves Christians! Humble followers of the Lord Jesus Christ!" Undaunted, he reconvenes the school a second time at the house of a free colored man. Recalling this struggle in the 1845 *Narrative*, Douglass is "almost ready to ask: Does a righteous God govern the universe? And for what does he hold the thunders in his right hand, if not to smite the oppressors, and deliver the spoiled out of the hand of the spoiler?"⁷⁹ The question resounds with an irony worth exploring, paraphrasing in tandem as it does Exodus 15:6 and Isaiah 33:1:

> Thy right hand, O LORD, is become glorious in power: thy right hand, O LORD, hath dashed in pieces the enemy.

And:

> Woe to thee that spoilest, and thou wast not spoiled; and dealest treacherously, and they dealt not treacherously with thee! when thou shalt cease to spoil, thou shalt be spoiled; and when thou shalt make an end to deal treacherously, they shall deal treacherously with thee.

Douglass's paraphrasing of the first line, second stanza from Moses's triumphant song celebrating Pharaoh's destruction alludes to the first occurrence in the Bible of that important anthropomorphic symbol of God's power, "Thy Right Hand," which in this instance both protects the faithful from their enemies and destroys them. Juxtaposing this with the paraphrase of Isaiah's address to the Assyrian conqueror, Sennacherib, warning of divine retribution for his rampage of destruction, underscores the righteousness of God's retribution, as well as the extent of his protective embrace of the faithful. Douglass's invocation of these two statements of the power of *God's Hand* to deliver the faithful from the enemies that threaten to destroy them, destroying them instead, parodies that power. It is the faithful who spoil; and God is either absent or unrighteous because they do so supposedly within his embrace. The irony is twofold. Bearing in mind that Christ is seated at God's right hand and that the church is Christ's body (Ephesians 1:20–23), Douglass parodies not just the authority of the church—whose support of slavery is exemplified in the assault by church-leaders, Fairbanks, and Garrison, on the Sabbath school—but also the redemptive power of the divine embrace. God's touch is supposed to give grace: "Now God, who justifies sinners, touches the soul causing it grace," Aquinas tells us. And so too, he continues, "the human soul in some sense touches God by knowing Him or loving Him."[80] Fairbanks and Garrison present themselves as "humble followers of the Lord Jesus Christ," in which case they are supposed to be like those in John 1:1, who, having touched flesh to flesh the incarnate God, know the incarnation to be the consecration of human flesh. In the body of Christ, the Word becomes flesh, which so consecrated enables the sacrament of the Eucharist, making it in Aquinas's Eucharistic theology, the perfect sign of Christ's Passion. We have the well-known passage from William Lloyd Garrison's Preface to the *Narrative* denouncing slavery as "that system, which . . . reduces those who by creation were crowned with glory and honor to the level with four-footed beasts, and exalts the dealer in human flesh above all that is called God!"[81] The implicit charge is that slavery, in its denial of the Negro's place in (divine) humanity, blasphemies against the idea of incarnation, of the Word become flesh. Even for an avowed Unitarian such as William Lloyd Garrison, for whom the Eucharist is a symbolic act commemorating Christ's sacrifice of the flesh without reactualizing it, such blasphemy is outrageous. Douglass reiterates this sense of blasphemous outrage in his "Reception Speech," when he exclaims: "What! God's own image bought and sold!"[82] Still recalling the Sabbath school experience, during which he planned his first attempt to escape slavery, Douglass furthers the thought that slavery is a blasphemy against the idea of incarnation, describing it as "a stern reality, glaring frightfully upon us,—its robes already crimsoned with the blood of millions, and even now feasting itself greedily upon our own flesh."[83] This gets slightly expanded in *My Bondage*, where, in the differentiation between the consumption of labor and that of flesh, he underscores the pure venality of the latter: "a stern reality, glaring frightfully upon us, with the blood of millions in his polluted skirts—terrible to behold—greedily devouring our hard earnings and feeding himself upon our flesh."[84]

Douglass is not being merely metaphoric here. The archive abounds with accounts of slaveholders consuming Negro flesh. Lydia Maria Child's *An Appeal in Favor of that Class of Americans Called Africans* has numerous reports of nearly ritualized butchery and torture of slaves. A particularly gruesome episode found there involves Thomas Jefferson's nephew by his sister, Lucy, Lilburn Lewis. In December 1811, Lewis, with the help of his brother, Isham, butchered alive his seventeen-year-old slave, George, in the kitchen cabin of his Livingston, Kentucky, plantation for accidentally breaking a water pitcher having belonged to Lucy. Child quotes the account written by Rev. William Dickey of Bloomingsburgh, Kentucky, to Rev. John Rankin of Ripley Ohio, which the latter published in his 1826 *Letters on Slavery*, the book Garrison credited with bringing him to the abolitionist cause. Dickey's account depicts the systematic ritualistic nature of the murder, including its homiletic aspect:

> The door [of the kitchen cabin] was fastened, that none of the negroes, either through fear or sympathy, should attempt to escape; he then told them that the design of this meeting was to teach them to remain at home and obey his orders. All things being now in train, George was called up, and by the assistance of his younger brother, laid on a broad bench or block. The master then cut off his ancles [*sic*] with a broad axe. In vain the unhappy victim screamed. Not a hand among so many dared to interfere. Having cast the feet into the fire, he lectured the negroes at some length. He then proceeded to cut off his limbs below the knees. The sufferer besought him to begin with his head. It was in vain—the master went on thus, until trunk, arms, and head, were all in the fire. Still protracting the intervals with lectures, and

threatenings [*sic*] of like punishment, in case any of them were disobedient, or ran away, or disclosed the tragedy they were compelled to witness. In order to consume the bones, the fire was briskly stirred until midnight: when, as if heaven and earth combined to show their detestation of the deed, a sudden shock of earthquake threw down the heavy wall, composed of rock and clay, extinguished the fire, and covered the remains of George. The negroes were allowed to disperse, with charges to keep the secret, under the penalty of like punishment. When his wife asked the cause of the dreadful screams she had heard, he said that he had never enjoyed himself so well at a ball as he had enjoyed himself that evening.[85]

As if to emphasize the ritual significance of Lewis's slaughter of George, Rankin adds in a *nota bene*: "This happened in 1811; if I be correct, it was on the 16th of December. It was on the Sabbath."[86] Child goes on to list other episodes of systematic devouring of Negro flesh, from the feeding of Negroes to blood-hounds in St. Domingo and the "negro hunts" of South Carolina, which were conducted like fox hunts, to the whipping to death of a mother and her newborn infant in Natchez, Mississippi. She likens those planters who advertise mothers to be sold separately from their children on the grounds of their right to dispose of their property right to Shylock demanding "his pound of flesh, cut nearest to the heart."[87] Child echoes reputable sources in regarding the slave system being sustained by consuming flesh—among them the physician Rev. Robert Walsh's *Notices of Brazil in 1828 and 1829* describing the system as "horrid traffic in human flesh"; and the Virginia General Assemblyman, Charles Faulkner's speech of 1832 referring to the "vigintial crop of human flesh."[88] Although those texts, including Garrison's preface, condemn slavery's consumption of flesh as unconsecrated, in contradistinction with the Eucharist, and so merely butchery and cannibalism, Douglass deploys the association to reproach American Christianity in toto. That reproach did not, however, cause him to dismiss the moral principles espoused in the Gospels, to which Americans fail to adhere. And so the epigraph on the title page of *My Bondage and My Freedom* reads:

> By a principle essential to Christianity, a PERSON is eternally differenced from a THING; so that the idea of a HUMAN BEING, necessarily excludes the idea of PROPERTY IN THAT BEING.

This line paraphrases a paragraph from *A Dissertation on the Science of Method*, which was published in 1818 as the introduction and first of the thirty-volume *Encyclopedia Metropolitana*. The paragraph in question occurs in section 2, where, having set out the philosophical principles of method in section 1, Coleridge provides illustrations of them in a historical sequence leading up to Francis Bacon's *Novum Organum*, which, serving as the portal to the modern era, receives the greatest attention. In that history of the *"education of the Mind,"* Coleridge comes to the Dark Ages of Europe, "which brought the countless hordes of sensual Barbarians from their Northern forest to meet . . . the spiritualizing influence of Christianity," as a period of virtually no significant innovation of mind except for one: "the gradual abolition of domestic slavery, in virtue of a Principle essential to Christianity, by which a *person* is eternally differenced from a *thing*; so that the *Idea* of a Human Being, necessarily excludes the Idea of property in that Being."[89] There is a significant difference in emphasis between the paragraph that occurs in the *Dissertation* and Douglass's paraphrase. Coleridge's italicizing *"person"* and *"thing,"* then capitalizing *"Idea"* and "Human Being" puts emphasis on Christianity as the source of the principle of inherent transcendent personhood at the foundation of our modern concept of freedom as an inalienable right. The modifications in Douglass's paraphrase—eliding the historicist periodization and allusion to the gradual abolition of European domestic slavery and then emphasizing in uppercase rather than italics "PERSON," "THING," "HUMAN BEING," and "PROPERTY IN THAT BEING"—amplify the indissoluble association of the idea of the rights of personhood with Christianity. They also relate Coleridge's *Dissertation* remarks to his earlier "Lecture on the Slave Trade," delivered on June 16, 1795, at the Assembly Coffee-House on Quay, Bristol, and the basis for the piece he published the following year in *Watchman*, "On the Slave Trade," in which he critiques slavery as un-Christian and, deploying the "blood sugar" topos, as fundamentally capitalist.[90] By the time Douglass would have read the *Dissertation*, the poet had already moved quite far into the opposing camp, using Christianity to justify his own increasing anti-black racism as well as slavery. Douglass's deployment of these lines, nevertheless, indicates his own continued investment in the Christian genealogy of the idea of inherent transcendent personhood. Clearly elaborating on Coleridge in the 1850 "The Nature of Slavery," Douglass declares:

> The Slave is a man, "the image of God," but "a little lower than angels"; possessing a soul, eternal and indestructible; capable of endless happiness, or immeasurable woe; . . . he is endowed with those mysterious powers by which man soars above the things of time and sense, and grasps with undying tenacity, the elevating and sublimely glorious idea of God. It is *such* a being that is smitten and blasted. The first work of slavery is to mar and deface those characteristics of its victims which distinguish *men* from *things*, and *persons* from *property*.[91]

And in that key, the distinction Douglass makes between humans, horses, sheep, and swine reverberates with the declamation from Genesis 1:26: "And

God said, 'Let us make a human, in our image [בְּצַלְמֵנוּ, *betsalmenū*], according to our likeness [כִּדְמוּתֵנוּ, *kidhmuthenū*], and let them dominate the fish of the sea and the birds of the skies and the domestic animals and all the earth and all the creeping things that creep on the earth." Read this way, Douglass's argument for the slave's inherent humanity entails a conception of "fleshliness" with theological provenance, according to which it is in opposition to the active divine intelligence. Fleshliness is the antithesis of thinking and so the earthly threat to being, to salvation of the immortal soul. Bear in mind, the postulate of transcendent personhood has remained fundamental to natural law/natural rights theory since, indisputably, Aquinas, and that it persists in post-Cartesian thought, including Kant's transcendental "I" as a regulative principle of rational morality and justice. The latter is arguably the philosophical source, by way of Emerson and the Transcendentalists, for Douglass's asserting the Negro's natural personhood as a moral being.

Having played along Douglass's line getting to here, Windham's "we should have our liberty cause . . . us is human flesh" is not, as first seemed, a simple elaboration on Douglass, but rather a riff on the same legal code, or at least the commonplace practice authorized by the code, to which Douglass alludes. Compared to Douglass's horses, sheep, swine and men trope, however, Windham's, "we should have our liberty cause . . . us is human flesh," strikes an altogether more strident note of discord with Lockean natural rights theory, postulating it is the person *of* not *in* the flesh who has inviolable rights. An additionally noteworthy detail of Windham's assertion in this regard is the complete absence of any theological reference. Entitlement to liberty is not based on divine endowment or any other claim of transcendent purpose, nor even on providential or evolutionary teleology. It simply is a fact of the very nature of human flesh. And so his privative rebuts the market evaluation without appealing to transcendence. Lacking as it does even a residual trace of the transcendent postulate, Windham's "us is human flesh" moves us away from the theological, as well as the metaphysical tendency of thought, the tendency to think the "I" that falls into the world of things having its reality beyond them.

Perhaps that is why Saidiya Hartman takes Windham's remark to be emblematic of the "basic assertion of colored folk's entitlement to freedom," glossing it to interpolate the underlying proposition: "The flesh, existence defined at its most elemental level, alone entitled one to liberty."[92] This interpolation is recognizably an invocation of Hortense Spillers's extended exploration of the relationship between fleshliness and persona—keeping in mind that *persona* connotes a determinate discursive sociality, rather than a state of nature—something she has been carrying out through a series of studies that focus on the issue of the black woman's embodiment in an effort to reimagine the question of community without adhering to the long-standing tradition of posting the *rift* between animality and generative intelligence as requisite for human sociality.⁹³ With that exploration in mind, we may well ask: What does it mean, however, to say flesh alone as existence defined at its most elemental level entitles one to liberty? What is the relationship between flesh and *one*? Is *one* predicable of flesh, or is flesh a predicate of the *one*?

A Semiosis of Flesh Thinking

In the context of Windham's testimonial narrative—the sociopolitical order of the New World, in which the modern capitalist institution of racial slavery is a fundamental constitutive element—the problematical rift is between sentient animality and fully entitled humanity, or, as Spillers aptly puts it, between "captive and liberated subject-positions." This particular rift is enacted and sustained through systemic techniques of severing the captive enslaved body from its motive will and active desire, the latter being markers of personhood. The purpose of the system is not to completely eradicate motive will and desire, but rather to circumscribe them within it, seizing their efficacy in the service of economic value. We can say, then, that motive-will and desire are distorted, not erased, by the rift, a distortion that has been called "civilization." On one side of the divide is the person captured, the particular process of whose personification as a social being is in relation to his or her physical presence *within* a grammar of sociality prior to capture. Whatever the particularities of that process of sociality, whatever its relational terms of identification, the persona articulated is its signifier. Simply put, the phenomenal body *purports* an order of signification, a semiological system, which is heterogeneous to that of New World slavery. In keeping with received representational practice, Spillers refers to this system and its sign as "West African." The rift demarcates civilization's interdicting the fluidity of this semiological system. Interdiction is not total eradication, however, and, *pace* Orlando Patterson's postulate of social death, elements of the "African" semiological system are subsequently iterated, albeit modified and adjusted on account of it: to wit, the barbaric elements "of purely African origin" in Negro-song to which both Allen and Lomax refer. What falls on the other side of the rift, then, is the *African* transformed in the interdiction of the semiological system for which the persona is a signifier into *enslaved captive body*, which is a signifier of particular value in the economy of slavery as an altogether alien order of meaningful sociopolitical living. We can express this relationship as *West African/enslaved captive body*. The dividing line is both conjunctive and transitive, symbolizing the activity of interdictory transformation. It presents the *West African* as such, which is to say as both the residual sign of a prior order of signification and a signifier of value in slavery's order. Yet, even though the "indigenous" meaningfulness is rendered inoperative, the efficacy of motive and desire implicated in it is not, becoming "liberated," as it were, from the first-order semiological system and made available to the economy of slavery in the form of the *enslaved captive body*. Spillers characterizes this semiological activity as the theft of the body, which can be read in the double sense of the physical capture of bodies from West Africa but also the *enslaved captive body*'s robbing the *persona* of its meaning.

The close resemblance this description of *persona/enslaved captive body* bears to how Roland Barthes defines the mythic signifier in "Myth Today" is understandable given Spillers's acknowledged conceptual indebtedness to his analysis there of the dynamics of myth as a semiological system.[94] Barthes's semiology is Saussurean, applying Claude Lévi-Strauss's structuralist study of myth to popular, chiefly French, cultural forms. Accordingly, his descriptive analysis of myth is patterned on the sign as expressing the correlation of a signifier and signified. The details of Barthes's semiology of myth need not overly concern us here, but what does is his construing the mythical signifier as having two aspects: one as the final sign of the linguistic system to which it has a parasitic second order semiological relation, called *meaning*; and the other as the first term of the mythical system, called *form*. So the mythical signifier straddles two semiological planes. On the plane of language, it is "full" (*plein*), belonging to a history comprised of a comparative order of facts, ideas, and decisions.[95] In other words, the *meaning* of the mythic signifier indexes the entire semiological system of language. On the plane of myth, the signifier is an empty parasitical *form* that does not suppress the meaning but rather impoverishes it, drawing nourishment to be put at the disposal of the myth's signified, which Barthes renames *concept* on the mythical plane. He then re-designates the third term in the triadic semiological correlation—what Saussure designated "sign"—as *signification*. Spillers's mapping of *persona/enslaved captive body*, or if you wish, *West African/enslaved captive body*, is analogous to this. Thus, when she recasts the rift as being "between 'body' and 'flesh,'" we should understand that *flesh*, in place of *persona*, functions as the metonymy for the pre-capture process of personification from which the *enslaved captive body* steals. "In that sense," as Spillers states, "before the 'body' there is the 'flesh,' that zero degree of social conceptualization that does not escape concealment under the brush of discourse, or the reflexes of iconography."[96] This sentence's phrasing so pronouncedly bears the markings of her already signaled indebtedness to Barthes that it warrants an interrogation pursuant, at least, with the concepts borrowed from his semiological analysis of myth. It also warrants such an interrogation because fathoming Spillers's conception of flesh might help us more fully appreciate how Windham's assertion of liberty offers a viable departure from the concept of proprietary personhood entailed in Douglass's line of thought. Put differently, it is a *particular* force of mythology that prevents us from recognizing the mythologizing force—why it is referred to as such becomes clear in due course—entailed in not only the collecting of Negro artifice, à la Lomax, Leiris, Allen, McKim, and Higginson, but also in the postulate of humanity supporting the line of liberation and rights traceable to Douglass, although not exclusively so.

We begin the interrogation by asking: What does it mean to state that before the "body" there is the "flesh"? Asking this, we note the adjective clause, "that zero degree of social conceptualization," evokes the title of Barthes's first book, *Le degré zéro de l'écriture* (The Degree Zero of Writing), the published English translation of which is entitled *Writing Degree Zero*.[97] In that work, degree zero is the conjunction of two distinct languages, or semiological systems, which Barthes situates in ordinal relationship, both historically and semiologically, as first and second. His example of this is the languages of classical and modern (French) poetry. In the first-order language of classical poetry, no word has any density by itself, but is rather the means of conveying connection, following the order of an ancient ritual to perfect the symmetry or conciseness of a relation, to bring a thought exactly within the compass of a meter. Connections lead the words on, carrying them toward an ever-differed meaning. In contradistinction, the second-order language of modern poetry releases words from connection, reducing the ancient rituals of symmetry while expanding the gratifying fulfilling force of words by themselves. *Degré zéro*, or "zero degree,"—taking into account the more idiomatic English-language placement of the adjective before the noun—designates this nonreferentiality of the word in modern poetry, in which "the Word is no longer guided in advance by the general intention of socialized discourse," becoming "encyclopedic . . . engorged with all past and future specifications at once."[98] Assuming Spillers's *flesh* to be structurally analogous to Barthes's *Word*, then it too, as zero degree, is "a generic form, . . . an unexpected object, a Pandora's box from which fly out all the potentialities of language." The pertinence of all this becomes clearer when we extend our interrogation of Spillers's engagement with Barthes's semiology to the two sentences immediately following the declaration that the flesh is degree zero of social conceptualization *before* the body: "Even though the European hegemonies stole bodies—some of them female—out of West African communities in concert with the African 'middleman,' we regard this human and social irreparability as high crimes against the flesh, as the person of African females and African males registered the wounding. If we think of the 'flesh' as a primary narrative, then we mean its seared, divided, ripped-apartness, riveted to the ship's hole, fallen, or 'escaped' overboard."[99]

In so extending our query, we should remark Barthes's insistence that in the well-developed myth the *meaning* of the signifier is never at zero degree, but is always there in full for the *form* to siphon off as nourishment for the *concept*. Barthes characterizes the perpetually emptying out of the meaning into form for the concept as robbery, calling myth "speech stolen and restored."[100] We should further note that, in illustration of how no language is safe from this theft, he offers modern poetry as an extreme instance of failed resistance. Modern poetry's fiercely refusing myth stems precisely from its being what Barthes calls *a regressive semiological system*, which contra myth, tries to regain pre-semiological state of language, a zero degree. In so doing, however, it surrenders to myth bound hand and foot. He illustrates the point by recasting his initial account of classical poetry from *Le degré zéro de l'écriture* as a mythology of literary language, making modern poetry a reading of the myth that seeks to destroy it by focusing on the empty signifier, letting the concept (literary language) unambiguously fill the form (the Word). Not even the zero degree can escape myth's process of theft. "What the form can always give one to read," Barthes determines, "is disorder itself: it can give a signification to the absurd, make the absurd itself a myth . . . [as] happens when common sense mythifies surrealism."[101] Arguably, we can infer this is what Spillers means by describing the flesh as "zero degree of social conceptualization that does not escape concealment under the brush of discourse," provided we attend closely to what is at stake in the two terms "escape" and "discourse." The inference holds if her "discourse" is taken to designate the determining principles of combination and order, which are actualized in forms of representation, codes, conventions, and habits that constitute a specific field of meaningful reality, a making of history in the very sense Aristotle understands *poiēsis* to be λέγειν γένοιτο (*légein génito*, "saying possibility"), in contrast to ἱστορία γενόμενα (*istoria genómen*, "the history of what happened").[102] We can say that *poiēsis* is the *historizing-occurrence* in the sense Heidegger uses the term *Geschehen*. The pertinence of that sense to our investigation will be explored as it unfolds. What matters right now is that when Barthes states, "le mythe est une parole [myth is a type of speech]," he is referring to myth as such an actualization.[103] As a type of speech, myth is a sign in a system of signs articulating a way of thinking and being in the world. The specificity of that system, what Barthes calls its arbitrariness or motive, has to do with its historizing-occurrence. And the function of myth, or rather the affectivity of its particular dynamic of signification, is to erase the historizing-occurrence of the semiological system by naturalizing its *concept*, not the *meaning* of its signifier, which provides the stolen nourishment for that concept.[104] If we then take Spillers to mean by "escape" an act of resistance to myth—keeping in mind Barthes's admonition "that it is extremely difficult to vanquish myth from inside, for the very effort one makes in order to be free [of myth] becomes in its turn the prey of myth"[105]—her stating the flesh does not escape concealment by the brush of discourse is to remark its being inevitably implicated with discourse as an essential element of signification. All this is confirmed by how her description of *flesh/enslaved captive body* is in accordance with Barthes's of the mythical signifier. So what the flesh does not escape, in fact, is mythical *parole*, which actualizes an expansive discourse of appropriation as value. Even though there is a sense of the inevitability of the flesh being inescapably captured in myth, Spillers's remark ought not be read as perennially pessimistic.[106] Barthes's admonition notwithstanding, Spillers's aim in remarking the inescapable captivity of the flesh is to demystify myth by exposing its semiological process, by revealing the action of its larceny. Before addressing the stakes, if not the efficacy of Spillers's move, we need to pause a moment and consider more carefully just what myth she is demystifying.

In our initial account of Spillers's *flesh/enslaved captive body* distinction, we overlooked the fact that she presents it in the context of reading Patrick Moynihan's 1965 *The Negro Family: The Case for National Action*, after having construed Moynihan's reference to "the Negro ethnic group," as a mythical signifier. More precisely, she takes *ethnicity*" to be a signifier of "memorial time," which is to say the formal aspect of the mythical signifier, *Negro* being its meaning. The resultant bi-dimensional mythical signifier, *Negro/ethnicity*, appropriates sustenance for the Moynihan Report's concept, *matriarchal family structure*, the sign, or mythical signification of which is *Negro social pathology*. Discovering the bi-dimensionality of the signifier weakens the myth exposing it as a representationally inadequate fiction, which, as Spillers puts it, "transports us to a common historical ground, the socio-political order of the New World."[107] The mechanism of that transportation turns on an implicit question: How does *Negro* mean *ethnicity*? It turns out that *Negro* as the meaning formally expressed as *ethnicity* is the final sign of another antecedent semiological system: what Spillers refers to as "the socio-political order of the New World," which can be further specified as the sociopolitical order of racialized capitalist modernity, or, following Michel Foucault's systemic analysis, the system of biopolitics, but is more aptly, albeit cumbersomely, referred to as the system of "biocentric ethnoclass."[108] That first-order semiological system also entails a pronouncedly predominant myth, the keynote signifier of which is *flesh/enslaved captive body*. We are now brought to ask an even more probative question: How does the flesh, formally expressed as the enslaved captive body, become Negro?

By focusing on the full mythical signifier—its meaning and form—and then drawing attention to *flesh* as a primary narrative, Spillers sets out to reveal how *enslaved captive body* robs from *flesh* the material needed to give *Negro* its meaningfulness. In the course of doing so, she proffers a pointed metaphor of signification, the hieroglyphics of the flesh, referring to the "undecipherable marking on the flesh" that renders the captive body as such.[109] Dr. Jonathan

Edward's somewhat detailed 1791 description of the lacerating and tearing out of small portions of flesh during the flogging of slaves is the occasion for the metaphor's application. Edward's description is reported by William Goodell in "Chapter XVII, Facts Illustrating the Kind and Degree of Protection Extended to Slaves," of his *The American Slave Code in Theory and Practice Shown by Its Statutes, Judicial Decisions, and Illustrative Facts*, as one in the list of eye-witness testimonies illustrating the "usual punishment" administered to slaves that Goodell compiled to establish the facts of the normative regularity of systematic and frequently fatal violence perpetrated on enslaved "negroes." With an eye toward this documentary aspect of the list, Spillers characterizes the lacerations and tears Edward describes as hieroglyphic marks that create the distance between culture proper—with its colluding instrumentalities of political economy, state, and civil society—and what she designates "cultural *vestibularity*."[110]

With this artful turn of phrase, Spillers transforms what is an architectural term, *vestibule*, designating an interior space, into an abstract noun of condition or state, thereby spatializing the process of mythic appropriation. But the vehicle of her spatial metaphor has a particular function and properties. The most ancient architectural usage is Roman, *vestibulum*, referring to the long narrow entrance-hall found in the type of ancient Roman upper-class house known as *domus*, leading from the front door into the *atrium*, the semipublic open central court of the house where guests and dependents (*clientes*) were greeted. Modern architectural usage of *vestibule* refers to an area immediately surrounding the exterior door, serving as an antechamber or foyer leading into a larger space such as a lobby.[111] The vestibule of the modern private residence is an entrance hall where the traces of being outside, such as shoes and outerwear, are left, usually in the coat closet, before gaining access to the domicile interior. This sense of the vestibule's function as a space of cleaning is connoted by the designation given the secondary more regularly used entryway in suburban American homes, "mud room." In opulent public buildings, the vestibule has a different function, that of transitional perspective. The contrast between its small space and the larger one into which it opens is designed to elicit a sense of anticipation while moving through the vestibule and grandeur on gaining access to the magnificent atrium or lobby. The length of the vestibule defines a buffer zone between the boundless exterior and the enclosed interior space, being the distance across which one must pass to gain proper admittance. Both the vestibule and the larger space into which it opens are inside the architectural space, so that the distance created by the hieroglyphics markings measures the flesh's passage through the vestibule, having already entered the cultural order, into its proprietary interior to become the *enslaved captive body*. Those markings are, in effect, indicial representations of the disciplining action of culture on the flesh. In other words, they have a real relation to it, like a weathercock to the wind. By that analogy, if the hieroglyphic markings are the weathercock and the sociopolitical order of racialized capitalist slavery the wind, *Negro* is the expression of that relationship. From this point, whenever this term is italicized, it is to keep an eye on its semiological function. As such, its representative function is something it is, not in itself or even in real relation to its object, flesh, but in relation to a particular train of thought. *Negro* expresses a general, conventional connection between the disciplining action of "culture" and flesh.

Giving due weight to Spillers's usage of Barthes's semiological analysis of myth, we can say that *Negro* is the signification of the mythical semiological system, the signifier and concept of which are *flesh/captive body* and *sociopolitical order of racialized capitalist slavery*, respectively. In this semiological system, *Negro* signifies slavery. We shall return to this momentarily, giving consideration to how, in that same system, *Negro* signifies other things related but not reducible to slavery. For now, the pertinent issue is that the sign of one semiological system, the first-order myth of the Negro, functions as the meaning of another, second-order myth, *Negro social pathology*. So that the myth of Negro social pathology derives its nourishment, via the formal dynamics of *ethnicity*, from the meaning of *Negro* as the signification of the first-order myth, which derives its nourishment, via *the captive black body*, from the flesh. There is, in other words, a double theft: *ethnicity* steals from *Negro*, which has robbed from *flesh*. As for the Moynihan Report, we can extend this to a third-order myth, in which *Negro social pathology* is the meaning of the form *the Negro problem*, the concept for this signifier being *widespread social disorder* and the signification Moynihan's "*case for national action*," which rather tellingly echoes Nathaniel Shaler's earlier pronouncedly Negrophobic description of the Negro problem as "a national danger."[112] This semiological order is represented schematically in Barthes's mode, as shown in figure 2.1. This tridimensional semiological order is what Spillers seeks to demystify, calling it "an American grammar," the provenance of which is the myth of the Negro, which is itself "really a rupture and a radically different kind of cultural continuation."

Because Barthes's semiological analysis of myth is the crucial theoretical touchstone in Spillers's demystifying this particular American mythology, it is particularly relevant that *Negro* functions as the meaning of a mythical signifier in one of the two key examples he gives to illustrate the relation of distortion constituting myth's signification. That example is taken from the cover photo of the June 25–July 2, 1955, issue of *Paris-Match*, which is of a young man from Wagadudu, Upper Volta, named Diouf, who is saluting during the opening ceremony of a "fantastic spectacle" put on by the French Army at the sports stadium—or so the caption accompanying the photo informs its

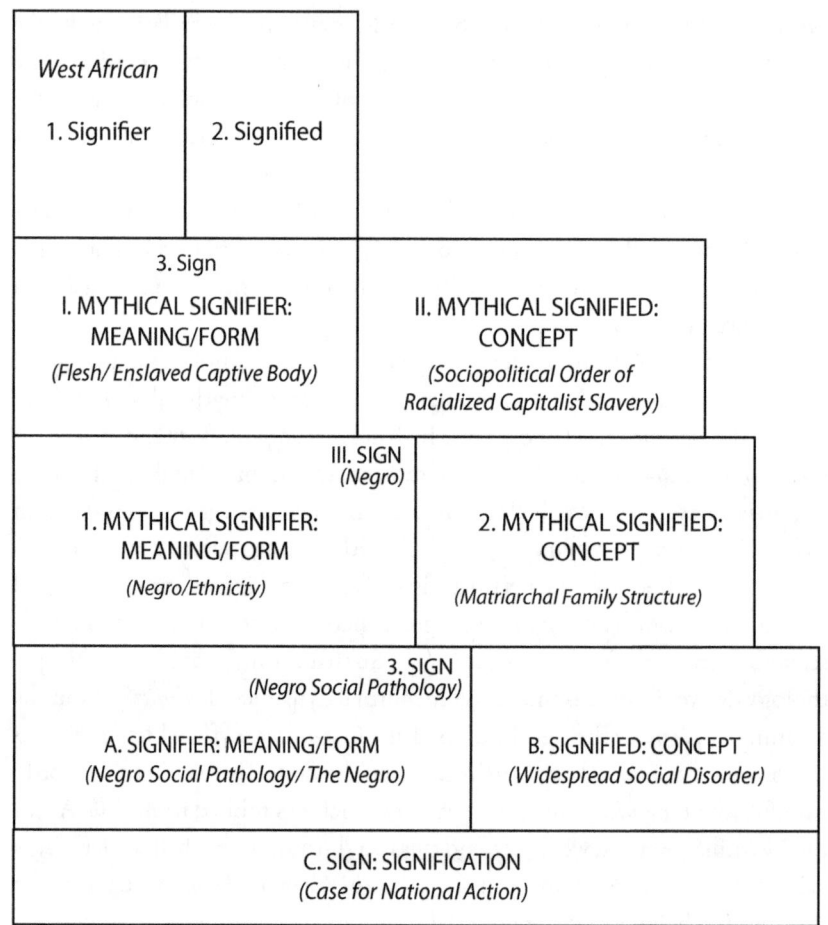

2.1 The Semiological Order of the Negro Problem

viewers. Caption notwithstanding, Barthes describes the photo as "a young Negro [*un jeune nègre*] in French uniform giving a military salute."[113] He then refers to it as "a black soldier [*un soldat noir*] is giving the French military salute," before settling on "a Negro [*un nègre*] is giving the French military salute," which is how it has come to be universally referenced.[114] All this warrants noting because in Barthes's example, "A Negro is giving the French military salute" functions as meaning *and* form. Arguable, "Diouf" is the first-order sign, the history of which is being impoverished by the form of the mythical signifier. Yet Barthes makes only the most elliptical of references to "Diouf," referring instead to "the history of the Negro" and "the biography of the Negro," which, in clear reference to the cover's caption, must be put in parenthesis.[115] *Negro* displaces "Diouf," and like the lion in Barthes's other example—*quia ego nominor leo* (because my name is lion), a Latin grammatical example—it is a collective generic noun.¹¹⁶ As a matter of history, it is a generic noun with a rather expansive connotation and so very narrow denotation. The term Barthes uses most consistently, *nègre*, was first codified in French with the Code Noir of King Louis XIV, the drafting of which was begun by Jean Baptiste Colbert in 1683 and completed by his son, the Marquis de Seignelay in 1685, when it was promulgated. With the two principal aims of regulating religion in the French New World colonies in favor of Catholicism, and slavery to secure cane sugar plantation economy on Saint Dominique, the code stipulates in article 2:

> All slaves on our islands shall be baptized and instructed in the Roman, Catholic, and Apostolic Faith. We enjoin the inhabitants who shall purchase newly arrived Negroes [*des Negres nouvellement arrivez*] to inform the Governor and Intendant of said islands of this fact within no more than eight days, or risk being fined an arbitrary amount. They shall give the necessary orders to have them instructed and baptized within a suitable amount of time.¹¹⁷

Having determined that *nègre* connotes slave, the Code Noir declares in its article 44: "Slaves are personal property, and enter into the community as such [*Les esclaves être meubles, & comme tels entrent en la communauté*]." This connotation of *nègre* as property within the economy of modern capitalist slavery does not dissipate with the subsequent use of the term to denote *les hommes de race noir* (the race of black men), or even more precisely *les hommes noir d'origine africaine* (black Africans). On the contrary, these usages underscore the immutable link between *nègre* and the slave trade.¹¹⁸

Let us digress a moment on a relevant point of translation. Leaving aside the dispute over the provenance of the English-language term *Negro*, its usage to designate property in the English colonies predates the Code Noir by twenty-six years. In 1659, the Virginia House of Burgesses enacted a law fixing the amount of tariff—two shillings per hogshead—to be imposed on "Dutch or other foreigners [who] shall import any negro slaves." The implicit identification of *Negro* as slave, regarded as property rather than person, is expressly established in what many regard as the earliest legal definition of *Negro* slavery in the English Empire, the 1661 the Barbados House of Assembly's "Act for the Better Ordering and Governing of Negroes."¹¹⁹ The Virginia General Assembly reinforced that connotation the next year, in 1662, when it adopted and applied the Roman juridical rule of *partus sequitur ventrem*, "offspring follows the mother," to the offspring of Negro women.¹²⁰ In Roman law, this rule applied exclusively to livestock and other nonhuman domestic animals and stipulated that the offspring of such animals belonged to the owner of the birthing female. The same assembly further reinforced the legal connotation of *Negro* as property when it enacted the aforementioned 1671 law—again predating the Code Noir, this time by fourteen years—establishing that "Negroes may be appraised" in kind with sheep, horse, and cattle. In 1705, using language reminiscent of article 2 of the Code Noir, the assembly enacted a law declaring Negroes to be real estate, following the example of South Carolina's earlier 1686 law defining Negro slaves as freehold property.[121] Arguably, the Virginia General Assembly's legal record alone is ample warrant for treating the terms *nègre* and *Negro* as cognate. Executing this warrant, we take note that *nègre*/*Negro* as an indicial signifier of property—more precisely, of the legal relationship *between* a person, the proprietary subject as responsible agent in and of the law, and some *thing* existing for the sake of that person—is a fundamental in capitalist modernity's formation, and that each occurrence of its expression indexes its genesis.

Point of translation taken into account, the consistency of Barthes's usage of *nègre* bears rather critically, in fact, on his own semiological project to understand how a society produces stereotypes as triumphs of artifice to be consumed as innate meanings, his analysis of mythical speech being a moment of that project. In light of Barthes's close attention to how the mythical signifier impoverishes the whole system of value—whether "a history, a geography, a morality, a zoology, [or] a Literature"[122]—if the statement *quia ego nominor leo* (because my name is lion) is a first-order sign, then we can ask: What of the Lion? Is *he* the victim of mythical theft? Is *he* subject to an insistent and dangerous stereotype?[123] We can ask the same questions about Diouf because Barthes presumes it is the biography and history of the sign *Negro*, which is distorted by the mythical signifier and not him. There is, however, a fundamental difference between *I am lion* and *a Negro giving the French military salute*, pertaining to the relationship of form to meaning in the mythical signifier. Whether taken from Victor Hugo's *Notre-Dame de Paris* or Gaius Julius Phaedrus's *Fables*, the form, *my name is lion*, is an apostrophic anthropomorphism; it is exclaimed by the lion.[124] And the richness of history being "outdistanced" by the exclamation is autobiographical: "I am an animal, a lion, I live in a certain country. . . . They would have me share my prey with a heifer, a cow, and a goat; but being stronger, I award myself all the shares for various reasons, the last of which is quite simply that *my name is lion*."[125] Humanizing the lion by giving it active voice highlights the work of mythical signification, expressly binding the meaning and form in name. The fact of the animal is displaced by the stereotype, which is the value of its name.[126] In contrast the form *a Negro giving the French military salute* is elliptical and even euphemistic: *Diouf* is elided as though it were an unutterable term. The history being emptied out is not that of "a young man from Wagadudu, Upper Volta, named Diouf who is saluting during the opening ceremony of a 'fantastic spectacle' put on by the French Army at the sports stadium," but rather "the biography of the Negro." Whereas being given active voice humanizes the lion, being rendered the object of passive voice dehumanizes Diouf. Someone else, Barthes in this instance, but always someone else speaks *Negro*, speaks of or for the *Negro*; and as Barthes explains, the removal of contingency, speaking of things rather than speaking things, celebrating things and no longer acting them is the business of myth as depoliticized metalanguage. Through his analysis of *a Negro giving the French military salute* as the mythical signifier's form that robs from *the biography of the Negro* to nourish the concept of French imperiality, we arrive at the signification of "the fact of French Empire," as shown in figure 2.2.[127]

Barthes's point in transcribing *Negro* over *Diouf* is that when looking at the *Paris-Match* cover photo what is seen is a Negro giving the French military salute as signifying the natural order of French Empire. Moreover, exposing the process by which such mythical signs (stereotypes) get produced and naturalized is a key "political" aim of his project, combining but not confusing Marx's and Engels's analysis of ideology with de Saussure's semiology in order to analyze mythology as a semiological system, as a formal science, and then identify it with ideology as a historical science. My point, however, and quite simply, is that from the very beginning of his own analysis, what Barthes sees is a *Negro*, doing whatever. Even when referencing the caption in parenthesis, he characterizes its information as "the Negro's biography." Clearly, then, *Negro* has a constancy of meaning, without contingency, across semiological systems, which suggests there is some stable phenomenal thing, let us refer to this as "the phenomenon of the Negro," which the sign *Negro* indicates. We encounter this constancy elsewhere in *Mythologies*, specifically in the essay "Bichon chez les Nègres" [Bichon among the Negroes], where Barthes reads another photo from *Paris-Match* as an instance of petite-bourgeois mythology's impotence to imagine the other.[128]

As with the 1955 cover, Barthes's reading of the Bichon photo exposes the values the compositional images embody iconically. As an iconic sign, *Negro* "has no full autonomous life; it is a bizarre object, reduced to a parasitic function, which is to distract the white man with its vaguely threatening baroque."[129] This is a mythical concept, driving the perception of its object, "the pathetic collusion of white flesh and black skin," the mythical formal expression of which is the *Negro*, *le nègre*, presenting an image produced according to "common sense." Barthes sets against this mythical iconic *Negro* the (scientific) knowledge of ethnologists such as Marcel Mauss, Claude Lévi-Strauss, and André Leroi-Gourhan in order to "demystify the Negro phenomenon [*démystifier le fait nègre*]."[130] But the ethnologists' work also situates the Negro iconographically. In this regard—that is to say, in Barthes's regard at the writing of "Bichon chez les Nègres"—the Mission Dakar-Djibouti comes to mind; as does Griaule's subsequent systematic typology of Dogon masque and analy-

1. Signifier (Paris-Match Cover Photo)	2. Signified (Young Man Named Diouf from Wagadudu, Upper Volta Saluting)
3. Sign (Negro) I. MYTHICAL SIGNIFIER (Negro Giving the French Military Salute)	II. MYTHICAL CONCEPT (French Imperial Colonialism)
C. SIGN: SIGNIFICATION (Case for National Action)	

2.2 The Semiological Order of French Imperialism

sis of their cosmology, along with Leiris's subsequent efforts at demystification. In full accord with the already noted avant-gardist ethnological primitivist motivations of the Mission, was the official motivation of symbolic imperial consolidation: to assimilate France's African territories into the empire by collecting "authentic" African Negro artifacts in metropolitan French museums, mainly the ethnographic Museé de l'Homme.[131] Those collected artifacts, in their status as specimens of the primitive and archaic, instantiate the order of acquisition's world-binding power. Leiris's journal record of the methods of force, coercion, and outright grand larceny by which the Mission collected its specimens reveals what Barthes characterized elsewhere as the obfuscated force generating symbolic representation.[132] In fact, recounting one episode of his forcibly taking in collaboration with Griaule what he calls "an African fetish," Leiris describes his action as "le rapt," which translates into English as "abduction," underscoring the resonance between Barthes's account of semiological theft and ethnographic collection.[133] By seizing Negro artifacts for the archive of human history, the ethnologist preserves the society that created them in an iconic relation of subordination, made eternal in the mythologizing of museum curation. Fascination with the object stems from its being perceived as vividly displaying in the details of its form the entire process of its creation: the execution of technique, as well as the elementals of conception.

Remaining attuned to resonances, this conception of the object exhibiting in formal detail the entire process of its creation is, on the whole, the sort of activity Aristotle described in the *Poetics* as μίμησις (mimesis): the activity by which humans represent to themselves materially the experience of being in the world. It is in this sense that Leiris regards the *objet d'art* as manifesting "the fetishism that is at the base of our human existence from the most ancient times."[134] That "true fetishism [*vrai fétichisme*] is the really *loving* love of ourselves, projected from the inside out clad in a hard shell and bound [*l'emprisonne*] within the limits of a precise thing and situation."[135] This assertion attributes to the fetish-thing an ultimate purpose, that it exists for our sake, it is made for us to make use of it; and in so existing, we are the ultimate goal of its making. We must pause here and do more than merely note that Leiris's sense of fetishism resonates with Aristotle's of mimesis as ἔργον (*ergon*, activity). What he is doing in *le rapt* of the African fetish, what he is doing *with it*, entails a powerful anticreative *ergon*. Adequately explaining just how his doing this accords with Aristotle's mimesis calls for some exposition, made all the more pertinent because Leiris's definition of true fetishism is proffered in regard to Alberto Giacometti's sculptures, and what he persistently abducts are sculpted pieces.

When Aristotle makes the statement in *Physics*, "τέχνη μιμεῖται τὴν φύσιν [*technē mimeitai tên phusin*], "art imitates nature," it is in the context of arguing that matter and form, while "two distinct aspects of nature [δύ αἱ φύσεις, *dio ai phúsis*]," are combined together as legitimate objects of the same discipline of knowledge.[136] Although this oft-cited passage—long regarded as a principal assertion in the history of Western aesthetic theory—seems to give primacy to nature, its function in the argument is to draw the analogy between physics and the arts as fields of knowledge (ἐπιστήμη, *epistēmē*), with the arts being the model for the conceptualization of how things are created. Let us not forget art (τέχνη, *technē*) refers to the requisite skills, procedures, and methods of deliberate human creation, in the sense Plato expresses when he has Diotima tell Socrates: "You know that creation [ποίησίς, *poiēsis*] is a thing of extensive meaning; for that which causes the passage of anything from non-being into being is altogether *poiēsis*, as are the processes of all the arts."[137] For Aristotle, all *technē* are creative arts (τέχνη ποιητική, *technē poiētikē*), "involving a true course of reasoning concerning making [ἕξις μετὰ λόγου ἀληθοῦς ποιητική, *hexis meta logou alêthous poietikê*]."[138] *Technē*, then, consists of a certain *know-how-in-a-certain way*. Aristotle uses the term *hexis* here in the specialized sense of a mental disposition assumed through, or by way of enacting a process. It is a disposition *in*, as well as *of* activity. We can say it is reached through the realization of that activity, in the sense it is the disposition that could only be articulated in the process of doing, πρᾶξις (*praxis*). This usage of *hexis* is on par with

Aristotle's conception of *enérgeia* (ἐνέργεια), which is commonly translated in English as "actuality," following the Latin rendering *actualitas*—although not quite because the full Latin sense of *actualitas*, which derives from *agere* (to put in motion, drive, conduct) and *actum* (a driving, impulse, setting in motion), is "that which makes a thing be real." *Actualitas* is that which has its origin in some type of human activity, approximating more closely Aristotle's conception of *enérgeia* than the common English sense of *actuality*—more closely, but not exactly, for *enérgeia* connotes action, a performative doing, or as Joe Sachs has proposed rendering it in English, "being-at-work-ness."[139] Aristotle contrasts this to *dunamis* (δύναμις), meaning a thing's constitutive capacity to be in a different, more complete state; as in the difference between being capable of seeing, even when one's eyes are shut, and seeing. We say, then, that *enérgeia* is the actuality-of-the-doing of seeing. On the grounds that such a doing is a means to an end, he further distinguishes two types of *praxis*: that praxis whereby the activity is in motion (ἐν κινήσει, *en kinísei*) without having achieved the objective of the motion is called *imperfect*; the perfect praxis is that which includes an end or τέλος (*télos*)—"to wit, at the same time we see and have seen [οἷον ὁρᾷ ἅμα καὶ ἑώρακε, *hoion horaō háma kai eórake*]."[140] Whereas the perfect praxis is what Aristotle calls *enérgeia*, he calls the imperfect praxis motion, or *kinesis* (κινήσεις).[141] In relation to *enérgeia*, *hexis* is the active disposition of humans-in-actual-doing. Its activity is that of cogitation (*logos*). In relation to *poiēsis*, it is the active disposition of knowing how to be-at-work-ness in creation. Aristotle tells us in the *Poetics* that what those who make mimesis, the μιμοῦνται (*mimoūntai*), are doing in this disposition is making mimesis (μιμούμενοι, *mimoumenoi*) of humans-in-actual-doing. Or, as the passage is usually translated, "artists imitate people in action."[142] The plural participle Aristotle uses in this passage, πράττοντας (*práttontas*), from the verb πράττειν (*práttein*), connotes "going through an action or state." Elsewhere, when identifying what he calls the active life (βίος ὁ πρακτικός, *bíos ho praktikós*) with happiness (εὐδαιμονία, *eudaimonía*), defined as well-doing (εὐπραγία, *eupragía*), Aristotle distinguishes between going through to get beyond (ἐξωτερικαὶ πράξεις, *exoterikai práxeis*) and going through when there is no beyond (οἰκείας τὰς αὐτῶν, *oikeías tas autōn*).[143] The latter corresponds with going through the motion, *kinesis*, of living, the former with actually having lived well.[144] In other words, perfect mimetic activity, as *enérgeia* entailing its object, mimics living people, where living is being-as-doing.

It is of no small moment, then, that in the passage from *Physics*, *technē* is, in fact, the subject of a conditional clause: "but if, on the other hand [εἰ δὲ ἡ, *ei de he*], art mimics nature."[145] This is further qualified in a way that establishes the epistemological stakes: "and it is part of the same discipline of knowledge [τῆς δὲ αὐτῆσ ἐπιστήμης, *tis de autēs epistēmēs*] to know both form and matter."[146]

The full conditional sentence is a paragraph long and gives parenthetically two examples of technical know-how (medicine and masonry), the consequence of which is: "It would be the part of physics also to know [τὸ γνωρίζειν, *to gnorizein*] nature in both its [formal and material] senses."[147] Aristotle's epistemological argument is deductive, working *from* the principle that art's processes of bringing into being what may or may not exist reiterates and complements (μιμεῖται, *mimeitai*) nature's processes of quadrated causalities (αἴτιας, *aitias*), which are: ἐνυπάρχοντος (*enyparchontos*), what we call *matter*; εἶδος (*eidos*), *form*; ἀρχὴ τῆς μεταβολῆς (*archē metabolēs*), "that which efficiates the complete transformation of matter, what creates what is created, and changes what is changed," generally referred to as *efficient cause*; and τέλος (*télos*), the *purpose* or *ends* for which the entire process is initiated.[148] The generative process of causing (αἴτιον, *aition*) a thing to be may begin with the existence of matter, "such as the bronze for the statue or silver for the phial," but it is the efficient cause, the at-work-ness of sculpting (τῷ ἀνδριαντοποιῷ, *te andriantopoiē*) that transforms the matter into the form specified by design serving a purpose.[149] The relationship between the four causalities is plainly teleological; and Aristotle conceived of the formal perfection of a thing to be attaining the fullest realization of function in capacity, which he called *entelecheia* (ἐντελέχεια) in both *On the Generation of Animals* and *On the Soul*. Aristotle uses *enérgeia* and *entelecheia* interchangeably, which is why the Latin translations of these works render it also as *actuallitas*, becoming *actuality* in English, and sometimes simply *entelechy*. In the course of elaborating his conception of formal perfection following function (ἐπιτελεῖσθε, *epiteleīsthe*), Aristotle asserts: "Generally art either works through [ἀπεργάσασθαι, *apergásasthai*] what physical nature cannot complete, or mimics [τὰ δὲ μιμεῖται, *ta de mimeitai*] physical nature."[150] If, then, artificial processes are purposeful, so are natural processes; for the relation of antecedent to consequent is identical in art and in nature. The two verbs ἐπιτελεῖ (*épitelei*) and ἀπεργάσασθαι (*apergásasthai*) are pivotal in this passage, which is generally taken to be an elaboration of the relation of causality, as well as fundamental to Aristotle's subsequent definition of mimesis in the *Poetics*. Both terms mean bringing something to perfection in the sense of fulfillment in execution in performance, with *apergásasthai* having the additional sense of working through. Hence, the arts work through to perfect completion, according to nature, but complementing its processes. Again, we are dealing with *enérgeia* in the sense of "being-at-work-ness," and it is this *enérgeia* that is the epistemological concern of both art and physics. We might say regarding the bronze statue by Polycleitus, which is one of Aristotle's examples of the being-at-work-ness of art, the relationship between the biological creature (ζῷον, *zōon*) called the person, Polycleitus, and the sculptor is coincidental insofar as "causing" the statue to be is concerned.[151] In that same vein, any other characteristics associated with the person are irrelevant to the *enérgeia* of causality.¹⁵² It is the *how* and the *why* of things coming into and passing out of being, or more generally, into the essential constituents of physical change that is under study, with a particular emphasis on the why (το διατί, *to diati*) predetermining the activity of how (αἰτία, *aitia*).¹⁵³ All references to *poiēsis* notwithstanding, the activity of scientific study (θεωρια, *theōria*), which is fundamentally philosophical, is dedicated to the process in abstraction; and the statue evokes that process.

For clarity, let us have recourse to Heidegger's explanation of this conception of formal causality, in which he elaborates on another of Aristotle's examples of causality mentioned in conjunction with the bronze statue, the silver phial, by translating it into the silver chalice used in the Christian ceremony of communion. The focus of Heidegger's commentary is the teleology, and so he gives emphasis to the *télos* determining at-work-ness of the efficient cause: from the selection of matter to its transformation. Regarding the chalice, this is the religious ceremony that requires the sacrificial vessel.¹⁵⁴ More in keeping with Heidegger's formulation we would say: this *télos confines* (*eingrenzt*) the chalice *in advance* into the realm of consecration and bestowal. Thereby, it is circumscribed (*umgrenzt*); and circumscribing (*Das Umgrenzende*) gives the thing its terminus, from which it begins to be what, after production, it will be. In describing the *télos* in this way, Heidegger recognizes the formal cause as entelechy.¹⁵⁵ This sense of formal cause compliments the tripartite aspect of mimesis Aristotle describes in the *Poetics*, drawing an analogy between mimetic media and material cause, mimetic object and formal cause, mimetic modality and efficient cause. Again, all of this is in theory, which is to say, it is the epistemological activity of philosophy that knows the universal process of at-work-ness exhibited with the work. *Poiēsis* may indeed be more philosophical and more serious than history because it exhibits the possible.¹⁵⁶ But it is *philosophy*, Aristotle's philosophy, that knows just how the universal process of at-work-ness is exhibited with the work, whether statue, phial, or chalice. And so too with ethnology, which knows just how the fetish exhibits the universal human activity of mimesis.

When Leiris speaks of true fetishism in terms of the really *loving* love of ourselves bound within the limits of a precise thing and situation, he echoes Heidegger's circumscribing. Although the resonance is likely coincidental, it is not just so. The objects Leiris values are those that attenuate circumscription, exposing interiority as its potent force; he calls such moments of exposure "crises... related to apparently trifling [*futiles*] events, devoid of symbolic value, and, if you like, gratuitous."¹⁵⁷ His identifying the fetish with trifling alludes to Kant's dismissal of what he took to be "the widespread religion of fetishism [*weit ausgebreitete Religion der Fetische*] among African Negroes [*Die*

*Negers von Afrik*a], founded on extreme triviality [*so tief ins Läppische sinkt*], consecrating with a few words a bird's feather, cow's horn, shells, or any other common thing into objects of veneration."[158] Leiris contradicts Kant's condemnation, however, by embracing, if not the consecration of common things as valuable in-themselves, their being the *material cause* of the mimetic process. Whatever the form—"Alberto Giacometti's fetish-like sculptures, or true idolized fetishes [*vrai fétiches qu'on peut idolâtrer*], meaning those that resemble us and are objectivized forms of our desire"—it is precisely the process of externalizing desire that is valued.[159]

Later in his life, Leiris would tell Sally Price and Jean Jamin that this investment in fetish was in rebellion against the so-called rationalism of Western society, fueling an intellectual curiosity about "peoples who represented more or less what Lévy-Bruhl called . . . *mentalité primitive*."[160] This was more a fascination than curiosity, which, as Leiris indicates in his Giacometti essay, began with his intense obsession with American Negro music. The first example he gives of moments of crisis related to trifling events is an encounter at night "on a luminous Montmartre street with a Negress (*une négresse*) of the Black Birds dance troupe, holding a bouquet of moist roses in both hands."[161] He offers another elsewhere. In the course of declaiming the tremendous influence on Western culture of jazz and the dances associated with it, which he describes together with Afro-American folk music, whether profane or religious, as "tasting like a distant whiff of Africa injected into our industrial civilization," Leiris recalls how "the image of a Josephine Baker abandoning herself [*se déchaînant*] to the Charleston is akin, under the sign of primitivism, to 'Christs all the same though of lesser obscure hope.'"[162] The quotation to which Baker is likened is all about the fetish. It is the last line in the last quatrain of Guillaume Apollinaire's poem "Zone":

> *Tu marches vers Auteuil tu veux aller chez toi à pied*
> *Dormir parmi tes fétiches d'Océanie et de Guinée*
> *Ils sont des Christ d'une autre forme et d'une autre croyance*
> *Ce sont les Christ inférieurs des obscures espérances.*[163]
>
> *You walk toward Auteuil you want walk the whole way home*
> *To sleep among your fetishes from Oceania and Guinea*
> *They are Christ of another form and another system of belief*
> *But Christs all the same though of lesser obscure hope.*

Leiris's position is complex here. Although jazz and its associated dances are emblematic of a primitivism that liberates from reason, this does not mean they are in any way simple or crude. Nor is African sculpture, the increased aesthetic appreciation of which has made it plain that "none of these people can be regarded as 'primitive' and it is recognized that many have a highly developed sense of values."[164] This is a distinction, rather than an outright contradiction. Leiris is distinguishing between *primitive*, in the Kantian sense of backward and uncultured, or Hegel's of those arrested in a permanent state of archaism, and his own sense of primitivism as the anti-rationalist exhibition of human creativity, indeed, as the manifestation of *poiēsis* liberated from philosophical speculation—which is to say, free of the circumscription of Western art theory and its history. So freed, the fetish is recognized not as simplistic and crude, but as manifesting the universal human activity of mimesis in the Aristotelian sense. It exhibits the worldly at-work-ness of humans with the associated *technē*, as well as *télos*. The material, "a coarse patch-worked canvas bag, covered in a bitumen of coagulated blood, inside of which are stuffed a disparate assortment [*hétéroclites*] of dusty things," is given a distinct form, "equipped at one end with a protuberance . . . and at the other a bell," to serve a purpose, blood sacrifice.[165] It is this *télos* that gives the simple, dirty, elemental abject object "the terrible force of religious emotion because it is the condensed absoluteness of these men, which they have imprinted on it with their own [human] force."[166] Something is amiss, however, because, while this *mimesis* of the fetish is a *technē poiētikē* actualizing some human conceptualization of the world, it is not necessarily theoretical; that is, its methodological knowledge, its *meta logou*, or meta-discourse, while accounting for the relationship between the how and the why, cannot account for the universality of the expression. Such an account requires the ethnologist, justifying his systematic pilferage. The *rapt* imbues the fetish with the universal voice that speaks volumes about the human condition and the fundamental capacity of human creativity. At the same time, it mutes the makers, those who have poetic cause (*poietikin aitia*, ποιητικὴν αἰτία), disregarding, if not altogether silencing their cosmology by failing to attribute to them any theory. The epistemological division is clear: the makers have know-how and *localized* why, which must be respected; the ethnologist has scientific knowledge, which circumscribes that know-how, placing it in its proper curated place in the museum of man.

We have, then, two orders of consecration, the primary one of the makers—the very description of the canvas bag seems tailored to neatly fit Kant's definition of fetish as trifling—and the second order consecration of the ethnologist, which makes the object into a fetish of his anthropology, "a faint breeze from distant Africa" that, wafting "into the midst of our industrial civilization," has the potential to redeem something supposed to have been lost. That potential is energized in the curated consecration, absolving all the sins of pillage and desecration enacted in acquisition. Haunting this consecrated redemptive fetish, just as Diouf haunts Barthes's reading of the *Paris-Match* photo, are the makers, whose poetic cause is sacrificed, just as their sacrificial *télos* is abnegated in the theft, to ethnological primitivism's *télos* of redemption. Primitivist *négrophile* is akin to the Eucharist with its salvation in blood sacrifice; an association Leiris explicitly makes when, describing his participation in a blood sacrifice while in Ethiopia, aimed at purging him of a *zâr* possession, he compares it to the Eucharist: "I felt very isolated, elected, and saintly. I thought of my first communion: if it had been as grave at this, perhaps I would have stayed a believer; but the true religion only begins with blood."[167] This reiterates what he wrote describing the Kono fetish he and Griaule had stolen earlier while in Mali: "Unfortunately, it was damaged, but completely covered in a coat of coagulated blood, which conferred to it the majesty that blood confers to all things."[168] Then again, he describes the "marvelous foundation" of an African village with its "rivulets [*ruisseaux*] of sacrifice."[169] Finding such blood sacrifice to be "the most intense and human poetry,"[170] Leiris captures its energizing force for his own personal purpose, which was an erotically infused desire to discover a "new personality" through returning to primitive Africa, the mother, in rebellion against modern Europe, the father.

The quest for personal redemption through the loving embrace of Negro things—"the really *loving* love of ourselves"—was one more thing Leiris had in common with Lomax, who was compelled by a nostalgic desire to find a childhood friend, Nat Blythe, the Negro from whom he learned his sense of rhythm and whom he loved as he had loved few people "with the fierce strength and loyalty of youth."[171] Traveling up and down the South on his phonographic expeditions of collection, he found himself "always looking for Nat."[172] In each instantiation of ethnological primitivism, however, whether Griaule's typology, or Leiris's and Lomax's respective participatory personal identification with the disappearing archaic Negro, the collector's motivation to redeem and conserve a lost, purer self fixates on the Negro artifice as the *archē* of what we have become, in accordance with the old sense of *translatio*, both *studii* and *imperii*—meaning that Atlantic modernity, in all its particularities, is the eternal *télos*, the ends and purpose of the transference of universal knowledge with its coordinate power. Only, instead of Greece, the Hellenophilia *archē* of universal knowledge, which then moves westward through Rome to the exclusion of Africa—this being the lineage of rational knowledge—Africa is postulated as the childhood home of our most primitive humanity, our affective engagement with the natural order of things before the advent and ascendency of reason. In this "Afrocentrism," the Negro is indissolubly African. However forcibly the Negro has been taken out of Africa, however enslaved and dehumanized, primitive Africa still reverberates in his artifice, which is what made Negro folksong such a valuable collector's specimen for Lomax, as well as a foundational inspiration for Leiris. As a quasi-positivist discipline—that is, as a systematic methodology of knowing that finds its objects given before it—

ethnology, including ethnographic folklore, is responsible for conserving the meaning, not only of cultural objects, but also of the culture in which they are made possible. Its task is to study the conditions of all historical signifying practices in order to answer the question: How have we come to be what we are now? But this is a question it is prepared to ask only dialectically: What is *ethnographizing* man as knowing-subject in relation to other types of men? Along such a line of inquiry, Negro artifice has universal meaning only as a specimen of archaic expression.

Coming back to Barthes, in contrasting the work of ethnologists with "l'opération Bichon," he seeks to draw attention to "the oppressive divorce of [scientific] knowledge and mythology" finding a way past the stagnation of the latter in the alacrity and straightforward path of the former (*vite et droit en son chemin*).[173] Yet, for all their "rigorous precautions . . . when obliged to use such ambiguous notions as 'primitive' or 'archaic,'" what the ethnologists are still said to be demystifying is the fact of the Negro phenomenon (*le fait nègre*). As though that was something supra-semiological, so to speak. Speaking in such a way, however, is still speaking *of* the Negro. This sense of the iconicity of the Negro is reiterated in Barthes's assertion regarding the cover photo that "the Negro who salutes is not a symbol of the French Empire; he has too much presence, he appears as a rich, fully experienced, innocent, *indisputable* image."[174] That iconicity is further reinforced in Barthes's comparing mythic signification to an ideogram and then pronouncing that "myth is a pure ideographic system [*système idéographique*], where the forms are still motivated by the concepts they represent." It may very well be that, historically, ideograms have gradually left the concept and become associated with sound, obscuring their conventionality by rendering it transparent and thereby naturalizing it. And even though the association of the term *Negro* with black skin is also naturalized, this is not achieved through its gradual distancing from the concept. On the contrary, *Negro* is indissolubly associated with the form and so the concept. In the example from "Myth Today," the association with the inviolable concept of French imperiality via the form (the image) of *a Negro giving the French military salute* gives us the *Negro colonial* as an iconic sign, evoking the semiological system of French Empire. The same evocation obtains in "Bichon chez les Nègres," where the form is simply the image of Negroes. Barthes's having to posit the fact of the Negro while earnestly seeking to demystifying it supports Spillers's assertion in the coordinating conjunction of the sentence we've been interrogating that the flesh does not escape concealment under "the reflexes of iconography," assuming what is meant by *iconography* is akin to what Barthes terms the *ideographic system of myth*. In that case, the association of *Negro* with the concept of the sociopolitical order of racialized capitalist slavery via the form of the enslaved captive body gives us the *Negro* as an iconic sign. In the ideographic system of colonial imperiality, as well as that of capitalist slavery, *Negro* is the sign of a distinctly alien life form, the value of which for the system can be determined only *within* the system, through its processes of appropriation.

Barthes correctly maintains that colonial imperiality has many other signifiers beside *Negro*, but it alone functions as the formal abstraction of the flesh as appropriate body in both the systems of colonial imperiality and New World slavery. With this singularity in mind, and taking into account that these are two of dominant modalities by which the complexly diffuse system of global capitalist modernity has become established, *Negro* can reasonably be construed as one of its principal icons. More precisely, it is an iconic sign of one of modernity's governing mythologies: the natural equation of individual freedom and property. The sign *Negro* invariably evokes this fundamental concept as the limit where the principle does not hold, either marking a type of being inherently incapable of purporting the principle, or that being whose inclusion under the principle through enculturation is requisite for universal justice and human rights. The question is, can *Negro* be such an icon and at the same time be another sort of sign altogether in relation to the flesh as well as the captured/colonized black body?

Having recognized the hieroglyphics markings as indicial signs of the disciplining action of culture on the flesh, Spillers ponders whether "this phenomenon of marking . . . actually transfers from one generation to another, finding its various symbolic substitutions in an efficacy of meanings that repeat the initiating moments." In this contemplation, the hieroglyphics of the flesh are regarded themselves as mechanisms of the torture the flesh undergoes, conferring on it the status of a particular type of body, the enslaved Negro body, particularly valued within the semiological system of racialized capitalist modernity. The contemplation, however, is contingent upon a reading, upon knowing how to recognize the marks as ideogrammatic signs in a system of signs, one in which the ideogram is phonemicized, "*Negro/nègre*," in a perpetual process of semiosis. What's more, it requires a, let us say, "phenomenological attitude," within which it is possible to discern and call out the intentionality of the process. In other words, to see the marks not merely as representations of experience of the socially ordered world where entities designated *Negro* are present, which they certainly are, but also as constitutive elements of that world, signifying the inextricableness of the perceptions and consciousness of those entities from the semiosis. Demarcating as they do the passage from being outside that system into it, these hieroglyphics are happenings in-the-way-of-becoming-with-the world; that is to say they are articulations *in* vestibularity. The articulated flesh, of course, is not tabula rasa. Human flesh, by definition, or at least by the definition taken from Windham's remark, is always already marked as interpolated in some signifying system, some thinking on the cosmic arrangement of things. Any discernable, not easily placed residuum of the dynamics of those systems at play in the flesh prior to its entering modernity's cultural vestibularity gets assigned as *African*. We might well take this as synonymous with Rousseau's hypothetical *savage*, the archaic human passing on the way to civilized society. Only, whereas Rousseau's savage is compelled by the interaction of exchange to make the passage in order to become a proprietary-social-subject, in this instance, the interaction *civilizes* the African *as* capital in an exchange system predicated on what Spillers calls "a protocol of 'search and destroy.'" The procedures of racialized capitalist modernity seek the *enérgeia* of motive-will and desire bound up with the flesh and body associated with the person of the prior *African* semiological system. The implication being that the modern capitalist semiological order acquires—or in Barthes's terms, steals—the potential of the prior system *in actuality* as the Negro body, *le nègre* with its deprecated person, as racialized human capital, which is an alienable asset used but not consumed in the production of goods and services, the appreciation and depreciation of which is calculated relative to real as well as prospective use.[175] What gets destroyed in that process, or rather what is supposed to be destroyed but is more aptly speaking parenthesized, is any semiological order that negates or otherwise compromises the Negro's capital value—that is to say, any articulation of person, including gender, that contradicts capital value. The procedural instrumentalities of this protocol—the economic, juridical, political, and religious discourses and practices constituting its apparatus—carry the female and the male in the flesh to the frontiers of survival, so that the captured body somehow "bears in person the marks of [this] cultural text."[176]

By Flesh Speaking Semiologically

It is important to note here that the persistence of prior semiology, the residuum acknowledged as *African*, prevents us from construing vestibularity as an event of assimilation or consumption. Granted, Allen and Higginson strove, in their Transcendentalist primitivism, to incorporate the non-Christian elements of the slaves' sonics into the civilized body by converting them into annotations and placing them within the long process of hominization as archaisms; the Negro is thus the historical event of transition from animal to human. They could not assimilate everything, however; what is registered as purely *African* qua *Negro* is a residuum that cannot be digested even by their extended ethnology and is transfigured in its exscription as an instantiation of the event of the primitive, the experience of which is supposed to somehow redeem us from the dehumanizing effects of modern civilization. In this attitude, *Negro* connoting primitive is placed in a perpetual moment of transitivity, and so is prior to the beginning of civilization. For it to serve that redemptive function, the residuum of the purely Negro *cannot* be entailed in the process designated by Hegel as *Erinnerung*, "recollection," whereby *Geist* incorporates history by assimilating its own past in a kind of "sublimated eating," to paraphrase Derrida.[177]

Continuing paraphrastically, in Hegel's infinite metabolism, everything is supposed to be digestible—his term for this is *aufheben*, which is usually rendered as "sublation," but he uses it, along with its noun cognate, *Aufhebung*, to connote the Christological sense of transubstantiation as formally analogous to the reconciliation of God's eternal nature with the world through incarnation.[178] *Geist* is supposed to incorporate everything external and foreign, assimilating it as something internal and its own—everything, that is, except African elementals, which stand out as singularly unavailable for transubstantiation, and so cannot be constitutively consumed into the body of history, leaving them particularly available to the technics of the body as a quasi-hominized animalistic thing. Remember, in the New World, since the colonial seventeenth-century juridical reforms, Negro conversion to Christianity did not suspend Negro thingness; in the Code Noir, just as in the 1667 and 1682 laws of the Virginia Assembly, the converted Negro is a Christian Negro, meaning a Christian thing.[179] Also remember that Spillers's contemplating whether the hieroglyphic mark gets exscribed in various forms of signification transmitted across generations suggests a semiosis in which a determinate noematic experience of Negro thingness, first inscribed on the flesh, is perpetuated. That "experience" is expressed in two ways. On the one hand, it is expressed in the sense of the intentional egoistic attitude toward things, whereby experience requires the ego, the "I" for whom the world is the common name for the things with which the subject loses (alienates) himself in order to live as himself. This is the "I" that *sees* things, grasping the world in a certain way. On the other hand, the noematic experience is of "me" being seen only *in the flesh* in relation to my body, and not the orthopsychic ego of specular doubling—seeing myself seeing me—Lacan elaborated, but rather in the sense of the sentient flesh whose self-awareness is concomitant with its knowing it is seen as a thing: "me" *seeing as seen*, dispersed among things. In the first sense, the hieroglyphs of the flesh are logograms, images of the act of expression (the violence by which the mark is made), which is interpolated as undecipherable into the semiological system of meaning—that is, the ideographic system (*système idéographique*) of the myth of the Negro.

To state, then, that *Negro* is the phonemicization of the ideogram means that the sign, whether phonemic of graphemic, functions as a glyph, is unavoidably ideographic. As Barthes would say, it is still motivated by the concept it represents. Elaborating further on Spillers's designation of physical torture's bodily marks as hieroglyphs, we can say that *Negro* is a taxogram, a determinative in the myth's ideographic system. In other words, it is a disambiguating sign, marking the semantic category, the proper context in which to situate the associated hieroglyphic marks: the mark of *Negro* work, that of *Negro* terror, and that of *Negro* flight. *Negro* as glyph is indissolubly associated with the image. The word cannot be dissociated from the image, and the image is always invoked by the word. This is what Barthes regards; and he regards it according to Edmund Husserl's phenomenology, attending to the intentional activity of the seeing ego-subject, the structures of consciousness constituting the experience of the image, rather than the image as representation of the world. In the terminology of photographic images Barthes develops subsequent to *Mythologies*, *Negro* is of the *studium*, which denotes those aspects of the image we *learn* (*une sorte de'éducation*) to see through our enculturation.[180] That *Negro* appears to us as it is, that we can decipher its determinative meaning is an effect of our cultural pedagogy, in the course of which, through repetitive, sustained exposure to received aesthetic forms, we assimilate the requisite consciousness to see it. It is a part of our consciousness. And it is so even as that aspect of the image Barthes calls in *La Chambre claire* the *punctum*—"a 'detail,' i.e., a partial object"—which disturbs the *studium* by leaping out of the image into us. "To give examples of *punctum*," he says, "is, in a certain fashion, *to deliver myself up*."[181] Barthes finds an illustrative example of such *punctum* in the photograph of a black American family (*famille noire américaine*) taken by James Van der Zee in 1926:

> The *studium* is clear: I am sympathetically interested, as a docile cultural subject, in what the photograph has to say, for it *speaks* (it is a "good" photograph): it utters respectability, family life, conformism, Sunday best, an effort of social advancement in order to assume the White Man's attributes (an effort touching by reason of its naïveté). The spectacle interests me but does not prick me. What does, strange to say, is the belt worn low by the sister (or daughter)—the "solacing Mammy"—whose arms are crossed behind her back like a schoolgirl, and above all her *strapped pumps* (Mary Janes—why does this dated fashion touch me? I mean: to what date does it refer me?). This particular *punctum* arouses great sympathy in me, almost a kind of tenderness. Yet the *punctum* shows no preference for morality or good taste: the punctum can be ill-bred.[182]

Pace Barthes's assertion that "the studium is ultimately always coded and the punctum is not," each of his efforts to describe the experience of *punctum* entails reference to codes of culture: "the 'solacing Mammy.'" *Le fait nègre* cannot escape the ambit of enculturation. Barthes himself is aware of this, and recognizing that *punctum* may very well be triggered by aspects of *studium*, he comes to consider *punctum* as supplementary, describing it as "a kind of subtle beyond [*de hors-champ subtil*], as if the image launched desire beyond what it permits us to see."[183] The determination to never reduce himself-as-subject, as subject-ego, to "the disincarnate disaffected *socius* with which science is concerned" notwithstanding,[184] by the second part of *La Chambre claire*, the earlier distinction between *studium* and *punctum* gets elided, so that the free transcendental ego—the objective of the Husserlian phenomenological reduction he seeks to evoke—even as a principle of thought necessary for the meaningful account of phenomenal existence, is exposed as a function of sociality, of accumulative communicate semiosis.

Reading Spillers's query about the semiotic transmission of the determinate noematic experience of Negro thingness concordantly with Barthes's taking up Husserl's phenomenological study of the structures of consciousness, brings to mind the latter's definition of culture: "If we speak of culture, we have in mind the signification-conferring structures [*Gebilde bedeuntungverleihender*], the performative activity of which [*Bedeutungsleistungen*] endows things with spiritual meaning [*vergeistigender*], as well as constituting spiritual connections of subjectivity [intersubjectivity]."[185] As a correction to Heinrich Rickert's neglect of historically active subjectivity in his theory of "world-experience" (*Welterfahrung*), Husserl asserts culture is adumbrated by and continuous with personal ego, *Ich*, which is the "*subject of an environing-world* [*Umwelt*]" foregrounding the ego, and not merely the totality of its potentialities.[186] "The environment is perceived *by the person* in his acts, is remembered, grasped in thought, surmised or revealed as such and such; it is the world [*Welt*] of which this personal ego is conscious, the world which is there for it, to which it relates in this way or that."[187] This environmental world and the ego are inseparably related to one another, such that "the world is only *for* an ego; that is, *without* an ego, the World is not."[188]

Focusing so ardently on the noetic constitution of the world as mental representation (*Weltvorstellungskonstitution*) leads Husserl to a Cartesian psychology, as we all know, in which the *mens sive, sive anima, sive intellectus* (the mind, or the soul, or the intellect) is the only certainty.[189] The sticking point here is the person in relation to the body. Although Husserl does not come to doubt the certain existence of the body, as did Descartes, he dismisses the naturalistic construal of the psychic ego-subject founded in and dependent on the body in a "real-causal way," as inadequate for understanding what we are as humans. Perhaps this is no more clearly laid out than in *Ideen II*, where Husserl draws a hard line between the naturalist anthropological, or more precisely zoological, attitude, in which the human body is a physio-psychic object, and the phenomenological personalist attitude, where the human person purports what he calls *der geistigen Welt* (the cultural, world of values and interests), which is fully psychological in the classical Aristotelian sense. He also characterizes this distinction as that between the psychic being of *animalia*, the psychic ego-subject as nature studied by the natural sciences (*Naturwissenschaften*), and the ego as *person* within the purview of the human sciences (*Geisteswissenschaften*), especially philosophy, sociology, and psychology, which, combined together, have assumed the task Bacon relegated to metaphysics in his *Novum Organum* at the dawn of our modernity. This is not tantamount to a dismissal or diminishing of the natural sciences. Instead, what the phenomenological attitude provides is a new psychology, "a universal science of the mind" that is neither psychophysical nor natural-scientific.[190] By the tenets of that science, consciousness can enter into the real world only by virtue of a certain participation in transcendence in its first and primordial sense as the transcendence of material nature.[191]

And yet, Husserl postulates, in accord with those same tenets, it is only through linking consciousness and body (*Verknüpfung von Bewußtsein und Leib*) into a natural, empirically intuited unity (*Naturalien, empirisch-anschaulichen Einheit*) that one, as a person, places oneself in the world in conversation of mutual understanding (*Wechselverkeher*) with other persons.[192] Only in that way, whereby in becoming one in "body and soul," as we might say, *one* becomes *person*, can every knowing-subject find a full world containing itself and other knowing-subjects, recognizing them as being like it, sharing the same world in common. Even the lived-experience of one's own physical body as foundational and constitutive of one's human being is the experience of the psychic ego-subject (*die Seelenerfahrung*).[193] The animate body comprising the strata of sensibility and free movement is the connecting bridge (*verbindende Brücke*) between agential intellectuality (*Geistigkeit*) and the realm of physical thinghood in nature.[194] The phenomenological attitude encounters this real constitution of lived experiences as being grounded in the subjective kinaesthetic-capacity (*Vermöglichkeit*) of the ego to take the world in a certain way.[195] Instead of the causal relation between subject and object, in which the objects of the surrounding natural order stimulate the human being as a psychophysical reality, there is the *relation of motivation* (*die Motivationsbeziehung*) between persons and things, such that the things do not exist of themselves in nature, but are experienced, thought, or in some other way intended; they are posited intentional objects of personal consciousness. Stimuli arise from things that are *meant* in the consciousness of personal ego as actually existing.[196] Such subconscious noematic unities—in Husserl's terms, they are quasi-presented in the background of consciousness (*Bewußtseinshintergrund vorschwebende*)—are points of departure for the ego's kinaesthetic-capacity. They stimulate its desire to delight in them, play with them, use them as a means, transform them to its purposes, or leave them alone. They function, at every level, as stimuli for the ego's being active or passive.[197] The knowing-perceiving-subject, then, *has* the body as a zero point of orientation: a *there*, the embodied *I* in the world (*Leiblichkeit*), displaced from the *here* of the ego, the *I* who *has* the world (*das Welthabende*).[198] What *I* finds in the world is not only things but also other ego-subjects, perceived as persons engaged in the world with *I*. Regarding those surrounding persons, the phenomenological attitude never inserts the intellect (*Geist*) *into* the body, never considers it as something *in* the body, as founded in it, or as belonging *with* the body.[199] To consider the intellect in that way, as something causally dependent on the body, upon which it seems grafted, would mean that humans themselves are posited as things. To be sure, modernity has evolved various ways in which humans are treated as mere things, but the two that have been most prevalent, in Husserl's assessment, are the juridical and the scientific. In the juridical context, to treat human beings as mere matter, as disposable things, is to not recognize them as subjects of rights (*Rechtssubjekt*), as members of the community-founded-in-law (*Rechtsgemeinschaft*) to which we all belong. It is, in other words, to recognize them as abstract indefinite persons, voided of any phenomenological experiential specificity.[200] The juridical deracination of experiential human personhood has dire consequences from a moral-practical standpoint—the standpoint predicated on the postulate that every possible act of willing is based on an act of valuation, from which derive all duties toward the human as a rationally self-conscious being obligated to the world and its perpetual emendation—because it entails deracinating the phenomenological agent of morality: the intellect as person (*Der Geist als Person*), coordinated with other persons in a linking association (*Personenverbandes*) constructing the world of rights.[201] As for the scientific treatment of humans as merely natural objects, Husserl deems it has legitimacy only if we acknowledge that the naturizing of persons and psyche in science may allow us to recognize only certain relations of dependency of objective existence and continuity that obtain between the natural world of things (*naturalen Sachenwelt*) and the personal world of intellect (*personalen Geistern*). Yet, he also acknowledges it is intellect as the subjective counterpart to things that makes apprehension of and research into the surrounding world possible. The naturalistic psychology, which sees nature only in the sense of natural objects, is blind to the sphere of intellect and cognition, and so cannot see persons, cannot "see the objects that depend for their sense on personal accomplishments—that is, objects of 'culture.'"[202] In Husserl's judgment, even though the scientific naturizing of person does not ostensibly share the "injustice" (*Unrecht*) entailed in denying human beings personal ego on moral or juridical grounds, by regarding humans as merely sentient flesh, it arrives at the same result: sentient flesh has no inherent rights because it has no independence from the mechanical causality of the world of things, which excludes it from the universal order of sociality grounded in the transcendental principle of freedom.

Husserl's insistence on the essentially fundamental role of the personal ego in the constitution of the world was a way to get some grasp on the processes by which individuation with consciousness—meaning the delimitation of a primal singular subjectivity—is actualized as the person who is linked to the body without being causally determined *by* the body. Culture is the ideographic system of actualization in the comprehensive experience of the other as personal subject related to the things of the surrounding world in common with one's own personal-ego. "We dwell communally in an image [*ein Bild*] that we see [*das wir sehen*]," Husserl says, emphasizing: "We *are* in that relation in common to the environing-world [*Umwelt*], and we *are* in personal association [*personalen Verband*]."[203] The two belong together, such that we cannot be persons for others if a common environmental world could not be experienced for us in community, in an intentional linkage of transcendental intersubjectivity (*Transzendentale Intersubjektivität*). This is how we experience our embodied self as person in the phenomenological reduction.[204] Should we concur with Jean-François Lyotard, then this phenomenological reduction, like all modern (post-Cartesian) philosophical conceptions of experience, is modeled on the Christian idea of salvation.[205] And in that vein, Husserl's *Epoché* is quite recognizably a rite of redemption, in which the flesh is directed phenomenologically to the subjective deep-structure of intentional consciousness as being in a transcendental community of "co-subjectivity" (*Mitsubjektivität*). The fleshliness of sentience—or rather the ego-subject's flesh-entanglement with the body—is *seen* (*gesehen*) clearly, so that it can then be parenthesized (*einklammern*) to achieve the sphere of transcendental experience (*transzendentale Erfahrungssphäre*). In the clarity of the phenomenological reduction, the flesh is experienced as the corpuscularity of the animate body (*Leibkörper*), which is *merely* the bridge connecting the ego-subject to its world of things, providing a point of orientation—that thing *I* is in constant proximate relation to, but not *what* is—for the ego-subject, whose worldly actuality (*Umweltlichkeit*) is very much a function of the transcendental community of intersubjectivity. That is why the juridical and naturalistic scientific treatments of the human being as just a physical body—valued as a dispensable source of productive energy—in negating the constitutional efficacy of personal-ego, threaten the very grounds of community, of human society, by progressively eroding the distinction between human and nonhuman animals long held in the tradition of Western jurisprudence, dating back to classical Hellenic antiquity, according to which every nonhuman animal has always been regarded as a *legal thing* that can be disposed of for the sake of *legal persons*, which are, by definition, full human beings. And in so doing, they have precipitated the crisis of European science qua modernity that so concerned Husserl and that the phenomenological attitude sets out to alleviate.

It is telling, however, that Husserl's concern remains in the abstract, seeing the feared tendency in the logical formations of positivistic science—perhaps even beginning with Bacon's rebellion against Scholasticism—with no clear reference whatsoever to the historical juridical definition of human beings as such things, which, as has already been noted, becomes a fact of law insofar as the definition of *Negro* in the seventeenth century is concerned. The fact that Husserl's admonition against the juridical treatment of human beings as mere things is made under the topic "The Person in Personal Associations [Die Person im Personenverband]," in the context of "The Spiritual Constitution of the Cultural/Intellectual World [Die Konstitution der Geistigen Welt]," where he provides an exposition of the new psychology of phenomenology, makes all the more relevant its alluding in form, without regarding the historical paradigmatic, to the jurisprudence of modernity, in which the *thingification* of a specific class of humans has been instrumental to intellectual (anthropological) as well as material progress.[206] The abstraction permits a "philosophical" forgetfulness of just how fundamental the deracination of personhood is to the *constitution of* human society in modernity. That forgetfulness is instantiated and perpetuated in the phenomenological reduction's circumscription of the flesh.

Taking all this into account refocuses our *quaestio* of Spillers's *flesh/enslaved captive body* distinction. There is a discernable reverberation of Husserl's project in her effort to reimagine the question of community through exploring the relationship between fleshliness and persona. Only, rather than the animate body as the zero point of orientation for the ego-subject of transcendental community, the flesh is the zero degree of social conceptualization. Its not escaping concealment under iconography is something like its being parenthesized. But as such, it is always inescapably present "for us" *in relation to* the iconography: meaning it is in the system of signification where the value of any given sign in relation to its object is determined by how it is communally interpreted—in this case, it is *Negro* as the determinative sign of the captive enslaved body. Accordingly, as a semiological system, the myth of the Negro articulates all the forms of representation: the codes, conventions, and habits of language that produce specific fields of culturally and historically located meanings. The rift between flesh and body demarcates the distance between culture and its antechamber. Because the flesh does not escape the circuit of iconography as a material of signification, the rift is not a singular event or action, but is rather an ongoing processual activity through and in which individual consciousness gets presented in the order of things. We can say, then, that individual consciousness is a cognitive articulation of some process of sociality—in Spillers's phrasing, it is the private particular space where biological, sexual, social, cultural, linguistic, ritualistic, and psychological fortunes converge—which is what is meant by the eventfulness of consciousness, its quality of being historically situated in the world.

Turning back on this point to what precipitated our interrogating Spillers's exploration of the relationship between fleshliness and person, Windham's assertion "us is human flesh" instantiates this eventfulness, which is to say it evokes the processual nature of the entire order of things. In a remarkably straightforward way, he is simply stating in respect to flesh: "us *is* it." The copula here functions as a sign of equality rather than attribution, situating person in some relational schema *with* things. In Windham's assertion of liberty, "us" is not *in this flesh*. By that same token, the living person is not predicable of the thingness of flesh; "us" is not *a piece of flesh*, but rather "us" *is* flesh. Pace Hartman's reading of it, to the extent Windham's "us is human flesh" implicitly postulates an irreducible elemental level of existence, it is *flesh/person*. This bifurcation is not to be confused with the one Barthes makes of the mythical signifier as meaning/form, in which the meaning is stolen from a prior first-order semiological system. Nor is it altogether identical with Spillers's flesh/body, precisely because the copula places emphasis on the conjunctive, over and against the transitive function of the dividing line.

Both Barthes's and Spillers's analyses focus on the signifier as the instantiation of a primary theft of meaning, the palimpsestic formal overwriting of one semiological system by another, subsequent, semiological system. Whether capitalist slavery, colonial imperialism, or modernity, the second-order system expresses a determinant order of thought that is, as Barthes puts it in his analysis of myth, ideological as a matter of historical science. By that analysis, the triadic signifying process of sign-signifier-signified expresses a mythological/ideological order of things, the reality of which derives from two activities. One is the seamless identification of the signifying process with the conceptual schema—the mythic signifier is determined by the mythic concept. The other is the sign's "naturalization" so that the process in which it is articulated gets obfuscated, making it simply an expression of the way things innately are. As we've seen, Barthes seeks to demystify the concept by exposing the teleology of mythical signification, according to which form follows function: the concept of *le nègre* is the final cause, the purpose or end of the mythic semiological system. And that system, it turns out, is a formalist abstraction, the meaningfulness of which is predicated on being disarticulated from external referentiality. For all the stalwart effort to demystify the mythology of the Negro, in the end, Barthes acquiesces to his own interpretive complicity by positing "the fact of the Negro phenomenon [*le fait nègre*]" as the starting point of mythic pilferage. In other words, there is a failure of differentiation precisely at the point Barthes seeks to expose the mythic failure of differentiation. His semiological analysis reveals how "the petit-bourgeois myth of the Negro [*le mythe petit-bourgeois du Nègre*]" fails to differentiate between the sign, *Nègre*, and *le fait nègre*, between *Negro* and the Negro phenomenon, construing the sign as being continuous in space and time with the object functioning as its signified, taking both to belong to the same general category of the world. Yet, his ethnologist-inspired effort to demystify the myth does the very same thing by confusing the sign, *nègre*, with the phenomenal entity, *le fait*, it is supposed to signify. Indeed, given the etymology and history of the sign as a term of legitimate propriety—"le nègre est un meuble"—to posit there is such a thing as the Negro in any way other than as a mythical signifier serving a mythical concept obfuscates the conventionality of the semiology. It naturalizes the semiotic epistemology, putatively subsuming all being to the totality of one world, one cosmos, which is adequately grasped only in this one single semiological system. Even granting that any phenomenal "fact" is determined in relation to the intersubjective constitution of the cultural/intellectual world (*Geistigen Welt*), all other semiological systems, all other cosmologies lead to this one, are comprehended in this one. At minimum, these are effectively parenthesized, concealed under the iconography of this phenomenology—"Diouf" is concealed under "la biographie du nègre." We are returned with Barthes, then, to Husserl's *Epoché* and consequently still well within the ambit of Kant's solution to the metaphysical problematic of the ethical grounds of freedom: the transcendental ego, which he shows in the "Transcendental Deduction" to be no more than a logical inference necessary for bringing unity to our empirical apperception of things.[207] Such an ego-subject can be conceived only through the thoughts it permits, offering in this way a "perpetual circle," within which the pursuits of metaphysical as well as theological knowledge—the soul, the world, and God—continue to function as regulative principles or goals for thinking.[208] In a telling, albeit seemingly ironic low key, Barthes's *le fait nègre* evokes the Western epistemological tradition's underlying presumption (inclusive of the entire range of the humanistic as well as natural sciences) that the world and consciousness are distinct orders of being, which the full force of philosophical/scientific thought must contrive to reunite—a way of thinking Maurice Merleau-Ponty once aptly characterized as "pensées de survol [fly-over surveying thought]."[209] Along this line of thinking, it is only within the purview of a particular subject-of-knowledge capable of seeing things that meaning is affixed to them, that their significance as things is determined *in being seen*. So, irony notwithstanding, the pertinent question in Barthes's semiological analysis is: What does *Negro* mean as a sign in our mythology *for us*? All in all, the conceptual orientation of this question is toward understanding the meaning of *Negro* as the sign of something external, some phenomenal corporeality to which we—and whoever "we" are, it is not, cannot be Negro—are in some relation that tests our ethical, anthropological, and even epistemic propositions. One cannot help but to wonder, if the lion could speak, would we be able to understand?[210] For that matter, why should it be presumed that "we" refers to all *humans*?

Windham's "us is human flesh" troubles this orientation in a way that cannot be easily dismissed. Rather than giving temporal primacy to flesh as the stolen sign, Windham's statement presumes that meaning and form are expressed spontaneously: the flesh is *with* and not *before* the body and person, and the body and person are *with* and not *before* or even *after* the flesh. Windham's person *is* in relation to his generally perceived fleshly thingness. It is not a representation of substance *for* some mind that, extricating it from the vagueness of things (the noumenality of being) through the transcendental activity of cogitation, might claim to *see* it. Neither is Windham's personal consciousness the expression of such transcendentality, parenthesizing the flesh so that the body can be experienced as the bridge connecting agential intellectuality and the world of physical things in communion with other embodied persons constituting the community of transcendental intersubjectivity in what is supposed to be the world of rights. The point is that Windham's person is inextricably *of* the flesh, lives life *as* flesh. The flesh about which Windham speaks is material, but it is not embodied, in the sense of corpuscles that combine to form a discrete entity. This flesh is not a fact or sum of facts. This flesh is not consecrated, nor could it ever have been consecrated. The long history of its consumption is not sacrificial, nor is it purely capitalistic. Douglass's distinction between devouring hard earnings and feeding on flesh catches the issue quite rightly. Returning, for a moment, to the legislated definition of *Negro* as alienable capital asset (*le nègre être meubles*)—the definition is somewhat scholastic; that is to say, it is a universal statement of species (*eidos*) essence, according to which being alienable capital asset is what differentiates Negro from other species in the genus *Homo*. This is the *differentia* because, even though the accident of color is initially associated with propertiness, it is a separable accident: *Negro* is not necessarily black. Propertiness is the defining essence of the species, *Negro*, which is predicable of individual hominids, differentiating them from other hominids regardless of any morphological resemblance. The hominid form may very well be necessarily predicable of *Man*—all men have bodies—but *Man* is not necessarily predicable of the individual hominid form—not all hominids are men. The force of necessity resides in the legal fiction: that hominid form to which the predicate propertiness is enforceable is designated *Negro*. Enforcing that predication is the gist of the clause Locke drafted in the 1669 *Fundamental Constitution of the Carolinas*, which stipulates: "Every Freedman of the Carolinas has absolute power and authority over his negro slaves, of what opinion or religion whatsoever." Once *Negro* is predicated on any hominid body, that body with all its inherent mental and physical capacities becomes a Negro body and is owned fully by its proprietor. Said proprietor also owns any use-value engendered or produced therewith, the commodification of which results in revenue (Douglass's "earnings") that is consumable by definition, leaving the body, a capital asset, to continue producing more over an extended time: a lifetime. The flesh of that same body, however, as a legal property of unfettered access, is the object of unbounded desire—the flesh of the slave is as much one's as is one's own flesh, there being no personal other associated with it who is necessarily recognized as having superior prerogative. *This is the gist of Husserl's objection to the juridical treatment of human beings as things: it undermines the person of intersubjectivity, which is to say, it ultimately interferes with the actuality of human community.*

Feeding on the flesh has no capital use-value. Whether done through sexual violence where the flesh feeds carnal desire as elemental, or through physical torture when pieces of flesh are cut away and discarded, cooked, or branded, or when such flesh is fed to dogs, worms, or even other human beings, the act of consumption belongs to a condition of pleasure that is fueled by and sustains structures of desire and imagination epiphenomenal to the capitalist economics of slavery. "Whipping darkies was the joy of the white man back in those days," an ex-slave told Ophelia Settle Egypt of Fisk University in a 1929 interview.[211] Such enjoyment was inseparable from the expenditure and ravishment of the flesh, to paraphrase Hartman.[212] For all the homiletic aspect and forced communion of Lilburn Lewis's butchering of George as a putative disciplining of the flesh, its driving force was expressly the pleasure derived from the consumption of flesh—an enjoyment greater than any dance ball. No redemption or salvation, just sheer delight in the consumption, which Abolitionists such as Child and Weld abhorred and denounced as non-Christian and corrosive to the moral and social fabric of the republic. What was less apprehensible to them was how the scale of the quotidian enactments of violence against the Negro body was a practical actualization of the underlying speculative epistemology of modernity, which operates on the basis of its presumptive capacity to assimilate everything, all existence, to its structures: Hegel's infinite metabolism of "recollection."

[2ND SET]

Sentient Flesh Dancing

Juba and the Buzzard Lope Play

As if in direct rebuttal to Lewis's finding greater pleasure in consuming Negro flesh than dancing, the slaves contested the actualization of that structure of pleasure in the very dances, or "frolics," as they were called, encouraged, by Douglass's account, on the Christmas through New Year holiday. He describes, in example of this contestation, what he calls "jubilee beating."[1] More generally known as "Juba beating," or "pattin' Juba," this was the practice of performing complicated polyrhythmic beats—most often 3-over-4—by simultaneously stomping the feet, hand-clapping, and slapping various parts of the body in musical accompaniment to the Juba dance, the polycentric movements of which respond to the patting rhythms.[2] Along with the beating, the performer, the "'Juba' beater," in Douglass's words, improvised sung rhymes with satirical jabs at the cruelty of slaveholders, with lines like: "You fry your meat. You give me the skin. And that's where mama's trouble begin."[3] Expressed jeremiad against "the palpable injustice and fraud of slavery" notwithstanding, Douglass assessed this dancing as carnivalesque, hence among the most effective means of suppressing insurrection by "authorizing" regular symbolic actions of resistance. We know from numerous other sources that these dances were held more frequently than just the holidays and were regular plantation events on Saturday nights and Sundays throughout the South. Henry Bibb, for instance, in his 1849 *Narrative*, refers to "pat juber" as one of the regular Sabbath day entertainments among slaves.⁴ Although not expressly concurring with Douglass's assessment of it being, in tandem with dancing, an instrumentality of oppression through directing potentially insurrectionist energies of imagination into diffusive symbolic action, Bibb thought it a singularly non-Christian form, practiced among those "who make no profession of religion," who do it out of ignorance of Scripture and so "want of moral education."⁵ The implication in both Douglass's and Bibb's assessments is that pattin' Juba and the Juba dance are expressions of an "African" symbolic order. Douglass signals this somewhat more than Bibb when, in the course of characterizing the frolics as conductors or safety valves used by the slaveholders to stave off the insurrectionary energies engendered by the cruelty of the system, he states: "It is plain, that everything like rational enjoyment among the slaves, is frowned upon; and only those wild and low sports, peculiar to semi-civilized people, are encouraged. All license allowed, appears to have no other object than to disgust the slaves with their temporary freedom."⁶ Douglass includes "jubilee beating" among the licentious act of this fraudulent liberty. Then again, the slaves' taking enjoyment from their own flesh by rhythmically beating it for entertainment during holidays from work was, as Hartman recognizes, the enactment of their "counterinvestment in the body as a site of pleasure and the articulation of needs and desires."⁷ Juba beating and dancing are indeed contradictory, in the sense that they operate a discourse of being-in-common contesting with the depersonalizing practices of slavery. In other words, the contestation of the flesh is between two distinct performative activities of signification. We are speaking here of signs and, in this context of beating the flesh, of sonic signs. The sounds made by striking the flesh signify something within some system of meaning. The crack of the whip on contact with the flesh, the thud made with the club and iron rod, producing the sound of shattering bone, the screams of anguish at the contact—all the noises made in violently assaulting the flesh are meaningful as signs, for the ear capable of hearing, that the system of slavery is working in proper time, disciplining the flesh into the body of propriety, into a fungible commodity producing consumable use-value. The hieroglyphs of the flesh are the score of these sounds, making them visible signs—for the eye capable of interpreting (reading) them as such—standing in relation to the sounds of at-slavery-work. In contradistinction, the sounds made by beating the flesh in pattin' Juba, extrapolating from slavery's work-time its own rhythms of pleasure, are meaningful signs, once again, for the ear capable of hearing, that a system contradictory and appositional to slavery is working *with* the flesh to express a body in free-play. Here, the flesh is beaten to produce the polyrhythmic flesh-sonics of Juba, which stand in isomorphic relation to the polycentric body-movement of Juba dance.

Were we to again put this in Husserl's phenomenological terms—something warranted perhaps by Hartman's characterization of practices like Juba as counterinvestments in the body as a site of pleasure, taking up and pushing the phenomenological reverberations in Spillers's work—there are two contesting operations of signification-conferring (*Bedeutungsleistungen*), expressing two distinct predications of value. In one, flesh is a fungible asset (*meuble*) that, like the land in Marx's "Trinity Formula," takes part as an agent in the production of use-value to be disposed of at its owner's discretion according to laws of property.[8] In another, flesh is human, to be enjoyed in and of itself in communion. Husserl called such predications of value "predicates of significance" and construed them to be of a hybrid nature inseparable from the crucial subjective psychological activity of conferring, which, whether undertaken individually or communally (intersubjectively), is transcendental in its articulations from external referentiality (the physical objects of nature) upon which it confers significance. The active subjectivity, especially in its intersubjective mode, constitutes the environmental world. It is a systemic apprehension of the world. In this respect, something is meaningful in relation to someone who determines it is significant. Even if we grant that this pertains to the two operations of slavery, disciplining the flesh and pattin' Juba, this is not an adequate account of what they do. True, in each operation, the crucial element is interpretation—something is meaningful in relation to somebody who hears or sees it in some way; but even the interpretant *I* is a function of the operation of signification-conferring, which, rather than being a product of phenomenological reduction, disarticulated from external referentiality (nature), is indissolubly engaged in things. The slaveholder wielding the whip, or burning tongs, or club, or rapacious physical force cannot transcend the flesh, which is why he must ingest it. And the slave has no desire to escape the flesh but wants to avoid its being digested. Instead of insight into a realm of the activity of transcendental intersubjectivity constituting the surrounding world, we get a profoundly material operation of significance-conferring, in which externality and interiority are constitutively inseparable. It is quite seeming, then, to refer to these operations as *semiosis*, in keeping with Charles Sanders Peirce's semiotic theory, emphasizing that they are interpretive operations of representation of reality that cannot be disarticulated from things. In other words, the ego-subject's flesh-entanglement with the body is not parenthesized in order to encounter "the real constitution of lived experience."

From here, Hartman's characterization of slave practices like juba beating as counterinvestments in the body as a site of pleasure is not so phenomenological after all, but about the semiosis of the flesh. There is neither slavery nor juba without the flesh. The difference being that, in disciplining the flesh, slavery seeks to denigrate its sentience and through the efficacy of law make it an elemental of the hominid body, which is placed in the modern taxonomy of being as primarily if not merely animal and thereby making the flesh legitimately available for consumption in labor and pathological pleasure. In contrast, juba beating the flesh expresses and enhances sentience, without denying the animal, moving in time, in contradistinction to standing as the zero degree from which space and time unfold. Time is not something *I*, Husserl's transcendental ego-subject, imposes on the fluid chaos of existence; but the ego is given by time, and so is an effect or function of the world as horizon. And the latter is historical, which is to say, actualized in the cumulative species activity of mimesis: we make the world, but do so as one of the actualizing forces (in Aristotle's sense of ἐνέργεια, *enérgeia*) on earth in *community* (in Kant's sense of activity in reciprocity, but without his regulating heteronomy) in time. Underlying Husserl's construal of culture as signification-conferring structures (*Gebilde bedeuntungverleihender*), as the process of subjectification of the world, is the problematic of animality and humanity. Still adhering to the line of thought laid out by Aristotle, the question for Husserl is: How do we pass from natural existence to symbolic being, from animality to humanity? Much like Kant's concept of culture as breeding (*Zucht*) the human from out of sentient animal flesh, Husserl's signification-conferring structures provide an intervention between natural animality and symbolizing humanity, thereby enabling the zoological *Homo sapiens* to form his supplementary anthropological symbolic order. In order for *Man* to become apparent as such, however, there needs to be posited that which may have the potential of becoming *Man* but is not quite yet there, that which has not fully subjugated animality. Such a being is how Aristotle construes the barbarian and modern philosophy, beginning with Kant and more emphatically and systematically elaborated by Hegel, construed the Negro. Just as the archive abounds with accounts of slaveholders consuming Negro flesh, it is also replete with accounts of the slaves having engaged this problematic on a regular basis in dance and song. A particular dance, the Buzzard Lope, involving pattin' the flesh with vocal accompaniment has particular pertinence here.

The earliest ethnological record of the Buzzard Lope is from the Georgia Sea Islands in Lydia Austin Parrish's 1942 book, *Slave Songs of the Georgia Sea Islands*.⁹ Parrish was an extraordinarily assiduous collector of Negro song specimen, whose collection falls well within the spectrum of taxonomic folklorist archiving undertaken by Lucy McKim, William Francis Allen, and Charles P. Ware in *Slave Songs of the United States*, a work Parrish made good use of while eschewing its designator "spirituals." She concurred with Allen's assessment of the secular "worldly" songs as most authentically Negro and took up, as did John Avery Lomax, his desire that someone should collect them. Her focus was on antebellum specimens she categorized as "Ring-Play, Dance, and Fiddle Songs," including the Buzzard Lope song. She sought to distinguish such ring-play from the religious ring-dance performed by African slaves in the West

Indies and the United States, in churches or praise houses, the participants moving in a circle counterclockwise, shuffling and stomping their feet, clapping and pattin'. Formally, this is a distinction without a difference, however. In fact, the Gullah-speakers of the Georgia Sea Islanders, among whom Parrish did her field work, are reported to have referred to the Buzzard Lope in Gullah as a *shout*.[10] Their referring to the Buzzard Lope as a shout is made all the more significant by Parrish's citation of the linguist Lorenzo Turner's tracing the Gullah word back to the Arabic etymon, شَوْط (*šauṭ*), referring to the counterclockwise circumambulation around the Kaaba that is part of the Hajj, the annual pilgrimage to Mecca.[11] Given this etymology, according to which the term has a primarily religious connotation (the circling of the Ka'aba during Hajj) and the apparent syncretic employment of it to Christian worship ritual among African slaves, the Sea Islanders' using it to denote an expressly worldly or secular performance is of no small moment. It suggests a fluid dynamic understanding of the correspondence between formal performance and being that is not readily reducible to a theological order. This is made all the more evident by the shout's performative identification with the animal, not by anthropomorphizing but by mimicking, by bodily assimilating animal movement. The animal being mimicked is, in fact, the vulture; the word "buzzard" refers in North America to the species *Cathartes aura*, idiomatically known as "turkey vulture." At the center of the shout ring, a solo dancer mimics the movements of a buzzard loping around an object in the center of the circle, usually a handkerchief, representing carrion.

Parrish was profoundly struck by the peculiarities of the Buzzard Lope's technique of mimicry. She regularly consulted the anthropologist Melville Herskovits for conceptual, if not methodological guidance to ensure the ethnological soundness of her field work among the Sea Islanders and thereby its reception as an authentic collection of African American folk music.[12] That collection began in earnest in 1912 when Parrish started spending the winter months on St. Simons, where she gathered the bulk of her material. She claims to have first learned in 1915 "that such a dance as the Buzzard Lope could be found in the neighborhood of St. Simons."[13] Yet, during years of asking to see it performed there, she was constantly told by "Negroes of that section . . . it was done on some far-off island such as St. Catherine's or Sapelo." Finally, in 1927, she was surprised to discover that Julia—the woman who had been in her service since 1912, first as her laundress between 1912 and 1914 and then as her cook from 1915—could do it "to perfection."[14]

Like her predecessor collectors McKim and Allen, Parrish grappled with the inadequacy of received musical notation to interpret the Negro's traditional music. In addition to the notorious impossibility of transcribing complex polyrhythm performed by pattin', foot-shuffling, and stomping, there is the difficulty of representing the performative choreography. So what she is reduced to collecting as representative specimen is the transcription of the Buzzard Lope's accompanying song along with a compromised notation. Also in suit with McKim's and Allen's bifurcating taxonomy, according to which those aspects of Negro music that are not readily subsumable to familiar European qua Christian forms are deemed to be residual Africanisms, as well as her own assessment of New World Negro forms as constitutively syncretic, Parrish describes the Buzzard Lope song as "an old religious song with narrative lines of a suitable character."[15] She names the song "Throw Me Anywhere," after one of its refrains and transcribes it as follows:

Throw me anywhere
    In that ole field
Throw me anywhere, Lord
    In that ole field
Throw me anywhere
    In that ole field
Throw me anywhere, Lord
    In that ole field
Members, you want to die, Lord
    In that ole field
Members, you want to die, Lord
    In that ole field
Members, you want to die, Lord
    In that ole field
Members, you want to die, Lord
    In that ole field[16]

Besides the already acknowledged difficulty of representing the Buzzard Lope's performative choreography on the page, there are some issues with the song Parrish transcribes. To start with, the lyrics she provides do not jibe with any of the numerous recorded performances of the Buzzard Lope. They do, however, echo those of "a lonesome melody" she heard sung by a woman she identifies as Susyanna, who learned it from her ex-slave grandmother, which Parrish characteristically names on the basis of its refrain, "In that old Field":

Throw me any way
    In dhat ole fiel'
Throw me any way
    In dhat ole fiel'.
In don' care whah you throw me
    In dhat ole fiel'

In don' care whah you throw me
In dhat ole fiel'.
Throw me ova hills an' mountains
In dhat ole fiel'
Throw me ova hills an' mountains
In dhat ole fiel'.
Sometimes I'm up sometimes I'm down
In dhat ole fiel'
But still my soul is heaven boun'
In dhat ole fiel'
Throw my mother out a doo's
In dhat ole fiel'.
Throw my mother out a doo's
In dhat ole fiel'.

The two songs transcribed by Parrish could be accounted for as versions on a theme, iterated in the recurrent refrain: "Throw me anywhere / In that ole field." In the version she titles after the refrain's first clause, "Throw me anywhere," and attributes to the Buzzard Lope dance—let us call this version A—that full refrain repeated in sequence makes up the first four of the song's eight lines. In the song she labels after the second clause, transliterated as "In that Old Field"—let us call this version B—the variant of the first clause, "Throw me any way," occurs only in the first two of nine lines, while the second clause is repeated in every line. The verb "throw," however, occurs in all but the fourth and third to the last lines, for a total of eight times, five of which entail the phrase "throw me." The overt Christian aspect of both Parrish's transcribed versions is minimalist. Version A has one line, repeated thrice, "Members, you want to die, Lord," which so elliptically alludes to the church that Parrish felt the need to add an extra-diegetic footnote of commentary explaining that "members" refers to deacons, preachers, brothers, sisters, and, strangely enough, mother. The reference to mother, of course, is a link she draws to version B, where the line "Throw my mother out a doo's" is repeated twice. That version, however, is even more minimal in its religiosity, with only one line without repetition, "But still my soul is heaven boun'," which could arguably be taken as a Christian reference. As thin a thread as these may be, they were enough to serve as the woof for Parrish's description of the Buzzard Lope song as an old religious song, the wrap of which was her unwavering certainty of the "remarkable musical gifts and deeply religious nature of the African slave," without which "there would be no soul-stirring sacred songs."[17]

In her assiduous effort to collect and preserve the most authentic specimens of these Negro songs, Parrish attempts to augment what is recorded of the musical performances in transcription as well as musical notation with photographs of dance performances, along with narrative descriptions. In the case of the Buzzard Lope, there are no photos complementing Parrish's transcription of the song "Throw Me Anywhere." But there is a brief narrative description of the dance performance, prompted by her encountering the Johnson family on Sapelo Island: "Of the twins, Naomi did the patting while Isaac did the dancing; and older brother rhythmically called out the cues in a sharp staccato, and another one lay on the floor in the wide veranda representing a dead cow."[18] In addendum to this description, she reports an exegesis of the symbolism of the dance's choreography apparently provided by one of the Johnson family dancers. Labeling the exegesis "directions" with parenthetical asides to help her understand and keep track, she is sufficiently taken aback by it to remark, "anyone who has seen turkey buzzards disposing of 'carr'on' will recognize [its] aptness," and to advise that "those who are at all squeamish had better skip this part."[19]

March aroun'! (the cow)
Jump across! (see if she's dead)
Get the eyes! (always go for that first)
So glad! (cow daid)
Get the guts! (they like 'em next best)
Go to eatin! (on the meat)
All right!—cow mos' gone!
Dog comin'
Scare the dog!
Look around' for mo' meat!
All right!—Belly full!
—"Goin' to tell the res.'"[20]

Aside from the warning, the only other remark Parrish makes directed at the Johnsons' exegesis is, "And with an eye to the dramatic exit, Isaac danced into the house." Both sets of remarks effectively mitigate the full significance of the exegesis, achieving a distancing from it. Having also characterized their performance of the Buzzard Lope as "a combination of the old dance form with rather more modern steps than the original African pantomime warranted," she adds the following footnote as if to enhance the aura of authenticity:

> In later years I saw the Buzzard Lope done by Isaac's teacher, Reuben Grovenor—a descendant of the Sapelo Bilali [Ben Ali], who wrote a "dairy" in Arabic. Many times have I seen others do this peculiar dance, but Reuben's performance is far and away the most finished. With effortless grace, he gives a stylized pattern of the bird's awkward steps, without any attempt

at realism. His is indeed a high form of rhythmic approximation, and those who have seen it at the Cabin are fortunate.[21]

Invoking a direct genealogical connection of Isaac Johnson's dancing to Bilali is in keeping with Parrish's grasp of Herskovits's theory of African survivals, as well as her acute interest in the Islamic elements at play in the Sea Island's forms. It enables her to definitively pronounce the shout's mimicry of the buzzard to be of African provenance.

One of the chief reasons she began corresponding with Herskovits in the first place was his 1934 work, *Rebel Destiny*, in which he describes a Kromanti obia dance performed by the Ashanti-descendants in Dutch Guiana to Opete—the Akan term for the vulture spirit, the sacred messenger who carries sacrifice to the home of the spirits—bearing some resemblance to the Buzzard Lope: "Those who danced for the buzzard had no machetes, but went about in a circle, moving with bodies bent forward from their waists and with arms thrown back in Imitation of the bird from which their spirit took its name."[22] There is also a resemblance between the Buzzard Lope and the dance of the Dahomey dedicated to Suvinenge—the earth spirit with a vulture's body and bald human head, who, besides carrying messages from the earth pantheon, Sagbata, to that of the sky, Mawu-Lisa, also carries sacrifice to its intended recipient. This resemblance in performance is given further pertinence by the Johnsons' exegesis of the Buzzard Lope symbolism, to which can be added that of Peter Davis, who was another of its well-known performers recognized by Parrish in her acknowledgments:

> Well, that's the way they [the slaves] feel, you see—according to how they were treated, you understand me. They said they were nothing but old dead carrion that they would throw away in woods someplace; and then the buzzard would come around, you know, and pick off the carrion. The angel was the buzzard that come pick up the soul out of the old dead carrion.[23]

Both the Johnsons' and Davis's exegeses accord with the function of Opete and Suvinenge as carriers of sacrifice. It is no small matter, in that regard, that for the same New World Akan in Dutch Guiana, Opete "took one of their warrior ancestors away from slavery across the river into the bush."[24] So too, the fact that Suvinenge takes the sacrificial offerings—the vulture's having eaten the carrion—is a sign of the prayer having been accepted. Discerning the similarities in performance and symbolism between Buzzard Lope, per Parrish's description, and these other dances led Herskovits to surmise it to be a New World iteration of the *voudun* cults. A surmise Parrish is quick to take up because it accords with her investment in preserving archaic Africanism, as well as her own assessment of the Buzzard Lope's syncretic nature: that it was a non-Christian performance "done for fun." This assessment, however, is an effect of prioritizing the collector's experience, which, as we pointed out regarding McKim's and Allen's work, is the true mimetic object, the true specimen being collected. This is evident in Parrish's skipping over the full significance of the Johnsons' exegesis as too vivid and dramatic. To be fair, in Parrish's case, as well as that of McKim and Allen, the underlying problematic is inherent to the media and modality of positivist mimesis: the attempt to transcribe experience in writing. Lomax's effort to get around that problematic with phonographic recording of in situ performance may have expanded the aesthetic spectrum of representation to include sound in action, but it still left intact the question of experience.

Turning to the phonographic record of the Buzzard Lope, the first known audio recording was made by Lomax's youngest son, Alan, on October 7, 1959. Alan Lomax had already been to St. Simons in 1935 as a twenty-year-old young man on a sound expedition for the Library of Congress, accompanying the more experienced anthropologist and folklorist Zora Neale Hurston, along with Mary Elizabeth Barnicle. Hurston, who studied with Franz Boas as well as Herskovits at Barnard College, was already an established anthropologist, having just completed her seminal collection of Negro folklore, *Mules and Men*. Racial and gender politics demanded, however, that Lomax be the official leader of the expedition. As an expedient to collecting, Parrish embraced the practice long established among the island's plantation owners of sponsoring the singing societies their black tenants would form among themselves, in order to help restore the prestige slave songs once enjoyed as genuine Negro music, which she considered "confronted by a real menace in the scornful attitude of those Negro school-teachers who do their utmost to discredit and uproot every trace of it."[25] With this attitude of preservationist dispensation, she began sponsoring the Spiritual Singers Society of Coastal Georgia in 1920. It was Hurston's prior familiarity with Parrish and the native St. Simons islanders that provided Lomax access to the Spiritual Singers Society of Coastal Georgia, which Bessie Jones had already joined just two years earlier in 1933. The 1935 Hurston, Lomax, and Barnicle expedition yielded recordings of several dozen performances of the Singers' sacred material, yet they did not record the Buzzard Lope or any other "worldly" music Parrish was striving so hard to collect for archiving.

Lomax had returned to St. Simons in 1959 as part of his year-long sound expedition making stereo recordings of black and white performers across the South in order to preserve what he regarded as the original American musical expression. To that purpose, he sought out the Spiritual Singers Society he'd recorded twenty-four-years earlier and was pleased to find the founding core members—Emma Ramsey, Henry Morrison, John and Peter Davis, Joe Armstrong—along with Bessie Jones still performing. The expedition recordings were released in

1960 by Prestige Record in the twelve-volume LP album set, *Southern Journey*, the first two of which, *Georgia Sea Islands, Vol. I*, and *Georgia Sea Islands, Vol. II*, contained the recordings done on St. Simons. The first track on the B-side of Volume II is Lomax's recording of the Singers performing the Buzzard Lope, led by Bessie Jones. The track is entitled "Buzzard Lope." There is more at stake than merely a difference in title between the song Parrish transcribes and the one Lomax records. At stake is the way Buzzard Lope gets entered into the archives of African American folklore and how it gets enshrined there as the earliest-known, or at least earliest-recorded specimen of archaic Negro music. We can begin to get a sense of that process by contrasting the full transcription of the song from the recorded 1959 performance with Parrish's:

>   *Throw me anywhere, Lord.*
>   *In that ole field.*
>   *Throw me anywhere, Lord.*
>   *In that ole field.*
>
>   *Don't care where you throw me.*
>   *In that ole field.*
>   *Since King Jesus own me.*
>   *In that ole field.*
>
>   *Throw me anywhere, Lord.*
>   *In that ole field.*
>   *Throw me anywhere, Lord.*
>   *In that ole field.*
>
>   *You may beat and bang me*
>   *In that ole field.*
>   *Since King Jesus saves me*
>   *In that ole field.*
>
>   *Throw me anywhere, Lord.*
>   *In that ole field.*
>   *Throw me anywhere, Lord.*
>   *In that ole field.*
>
>   *Don't care how you treat me.*
>   *In that ole field.*
>   *Since King Jesus meet me.*
>   *In that ole field.*
>
>   *Don't care how you do me.*
>   *In that ole field.*

Since King Jesus choose me.
In that ole field.

Throw me anywhere, Lord.
In that ole field.
Throw me anywhere, Lord.
In that ole field.

Throw me anywhere, Lord.
In that ole field.
Throw me anywhere, Lord.
In that ole field.

Throw me anywhere, Lord.
In that ole field.
Throw me anywhere, Lord.
In that ole field.

Don't care where you throw me.
In that ole field.
Since King Jesus own me.
In that ole field.

Don't care how you treat me.
In that ole field.
Since King Jesus meet me.
In that ole field.

Don't care how you do me.
In that ole field.
Since King Jesus choose me.
In that ole field.

This song shares the repeated refrain, "Throw me anywhere / In that ole field," with the two transcribed by Parrish; and can arguably be regarded as combining elements of both into a variation with more explicit and frequent Christian reference. The refrain, "Since King Jesus," occurs in seven out of the thirteen stanzas, and is given four verbal aspects: "own," "saves," "choose," and "meet." Yet, while it can obviously be taken as alluding to the Gospel of Matthew, given the expressly non-Christian context of the Buzzard Lope—it is for "fun" or worldly—as well as the reverberations in it of Opete and Suvinenge, it could just as well be an allusion to the Buzzard itself as king of the birds, Fene-Ma-So, carrying the sacrifice home. Indeed, Jesus could well be identified with Lisa in the Dahomean pantheon, per Herskovits's citing Henri Labouret and Paul Rivet's claim that in the Capuchin monks' 1658 translation of *Doctrina Christiana* into Fon, Mawu (the creator goddess) was employed for the Christian God, and Lisa (her brother-consort) as equivalent to Jesus.[26] Lomax, in his liner notes to the Prestige release, however, focuses on the Buzzard Lope's authenticity as an archaic African form still performed on the Georgia Sea Islands. His investment in that proposition led him to return to St. Simons in 1960, looking for musicians who could perform such authentic Negro music for a film, *Music of Williamsburg*, being directed by Sidney Meyers in Williamsburg, Virginia, on colonial era music. As one of the film's two musical directors, Lomax was responsible for coordinating the performances of traditional popular music of the era. In that capacity, he recruited musicians from across the southeastern United States in order to reconstruct the sort of musical performance that might have occurred in colonial Williamsburg. Those he gathered together included the Mississippian flutist Ed Young, who played the slave-era fife; the Bahamian drummer Nathaniel Rahmings, who played the one-headed drum once used on St. Simons and still played in the Bahamas; and playing a reconstruction of the four-string fretless African banjo was the legendary southwest Virginia mountain banjoist Hobart Smith, who learned his double-noting style of banjoing as a youngster from John Greer, who in turn learned it from the black banjoist Henry Hays of Laurel Fork, Virginia.[27] After the filming was completed on April 27, 1960, the musicians stayed on an extra day so Lomax could record the Spiritual Singers performing with the slavery-era instrumental accompaniment. During this session, they performed the Buzzard Lope, led this time by John Davis. The recording of this performance was subsequently included on *The Alan Lomax Collection: Southern Journey, Vol. 13—Earliest Times*, released by Rounder Records in 1998. Running five minutes and twenty-two seconds, the Davis-led version is considerably longer than the earlier recorded Jones-led performance, which ran one minute forty-seven. The difference between the Davis-led performance and that of Jones was not just due to the fact it had instrumental accompaniment, while hers was *accompanied throughout by polyrhythmic pattin'. There is also an overall* affective difference between Davis's shout and Jones's singing that is *discernable even in transcription*:

> *Throw my body anywhere*
> *In that ole field.*
> *Throw my body anywhere*
> *In that ole field.*
>
> *Throw my body anywhere*
> *Lord, in that ole field.*
> *Throw my body anywhere*
> *Lord, in that ole field.*

Don't care where you throw me.
Lord, in that ole field.
Don't care where you throw me.
Lord, in that ole field.

Throw *my body* anywhere
Lord, in that ole field.
Throw *my body anywhere*
Lord, in that ole field.

Throw *my body* anywhere
Lord, in that ole field.
Throw *my body anywhere*
Lord, in that ole field.

So long Jesus love me.
Lord, in that ole field.
So long Jesus love me.
Lord, in that ole field.

Throw my body anywhere
Lord, in that ole field.
Throw my body anywhere
Lord, in that ole field.

Throw *my body* anywhere
Lord, in that ole field.
Throw my body anywhere
Lord, in that ole field.

Don't care where you throw me.
Lord, in that ole field.
Don't care where you throw me.
Lord, in that ole field.

So *long Jesus love* me.
Lord, in that ole field.
So long Jesus love me.
Lord, in that ole field.

Throw *my body* anywhere
Lord, in that ole field.
Throw *my body* anywhere
Lord, in that ole field.

Throw *my body* anywhere
Lord, in that ole field.
Throw *my body anywhere*
Lord, in that ole field.

Don't care where you throw me.
Lord, in that ole field.
Don't care where you throw me.
Lord, in that ole field.

So long Jesus love me.
Lord, in that ole field.
So long Jesus love me.
Lord, in that ole field.

Throw my body anywhere
in that ole field.
Throw my body anywhere
Lord, in that ole field.

Throw my body anywhere   [crescendo musical instrumentation
   and
Lord, in that ole field.   decrescendo singing for next 9 stanzas]
Don't care where you throw me.
Lord, in that ole field.

Don't care where you throw me.
Lord, in that ole field.
Don't *care where you throw me.*
Lord, in that ole field.

Don't care where you throw *me.*
Lord, in that ole field.
Throw *my body anywhere*
Lord, in that ole field.

So long Jesus love me.
Lord, in that ole field.
So long Jesus love me.
Lord, in that ole field.

Throw my body anywhere
Lord, in that ole field.
Throw my body anywhere
Lord, in that ole field.

Throw *my body* anywhere
Lord, in that ole field.
Throw my body anywhere
Lord, in that ole field

So *long Jesus love* me.
Lord, in that ole field.
Don't care where you throw me.
Lord, in that ole field.

Throw my body anywhere
Lord, in that ole field.
Throw my body anywhere
Lord, in that ole field.

Throw my body anywhere
In that ole field.
Throw my body anywhere
In that ole field

[28 second fife, drum, and banjo instrumental break]

Throw me anywhere Lord.
in that ole field.
Throw me anywhere Lord
Lord, in that ole field

Throw *my body* anywhere
Lord, in that ole field.
Throw my body anywhere
Lord, in that ole field

Don't care where you throw me.
Lord, in that ole field.
So long Jesus love me.
Lord, in that ole field.

Throw my body anywhere
Lord, in that ole field.
Throw my body anywhere
Lord, in that ole field

Throw my body anywhere
Lord, in that ole field.
Throw my body anywhere

> *Lord, in that ole field*
> *[28 second fife, drum and banjo instrumental finale,*
> *with fortissimo fife]*

This Davis-led version is as minimalist in its Christian aspect as the version Parrish transcribed, having only one line, "So long Jesus love me," repeated in five out of thirty stanzas. Granted, the emphatic contrast between "*Throw* my body *anywhere*" and "*So* long Jesus love *me*" suggests that between body and soul. Nevertheless, the far more repeated emphasis on *throw* and *anywhere* accords with John's brother Peter's exegesis of the Buzzard Lope as a coded jeremiad condemning slavery's unsanctified consumption of flesh. In 1977, New World Records released *Georgia Sea Island Songs*, which would become a crucial document in the study of African survivals in American Negro music. In compiling the album, Lomax assembled a selection of performances by different configurations of the Spiritual Singers, which he labeled Group A, for the recording made on the 1959 expedition; Group B for those made on his 1960 recruitment trip for the Williamsburg film; and Group C for those recorded during the post-filming session. The preponderance of performance featured on the album are by Group A: all eight of the spirituals on side 1, and five of the nine secular songs on side 2, including the Buzzard Lope. Of the remaining four secular songs, two are of Group B, and two of Group C. The reason for this distribution can be accounted for in terms of Lomax's commitment to two fundamental ideas, both of which derive from Herskovits's conception of African survivals. As can be gleaned from his liner notes to *Georgia Sea Island Songs*, Lomax, like Herskovits and Parrish, whom he cites, presumes the syncretism of New World Negro religiosity, particularly the combination of residual *voudun* cults with Christianity. The second fundamental idea is a necessary corollary: the authenticity of Africanism must be determined. In the case of the songs of the Spiritual Singers Society of the Georgia Islands, he credits Parrish with having so determined. The imperative for authenticity drives the investment in the Georgia Sea Islands as being sufficiently remote to ensure uncontaminated continuation of African practices. This has considerable bearing on how Lomax recalls the post-film Williamsburg session in his liner notes:

> After the picture was shot, members of its folk-music cast stayed on for an extra day, and the islanders had the opportunity to sing with the sort of accompaniment the slaves sometimes had—a cane fife, a one-headed drum of the type still used in the Bahamas, and a reconstructed fretless, bowl-shaped "slave" banjo, played with abandon, and with the total approval of the black cast, by white Hobart Smith. I cannot swear to the authenticity of this reconstructed music, but there can be no question that the conservative Sea Island Singers gave it their enthusiastically approved of it.

These comments are repeated with some modifications in the 1998 Rounder release liner notes. The reference to Smith's race and the blacks' approval of his presence is removed. Instead, there is a straightforward nonracial listing of instrumentalist: "Hobart Smith picked the bow-shaped 'slave' banjo with abandon, Ed Young blew thrilling litany phrases on his cane fife, and Nat Rahmings played a drum of a type once used on St. Simons and still played in the Bahamas." But the concluding sentence, which is the focus of our concern because it is about judgmental authenticity, stays essentially the same with the addition of a qualifying adjective, "the *musically* conservative Sea Island Singers," and the transformation of the adverb/verb coupling "enthusiastically approved" into an adjective/noun "enthusiastic approval." In both formations of the sentence, the implication is clear: the participation of musicians from the mainland, including one white, may entail innovative elements that could compromise authenticity from the expert perspective, the Sea Island Singers' enthusiasm notwithstanding. Before carefully considering the significance of this distinction in judgment, we should point out the relevant fact that the 1959 Bessie Jones–led version of the Buzzard Lope became iconic among folklorist, due, in large measure, to Lomax's repeated re-releasing of it in numerous albums over three decades, including the oft-cited 1977 New World Records *Georgia Sea Island Songs*, as well as the 1998 Rounder release, where it is the second of twenty-one tracks and the Davis-led recording is the last. In this, Lomax was diligently promoting both his and Jones's aspiration to take the heritage of the Georgia Sea Islanders to the greater world. The first opportunity to do so presented itself not long after the 1960 Prestige release of *Southern Journey*.

Ethnographic Epistēmē Abuts Performative Technē Poiētikē

In May 1962, CBS Television contacted Lomax, who was doing field work in Trinidad, about a new show they were developing called *Accent*, in which its host, the poet John Ciardi, was to take viewers on a guided tour of various locations in the United States exploring ideas about American culture. Lomax was invited to participate as music coordinator of the series' second episode, set on St. Simons Island and featuring the Spiritual Singers as representing the culture and song heritage of America's earliest slaves. The segment aired on June 14, 1962, with the title "The Golden Isles: Cradle of American Song," featuring Lomax as co-host. The naturalistic conceit of the segment was a "true Georgia fish-fry" being held by the local Negro, which Ciardi drops in on to watch up close along with Lomax serving as his guide. That this is a proximate but carefully mediated spectacle is firmly established by Lomax's providing running expert commentary, explaining to Ciardi and the viewing audience the meaning of what the Spiritual Singers dance and sing. The preponderant mode of commentary is a casual onscreen conversation with Ciardi, during which the two men focus intensely on one another, while the Spiritual Singers dance and sing, for the most part, off-camera. The manner in which Lomax and Ciardi's exchange stands in relation to the Singers' performance warrants full exposition because of how it so exemplifies the interpretive paraphrasis of collection to which we have been attending, and how it speaks as well to the stakes at play in the aforementioned differentiation Lomax makes between his judgment and that of the Singers about the authenticity of the Davis-led performance of the Buzzard Lope.

Having already spent quite a few minutes explaining to Ciardi the context of the preeminence of undiluted Africanisms among the Georgia Sea Island Negro, thereby establishing their value as authentic specimen, Lomax calls Bessie Jones over to where he and Ciardi are standing so he can introduce her to him as "one of the people who really knows the old songs here." He then asks her: "Bessie what's gonna happen next?" To which she responds: "The fish-fry, we have the Buzzard Lope next in the fish-fry." This momentary, somewhat awkward exchange is the only occasion in the half-hour segment when Jones or any of the other the Singers speak directly to Lomax and Ciardi. Whatever knowledge she is purported to have is expressed in the performance only and not in any form of explanatory commentary. That is the exclusive purview of Lomax, who, as Jones goes off-camera joining the rest of the Singers to start the dance, continues his interpretive commentary with Ciardi, saying: "John, this Buzzard Lope is really a fascinating thing, it's probably the oldest surviving African dance on the continent. In the dance, the principle solo dancer leaps out into the dancing circle and mimes the actions of a buzzard after carrion. You'll see it all in a moment." Lomax then takes a page out of Parrish's book and immediately draws attention to song: "But, the exciting thing about this dance is the text, probably. The text says: 'Throw me anywhere Lord in that ole field I don't where you throw me in that ole field.'" As though on cue, the Singers begin singing the song, still heard off-camera in the background. Neither Lomax nor Ciardi look in the direction of the singing. In fact, Ciardi's attention has remained riveted on Lomax, who now gives an exegesis of the song: "It's pulling right out of the heart of the oppressed slave. He's saying 'I'm just to you as a piece of carrion, but I'll survive somehow.' And as Bessie has told me, her ancestors told her..."—at this point the camera fades to a wide-angle of Peter Davis flapping his arms and hopping around in mimicry of the buzzard while Lomax continues to talk commentary in the background as the camera first zooms in on Davis's flapping then back out to a wide-angle shot of the full singing circle with him dancing in the center—"... her grandparents told her that when they sang that song they identified themselves with Jesus who was buried in the field." Ciardi's now says, again in the background: "So the Buzzard is kind of a rival of judgment. I'd like to see this." They both then fall silent, as the wide shot of Peter Davis doing his solo in the circle continues. The camera then fades to a close-up of Jones singing and clapping, only to fade back out to a wide shot of Peter now joined in the circle by his brother, John, who will eventually swoop down and take up the shirt in his mouth as the dance ends. The overall performance time of Bessie Jones and the Spiritual Singers doing the Buzzard Lope is one minute fifty-two seconds, the first fourteen seconds of which is off-camera, dominated by Lomax's commentary exchange with Ciardi, followed by eighteen seconds of on-camera dancing, during which Lomax continues his commentary. Then there is one minute and twenty seconds of the Singers in on-camera performance free of commentary. Even though the commentary-free performance is given the greater onscreen time, it is the commentary that defines the form through its expertise. Once the dance ends, the camera goes straightway back to Lomax and Ciardi, with the latter rather jocularly punctuating the performance, toward which he is now looking: "And off goes the buzzard."

The following exchange, which begins and ends with Lomax, situates that performance canonically in the overall curated collection of Negro expression:

"Yes John, there you see the most primitive dance probably on this continent except among the American Indians."

"Are all the dances African in origin here?"

"Well really of course they are. But this one with its typical African circle, the singing leader, and the dancer involved with his whole body and dramatizing, this is really African transported to America. Now, in these dances you can see the origin of the things that came later in the minstrel show, the Negro reel, the ragtime, jazz, on up to the twist. You can see those elements. But in a cruder form because these country people still have the agility to dance to this polymeter that you saw them clapping."

Lomax's televised expert pronouncement, situating the Buzzard Lope in the genealogy of Negro expression as an archaic African survival at risk of disappearing into the dynamics of modern civilization, not only echoes Parrish's construal (à la Herskovits), it also exhibits the same primitivist Negrophilia driving her curatorship of Negro expression, as well as that of Allen, Leiris, and his father, John Avery Lomax. What comes into sharp focus here, however, is the implicit presumption that *African* is the opposite of modern civilization. A presumption enhanced by the scene's compositional elements: the full two shot of Lomax and Ciardi conversing while the Singers can be heard performing off-camera, the cutaway to Davis mimicking the buzzard that zooms in, then back out to a wide-angle shot of the Singers' performing the shout, with the circle opened at the bottom of the shot where the camera is viewing Davis dancing in the center joined by his brother and two other dancers, during the first few seconds of which the two white men are heard but not seen and then shown silently watching.

Because Lomax and Ciardi are identified with the camera perspective during the Singers' onscreen performance, the overall effect is a rather well-curated diorama, with the Buzzard Lope, which has its own choreography—key elements of which, such as the beating broomstick and pattin', are missing in the televised performance—set in a pastoral scene of native islander celebration, the fish-fry. We are supposed to be watching the performance of a pure Africanism on the verge of becoming extinct with the islanders' increased integration into mainland culture. In fact, the performance is choreographed according to the dictates of recording, which complements the ethnological story that is not addressed to the Singers, or even in conversation *with* them, but at the "broader audience" for whom the Buzzard Lope is presumed to be something precious in its archaism; a presumption that is underscored by the ethnologist's absolute control over the interpretive narrative. These "country people" may be the keepers of the tradition in practice, but they are not its expert interpreters. This is to suggest, moreover, that there is no transmission of conceptualization with the modification of form. What we would consider improvisation is cast by the ethnologist as degradation. Parrish recounts a story about a "Northern Negro composer, unfamiliar with the traditional songs of his race," who, upon hearing a washerwoman singing the spiritual "By an' by-e I'm Goin' t' See the King" while working, "innocently believed her when she claimed she had made it up, and told reporters that new spirituals are born every day." It was on the strength of her deep familiarity with the archive of Negro song she'd compiled that Parrish knew the truth, having heard the song long before our composer was born. The ethnologist collector has true knowledge of the authentic form and lines of transmission, which are preserved through her constituting the archive, and then providing masterful analysis of its contents. Whatever that washerwoman and composer think she is doing and where its coming from, it was not an authentic line of transmission until judged so by Parrish.[28]

What are we to do, then, with Samuel Floyd's account of the way in which the performative style—that is to say, the *technē poiētikē*—of shouts like the Buzzard Lope are constitutive elements in a transmitted understanding of human existence in the world, which he designates "Call-Response"?[29] Are we to simply ignore, for that matter, Sterling Stuckey's hypothesis that the shout was "the main context in which Africans recognized values common to them—the values of ancestor worship and contact, communication and teaching through storytelling and trickster expressions, and of various other symbolic devices. Those values were remarkable because, while of ancient African provenance, they were fertile seed for the bloom of new forms."³⁰ The emphasis here is on new forms, spirituals being one of the forms invented through the shout. Contra the Allen-Parrish hypothesis, according to which the shout is taken to be a Christianization of an African form, with the spirituals being the modality of that Christianization, Stuckey argues that it should be considered as an Africanization of Christian symbolism, with the technique of the shout being the modality of invention. Both Stuckey and Floyd construe the preeminence of the shout among the various peoples brought from the continent of Africa into New World slavery as a new form created by and instrumental in the proactive creation of a people newly formed in the vicissitudes of modern capitalist slavery.³¹ Stuckey calls this process "pan-Africanization," by which he can be taken to mean something akin to Édouard Glissant's *créolisation*; that is to say, "a mode of forming a complex mix [*l'emmêlement*] that is only exemplified by its processes and certainly not by the 'contents' on which these operate.'"³² It can be said that the people invented through the systematic violence of modern capitalist slavery, designated *Negro*, invent; and that process of invention is what we call *poiēsis*, indicating a particular semiosis articulating a particular understanding of human existence that is not altogether circumscribed by the ethnologist's knowledge.

Fred Moten remarks how Glissant's account of *creole*, beginning with the imposition of sound on the enslaved body—the *Negro*—instigates a semiosis, in which, pace Ferdinand de Saussure, phonic materiality, noise, is meaningful in itself. The pitch, tonic color, repetition, and so rhythms of noise articulate a movement of relationality. It can be said, *parole* enables, indeed, engenders language; it is not the corrupting derivative material enunciation. In terms of scientific linguistics, creole is a synchronic prototype. More to the point for Moten, this making of noise is an inaugural moment in "the animative materiality—the aesthetic, political, sexual, and racial force—of the ensemble of objects," which he says might be called "black performances, black history [or] blackness."³³ Our designating this *poiēsis* does not contradict the word or gist of Moten's saying. On the contrary, it does justice to his further describing the generative and transformative force of the scream attending the imposition of noise, the congruence of song and speech, referring to Abbey Lincoln's punctuating screams over Max Roach's intense percussion on "Protest," putting it in the lineage of Aunt Hester's scream recounted by Douglass, the echo of which haunts Albert Ayler's "Ghosts," as well as James Brown's "Cold Sweat"—the examples proliferate: "Where shriek turns speech turns song—remote from the impossible comfort of origin—lies the trace of our descent."³⁴

This brings us back to Lomax's remark about the authenticity of the Davis-led Buzzard Lope performed at Williamsburg on April 28, 1960. What does it mean to say that *he* cannot *swear* to the authenticity of this reconstructed music performance? By "reconstructed," he is referring to his role as music director for the film, putting together the Spiritual Singers of St. Simons with musicians from elsewhere to recreate the sort of musical performance, including the likely instrumental accompaniment, slaves might have done in the colonial era. This was a function of curation, which may not have been in keeping with Lomax's own ethnomusicological criteria for collecting authentic specimen. We can reasonably take this to be what he means by not being able to swear to its authenticity of the performance. He seems to be marking a distance between his expertise as an ethnomusicological archivist and the event of the performance. But is he? At the same time he claims to be incapable of vouching for the performance's authenticity, he apparently defers to the musically conservative Sea Island Singers' enthusiastic approval. This presents two more terms to trouble here besides "reconstructed," "swear," and "authenticity." They are "conservative" and "approval."

Saying the performance cannot be vouched for as authentic from the perspective of the ethno-anthropologist committed to finding and preserving specimen that are authentic in form and execution presumes having definitive, indeed commanding knowledge of the provenance of such specimen, which means a genealogical narrative of origin. With respect to the Buzzard Lope, that is a twofold task, one of location, the other of form. As for location, the fact that the Georgia Sea Islands were isolated from the mainland, with minimal white presence is supposed to mean that the African slaves were left, in good measure, to themselves. In their relative isolation, the Negros on islands such as St. Simons and Sapelo "reconstituted their African culture," as Lomax put it, "continuing a strongly African nonverbal culture in music, dance, and interaction pattern," which was "pan-African or pan–West Central African," since the people on the island plantations were of various ethnicities from that region. In support of the proposition that such African survivals abound on the islands, Lomax, like Parrish, cites Herskovits, this time his polemical *The Myth of the Negro Past*. The evaluation of the Georgia Sea Islands as containing a trove of remnant of African ways of life continuing into the present is complicated, however, by Lomax asserting the islanders "reconstituted their African culture" and that it was "pan-African or pan–West Central African." Two contradictions are readily apparent. First, if the plantation population consisted of diverse ethnicities, this means, in ethnographical terms, there were diverse cultures and not a singular African culture. Paradoxically, that contradiction is mitigated by the second. If the authenticity of the islanders' music stems from the fact that it is a continuation of African forms, then what does it mean to say these were "reconstituted"? To say that presupposes those forms were otherwise forgotten or dispersed. Undoubtedly, the Middle Passage—the metonym for the systematic transport of masses of peoples from Africa across the

Atlantic into New World slavery undertaken by corporate European interest—was a traumatic event for those individuals wrenched from their natal cultural milieux and the geographic, as well as geopolitical horizon of their communal semiosis. That would account for a certain dispersal in which Fon, Yoruba, Pular, Wolof, Mandinke, and the like find themselves forced together under a new common category, *African* and *Negro*. Imposition of this category does not mean, however, that the Passage simply eradicated their various semiosis. Rather, and this is a central aspect of Herskovits's work, beginning in the hold of the slave ship, an amalgam of semiosis occurs, one in which the enslaved "as creative human beings," to quote Lomax, "were constantly inventing and remaking a new lifestyle out of their experience in this new environment." He uses this language to describe the nature of "pan-African southern-black folklore." It is the description of a process of constituting, of creating a culture, and not of reconstituting it. Moreover, given that the category *African*, like *Negro*, is a function of the semiosis of capitalist slavery, as has already been pointed out, to say the Sea Islanders "reconstituted their African culture" is confused at best. At worst, it is to further impose upon them an abstraction that negates the very human activity of dynamically creating ways of living in practice Lomax seeks to preserve *for the record*. Here is the crux of it: preservation for the record is not a conservative endeavor; that is to say, the archive collects and monumentalizes, fixes on vinyl or celluloid, a moment of performance that is labeled authentic in its archival collection. Archival authenticity is categorical; the strictures and imperatives by which the true specimen of "pan-African southern-black folk" is secured overrides the dynamic performance, disregarding the careful semiosis, the thinking-in-action manifest *with and by* pan-Africanization. This is meant in Stuckey's sense of a process of constitutively admixing forms, that they are *in and by way of* formal admixture. Again, in a manner akin to Glissant's *créolisation*, Stuckey's pan-Africanization is not a process of miscegenation (*métissage*) in that it does not predict an outcome of amalgamation predicated on anterior heterogeneous purity. It is more syncretic, but only to the extent that, taking some liberty with Stuckey's conception, syncretism is construed as an unpredictable process of facilitating coexistence without positing an underlying essential unity. This semiosis of pan-Africanism is arguably what the Spiritual Singers are "conservative" about. They are conserving a way of existing in the flow of, to paraphrase Lomax again, constantly inventing and remaking new lifestyle out of new experience. This is arguably what they enthusiastically approved of in the April 28 performances, including the Davis-led Buzzard Lope.

The distinction Lomax makes between his inability to vouch for the performance's authenticity and the Singers' approval unfolds along the lines of the earlier discussed Aristotelian distinction between *technē poiētikē* and *epistēmē*, between the technical know-how of the artist and the theoretical knowledge of the ethnologist. We get a sense of this when we attend to the first six seconds of the recorded performance, where Nat Rahmings is giving Ed Young orchestral direction:

RAHMINGS: "He start it . . ."
YOUNG: "That's right . . ."
RAHMINGS: ". . . he comes in with the flute . . ."
YOUNG: "That's right . . ."
RAHMINGS: ". . . I come in with the drums and that's it"
YOUNG: "That's right I knew that."

We can make out the Singers in the background concurring. This is precisely what it sounds like: a group of musicians who are all familiar enough with the form to play together without needing extensive instruction. Young's repeatedly saying "that right" to each of Rahmings's directions, and then concluding with "I knew that" evidences a shared *technē poiētikē*. We must ask ourselves, which mode of knowledge, the performers' *technē* or Lomax's *epistēmē*, determines lines of transmission. In other words, which lineage of transmission matters? Is it the transmitted know-how in performance, which is apparently fairly widespread among black musicians, pace Lomax's claims about St. Simons's distinctness in isolation, that conserves a tradition in action. Or is it the ethnomusicological archivist's "scientific" method of collecting?

This, of course, is a question of authority and disregard of authority, of the ethnologist's authority to taxonomize and the black resistance to taxonomization. One of Parrish's chief complaints was that "the secretiveness of the Negro . . . is the fundamental reason for our ignorance of the race and its background, and this trait is in itself probably an African survival."[35] In support of this conclusion, she adduces evidence from her default expert, Herskovits, who quotes a Dutch Guiana Bush Negro as saying: "Long ago our ancestors taught us that it is unwise for a man to tell anyone more than half of what he knows about anything."[36] Yet, in her three-page exposition of how Negro secretiveness hinders ethnographic work, Parrish suggests the underlying struggle against power:

However, it is just possible that an age-old compensation complex explains the situation. I am convinced that the average Negro enjoys intensely knowing something that the white man does not, and the exquisite delight he derives from realizing that the white man has been bested in a little game makes up for any loss or indignity he may be obliged to endure. . . . That such tactics may have a less pleasant side—aimed at the eventual discomfiture of an exacting employer—it may be well to remember. . . . The inquisitive college professor is particularly vulnerable, and when he becomes authoritative he is giving the Negro the opportunity he relishes above all things to laugh up his sleeve at the white man's gullibility.[37]

Parrish found the Buzzard Lope to be a form shrouded in a particular secretiveness the reason for which she simply could not fathom. "It took me three winters on St. Simon's to hear a single slave song," she says, "three times as many winters to see the religious dance called the ring-shout, still more winters to unearth the Buzzard Lope and similar solo dances, and the game songs known as ring-play." Besides referring twice to how her cook, Julia, kept from her for twenty-two years that she knew the Buzzard Lope shout, Parrish offers up as illustration of the extent of Negro secretiveness the case of a white planter "Uncle Scotia, when he saw the Buzzard Lope—for the first time in his life—done by a Negro woman he had known for more than fifty years."[38] The shrouding has everything to do with the black understanding of this shout as a form of resistance, something indicated by Peter Davis's exegesis. It also speaks to the struggle between *technē poiētikē* of and the *epistēmē* of ethnology, which we see at play in the difference between Lomax's account to Ciardi of what Bessie Jones told him about the significance of the Buzzard Lope and the account she provides directly in her autobiographical memories, *For the Ancestors*, where she recounts what her maternal grandfather, whom she called "Pa," told her was the reasoning behind the Buzzard Lope song:

> So in those days, they had those things they call "boneyard," where if a cow or a hog or a mule would die, they would carry it down to the edge of the woods and leave it for the buzzards. And Pa said they'd seen how white folks were buried and they knew how they were buried, and in their minds they talked it over and thought they might just be carried down there and put on the side of the woods so the buzzards could pick them. So this is why they made up a song, "Throw me anywhere, Lord." They were talking to the white folks "you might as well throw me out in that old field, 'cause you ain't doing me right nohow."[39]

She then explains the relationship between the song, clapping, and dancing as an act of subversive resistance, providing a description of the dance's choreography entailing elements of the Johnsons' and Davis's exegeses:

> Now about the clapping: we clap our hands and whether it's in church or anywhere else, they're on time.... Pa and them would clap and get to set-dancing, and they'd do "The Sand," "The Buzzard Lope," and other dances like that, clapping themselves and getting into it. They did the lope dance to keep the people from understanding the buzzard lope song they were singing. But they were talking to them, that's what they were doing. And

they made up something that kept old massa and old missus from knowing directly what they were talking about. And it would be funny to them, because the whites would come out there doing that dance, and that tune, trying to see how good they could sing that song. They didn't know what they were talking about. And in doing the dance, doing the buzzard lope, they would spread something out—like an old shirt or a hat—and they had a way of coming down to this thing. The main buzzard, he comes down, looks around, picks around, jumps over it, then he gives out that "Caaww!" and the rest of them come down and then dance around. Pa and them marked how the buzzards did it and they did it the same way, and it was funny to them to have the white folks doing the dance, because in it folks were telling them.[40]

At this point, Jones repeats the full song, which is the version transcribed by Lomax, only to conclude: "Look like people could see it, don't it? But they couldn't see it." This sense of resisting white people's understanding of things is also conveyed in Cornelia Bailey's recounting the significance of the Buzzard Lope shout her father and his friends used to perform on Fridays when she was a child in the 1950s. This recollection, which comprises the whole of chapter 18, "The Buzzard Lope," in her book, is one of the fullest insider accounts of what the shout was about.[41] Careful storyteller that she was, Bailey describes the scene of those gatherings where the men got together at one another's house to drink and have a good time, and "once they really hit the bottle their anger at buckra [whites] for all they'd put up with that week would spill out." They would save the Buzzard Lope until they were well into the evening because it was not easy to do. Bailey tells us that a lot of men on the Sea Islands knew the Buzzard Lope, but its performance had become less frequent by the time she came along so seeing her father do it was so special a thing that she describes his performance in some detail, after which she explains its meaning:

> There's a story that goes with that dance and it is from the days of slavery. From a time when the people who were enslaved had a hard taskmaster, a very hard taskmaster, and they were working in the fields, in the sun, in the summertime, and that heat got to someone. It got to him bad, or maybe he was feeling poorly already, and the heat made him that much worse, and he fell over dead in the field. The master wouldn't let the workers stop. He wasn't going to let two or three people stop to bury their family member until it was dark and they couldn't work any longer. But a whole day in August was a lifetime, and the buzzards came, and they circled around, and the head buzzard came in and checked out the prey and the other buzzards joined him, and they started their natural thing of cleaning up the earth.

> If you're in a group and you hear a story like the one that goes with the Buzzard Lope, everyone instantly feels the same thing. Your heart goes out. This awful feeling comes over you and you become one for that instant. That's how it was with Papa and his buddies. The men had a camaraderie out of this world when they were together, a sharing from the soul.⁴²

Bailey's "story that goes with the dance" is an extended narrativization of the song by a knowledgeable Sea Islander, from the perspective of that knowledge, accounting for the way the Buzzard Lope articulates an affective community, a being together in the world. Bailey's account of the significance of the shout is pointedly secular or worldly. But it is also an eloquent account of the animal mimicry at its heart:

> You could hear the beating of the stick good on the wooden floor. The sound can fill up a room, now, and the men were moving in the circle. Their arms stretched out wide, gliding like a buzzard, because a buzzard can glide on that air current a long time, soar in that sky a long time, without flapping its wings Papa and the other men kept their arms out in that open fluid way, flapping their wings once in a while, moving their feet in a certain way, and going around and around in that circle, like buzzard circling its prey. I was just amazed, I was going, "how can they be in their rough work clothes and be so fancy at the same time?" They were acting just like the buzzards do in real life.⁴³

The Buzzard Lope is not just about identifying with the carrion, the prey; it is about becoming the buzzard, and in so doing becoming free to fly effortlessly and long on the currents. As a form of performative animal mimicry, the Buzzard Lope obviously entails a *technē poiētikē*, a know-how of *poiēsis*, as well as a cunning with respect to the performance of that *poiēsis* before whites, what we could call μῆτις (*mêtis*), drawing attention to the classical association of such cunning with the sort of sharp intelligence evidenced in Bailey's account of their privately laughing at whites. Recall that in ancient Greek mythology, the goddess Μῆτις (Mêtis)—daughter of the Titans, Okeanos and Tethys, Zeus's first wife and Athene's mother—was the mother of wit and deep thought, as well as magical cunning, thus equally equated with the trickster powers of her cousin Prometheus and the royal wisdom of Zeus, μῆτιετα (Mêtieta, "the wise counsellor"). Given the high value placed on *mêtis* in the social and spiritual life of ancient Greece, Aristotle was compelled to displace and devalue it by separating it from prudence (φρόνησής, *phronesis*), which he argues is more closely connected with *epistēmē* regulated by *virtue* and wisdom (σοφία, *sophia*).⁴⁴ There is no doubt *mêtis* is a type of somatic thinking and intelligence, or we would say, fleshly intelligence; it is just not recognized as capable of theorizing or sustained speculation of its own possibilities.⁴⁵ Davis's commentary and Bailey's account, however, make obvious the Buzzard Lope *technē poiētikē* also entails a knowing-whereby, as in a fleshly cunning theory of purpose. The relationship between purpose and form is not the strongly teleological one detailed in Aristotle's account of *poiēsis*, however. Should we accept Herskovits's assessment about the African provenance of fundamental elements in the dance, those may very well have been, in their originary context, teleological, with the form following the function of sacrifice. In the context of New World slavery, the form, while still expressing a purpose, is not derived or created *for* that purpose. That is quite obvious with the Buzzard Lope. All its formal resemblance to the Opete performed in Dutch Guiana and the "John Canoe" in Cuba strongly suggests a common formation originating in the sacrifice rituals of the vulture determined by the *télos* of the cosmology shared by the Ashanti, Dahomey, and Fanti peoples. Nevertheless, by circumstantial necessity, its performance in the Georgia Sea Islands, Virginia, and the Carolinas uproots the form from its fundamental purpose without effacing the common formal elementals, freeing it in a manner akin to how Barthes construed the zero degree of modern poetry. This is the creating of new forms Stuckey refers to, which we again call *poiēsis*, foregrounding its perpetually dynamic semiosis. Formal innovation becomes determinate, indeed becomes the purpose of performance, in which the Buzzard Lope, along with its pattin', energizes a semiosis of flesh that not only de-commoditizes it, but makes manifest the conventionality of the process that fetishizes the commodity as something of objective value.

When effective, Marx tells us, fetishism of the commodity is the obfuscating of its consecration as a thing of value; that consecration itself enshrouds the activity of human production in a mystery of self-presentation. Casting this in religious terms, somewhat along the lines he does, just as the eternal blood and body of Christ are present in the elementals of the Eucharist, whenever they are regarded as the "Blessed Sacrament," having been actualized as substance with the performance of the liturgical rite, so too labor in the abstract is present in the elemental Negro, having been actualized in the political economy of modern racialized capitalist slavery. In both the Eucharist and slavery, the species—bread and wine in the one, flesh in the other—remain materially unchanged, and their signification apart from their actualized essential substance is disregarded. There is a crucial fundamental difference, however. Whereas the Eucharistic transubstantiated substance of bread and wine *are* metabolized on their ingestion, the flesh of slavery is not; and its substance, labor, gets consumed in the production of use-value, without being digested.⁴⁶ There is an additional crucial difference. The substantive agency of the Eucharist is fully ideological, regardless of whether one believes in its reality; that is to say, it is a sign-function *of semiosis*, the material manifestation of which is in the elemental species, given its significance by way of the liturgical semiotic act of the Eucharist rite. In contrast, the productive agency of the Negro slave is corporeal and, while significantly expressed within the semiosis of society in general, would still exist as a fundamental species activity absent that semiosis. Marx referred to this as "the productive activity of human beings in general [*die produktive Tätigkeit des Menschen überhaupt*]" that is behind the abstraction of labor. It is the activity by which humans "promote the metabolic interchange with nature [*den Stoffwechsel mit der Natur*], divested not only of every social form and well defined character, but even in its bare natural existence, independent of society.... [It is] an expression and confirmation of life that the still non-social [qua primitive] man in general has in common with those who are in any way socially determined."[47] In the earlier critique of Leiris's fetishism of the Negro, we called this activity *poiēsis* in the most capacious sense of poetic causality (*poietikin aitia*), bringing into being something with significance, something invested with value. Regarding the commodity-fetish, this activity has only a spectral, abstract presence, with the semiotic value it generates misconstrued as being inherent to the commodity form *having* objective value. Marx's heuristic de-fetishizing example is the speaking commodity that says: "Our use-value (*unser Gebrauchswert*) [which] may be a thing that interests men ... is not part of us as objects. What does belong to us as objects, however, is our value (*unser Wert*)."[48] By the same example, we understand that semiosis is not a commodity but gets identified with the modes of production, which are naturalized *in* the commodity, obfuscating the social dynamics of production. In other words, the commodity-fetish indexes a semiosis of human sociality—in Marx's terms a system of social relations. A commodity may have semiotic value, it may be an indicial embodiment of the relational social order of capitalist slavery, but it possesses in itself no agency of signification. Its fetishism is a function of structures of imagination and desire, circumscribed, in Heidegger's sense of *Umgrenzende*, by the *télos* of capital. The tendency in the context of racialized capitalist slavery is to concentrate all human forces on structural work, and the predominant *poiēsis* is the economical-practical: the transformation of the flesh into the Negro body as a fungible repository of labor power. All the force of law, all the technologies of torture, and the economics of consumption deployed in the better ordering and governing of Negroes had as a primary and essential purpose the disciplining of motive will into manageable forms of desire. The purpose of *permitting* Juba and dancing, then, was to control imaginative potential by directing it away from actualization in the disruptive physical action of rebellion into aesthetic expression in a regularized carnivalesque-time. Hence both Douglass's and Bibb's disgust at the planter-sanctioned Saturday and Sunday dances as instrumentalities of slavery.

While that may very well have been the *télos* of capitalist slavery in sanctioning, even encouraging pattin' Juba and dancing the Buzzard Lope, in their so circumscribed performance, they attenuate that circumscription from within, exhibiting a formation of imagination that is in direct contestation with that of capitalist slavery. Arguably, this is how Leiris construed the workings of "true fetishism," in opposition to philosophy's dismissal of fetishism as the logical mistake of hypostasis, stemming from the undeveloped imagination lacking, as Hegel claimed, the principle of universality.⁴⁹ Except the Juba and dancing, rather than engaging in what is supposed to be a *liberating* fetishism of the flesh, are performances in fleshly sentience. Their *technē* is a materialism that is not only in conflict with capitalist slavery and its attendant philosophical tradition, but also incompatible with teleology, Christian or otherwise. This is what we mean when stating that pattin' Juba and dancing the Buzzard Lope energize a de-fetishizing de-commoditizing semiosis of flesh. The flesh is not beaten in Juba and contorted in dance to sacrifice for the gods, or even the ancestors, who are always present. Rather, it is worked in semiotic contestation. No matter the slaveholder's recognizing the potentiality of pattin' and dancing as an instrumentality of property management—their doing so speaks more to the severe limitations of *their* conceptualization, as well as power to control semiosis, than it does to the efficacy of the *poiēsis* of pattin' and dancing in constituting a viable way of being communally—that is, being-at-work-ness-in-common-in the flesh of the environmental world. Every performance of the polyrhythmic flesh-sonics of pattin' and the polycentric body-movement of dance makes manifest the persistence of a heterologous fleshly sentient capacity, which not only exceeds the individual but constitutes the very conditions of individuation, instantiating what I will now call *poiēsis in black*.

In the formulation *poiēsis in black*, the emphasis is on *poiēsis* as a dynamic process of inventing infinite possibilities associated with human imagination in general, with the preposition linking that species activity to a particular tradition of performance. Accordingly, performances such as Juba and Buzzard Lope are instantiations of the essential species activity of *poiēsis*. All that differentiates them from other such instantiations is their association with those human beings historically denoted as *Negro*. And to repeat what was remarked a bit earlier, those performances, in that association, is what Moten terms *blackness*. Let us construe this to denote the critically self-reflective way of being *appositional* to the capitalist slavery semiosis of individuation as either fungible object or exploited alienated subject. *Apposition* is pointedly not being used here in the rhetorical sense of ἐξήγησις (*exígisis*, "exegesis"), which would suggest that *blackness* is an explanation of *Negro*, when what is meant is something else that those decreed *Negro* do besides, as in not defined by, that decree. Rather, it is used in a polyvalent sense of juxtaposition. Besides the general grammatical sense of being in juxtaposition, side by side in close proximity, or parallelism, *apposition* has five meanings in medical terminology, three of which share the connotation of juxtaposition: the placing in contact of two substances, the condition of being placed or fitted together, and the relation of fracture fragments to one another. Of the remaining meanings, the one most germane to us here is the process of thickening a cell wall known as "appositional growth," accomplished by the addition of new layers to those previously formed: for example, the addition of lamellae in the formation of bone, by which nutritive matter from the blood is transformed on the surface of an organ into solid unorganized substance. Such growth is the characteristic mode when rigid material such as bone is involved.[50] This is also the meaning of "appositional growth" in cell biology, where it denotes the deposition or accretion of additional layers of cell wall material onto a preexisting cell wall; and in botany, where it is the deposition of successive layers of cellulose onto those already present on the inner surface of a plant cell wall, a process that strengthens the overall cell structure.[51] Combining the grammatical, medical, and biological senses underscores the concomitance of dynamic processes of intra-elemental transformation within the semiosis of capitalist slavery and that of *poiēsis in black*, and their respective parallel systemic extension. In other words, *Negro* and *blackness* are co-articulates in a system that is multilineal as well as polymorphous. There are points of convergence or contact articulating transient forms, such as bodily representation, without necessary identity or meaning. Such contact points manifest *poiēsis* in the Aristotelian sense, accounted for earlier, of saying possibilities. And, in that sense it is the dynamic process Glissant designates as *créolisation*, also accounted for earlier, which is, to repeat, "a mode of forming a complex mix that is only exemplified by its processes and certainly not by the 'contents' on which these operate." Further repeating what was said before, this is the process of invention, indicating a particular semiosis articulating a particular understanding of human existence. That semiosis is not instigated by the system nor altogether circumscribed by it, although it may be interpolated into the system as *Negro* and imbricated therein, with *black* overlapping *Negro*.

It bears pointing out that *poiēsis in black*, as instantiated with Juba and the Buzzard Lope, is not an interdiction *against* individuation and subjectivity; rather, it is a *process* of dynamically differentiated self-consciousness, in the sense of a consciousness of being-presented-in/by the performance, in the poetic activity of whatever form of *technē*, without grounding in a transcendental principle of identity. Let us call this the performance of persona *occasioned* by ancestral forces sustained formally in the stylistic conventions of that performance. For instance, in the stylized beating on the body for musical rhythm in Juba, as well as the solo of the Buzzard Lope dance, when a player presents before the other players as a differentiated individual, that individuality exhibits the grammar of the situation, the rules of play Bessie Jones described to Bess Lomax Hawes. The individual's self-consciousness as a soloist, even one who strives to differentiate him- or herself as a radical improvisationist, is inextricably expressed in relation to the situational grammar. That moment of the solo spotlights "the ineluctable modality" of being-in-semiosis; even the most pronouncedly innovative solo, expressing the most profound desire to differentiate oneself from others, is an experiment in form, projecting the possibilities of being articulable *within* the semiosis. Because semiosis is a dynamic system entailing an enormous number of possible configurations of the individual performances, any given solo can be regarded as random or indeterminate. As Albert Murray once said to Don Noble, explaining the formal experimentation in three of his works, *Train Whistle Guitar*, *South to a Very Old Place*, and the *Spyglass Tree*:

> I now think in terms of particles and/or waves. That's the way we conceive of entropy, which is chaos, and the one thing we have or the only thing we can do about it is to use that endowment that we have that Joyce was talking about when he referred to the "ineluctable modality" of the visible, of the audible, of the conceptual. The concept is an attempt to bring some form. Without that, you just have chaos. So, you've got to have some sense of form, whether it's up, down, outside, inside, round, square, or whatever.[52]

We can take him to mean here *style*; and so the solo provides a style of thinking in the disorder of entropy. Furthermore, because the semiosis is itself an indeterminate dynamic of transient form in disorder, it is perpetually reorienting with each innovative performance without losing the coherence of its play, its momentum. Murray helps us understood the performative style of black musical practices not as a projection of the primal unity of subjective will or ego, but as the eventful dynamic of perpetually transitive and transitional consciousness. Although his illustrations of this style of thinking in disorder were primarily focused on the Blues and Jazz, he thought it evident across mimetic forms: "All poetic expressions represent or express human feeling, how humans are constituted affectively and so what they are aware of."[53] This applies, unquestionably to Juba and other such performative activities of collective dynamics associated with the Negro.

Shifting the analogical context to cellular biology—not at all inappropriate, given our concern here with flesh's embodiment—think of the solo as an event of interstitial growth in which the fluid exchange of material from different centers of play (the different singing voices or dancers in the ring) increases the combinatory range of the auditory and visual mix, extending or lengthening the semiotic field. With each solo remix, the surface contours defining the specific form increase their permeability, permitting the inclusion of new material from "outside," adding an additional layer in appositional growth, while also synthesizing and releasing elements of its internal matrix, thereby contributing to the dynamics between parallel semiosis. As the field of semiosis grows in extension, it acquires greater density in relation to parallel semiosis. We see this in the "development" of musical form from Spirituals and Gospel, to Blues and Jazz, from R&B to Rock & Roll, and Soul. Being in the concomitancy of interstitial and appositional growth is what James Baldwin depicted as being in the beat and Ralph Ellison as perpetual movement in space and time.

No analogy can be drawn between the sentient flesh of *poiēsis in black* and the "speaking implement" of Marx's oft-cited footnote.[54] That note, which occurs in the second section of chapter 7 in volume 1 of *Capital* under the rubric "Production of Surplus-Value [*Verwertungsprozeß*]," is in reference to ideal conditions under which labor is carried out in the production of surplus-value and the necessity for high-quality labor. Elaborating on that argument, Marx presents slavery (*Sklaverei*), as the counterexample of high-quality profitable labor, stating: "The laborer here is, to use a striking expression of the ancients, distinguishable only as *instrumentum vocale* [speaking tool, *sprachbegabtes Werkzeug*], from an animal as *instrumentum semi-vocale*, and from an implement as *instrumentum mutum*."[55] The ancient expression refers to Varro's *Rerum rusticarum*, in which he uses the phrase *instrumenti genus vocale*, "the class of speaking instruments," to distinguish human labor from that of animals and tools.[56] Although Varro includes the labor of slaves and freemen in the class of speaking instruments—both being humans, distinguished only in terms of social, and not ontological situation—Marx uses it exclusively for slavery. Distinguishing slavery from wage-labor, he describes it as a primitive form belonging to a pre-capitalist social order; and so the slave's attitude is not conducive to the production of surplus-value. "He [the slave] convinces himself, as a matter of self-esteem [*Selbstgefühl*], that he is different [from both beast and implement], by treating the one unmercifully and damaging the other *con amore*," Marx writes, offering in illustration Frederick Law Olmsted's journalistic secondhand reports from slaveholders of the treatment farm animals "get from Negroes."[57] In Marx's analysis, capitalism's demand for the most cost-efficient production of surplus-value eliminates the need for, indeed any conceivable economic benefit of, slavery. Marx's argument in this footnote effectively deracinates slavery from the history of capitalist development, except as an archaism, being displaced in actuality by the structures of capitalist labor markets. A corollary of this analysis is the disregarding of the long tradition of black critiques of the capitalist system, what James Ford calls *fugitive discourse*, taking Frederick Douglass as his primary example of such.[58] In a close reading of the footnote, he persuasively links Marx's speaking-implement argument to the tendency among Douglass's white fellow abolitionists to introduce him on the occasions of his public speaking as "chattel," encouraging him to not sound intelligent because that would discredit the authenticity of his claim to have been a slave. The link is reinforced with reference to Marx's aforementioned subjunctive example of the speaking commodity, which, recall, is meant to underscore the fact that commodities cannot speak in critique of the commodity-fetish. Here Ford follows Moten, who argues that Marx's supposition denies the "historical reality of commodities who spoke—of laborers who were commodities before, as it were, the abstraction of labor power from their bodies and who continue to pass on this material heritage across the divide that separates slavery from 'freedom.'"⁵⁹ Contradicting Marx's assumption that commodities cannot speak brings to the fore a radical material theory of value that is in contrast to Marx's and, by Moten's account, animates black performances as a perpetually expressed "freedom drive" informing a radical understanding of social change.⁶⁰

When we factor pattin' Juba and the Buzzard Lope shout into this analysis of black performance, they are readily recognizable as a practice and theory of value and freedom that disrupts the capitalist sociopolitical economy within which it is circumscribed, articulating a radical sociality. Still, it behooves us to bear in mind that the semiosis by which this occurs, because it is heterologous to that of capitalist slavery, fundamentally contests the efficacy of its claiming to circumscribe the flesh. Marx is correct, in other words—commodities *cannot* speak—and the persistent immanence of the un-arrested *poiēsis in black* makes manifest the fact that semiosis-engendering sentient flesh is not properly commodifiable. The body, which is already an abstraction predicated on the presumptive stealing of the flesh, may very well be a commodity in precisely the way Marx's defines commodity—which is to say it is an expression of value within a semiotic order into which the flesh is interpolated. That interpolation, however, is never absolutely completed, and the residuum of heterologous semiosis still engages the same flesh. What is from the perspective of racialized capitalist slavery, to paraphrase Moten, "stolen life"—meaning life in escape from the order of things—from that of the heterologous *poiēsis in black*, is the *un-stealable life*, articulated in the semiosis of sentient flesh. Nor is this akin in any way to bare life, neither in the sense of the simple biological existence, ζωή (*zōē*), of Aristotelian lineage so valued by Hannah Arendt, contrasted with the political life of speech and action, βίος (*bios*), nor that in Agamben's thinking, according to whom bare life is the remainder of destroyed political *bios*. The difference from the first of these conceptions of bare-life is clear, because the sentient flesh is always already *in relation with* semiosis, in sociality.⁶¹ The difference from Agamben's conception is more nuanced and stems from his account of bare life as "a zone of indistinction and continuous transition between man and beast" being the consequence of destroyed political *bios*, with all that entails about the presumptive priority of citizenship as the condition of rights.[62] As has been made plain in our account of the know-how and theory, the *technē poiētikē* of Juba and the Buzzard Lope, the zone of transition, vestibularity, is not arrived at in the wake of the loss of *bios*; it is the condition of being articulated already in the residuum semiosis, which is not remnant, in the biblical sense of an enduring core seed from which the original people can reemerge, implied in Agamben's sense of bare life as remainder.[63] As has also already been noted, in dances such as the Buzzard Lope, John Canoe, and Opete, the movement is not to anthropomorphize the animal, nor is it to bestialize the human. It is to, in mimicry, be human *with* the animal. And this is not merely, or even primarily in mockery of the capitalist construal of the Negro as akin to the sheep, horse, cow, and swine. These forms express a conception of the animal human in vestibularity.

Windham makes no explicit reference to pattin' Juba or Buzzard Lope. Nevertheless, his "us is human flesh" reverberates with the same sense of the indissoluble animality of the human; "us" connotes the kinesis of human flesh thinking in the world and expresses that thinking in a communicative system of meaningful signification of the world. Vestibularity. "Us" is what Spillers calls performing subjectivity, which, in contradistinction to Husserl's transcendental ego-subject, does not ground sociality but is articulated by and in relation to it. The myriad actualizations of us are in accord with the myriad possibilities of the world-in-motion, within its horizons, so to speak; and so speaking is to speak of a *nonegocentric* world. This is not to say that there is no ego-subject, but that it does not exists a priori, or prior to the world, and is, in fact, given by the world in the continuous dynamic process of the meaningful signification of reality as *semiosis*. Us is there where us is. This has obvious resonance with Jacques Lacan's conception of the subject as being nothing but an effect of a system of signifiers—a conception that shall be critically taken up presently. For now, the resonance is merely marked in passing, on the way to underscoring that *us* is fully cosmological, exscribing being *in* the world while simultaneously being elemental *to* the world. The word need not become flesh; it was already flesh. Nor need flesh become parenthesized in order that the word, the transcendental ego-subject, can be seen in an attitude of mystical discovery. It is not about seeing, or even touching the flesh. It is about being flesh. To restate this for the sake of a certain clarity, flesh *represents* nothing but *signifies* everything, including an unassimilated semiosis, not fully digested into the anthropology of "Man," which can only imagine the world as constituted in a process of production, whether called that or called providence, or nature, over which Man is destined to acquire mastery. It can be said that in his taxonomy of sentient flesh, Windham's anthropological distinction demarcates a profoundly semiotic *form of life*, within which existence is meaningful. Going one step further, it can also be said that cognition and consciousness are articulated *with* semiosis, in which our concepts and ideas are signs. Cognition as semiosis is neither an a priori—as in divinely revealed, or providential—nor merely an epiphenomenon of the flesh; it is being-in-the-process, the kinesis of semiosis. Human flesh is sentient *in semiosis*—or to use a more familiar, although no less daunting expression, in its language-games. That is what is meant by individuation as a historical process of mimesis, in which person is a performative action indicative of the *enérgeia* of signification. The phenomenological attitude addresses the question: What are "we/I"? The semiotic attitude ponders: How is "us"? What we are is clear: flesh and blood animals. The question is: How are we human flesh?

Poiēsis in Black

Consciousness Articulated with Semiosis

Windham's basic assertion of colored folk's entitlement to freedom does much more than call into question the rationales that legitimated the exclusion of black bodies from the purview of universal rights and entitlements. It calls into question the entire modern philosophical discourse—from metaphysics to ethics, as well as politics—of the distinction between animal and human. The proper name modern philosophy has given this distinction is *Negro*, designating that animal thing, the ingestion of which has been a necessity in the realization of modernity's material world, but which cannot be assimilated, cannot be properly digested, although it is ceaselessly consumed. *Negro* connotes the defaillance of what Jacques Derrida called "the trope of cannibalism." Du Bois insisted on sticking with this designation precisely because, in connoting that defaillance, it exposes the occurrence of a particular instantiation of "intellect-in-action."

We understand from glancing at the late seventeenth-century laws governing the Negro slave, that the word is a neologism coined in the novel historical situation of seventeenth-century mercantile capitalist slavery emerging as the compelling force in the inhabited extraordinarily intercultural spaces of the colonies of the North Atlantic world. In its initial usage, it indexes the emergence of a new problematic concerning the capacity of the flesh to embody value, to signify, a problematic that entailed noncommercial, as well as commercial value. In other words, *Negro* indexes the problematic of the capacity of the flesh to embody values of *person* in accord with the semiological system of emergent Enlightenment Europe—self-awareness, full self-possession of motive will and desire, liberty—while also, in accord with that same order, to embody values of property—real estate, personal, and chattel property—as well as whatever the values of whatever semiological order in which the flesh was already interpolated before capture. When we call these latter values "African" we are indicating the full ambit of the North Atlantic world—that is to say, the full range of spatiotemporal movement, encompassing myriad semiologies constantly converging and crossing one another. In that movement, *Africa* is not so much the name of a geographical place of origin, but more a chronotopic index for the originary dynamics of various semiologies ingested but not fully digested into the capitalist order. In that order, the residuum of those semiologies of the flesh are manifest as aesthetic, libidinal, and spiritual—in the sense of *Geist* more than religion in the modern connotation, which is that against which commodity logic is opposed—as values.

My point here is that, per William Pietz's aforementioned argument on the origin of the fetish, the genesis of *Negro* is in conjunction with the emergent articulation of the ideology of the commodity form, which defined itself within and against the social values and ideologies of different types of noncapitalist societies—inclusive of the various ostensibly European socialities undergoing commoditization (the century-long system of indentureship, along with the two-century-long one of piracy), the various indigenous American systems, as well as the various African systems, both Islamic as well as non-Islamic—as they encountered each other in an ongoing transcultural situation. This, too, is readily tractable in the history of the word itself, as it developed from the Portuguese and Spanish *negro* to the Dutch *neger*, the English *negro*, and the French *nègre* to the seventeenth-century legal designation for the human being as fungible commodity. The institution of law, in defining the neologism *Negro*, was compelled to undergo some foundational transformation in respect to its conception of the human, as well as property, the compulsion coming from the scale of the emerging commerce in slaves from Africa, whose hitherto presumptive humanity conflicted with the commercial need to use them as fungible and disposable property. Better put, the emerging systematic practices of consuming the flesh in increasingly industrialized plantation labor for profit (surplus-value) conflicted with the centuries-old legal, as well as religious, conception of humans.

Accordingly, *Negro* refers to that which has no *proper* historical field other than the history of the expression, which is indicial to the world of its expression. In this sense, *Negro* is an indicial sign of the perpetual activity of translation and transvaluation constituting the North Atlantic world of modernity.

This is Du Bois's point when he states in his correspondence with Barton: "'Negro' is quite as accurate, quite as old and quite as definite as any name of any great group of people."[1] Something we did not attend to in our earlier consideration of the Barton–Du Bois correspondence is rather pertinent in this context, which is that the fundamental issue at stake in their exchange is the relation of what *Negro* denotes (extension) and what it connotes (comprehension). Arguing that the word *Negro* is preferable on phonetic, as well as philological grounds—it names blackness with relatively the same pronunciation across three of the major languages of the New World, English, Spanish, and Portuguese—Du Bois supposes that, for Barton, it has a rather narrow connotation of racial physiognomy: "Your dislike of the word Negro is easily explained: 'Negroes' among your grandfathers meant black folk; 'Colored' people were mulattoes. The mulattoes hated and despised the blacks and were insulted if called 'Negroes.'"[2] In accordance with the logical law of inverse variation, the narrow connotation has a wide denotation: all black-skin-colored humans. For Du Bois, the connotation is increased, or wider, as he puts it: "those descendants of dark slaves [regardless of their subsequent physical appearance] who are largely excluded still from full American citizenship and from complete social privilege with white folk."[3] This has narrower, or decreased, denotation than Barton's, which is: those historically enslaved in the Atlantic world colonies and defined in law as property. There is an additional aspect to this denotation, which is: said people who concomitantly formed a particular cultural heritage in and of resistance to slavery. In denoting that particular class of individuals, *Negro* connotes not just the formations of political economy in the Atlantic world in modernity, but also of the particular historical practices of creative, dedicatedly emancipatory knowledges, the conceptual speculations and reflections—theories—of which are irreducibly coincidental with, although not necessarily reducible to, those formations. To elaborate on something stated earlier, *Negro* designates the historical material process of individuation articulated in the movement from African to slave to freedmen concomitant with the emergence of the U.S.-centered anti-imperialist international financial system.

The Americas-centric nature of this denotation seems to limit its significance in the larger world. Except that it coincides with Du Bois's overall analysis of the contraction of European imperialist colonialism and American racialized slavery after the U.S. Civil War. Emerging in that contraction was a global order of capitalist exploitation, predicated on the racialization of labor, which Du Bois correctly construed as the Americanization of the world, or at least the world's circumscription within the American order of things. The signature motto of this being the subordinate clause at the end of the opening paragraph of *The Souls of Black Folk*'s Forethought: "for the problem of the

Twentieth Century is the problem of the color-line."⁴ Along those lines of reasoning, the populations that had been forged in that order and had formulated a heritage of practices of resistance were to be the vanguard in the formation of a global heritage of resistance to this emergent imperialism. This was the agenda of what Du Bois initially called "Pan-Negroism."⁵ Even in its initial use in his 1897 American Negro Academy occasional paper, "The Conservation of Races," the emphasis of which was on "the 8,000,000 people of Negro blood in the United States of America," "Pan-Negroism" referred to worldwide movement, within which the American Negroes were "to take their place in the van."⁶ By 1928, after the shift to "Pan-Africanism," the connotation had expanded to include all peoples of the world subjected to the emergent racialized imperial order. In the November 1933 issue of *Crisis*, Du Bois wrote the article, "Pan-Africa and New Racial Philosophy," in which he asserts:

> It is, therefore, imperative that the colored peoples of the world, and first of all those of Negro descent, should begin to concentrate upon this problem of their economic survival, the best of their brains and education. Pan-Africa means intellectual understanding and cooperation among all groups of Negro descent in order to bring about at the earliest possible time the industrial and spiritual emancipation of the Negro peoples.⁷

There is an inchoate theory of signs at play in Du Bois's response to Barton, that bears a remarkable resemblance to Charles Sanders Peirce's, according to which a sign—in this instance the word *Negro*—is something that stands in some relation to something else, some object, for someone capable of interpreting that relation. Barton's problem is that he misconstrues the nature of the relation between the word, *Negro*, and its object. In accord with Du Bois's response, the word, in its material qualities as a sign—the phonemes or graphemes constituting it—has nothing to do in and of itself with its representative function. It has no shared quality with its object; there is no existential fact or necessary causal connection between them. The word is not really connected with the very thing—that particular fleshly form—it putatively references, which means there is no purely demonstrative application of the sign. The objection that *Negro* is a white man's term to insult us suggests, however, that there *is* a causal connection between the phenomenal event of black-skin and Negro. Du Bois strongly disputes that presumption when he states: "The feeling of inferiority is in you, not in any name. The name merely evokes what is already there. Exorcise the hateful complex and no name can ever make you hang your head."⁸ Evoking "what is already there" draws attention to our knowledge of reality being constituted in a cumulative relation of thoughts shared in common over time. "Names are not merely matters of thought and reason," Du Bois writes, "they are growths and habits. So long as the majority of men mean black or brown folk when they say 'Negro,' so long will Negro be the name of folks brown and black."⁹ Even though the sign, in its conventionality, can only point at the what is already there that it does not totally comprehend, its epistemic efficacy remains potent: "Suppose we arose tomorrow morning and lo! Instead of being 'Negroes', all the world called us 'Cheropolidi',—do you really think this would make a vast momentous difference to you and to me? Would the Negro problem be suddenly and eternally settled?"¹⁰ In the dynamics of the triadic relationship of signification Du Bois is purporting, the crucial element is interpretation, which determines the nature of the sign's connection with its object, establishing not only that the sign is meaningful, but also precisely the way it is meaningful. The name *Negro* expresses a general, conventional connection between it and its object. That convention is a function of some common agreement of designating interpretation, what Du Bois refers to as "the name-habit," which is a systemic thinking of the world, a common held belief regarding the relationship between signs as representations and the things they reference. In other words, *Negro* is a sign in the dynamic process of meaningful signification (semiosis) of reality. As such, it is an element in the articulation of the world-in-common, or thinking in the world. The world, by this account, is the complexity of material environmental forces, including the activity of humanity that constitutes and sustains society and its various institutional practices.

In Du Bois's theory, the name *Negro* signifies the various social practices and cultural institutions that give it meaning, the full spectrum of semiosis. *Negro*, in a very specific way, is and is not a weathercock. Du Bois's principal argument in his exchange with Barton is that it is not really connected with the very thing—that particular type of flesh—it putatively signifies, which means there is no purely demonstrative application of the sign. Saying, "Look, a Negro," is not the same signifying action as seeing a weathercock turning in the wind. In fact, it is the causal connection between the weathercock's turning and the wind that brings us to say it is a certain index of the way the wind blows. The relationship between *Negro* and its putative object is of an altogether different order; it is a conventional connection of imputed character that is a function of some common agreement of designating interpretation. It is a symbol, and what it symbolizes, blackness of skin, is already itself thought to signify the opposite of virtue and full humanity within a specific semiotic order. That stated, at the same time *Negro* is necessarily connected to that order; its expression indicates the working of that order. In fact, there is a direct causal connection between that working order and the expression. So *Negro*, while being a conventional symbol, also indexes the momentum of the convention; it shows which way the semiosis is flowing. *Negro* does not designate any *thing*, it has no proper object; rather it indexes *positioning in the order of things*. This is why its usage is always attended by the question, Where am I in relation to that position? Recall the "pertinent" question asked about the Negro in Barthes's semiological analysis of myth: What does *Negro* mean as a sign in our mythology for us *who are not Negro*? This is precisely, of course, what Du Bois dismisses as perpetuating an anthropological and epistemic fallacy when he parodies the question: How does it feel to be a problem? The thrust of his parody is plain: "problem" for whom? His even more challenging and generative response is to change the question: What is the meaning of being black?

There is a fundamental point about cognition and semiosis entailed in the pursuit of this question, one that is along the lines traced from Windham's taxonomy of sentient flesh: cognition and consciousness are articulated *with* semiosis. Shifting the orientation from the semiology of presumptive fixed exteriority to the dynamical semiosis of consciousness brings us to ask what the three correlates are to which *Negro* refers, which is arguably the gist of Du Bois's use of Negro double consciousness. There the question is: When we think *Negro*, to what thought does the sign that is our self address itself? This is not at all simply a matter of Cartesian introspection. We always address our self to thought of another person, which is to say, it is always in relation to other thoughts constituting a stream, or train, of thought. As for what the thought-sign names, what object it stands in relation to, even that relationship is determined by previous thoughts of the same object. It follows that the thought "I am Negro" entails two signs, *I* and *Negro*, connected by a third, the copula *am*. That connection leads us to imagine *Negro* is a predicate of *I*; and it is readily apparent that different predicates may be attached to this same subject, with each making applicable to it some conception. Because each predicable is thought to be true of the same subject, we are lead to imagine the constancy of the subject; and when thinking metaphysically we regard this as that being among beings that contemplates being qua being. More simply put, *subject* is the sign for that entity capable of thinking about its own existence in the context of existence in general. Bearing in mind that the conception is about a sign, its constancy is in its mediate application to things—it is the same subject for a variety of predicables. It is this variety of predicability that leads us to imagine something is true of the subject, which is constant in its receiving predication—what Kant recognized as its logical necessity as a regulative principle of cognition (the transcendental I). Being, then, may be defined as a function of semiosis. Peirce gives an illustration of this with an example most pertinent to our topic.

> Let us suppose, for example, that Toussaint is thought of, and first thought of as a *Negro*, but not distinctly as a man. If this distinctness is afterwards added, it is through the thought that a *negro* is a man; that is to say, the

subsequent thought, *man*, refers to the outward thing by being predicated of that previous thought, *Negro*, which has been had of that thing. If we afterwards think of Toussaint as a general, then we think that this negro, this man was a general. And so in every case the subsequent thought denotes what was thought in the previous thought.[11]

The pertinent point Peirce is illustrating, undisputable racism notwithstanding, is how the representative function of a sign is something it is, not in itself or in a real relation to its object, but in relation to a train of thought. Its pertinence is amplified by the fact that the concept *Negro*, predicable of the subject Toussaint, is not a conception formed by the connection of the two concepts *man* and *black*. The concept man is, instead, predicable of the subject *Negro*: "a *negro* is a man." And it is this predicability that refers to the "outward thing," Du Bois's "what is already there." But the extent to which what is already there has presence in our cognizance, it is a presence *for us*, whatever else it may or may not be independently from us as a community of interpreters. The difficulty has to do with the indeterminacy of the designation *that*, which is not necessarily *this*. What matters is the representative function of the sign. The implication of Du Bois's semiotics of *Negro* as a mode of being is that being is a factitious universal; it is solely a human thinkable, and not a universal, necessary thinkable.[12] Often characterized as "race-consciousness," other times as being obsessed with or fixated on race, and in an older discourse as "knowing one's place" in the order of things, Du Bois's calling Negro double consciousness a "second sight" underscores that semiosis is the articulation of a dynamic community of interpreters. What's more, it is the community's *becoming-in-the-ordering-of consciousness*. That is what *Negro* indexes if it indexes anything at all.

These, then, are the stakes in Du Bois's effort to provide an exposition of *Negro* interiority as illustrative of how subjective consciousness is socially extended, and not in the mode of Husserl's transcendental community, but in the being-at-work-ness of semiosis. A similar proposition is entailed in what we called "a grammar of sociality" when reading "Of the Coming of John," remarking the historizing occurrence of Jones's consciousness as an orientation of cognizance, extending a particular systemic societal dynamic. The proposition that consciousness is socially extended is in back of Du Bois's reference to the thousand and one little actions that make up life into a particular order of conceptual schemata of being in the world, a distinctive pattern of thought and feeling. It is not so much that Negro double consciousness is *exceptionally* socially extended—constituted, or otherwise determined (established) by the symbolic order in various social practices occurring within social and cultural institutions. It is rather that *Negro* signifies a particular variation of conscious agency, or will, realized in the world. Addressing the matter of consciousness is inevitably about probing existence and the nature of the world humans live in, pondering what humans do in and to the world. It is to ask: What changes, if any, result from human being, and whether human action can be evaluated as meaningful in its existence? Formulated in terms of criticism—that is, judgment in the performance of critical thinking, following a particular lineage of practice and techniques of intellection and imagination—in relation to the black community, Du Bois takes up the issue in terms of thinking as a decisive human activity in the world. In this regard, Du Bois's *quaestio* of the Negro is fundamentally an inquiry into the constitutive role of dynamic human intelligence in the formation and sustainability of a universal ethical community not grounded in a transcendental principle, whether theistic or metaphysical. A fuller sense of this is gained when we return our attention to the 1956 Aptheker letter.

Recall Du Bois's stating he gave up the search of absolute "Truth," having arrived instead at firm belief "that gradually the human mind and absolute and provable truth would approach each other and like the 'Asymptotes of the Hyperbola' . . . would approach each other nearer and nearer and yet never in all eternity meet. I therefore turned to Assumption—scientific Hypothesis." In Du Bois's view, hypothesis is a general proposition: "Whenever something of the kind *A* is done, there is a result of kind *B*," which he describes as the workable logic of its truth. Since he held this general proposition to be universal, the firm belief he reports to Aptheker is in the reality of generals or, in older language, universals. The increasing proximity of inductive hypotheses, their efficacious provable "facts," and the "truth" of existence, is the very process by which the existent progressively embodies those universals. Universals, accordingly, are not transcendental givens, nor are they hypostatized substances; rather, they are truths in the sense they are the instantiations of the cumulative thinking over time of a community of interpreters, which, again, is not transcendental but a community *in* and *of* motion. Clearly, Du Bois is not interested in taking up Platonism, but rather seems to be siding with Aristotle when he states in the same letter that he set out to "make a scientific study of human action, based on the hypothesis of the reality of such actions, of the causal connections and of their continued occurrence and change because of Law and Chance." He means that human action (*enérgeia*) is a τρίτον τι (*triton ti*), or as the Latins put it *tertium quid*, is a third element beyond necessity (ἀνάγκη, *anagkē*), the determinism of Democritus's atomistic physics, and absolute arbitrariness or fortune (τύχη, *tyche*). But, whereas for Aristotle, that *enérgeia* unfolds teleologically, according to its constitutive *entelecheia*, in Du Bois's account, it is probabilistic; that is, it is a contingency in relation to law and chance. When we pay careful attention to his wording—"the reality of such actions ... and their continued occurrence and change because of Law and Chance"—clearly it is not quite right to say that, in Du Bois's account, human action is a third element beyond necessity and absolute arbitrariness. Rather it is *because* of these parallel dynamics, and is in apposition to them. Still bearing in mind the mathematics invoked by Du Bois's asymptotes of the hyperbola analogy, we can understand his postulate of human action as contingency in terms of Abraham de Moivre's doctrine of chances, or Pierre Simon Laplace's "calculus of probabilities," derived mathematically in the de Moivre-Laplace Theorem for binomial distribution, which Peirce named, following Gauss, "Normal Distribution."[13] Understanding the meaning in normal distributions of random events was a chief problematic for social statistics in the nineteenth century, and many maintained that chance is merely epistemic. "Chance" is the metonym for our ignorance of the causes of the phenomena we observe to occur successively without apparent order, to paraphrase Laplace. The implication being that all chance events are driven by underlying laws that ensure the observed statistics of the normal distribution. Contra this position, while recognizing a priori probabilities as theory—*hypothesis* is his term—Du Bois maintains, along with William James, that absolute chance (*tyche*) is real, and furthermore, along with Peirce, that it is a primary dynamic, beside the deterministic laws of nature, driving change and increasing complexity. The hypothetical understanding of the constitutive dynamic relation between law, chance, and human action Du Bois shares in his letter to Aptheker echoes what Epicurus stated in his letter to Menoeceus: "some things happen of necessity [κατ' ἀνάγκην, *kat' anagkēn*], others by chance [ἀπό τύχης, *apó tyches*], others through our own agency [παρ' ἡμᾶς, *par' hēmās*]."[14] In that same Epicurean regard, it is understood "that necessity [ἀνάγκην, *anagkēn*] negates responsibility, and chance [τύχης, *tyches*] is inconstant; whereas our own actions are autonomous [ἀδέσποτος, *adéspostos*], and it is to them that praise and blame naturally attach," which is to say it is the autonomy of human action that gives us the sense of moral responsibility.[15] Recalling for a moment in that regard our earlier exposition of his critique of statistical sociology, we can see Du Bois is working from the postulate that human beings can alter and redirect the course of events so as to better human conditions relative to the understanding of natural law. Inquiry into these occurrences is experimental and uncompromisingly committed to empirically verifiable evidence. And the evidence pointed consistently to decisive human action, leaving aside as irrelevant the possibility of divine purpose or teleology, that "some God [was] also influencing and directing human action and natural law." Du Bois held, as a corollary, that because manifestations of decisive human agency are limited by environment, inheritance, and natural law, "from the point of view of science, these occurrences must be a matter of chance and not law." Rehearsing and embellishing on those same earlier remarks apropos the teleological question just raised, this confluence was at the core of Du Bois's maintaining sociology to be "the measurement of the elements of Chance in Human action," going so far as to claim that "true students of sociology [assuming] a world of physical law, peopled by beings capable in some degree of actions inexplicable and uncalculable according to these laws . . . [seek] to measure, if you will, the Kantian Absolute and Undetermined Ego."[16] Measuring the "Kantian 'Absolute and Undetermined Ego'" is tantamount, of course, to turning Kant's transcendental critique on its head. Rather than seeking the grounds of the ego in a transcendental order, accounting for its operations in terms of a teleological principle, Du Bois's sociology recognizes the operations of the ego as emergent with and in the order of things, accounted for in terms of materialist phenomenology, its "deviations" from the established understanding of how things work (law) being innovations in the law. The relational dynamics of chance and law, then, are the process of evolution whereby the existent comes more and more to embody the universal. We can say that thinking controlled by hypothetical experimental reasoning—and it should be noted that Du Bois's identifying "assumption" with scientific hypothesis suggests the latter involves abduction as well as inductive a deductive reasoning—follows a pattern that, while not teleological in the Aristotelian sense of a circumscribing *télos*, determines certain habits of conduct as conditional for arriving at truth. This is what he means by scientific method, which in its autopoetic processes of innovation—what we have become habituated to call "paradigm shifts"—constitutes an ongoing community of investigators, or, if you will, interpreters, the activity of which is deliberative, and so conventional. If we say that those habits of conduct, of action, are destined, it is in the sense that they are circumscribed and dictated by the processes and must follow the trajectory they set out. They are functions of a line of flight that is conceptually perpetual and, again, asymptotic.

Assessed in these terms, the Negro population's being constituted immediately in the engagement of sociopolitical and economic forces with human will, both the subjugating and the subjugated, provides a direct empirically verifiable instance of the processes *in concreto situ* by which the person is *made* in the dynamic interaction of the material forces of society. So the methodologically rigorous inductive analysis of Negro sociality would yield a model of sociopsychological development with universal significance. As Du Bois states, again, writing to Aptheker, this was one of the reasons he began in 1896 to "count and classify the facts concerning the American Negro and the way to his betterment through human action."[17] The date refers to when he undertook the yearlong research project, on commission from the University of Philadelphia, to gather and analyze data on the social condition of the Negro in Philadelphia.

By the time its results were published in 1899 as *The Philadelphia Negro*—one of the first monographs in statistically based sociological science—Du Bois was already two years into his directorship of the annual conferences at Atlanta University, which had been instituted in 1896 by the university's president, Horace Bumstead, and a trustee, George Bradford, as "The Atlanta University Studies." They were conceived of, from inception, as a program in inductive sociological analysis of urban Negro problems conducted annually, comparable to what was being done for rural districts at Tuskegee Institute. Du Bois assumed directorship with the 1897 conference, and held it until 1914.

Refining the methodology of data-gathering and inductive analysis, Du Bois organized the conferences into a long-term research program of inductive statistical analysis of the changing social conditions of the Negro population. During his directorship the conferences gathered data across the urban South in a ten-year longitudinal study and published its findings in eighteen papers.[18] Demystification of the "Negro problem" with science was the impetus driving Du Bois's directorship of the Atlanta Conferences project. As he put it in a retrospective description: "Carefully gathered scientific proof that neither color nor race determined the limits of a man's capacity or desert ... [would achieve] the long-term remedy [to racism]. ... 'The Truth shall make ye free.'"[19] Du Bois's faith at that time in empirical research as an instrument for social reform was the effect of his work with Gustav von Schmoller, who directed his dissertation at Berlin University. He was particularly influenced by Schmoller's postulate that measurable data from historical experience provides firm grounds for logical induction about social dynamics and conditions, which, in turn, form the basis for normative laws. This was predicated on rejecting classical economics' method of deriving rules from axiomatic first principles deduced from universally valid precepts of human action.[20] Du Bois carried Schmoller's rejection of the axiomatic-deductive method in favor of inductive analysis of carefully gathered empirical data over into the field of sociology. It is a well-rehearsed story that by 1903, just four years into his directorship of the Atlanta Conferences, Du Bois encountered methodological problems of measurement and interpretation. The accumulated data, which he characterized as "a growing tangled mass of facts," was already so immense and variegated that the analyses were indeterminate, making it nearly impossible to produce anything like a systematic meaningful account of the Negro's social condition. The resulting inability to arrive at a meaningful account of the data meant real delay in developing a scientifically based prescriptive program of social improvement. What's more, Du Bois had concluded by 1944 that "the majority of men do not usually act in accord with reason," but are driven by psychologies so naturalized through habituation and so regularized by the rhythms of political economic life that something cataclysmic is required to achieve the radical reform necessary for realizing universal freedom.[21] From his remarks to Aptheker in the 1956 letter, however, Du Bois clearly remained committed throughout his long career to the proposition that inductive analysis of determinant historical human action could shed considerable light on processes of social institution, and even the activity of individual agency.

If we elaborate Du Bois's asymptote of the hyperbola analogy, assuming the hyperbolas to be human knowledge and truth, with "Law" the transverse axis and "Chance" the conjugate, then ethics is the point at the center of the hyperbola where they meet, from which are plotted the oblique asymptotic lines of continuous thinking along which the branches of the hyperbola move toward infinity, with the hyperbola vortices approaching one another in the evolutionary process that is the history of thought. Concluding the letter, Du Bois raises the issue of ethics, describing those of his colleagues in sociology who refute the hyperbola analogy's epistemological implications as having "reverted to firm belief in unalterable Law, thus to my mind changing Man to an automaton and making Ethics unmeaning and Reform a contradiction in terms."[22]

Doctrine of Submission with "The Renaissance of Ethics"

The reversion in ethics he has in mind is the one he critiques in the previously mentioned unpublished 1889 essay, "The Renaissance of Ethics," which he postulates results from the fact "that modern systematic ethical study has practically made but little advance upon the Scholastic method," meaning theistic teleology.[23] And, as he argues there, the continued grounding of ethics in such teleology hinders the development of an ethics predicated on an empirical "science of mind." The question behind the so-called Negro problem is: What would real social change be? The question behind that is: What is the worldly basis of human society, for interpersonal human relation? Pursuing that, we are brought to ask: Can there be a "science of duty"?[24] And behind that is the fundamental epistemological question: What is the relation between science and teleology?[25] Addressing this fundamental question, Du Bois ventures an analogy:

> Suppose a man has before him a piece of finely wrought lace; he asks two questions: What? and Why? What is this, why is it such as it is? There are two methods he may pursue: he may guess at why it is, or he may systematically and carefully find out *what* it is in order that facts may guide his guesses and ultimately lead him to the truth. Manifestly, if his work is anyways intricate, and if *it is of any moment whether he arrives at the truth or not*, he should take the latter method: true it may never lead him to the truth, but

it will lead him nearer than any other path. He will in pursuing this method strictly separate inquiring into the What from inquiring into the Why—this was indeed the very gist of his method. He searches the What *for* the why, and cannot consequently use the *why* to search with. If, however, by strange oversight or ignorance, he does mix them; explains an isolated fact by a wild unbridled guess instead of bridling the hypothesis by multitudinous systematized facts; speculates when he should search; what happens? Scholasticism. If now he separates his piece of lace into two parts; on one part still pursues his mongrel method, on the other confines himself to a strict search for the *what*—what then? On one side advance; on the other side Scholasticism. Now apply this to the World: science on one part of the lace, metaphysics on the other. Since it first saw the sunrise the world has wondered—has asked What and Why. First it wondered, then it guessed a thousand years, and finally began a systematic search for truth—on half the lace. It has partially come to the conclusion—it must finally come to the conclusion, that the only way to find *why* the world is [as it is] is to find *what* it is—the only path to teleology is science. . . . In the world then—to us, is it of any moment whether we arrive at the Truth or not? Yes, answers the philosopher, "we want Truth for its own sake"—not so answers, has already answered, the world: "Nay, Truth is not our End"; we worship not a fetish of bare fact; the very situation of *not knowing* the *why* of a mockingly mysterious universe, of not knowing how vast or how slight is the difference between the Best and the Worst that universe can be by our own efforts, makes the question What is the End? a question that touches the deepest depths of our souls, that overshadows the awfulness of life and Death itself in the greater question of Heaven and Hell. The object, then, of science is Truth, *Truth is the one path to teleology, teleology is ethics.*[26]

With this lace analogy, Du Bois lays out the terms of his argument for discovering a secular ethics. His invoking this same argument sixty-seven years later, in the last decade of his life, is as certain an indication as any of its continued centrality in his thinking. Its formulation in "The Renaissance of Ethics" is arguably the earliest and perhaps the most systematic presentation by Du Bois we have of his critique of Christian theology, in particular its theistic teleology. That critique is a fundamental aspect of his overall project. As noted earlier, Du Bois wrote "The Renaissance of Ethics" as the final paper for the course "Philosophy IV," which he took with William James at Harvard during the 1888–1889 academic year. James taught this course only that once in his entire career, and did so as a last-moment replacement for its regular instructor, his colleague and friend Josiah Royce, who was on sabbatical leave in Australia. Under James, the course was chiefly a close reading of two James Martineau works, one per semester. The fall 1888 semester was dedicated to volume 2 of *Types of Ethical Theory* and the spring 1889 semester to volume 1 of *A Study of Religion, Its Sources and Contents*. Du Bois's essay engages the second semester's reading, *A Study of Religion*, in which Martineau, postulating two fundamental sources of religion—human curiosity about the origin and end of things and "the consciousness of what *ought to be* beyond anything *that is* as a moral or ethical rule—expressly aims to vindicate the teleological interpretation of nature, otherwise known as the physico-theological argument for God's existence, after its "opprobrious treatment" in the wake of Bacon's restricting it to metaphysics.[27] Martineau is especially concerned with the condescending dismissal of William Paley's argument from design, resulting from the displacement of final causes, or deliberative purpose (*télos*), with causality as "a rule of time-succession traceable in the order of phenomena."[28] Hume, Brown, and both Mills are held to have participated in this displacement, but the chief culprits are Kant and Comte. Although he gives Comte's Positivism its due attention as one of the more fashionable trends in "Advanced thought" dismissive of the argument from design, it is Kant who is singled out as the principal fount of condescension. This is largely because it was he who presented the most systematic critique of metaphysics, which was elaborated on not only by Comte, but also the Utilitarians, Darwinists, and Pragmatists—all of whom Martineau identifies as opponents of the natural theology associated with Paley and the Bridgewater Treatises. Kant's epistemology sets the stage for Comte's subsequently expunging the language and ideas of causality from scientific analysis of the phenomena of nature. Hence, Martineau in his rebuttal of Comte, charts a history of ideas from Kant to Royce, in which he demonstrates how inescapable the teleological argument is as he essays what he terms a critical metaphysics that recombines "the intuition of Causality as the grounds of natural phenomena, and that of Right as the ground of Moral."[29] On the thesis that "metaphysics are sure to end in a Theology," Martineau's plan is to protect natural faith by countermining the hostile lines of philosophical thought that approach its foundation.

Judging from Du Bois's notebook for Philosophy IV, which is an orderly lecture-by-lecture transcription of the course, James followed the book's itinerary rather closely, all the while consistently challenging Martineau's efforts at countermining in keeping with his own effort to displace metaphysics for what he would eventually come to call "Radical Empiricism."[30] According to its opening paragraph, "The Renaissance of Ethics" resulted from an extended study of Scholastic ethics prompted by skepticism about the modern dogma of anti-Scholasticism—hence the essay's subtitle: "A Critical Comparison of Scholastic and Modern Ethics." Conceivably, the beginning of that study antedated Du Bois's taking the philosophy course with James. He came to

Harvard consequent to his having "determined to go to the best university in the land and if possible the world, to discover Truth." That determination was precipitated by his experience at Fisk, where in the last semester of his senior year he took a philosophy course that, as he told Aptheker, "was ruined by the interpolation of religious dogma and inexcusable contradictions of logic in reasoning" of its professor, Erastus Cravath.[31] The course with James, then, provided a sought-after occasion to bring thinking to some fruition. So it is not at all surprising James found the handwritten fifty-five-page course essay to be, as he says in his final comments, "a very original thesis, full of independent thought and rigorous expression."[32] Even more interesting, however, are the clear points of disagreement between the professor and the young scholar evident in James's marginal commentary, but also in Du Bois's notebook. Those disagreements reveal just how qualified and nuanced Du Bois's vaunted turn to James's pragmatism was. Particularly pertinent to our concerns here is their disagreement about the possibility of a "science" of ethics. Commenting on Du Bois's attributing to him and Royce the attempt to base ethics on matters of fact and make it a science, James writes in the essay's marginalia: "I doubt we do seek to make it a 'science'—to me, that seems impossible."[33] In his insistence on a scientifically based ethics, however, Du Bois approaches Peirce's first formulation of the pragmatist maxim—"By their fruits shall ye know them"[34]—rather than James's interpretation of it. Peirce consistently contested that interpretation and eventually abandoned the term of his coinage, "*pragmatism*," as a result of James's popularization of it, for "pragmaticism," quipping, "it is ugly enough to be safe from kidnappers."[35] What I mean is that Du Bois is working from the same premise as Peirce that the entelechy of mind is the process of contiguous semiosis over time. As Peirce put it in a later formulation of the maxim: "The pragmaticist does not make the *summum bonum* to consist in action, but makes it to consist in that process of evolution whereby the existent comes more and more to embody those generals which . . . [are] now said to be destined, which is what we strive to express in calling them reasonable."[36] The significance of this language to Du Bois's thinking will become apparent as we attend more closely to the text of "The Renaissance of Ethics," along with the notebook, from which much of the substance of its argument is taken. It suffices to point out now that it bears directly on the way Du Bois's critique of theistic teleology relates to his critique of Kantian transcendental philosophy, and how the problematic of sentient flesh is involved in his theory of the Negro as an exemplary of a global type expressed in the historical social order of capitalist modernity, a theory that is itself a paradigmatic articulation of the poetics of black being.

The full wording of the essay's governing thesis is: "that the Renaissance of ethics has not yet wholly passed, i.e., that modern systematic ethical study has practically made but little advance upon the Scholastic method."³⁷ The renaissance in question was supposed to have occurred in the sixteenth and seventeenth centuries, beginning with Bacon's elaboration and application of inductive reasoning in his *Novum Organum Scientiarum*, followed by Descartes's *Meditationes de prima philosophia*. Du Bois starts out by tracking the conceptual lineage defined by the Neo-Platonist contention between reason and revelation as sources of knowledge posited with Origen's initiation of systemic Christian theology. The salient point of note is how Origen's effort to reconcile the deliberate intelligence of Plato's demiurge with the intrinsic causality of Aristotle's entelechy in support of Christian faith achieved a "theistic teleology of the most mundane character . . . that resulted in the subjection of reason to dogma."³⁸ Situating Scholasticism in this genealogy, Du Bois then presents an itinerary of thought that traverses the span from Erigena in the ninth century until Aquinas in the thirteenth with two in-tandem movements of inquiry: "the what and why of the universe." Carefully following the way he tracks that history of thought helps to clarify how his *quaestio* of the Negro entails critically overturning the Western theological-philosophical tradition's conceptualization of human being.

Acknowledging Scholasticism's ambition as "a wonderful example of that force which impels the mind to the Unity of Truth," Du Bois critiques its methodological flaws, chief among which is continued adherence to the dogmatic proposition that divine revelation has priority as *the* source of true knowledge about the universe. This is clearly the case with Erigena's reiteration of Augustine's engagement with Neo-Platonism, as well as Abelard's enhancement on it. Even Aquinas's subsequently acknowledging two parallel sources of knowledge—which, in Du Bois's account, is the first epistemological shift leading to modern thought—merely secured "the right of reason to an equal place with dogma."³⁹ Epistemologically, this eventually allows natural philosophy, or "science" as Du Bois puts it, a tangential course in relation to revelation; but it does not emancipate it from the constraints of dogma. Following Augustine in construing all principles of demonstration and all demonstrative propositions (apophantic reasoning) as necessary truths "only because they exist in the eternal mind which is the divine intellect alone," Aquinas makes science the handmaiden of revelation.⁴⁰

We should pause a moment and give careful attention to Du Bois's characterization of the ethical stakes in Aquinas's ordering of intelligence because it is central to how he construes the effect of the second epistemological division that occurs with Bacon and Descartes and inaugurates modernity. With Aquinas's bifurcation, dogmatic Christian theology is secured as the higher parallel path of knowledge. Whether the methods of natural philosophy provide a true account of what and how things are in the world is measured by their agreement with theistic account of why things are so in the world, which is to say, divine final cause, God, the universal author of all things good, the highest good or *summum bonum*. Du Bois's paraphrase of Scholasticism's taxonomy of the good in this regard is well worth quoting at length here:

> There are two kinds of good, the uncreated and eternal—God, and the created and temporal, viz.: (1) goods of fortune, (2) goods of body, (3) goods of soul. Some place the Highest Good among these latter, but it cannot be among the goods of fortune, because this leaves out Health, Reason, and Virtue; nor among the goods of body because the body is lower than the soul, and the Highest Good can be lower than nothing; nor among the goods of soul because they can be attained only by a few and then imperfectly, and abstract virtue is impossible. Therefore, the Highest Good is God, who is perfect, comprehends all goods, and only in him is man perfect. Man may strive after God implicitly, i.e., after happiness, or explicitly, through free will. All other goods in the world are *bona utila*, means to the Highest Good. The subjective Highest Good is, consequently, the knowledge and love of God. If man seeks the Highest Good, he will make his life like God's. This depends on action and the action must be the highest and noblest, and on the highest object, i.e., knowing God; this, according to the definition of Highest Good, should make man perfect, which it does, but not in this world—only in the higher life, which must be eternal, least the fear of losing it impair the happiness: this life, then, is only relative to the next. In this life, however, a man must have a life-work, on the fulfilling of which depends his hope of the life to come, in doing this there is a temporal happiness, viz., the goods of body and fortune, and especially the goods of the soul, which give us knowledge of truth, i.e., God, who is eternal truth. Without freedom of will ethical conduct is impossible. There is a difference of good and bad in men's actions for . . . reason makes certain demands on the will and it makes a vast difference whether they are fulfilled or not. . . . We need a moral rule to point out this difference. This rule must not only direct but compel, and thus we have it divided into the *norma directiva* and *norma imperata*; we ask what is the *norma imperata*? There are three false theories: the Excessive Supernatural (direct command of God), the Subjective Rational (Kant's), and the Materialistic (Utilitarian). The real rule is the moral hierarchy of inner motives, supplemented by Divine intelligence as far as revealed in man. The *norma imperata* is the reason. A law implies a law-giver—a moral law a legitimate law-giver, a universal law, and one for the highest good of all. God is the author of all the laws underlying the natural moral order. The obligation to obey these laws lies not in the

reason, but in the will of God. It does not, however, depend on his free will because having made a free choice he must carry it out.⁴¹

Correlating eternal happiness with knowing and loving God recalls Augustine's pronouncement that virtuous love of God, *caritas*, is key to salvation, about which we will have a great deal to say later. Right now, in the course of our engaging Du Bois's paraphrasis of Scholasticism's taxonomy of the good, the pertinent issue, with respect to the *norma imperata*, is the relationship between duty and happiness: What ought to be done in order to secure future salvation? "Given a universe with two possible futures and the question becomes to each individual, How much difference will it make if this be tomorrow's universe rather than that?"⁴² Because the difference between these two possible futures for Scholasticism is the difference between Heaven and Hell, the question of duty is settled. It hangs upon the *summum bonum* as "the cause and purpose of this great drama we call life; in fine, to understand duty, we must know ends, . . . for the very idea of duty depends entirely on what is the teleological base, the end of existence."⁴³ With this identification of the *summum bonum* and final cause as the basis for explaining the world of existence, Scholasticism becomes "an imposing edifice that sought to enclose in its four walls the whole universe of teleological truth," placing ethics in the line of pursuit for uncreated eternal happiness (unity with God) in opposition to the pursuit of earthly happiness, that of the flesh and world.⁴⁴ At the vortex of Scholasticism's methodological error is the imperative to constrain science—the impulse toward systematic knowledge about the *what* and *how* of reality—according to dogmatic understanding of revealed theistic teleology. Consecrated as dogma, teleology curtails speculative imagination and "usurps science."⁴⁵

The second epistemological shift, precipitated by Bacon and Descartes, liberated natural philosophy from "the mischief of Scholasticism," bifurcating it into physics and metaphysics. Yet, while physics as natural science abandoned inquiry into final causes in favor of efficient causes, metaphysics remained overtly invested in teleology; and that investment continued to provide conceptual footing for the new, modern science. The persistence of this teleological principle into the modern era, albeit stripped of theistic dogma, contributes to the failure of the renaissance of ethics. Ample archival support for Du Bois's reading is readily at hand. For instance, Bacon's oft-cited remark in *Advancement of Learning* that "the inquisition of Final Causes is barren, and like a virgin consecrated to God produces nothing," aimed at excluding such investigation only from physics, while he expressly maintained it to be the "second part of metaphysics."⁴⁶ Descartes also emphatically eschews final-cause explanation in natural philosophy, but then proceeds to provide an apparently

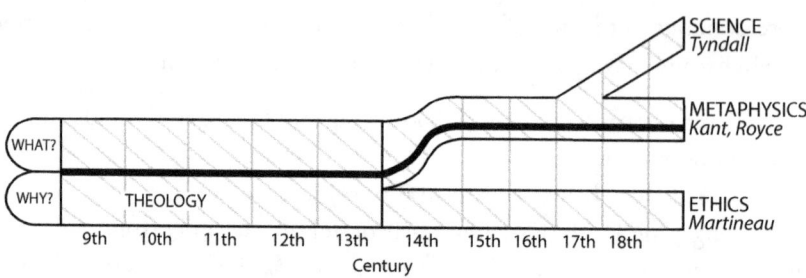

4.1 Du Bois's Chart of the History of Thought in Western Christendom

teleological account of the biological functions of sensation in Meditation Six.[47] Nor does Descartes deny that God acts from ends, but rather that man cannot ever discover that purpose, and so consideration of it must be excluded from the field of physical inquiry, where only efficient causes can be determinately known. In Du Bois's judgment, the primary contributing factor in the persistence of teleology in metaphysics was precisely the hard distinction between mind and matter as objects of study resulting from the Baconian and Cartesian epistemologies. "Only matter was capable of scientific treatment, and consequently science ... strictly confined itself to matter, while in metaphysics and ethics science and teleology have remained blended."[48] Du Bois presents a diagram charting the history of thought in Western Christendom from the ninth through to the nineteenth century, articulated as the two questions of "WHAT?" and "WHY?" (figure 4.1).

This diagram shows the continuity of theistic teleology in the history of modern thought, despite the two epistemological bifurcations. At the first, occurring in the thirteenth century with Aquinas's *Summa Theologica*, theistic teleology is differentiated from science, which retains an aspect of teleology, the two becoming parallel sources of knowledge. The resultant line of theistic teleology continues unadulterated by scientific reasoning for the full duration from Erigena to Martineau. The second bifurcation occurs in the early seventeenth century, coincident with the publication of Bacon's *Novum Organum Scientiarum*, when the line of science branches into natural philosophy (science), leading to Tyndall, and metaphysics, leading to Kant and Royce. We can readily see, then, how material science may have advanced with the Baconian and Cartesian epistemological bifurcation, but the resulting metaphysics remained in the grip of Scholasticism. Whereas "science is daily narrowing the field for available hypotheses," and so progressively approaching truth, "metaphysics is widening hers, [generating] new and bewildering theories, nice hairsplitting and words, words, words," in the course of which its divergence from the world humans live in increases.[49] "The history of modern metaphysics from Kant to Royce," Du Bois declares, "is not a whit less unavailing than scholastic science from Abelard to William Ockham; both [metaphysics and Scholasticism] labor under the same mistake; to both, unity seemed impossible; with each, science and teleology, fact and ultimate cause, were indissolubly bound and knit up together in a manner positively forbidding advance."[50] More troubling even than the Scholasticism of modern metaphysics was the development of two "almost antagonist" lines of inquiry: the scientific and the theological.

> The physicist, making all the advance made anywhere, not unnaturally concluded that the science of matter was all the world, and consequently began to evolve the world ethics and all therefrom. On the other hand, Christian ethics remained practically untouched, except a necessary retreat from dogma to faith. Science, however, was not satisfied—there must be found a "scientific" basis for duty, and pleasure, life and chance were, at different times, called into requisition; so far so good: for either stand had the questionable advantage of not being "disprovable" (to coin a word); but they went one step further and demanded *either* that man should follow pleasure or life with the same deep moral sense as he follows God, i.e., that like and dislike be right and wrong, *or* that man have no moral nature at all. This was demanding an impossibility: for the very idea of duty depends entirely on what is the teleological base, the end of existence; consequently, the deep moral faith of the world found no resting place here, but clung to the scholastic God. The Christian ethical philosophers, on the other hand, in formulating their moral philosophy, approximated the truth more nearly; indeed, were only kept from it by the strange oversight which in these days has bound together in metaphysics, science of mind and teleology of the universe. "Act," says Martineau and his school, "in accordance with the highest motive," which is but a subjective statement of the Scholastic "Seek the Highest Good," a rule which, to anyone *having faith* in a certain teleology, is as ultimate as possible.[51]

Before metaphysics can get on par with natural philosophy and slip the yoke of theology it must "banish teleologic guesses and dogma, whether true or false, from its the domain," just as the material sciences had done.[52] Once emancipated form Scholastic teleology, metaphysics, "instead of inquiring into the categories of the reason, space-perception, and the authority of conscience . . . shall systematically study the mind's actual manifestations just as the physicist studies heat not by its inner consciousness, but by what it does."[53]

We come, then, to Du Bois's assertion in the essay about William James's and Josiah Royce's respective projects being in search of science of ethics:

Lately, however, with Professors James and Royce, a variation of this comes in; another attempt to base ethics upon fact—to make it a science. This theory may be so stated: the attempt to unify goods and find a *summum bonum* is fruitless and impossible; there is therefore no *summum bonum* and one must strive to realize all that anyone anywhere calls good.[54]

James's dissent from this assessment of his and Royce's work aside, bundling them together as proponents of an ethics with no use for a *summum bonum* is rather perplexing, given their pronounced polemics on the matter. While James's critique of metaphysics clearly informs the historical analysis in "The Renaissance of Ethics," the function Josiah Royce plays here is complicated and contradictory, if not simply confusing. All the more so given the text read under James's tutelage that precipitated Du Bois's critique of Christian teleology, Martineau's *A Study of Religion*, is the same work that prompted Royce to ask: "In what sense, if any, can the modern man consistently be, in creed, a Christian?"[55] This is the principal question posed in *The Problem of Christianity*, where, working from the hypothesis that the human race has been subject to a more or less coherent process of education in which Christianity is a paradigmatic pedagogical moment, Royce elaborates a metaphysics of community through philosophical treatment of the Pauline conception of the church as the universal community of love. He gains this through interrogating the way in which Paul's idea of salvation from original sin through grace and loving union with the spirit of Jesus Christ is inseparable from his regarding the church as the visible worldly body of Christ. In point of fact, Du Bois found the solution to theistic teleology in Royce's project somewhat farfetched. Yet, he tells us in "My Evolving Program" that in the course of searching for a science of ethics (the "scientific law of action"), he "fell back upon my Royce and James," through whom he discerns the operation of chance in the ordering of human life. "This," he concludes, "was the Jamesian pragmatism, applied not simply to ethics, but to all human action, beyond what seemed to me, increasingly, the distinct limits of physical law."[56]

To better appreciate Du Bois's associating Royce with James in seeking a science of ethics we need have recourse to his course notebook for Philosophy IV, where we find the entry for "Lesson IV" beginning with the statement: "Royce's argument for idealism is a new original argument which I cannot shake."[57] This is followed immediately with the diagram shown in figure 4.2. Du Bois then gives this narrative analysis of the diagram: "WJ to correspond with the other WJ except as the over-soul comprehends them as objects & makes them by thinking. This provides for truth and error." Bear in mind, this is a notebook, paraphrasing James's course lectures. And it is critical paraphrasing, meaning there are notes of disagreement, as well as elaboration in clarification—a sort

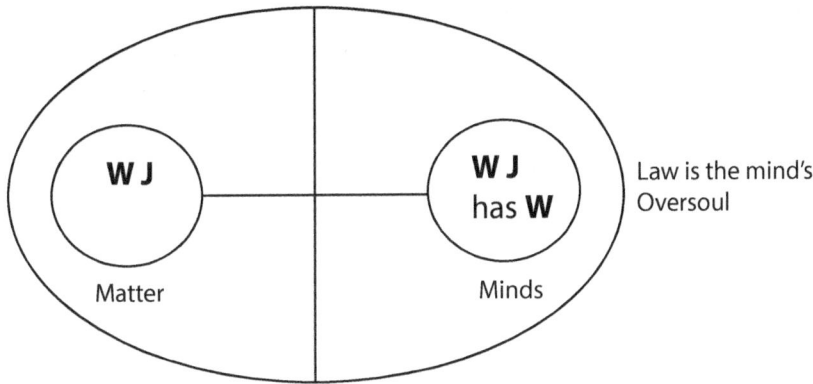

4.2 Du Bois's "Lesson IV" Diagram

of thinking through and grappling with the lecture points. This is clearly the case with regard to the statement about Royce's idealism. The statement itself is a report of James's assessment of Royce's philosophical project, echoing what he stated in his 1885 *Atlantic Monthly* review of *Religious Aspect of Philosophy* as: "Dr. Royce's new and original proof of idealism is so far as we know, the most positive and radical proof yet proposed."[58] James was an ardent critic of the absolute idealism that Royce spent most of his career arguing for, so his being unable to shake that argument was a testimony to its force and insight. As he states in the review:

> The more one thinks, the more one feels that there is a real puzzle here. Turn and twist as we will, we are caught in a tight trap. Although we cannot help believing that our thoughts *do* mean realities and are true or false of them, we cannot for the life of us ascertain how they *can* mean them. If thought be one thing and reality another, by what pincers, from out of all the realities, does the thought pick out the special one it intends to know? And if the thought knows the reality *falsely*, the difficulty of answering the question becomes indeed extreme. Our author calls the question insoluble on these terms; and we are inclined to think him right, and to suspect that his idealist escape from the quandary may be the best one for us to take.[59]

That the diagram, although most likely Du Bois's, is still a Jamesian elaboration of Royce is signaled by the use of the term, "over-soul," in it and the subsequent analysis. James uses this term in the review to rename what Royce designates varyingly in *The Religious Aspect of Philosophy* as "Universal Will," "Universal Reason," "Universal Consciousness," and "Universal Thought." Paraphrasing Royce's argument for a Universal Thought in which all particularities exist, he writes: "An 'Over-soul,' of whose enveloping thought our thought and the things we think are alike fractions—such is the only hypothesis that can form a basis for the reality of truth and of error in the world."[60] Deployed in this way, the term, which James takes from the title of Emerson's renowned 1841 essay, suggests an affinity between Emersonian Hegelianism, otherwise known as Transcendentalism, and Royce's absolute idealism.[61] Yet, even if James judged such absolute idealism "insubstantial and unreal enough" and was certain that the Hegelians qua Transcendentalists would be pleased with Royce's book for reaching results similar to theirs, he thought Royce's method superior because it is "entirely free from that identification of contradictories which is the great stumbling-block in the Hegelian system of thought."[62] The upshot of Royce's absolute idealism is "that all truth is known to one Thought, that is infinite, in which the world lives and moves and has its being."[63] Characterizing Royce's Universal Thought as "pantheistic monism," the ordinary objection to which is the ethical one—"that it makes all that happens a portion of the eternal reason, and so must nourish a fatalistic mood, and a willingness to accept and consecrate whatever is, no matter what its moral quality may be"[64]—James thinks Royce far more serious and rigorous than the Hegelians in attending to the problem of evil, providing in the last chapter of his book "as original and fresh a treatment of the subject as we know."[65]

The context for the reported statement and the attending diagram is defending Royce's idealism from precisely the ethical objection, which is what Martineau provides in *A Study of Religion*. Du Bois records in his notebook the effort, carried out across three lessons thus far (III, IV, and V), to counter Martineau's erroneous characterization of Royce's concept of "Universal Thought" as a repudiation of the category of causality. What is pertinent to our concerns is how in the notebook, Du Bois does not merely record James's defense of Royce against Martineau, but, in elaborating Royce's argument for error, sets out the groundwork for his own critique of theistic teleology, which is the thrust of "The Renaissance of Ethics" and, as shall be seen, pivots on the diagram. Let us note that the scope of James's correction covers book 2 in volume 1 of *A Study of Religion*, "Theism," where Martineau presents a sweeping expository review of the history of philosophical theories of causation, arguing that causality in some form or another is essential to our perception and understanding of things in the world, and that when we know something other than our own states of consciousness, it is in relation to causality.[66] On this basis, he postulates that the "Infinite Being presupposed in all phenomena must be sought in the field of his *Causality*," through the exploration of which can be found his singular will.[67] This is central to Martineau's defense of theistic teleology in particular and theism in general. His issue with Royce's *The Religious Aspect of Philosophy*, which he erroneously recognizes as a "new version of Theism," is that it "divests the Divine Mind of all causality, and finds its perfection in the exact correspondence of its consciousness with facts as they are: All seeing, all-judging, right-thinking, but doing nothing and preventing nothing, it is the infinitude of Reason and the negation of Will."[68] Martineau is contesting Royce's proposition that "in the midst of the warfare of individual wills, we have caught sight of an Universal Will," resulting in a moral doctrine, the maxim of which, briefly stated, is: "Act always in the light of the completest insight into all the aims that thy act is to affect."[69] In critique of Royce's idealism, Martineau proffers a critical paraphrasis of Royce's argument for community as the fundamental philosophical principal in ethics, which is quoted here at length because it is the context of Du Bois's engagement with Royce *in critique* of Martineau.

> If I fling myself into the throng of life, to consult the dominant aims of other men, I am confused by the din of clamorous demands, tormented by the "warfare of ideals," and borne hither and thither by their "instability." There will be no want of advisers willing to rescue me and set me clear; the dogmatist inviting me into his patent ideal, to drive off with him through the crowd of impostors that fly at his approach; and the sceptic [sic] bidding me disregard the rival pretensions of all, and believe one as good as another, and each best as the fancy takes me. Professor Royce requires me to reject the one as a false redeemer, yet not despair, in spite of the other, of still determining a "highest aim" of human activity. The very hopelessness into which I am plunged by the conflict of incompatible ends of human life, betrays the secret of an ideal beyond them all, and marks the first stirring of a "moral insight" stealing towards that ulterior light. If there were nothing to choose among them, why should I care about their strife? If all are legitimate alike, no one is the worse for their dividing the wills of men among them, and my despondency at the sway of "chance desires" is unmeaning. That I cannot part with it shows how I am haunted by a dream of *harmony*, as the over-topping crown of all ideals, the τέλος τελεότατον [perfect end] of a "Universal Will." The hindrance to the attainment of this end is the preoccupation of each will with its own particular aim, and the unsympathetic gaze at the different drift of his neighbour's movement. The remedy is plain: break the bonds of your individuality; plant yourself in his enthusiasm; nay, realize all the several aims that engage the lives of others; let them be admitted to your thought on equal terms, as if the many wills had coalesced in one; and in this unification, the conflict will have died away: the moral insight into all human ends will have conquered a peace for each; and your rule will henceforth be, "Having made myself, as far as I am able, one with all the conflicting wills before me, I must act out the resulting

universal will as it then arises in me." This "realization of others' life" is to be more than an imaginative representation to yourself of others' type of character; more even than sympathy with it as a foreign sample of heroism; it must be an entry on your part into their inner consciousness,—a fusion of your personality with theirs, so complete as to annul the difference between the *meum* and *tuum* of aim and experience, and gather all agency into one. By this "moral insight" you are lifted above the very antithesis between Self and Not-self: it says to us all, *act as one* being; the universal will of the moral insight must aim at the destruction of all which separates us into a heap of different selves, and at the attainment of some higher positive aim: the undivided soul we are bound to make our ideal; and the ideal of that soul cannot be the separate happiness of you and of me, nor the negative fact of our freedom from hatred, but must be something above us all, and yet very positive.[70]

The argument Martineau is paraphrasing occurs in chapter 6 of Royce's *The Religious Aspect of Philosophy*, "The Moral Insight." After having undertaken a thorough skeptical interrogation of ethical doctrines from Plato, the Stoics, and Christianity to Hobbes, Kant, and Schopenhauer, Royce turns to interrogate the skepticism itself. Distinguishing between the "mental death [of] ... unreflective, self-satisfied skepticism" and that which he calls "self-critical theoretical skepticism" and claiming the whole of *The Religious Aspect of Philosophy* to be an illustration of the latter, he asks: "What is the sense of this theoretical skepticism of our present attitude?"[71] The attitude, of course, is the one taken toward ethical doctrine across the first five chapters of the book. Proclaiming that his entire enterprise turns on it, Royce gives his reply to this question:

> This skepticism expresses an indifference that we feel when we contemplate two opposing aims in such a way as momentarily to share them both. For the moment we realize equally these warring aims. They are ours. This conflict is in us. The two wills here represented are our will. And for this reason, and for this only, can we feel the skeptical indecision. Had we only the will to choose the one end alone, we should unhesitatingly choose it, and should not see enough of the opposing will to be skeptics. Had we only the will that chooses the opposing end, we should feel equally indifferent to the first. Had we neither will at all in mind, did we realize neither one of the opposing ends, we should be feeling no hesitation between them. Our doubt arises from the fact that momentarily and provisionally we are in the attitude of assuming both.[72]

Royce's treatment of all known historical ethical doctrines as entailing, or at least indicating, a relation to some truth about our humanity, interpolates his skepticism as an ethical act precisely because it is predicated on an unwavering investment in the possibility and importance of arriving at a universal ethical proposition. "Our indifference is not the indifference of ignorance," he states, "but of knowledge; not of failure to understand either end but of readiness to realize both ends. Hence it follows that moral skepticism is itself the result of an act, namely, of the act by which we seek to realize in ourselves opposing aims at the same time."[73] Self-critical theoretical skepticism reveals "the supreme End that makes skepticism itself possible."[74] What's more, in the course of his applying it to known ethical doctrines, Royce discovers that "ethical aims themselves are all of them the expression of somebody's will."[75] Having reduced ethics to a question of will, Royce then formulates it as an epistemological question: "How can I know that there is anywhere a will, W, that chooses for itself some end, E?"[76] Two possible responses are proffered, one psychological and the other philosophical. According to the psychological explanation, to really know there is will is a function of imitation. "One must repeat in one's own mind more or less rapidly or imperfectly this will, W, that one conceives to exist in somebody else."[77] Royce means by imitation here mimesis in both the sense of mimicry and representation, which he takes, following Alexander Bain, to be a faculty of mind. The argument is rather along the lines set out by Plato in *The Republic* regarding the cognitive effect of mimicry, which is that in imitating the actions of others, one assimilates their thinking. As Royce puts it: "If one were to dwell upon the nature of this act [being imitated], and were fully to realize its nature in his mind . . . if two opposing fashions of action are present to the mind, and if mentally we are trying to realize them both, then mentally we are seeking to reproduce them both."[78] Skepticism, then, is the expression of our effort to mentally assimilate two contesting ways of thinking. The philosophical explanation begins with three questions: "What represents a Will but a Will? Who could know what it is to have an end unless he actually had ends himself? Who can realize a given aim save by somehow repeating it in himself?" The response to these also adheres to Plato's psychology of mimesis: "And so it is rationally and universally necessary that one shall realize the end of a moral system by reproducing in himself the will that accepts this end. . . . . In so far forth as he reproduces this will, it is his will. And the end is his end."[79] Again, skepticism is the effect of trying to assimilate simultaneously opposing wills. The upshot of both these explanations is that "absolute ethical skepticism, if it were actually possible without self-destruction, would still presuppose an end, namely, the effort to harmonize in one moment all the conflicting aims in the world of life. . . . Absolute skepticism would thus be founded on absolute benevolence. Its own aim would be harmony and unity of conduct."[80] This means that the so-called skepticism is, in the end, predicated on the hope of a universal ethical doctrine, which differs from those doctrines that struggle to bridge the divide between the world of facts and moral doctrine by instead considering the ethical question in relation to the world of ends, and to consider that world not in detail but as a whole. The skeptical question becomes, "What highest end is suggested to him who realizes for himself this whole world of ends?"[81] On the assumption that such a seeker assimilates the ends of all the conflicting ethical doctrines as his own, the highest end, which Royce also calls the Higher Good, translating the Scholastic *summum bonum*, is the absolute harmony of the conflicting ethical systems. Hence, having reduced ethics to will, Royce's claims to discover the Universal Will "in the midst of the warfare of individual wills" and his new moral doctrine, the maxim of which is, as we've already noted: "Act always in the light of the completest insight into all the aims that thy act is to affect."[82]

Martineau grants that Royce's epistemological argument about the will, with its postulate that other life is as my life, has the advantage of insight over "the 'individualism' of the hedonist, of the sentimental cultivator of his own 'beautiful soul,' or the defiant Titan towards all that resists his fixed intent." His objection is that this is not a "*moral* insight" precisely because it erases the argument for divine causality.[83]

> The process of thought indeed which Professor Royce commends to us, viz. of merging our separate selves, of turning our *relations* to other minds into *fusion* with them, and losing our finite being in the life of one Universal Will, conducts us, I should say, right away from every possibility of Morals, instead of giving us the key of entrance to them. By attempting to erase from the world its highest fact,—the existence of Personalities, as distinct creative centres, with individualized reason and choice,—it removes the conditions of ethical obligation, and treats its enthusiasm as an illusion of human childhood. Its professed end is unification of life, not harmonious differentiation of excellence; in forgetfulness of the certain fact that, even if it were possible for individual agents to melt themselves into a single being, neither they, nor the "One Universal Will" compounded out of them, could have the slightest power to withdraw our moral interest from the impassioned drama of *personal* intelligence and character. Such suppression of individuality in homage to an "impersonal" social organism is a relapse into the ruder tribal life, out of which personality is evolved as the higher stage, with its noble characteristics of inalienable trust and imperative Duty.[84]

This argument is in accord with Hobbesian anthropology. Society is made by individualistic *Man*, whose natural anarchic tendencies are requisite for morality. The imperative to duty stems from the fact that "*emphatically* it is, this sense of 'other life which is *not* as my life,' which supplies the 'positive' contents of all moral affections and righteous action."[85] Conflict of disparate, mutually incomprehensible wills is the dynamic force of historical change; and it is only in voluntary submission of one's will in duty to a superior intelligence and will transcending all other wills that ethical action becomes possible. The truth is found with the living God whose existence transcends all his creation and so cannot be directly known, but whose agency in the world is. What Martineau contests is Royce's argument for "Universal Will" as the expression of the composite "Universal Thought." According to that argument, "God" is a convenient designation for this Universal Thought, the moral insight of which is to "aim at the destruction of all which separates us into a heap of different selves, and the attainment of some higher positive organic aim," what Royce calls, misquoting the last act of Shelley's lyrical drama, *Prometheus Unbound*, "one undivided soul of many a soul."[86] As Martineau notes, Royce is seeking to "break the bounds of subjective Idealism on this track"; and so noting, judges him to have failed because of "his repudiation of the category of causality, as absolutely inapplicable to transcendental thought and religious use."[87] Without grounding in theistic teleology, there can be no universal determination of ethical truth, of what is absolute duty for all humanity. Rather than teleology as the beacon of truth, Royce postulates that the existence of error involves the existence of truth, in relation to which alone it declares itself to be error. Martineau succinctly paraphrases the theory of error as:

> Truth is true thought, the apprehension of reality. But we, as subjectively limited to our own ideas, and unable to compare them with anything beyond, are placed out of reach of this, in common with all created minds. There must therefore be, a seat of truth, a universal "containing mind," the measure of all thought. In the author's words, "the agreement or the disagreement of my judgments with their intended objects exists and has meaning for an actual thought, a consciousness, to which both these related terms are present, viz. both the judgment and the object with which it is to agree."[88]

The fact that it is on the strength of this argument for the possibility of error as the condition of truth Royce can "pass from idealism as a bare hypothesis, expressing postulates, to idealism as a philosophical doctrine" does not escape Martineau's attention.[89] Indeed, here lies the crux of his critique. Royce's "leap out of his subjective idealism to the all-containing Reason as the complementary reality cannot," Martineau believes, "be made good"; because although "the existence of error no doubt implies some *reality* which is misconceived, and which, to better intelligence, might become rightly conceived . . . it does not imply the presence of such intelligence, therefore not the existence of *truth*, which is *apprehended reality*."[90] Du Bois has warrant when he writes in his notebook, regarding this passage that, "Martineau makes a common blunder in regard to Royce's theory," which states, Du Bois recalls, that a "3rd mind [Royce says "third and higher thought"[91]] is necessary to find error. Royce's argument proves that error can't *exist* unless the third mind is there—for the very *constitution of error*, a third mind *must be*. The world is the dream of the infinite."[92]

Du Bois's investment in marking Martineau's misconstruing the argument for error becomes clear when we attend to the argument as Royce presents it:

> To explain how one could be in error about his neighbor's thoughts, we suggested the case where John and Thomas should be present to a third thinker whose thought include them both. We objected to this suggestion that thus the natural presupposition that John and Thomas are both separate self-existent beings would be contradicted. But on this natural presupposition neither of these two subjects could become object to the other at all, and error would here be impossible. Suppose then that we drop the natural presupposition, and say that John and Thomas are both actually present to and included in a third and higher thought. To explain the possibility of error about matters of fact seemed hard, because of the natural postulate that time is a pure succession of separate moments, so that the future is now as future non-existent, and so that judgments about the future lack real objects, capable of identification. Let us then drop this natural postulate, and declare time once for all present in all its moments to an universal all-inclusive thought. And to sum up, let us overcome all our difficulties by declaring that all the many Beyonds, which single significant judgments seem vaguely and separately to postulate, are present as fully realized intended objects to the unity of an all-inclusive, absolutely clear, universal, and conscious thought, of which all judgments, true or false, are but fragments, the whole being at once Absolute Truth and Absolute Knowledge.[93]

Precisely this sort of reasoning is what prompts Du Bois to declare, "Royce is a type of Absolute Idealist."[94] Yet that idealism is worth embracing precisely because it is, as Martineau claims in his critique, anti-theistic in postulating that what we call "God" is simply Universal Thought as pure cognition, which has infinitude only in the intellectual dimension: insight without agency.[95] The charge of anti-theism, in the sense Martineau means, has merit, considering what Royce states in the book's epilogue:

> There are writers who have undertaken to defend Theism, and who have actually in all sincerity argued for the necessity of the Universal Thought. The plain people have reason to suspect such of trying to substitute for the "God of our Fathers" something else, to be called by the same name, and so to be passed off for the same thing. We therefore answer very plainly that

we desire to do nothing of the sort. If in the foregoing we have on occasion used the word God, no reader is obliged to suppose that our idea agrees with his idea, for we have fully explained what our idea means. We repeat: As my thought at any time, and however engaged, combines several fragmentary thoughts into the unity of one conscious moment, so, we affirm, does the Universal Thought combine the thoughts of all of us into an absolute unity of thought, together with all the objects and all the thoughts about these objects that are, or have been, or will be, or can be, in the Universe. This Universal Thought is what we have ventured, for the sake of convenience, to call God. It is not the God of very much of the traditional theology. It is the God of the idealistic tradition from Plato downwards.[96]

We can glean from this passage the basis for Du Bois's engagement with Royce's argument for idealism, specifically, his proposition that the ethical imperative is contingent on the actualization of human community in the semiosis of thinking; which is to say, contra Martineau's claim, that thinking is material agency. A good deal of Du Bois's notebook is concerned with determining, in dispute with Martineau, the causality of human action in the world in order to discover, in disagreement with James, the scientific, nontheological grounds of ethics. In that pursuit, Du Bois writes regarding the Humean postulate of antecedents and consequents, "Hume says the word *cause* covers the word *law* and not entity, and this is the boast of modern science."[97]

Having dismissed Martineau's theory of mutually resisting causation as derivative and little more than the identification of causality with divine will in Lesson IV of the notebook, he continues the exposition of the scientific accounts of cause in Lesson V, proclaiming: "Cause is as it were an altar to an unknown god—an inquiry for rational grounds upon which to base observed sequence. This ground may be (1) uniform sequence, (2) identity, (3) force."[98] After then identifying the first option as Hume's, and the second as the logistic neo-Kantianism of Alois Riehl, he finds the third option, force, to be "nothing more or less than desire. . . . Cause in philosophical discussion is nothing more than *desire*."[99] And so we are brought to Lesson VI and Du Bois's diagram, in which the value of the sign "WJ" appearing in both the circles within the oval has the value, personhood—the initials for William James being a heuristic symbol. Such that the "WJ" of the circle in the left-half of the oval labeled "matter" is individuated embodiment or incarnation, which we can designate, "WJ^e"; and the one in the right-half of the oval labeled "minds" is cognitive self-consciousness, which we designate, "WJ^c". The side-bar, "law that is the mind's over-soul," references causality according to Hume's postulate, which is to say, the comprehensive relation of common cognition, what Royce calls "Universal Thought" and Martineau characterizes as "pure cognitive intelligence." Picking up the thread of Du Bois's analysis from here, WJ^e corresponds with WJ^c only when WJ^e and WJ^c equal elements of the Universal Thought.

Martineau is not quite right in construing Royce's idealism to be a version of Spinoza's pantheism, according to which God exists only in thought. Spinoza's "God" is the Absolute eternal substance in which all reality, everything, exists necessarily as modalities or attributes; so that there is no contingency or spontaneity to the actual world—it is not brought into being by God out of nothing in an act of divine free will—meaning there are no alternatives to the actual world. On the contrary, Royce's "Universal Thought" is the dynamic unfolding of the world as contingency, the culminating effect of human cognitive activity in common relation to things, including itself. Can the modern man consistently hold a Christian creed? This is the question Josiah Royce pondered while reading Martineau's *Types of Ethical Theory*, a reading prompted by Martineau's critique of *The Religious Aspect of Philosophy*. That pondering finds a sustained public expression in *The Problem of Christianity*, where "modern man" condenses into the hypothesis that the human race has been subject to a more or less coherent process of education, according to which Christianity is a pedagogical moment in that process, which, via mimicry of Jesus, brings the individual into community. The necessary condition for the individual's salvation is membership in a certain spiritual community in whose life-practices the Christian virtues reach the highest expression. Royce contemplates the issue of salvation through interrogating the way in which Paul's idea of salvation from original sin through grace and loving union with the spirit of Jesus Christ is inseparable from his regarding the church as the visible body of Christ. Analyzing this as a historical interpretive activity rather than a theological proposition or doctrine, Royce came to regard it in terms of Peirce's concept of *agapism* or "evolutionary love." As an orienting principle, agapism directs the Universal Thought asymptotically, providing a certain coherence and contiguity to the actualities of communities in interpretation; that is the way in which each realized moment of interpretation relates to those that came before it, the past, and will follow from it, the future. Royce called this "the Will to Interpret."[100] Perhaps this Peircean via Royce agapism is what was on Du Bois's mind when, three fourths of the way through "The Renaissance of Ethics," in the course of arguing for a materialist science of mind as the basis for a science of ethics, he remarks, in a non sequitur in passim: "One momentous fact, however, future science must not forget: Christian teleology is the only one yet presented which seems worthy of a man."[101]

There is a remarkable resonance between Royce's Universal Thought and Du Bois's intellect-in-action; both propositions focus on the *enérgeia* of thinking as the constitutive action of community. Before taking this to indicate a common conception of community, however, we should consider what Du Bois writes in the notebook, glossing his own analysis of the "Lesson IV" diagram: "If this is the fount of our knowledge, then the greatest evolution of our minds is to attain to the universal mind. Suppose the words of a sentence have minds, then you are the universal mind, etc. [but how about the error of the U. mind?]." The inclination to read this as a transcription of James's lecture is prompted by the bracketed interjection, which is clearly Du Bois's query of what has just been stated. Regarding that statement, the second sentence suffers an incoherence that is resolved by transposing its two verbs, assuming their original placement to be an error of transcription. We get then, "Suppose the words of a sentence *are* minds, then you *have* the universal mind, etc." With this adjustment for coherence, we can infer that the universal thought is syntactic, which is fully in keeping with what follows the bracketed interjection: "By this, cause & effect is a thought-relation: as in *vir bonus*: alter *bonus* to *bona* [and] *vir* is changed—this causal nexus is a logical or rational nexus. Force is the cause of the materialistic world, Reason of Idealism." The bracketed query takes up Royce's theory of error as a function of syntactic irregularity, a fault that makes evident the integrity of the overall structural relation, which he acknowledged was derived from Peirce's theory of semiosis. With Du Bois, rather than accounting for intelligence on the basis of a foundationalist construal of reality—whether materialist or idealist—according to which it is substance (πνεῦμα, *pneuma*), intelligence is described in terms of a notational system expressing dynamic relation of reciprocity (in Kant's sense). Still following the asymptotes of the hyperbola analogy, intelligence is *indeterminate enérgeia*—and what I mean by this is that its articulations are not necessary determinate actualizations of a teleological dynamics, but are actualities-in-action, fleeting and myriad if not infinite. Intellect-in-action is being-in-worked-ness without a governing blueprint, which is why its articulations express the perpetually emergent conjunctions of chance and law. And in that vein, causality is a function of logical relation in thinking; that is to say, perceived accidental change is an issue of perspective, and not structural relation in necessarily actualized position.

The case Du Bois proffers in proof, altering *bonus* into *bona*, changes the terms of relation; in accordance with Latin syntax, making the adjective feminine in this phrase dictates that the noun *vir* (man) becomes *mulier* (woman). It does more, however, much more, given the provenance of the phrase, according to which the meaning of its noun is paramount. In classical Latin, *vir* means interchangeably "hero," "man," "grown man," and "husband." *Vir bonus*, "the good man," belongs to the discourse of public conduct, as in Cato the Elder's oft-cited maximum to his son: "Orator est, Marce fili, vir bonus dicendi peritus [An orator, my son Marcius, is a good man skilled in speaking]." Quintilian takes considerable care to make it abundantly clear this is about character, emphasizing that what Cato places as the first quality the orator must possess is "in the very nature of things the greatest and most important, that is, he must be a good man [*utique vir bonus*] . . . no man can be an orator unless he is a good man [*sed ne futurum quidem oratorem nisi virum bonum*]. For it is impossible to regard those men as gifted with intelligence who on being offered the choice between the two paths of virtue [*honestorum*] and vice choose the latter."¹⁰² The *Vir bonus* has *virtus*, an abstract noun derived from *vir*, connoting valor, courage, excellence, and character—all qualities associated with overall manliness in public conduct specific to free adult Roman men. Although regarded by the Romans as *homo*, human beings in the Greek sense of *anthrōpos* (ἄνθρωπος), the male slave was not *vir* but *puer* (boy), and so, like a child, was incapable of *virtus*. The highest public conduct of Roman women was *pudictia*, "modesty" or "chastity." Granted, Cicero at times attributes *virtus* to women, most famously in his speech defending Sextus Roscius Amerinus, where he praises Caecilia Metella Balearica as "a woman, in whom [*in qua muliere*] traces of the old-fashion virtue remain [*vestigial antique office remanent*]. By her virtue, loyalty, and diligence [*eius virtute, fide, diligentia*] Sextus Roscius is a living man among the accused rather than a dead man among the proscribed."¹⁰³ When he does so, however, he is attributing to her a masculine characteristic, even grammatically; while *fide* and *diligentia* are both feminine ablatives, *vitute* is masculine. Changing the noun from *vir* to *mulier*, based on altering *bonus* to *bona*, gives us *mulier bona*, "good woman," which is not the same as Cicero's attributing *virtus* to a woman. By feminizing the good, Du Bois's conjectured alteration challenges the presumptive provenance of goodness in the heroic, opening up the ethical question in a radical way that entails far more than a realignment.

It has been suggested that the study of etymology may throw light on the history of the evolution of moral concepts.¹⁰⁴ In this case, the etymological itinerary of *vir, virtus* that Du Bois's suppositional alteration set us on is particularly relevant to his critique of the persistent investment in the *summum bonum*, from Scholasticism up until James and Royce. The historical scope of that critique extends back beyond Scholasticism or even Christianity, however, when we recall the provenance of the phrase *summum bonum* is Cicero's *De Finibus Bonorum et Malorm* [On the Ends of Goods and Evils], where it is the Latin translation for the Greek term, εὐδαιμονία (*eudaimonia*). So Du Bois's subjunctive alteration goes to the foundations of the millennia-long tradition of moral philosophy inaugurated with Plato's idealization of ἀρετη (*areté*), "excellence-in-action." In Homeric Greek, this connoted primarily manly martial valor (ανδρεία, *andreia*), and so is analogous to Roman *virtus*; as in Poseidon's telling Idomeneus: "Success [ἀρετη, *areté*] comes when even very poor warriors [ἀνδρῶν, *andrōn*] are together, but we two know well how to do battle even with men of valor [ἀγαθοῖσιν, *agathoīsin*]."¹⁰⁵ Staying on the etymological course, it is significant that the Homeric term used in this passage, ἀγαθοῖσιν (*agathoīsin*), which is the masculine plural of ἀγαθός (*agathos*), "the good," when applied to persons in reference to attributes, shares the same connotation as ἀρετη (*areté*). For instance, Agamemnon, rebutting Achilles, says, "mighty [ἀγαθός, *agathos*] though you are, godlike Achilles [θεοείκελ᾽ Ἀχιλλεῦ, *theoeikel' achilleu*]"[106] When applied to persons in reference to birth, however, *agathos* meant "noble" or "high-born," in contrast to the κακός (*kakos*), "low-born" or "commoner," as in Diomedes's declaring to be, "born of a goodly noble father [πατρὸς δ᾽ ἐξ ἀγαθοῦ, *patros d' ex agathou*]."[107] The superlative of *agathos*, ἄριστος (*aristos*), connoted the best and most excellent, nobility. Speaking to Priam, Argeiphontes says of Hector: "The noblest of all men [τοῖος γὰρ ἀνὴρ ὤριστος, *toios gar anér aristos*], has perished."[108] In the dialogue *Meno*, Plato attributes to the Sophist, Gorgias, the following statement: "A man's virtue [ἀρετη, *areté*] is in managing political affairs to benefit his friends and harm his enemies, without harming himself; whereas a woman's is in good domestic management and obedience to her husband. The child's virtue [ἀρετη, *areté*] is another thing, depending on gender. Another still is that of the elderly man, or the low-born freeman, or the slave."[109] In arguing against this conception, Plato has Socrates instruct Meno in what has come to be known as the Unity-of-Virtue doctrine, according to which real virtue is the same thing whether it is manifest in a man, woman, or child; and all the pluralities of type—courage, righteousness, piety, etc.—are merely parts or aspects of it. Rather than one's social role or function determining one's virtue, it is the universally distributed *capacity* to have a virtue that determines suitability for that social function. Plato argues along the same line in Πολιτεία (*Politeia*)—the work we call in English *The Republic*—concluding that even though women are physically weaker than men, "There is no administrative pursuit of a state that belongs to a woman because she is a woman or to a man because he is a man. Rather the natural capacities [αἱ φύσεις, *ai phuseis*] are distributed alike among both creatures, so that women and men naturally share in all pursuits."[110] Having thus idealized ἀρετη (*areté*), Plato identifies it with εὐδαιμονία (*eudaimonia*), which we could literally translate as "good [εὖ/*eu*] spirit [δαίμων, *daimon*]," drawing attention to the fact that the prefix, εὖ (*eu*)—derived from the noun, ἐΰς (*eÿs*), meaning "good," "brave," or "noble"—shares the same connotative expanse with *agathos* and *areté*. The Platonic *Definitions* defines it as "the good [ἀγαθόν, *agathón*] composed of all goods [ἀγαθόν ἐκ πάντων ἀγαθῶν, *agathōn ek pantōn agathon*]; the sufficient resources for living well; perfection [τελειότης, *teleiotés*] in respect to virtue [τελειότης κατ᾽ ἀρετήν, *teleiotés kat aretén*]; what is enough for a living creature to have."[111] This, of course, is τοῦ ἀγαθοῦ ἰδέαν (*tou agathou idéan*), "the Idea of the Good" that makes the truth of things intelligible.[112]

Labeling this Platonic concept "Universal Good" (καθόλου βέλτιον, *katholou beltion*), Aristotle dismisses it as pure idealism, arguing that if such goodness really exists separately and absolutely, it clearly is not practicable or attainable by humans.[113] The good that *is* within reach is that which every art (τέχνη, *technē*) and every scientific inquiry (μέθοδος, *méthodos*), as well as every practical moral choice (προαίρεσις, *prohairesis*) aims at.[114] Each of these, the arts, sciences, and ethics, is an intentional activity (ἐνέργεια, *enérgeia*) in the being-at-work-ness of the human (τὸ ἔργον τοῦ ἀνθρώπου, *tó érgon toū anthrōpou*).[115] That is to say, they are the *enérgeia*, the doing of the human as a particular animal life form (ἔργον ζωήν, *érgon zōēn*) being-in-possession of reason (τοῦ λόγος ἔχοντος, *toū logos échontos*).[116] The human is a life form composed of soul and body (ψυχή καὶ σῶμα, *psychē kai sōma*).[117] All natural composite structures and life forms, Aristotle postulates, where a plurality of parts, whether continuous or discrete, is combined to make a single common whole, always entail a ruling (ἄρχον, *archon*) and a ruled or subjugated (ἀρχόμενον, *archómenon*) factor.[118] All animals, not just humans, have soul, which rules the body as a despotic master (ἄρχει δεσποτικήν, *archei despotikín*).[119] We can take this to mean what we've referred to previously as sentience, which is precisely how Aristotle refers to it: "the sentience [αἰσθητική, *aisthetikí*] that appears to be shared by horses, oxen, and animal life in general [παντὶ ζῴῳ, *pantí zoē*]."[120] In a way distinct from that of other animals, however, the human *psychē* entails two related but different parts, the irrational (ἄλογον, *álogon*) and the rational (λόγον, *logon*), each of which bifurcates as well.[121] A part of the irrational is the rudimentary capacity to perceive and respond to the environment sufficiently enough to live actively, what we referred to earlier as the reflex arc of perception, cognizance, and behavioral response and Aristotle calls the vital capacity (δύναμιν, *dynamin*) that does not engage at all the rational—or, as we would say these days, is precognitive.[122] Besides this part of the irrational, there is another called the appetitive (ὀρεκτικὸν, *oretikon*) that is the seat of appetites and desires (ἐπιθυμητικὸν, *epithumitikon*), which Aristotle recognizes can also be construed as participating with the rational because it is responsive to and can be subjugated by reason.[123] Thus, the rational bifurcates into one part that is obedient to reason (ἐπιπειθὲς λόγῳ, *epipeithés logō*) as though to a father, and the other that, exercising intelligence, is the active faculty of reason (λεγομένης τὴν κατ' ἐνέργειαν, *legoménēs tén kat' enérgeian*), and so is reason in the ultimate, or proper, sense.[124] Adhering to this hierarchy of ruler/ruled binaries, the doing-of-being-in-possession of reason that is the human disposition is the active exercising of the psychic faculties (ψυχῆς ἐνέργεια, *psychēs enérgeia*) in conformity with the ultimate rational principle. In that regard, the function of a good man (ἀνδρὸς εὖ, *andros eū*) is to perform these activities beautifully (καλῶς, *kalōs*) according to their proper excellence (τὴν οἰκείαν ἀρετήν, *tén oikeian aretēn*).¹²⁵ Such exercise in excellence of the cognitive faculties serves the overall good of humanity (ἀνθρώπινον ἀγαθὸν, *anthrópinon agathon*).¹²⁶ In so doing, it is striving for the good of all good (τἀγαθὸν καὶ τὸ ἄριστον, *tagathon to ariston*), or, as we say, "the Supreme Good."¹²⁷ When Aristotle calls achievement of the Supreme Good εὐδαιμονία (*eudaimonía*), he shifts the connotative register of this term from Plato's idealism to practical, albeit speculative, ethics.¹²⁸ It has long been the practice with respect to Aristotle's use of εὐδαιμονία (*eudaimonía*), to render it into English as "happiness." The aforementioned etymology, however, suggests that in idiomatic Greek it meant something along the lines of "living in a way that is well-favored by a god," or "blessed." Thus, Rackham, who throughout his translation gives it as "happiness," was compelled to add a footnote in which he regrets that this translation "can hardly be avoided," but that a more accurate rendering would be "well-being or prosperity, remarking further that Aristotle "does not interpret it as a state of feeling but as a kind of activity."¹²⁹ This point is reinforced by Aristotle's remarking that in everyday speech, εὐδαιμονία (*eudaimonía*) is synonymous with "'the good life in general' [εὖ ζῆν ὅλως, *eu zēn holōs*], and 'doing-well' [εὖ πράττειν, *eu práttein*]."¹³⁰

In fact, working from the more prevalent somewhat reasoned *doxa* about what εὐδαιμονία (*eudaimonía*) means, Aristotle delineates three connotations, associated with three ways of life: the life devoted to enjoyment (τὸν βίον ἀπολαυστικόν, *ton bion apolaustikon*), that of politics (πολιτικὸς, *politikòs*), and that of contemplation (θεωρητικός, *theoretikós*).¹³¹ Attending to the first two of these, he notes that the multitude and vulgar among the elite, who are utterly slavish in pursuing what he characterizes as a life for cattle (Βοσκημάτων βίον, *boskimáton bíon*), identify the Supreme Good with sensual pleasure (ἡδονήν, *hēdoné*). In contrast, men of refinement and action (χαρίεντες καὶ πρακτικοὶ, *charíentes kai praktikoí*) seeking honor (τιμήν, *timín*) think the Supreme Good is virtue (ἀρετή, *areté*) because that, even more than honor, is supposed to be the *télos* of the political life (πολιτικοῦ βίον, *politikoú bion*).¹³² In that vein, virtue is differentiated, in correspondence with the hierarchical bifurcation of the human soul, into two categories, the ethical (ἠθικάς, *ethikás*) and the intellectual (διανοητικὰς, *dianoitikas*). Liberality (ἐλευθεριότητα, *eletheriótita*) and even-temperance (σωφροσύνην, *sōphrosynin*) are ethical virtues, while wisdom (σοφία, *sophia*) or mother-wit and prudence (φρόνησής, *phrónesis*) are intellectual.¹³³ As with all Aristotle's binaries concerning the human soul, there is a hierarchical relation between these two modalities of virtue. In describing a man's ethical character (ἦθοσ, *ethos*), it is not said that he is wise or intelligent, but that he is gentle or temperate (πρᾶος ἢ σώφρων, *práos í sōphron*). A wise man (σοφὸν, *sophon*), however, is praised for his disposition (ἕξιν, *hexin*); and praiseworthy dispositions (ἕξεων δὲ τὰς ἐπαινετὰς, *hexeon de tas epainetàs*) are called virtues (ἀρετὰς, *aretàs*).[134] Here we encounter again Aristotle's concept of *hexis* as a mental disposition achieved in the actuality-of-the-doing. Rather than being a natural quality of the superior man—as in Heraclitus's of-cited aphorism, "Man's character is his divinity [ἦθος ἀνθρώπῳ δαίμων, *ēthos anthrōpō daimōn*]," meaning his divinely ordained destiny—ethical virtue is a disposition of habitus (ἐξ ἔθους, *ex ethos*), according to Aristotle, who derives the term ἠθικάς (*ethikás*) from ἔθους (*ethos*).[135] As for intellectual virtue, its genesis and development is in instruction, requiring experience over time. The probability of Aristotle's etymology notwithstanding, both modalities of virtue are actualities-of-doing what is humanly possible; that is to say, they actualize the dynamics of inherent human capacities and are aspects of a human being-at-work-ness-in-common. As in the arts, the disposition of a virtue is acquired by having actually practiced that virtue. It is in the doing of temperate things that one becomes temperate.[136]

Because the genesis of virtuous dispositions corresponds with actuality-in-doing (ὁμοίων ἐνεργειῶν, *homoiōn energeiōn*), acquiring them is contingent upon controlling the character of conduct, which means the way in which one is socially accustomed to act from childhood is of paramount importance.[137] Achieving ethical disposition, then, is very much a function of knowing how to conduct oneself in conformity with a principle of correct or right action (ὀρθὸν πράττειν, *orthon práttein*) held in common (κοινὸν, *koinon*).[138] Because achieving an ethical disposition is an issue of sociality, of gathering together in collective fellowship or community (κοινωνία, *koinónia*), and insofar as all community is formed in order to fulfill some human expectation of the good, *agathos*, knowing the principle of right is part and parcel of achieving that good. As the supreme form of community with the greatest power, the city-state, the πόλις (*polis*), strives to realize the most supreme of all good, εὐδαιμονία (*eudaimonía*).[139] Accordingly, the aim of all political legislation is to make citizens good by accustoming them to right action. Failure to do so is what distinguishes a nefarious political constitution from a good one, demonstrating that the same actions through which any virtue is engendered are also those through which it is destroyed.[140] "Acting in conformity with right principle [οὖν κατὰ τὸν ὀρθὸν λόγον, *oun kata ton orthón lógon*]" is a formulaic statement (εἰρημένον, *eirēmenon*), a saying, Aristotle abbreviates as ὀρθός λόγος (*orthós lógos*).[141] This is generally rendered in English as "right principle," but could also be given as "right [ὀρθός, *orthós*] reason [λόγος, *lógos*]," the latter of these picking up on the broad philosophical connotation of *lógos*. Both renderings, however, elide the active performativity as a speech act grounding a discursive field, that it is a way of talking.[142] In order to keep that discursivity in play, ὀρθός λόγος (*orthós lógos*) is rendered here instead as *right-principle-discourse*, connoting a manner of talking. The warrant for foregrounding the discursive aspect of Aristotle's expression with this somewhat cumbersome English-language formulation shall become apparent as we move along. Returning to the point more immediately at hand, determining *right-principle-discourse* is the practical business (πραγματεία, *pragmateía*) of speculative contemplation (θεωρία, *theoría*).[143] More precisely, it is the business of a discourse of conduct (πρακτῶν λόγος, *praktōn lógos*), belonging to the universal formulae (καθόλου λόγου, *kathólou lógou*) of ethics, which, unlike other fields of speculative contemplation, has a practical aim in knowing what ethical virtue is in relation to the quality of acting in common, especially in the political commons.[144]

Defining the right principle, as well as what is the standard by which it is determined, requires a further bifurcation of the rational half of the human psyche into separate faculties: the scientific (ἐπιστημονικὸν, *epistemonikón*), which contemplates (θεωροῦμεν, *theoroūmen*) things and the first principles of things that are invariable; and the calculative (λογιστικόν, *logistikón*) or deliberative (βουλεύεσθαι, *bouleuesthai*), which contemplates those things subject to variation.[145] Both faculties are concerned with attaining truth. The object of scientific contemplation exists of necessity; its first principle or universal is either supplied by induction, or is the starting point (ἀρχὴ, *archē*) for deduction.[146] Knowing the conclusions that follow from first principles and also having a true conception of those principles is wisdom, *sophía*, which is the most precise mode of epistemic knowledge because it combines intelligence (νοῦς, *noūs*) and science (ἐπιστήμη, *epistēmē*).[147] The deliberative faculty is concerned with two distinct sorts of things that admit variation, created things (ποιητὸν, *poieton*) and things to be done (πρακτὸν, *prakton*).[148] As noted earlier in reference to Leiris regarding the *objet d'art* as the true fetishism at the base of human existence, Aristotle defines the creation of things (*poiēsis*) as the activity of causing something to pass from nonbeing into existence, the efficient cause of which is in the creator not the thing. The pertinent point here is that, in contrast to the object of science, that of art has no necessary existence in-of-itself; and it is in this sense that it admits of variation. The disposition of the deliberative faculty regarding *poiēsis* is art, *technē*, and it is altogether different from that of deliberating on things to be done, which is *phrónesis* and is about making a choice of action, *praxis*, in relation to what is good and advantageous for oneself as a means to the good life in general.[149] Being able to deliberate well about what is good and advantageous is deliberative excellence (εὐβουλία, *euboulía*).[150] Such deliberation may well imply investigation as well as calculation, but it is investigation of a very practical thing, matters of conduct, *prakton*, and not apodictic universal first principles, which belong to the purview of science.[151] Nor is it skill in conjecture (εὐστοχία, *eustocxía*) or quickness of mind (ἀγχίνοια, *agxínoia*), both of which are rapid apprehension without conscious calculation. Deliberative excellence is correctness in thinking that arrives at the good in determining what is to be done. It turns out, then, that ethical virtue ensures the rightness of the ends of action, and intellectual virtue ensures the rightness of actions as means to those ends. Together, they determine the complete performance (ἀποτελεῖται ἔργον, *apoteleītai érgon*) of human being.[152] Deliberative excellence is where the political life *in* action directly engages the contemplative life *for* action. The conjunction of the active and the contemplative life is the actuality-in-doing that both enables and is enabled in the political constitution. It is only in the *polis*, the most advanced or "supreme" form of community, that the fulfillment of human being is in conformity with excellence or virtue.

This is why we must not forget that, for Aristotle, the ideal political constitution was one in which the best-born, the ἀριστοκρατία (*aristokratía*), rule, where citizens are fundamentally excellent in virtue (ἁπλῶς κατ᾽ ἀρετὴν, *aplos kat' aretēn*) and not just deemed "good men" (ἀγαθῶν ἀνδρῶν, *agathōn andrōn*) according to some customary standard.[153] Under aristocracy in the fullest sense, the excellent man *is* the good citizen, and honors are distributed *according* to excellence of virtue.[154] The ideal polity, then, is, then, is one in which righteous rule is enacted in accordance with prudence (φρόνησής, *phronesis*) and philosophy. This is indeed an ideal, given that the actual forms of rule most approximating it are constitutions of diverse elements—they are often an admixture of wealth, virtue, and the common people, as in Carthage, or virtue and the common people, as in Sparta—differentiating between aristocratic virtue and that of other classes is of paramount importance.[155] In keeping with his critiquing Platonic forms, Aristotle disposes of the Unity-of-Virtue doctrine in his Πολιτικά (*Politikā, Politics*), taking up Gorgias's proposition, expressly contra Socrates, that virtue follows function.[156] A particularly vexing ethical problematic that results is the legitimacy of the absolute power of the master (δεσπότης, *despotés*) over the slave (δοῦλος, *doūlos*), who is instrumentalized in the service of securing the ideal political situation for attaining εὐδαιμονία (*eudaimonía*). Does a slave possess any of the virtues of the freemen, such as temperance, manly valor, and righteousness, or does he have no other virtue beside that of his bodily instrumentality (ὀργανικὰς, *organikas*)? If the slave's only virtue is bodily instrumentality, to the exclusion of all else, then another problem presents itself, given that the slaves are still human beings capable of participating in reason (ἀνθρώπων καὶ λόγου κοινωνούντων, *anthrōpōn kai logou koinwnoūnton*).[157] The issue at hand is the nature of despotism, or more precisely the distinction between the absolute autocratic power of the master over the slave, and that of despotic tyranny, which is unrighteous precisely because it is not natural for one person to have absolute sovereignty over all the citizens where the *polis* consists of men who are no different in nature—that is, in being human, ἄνθρωπος (*anthrōpos*), a genus including women and children, as well as noble and low-born men and slaves. In that regard, Aristotle proceeds to address the general problematic of slavery by defining the essential quality (δύναμις, *dynamis*) of the slave, which is a human being belonging by nature not to himself but to another human as an animate article of property that is an instrument of action (ὄργανά πρακτικόν, *organa praktikón*) necessary in the maintenance of life (πρὸς ζωὴ ἀναγκαίων, *prós zōē anagkaion*) and useful for the community of polity (χρησίμων εἰς κοινωνίαν πόλεως, *chrisímon eis koinōnían*).[158] Defining the slave as a human being compounds matters even further, however, because subordinating fully rational humans to the absolute abjection of slavery would be unrighteous.

Aristotle finds the solution in the aforementioned teleology of hierarchical bifurcation of ruler and rule in nature. Just as it is natural and expedient that the soul rules the body as a master, so too is it for the active rational intellect to rule the irrational passions (πάθη, *pathē*). By logical analogy, those among humans with the greater proportion and most developed active intellect are the natural rulers of those who are stronger in body and passion than soul, who are naturally submissive, and thus suited in their teleological function to be slaves. Because they lack a class of natural rulers, barbarians are slaves in nature: "ὡς ταὐτὸ φύσει βάρβαρον καὶ δοῦλον [*hōs tautó physei bárbaron kai doūlon*]."[159] Still caught in the passionate drives of animal nature, the barbarian needs the discipline of a master in order to be of service to civilization. Hence, their proper status in the *polis* as slaves who, while being instrumentally essential to its maintenance, are not *of* the political community, which by definition is the supreme institution of human fulfillment. Granting this anthropological difference in kind between the natural ruler and the naturally submissive, in order for the ruler to rule justly and the slave to obey well, they must both be capable of some form of moral nobility (καλοκἀγαθίας, *kaloagathías*), each according to the proportion of the two kinds of intellect naturally preponderant in his soul. The slave qua barbarian has no deliberative part at all, being overwhelmingly pathetic, whereas "the ruler must possess total cognitive virtue (διανοητικὴν ἀρετήν, *dianoitikín aretēn*). As for free women—the female slave does not figure in Aristotle's calculations—they have the deliberative faculty in full, but without full authority, which is why they must be ruled "in the republican way [τρόπον πολιτικῶς, *de trópon politikós*]."[160] In Aristotle's revaluation of manly virtue (τοῦ ἀνθρώπου ἀρετήν, *toú anthrōpou aretín*), it is a particular disposition of the psyche he calls μεσότης (*mesotēs*, "the intermediate"), which, insofar as it is a contemplative activity, aims at and achieves what is μέσον (*méson*, "the mean")—that point which is precisely equidistant from excess and deficiency in relation to anything that is continuous and divisible.

This is the absolute point of proportion, which can be expressed arithmetically (ἀριθμητικὴν ἀναλογίαν, *areithmetikin analogian*): for example, 6 is the mean when 10 is the point of excess and 2 deficiency, "since 6 − 2 = 10 − 6."[161] The mean is the determining point of arithmetic proportion, the point of measure that cannot be measured and is neither augmented nor decreased. There are many ways to miss the mark, given that the form of evil is infinite. But because the good is a finite accomplished point (πεπερασμένου, *peperasménou*), there is only one way to arrive at the μεσότης (*mesotēs*) of virtue.[162] And it is hard to find without adequate knowledge; just as finding the center of a circle requires knowledge of geometry.[163] More precisely, ἀρετη (*aretḗ*) is the activity of aiming at and achieving the intermediacy of psychic being, which is to say that virtue is being in the active interval that is proportionate, neither too much or too little, but just right. It is thus found in what Diogenes Laertius calls, referring to Aristotle's work, μετριοπάθεια (*metriopatheia*), the golden mean between excess and deficiency of emotion.[164] Virtue is in the proper management or moderation of *pathē* rather than their elimination in what we have come to know, after the Stoics, as apathy (ἀπάθεια, *apatheia*). "He who fears absolutely nothing and abides and confronts everything is overly bold, which is to say rash," Aristotle tells us.[165] "Likewise, he who indulges every pleasure (ἡδονῆς, *hédonēs*) without restraint becomes intemperate (ἀκόλαστος, *akólastos*), and he who flees (φεύγων, *feugon*) from all pleasure is witless (ἀναίσθητός, *anaisthetos*). Thus temperance and courage are destroyed by excess and deficiency, and preserved by the mean [μέσον, *méson*]."[166] The μέσον (*méson*), then, is about achieving the right proportion of pleasure and pain; it is the disposition of reasoning intelligence facilitating the theoretical worldly wisdom deployed in securing the good living (ζῆν καλῶς, *zēn kalōs*) that enables the broadest possible achievement of εὐδαιμονία (*eudaimonía*). That disposition, however, is available only to the man of goodness (ἀνδρὸς ἀγαθοῦ, *andros agathoú*) in the *polis*, who, talking ὀρθός λόγος (*orthós lógos*), right-principle-discourse, is free and fit for politics as a citizen (οὐδὲ τὸν πολίτην, *oude ton politēn*).[167] The emphasis here is on ἀνδρὸς (*andros*, man) as a particularly valued supreme form of ἄνθρωπος (*anthrōpos*, the human) in contradistinction to other forms; and talking right is what delineates civilized man from the barbarian qua slave who is not fully out of nature and animality nor in civilization. So, Cicero's rendering of ἀνδρὸς ἀγαθοῦ (*andros agathoú*) as *vir bonus* is an elaboration in translational paraphrasis of the Greek philosophical discourse of manly virtue, ἀρετη (*aretḗ*), as the yield and instrumentality of supreme human fulfillment in polity, the Supreme Good. We can, accordingly, reasonably render *zēn kalōs* as "civilization." Civilization is thus hierarchical, and the virtuous aristocratic intelligence needs the activity of maintaining bare life just as the activity of maintaining bare life needs its rule to function. As the disposition of intermediacy (μεσότης, *mesotēs*), ἀρετη (*aretē*) is a homeostasis of mind that is tightly regulated through ὀρθός λόγος (*orthós lógos*), the right principle discourse, which aims to conserve a specific balance of energy within the system. This abstraction of virtue as a disposition of mind toward which all rational men aspire is fundamental and foundational to the millennia-long tradition of moral philosophy as virtue ethics, whereby civilization is engendered and sustained through the activity of virtuous men authorized and empowered to enforce the right principle discourse. To put this in more pointedly Roman terms, civilization is founded and maintained on the authority (*auctoritas*) of strong men emanating from their virtue (*virtus*)—who have the power (*potestas*) to enforce the fair and good (*aequum et bonum*) order of things in law (*ius*). Regarded in this way, civilization is the auto-legitimating exercise of power by *boni viri*, brave qua good men of honor.

Regaining our bearings, we come to this understanding of the identification of virtue-ethics as civilization by following the etymological itinerary indicated by Du Bois's conjectured alteration of *bonus* to *bona*. That way elucidates how his proposed feminization of the good begins to unsettle the traditional understanding of civilization by undoing its identification of the goodness of human being with masculine virility. There is a good deal at stake in that identification. A corollary to Aristotle's revaluing the ancient aristocratic virtue into the attendant psychic disposition of civilization is an anthropology that naturalizes this concomitancy as the actuality-of-doing what is humanly possible. Civilization is the teleological *enérgeia* of human being, which is to say it is the entelechy of the human. An implication of Aristotle's applying his theory of the ubiquity in nature of hierarchical binaries to human polity is that the civilization of virtuous strong men conquering all other forms of community and subjugating them to its activity, its regulating homeostasis of μεσότης (*mesotēs*), is inevitable human destiny. It is the natural fulfillment-in-actuality of human being as a particular animal life form. In a sense, Aristotle provides a primary theoretical account of the strong man as agent of civilization, according to which the strong man is human apotheosis. As stated at the beginning of our reading of "The Renaissance of Ethics," one of the principal questions entailed in the "Negro problem" is: What is the worldly basis of human society? Having attended to how Du Bois approaches this as a question of ethics, we find ourselves once again butting up against the anthropological question posed by Windham's assertion of human flesh: What is the human? Or more precisely, in the ethico-political line we've been tracking with Du Bois, Who can legitimately say what is human? The question of legitimacy is vexing because it is the question of civilizational authority, the authority to promulgate a narrative of human-being that is broadly compelling. Who can speak for the human, and from where does the authority to do so come? Du Bois asks this very question in an extraordinarily publicized way just months after writing "The Renaissance of Ethics" essay in his highly acclaimed and oft-cited 1890 Harvard commencement speech, "Jefferson Davis as a Representative of Civilization," in which he troubles the traditional conception of civilization being advanced through virtuous coercive power and does so in a way directly linked to the critique of virtue ethics elaborated from the Philosophy IV course notebook.

Du Bois's 1890 Harvard address merits careful attention because of how it so concisely presents the terms of the matter at hand, as well as what is at stake with those terms. The acclaim it garnered was due in large measure to the fact that he was the first black to ever speak at Harvard's commencement-day exercise. We now know, thanks to Bruce Kimball's research, that the seven-member faculty committee charged with selecting the student graduation speakers initially chose two blacks, Du Bois and Clement G. Morgan, to be among the six speakers selected from the forty-four honor students who competed for the distinction.[168] Their selection was supposed to be concrete evidence of Harvard's commitment under President Charles Eliot to academic meritocracy, wherein academic achievement trumped personal characteristics such as social rank and pedigree as the measure for evaluating students and faculty. In this case, the distinction of being a student commencement-day speaker entailed two other prerequisite distinctions: the student's attaining a grade-point average of academic honor determined by his department, resulting in the dean of the college's invitation to write a "commencement part," which earned the graduating student a place on the official list of scholarly distinction in the university catalog. Upon achieving these two distinctions, the student qualified to vie for one of the six student commencement-day speaker slots. That competition entailed orally presenting the "commencement part" to the selection committee in a two-day competition, which was held from May 23 to May 24. Both Du Bois's and Morgan's presentations fared quite well in that contest. Du Bois was the only student out of the forty-four competitors to be unanimously chosen by the seven-member selection committee, five of whom ranked him first, while Morgan received a slim majority of four out of seven. Yet, what was to have been a very public triumph of absolutely unbiased academic meritocracy was itself infused behind the scenes with racial tension. Concerned that white racists' sensibilities would be ruffled by there being two black speakers at the commencement ceremonies, committee member Francis G. Peabody, the Plummer Professor of Christian Morals, moved that the selection be vetted by the Harvard Corporation. The unprecedented motion split the committee, necessitating an additional day of deliberation on May 25. The evening before that meeting, Peabody privately solicited President Eliot's support for his concern. Eliot, whose stance on the Negro question was "accommodation and compromise," concurred with Peabody, and the next day Morgan was removed from the list. Among the arguments made to justify this other-than-meritocratic decision was that having two black speakers at the commencement exercise would offend members of the graduating class, especially because Morgan had already been selected by the senior student body, with some acrimony, to be the first black to speak at the class day exercises held the Friday before commencement. In point of fact, that was less of a distinction than his having a place on the official list of scholarly distinction, which had qualified him to compete for a commencement speaker's slot. Writing in his personal journal about the selection committee's deliberations, committee member James B. Thayer, a law professor, who found the entire affair "pitiable," sums up the gist of Morgan's removal: "He loses his fairly won place there because he is black or, to put it in its mildest form, because somebody else is black."[169] A factor in the selection committee's choosing Du Bois over Morgan as their token Negro speaker was their approval of the way he handled his timely subject, Jefferson Davis, who had died just five months earlier on December 6, 1889. In keeping with the attitude of accommodation and compromise, they misconstrued Du Bois's handling of Davis as respectful and somewhat deferential.

Du Bois was apparently unaware throughout his long career that his singular distinction as the first black Harvard commencement speaker was because of this accommodation to racism. He certainly had no knowledge of it when he presented himself on June 25, 1890, to the Harvard graduating class, university president Charles Eliot, and his distinguished guests—among whom were Massachusetts governor John Q. A. Brackett, First Lady Francis Cleveland, and the Episcopal bishop of New York, the Right Reverend Henry C. Potter. Even without knowing about the racism vexing his selection, however, he opens his speech with a series of emphatically provocative pronouncements, contradicting the, unbeknownst to him, selection committee's construal of his attitude toward his title subject:

> Jefferson Davis was a typical Teutonic Hero; the history of civilization during the last millennium has been the development of the idea of the Strong Man of which he was the embodiment. The Anglo-Saxon loves a soldier—Jefferson Davis was an Anglo-Saxon, Jefferson Davis was a soldier. There was not a phase in that familiarly strange life that would not have graced a mediaeval romance: from the fiery and impetuous young lieutenant who stole as his bride the daughter of a ruler-elect of the land, to the cool and ambitious politician in the Senate hall. So boldly and surely did that cadaverous figure with the thin nervous lips and flashing eye, write the first line of the new page of American history, that the historian of the future must ever see back of the War of Succession, the strong arm of one imperious man, who defied decease, tramples on precedent, would not be defeated, and never

surrendered. A soldier and a lover, a statesman and a ruler; passionate, ambitious and indomitable; bold reckless guardian of a peoples' All—judged by the whole standards of Teutonic civilization, there is something noble in the figure of Jefferson Davis; and judged by every canon of human justice, there is something fundamentally incomplete about that standard.[170]

Having thus cast the title subject of his address in sharp relief, Du Bois then, in an abrupt appositive marked in the speech transcript by a hard dash, changes focus to the title's prepositional clause, and with truly subtle deftness contextualizes what he has just said in a way that seriously troubles it: "—judged by the whole standards of Teutonic civilization, there is something noble in the figure of Jefferson Davis; and judged by every canon of human justice, there is something fundamentally incomplete about that standard." If the tenor of public praise heaped upon Du Bois's address is anything to go by, his audience seems to have joined the selection committee in miscomprehending the critical thrust of his remarks. Reviewing the Harvard commencement ceremonies in its July 3 issue, the *Nation Magazine* lauded Du Bois for handling the "difficult and hazardous subject [of Jefferson Davis] with absolute good taste, great moderation, and almost contemptuous fairness." The October issue of the preeminent periodical *Kate Field's Washington* followed suit, reporting that Du Bois was judged by all to have been the star of the commencement ceremonies, and observing "how remarkable it was to hear a colored man deal with Jefferson Davis so generously [using] such phrases as a 'great man,' a 'keen thinker,' a 'strong leader.'" Not only did these firsthand reports on Du Bois's commencement speech miss the irony in his characterization of Davis's life as a medieval romance and description of him as "cadaverous," but they seem to have stopped listening altogether right at the appositive. Because, at that point, it was very clear absolutely nothing about Du Bois's remarks made on that June day in 1890 could be even slightly construed as eulogizing the recently deceased president of the Confederate States of America. In fact, having just cast doubts on the very standards by which Davis is celebrated, Du Bois explicitly states he wish is "to consider not the character of the man, but the type of civilization which his life represented."[171] More precisely, the focus of his reflections was that civilization's foundational "idea of the strong man—individualism coupled with the rule of might," the standard by which it is conceivable to judge Jefferson Davis as noble. It is this idea, Du Bois declaimed, "that has made the logic of even modern history, the cool logic of the Club. It made a naturally brave and generous man, Jefferson Davis—now advancing civilization by murdering Indians, now hero of a national disgrace called by courtesy, the Mexican War; and finally, as the crowning absurdity, the peculiar champion of a people fighting to be free in order that another people should not be free."[172] Du Bois is no more invested here in vilifying Jefferson Davis as a singular individual than he was in eulogizing him. Rather, his aim was to critically explicate how the idea of the strong man and his mighty right arm "has found an even more secure foothold in the policy and philosophy of the State [where] the Strong Man and his mighty Right Arm has become the Strong Nation with its armies."[173] And the stakes of this explication are global because, "however a figure like Jefferson Davis may appear, as a man, race, or nation, his life can only logically mean this: the advance of a part of the world at the expense of the whole; the overweening sense of the I, and the consequent forgetting of the Thou."[174] This is the conception of civilization Jefferson Davis represents. The fundamental incompleteness of its standard stems from being "handicapped by shortsighted national selfishness," fostering a system of culture predicated on the principle that "the rise of one race on the ruins of another" is the definitive arch of civilization."[175] And let us note in passing the reverberation of that principle in Adorno's earlier-mentioned reformulation of Michelet's aphorism: "The recent past always presents itself as if it were annihilated by catastrophes." On that score, Du Bois thinks, it is virtually impossible "to introduce a new idea into the world except by means of the cudgel," which reduces civilization to little more than a "field for stalwart manhood and heroic character, and at the same time for moral obtuseness and refined brutality."[176] Even if the world "has needed and will need its Jefferson Davises," his type "is incomplete and can never serve [civilization's] best purpose until checked by its complementary ideas." What is required is a more capacious concept of human history and civilization, a different narrative. And so, Du Bois poses the question: "Whence shall these [ideas] come?" Question posed, it is directly answered:

> Through the glamour of history, the rise of a nation has ever been typified by the Strong Man crushing out an effete civilization.... Not as the muscular warrior came the Negro, but as the cringing slave. The Teutonic met civilization and crushed it—the Negro met civilization and was crushed by it.[177]

This is not to suggest that the Negro possessed no martial valor. Du Bois was well aware that they did. In chapter 3 of *The Souls of Black Folk*, he mentions "all the leadership or attempted leadership," which, as he says, was driven by "the one motive of revolt and revenge,—typified in the terrible," referring in illustration to Cato, who led the Stono Rebellion of 1739 in South Carolina.[178] If we cast our net farther afield across the Americas in general, we find the examples of Marcos Xiorro in Puerto Rico, Ventura Sánchez in Cuba, and Domingo Bioho in Columbia, as well as Ahuna, Manoel Calafate, and Dandará of the 1835 Malê Revolt in Bahia Brazil, and François Mackandal in Haiti. Du Bois is not overlooking such individuals when he says, "In the history of this people, we seek in vain the elements of Teutonic deification of Self, and Roman brute force."[179] Rather, his point is for all the motivation of terrible revolt and revenge even in such cases, violence is not enacted in pursuit of individual vainglory. We do not find the likes of such figures as Egil, or Ragnar Lodbrok of the *Völundarkvitha* (the Icelandic saga). Instead, what is celebrated about these black heroes, by and large, is their sacrifice in pursuit of collective freedom, which is precisely what Du Bois characterizes as "the submission of the strength of the Strong to the advance of all."[180] His designation for this is "the doctrine of the Submissive Man," which is contradistinct to the Teutonic Strong Man's egotistical self-aggrandizement and assertion of the I. As Du Bois spells it out:

> The Teuton stands today as the champion of the idea of Personal Assertion: the Negro as the peculiar embodiment of the idea of Personal Submission: either alone, tends to an abnormal development—towards Despotism on the one hand which the world has just cause to fear, and yet covertly admires, or towards slavery on the other, which the world despises and which, yet is not wholly despicable.[181]

Bear in mind that all of this is figurally speaking. Jefferson Davis is an exemplum of a figure, "the Teutonic Hero," which is synonymous with "the Strong Man," itself a figure identified with the foundational ideal of a type of civilization whereby the ascendency of mighty individualism is the supreme mode of freedom. That ideal as the compelling force of modern history is the topic of Du Bois's Harvard oration. The issue at hand is not just what is wrong with Teutonic civilization judging Davis noble, but what is wrong with the very concept of "Teutonic civilization," or more precisely, with the historiography of civilization predicated on the apotheosis of the Strong Man as its providential agency. In counterpoint, the Negro Submissive Man is a figure of *being-in-common-with-one-another* as the basis for viable, sustainable worldly collectivity. We have, then, two figural dyads: Strong Man/Submissive Man, Teutonic/Negro. And there is a struggle of concepts being waged with these figures.

A complicated relationship between figure and concept—between the dynamic movement of language as poetry, and the fixedness of concept as determinate definitiveness with its demands of demonstrability, or apophantic truth—is at play in these two dyads. The complexity of this relationship requires we attend just as carefully to the expressions of figure as to the logical relations of concept. We must carefully interrogate what Du Bois is connoting when he maintains that the appeal of the strong man "always arises when a people seemingly become convinced that the object of the world is not civilization, but Teutonic civilization."[182] We must just as diligently interrogate what he is talking about when he says, "In every Southern country . . . destined to play a future part in the world—in Southern North America, South America,

Australia, and Africa—a new nation has a more or less firm foothold. This circumstance has, however, attracted but incidental notice, hitherto."[183] Or when he then declaims, "In the history of this people, we seek in vain the elements of Teutonic deification of Self, and Roman brute force, but we do find an idea of submission apart from cowardice, laziness or stupidity, such as the world never saw before."[184] Pursuing this line of inquiry raises two questions. What is this concept of civilization Du Bois refers to as "Teutonic," the fundamental principle of which is "the overweening sense of the I, and the subsequent forgetting of the Thou"? And what is this doctrine of the Submissive Man, exemplified by the Negro that is "at once the check and complement of the Teutonic Strong Man?"[185]

There are those in Du Bois scholarship who are inclined to discern a pronounced Hegelian tendency in his early work, and so describe the doctrine of the Submissive Man as "a kind of Christian-Hegelian recognition of duty and collective debt as the basis of the state—not subservience."[186] Accordingly, the Strong Man/Submissive Man dyad is taken to be an iteration of the well-known *Herrschaft und Knechtschaft* dialectic—which we render as "lordship and bondage," following Baille's and Miller's translations, rather than the more recent common-place Kojève-influenced "master and slave"—and the *Teutonic/Negro* dyad gets construed as Du Bois transferring that Hegelian scenario of the struggle for recognition (*Anerkennung*) onto the landscape of American race relations.[187] Having learned German at Fisk, Du Bois read Hegel's *Phänomenologie des Geistes* in that language with George Santayana while at Harvard, and maybe even discussed it with Royce, who had already begun to interpolate his own interpretations of the *Phenomenology* into his lectures during the period Du Bois interacted with him. Moreover, there is ample enough evidence in Du Bois's Harvard course notebooks of a struggle with and critique of Hegel's idealist teleology, in which the question of the etiology of self-consciousness set out in chapter 4 of the *Phenomenology*—where we find the *Herrschaft und Knechtschaft* dialectic in the subsection titled "Selbstständigkeit und Unselbstständigkeit des Selbstbewußtseins; Herrschaft und Knechtschaft"—is in play. The question is whether the terms of Hegel's dialectic do indeed map onto Du Bois's "Strong Man/Submissive Man" and "Teutonic/Negro." It is useful, with respect to this question, to consider briefly Hegel's usage of *Herr* and *Knecht* across his work, from the *System of Ethical Life* to the *Philosophy of Right*, the *Philosophy of Mind*, and the *Phenomenology of Spirit*.

As Hyppolite points out, Hegel's usage reflects the etymological provenance of the two terms. For instance, *Knecht* in Old High German, where it is *kneht*, meant "boy" or "child." Sullivan reports that this connotation expanded rather early on so that Notker the Stammerer (ca. 840–912 AD) uses it to mean "warrior." In Middle High German, where it is *knëht*, it connotes "male servant," particularly on a farm—so "male farm laborer." It was at times also used in a way synonymous with the legal term *scale*, referring to a slave, serf, or unspecified servant status—in other words, some sense of "unfree" akin to the Latin *servus*. But when modified by either the adjective *gout* or *tiure* (worthy), it usually meant "knight." Sullivan speculates that the confusion between *scale* as a legal term for *servus* and *kneht* as a martial term for warrior was traceable to the unfree status of feudal German knights or *ministeriales*.[188] *Herr* is far less ambiguous. Derived from the Middle High German *hêrre*, which in turn comes from the Old High German *hêriro*, a loan word from the Latin *senior*, it consistently connotes a "lord," whether religious or secular, in contradistinction to his vassals. As Andrew Cole has argued, Hegel consistently used *Herr* and *Knecht* across his writings in specific reference to feudal relations; whereas when discussing Greek and Roman society, he regularly uses the term *Sklave* for slave.[189] At issue for Hegel is the very concept of "man," as is evidenced in his discussion of the dangers of legal definition, *Omnis definitio in jure civili periculosa*, in the introduction to the *Philosophy of Right*: "Thus, in Roman law, for instance, no definition of man was possible, because it excluded the slave [*Sklave*]. The conception of man was destroyed by the fact of slavery."[190] Hegel is refuting the principal precept of the Roman *De Jure Personarum* (The Rights of Persons) from the *Corpus Juris Civilis*, which states: "The chief division of rights of persons is this: all men [*omnes homines*] are either free [*liberi*] or slaves [*servi*]."[191] It then states: "Freedom, . . . as applied to men, is the natural power of doing what one pleases, insofar as one is not prevented by force or law. Slavery is an institution of the laws of nations, whereby one man is subject to another's dominion, contrary to natural right [*naturam subicitur*]." Because it is contrary to natural law, *jure naturali*, which nature teaches to all animals (*omnium animalium*), including humans, slavery (*Servitus*) destroys the conception of man-in-and-of-himself. Hegel charges the Roman legal conception with positing the individual as an "unfulfilled abstraction" that cannot attain unity by the sheer plurality of its legal personage. In fact, under the topic "Acts of Possession" in *Philosophy of Right*, he uses *Herrschaft* deliberately in contrast to *Sklaverei* when discussing the difference between how slave masters and feudal lords justify their despotism.[192] In the same paragraph, he goes on to make a distinction between the "false, comparatively primitive phenomenon of slavery [as] one that befalls mind when mind is only at the level of consciousness," when the human exists only as a natural thing, without the concept of "human"—that is to say, without the concept of itself as itself apart from the concept—and the position of the free will when the mind "consists precisely in its being no longer implicit or as concept alone, but in its transcending this formal stage of its being, and *eo ipso* its immediate natural existence, until the existence that it gives to itself is one that is solely its own and free."[193] It is at this stage, where the science of right begins, that the dialectic of the concept and of the purely immediate consciousness of freedom brings about "the fight for recognition and the relationship [*Anerkennen und das Verhältnis*] of Lord and bondage [*Herrschaft und der Knechtschaft*]." On this point, Hegel cites the *Phenomenology* for further elucidation, where he pays particular attention to the feudal sense of the terms *Herr* and *Knecht* as a part of his acute interest in feudal forms of possession. A parallel can be drawn, indeed Hegel is drawing it, between the dialectic of mind and the history of tenth-century Europe, when, in the German speaking lands, the ancient Greco-Roman institution of slavery gave way to the feudal system of bondage. All of this provides a firm basis for rendering these terms into English as "Lord" and "bondsmen," and certainly not "master and slave." It also helps clarify that Du Bois's figural dyads are not at all Hegelian.

Now, perhaps it can be supposed there is an analogy between the transition from slavery to feudal bondage in Europe and the end of slavery to sharecropper peonage in the United States. In which case, by construing Du Bois's dyads to be suggesting the Negro freedmen are analogous to the European serfs, it could still be argued that he is mapping the Hegelian dialect onto the North American scene. Two problematics immediately confront that supposition, however. The first has to do with the distinction between law of social status and law of ontological being. Unlike the Roman law Hegel adduces, whereby the person is a legal entity distinguished into three classifications of status—*liberatus* (freedom), *civitas* (citizenship), and *familiae* (family)—modern Western law, as has already been noted, defined "Negro" as a singular *non-persona*, human property. And it did so well after the moment in time—circa tenth century—in Europe when *servitus* is abolished and the *Sklave* becomes *Knecht*, which, by Hegel's account, is the moment of the dialectic process when the mind comes to conscious fulfillment of itself as and for itself in the world. In other words, the moment when *Man* becomes possible, entering into the realm of communicative human relationship that is to become the public sphere, the grounds for which supersede those of the state, *polis*, and *civitas*. This is the realm in which *Negro* is defined in law as something within it but constitutively and supposedly conclusively outside that human relationship—such is the thrust of the 1662 Virginia law of *Partus sequitur ventrem*—as something other, a type of human that, in accord with Aristotle's theory is lacking in full human cognition and so naturally disposed to being property. The moment of modern law, the *juris gentium*, certainly does surmount the Roman *De Jure Personarum*, giving instead the rights of man, attended by a sharp ontological division. The Negro, however, is *construed* as a different sort of being. That perceived ontological status, although conceived with slavery, is perpetuated well beyond the legislation of the Thirteenth, Fourteenth, and Fifteenth Amendments. Post-Abolition, the Negro remained *Negro*, unlike the *Sklave* who become *Knecht*. With respect to the dialectic of mind, it could be argued that the freedman is analogous to the *Knecht*, this again being an issue of the stage of mind-in-the-world, and not social status. If one takes into account the legal and social structures of post-Reconstruction Jim Crow—the Black Codes and convict leasing system—as a form of bondage, then the analogy of consciousness gets some purchase. This is slim purchase, however, because the whole point of Du Bois's elaboration of the doctrine of submission is that the Negro manifested its qualities *already while enslaved*.

We come, then, to the second problematic. There is no analog for *Herrschaft* in Du Bois's 1890 Harvard commencement address. He does not refer to slave masters let alone lords, but rather to the Strong Man as the type checked by the Submissive Man in a relationship of complementarity. Nor should we mistake the relationship of check and complementarity between the Strong Man and the Submissive Man as resembling that particular moment in the dialectic of mind when the relationship between lord and bondage and the fight for recognition is manifested, beginning the long unfolding of bourgeoisie consciousness in which full commensurability of authority and responsibility is the *télos* of mind's actualization. The dyads Teutonic/Negro and Strong Man/Submissive Man are not dialectic in that way. The Negro is not the antithesis of the Teutonic, nor the Submissive Man that of the Strong Man. Neither of these dyads is a movement toward synthesis; rather, they are nonsynthetic contestations of distinctly different ways of being brought into correlation. In a recognizable, albeit somewhat elliptical, allusion to Hegel's *System der Wissenschaft* (System of Science), of which the *Phenomenology* was the first part, Du Bois states: "For wherever the Negro people have touched civilization their rise has been singularly unromantic and unscientific."[194] Thus, the consciousness signaled by Du Bois's doctrine of Submissive Man is not an articulation of the Hegelian dialect of mind. Rather, it is emphatically an order of consciousness that is heterogeneous and even anachronic to that dialectic. What's more, Hegel's hypostatizing the events of European history as actualities in the dialectic *translatio* of an ultimately singular mind (*Geistes*) moving toward the *télos*, the bourgeoisie—a historiography that finds inspiration in the figure of Napoleon astride Marengo riding out of the city Jena on October 13, 1806[195]—is precisely what Du Bois is challenging when he says his doctrine of Submissive Man is predicated on "recognizing the fact that 'To no one type of mind is it given to discern the totality of Truth.'"[196]

Having argued, *pace* the consensus reading, that the conceptual struggle over civilization at play with the figural dyads, Strong Man/Submissive Man and Teutonic/Negro, is *not* waged in terms of the Hegelian dialectic, it remains to determine in what terms it is being waged. For that, let us bear down more carefully on the first of our two questions: What is this civilization he refers to as "Teutonic," the fundamental principle of which is "the overweening sense of the I, and the subsequent forgetting of the Thou"?

At one point in "Jefferson Davis as a Representative of Civilization," Du Bois remarks: "The Teutonic met civilization and crushed it," which is in reference to the myriad Teutonic peoples who overran the western part of the Roman Empire in the fifth century AD. At another, he characterizes the Teutonic as the hero of civilization, epitomizing its highest ideals, saying: "The Teuton stands today as the champion of the idea of Personal Assertion . . . the hero the world has ever worshipped, who gained unthought of triumphs and made unthought mistakes." This description of the Teutonic as crusher cum principal agent of civilization is concordant with, if not simply an allusion to, Edward Gibbon's assessment in *The Decline and Fall of the Roman Empire*. Expanding on Longinus's metaphor that the Romans had become pigmies as a result of "the introduction, or at least the abuse of Christianity," Gibbon refers to "the revolution of ten centuries," meaning the thousand-year span from Odoacer's deposing the last Western Roman emperor, Romulus Augustulus, in 479, up to Martin Luther's Reformation, in the course of which the Christian Church, unable to extinguish the Teuton's ferocious brutality, absorbed it, converting its energy into the driving force of a renewed, faith-based imperial expansion.[197] Gibbon is being characteristically ironic in claiming that the manly spirit of freedom with which the conquering Teutonic infused Christianity "became the happy parent of taste and science." As he is further on in his *History* when, after extending the Christian Teutonic revolution to fourteen centuries—effectively adding the period from the so-called Age of Discovery up to the Enlightenment and close of the eighteenth century—he says, "by the industry and zeal of the Europeans," Christian civic virtue was "widely diffused to the most distant shores of Asia and Africa; and by the means of their colonies has been firmly established from Canada to Chili [sic], in a world unknown to the ancients."[198] After all, Gibbon's own description of the story he tells is "the triumph of barbarism and religion," and he regards it as a story of progressive retrogression from the archaic conception of heroic martial excellence that the Romans termed *virtus*, which had been a key element in the millennium-long development of classical civilization. This story of retrogression, whereby the myriad conquering Teutonic peoples merge with the Church of Rome to constitute the Germanic Holy Roman Empire, followed by the Westphalian system of sovereign nations, and eventually the international system, is the history of Europe as perpetual, ever-expanding conquest, which certainly warrants Du Bois's label, "Teutonic civilization." His designating it so reverberates with Gibbonesque irony, as does his characterizing it as a field for stalwart manhood and heroic character infused with moral obtuseness and refined brutality. Along these lines, I take Du Bois to be alluding in rebuttal to Gibbon's *History* when he then says, "Through the glamour of history, the rise of a nation has ever been typified by the Strong Man crushing out an effete civilization. That brutality buried aught else beside Rome when it descended golden haired and drunk from the blue north has scarcely entered human imagination." His description of the nation rising brutal, golden haired, and drunk from the north to crush an effete civilization calls to mind another reader of Gibbon, Friedrich Nietzsche, who also speaks of the Teutonic peoples who crushed Rome as *der blonden germanischen Bestie* (the blond Germanic beast). At other times, he refers to them as *alten Germanen* (ancient Germans, or Teutons), in distinction from what he terms *uns Deutschen* (us Germans), by which he means the degenerate fruit of the very centuries-long Christian tempering of the Teutons Gibbon recounts.[199]

There is no need here to speculate whether Du Bois had Nietzsche in mind when, invited by the dean of Harvard College to write a "commencement part," he composed "Jefferson Davis as a Representative of Civilization."[200] It suffices to take note of the resonance in figure and attend to the conceptual reverberations regarding the question of civilization. In so doing, it is also worth bearing in mind that James grappled with Nietzsche's views about ethics and action in his 1884 essay, "The Dilemma of Determinism." That grappling's coming into play in the yearlong lecture course on ethics, "Philosophy IV," he conducted during the 1888–1889 academic year is strongly suggested in Du Bois's course notebook, where Nietzsche's concepts and issues regarding the "Science of Morals" were matters of some moment between the professor and young scholar. Those same issues were more fully taken up by Du Bois in "The Renaissance of Ethics" essay. We have already given rather careful attention to both the course notebook and the essay; what makes them germane here is the fact that together they provide a detailed presentation of the thinking and theoretical argumentation behind the doctrine of Submissive Man Du Bois presents in his Harvard commencement oration. We learn from them that by the end of James's course in ethics, Du Bois had determined there is no free will, no human will, except in action. This lays the basis for the line of thinking about the nature of freedom and the history of human civilization intimated in the commencement address, the first principles of which are quite plainly set out in the closing pages of the notebook, which pose a series of questions very much aligned with Nietzsche's:

> Philosophy gives up the settling of the problem. The partial man, scientific, he goes on. The philosophical man is halted and the question of possibles [*sic*] comes up—is it possible that all is unity and bad is good, or

that good & bad *are* & plurality is true? She [philosophy] must give up some of her ideal, [*sic*] as clearness, unity, etc., and taking a stand believe in it. This is the attitude of Hegel—mysticism, which in ordinary life is the peaceful religious attitude (no gas) which left on me an impression that our consciousness is but an island in a vast sea-floor of consciousnesses. We must take account that there is little we know, & more knowledge may do away with contradictions. All this is open faith but not philosophy—which shall we embrace? If we take p[hilosophy], we give up unity, but is this sacrilege? I think it nothing but an aesthetic demand & [it] has no right to drive out everything else. I find that I must turn my back on unity for the sake of clearness & though I lose something—a great deal, I think I gain more: goodness, personality, possibility, as real things. I gain too the unity of continuity. The lowest possible terms of my universe are many—it is a plurality, [and] cannot be written down in one formula. One contradiction cannot itself explain another. We thus avoid the contradiction of finite & infinite by saying there are first beginnings, new things come. Actual God is finite though possibly potentiality infinite; he may be one of many powers—in other words, polytheism is an attitude—the normal attitude of the human mind. This, then, gives us the reality of the moral life—bad things are not good because God made them—he didn't make them. Thus philosophy come back to the path of ordinary commonsense & ordinary religion. Life becomes a militant fight v. bad, with a power to look out for the good & not responsible for the bad. The facts, then, of the world are psychic facts and scientifically don't compel us to believe in a God. We believe in one because our religious nature demands it. There is no coercive philosophy of religion. In all our logical dealings with the world, we make the mistake of *illicit process*. Shall, then, I believe in God? Am I wise in believing anything beyond the evidence? Is faith in what we wish a legitimate philosophical attitude? But the whole stirring of our activity, scientific & otherwise, are [*sic*] founded on a faith in something we want, & therefore, the attitude of faith is honorable & right. It is simply the courage to risk life on a possibility & differs much from dogmatic theology & intolerance. This [is] the world become a republic. The only way to prove an assumption is to act upon [it], in science or any other [field]. Act, then, on this hypothesis in order to prove God—this [action] is the only *proof*. But the dilemma is: either never know or know this man. This is a place to know & not to be agnostic. *Man must act*. (Voluntary action in optimism & pessimism).[201]

The notebook's last words, "*Man must act*," summing up his argument against confusing cause and effect, are fully consonant with Nietzsche's condemnation of free will as a theologian's artifices: "its originators, the priests at the head of ancient communities, wanted to create for themselves the right to punish—or wanted to create this right for God. Men were considered 'free' so that they could be judged and punished."²⁰² For both Du Bois and Nietzsche, contra this psychology of punishment, there is no willing subject as substratum behind the doing of action; there is only the *doing*, which articulates and sustains what is called the subject but is more aptly taken as the *persona* of doing. Further resonances between Nietzsche's and Du Bois's thinking can be found throughout the course notebook. Both are critical of moral philosophy for its persistent adherence to theistic teleology, resulting in its untenable propositions regarding human agency, most pointedly, that of free will, predicated on the concept of causality. Nietzsche finds Kant's categorical metaphysics to be a chief culprit for the mess for reasons very similar to those prompting Du Bois in "The Renaissance of Ethics" to count Kant's categorical imperative among the "false theories" of ethics. Near the end of that essay, as though responding directly to Nietzsche's admonishment to abandon the metaphysical account of the soul altogether in favor of a scientific analysis of the socio, as well as ontogenesis of the mind—the practitioner of which Nietzsche christens the "*new* psychologist"²⁰³—Du Bois calls for an ethics based on a science of mind, saying:

> The "new" psychology and the modern effort at physical research are tentatives in that direction, but one is more a science of brain, the other very analogous to a study of the human body which should begin with the investigation of the most glaring monstrosities: of great use no doubt but never destined to reveal its true value until the type of which it is a caricature is more thoroughly known.²⁰⁴

The remark about type, with respect to a science of ethics, goes directly to Nietzsche's assertion that in order to achieve a "Science of Morals," there must first be a comprehensive survey and classification of the immense varieties of actual common forms of so-called ethical practice, culminating in a "*theory of types* of morality." Properly attending to this resonance requires that we briefly recount some of the more germane points in Nietzsche's typology, so as to show just how, resonance notwithstanding, Du Bois's doctrine of Submissive Man challenges it.

More emphatically, or perhaps better to say, less ironically, than Gibbon, Nietzsche construes the distinction between the Teutonic people who conquered Rome and those who came afterward as one of existential moral character. This is in keeping with his premise that moral judgment and evaluations are "only images and fantasies based on a physiological process unknown to us."²⁰⁵ Or, as he also puts it, they are "only a sign language [*Zeichensprache*] of the affects."²⁰⁶ In either case, the particular types of morality "may always be considered first of all as the symptoms of certain bodies [*bestimmter Leiber*]."²⁰⁷ A naturalistic taxonomy of human types underlies Nietzsche's theory of moral types, according to which there are types of persons engendered by natural and civilizational forces.²⁰⁸ Among these is the predatory strong man type Nietzsche famously describes as the "*schweifende blonde Bestie* [lustfully roving blond beast]"—Nietzsche's metonym for the lion as the *par excellence* figure of the predatory animal, which when applied to this type can be understood to mean something like "lion-hearted."²⁰⁹ He postulates this is the primal type of man "at the bottom of all the noble races," telling us in in *Genealogy of Morals* that these include "the Roman, Arabian, Germanic, and Japanese nobility, Homeric heroes, and Scandinavian Viking." Also included among the noble races are "the Athenians [in their] ραθυμία (*rathymía*)—indifference and contempt for safety, life, and body with a terrible gaiety and profundity of delight in all destruction, in all blisses of victory and cruelty." Nietzsche reaches further back than Gibbon's Roman *virtus* to adduce as the principle example of a noble morality, *Vornehme-Moral* the Homeric ἀρετή (*areté*)—the excellence of strong men of instinct and vital desire exhibited in martial conflict. For such aristocratic souls, whoever has the power to repay deed for deed, being grateful and vengeful is called *good*; whoever is powerless, incapable of repayment, is *bad*. The good belongs to a community of the powerful, and so to be good is to have communal feeling (*bonus = communitas virtutis = sensus communis*), which is to be beautiful, happy, and loved by the gods. The bad, *malus*, belong to the group of those subjugated, who, being impotent, cannot constitute a community in action and so cannot have communal feeling (*malus = homo impotens = missis subjugavit = sine communi sensu*).²¹⁰ These strong men of courage were the ἀνδρὸς ἀγαθοῦ, men of excellence, that both Plato and Aristotle postulate as the ideal type of human on which to base the ideal community. Along their philosophical lines, Homeric ἀρετή (*areté*) is transvalued into a universally distributed *capacity* for excellence-in-action, thereby subjugating the men of excellence's ferocity to reason in service to the righteous polity. Calling this "Socratic moralism," Nietzsche dismisses it as "a self-deception on the part of philosophers," and regards the Platonic equation—"Reason-virtue-happiness [*Vernunft* (λόγος, *logos*)] = *Tugend* [ἀρετή, *areté*] = *Glück* [ευδαιμονία (*eudaimonia*)]"—to be symptomatic of a pathological condition, which is only exacerbated by Aristotle's epistemic absolutism.²¹¹ The truly devastating effects of this pathology become manifest once it is taken up by Romanized Christianity, in part through the Neoplatonist efforts of Origen and Augustine:

> The nobility of instinct, the taste, the methodical research, the genius of organization and administration, the faith in, the will to, man's future,

the great Yes to all things, become visible in the *imperium Romanum*.... Christianity found its mission in putting an end to precisely such an organization *because life prospered in it*.... These holy anarchists made it a matter of "piety" for themselves to destroy "the world," *that is*, the *imperium Romanum*, until not one stone remained on the other, until even Teutons and other louts could become masters over it.[212]

What troubles Nietzsche most is that under the dominion of the Roman Church, the ethics of heroic excellence had succumbed to a protracted "slave insurrection in morals," which, having been spawned in the *ressentiment* of the *missis subjugavit*, the subjugated masses, finally made the slave-morality (*Sklaven-Moral*) predominate throughout the imperium. Accordingly, the aristocratic equation "good = aristocrat = beautiful = happy = loved by the gods" is replaced with the contrary equation, "the wretched are alone the good; the poor, the weak, the lowly, are alone the good; the suffering, the needy, the sick, the loathsome, are the only righteous ones." This is more than merely an inversion of position. It accomplishes the transvaluation (*Umwertung*) of heroic ethics.[213] Whereas for the aristocratic soul, the good was in the public action of virtuous men, whose doing was the manifestation of their goodness, and the bad was merely that which was lowly and wretched, the noncommunal, but still human, mass. For the Christian, one cannot be good or bad by what one does; one *is* either good or bad by the grace of God. Christianity hypostatizes the ethical hierarchy as eternal, such that the lowly soul is quintessentially good and the aristocratic quintessentially evil, and the suffering pitiful are the only ones who are blessed, for them alone is salvation.[214] Powerlessness, thus, acquires moral force in the Christian virtue of pity, which Nietzsche calls "the practice of nihilism," multiplying and conserving misery as piety on the premise that all humans are the children of God, the banner motto of which is "the beloved community." In this vein, the ancient Roman virtue *fides* (the reciprocal trust between two parties) is revalued as the Pauline virtue *faith* (belief in the truth of the promised kingdom to come beyond this world that can be known only after death, and access to which is contingent upon obedience to the church). Hope of happiness in the future world displaces fulfillment achieved through heroic virtue, so that the *summum bonum*, the Supreme Good, is actual only after death. This same Christian *hope*, as a disposition of the soul, also replaces *phronesis*; and the happiness of *evangelizo vobis*, "glad tidings" proclaimed in Luke 2:10, is received by living in love without subtraction and exclusion, without regard for station because everyone is the child of God. This profoundest and sublimest kind of love, which transcends the *eudaimonia* of the *polis*, is what Paul calls ἀγάπη (*agapē*), glossing the Alexandrian diaspora Septuagint rendering of the Torahic "אהבה (*ahava*)," as in Leviticus

19:18: "καὶ ἀγαπήσεις τὸν πλησίον σου ὡς σεαυτόν [*kai agapēseis ton plésion sou hōs seautón*, but thou shalt love thy neighbor as thyself]."[215] In its displacing *fides* with pity and *phronesis* with glad tidings, Paul's doctrine of love changed the purpose of action from working to constitute the world to working for its end, ἔσχατον (*eschaton*). The only hope for salvation is in Divine *agapē*, which, because it is spontaneous and unmotivated by anything in humanity, says nothing about what humanity is, except the recipient of this unsolicited Divine love. As such, it is the opposite of the ἔρως (*éros*) Plato espouses in the *Symposium*, which is all about the physically motivated human acquisitive desire becoming spiritualized, per Diotima's *scalia amoris*, whereby a virtuous man moves *from* physical desire *to* metaphysical contemplation of the Divine.[216] Platonic *éros* accounts for everything about the capacity of human desire to ascend and transform along Epicurean lines—that is to say, παρ᾽ ἡμᾶς (*par' hēmās*, from our own volition)—and nothing about the Divine except that it is the most exulted object of human desire. *Éros* is the expression of the human will to make ourselves more than we are now, to aspire toward more fulfillment in life (*eudaimonia*).[217] And it is precisely because *agapē* is profoundly *inhuman*—the spontaneous unmotivated love of God manifested in the Passion of Christ, which is to be the initiator of community, the fellowship with God in love—that Nietzsche finds it fatal. His expression of this is clarifying:

> Jesus had abolished the very concept of "guilt"—he had denied any cleavage between God and Man; he *lived* this unity of God and man as his "glad tidings." And *not* as a prerogative! From now on, there enters into the type of the Redeemer, step by step, the doctrine of judgment and return, the doctrine of death as a sacrificial death, the doctrine of the *resurrection* with which the whole concept of "blessedness," the whole and only actuality of the evangel, is conjured away—in favor of a state after death.[218]

Once that occurs, "World," connoting the polygenous, polymorphous human-being-in-work-ness on earth, the end of which Paul was certain would occur presently, becomes an opprobrium.[219] And, thus, the Roman *vir bonus* of heroic excellence in action, *virtus*, is transformed into the civilized "'Man' [*Mensch*]" of Christian piety.[220] With that conquest, Christianity was confronted with a different type of beast of prey, the "inwardly wild and self brutalizing, strong but flawed [*missrathenen*] men, whose dissatisfaction with their self was not due to an excessive sensitivity and susceptibility to pain, but to an overpowering desire to inflict pain, finding an outlet for inner tensions in hostile acts and ideas."[221] To overcome such barbarism, the church utilized its own barbaric force of the Passion and Eucharist, consumption of the sacrificed flesh and blood, to seduce these Teutonic beasts and achieve mastery over them. Once they assimilated the principle Christian tenet of man's ignominy

(*Schande des Menschen*), they were weakened and made sick psychologically.[222] Nietzsche's point here is that "enfeeblement [*Schwächung*] is the Christian recipe for *taming* [*Zähmung*], for 'Civilization,'" which he, like Gibbon, views as "the regression [*Rückgang*] of mankind" rather than improvement.[223] The moral type it induces is what he calls the *décadence* type of man.[224] The splendid Teutonic blond beasts who waged war in the conviction that the excessive wantonness and equanimity of their murderous, destructive violence would inspire poetic celebration were transformed into faithful Christian warriors who wage war in the conviction that their violence will establish God's rule on earth, in hope of eternal redemption in the afterlife. The ferocity and violence of these civilized and civilizing Teutons is just as wanton and impartial, only now it is an act of piety; redemption is found in killing under the Latinate motto *pro Christo et Ecclesia*, "for Christ and Church." The noble heroic strong man is, thus, displaced by the pious religious strong man, for whom truly heroic virtue is inaccessible. Contra Ernest Renan's claims, "if anything is unevangelical it is the concept of the hero," whether in the Roman form, *vir bonus*, or the Teutonic blond beast.[225] Nietzsche's typology of morals, thus, gives us two related but distinct connotations of "Teutonic"—the *alten Germanen* who, possessing a ferocious freedom akin to the classical Homeric ἀρετή and Roman *virtus*, crushed Rome, and the Christian-tamed, civilized, civilizing *Deutschen*, who are a mongrel retrogression from the noble blond beast.

Turning our attention back to Du Bois's Harvard commencement address, it becomes clear that he uses "Teutonic" to connote the *alten Germanen*, but also as a synonym for Nietzsche's metonymic "lustfully roving blond beast." And he uses "Teutonic civilization" in reference to the Gibbonian story of Western European civilization, according to which the blond beast is the catalyst and bearer of civilization. As for his doctrine of Submissive Man, despite being formulated in the very processes of European capitalist slavery, it is not a version of what Nietzsche characterizes, *per* Christian piety, as a slave-morality based on *ressentiment*. In fact, Du Bois's doctrine of Submissive Man is expressly opposed to the disposition of pious sacrifice. By that same token, in contrast to the Teutonic—who, having invaded and conquered the Roman imperium by force, were assimilated by Christian civilization in spirit—the Negro of Du Bois's description, although subjugated in modern Western capitalist Christian civilization to an intensely systematic, sustained economy of force, is never fully assimilated nor entirely stripped of prior so-called "African" ways of being. Not because the Negro is inherently *malus*, congenitally incapable of assimilating civilization; rather, the Negro's being neither *vir* nor *bonus* is a function of the severely limited syntax of Western civilization's conception of the human.

In this respect, the ethics of submission Du Bois proposes does indeed regress from Nietzschean *mankind* (*der Menschheit*), disgracing the noble hero at the foundations of virtue-ethics. Although using the term "Man," Du Bois seeks to dispense with the hero worship of virility; or rather, he thinks the Negro's systematic exclusion from it presents an occasion for a radically different conception of the human. Thus, in accord with Du Bois doctrine, *Menschheit* is subordinated to *Humanität*, a sound German term that is derived from the Latin *hūmānitās*. "When one speaks of humanity [*Humanität*]," Nietzsche once wrote, "the idea is that it may be what separates and distinguishes man [*Menschen*] from nature. But such a separation is not given in reality: 'natural' properties and the actual 'human' [*menschlich*] are inseparable."[226] Relating this to Windham's taxonomy of sentient flesh, we can say the Negro manifests a robust *Humanität* that, rather than being in opposition to nature, is an animal *enérgeia*, a being at-work-ness of the human solely and wholly *with* the flesh. Accordingly, Negro *Humanität* is profoundly human (*menschlich*). If we think about this concordantly with Du Bois's description of "the Negro as the peculiar embodiment of the idea of Personal Submission" in his doctrine of Submissive Man, then it becomes quite clear that *Negro* signals a concept of human being that pointedly contradicts what Nietzsche takes to be the "natural man," whose "terrible and inhumane [*unmenschlich*] capacities," manifested in impulsive actions such as the ancient Greek *rathymía*, "are the fertile grounds from which alone all humanity [*alle Humanität*] grows."[227] The discord here is over whether cruelty is the necessary primal force in forming human community.

Nietzsche aspires to the virile Greek *Humanität*, with its "strand of cruelty and tiger-like [*tigerartiger*] desire for destruction," mixed proportionately with reasoning intelligence (*phronesis*) and theoretical worldly wisdom (*sophia*) in well-balanced mean. Roman *pulcer* (noble excellence), which he renders as *Stärke* (strength), is heir to this Greek virility. And that lineage of the eudaimonic strong man (*andros eū*) of civilization, the noble beautiful fulfilment of human being, he contrasts to the German *Glänzende* (glitzy sparkle), which is an expression of "the soft concept of modern *Humanität*,"[228] which so prides itself, on its mastery over the savage cruel beast.[229] Yet, the cruelty of the savage beast persists, and not only in some faint residual tendencies or momentary outbursts, but

> everything we call "higher culture" is based on the spiritualization [*Vergeistigung*] and profundity of cruelty. From the painful voluptuousness of tragedy to everything sublime up to the highest most delicate shutters of metaphysic, from the Roman circus to the Christian ecstasies of the Passion, to Wagner's *Tristan and Isolde*; each of these rites "receive its sweetness [*Süßigkeit*] solely from the admixture of cruelty."[230]

Cruelty, Nietzsche argues, belongs to the most ancient festive joys of mankind, where, in a "horrible mixture of sensuality," it is what he calls *Dionysian*: that intoxicating draught that, like a suddenly swelling flood, subsumes everything subjective, every individual wave into its momentum.[231] It is the titanic urge (*Drang*) to not only unify every individual human into a mass, but to reconcile that humanity with the phenomenal world, with nature, which has become alienated, hostile, or subjugated. This is the intoxicating draught expressed in the songs of all primitive men and peoples, Nietzsche insists, the intensity of which engenders an ecstasy that breaks all the rigid barriers fixed between men, "as if the veil of *Māyā* had been torn aside," so that each feels himself not only united, reconciled, and fused with his neighbors, but as one with them in a primordial unity.[232] For the Dionysian, cruelty is an element of the capricious violent forces of life in the world; and the community it founds and sustains is that of the throng perpetually on the verge of chaos, embracing the passion for destruction and making-suffer, for intoxicating excess. Contrasting this primal unity of the throng is that of the *Apollinian* dream, which Nietzsche likens to what Schopenhauer describes, speaking of the man *wrapped in* the veil of *māyā*: "'Just as in a stormy sea that, unbounded in all directions, rises and drops mountainous waves, howling, a sailor sits in a boat and trusts in his frail bark: so in the midst of a world of torments the individual human being sits quietly, supported by and trusting in the *principium individuationis* [principle of individuation].'"[233] The Apollinian, as apotheosis of this individuation, "knows but one law—i.e., the delimiting of the boundaries of the individual, *measure* in the Hellenic sense," which is to say the homeostatic intermediacy Aristotle termed μεσότης (*mesotēs*) that subtends the civilized individual.[234] Side by side with aesthetic necessity are the imperatives γνῶθι σεαυτόν (*gnōthi seautón*) "know thyself" and μηδὲν ἄγαν (*midén ágan*), "nothing in excess." Consequently, the excesses wrought by the Dionysian, for the Apollinian, belonged to the pre-Apollonian age of the Titans; and, as we saw with Aristotle's *Politics*, that is the world of the barbarians. They are manifestations of the bad, *malus*, the nonpolitical qua noncommunal mass in the sense of the mob determined by animality and lacking *sensus communis*. But the same Aristotle, in his *Poetics*, recognized that even the Apollonian needs the entire world of suffering—spiritualized through the aesthetic forms of tragedy, the beautiful staging of the moment when terror is unleashed—in order for the primal unity of the individual to be consummated in a moment of "redeeming vision," to see itself as "sitting in a little boat . . . amidst the furious torments of the world," tranquilly certain of its sufficient reason.[235] In the last analysis, the "titanic" and "barbaric" are as necessary as the Apollinian. Simply put, the dynamic tension between these two cosmogonies is at the origin of Western civilization and its philosophical tradition, both of which turn on the generative force of cruelty, the pleasure (*Wohlgefühl*) of making suffer (*Leiden-machen*), that is "*a right of the masters [Herren-Rechte]*."[236] If we are to believe Nietzsche, cruelty is to be accepted "as a normal quality of man—and thus as something to which conscience cordially *says Yes*!... To see others suffer does one good, to make others suffer even more.... Without cruelty there is no festival... and in punishment there is so much that is *festive*!"[237]

"Negro" is not found in Nietzsche's list of beautiful predatory beasts at the foundation of all noble races. Perhaps that is because, as already noted, it is the synecdoche for a process of constitution incomprehensible in term of the binarisms, noble/slave, *virtus/malus*, as well Dionysian/Apollinian. Yet, in vilifying the modern notion of humanity, whereby suffering is the principle argument against existence, Nietzsche adduces "the Negro [*der Neger*] (taken as the representation of prehistoric man [*vorgeschichtlichen Menschen*])," in their apparent greater capacity to endure severe physical pain without distraction than "the best constituted European" as evidence that archaic man "was unwilling to refrain from *making* suffer and saw it... a genuine seduction to life because pain did not hurt as much as it does now."[238] *Negro* here connotes a congenital biophysical capacity of primitive man to not only endure cruelty but to thrive on it. The implication is that *Negro* connotes a type of human animal less predatory than the noble races, which, in its capacity to thrive in physical suffering, affirms the natural order of cruelty. Let us never forget, however, that this inception of *Negro* as a type of human animal constitutively inured to endure cruelty is in the originary confluence of Western modernity's juridical, economic, and political energies. Simply put, it is a primal instance of the modern *Humanität* differentiating itself from the human animal. Be that as it may, Nietzsche invokes the phenomenal Negro in evidence that being predatory is undoubtably a prominent aspect of the human animal at large, and so too is finding common ground in the pleasure of predation's cruelty. This amounts to situating the ritualized systematic violence of modern capitalist slavery in relation to the antiquity and ubiquity of blood-sacrifice rites throughout the species. In a way that foreshadows Saidiya Hartman's construal of the significance of repeatedly attending to the scenes of Negro subjugation, Nietzsche recognizes the regularized cruelty to the Negro to be fundamental to social cohesion. Revisiting cruelty to the Negro is elemental to civilization.

Du Bois's proposition, in contradistinction, is that cruelty is not necessarily the excellence (ἀρετή, *areté*) of our nature, nor the determinate of our destiny. The impulses of imagination and cogitation are equally animal, equally generative as the predatory; and these, *pace* Aristotle, are not most excellently fulfilled *only in the polis*. Other orders of sociality or community achieve sustainable ways of being-human-in-the world beyond the comprehension of philosophy and virtue ethics. To paraphrase Du Bois's Harvard commencement speech, when it descended golden haired and drunk from the blue north, Teutonic cruelty "buried aught else besides Rome."[239] In other words, the Negro is neither Dionysian nor Apollinian, is simply not Greek, Roman, or Teutonic.

Du Bois undermines the glamour of the strong man history with his conjectured alteration of *bonus* as *bona*. So, when, near the end of his course notebook, he calls for a science of ethics based on the science of mind that promises a better conceptual understanding of human type, he is challenging, not echoing, Nietzsche. Juxtaposing their respective sciences of ethics and typologies brings to mind Cedric Robinson's elaboration of "the principle of incompleteness" in *The Terms of Order*, when, in the course of critiquing Max Gluckman's account of the Tonga conception of *mukowa* in his *Politics, Law and Ritual in Tribal Society*, he writes: "If, in some spiteful play, one were compelled by some demon or god to choose a transgression against Nietzsche so profound and fundamental to his temperament and intention as to break apart the ground upon which his philosophy stood, one could do no better than this: a society which has woven into its matrix for the purpose of suspending and neutralizing those forces antithetic to individual autonomy, the constructed reality that *all are equally incomplete*."[240] There are "types" of human being that cannot be comprehended by the binarism of dialectic relation; and *Negro*, in the Du Boisian sense, connotes such. *Negro* is an articulation of and articulates a capacity of endurance, of moving fluidly in engagement with inevitable force and utilizing it in realization of living potentiality. "Dogged patience bending to the inevitable" is how Du Bois characterizes this dynamic; and then, referring to it as "the cool purposeful 'Ich Dien' of the African,"[241] insists it is not to be regarded with "sentimental interest [or] sentimental duty," but as a constitutive expression of the human, manifest in relation to civilization and on par with and "at once the check and complement of the Teutonic Strong Man."[242]

Du Bois's critique of the strong man theory of civilization as being woefully inadequate and bad historiography entails a corollary critique of the modern concept of sovereignty. More precisely, when "Jefferson Davis as a Representative of Civilization" is considered in tandem with "The Renaissance of Ethics" and Du Bois's course notebook, what comes into play is a critique of the dominant tendency in political theory to confound the exercise of force emanating from the individual will across space with authority—in other words, to equate authority with sheer coercive force, collapsing that composite into the figure of the sovereign person. Du Bois's Strong Man/Submissive Man dyad pushes back against confusing political institutions, including law, with human society. Contra Hobbes's claim to have radically broken with classical political philosophy, Du Bois regards the sovereign of modern discourses of power as an iteration in the long tradition of virtue ethics, with its underlying Aristotelian conception of the human. His contending that the Negro "has illustrated an idea which is at once the check and compliment of the Teutonic

Strong Man" is a gesture toward a reconceptualization of the relationship between society and its political institutions, predicated on the question of governance being regarded in terms of communal authority rather than sovereign power. Du Bois does not, with that gesture, abandon the concept of human fulfillment. Rather, in critiquing the tradition of virtue ethics, and by implication its derivative political theory, he rejects the proposition that authority is necessarily founded on brute force and maintained by the coercive enforcement of political and juridical institutions. Arguably, at the crux of Du Bois's doctrine of the Submissive Man is the implied proposition that, to paraphrase Michel Foucault, "sovereignty is never shaped from above by a decision of the strong man, the conqueror; rather, it is always shaped by the confluence of multiplicious spheres of authority." In this paraphrasing of Foucault to suit Du Bois, however, the dynamics of confluence displaces Foucault's phrase *par en dessous*, "from below," and elides altogether his prepositional *de ceux qui ont peur*, "from those who are afraid."[243] The former is displaced and the latter elided because Du Bois's doctrine is pointedly nonhierarchical, emphasizing instead appositionality; accordingly, the Negro articulates "an idea of submission apart from cowardice, laziness or stupidity."[244] The point is not merely to remark that Du Bois's gesture toward a critique of sovereignty anticipates Foucault's by eighty-six years, or, for that matter, Hannah Arendt's by some forty-one.[245] It is to highlight how, merely with that gesture, he does something neither of them deign to do; and that is situate the Negro created by capitalist slavery as a central factor in the modern discourses of power. Or, more precisely, he identifies the activity of those called *Negro*, in response to and aside from that designation, as providing the basis for reimagining the order of human sociality, governance, and being.

Let us return for a moment, in this context, to our earlier construal of Du Bois's calling Negro double consciousness a "second sight" to be implying that semiosis is the articulation of a dynamic community of interpreters, and that, accordingly, it articulates a particular community *becoming-in-the-ordering-of consciousness*. The fundamental problem with so construing Negro double consciousness, even as a factitious universal, is that it perpetuates the normative tyranny of binarism in the conception of civilization: ruler and ruled; master, whether despotic or benevolent, and subjugated. In postulating the doctrine of Submissive Man, Du Bois seeks to unseat that binarism. The absence of *Negro* from Nietzsche's list of noble races does not preclude its expression *within* modern civilization, according to the syntax of which it remains primarily comprehensible as a phenomenon in relation to capital investment. Nor does *Negro* not being accounted for in terms of "Teutonic deification of self" elide its expression as something other than that, as sentient flesh. Such self-expression is a violation of that syntax, which heralds a semantic, and so conceptual, transformation of civilization. Rather than the strong subjugating all in the name of unilinear universal progress toward a *télos*, a purposeful ending resolution, civilization is recognized as the perpetual challenging of egotistical strength—in all its variety, and not just those of ἀρετή (*areté*) and *virtus*, piety and faith, or providence and destiny. Elaborating this change in conception of civilization, Du Bois says "that not only the assertion of the I, but also the submission to the Thou is the highest Individualism."[246] This statement is concordant with the earlier-discussed remarks he made in the 1897 *Atlantic Monthly* essay, "Strivings of the Negro People," attributing to the enslaved Negro a concept of freedom more radical than that of "eighteenth-century Rousseauism."[247] Our focus in that discussion was on Rousseau's *Social Contract*. Here, it is on his *Discourse on the Origin and Foundations of Inequality among Men*, where he postulates that primordial man in the state of nature is, contra Hobbes's impassioned, hyperaggressive, warring brute, a self-sufficient individual, whose aggression is primarily driven by a keen sense of self-preservation (*l'amour de soi-même*) tempered by compassion (*pitié*).[248] While this postulate, along with his critique of proprietary heroic virtue (*l'amour propre*) as a destructive social artifice, is resonant with Du Bois's doctrine, Rousseau maintains, along the same lines as Hobbes nonetheless, the individual's being antecedent to community, which results from an aggregate of individuals forming an association that will defend and protect with all the common force the person and goods of each associate. What makes Du Bois's doctrine of Submissive Man radical is not its proposition that brute strength is never enough to claim mastery, that the strong man must surrender his strength in service of the general will; nor is it the corollary proposition that submission to force is an act of necessity, not of will—the enslaved do not, in fact, lose their social self but, in prudent submission to violent force, perpetuate variegated possibilities of sociality. Both of these propositions are held by Rousseau, after all—even Hegel argues that in submitting to force, the bondsman does not become alienated from himself; on the contrary that submission facilitates the unfold of the true self. What makes Du Bois's doctrine of Submissive Man more radical is its proposition that community is not constituted by way of subjection—even according to an intersubjective social contract whereby individuals precede community—but rather, individuals are coarticulated *beside one another simultaneously* in community. This is not to suggest the doctrine of Submissive Man is some sort of quietism. Du Bois was not, *pace* Wilson Moses's charge, "fascinated by the idea of redemption through suffering."[249] Nor was he only occasionally hostile to Christianity, as Moses also states. On the contrary, Du Bois was consistently critical of what he termed "the doctrines of passive submission embodied in the newly learned Christianity," referring to the Second Great

Awakening, when slaveholders authorized Baptist and Methodist preachers to convert their slaves. As he says in "Of the Faith of the Fathers":

> The long system of repression and degradation of the Negro tended to emphasize the elements in his character that made him a valuable chattel: courtesy became humility, moral strength degenerated into submission, and the exquisite native appreciation of the beautiful became an infinite capacity for dumb suffering. The Negro, losing the joy of this world, eagerly seized upon the offered conceptions of the next; the avenging Spirit of the Lord enjoining patience in this world, under sorrow and tribulation until the Great Day when He should lead His dark children home—this became his comforting dream. His preacher repeated the prophecy, and his bards sang—
>
> *Children, we shall be free*
> *When the Lord shall appear.*
>
> This deep religious fatalism, painted so beautifully in "Uncle Tome," came soon to breed, as all fatalistic faith will, the sensualist side by side with the martyr.[250]

In the effort to conceive of community as a style of thinking-in-action improvised according to expressive possibilities that are contingent and not necessary, Du Bois's doctrine of submission expressly eschews martyrdom and sentimentalist abandonment of this world. Grappling with the concept of community entailed in the doctrine means engaging with the *persistent dynamic* of being-in-common in which, as was already remarked regarding the dynamics of pattin' Juba and dancing the Buzzard Lope, subjectivity—even in the most robust sense of Nietzschean will—presents in the performance, the poetic activity of whatever form of *technē*, without grounding in a transcendental principle of identity. As with Husserl's transcendental intersubjectivity, the primal experience of one's self is *in* the activity of engaging other people and things. Unlike Husserl's transcendental intersubjectivity, however, the primal unity of the subject *does not ground* the activity. It is not the collective action of already differentiated subjects that constitutes the activity; rather, the subjects are differentiated in and by the activity. It is the activity that articulates the differentiation and so the subjects, who are in-relation-beside one another in a semiosis that is in-relation-beside the flesh.

Regarding this activity as an aspect of *poiēsis in black*, we may very well say it instantiates *para-semiosis*; that is to say, multiplicious vectors of performance-in-referentiality. These vectors, in turn, may be regarded metaphorically as topological long lines, such that, although roughly homomorphic to one another, the characteristic of the lines' relationality is apposition, or *being-in-appositionality*—just like with Juba and the Buzzard Lope—*whereby* multiple orders of referentiality converge without synthesis, entailing dynamic properties of infinite diffusion, according to the flow of which a function may be expressed in infinite divisibility. We could think of this in terms of Dedekind cuts, and as with the cut, the expression of function in the multiplicious lines of *para-semiosis* is always in dynamic relation-in-action; so that what is paramount is not the individual elements, but the dynamic of signification in referentiality they exhibit in common. In this respect, Du Bois's doctrine of the submissive deconstructs individuation, exposing what can be called para-individuation: the person indexes the multiplicious fluidity of semiosis as a *contingent*, and hence infinitely divisible orientation. This divisible person goes to the heart of what is at play with the concept of civilization Du Bois presents in "Jefferson Davis as a Representative of Civilization." It is not just that "submissive man" as divisible person is contrasted to the "strong man" so as to become the basis for an alternative civilization. Du Bois's point is that community consists of multiplicities of heterogeneous dynamic elements in *relation with* one another, and not the aggregation of a priori integral subjects. The challenge is to reimagine the individual by reimagining community. In other words, Du Bois's 1890 Harvard commencement speech calls us to abandon the processes of individuation predicated on the Western philosophical tradition's account of being qua being, otherwise known as ontology. In order to adequately exposit how that is the issue at hand, a more careful elaboration of what is meant by *para-semiosis* is in order.

Para-Semiosis

To begin with, it should be noted that my use of the prefix *para-* is in a manner somewhat akin to what Nahum Chandler has termed *para-literacy* to name a "'universal' inhabitation of thought and culture arising by way of its double position as simultaneously both within and outside of the 'mainstream.'"[1] The prefix *para-*, in Chandler's terms, marks the generatively transgressive as a problem for the practice of critical thought, indicating "the need for thinking the whole" without appealing to some transcendent point of "neutral" adjudication.[2] It is the problem of thinking from nowhere in a way that "overturns existing claims of the relation of the universal and particular . . . and resituates such claims in a larger, perhaps illimitable frame."[3] This new epistemological construal is "the very pathway of the articulation of a critical self-consciousness of an African American intelligentsia," Chandler says, paraphrasing Spillers on the performative work of the black creative intellectual.[4] So saying, he then situates Du Bois's 1899 address to the Third Annual Meeting of the American Negro Academy, "The Present Outlook for the Dark Races of Mankind," in a lineage of discourses operating in the domains of treatise, oratory, or sermon simultaneously; from Absalom Jones and Richard Allen, to Walker's appeal and Anna Julia Cooper's.[5] The largess of this discourse's epistemology stems from the force of its particularity. "The African American problematic," Chandler says, "is, from its inception, a displacement from putative primordial origin . . . [T]he situation specific to African Americans, and there is always such specificity, comes about only by way of social processes that are excessive to any locality, no matter how locality is defined."[6] This very particularity of situation "sets in motion, or calls for, a form of supra-inhabitation of thought or demands that a certain meta-perspective take shape right in the midst of experience, self-consciousness, or the particularities of existence. It solicits the development of a paraontological discourse."[7] As with *paraliteracy*, the prefix, *para*, here denotes this discourse's transgression beyond, or beside the ontological, which is itself a way of talking (λόγια, *lógia*) about being (ὄντος, *óntos*). But what is this paraontological discourse about? Some clarification of what this might be is provided by Fred Moten's subsequent elaboration of Chandler's concept of the paraontological, which he refers to in the course of reflecting on Frank Wilderson's Afro-pessimist pronouncement that blackness, his own and all others, is nothing. Grappling with the severity and intensity of that pronouncement, Moten is compelled

> to consider *what nothing is*, not from its own standpoint or from any standpoint but from the absoluteness of its generative dispersion of a general antagonism that blackness holds and protects in as critical celebration and degenerative and regenerative preservation. That's the mobility of place, the fugitive field of unowning... the mobility of place, from which we ask, paraontologically, by way of but also against and underneath the ontological terms at our disposal: What is nothingness? What is thingliness? What is blackness? What's the relationship between blackness, thingliness, nothingness and the (de/re)generative operations of what Deleuze might call a life in common?[8]

Moten's four questions add another dimension to Chandler's notion of displacement from any putative primordial origin, one in which *place* is wherever us is moving in space and time, and not a settled or to-be-settled geographical location. This aligns somewhat with my earlier formulation regarding Du Bois's insistence on using the term, *Negro*: "*Negro* refers to that which has no *proper* historical field other than the history of the expression, which is indicial to the world of its expression." In denoting displacement, *Negro* manifestly invokes the totality of placement at work, exhibiting what Chandler refers to as the problem of thinking the whole differently from a meta-perspective, a supra-inhabitation of thought that solicits a paraontological discourse. Assuming that supra-inhabitation of thought is akin to what we are calling *poiēsis in black*, we might well ask, how is it paraontological? And asking that prompts us to probe even further what paraontology is about.

In light of Chandler's claiming the development of paraontological discourse is solicited by that of that *paraliteracy*, we should take careful measure of his describing the latter as, "a disposition and possibility... the proposition of a double or redoubled understanding—a remark of both sides of a limit, so to speak—of various forms of limited and parochial understandings of the world that have been promulgated as universal such that the layers of sedimentation in which such distinctions would ostensibly be secured can be rendered susceptible to a certain desedimentation."⁹ There is a hard to disregard resonance between this sense of *paraliteracy* and the disposition Jacques Lacan calls "le par-être," meaning "the being '*para*' that is being beside [*l'être à coté*]."¹⁰ Lacan takes care to note that he is saying *par-être*, and not its homonym, *paraître*, used in the philosophical sense of "phenomenal appearance," translating the German, *Erscheinungen*, beyond which there is supposedly the noumenon, or *thing-in-itself*. Lacanian *par-être*, the being *para*, is neither phenomenal or noumenal, but rather has to do with the way the question of being presents itself in the paradoxes springing up with respect to everything that manages to be formulated as the effect of writing. As such, it indicates the contingency and materiality of the letter, uncovering its *envers*, its other side. The work of both Chandler's *paraliteracy* and Lacan's *par-être* is expositing a discourse of being that, while not ontological in the strict sense of a particular philosophical project—the study of being *qua* being—has a *lateral* relationship to it, which is signed by the *para*. Taking into account Lorenzo Chiesa's recognition that Lacan's *par-être* as lateral discourse entails "the elaboration of a new ontology, or better, a para-ontology," amplifies the resonance between it and Chandler's paraontological discourse.¹¹

Two crucial insights result from recognizing this reverberating resonance. The first is that, even though there is some confluence in the attention given to the dynamics expressing system and subject—the grammar of discourse—between the use of *para* in the Chandler/Lacanian *para-ontology* and in what I've designated *para-semiosis*, there is also a conceptual difference; one which is remarked with Lacan's saying: "What we must get used to is substituting the *le par-être*—the being *para* [*l'être* **para**], the being beside [*l'être à côté*]—for the being that would take flight [*fuirait*]."¹² The referenced being that would take flight is akin to Kracauer's fleeing bourgeois traveler. But this is not to be confused with *Negro* being-in-flight emblemized by John Jones. Kracauer's traveler flees *from* mechanized capitalist commodification in order to redeem the inherent integrity of being that has been lost to it. *Negro* being-in-flight is *being-in-appositionality*, and so is neither a flight *from* (capitalist modernity) nor *toward* (redemption of a lost self). This conceptual difference is crucial enough there is a fundamental incompatibility between *poiēsis in black* as *para-semiosis* and the paraontological discourse adduced by Chandler. That incompatibility lies in what is prefixed by *para*. Gaining this first insight, however, depends on the second, which is that Chandler's claiming the situation specific to African Americans solicits development of a paraontological discourse brings into play a particular lineage of mid-twentieth century Franco-German thought beginning in 1927 that is trackable by way of Lacan. We cannot sufficiently appreciate what is at stake in the difference between what is to the right of the *para*—semiosis or ontology—without carefully considering that lineage guided by a set of questions. The first of these has to do with the putatively universalist discourse whereof being has place: the discourse known as ontology, which paraontology seeks to challenge with *displacement*. The challenge involves questions of the *transcendence*, *worldliness*, and *historicity* of being; all three of which turn on the relationship between being, self, and things, prompting an adjusted version of Moten's fourth question: What is the relationship between thingliness, worldliness, and the semiosis of human living-in-common? With respect to the lineage of paraontology, that turn hinges on the question: What is the primitive? And in the lineage of thought evoked with Chandler's paraontological discourse, that question gets expressly identified with the Negro. Historically, the Negro stymies paraontology, raising the perennial question implied by Windham: What is me in relation to we?

All That Comes with Paraontology

In addressing the question of the displacement of being, we may as well begin with Jacques Lacan as the link connecting Chandler's paraontological discourse to the chain of paraontology's conceptual transmission. Lacan's *par-être*, as the effect of writing, seeks to exorcise the philosophical ontological use of the copula as an isolated signifier. It suffices to do so, Lacan suggests, by simply considering that "when we say about anything whatsoever that it is what it is [que ce soit que c'est ce que c'est], nothing in any way obliges us to isolate the verb 'to be' [être]." To make this point he proffers a pointedly French play on words: "That is pronounced, c'est ce que c'est ['it is what it is'], and it could just as well be written, *seskecé* ['idizwadidiz']."[13] Lacan's point being that the only reason we see meaningful relation in these enunciations is due to our use of the copula. Without it we would see nothing at all. And the only reason we see something with the copula is because the discourse of the master (*maître*), of "to be myself" (*m'être*), has emphasized the verb "to be" (*être*) and imposed it upon us.

Philosophy, accordingly, epitomizes the discourse of being the master of myself (*m'être*), of being-me-to-myself (*m'être à moi même*), which is what Lacan calls "I-cracy" [*Je-cratie*] meaning "the myth of the ideal I [*Je idéal*], the I that masters [*je qui maîtrise*]."[14] His quip about *que ce soit que c'est ce que c'est* and *c'est ce que c'est* is in reference to the Scholastics' rendering of Aristotle's two phrases, τό τὶ ἐστι (*to ti esti*, that is what it is), meaning the nonqualitative property of a thing determining its individuation, and τo τὶ ἦν εἶναι (*to ti én einai*, the what it was to be a given thing), meaning the generic qualities a particular thing shares with other things, as haecceity (*thisness*) and quiddity (*whatness*) respectively. In a contradictory usage of this Scholastic terminology, however, Lacan construes τό τὶ ἐστι (*c'est ce que c'est*) as *quiddité* (quiddity), maintaining that Aristotle sets this in opposition to the *entity* designated in the phrase, το τὶ ἦν εἶναι (*to ti én einai*, the what it was to be a given thing), which he translates as "ce qui serait produit si était venu à être, tout court, ce qui était à être [what would have been produced if that which must have been tout-court had come into Being]."¹⁵ Lorenzo Chiesa's point in identifying Lacan's mislabeled *quiddité* as "para-ontology" and that from which it is differentiated "ontological being" is to distinguish philosophical ontology—here, I would simply say ontology—as the discourse of the masterful *I* that has inscribed itself into the much richer field of language in an effort to master the universe—"I am the master of myself [m'être de moi] as I am the universe"—from another discourse running beside it, the aforementioned being beside (*l'être à côté*), or para-being (*par-être*).¹⁶

What Lacan proffers is the *autre lecture*, psychoanalysis as the antiphilosophical "other reading" of being, which never quite leaves off *being* at the heels (*à la botte*), at the order of the master. He tries to slip that yoke by focusing on the function of the written in analytical discourse, by reading being as a letter, A, which he then makes "a function . . . of the proposition that only takes the form of a written formula, and that is produced by mathematical logic." Lacan goes on to say, emphasizing the mathematical point: "Following the thread of analytic discourse tends towards nothing less than breaking up anew [*rebriser*], inflecting, marking with its own curvature—a curvature that could not even be maintained as that of lines of force—that which produces the cut [*la discontinuité*]."¹⁷ Any doubt that is a rather elliptical reference to the Dedekind cut is redressed by his next sentence: "Our recourse is in *lalangue*, which breaks [*brise*] it."¹⁸ The neologism *lalangue*—a compound of the feminine definite article, *la*, and the noun, *langue*, meaning spoken language in the sense of spoken tongue—connotes what happens acoustically when one syllable of a word gets repeated endlessly (the example given is: "la, la, la . . ."), revealing that polysemy is possible due to the existence of homonyms. From here, Lacan engages arithmetic logicism's symbolic representation of function by the letter, underscoring the connection he is making between mathematics and *par-être*. The use made of the letter by mathematics reveals what is called in discourse *grammar*; "and grammar is what is revealed in language only in written form. Beyond language, this effect, which is produced solely with support of writing, is certainly the ideal of mathematics."¹⁹

Having thus aligned, by way of the letter, mathematics in relation to *par-être*, Lacan turns to questions of grammatology and from there to set theory:

There is a lot to learn here . . . by regarding more closely what mathematicians have been doing with letters since, in defiance of a certain number of things, they began, in the most well-founded of ways, under the name of set theory, to perceive that the One could be approached in another way than the intuitive, fusional, amorous. The One that is always talked about is, first of all, a mirage of the One that one thinks oneself to be. Not to say that this is the whole horizon. There are as many Ones as you like—they are characterized by the fact that none of them resemble any of the others in any way—see the first hypothesis in the *Parmenides*. Set theory breaks out of all that—let us speak about the One for things that are strictly unrelated to each other. Let us put together objects of thought, as they are called, objects of the world, each of which counts as one. Let us assemble these absolutely heterogeneous things, and give ourselves the right to designate this assemblage by a letter. This is how set theory expresses itself at the outset, that theory, I mentioned last time in relation to Nicolas Bourbaki.[20]

Although Lacan cites the collective pseudonym under which a group of French mathematicians published their influential twelve-book series, *Éléments de mathématique*, referencing his earlier mention in the previous seminar session of the first volume from that series, *Théorie des ensembles* (Set Theory), as a definitive text in set theory, his description of set as "put together objects of thought" echoes the one Dedekind provided in *Was sind und was sollen die Zahlen?*—which, as Zermelo proclaimed, was indeed "at the outset" of set theory. Arguably, Dedekind's definition of "every object of our thinking as a thing [*Ding*] . . . we designate by letters" informs Lacan's identifying letter with number and his formulaic use of letters in the fashion of mathematical logic.[21] We have already encountered the relevant Dedekind passages in our earlier discussion concerning Du Bois's problematic invocation of the arithmetization of analysis.[22] It will suffice to recall here that our interrogation of that invocation highlighted his critique of ontology, a nontrivial fact with respect to Lacan's emphasizing, contra Bourbaki, that letters do not designate sets, "letters *constitute* [*font*] sets . . . they are sets."[23] That emphasis has some bearing on the distinction I am making between the *being-beside* of *par-être* as paraontology and the *being-in-appositionality* of *para-semiosis*. At this juncture, it is clear the difference is not just about what is to the right of the *para*, but also the work of the hyphen itself, which is Lacan's innovation in the conceptual genealogy, underscoring the space of parallelity; something also in play with *para-semiosis*.

In paraontology, the hyphen indicates the break between philosophical ontology and psychoanalysis, but also their conjunction. With the break, the *par-être* presents in the paradoxes of writing. We should learn to conjugate that appropriately Lacan says: "I *par*-am [*je par-suis*], you *par*-are [*tu par-es*], he *par*-is [*il par-est*], we *par*-are [*nous par-sommes*], and so forth."²⁴ By this suggested conjugation, every occurrence of the hyphenated *par* signifies both the distinction and correspondence between the elements of two distinct domains of meaning. To the right of *par-* are the elemental signs {am [*suis*], are [*es*], is [*est*], are [*sommes*]...} belonging to the domain of traditional ontology, the discourse of mastery in which the verb "to be" is isolated as a signifier. To the left of *par-* are the elemental signs {I [*je*], you [*tu*], he [*il*], we [*nous*]...} belonging to the domain of being articulated beneath the discourse of mastery. Continuing to underscore the connection Lacan makes between mathematics and *par-être*, let us notate these two domains as $\mathcal{X}$ and $\mathcal{Y}$ respectively, and the *par-* as $\mathfrak{f}$. Along this line, operates a bijective function, pairing each element of $\mathcal{X}$ with those of $\mathcal{Y}$. If we express Lacan's conjugations in functional notation, we get $\mathfrak{f} \cdot \mathcal{Y} \to \mathcal{X}$, defining the being articulated beneath the discourse of mastery as the starting domain and ontology as the codomain. This accords with his argument that there is no necessity for the copula in expressing being beyond that imposed by the discourse of philosophical ontology, which is what psychoanalysis, augmented by arithmetized analysis, is supposed to counter. Precisely because the point of departure is to counter, to be the antiphilosophical discourse of being, the arrow of the functional notation can be turned around, so to speak, inverting the relation of domain to start in $\mathcal{X}$, ontology: $\mathfrak{f} \cdot \mathcal{X} \to \mathcal{Y}$. Lacan's *par-être*, then, itself runs the risk of turning into some form of necessary ontology so that even his psychoanalytic discourse remains on some level a discourse of *Ur*-mastery. This risk stems from Lacan's effort to renounce the reflexive subject of philosophical ontology as the center of all experience, while at the same time conserve the category of the subject in order to renew it from the ground up as the function of irreflexive transindividual structure. Here is the point of conjunction between philosophical ontology and Lacan's paraontology of psychoanalysis. Lacan's construal of subjectivity as a function of one signifier representing to another in a metonymic chain simply displaces the old metaphysical problem of how there can be spirit beside matter with the question of how there can be signs beside things.²⁵ The turn to set theory reinforces the conjunction. For, as we saw with Dedekind, the mapping (*Abbildung*) of a series (*Menge*) sustains an ontological space within which subjectivity presents as the event of willful decreeing of sets, the cut. In Lacan's analysis, this is an effect of the *Real* (*réel*), the encounter with the absence of meaningful relation directing desire, which remains in excess of representation.

We have returned, and in a way that is not at all willy-nilly, to the Du Boisian paradox of the calculable and the uncalculable and how the Negro's uncalculability short-circuits the coordinated movement of philosophical ontology. Like Du Bois before him, Lacan is critical of the promise made by the great European traditions in ethical and political theory regarding the telos of human-life—the promise of *eudaimonia*, happiness in fulfilment of human being—which Du Bois in his critique refers to as the *summum bonum*, and Lacan as *Souverain Bien* (Paramount Good).[26] Giving Aristotle's *Nicomachean Ethics* an important place in his critique as "the most exemplary and valid analysis" of ethics, Lacan pays careful attention to Aristotle's account of the reasoning subject's management of desire according to the deliberative contemplation, the theory-work of ὀρθός λόγος (*orthós lógos*), *right-principle-discourse*. Of particular pertinence is Aristotle's expressly elaborating that this way of talking as the discourse of mastery, in the double-sense of its being the discourse of and for the master (*despotés*), as well as the discourse of reason's mastery over intemperance, is what secures the ideal political situation for attaining *eudaimonia*. This Paramount Good, which legitimates the discourse of mastery, is an expression of that very same discourse. In other words, it belongs to the symbolic order of the master as the signifier of its teleological limit: virtuous men strive for the Paramount Good, and striving for the Paramount Good is virtue.

All said and done, the only *good* Lacan recognizes is "the price one pays for access to the truth of one's desire," the fixed vanishing point of all desiring, that which he calls, paraphrasing Freud, "*das Ding* (*la Chose* [the Thing])." In the later development in his theory of the three registers of the Imaginary, Symbolic, and Real, the Real referred to the Thing as the forever unattainable that resists all symbolization and cannot be the signified for any signifier, which is where he situates the Paramount Good. This has to do with the distinction between what discourse makes explicit about itself and its meaning, as when Lacan states regarding the letter, "Language, in its meaningful effect [*effet de signifié*], is never but beside the referent [*à côté du référent*]."[27] This aspect of Lacan's analysis can well be designated the logic of the signifier, whereby the true nature of desire is repressed by denoting it in a chain of signs that indicate the signifier as the element that is lacking.[28] If we regard, à la Jacques Alain Miller's reading of Lacan, the specific function constituting the relation of the subject to the chain of its discourse as a suture—that is, as a row of stiches—then an analogy can be drawn between it and Frege's function of equinumerosity (*gleichzahlig*), with which the number zero is deduced. Accordingly, Lacan's concept of non-identity-to-self is assigned (in Frege's sense of *Umfang*) by the number zero, which sutures the logical discourse.[29] And just as Frege's *o* effects the disappearance of the thing that is but cannot be—the nothing not identical to itself—engendering the progression of the number series and misrecognizing the function of the subject as purely logical, so too the logic of the signifier, by way of the sign of the signifier, effects the disappearance of the real that is the impossible object of signification. In other words, the sign of the signifier is the subject (I, you, he, we, etc.), which works exactly like numbers in both Frege's and Dedekind's theories. This puts Lacan's critical reading of Aristotle's ὀρθός λόγος (*orthós lógos*), *right-principle-discourse*, in a particular perspective relative to the concept of *being-beside* as an aspect of *poiēsis in black*.

As noted earlier in our reading of Du Bois's essay "The Renaissance of Ethics," Aristotle deploys ὀρθός λόγος while attempting to resolve the ethical problematic of despotic legitimacy over the human slaves in order to secure the possibility of the man of goodness (ἀνδρὸς ἀγαθοῦ, *andros agathoū*), for whose benefit the promise of the Paramount Good is taken up. That possibility is an effect of the logic of the signifier; which is to say, to the extent the abstraction, *Man*, is a human subject, it is nothing but a result of the system of signifiers constituting the objective, as in nonegoistic, symbolic order. The exemplary virtuous man, the ἀνδρὸς ἀγαθοῦ (*andros agathoū*) of polity, and the *vir bonus* of *civitas* are both enunciations of the symbolic order—the philosophical qua master discourse of polity dedicated to realizing εὐδιμονία (*eudaimonia*)—which enunciate that order. As such, *Man* denotes the human subject's being constitutively the speaking subject (*parlêtre*) circumscribed by that order. And what is spoken is λόγος ἀποφαντικος (*lógos apophantikos*, apophantic speaking), a modality of which is the *right-principle-discourse*, whereby *Man* is deduced in the arithmetic proportional mean (μεσότης, *mesotēs*) of pleasure and pain. Assuming that all species of human being are speaking (*parlêtre*), are effects of some symbolic order—and there are multiple multiplicities of these, not all of which are translatable or even fully comprehended by a universal symbolic order of structure in abstraction—there is no absolute necessity for deducing *Man* from sentient flesh. Along these lines, Lacan's psychoanalysis plays on the equivocity of the signifier and the concomitant plurality of interpretations and in so doing demolishes a fundamental conception of philosophical ontology since Aristotle: the univocity of being. Setting the path of the psychoanalytic cure in the realm of equivocity, of hermeneutic ambiguity, Lacan opposes the philosophical construal of the meaning of truth (*sens de la vérité*) as the identity of thinking and being enunciated in the formulae of knowledge. Recall also from our reading of "The Renaissance of Ethics" that Aristotle's ὀρθός λόγος (*orthós lógos*), *right-principle-discourse* is not just a formula; it is a way of talking, a saying that opens onto a discursive field of scientific (ἐπιστημονικὸν, *epistemonikón*) theorization and knowledge. Yet, for all his arguing that psychoanalysis is antiphilosophy, Lacan's expressed ultimate goal is an integral unequivocal transmissible knowledge without residue, an order of symbolization he calls *formalisation correcte* (correct formalization). To reiterate with amplification, Lacan may very well seek to demolish that univocity of formulaic *right-principle-discourse*, the formula that grounds care of the self in knowledge of the truth of being, but he does not eschew univocity or formulae altogether. That is to say, he does not eschew the univocity *of* formula, but reaches for it in his *mathème*.

Precisely what is at stake in this question of the formula is brought to the fore with Lacan's 1973 essay "L'étourdit" (The Said Turn), where he provides what he calls "formulas of sexuation."[30] There are four mathematically notated formulae of sexuation in which the phallic function, that is to say, the possible, is identified with Frege's Leibnizian-derived definition of zero, notated as Φx. The first two of these formulae utilize received notations, ∀ for universal quantification: "for all" or "for every"—Lacan's neologism for which is *pourtout* (forall)—and ∃ for existential quantification: "there is." So, we have, in order of appearance, $\forall x \cdot \Phi x$ (for all x Φx is satisfied), which Lacan further translates as T, notating truth-value; and $\exists x \cdot \overline{\Phi x}$ (there is at least one x for which Φx is not satisfied). The remaining two formulas, $\overline{\exists x} \cdot \overline{\Phi x}$ and $\overline{\forall x} \cdot \Phi x$, utilize an idiosyncratic Lacanian notation, with the bar above the quantifiers functioning as negation, so that $\overline{\exists x}$ notates "there is at least one x that is not," and the $\overline{\forall x}$ notates "the forall that is not."[31] Lacan presents these formulae pursuant to his interrogating what is a formalization, an interrogation that begins with his meditation on the banderole for a news-flash on the psychoanalytic discourse: "That one says [*Qu'on dise*] remains forgotten behind what is said [*ce qui se dit*] in what is heard [*ce qui s'entend*]."[32] He takes care to point out that he had previously given this formulaic statement (*énoncé*) in one of his seminars as a speech (*de ce que j'y porte de parole*), wanting to demonstrate by attending to the structural relation of its clauses, the meaning they take on from psychoanalytic discourse. This touches on the opposing of psychoanalytic meaning to that of philosophy, to the difference of *meaning* in the master's discourse and the analyst's discourse. Whereas both discourses may touch on the Real from logic, psychoanalysis does so "by encountering it as impossible."[33] Lacan's saying, then, is an assertion of truth enunciated in the form of the type of proposition described as universal in logic. For what is said (*dit*) to be true, one must still say it (*qu'on le dise*), there should be a saying (*dire*). So the truth cannot be said without saying, and the saying enunciates the possible in response to what is impossible to say. As for what is said as truth (*dit de vérité*) in this way, "It is existence that makes it respond from its saying [*dire*], not by making this saying exist, since it simply names it, but by denying its truth—without saying so."[34] Extending this, he comes to his own formula that "there is no universal that must not be contained by an existence that denies it," further undermining philosophy by exposing "that the stereotype that every man is mortal is not stated from nowhere."[35] This nullibility, this claim that truth simply is and *comes* from nowhere, indeed, the very claim that there is nowhere, is an alibi created to legitimate the discourse of the master. There is no saying from nowhere, but only and always from somewhere, which is not to say somewhere *is*, but rather somewhere never is without saying. It is from that place, where philosophical logic turns, that the discourse of the master "must take great pain . . . to notice what is its own quotidian resource: that nothing hides so much as that which unveils [*dévoile*], that truth, ἀλήθεια = *Verborgenheit* [concealment]."³⁶ Lacan is alluding here to a saying of Heidegger's from *Being and Time*. Yet, his use of Heidegger's neologism, *Verborgenheit*, to mean truth is the exact opposite of what Heidegger says regarding truth *as a way of saying*.

With this, we arrive at the second link in the chain of conceptual transmission we are tracing back from Chandler's paraontological discourse. In a way that clearly informs Lacan's critique of Aristotle's ὀρθός λόγος (*orthós lógos*), Heidegger construes the philosophical concept of λόγος (*lógos*) handed down from Plato and Aristotle to connote talking or discourse (*Rede*), noting how both of their terminological usages retain the sense Heraclitus gave the term: to make manifest (δηλοῦν, *diloún*) what is being talked about, so that it is seen (φαίνεσθαι, *phaínesthai*) for the speaker and those who talk with one another. As with Lacan, this is about the referentiality of words, about how we talk; and talking is talking about something, according to which "there is something said-in-the-talk as such."³⁷ More precisely, Heidegger's talking about *lógos* as *alétheúein* repeats an ancient prephilosophical (*vorphilosohischen*) Greek referentiality of ἀλήθεια (*alétheia*). By referring to the ancient Greek referentiality of ἀλήθεια (*alétheia*) as prephilosophical, he distinguishes it from the way of talking inaugurated by Plato and Aristotle, who are first to develop and master a conspicuously conceptual mode of investigating extant entities as a branch of knowledge by skipping over [*überspringen*] the question of existence. Even with that mode, however, the prephilosophical signification of οὐσία (*ousia*) as *Anwesenheit* (being as coming-to-presence) was still in play.³⁸ Bear in mind that Aristotle, drawing on the classical Athenian legal term ἀποφαίνεσθαι (*apophaínesthai*), meaning "making known in an evidentiary report," coins the philosophical term ἀποφαντικός (*apophantikós*), which is anglicized as "apophantic," to designate the kind of discourse that makes something be seen *from the very thing being talked about*. In defining λόγος ἀποφαντικός (*lógos apophantikós*) as categorical or propositional statement, he divides it into two kinds, κατάφασις (*cataphasis*, countable) or positive proposition—Zora Neale Hurston was a Negro—and ἀπόφασις (*apophasis*) or negative proposition—Zora Neale Hurston was not a Negro—either of which can be true or false. Moreover, the Greek term, ἀλήθεια (*alétheia*), along with its verb, ἀληθεύειν (*alétheúein*), is the negation of λανθάνειν (*lanthánein*: "to escape notice, be unseen") and λήθη (*léthē*: "forgetting, forgetfulness"). All this is at play in Heidegger's saying: "The 'being-true' [*Wahrsein*] of the λόγος as ἀληθεύειν [*alétheúein*] means the entity talked *about* in λέγειν [*légein*, speaking] as ἀποφαίνεσθαι [*apophaínesthai*] is taken out of its concealment [*aus seiner Verborgenheit herausnehmen*]; one must let them be seen as something unconcealed [*Unverborgenes*] (ἀληθές, *aléthés*); that is, they must be *discovered* [*entdecken*]."³⁹ He says further on, in reference to Aristotle's equating the ἀλήθεια (*alétheia*) of λόγος ἀποφαντικός (*lógos apophantikós*) with πρᾶγμα (*pragma*, things done), and φαινόμενα (*phenomena*), that "it lets entities be seen in their unconcealment [*Unverborgenheit*] (discoveredness [*Entdecktet*]), taking them out of their concealment."⁴⁰ Lacan's antonymic substitution of *Unverborgenheit* with *Verborgenheit* as the translation of ἀλήθεια thus seemingly rebuts by parody Heidegger's saying. Yet, the force of that rebuttal is complicated, maybe even compromised by Lacan's immediately refusing to renounce his brotherly attachment to Heidegger's saying: "So, I do not renounce fraternity with this *saying* [*dire*], since I only repeat it on the basis of a practice that, situated from another discourse, renders it incontestable."⁴¹ Arguably, the other discourse that renders Heidegger's saying "incontestable" is philosophy, which his "'definition' of truth does not *shake off* ... but rather is its primordial *appropriation*."⁴² On the way to this appropriation, however, Heidegger also says with respect to Aristotle's elaboration of *lógos* as apophantic: "Thus unconcealment [*Unverborgenheit*], ἀ-λήθεια [*a-létheia*], belongs to the λόγος. To translate this word as 'truth' [*Wahrheit*], and what's more, to define this expression conceptually in theoretical ways, is to conceal (*verdecken*) the meaning of what the Greeks posited at the basis, as self-evident and as pre-philosophical, of the terminological use of ἀλήθεια. In citing such evidence, we must guard against unrestrained word-mysticism [*Wortmystik*]."⁴³

The ancient Greek cognizance of ἀλήθεια (*alétheia*) has been obscured or simply spoken-over and concealed by the discourse of philosophy. Yet, while the beginning of philosophy's talking-over the ancient Greek way of talking about being was in Plato's and Aristotle's naïve skipping over the question of existence, the cutting-off from access to this cognizance became pronounced only after the language of philosophy shifted to Latin, particularly with the late Scholastics. By the seventeenth century, this concealing philosophical talking-over is given its proper name, *Ontologie* (ontology).⁴⁴ Taking care not to slip into unrestrained word-mysticism, Heidegger dissects this modern term into its putative Greek etymons, of λόγος (*lógos*), emphasizing the ancient meaning as *speaking to* (*Ansprechen*) by recalling its verb, λέγειν (*légein*, to say, converse, tell a story), and ὄντος (*ontos*), the genitive of ὄν (*ón*), which is the present participle of the verb εἰμί (*eimí*) meaning to be, exist. This achieves a retrieval in renovative construction of the "*power of the most elemental words*" of ancient Greek cognizance; so that *ontology* denotes a way of speaking to, as in addressing, entities as existent.⁴⁵ It is a theoretically and conceptually developed way of talking about entities as existing in general; "but it is also that *to which* those entities are speaking [*angesprochen*] (λεγόμενον, *legómenon*)."⁴⁶ The implication is that all expressive modes of human existence are ontological in this capacious sense of a talking about and to entities whereby that talk exhibits a way of being in the world that understands itself as such.

Heidegger mitigates the harmful effects of philosophy's talking-over ancient Greek talking about being by postulating the "ontological difference" (*ontologische Differenz*), described in his essay "Vom Wesen des Grundes" (The Essence of Causes) as "the Not between [*das Nicht zwischen*] entities [*Seiendem*] and existence [*Sein*]."[47] The difference is between that which exists phenomenally, entities, what Heidegger calls *ontische* (ontic or ontical), and that which makes the ontic intelligible as existence, what he calls *ontologische* (ontological). To put it another way, paraphrasing his 1927 lecture, "The Basic Problems of Phenomenology," on the one hand, there is our experience of entities, and on the other, the understanding-of-existence itself (*Seinsverständnis*), which makes us able to experience them as such. What is fundamental here is the entity that *has* the experience of entities as existing, including itself as such—that is to say, the experience of there-being, of *Dasein*, the investigation of which Heidegger calls fundamental ontology (*Fundamentalontologie*), meaning the ontological analytic (*ontologische Analytik*) of Dasein's preconceptual function and understanding of existence.[48]

In light of the *ontological difference*, the task Heidegger sets for himself is to retrieve the ancient pre-ontological, or proto-ontological Greek investigation of existence. Insofar as the term *ontology* connotes the philosophical talking-over the ancient Greek talking, retrieving the question of existence requires deconstruction (*Destruktion*) of the content of traditional philosophical ontology so as to "arrive at those primordial experiences in which the first, and subsequently guiding ways of determining the nature of existence were achieved."[49] And insofar as the understanding-of-existence itself is the determining character of Dasein, then the term *existence* (*Existenz*) cannot have the same connotation as the traditional philosophical ontological term *existentia*, used by Suárez, to connote objective presence.[50] In the interpretive terminology of Heidegger's fundamental ontology, such objectively present entities are *present-at-hand* (*Vorhanden*), while the term *Existenz* is allotted only to Dasein and so is often rendered in English as *Being*.[51] The context of the structures of existence, of its varied ontic as well as ontological possibilities Heidegger calls *Existenzialität* (existentiality); and the careful effort to understand it theoretically is *existential analytic* (*existenziale Analytik*). "Thus, *fundamental ontology*, from which alone all other ontologies can emerge, must be sought in the existential analytic of Dasein . . . which comes before any psychology or anthropology, and certainly before any biology."[52] The thing to underscore here is that, through retrieval of the ancient Greek talking, Heidegger aims to redeem philosophy by making its "ultimate business [*Geschäft*] to *preserving the power of the most elemental words* in which Dasein expresses [*ausspricht*] itself, protecting them from being flattened by the common understanding to the point of unintelligibility, thus becoming a source of illusory problems."⁵³ In that vein of retrieval and preservation, Heidegger maintains that the primordial prephilosophical understanding of truth somehow endured even the concealment (*Verdeckung*) implicit in the philosophy of Aristotle, who he claims never defended the thesis that the primordial "locus" of truth is apophantic judgment, but rather that "λόγος [*lógos*] is the way of being of Dasein that can either uncover [*entdeckend*] *or* conceal [*verdecken*]. This *double possibility* is what is distinctive about the being-true of the λόγος, it is the comportment that *can also conceal*."⁵⁴

So, what initially seems rebuttal on Lacan's part turns out to be an insightful reading: the "truth," ἀλήθεια (*alétheia*) of traditional philosophical ontology does equal concealment (*Verborgenheit*) of the fundamental understanding of human existence, Dasein; the unconcealment (*Unverborgenheit*) is achieved through Heidegger's existential analysis of that existence. However much Lacan's fraternity is with the deconstruction of traditional philosophical ontology he recognizes in Heidegger's saying, he remains opposed to its project of renovating the philosophical discourse of mastery. The gist of Lacan's antonymic substitution of *Unverborgenheit* with *Verborgenheit* as the translation of ἀλήθεια is critical editorial engagement with Heidegger's project, effectively saying: "Stop at the deconstruction." Lacan's dismissal of the renovative retrieval project notwithstanding, his embracing Heidegger's deconstruction of philosophy for exposing its long-standing project of concealing the nature of human existence—a primordiality psychoanalysis simply lets be—resembles, to the point of evocation, an earlier extended engagement by Heidegger's longtime friend and colleague, the mathematician Oskar Becker.⁵⁵ The provenance of the *para* prefixed to ontology lies in the course of that engagement. In fact, it is Becker who first gives us the term *paraontology* as a result of his long effort to elaborate a phenomenological investigation of mathematical space and its objects—the axiomatic foundations of geometry—following Husserl's definition of eidetic phenomenology as a "descriptive theory of the essence [*deskriptive Wesenslehre*] of pure lived-experience," which investigates not the experience (*Erfahrung*) of the individual object, but the whole essential content (*ganzen Wesensgehalt*).⁵⁶ Becker's most coherent and cogent presentation of this phenomenology was his magnum opus, *Mathematische Existenz* (Mathematical Existence), which appeared alongside Heidegger's *Being and Time* in the same 1927 volume of *Jahrbuch für Philosophie und Phänomenologische Forschung*.⁵⁷ The phenomenological investigation Becker postulates, however, pushes past Husserl's transcendental idealism, concurring with Heidegger that intentionality is already an activity of performative interpretation and not a transcendental ground of understanding. But he then counters Heidegger's displacement of the eidetic, by reconstructing *eidos* as a prehistorical point of investigation, the primordial instance when the possibility of interpretation is presented, which he calls *Mantik* from the Greek μαντική (*mantikē*), meaning divination, a designation he justifies on the grounds that mathematics, as well as the natural sciences and medicine historically arise from the archaic arts of divination and magic. This sense of *Mantik* aligns somewhat with Husserl's construal of mathematics as an exact science of essence—which is to say, its procedure is exclusively eidetic, studying not actualities but ideal possibilities, not actual but *essential* relationships—a procedure Husserl calls interchangeably, *Wesenserschauung* (essence-intuiting) and *unmittelbare Sehen* (immediate seeing), in the sense of a primordially imaging (*gebendes*) consciousness of any kind whatsoever.[58] Although Becker will abandon the term *Mantik*, in subsequent publications, he further expounds on the concept of the primordial presentation of presentation in his 1937 essay "Transzendenz und Paratranszendenz" (Transcendence and Paratranscendence), renaming it *Paraexistenz* (paraexistence) and its phenomenological investigation *Paraontologie* (paraontology), intending the latter to be a corollary improvement on (*Überbietung*) Heidegger's phenomenological hermeneutic of facticity (*phänomenologische Hermeneutik der Faktizität*).[59]

Having thus arrived at the first link in the chain of conceptual transmission we are tracing from Chandler's paraontological discourse through Lacan and Heidegger, it behooves us to give careful attention to way in which Becker's paraontological amendment to the existential analytic of Dasein exposes just how incapacitating is Heidegger's admission that the analytic "cannot provide orientation for an interpretation of the primitive world, let alone the ontology of thingliness." The primitive looms large in Heidegger's phenomenological hermeneutic of facticity as a figure of ethnography but also in the ontological analysis of human signification, semiosis, as what structures the world. In both figural aspects, Heidegger's heuristic for the primitive is the Negro. Rather, for him, the Negro as ethnographic object provides evidence of still extent primitive Dasein, and the Negro fetish evidence of the impenetrability of primitive semiosis for the existential analytic. Heidegger's admitting the incapacity of the analytic to surmount the Negro as an epistemic limit fatally undermines its pretensions to a universal account of being qua being, and in so doing reveals Heidegger's project of reviving fundamental ontology as a dead-end. Becker's paraontological adjustment provides a way out by aligning the opacity of the primitive fetish, construed as mantic, with mathematics. But this is at the price of racializing Dasein and is an expression of primitivism, whereby the Negro is cast as perennially at the cusp between animality and full humanity in order to serve both as a sign of the mystical origins of scientific knowledge and as a sign of the developmental superiority of European—for Becker, that is expressly Nordic—Dasein. Supposing the fetishistic semiosis Heidegger refers to is an instantiation of *para-semiosis*, its opacity to the existential analytic clearly indicates the uselessness of fundamental ontology for understanding *poiēsis in black*. By that same token, the primitivism of Becker's paraontological adjustment makes it equally as inapplicable. With respect to the question of how *poiēsis in black* might be paraontological, then, the answer is it is not, and fundamentally so. In order to demonstrate this, and not merely assert it, we need to recall some of the details of Becker's engagement with and adjustment of Heidegger's investigation, thereby establishing the relevant link to our interrogation of the distinction between *para-semiosis* and the paraontological.

There are three main focal points of Becker's paraontological engagement with Heidegger. These are the questions of essence in relation to transcendence, worldliness, and historicity, all of which lead to a principal problematic between them, the nature of primitive Dasein. Let us start by considering what Heidegger has to say about these questions, beginning with the first, essence in relation to transcendence. Heidegger rather perfunctorily begins "Vom Wesen des Grundes" (The Essence of Causes): "Aristotle sums up his classificatory explication [*Auseinanderlegung*] of the manifold meanings of the word ἀρχή (*arché*): πασῶν μὲν οὖν κοινὸν τῶν ἀρχῶν τὸ πρῶτον εἶναι ὅθεν ἢ γίγνεται ἢ γιγνώσκεται [It is indeed a common property, then, of all beginnings to be the first point from which something either already exists, comes into existence, or becomes known]."[60] He reads this passage to be an account of the various kinds of causes [*Grund*] for what an entity is.[61] Heidegger's classification is threefold: "the cause [*der Grund*] for what an entity is [*Was-seins*], for its facticity [*Daß-seins*], and for its being true [*Wahr-sein*]. Their κοινὸν [common property] is in τὸ πρῶτον εἶναι ὅθεν [being the first point]."[62] This threefold classification along with the fourfold divisions of causes—material, formal, efficient, and final—plays a prominent role in the subsequent history of metaphysics. Leibniz, for instance, reformulates the problem of causes as the question of *principium rationis sufficients* (principle of sufficient reason), which he gives in German as "der Satz vom Grunde," with Heidegger following suit, which, keeping in consideration Lacan's "L'étourdit," we render as "the statement of sufficient cause." Heidegger abbreviates this negatively as *nihil est sine ratione*, "nothing is without cause," and positively as *omne ens habet rationem*, "every entity has a cause,"[63] the latter of which paraphrases John Duns Scotus's Scholastic saying: *omne ens habet rationem objecti intelligibilis* (every entity has an understandable cause).[64]

Taking all this in stride, the statement of sufficient cause says something about entities in relation to understanding. It is apophantic in Aristotle's sense of a statement, the predicate of which may be logically attributed to its subject—"all men are mortal." And in that sense, it is a way of determining truth in relations of identity a priori. If taken thus as the essence of propositional truth, *identity* means *unity*, in the sense of that which belongs together. According to Heidegger: "Truth, therefore, means unanimity [*Einstimmigkeit*], which in turn is only in consonance with what manifests itself in identity as a whole. By their very nature, 'truths'—i.e., true statements [*Aussagen*]—refer to something *by cause of which* [*auf Grund wovon*] they can be unanimities."[65] There is an essential relationship to cause at the very heart of truth as such. Yet, in the case of the saying, "Every entity has a cause," the propositional truth, whereby entity is the possible subject of the predicative definition (cause), is rooted in a more primordial ontical truth (*ontische Wahrheit*): the pre-predicative manifestness of entities as present-at-hand (*Vorhandenen*), available things. This manifestness is, in turn, "already guided and clarified by an understanding of existence (existence-constitution [*Seinsverfassung*]): the what and how of entities."[66] Here is where the investigation predicated on the *ontological difference* gives priority of importance to ontology. "*It is the unveiledness of existence* [*Enthülltheit des Seins*] *that first enables the manifestness of entities.* . . . This unveiledness is called *ontological truth*."[67] Both the ontical and ontological truth concern entities *in their existence*, as well as the *being* of existence. "They belong together be-cause of [*auf Grund*] their relationship to *the difference between Being and entities* (the ontological difference). The essence of truth, which is necessarily bifurcated ontically and ontologically, is only possible given this difference."[68]

If, as Heidegger claims, the hallmark of human being, Dasein, is to behave in relation to entities by understanding existence, then the ability to distinguish, in which the ontological difference becomes actual, must have the roots of its possibility in the ground of the essence of Dasein—that is to say, "the cause [*Grund*] of the ontological difference," which is the transcendence of Dasein.[69] This shifts phenomenological analysis away from the study of the a priori categories describing objects according to our judgments and perception—the consciousness of objects Husserl called *intentionality*, which was so fundamental to his transcendental phenomenology—toward the interpretation of the pretheoretical conditions enabling such intentionality. "If one characterizes every *way of behaving* [*Verhalten*] toward entities as intentional, then intentionality is only possible *on the basis* [*auf dem Grunde*] *of transcendence*, and is neither identical with, nor even that which enables transcendence [*Transzendenz*]."[70] Heidegger specifies transcendence to mean "surpassing" (*Überstieg*), in the sense of a relationship of some entity going beyond something toward something else. We can say, then, that there is that *toward-which* (*woraufzu*) surpassing occurs, and that which is surpassed (*überstiegen*). The concern here is not with surpassing as a kind of spatial occurrence, but rather as signifying what is appropriate to human Dasein, not in the sense of one among other possible and occasionally executed modes of behavior toward entities, "but rather as the *basic constitutive feature* [*Grundverfassung*] *of this entity, happening prior to all behavior.*"[71] *Transcendence*, in this usage, denotes "the surpassing [*Überstieg*] that makes something like existence, and therefore also moving-in-space itself [*Sich-bewegen-im-Raume*], at all possible."[72] Nor is this transcendence defined as a subject-object relationship. Transcendent Dasein does not surpass (*übersteigt*) some barrier at the edge of the subject forcing it to remain somehow immanent or some gap separating it from the object. Objects, as in objectified entities, are not that toward-which surpassing occurs. Insofar as Dasein is a surpassing, what it surpasses is simply existence itself, which is to say, every entity that can be or become unconcealed (*unverborgen*) to Dasein, including Dasein as it exists itself. This sense of transcendence as surpassing is crucial here, for, in the fundamental ontology, only by way of surpassing is it possible to distinguish and decide within existence who and how a "self" is and what is not.

Heidegger is at odds with the received reading of Plato, which construes his concept of ἐπέκαινα (*epékeina*) as "transcendence." By that reading, Plato's saying in the *Republic*, "οὐκ οὐσίας ὄντος τοῦ ἀγαθοῦ, ἀλλ ἔτι ἐπέκαινα τῆς οὐσίας πρεσβείᾳ καὶ δυνάμει ὑπερέχοντος, oúk ousías óntos tou agathou, all éti epékeina tís ousías presbeía kai dynámei uperéchontos," is rendered as: "though the good itself is not essence but still transcends essence in dignity and surpassing power."[73] Quoting verbatim only the phrase ἐπέκαινα τῆς οὐσίας, *epékeina tís ousías* (essence of the being-presence), Heidegger states that the term ἐπέκαινα (*epékeina*) in this passage cannot be interpreted as the transcendence of Dasein because the problem of ἀγαθόν (*agathon*, the good) that Plato is discussing is "merely the culminating point of the central, very concrete question about the basic possibility of the *existence of Daseins* in the *polis*."[74] It is a matter of political and not existential existence. Be that as it may, Plato's tripartite characterization of ἀγαθόν (*agathon*) still leads to the question of the primordial unified ground of the possibility of truth, understanding, and being. Taking this to be in reference to "the disclosing project of being as the originary action of human being, in which all existence must be rooted in the midst of entities," Heidegger argues that for Plato, "the ἀγαθόν [*agathon*] is, thus, the one ἕξις [*hexis*] (*Mächtigkeit* [cardinal-power]) that is powerful [*mächtig*] in the possibility of truth, understanding, and even being; indeed, of all three at once."[75] His gloss of ἕξις (*hexis*), "disposition," as *Mächtigkeit* is more in line with Aristotle's usage than Plato's, however. That is to say, *Mächtigkeit* is assumed through, or by way of, the activity of causing (αἴτιον, *aition*), taken precisely in Heidegger's sense of *Grund*, the passage into being; it is, as Aristotle might say, the disposition that "works through" (ἀπεργάσαθαι, *apergásasthai*), goes beyond what nature cannot complete.

On that point, we should not lose sight of our earlier reading of Aristotle apropos the Negro and primitivism. Heidegger's intentionally reading *hexis* in the Aristotelian sense is confirmed by the marginal note added to this passage in his personal copy of the 1931 edition of "Vom Wesen des Grundes": "No! Dasein is not grasped and not experienced. Επέκαινα [*Epékeina*] is also not transcendence, but ἀγαθόν [*agathon*] as αἰτία [*aitia*]."[76] So, "the essence of ἀγαθόν [*agathon*, the good] lies in the cardinal-power [*Mächtigkeit*] as its own οὗ ἕνεκα [*oú heneka*]—as the *for-the-sake of* [*Umwillen*] . . . , it is the fountain-head [*Quelle*] of possibility as such."[77] Or, as Plato says in the passage of reference: "You must affirm the idea of the good as the cause [αἰτάν, *aitán*] of knowledge and truth insofar as they are thinkable."[78] In the Platonic doctrine, the *for-the-sake of*, which is the ἡ τοῦ ἀγαθοῦ ἕξις (*hé tou agathoū hexis*, "the disposition of causality of the good," as an ἰδέα (*idéa*) is an apprehended aspect of εἶδος (*eidos*), "essence"—no absolute distinction can be drawn between them—remaining in the ὑπερουράνιον τόπον (*hyperouránion topon* [place beyond heaven]).[79] By contrast, in the Aristotelian epistemology, *hexis* equates with what Heidegger's analytic discovers is the primordial projection of Dasein's possibilities, its potentiality-of-being (*Seinkönnen*) toward itself in-the-world, for the sake of itself.

The resonance of *hexis* and Dasein is amplified by Aristotle's definition of *mimesis* in the *Poetics* as the generative activity whereby humans represent to themselves materially—that is, in entities—the experience of existing in the world. If "working through," ἀπεργάσαθαι (*apergásasthai*), is taken as synonymous with *Übersteig* (stepping over), then the existence Dasein surpasses is not a random aggregate of objects; no matter how that existence is defined and articulated, it is always surpassed *in a totality*. Continuing with Husserl's conception of human being in an environing-world (*Umwelt*), Heidegger calls that totality "*toward-which* [*woraufhin*] Dasein transcends, the *world* [*die Welt*]"[80] Accordingly, "World co-constitutes [*macht . . . mit aus*] the unitary structure of transcendence; because it is part of this structure, the concept of world [*Weltbegriff*] is called *transcendental*," with transcendence construed as an indicator of Dasein's finitude.[81] Heidegger arrives at this particular elaboration on Kant's postulate that the concept of the world (*Weltbegriff*) is a transcendental ideal by recalling the ancient Greek concept of the κόσμος οὗτος (*kósmos ontos*), "worldliness of the world," which he construes as contemplation of the condition or state of affairs as the *how* (*Wie*) whereby being is in its totality. The *how* in its totality is itself relative to human Dasein, is equiprimordial with it, which is why Heidegger considers the Greek meaning as existential; "Thus the world belongs strictly to human Dasein, although it encompasses [*umgreift*] all being, including Dasein, in its totality."[82]

WORLDLINESS

This concept of the world is given a Christian focus and clarification by Paul, who uses the term κόσμος (*kósmos*) to mean "the being of man in the *how* of a way of thinking that is estranged from God."[83] That connotation carries over into Jerome's Vulgate term, *mundus*. Concurrently, Augustine refers to *mundus* to mean the whole of creation, but also to stand for *mundi habitatores*, "inhabitants of the world," which is a term of disposition having the sense of those who delight in the world, the impious, the carnal, the *amatores mundi*, "lovers of the world," or worldly.[84] In Scholastic metaphysics, *mundus* becomes synonymous with *universum* (the sum of existing things), or *universitas creaturarum* (the totality of created beings), as well as *saeculum* (an age, or time), which Heidegger glosses as *weltliche Gesinnung* (worldly way of thinking), signaling the temporality of human Dasein's worldliness. Suárez places *world* under *metaphysica specialis*, the study of the sum of all types of beings, in contrast to *metaphysica generalis*, which is the study of being qua being, or general ontology. Leibniz's conception of "the universe as only a certain kind of collection of all possible existents" is of less pertinence to Heidegger's consideration of how the ancient *kósmos* gets reworked in Western intellectual history than is Christian Wolff's adaptation of it.[85] In that adaptation, Wolff further clarifies and systematizes Suárez's distinction by first innovatively redefining philosophy as the science inquiring into possible being, insofar as it is possible: "Philosophia est scientia posîbilium, quatenus esse possunt."[86] He then orders it into three divisions: natural theology, the object of which is the possibility of God (*quæ per Deum possibilia sunt*); psychology, the object of which is the possibility of the human mind (*quæ per animam humanam possibilia sunt*); and physics, the object of which is the possibility of bodies (*quæ per corpora possibilia sunt*).[87] Physics divides further into general and special. Wolff calls that division dealing with bodies in the world as a whole (*quæ corporibus mundi totalibus*) *cosmologia*. Defined in cosmological terms, the world is "a series [*Reihe*] of mutable things that are next to each other, follow upon one another, but are in total interlinked [*verknüpfst*] with one another."[88] Punctuating this line of thinking, Baumgarten defines "*Mundus [die ganze Welt]* (*universum, pan*) as the series (*multitudo totum*) of actual finite things that is not equivalent to something else."[89] Disputing the Leibniz-Wolff conception, Christian Crusius holds that equating the world with the entirety of that which is *ens creatum* (creatures) means grasping the concept of the world requires understanding the essence and possibility of the proofs of God's existence. Crusius, thus, returns to the Pauline doctrine, whereby God is set over against the world as the unity of the entirety of created being. Kant, in his critical engagement with Wolff's structuring of metaphysics through Baumgarten and Crusius, reorganizes it into the subdisciplines of *theologia rationalis, cosmologia rationalis,* and *psychologia rationalis,* which requires that the concept of world assumes a different form. With the *Critique of Pure Reason,* the classical Greek "existential meaning of 'world' reappears, freed from its specific Christian coloring [*Färbung*], alongside the new "cosmological" meaning: "The concept of world [*Weltbegriff*] is that transcendental ideal whereby the absolute totality of objects accessible in finite knowledge—the sort of entities accessible only in sensory reception (in finite intuition [*endliche Anschauung*]) as appearances, phenomena [*Erscheinungen*]—can be represented a priori."[90]

According to the analysis of Kant's transcendental idealism, the aggregate of all appearances is the aggregate of all possible experience, the synthesis of which *world* denotes; that is to say, *world* means "the absolute totality of the aggregate of existing things," and with its usage, "we direct our attention solely to the completeness of the synthesis (although actually only to the regress to conditions)."[91] The parenthetical qualification underscores that the concept of world is not, as Heidegger puts it, "an ontical linkage of things in themselves but a transcendental (ontological) aggregate of things as appearances."[92] The world is, therefore, an idea or pure synthetic concept of reason, belonging to a class of transcendental ideals.[93] This is the point Heidegger wants to stress, when he says, "World as idea is transcendent; it *surpasses* [*übersteigt*] appearances in such a way that, as *their* totality, it is *referred back* [*zurückbezogen*] to them. Transcendence, in the Kantian sense of the surpassing of experience [*Übersteigens der Erfahrung*], is ambiguous, however."[94] The ambiguity stems from Kant's using the word in two ways. On one hand, he uses it to mean that which exceeds (*überschreiten*) the manifold of phenomenal appearances (*Erscheinungen*) given *within* experience. This sense applies to the representation (*Vorstellung*), "world." On the other hand, Kant uses *transcendence* to mean that which emerges from (*heraustreten*) phenomenal appearance as finite knowledge in general, referring to the possible entirety of all things as the "object" (*Gegenstand*). The transcendental ideal arises from this latter sense of transcendence, in contrast to which the world presents a limitation (*Einschränkung*) and denotes finite human knowledge in its totality.

Regarding this ambiguity, Heidegger concludes that, after Kant, "the concept of world stands, as it were, *between* [*zwischen*] the possibility of experience and the transcendental ideal. So, it ultimately signifies the totality of the finitude of the human essence."[95] In an ironic paraphrasing of the *Critique of Pure Reason* that is also a not-so-subtle dig at Husserl, he then says: "The 'transcendental Ideal' goes together with the *intuitus originarius*."[96] This reiterates a line from his earlier work, *Kant und das Problem der Metaphysik* (Kant and the Problem of Metaphysics),[97] which considers the distinction Kant makes in the "Transcendental Dialectic" between *Anschauung* (intuition), *Erkenntnis* (cognition or knowledge), and *Denken* (thinking) with regard to *Vorstellungen* (representations).[98] With respect to this distinction, Heidegger draws attention to the first sentence of *The Critique of Pure Reason*: "In whatever manner and by whatever means a cognition [*Erkenntnis*] may relate to objects, that through which it relates immediately to them, and at which all thinking [*alles Denken*] as a means is directed, is *intuition*."[99] In quoting these lines, he emphasizes *intuition* to drive home the point that cognition is primarily intuiting and that taking care of this fact is requisite to understand the *Critique of Pure Reason*. "From this," he asserts, "it at once becomes clear that the reinterpretation of cognition into judging [*Urteilen*] (thinking) is contrary to the decisive meaning of the Kantian problem."[100] Heidegger's use of the term *Urteilen* here is consistent with his taking Kant's formulation of the question—"How are a priori synthetic judgments [*Urteile*] possible?"—to "conceive cognition as judgment [*Erkennen als Urteilen*]."[101] He reads Kant to be maintaining that all cognition is in service of intuition, such that thinking is not only present alongside intuition, but rather, according to its own internal structure, serves that to which intuition is primarily and constantly directed. Holding thinking and intuition to be essentially related in this way presumes their having a certain inherent kinship (*Herkunft*) that allows their unification, which is manifested in their sharing representation (*Vorstellung*) in general as the genus of cognitive expression. Heidegger has in mind the concluding passage of section I, book I, of the Transcendental Dialectic, titled "On Ideas in General," where, in order to protect scientific understanding of the various types of representations from careless disorder, Kant maintains a hierarchical distinction between "representation in general (*repraesentatio*) and representation with consciousness (*perceptio*)."[102]

Bearing in mind, as Heidegger does, that Kant uses representation (*Vorstellung*) in the broad sense of one thing indicating (*anzeigt*), announcing (*meldet*), or presenting (*darstellt*) another, when such representing takes place with consciousness, there belongs to it a cognizant-recognizing (*Erkennen*) of the announcing (*Melden*) *and* the having-been-announced (*Gemeldetsein*) by something.[103] According to the opening sentence of the *Critique of Pure Reason*, cognition is a thinking intuition (*denkendes Anschauen*). Yet, thinking as general representing is in service of the single object in its immediacy. This suggests that while both intuition and thinking are representation (*Vorstellung*), they are not cognition (*Erkenntnis*). Kant makes precisely this point in "Welches sind die wirklichen Fortschritte" (What Real Progress Has Metaphysics Made in Germany), where he calls representation in general through concepts (*Begriffe*) "thinking" (*denken*), in contrast to the immediate individual representation of intuition, and the capacity to think, "understanding" (*Verstand*). He says accordingly that "cognizance [*Erkenntniß*] through concepts is called *discursive* [*discursiv*] and that through intuition [*Anschauung*] intuitive [*intuitiv*]; both combined together are required, in fact, for there to be any properly named cognition."[104] In other words, an object is known (*erkannt*) only when an intuition accords with a concept. Heidegger takes this to justify inferring a reciprocal and completely balanced relationship between intuiting and thinking, concluding on that same warrant, "Knowing is intuitive thinking [*anschauendes Denken*]; that is to say, basically [*im Grunde*] judgement [*Urteilen*]."[105] This bears on his earlier-remarked quip aligning the transcendental Ideal and *intuitus originarius*, which has to do with the distinction Kant makes between the idea of infinite godlike knowledge, a knowledge in general, and finite human knowledge. The problem Kant confronts is determining how a priori synthetic judgments are possible for humans in accordance with the mental faculties they possess by virtue of which they are capable of expanding their knowledge a priori, that is to say, the faculties of pure reason (*reinen Vernunftvermögens*). But he also says, regarding such cognition, "If by a pure reason of a being in general, we understand the faculty of knowing things independently of experience, and therefore of the sense-representations [*Sinnenvorstellungen*], then it is not at all determined in what way such cognition is generally possible in such an entity (e.g., in God or another higher spirit [*höheren Geiste*])."[106] The implication is the cognizance of such a being must be intuition (*Anschauung*)—an *intuitus originarius*, an "original intuition," that creates its own objects and is not received from them—and not thinking, which always proves itself to be finite. God does not need to think, thinking being indicial of finitude. Man, by contrast, has only *intuitus derivativus*, intuition that is received from objects and does not create them. If, as Heidegger claims, the decisive difference between infinite and finite knowledge is not that the godlike knowing is only intuition while finite human knowing is a thinking intuiting, but rather it lies primarily in the intuiting itself—since properly speaking, even knowing entails intuition—then the cause (*Grund*) of human cognition must be sought in the finitude of its intuition. "That a finite knowing entity [*erkennendes Wesen*] must 'also' think is an essential consequence of the finitude [*Endlichkeit*] of its own intuiting. Only in this way does the essentially subordinate service of 'all thinking' come into the right light."[107] It is the finite being that thinks infinity, and not the infinite being, which does not think at all. In that same vein, it is the finite being that is in-the-world, and thinks it. Finitude is requisite for the transcendence that enables the concept of the world as a totality.

What begins as a question of the essence of causes flows into the investigation of transcendence and then into that of the concept of world, which turns out to be about human finitude. To quote Kant from the opening paragraph of his *Anthropologie in pragmatischer Hinsicht* (Anthropology from a

Pragmatic Point of View): "Recognizing Man [*Mensch*], according to his specie, as an earthly being endowed with reason [*Vernunft*] deserves especially to be called knowledge of the world, [*Weltkenntnis*], even though he is only one part of the earthly creation."[108] Kant, of course, bifurcates anthropology as the systematic theorization of knowledge about man into the physiological and pragmatic. Physiological anthropology investigates "what nature makes of man in relation to other things in the world, such as animals, plants, and minerals in various lands and climates"; pragmatic anthropology investigates "what man can or should make of himself as a free-acting being [*freihandelndes Wesen*]."[109] When he says, then, that knowledge of man (*Menschenkenntnis*) is knowledge of the world, he means the pragmatic anthropology exclusively; and "it is properly pragmatic only when it entails knowledge of *man as citizen of the world (als Weltbürgers)*."[110] In illustration, Kant remarks that "even raciology [*Kenntnis der Menschenrassen*], which regards races as products of the play [*Spiel*] of nature, is not counted as pragmatic, but only theoretical knowledge of the world."[111] The point being that the proper task of the pragmatic anthropologist is not taxonomy, but rather to engage the conceptual/discursive realm of everyday interaction of human being. Kant underscores this by commenting on two idiomatic expressions: "He knows the world [*Welt kennen*]" and "He knows his way around the world [*Welt haben*]." He glosses the first as tantamount to saying, "One only understands the game as spectator [*zugesehen*]," and the second as "One is an active player in it [*mitgespielt*]."[112] Heidegger takes the invocation of these expressions to indicate Kant's having an existential concept of world, referring to the existence of man *within* his historical community and not his presence in the cosmos as a species of living creature. He thus extrapolates, "'World' is the name for the 'game' of everyday Dasein, indeed of Dasein itself.... 'World' is the designation for the essence of human Dasein."[113]

Kant's usages of *world* signifies an ontological-existential concept of the milieu *wherein* a factical Dasein *lives* as Dasein, and not the totality of extent present-at-hand entities. Human Dasein, as an entity situated in the midst of entities, relating itself *to*, behaving *toward* (*verhaltend*) those entities, exists in such a way that the entirety of existence is always already manifest as a totality. That totality, in all its variability, is understood without needing to grasp or even *completely* investigate the entirety of manifest entities in all their connections, spheres, and strata. This anticipatory comprehension of the totality is what Heidegger means by Dasein's being-in-the-world (*In-der-Welt-sein*) is a "surpassing *to* the world [*Überstieg zur Welt*]."[114] After Kant, it would be in error, he warns, to use the expression *world* as a name for the entirety of natural things. Kant's usages of *world* signify an ontological-existential concept of the milieu *wherein* a factical Dasein *lives* as Dasein, and not the totality of extent present-at-hand (*Vorhanden*) entities. World as a totality is not a particular entity qua thing, or even the sum total of such entities, but is that from which Dasein *"gives itself to signify [sich zu bedeuten gibt],"* meaning in coming-out (*Auf-es-zukommen*) through the world, Dasein "makes a *self* of itself as a being that is given over *to be [zu sein ihm anheimgegeben ist]*. Its existence lies in *its potentiality-of-being (Seinkönnen)*. Dasein exists *for-the-sake of [umwillen]* it."¹¹⁵ Even if it is granted the world is that in the surpassing (*Überstieg*) toward which selfhood first emerges, then it is *also* that for the sake of which Dasein exists. Indeed, the fundamental character of the world is the *for-the-sake of*, in the primordial sense that it ensures the inner possibility of every actualized "for your sake," "for his sake," "for its sake," et cetera, so that world, indeed, belongs to selfhood; they are essentially the same. As the totality of what exists for the sake of a Dasein, the world is brought by Dasein before Dasein itself. This bringing-itself-before-itself (*Vor-sich-selbst-bringen*) is the primordial projection of the possibilities of Dasein, insofar as it behaves toward entities in the midst of being. Dasein by its existence provides the *opportunity* for entities, or nature in the widest sense, to be manifested. Heidegger speaks of this in terms of "entities possible and occasional world-entrance [*Welteingang*]." And entering the world is what happens (*geschieht*) *with* the existence *of* Dasein. "An entity becomes 'existent,' the hour and day it enters the world by way of Dasein's temporalizing [*Zeitigung*]. Only with the occurrence of this primeval happening [*Urgeschichte*], which is transcendence, is it possible for existence to reveal itself."¹¹⁶ It occurs with the throwing (*Überwurf*) of the projected world over being, enabling it to manifest itself in form, much like a proper mantle (*Überwurf*) outlines the form of what it covers. When Heidegger says, then, "Dasein transcends," he means it is *world-forming* in the essence of its being. Indeed, it "'forms' the world in the sense it lets the world take place, and with the world gives itself a primordial scene (*tableau*) that although not specifically grasped, nevertheless functions as pre-image [*Vor-bild*] for all manifest entities, including Dasein itself."¹¹⁷

Understanding the transcendence of Dasein is inextricably bound to the ontological investigation of the world, which, in turn, belongs to the existential analytic of Dasein itself as being-in-the-world in everydayness. And that existential analytic starts with those entities nearest to us in the proximate environmental world (*Umweltlichkeit*) encountered in our everyday activities of doing and making things. These entities are not objectively *present-at-hand* (*Vorhanden*), but rather are *ready-to-hand* (*Zuhanden*), things used and produced by human artifice. Classical Greeks called such entities πράγματα (*pragmata*), meaning the things or stuff used in πρᾶξις (*praxis*), which Heidegger glosses as *besorgenden Umgang*, and we render as "careful-dealing," in the sense that their usefulness matters to us and we are invested in them. In keeping with the Greek sense, Heidegger calls these *Zeug*, literally "useful stuff"—but we might say "useful things," or "instruments"[118]—the analysis of which is extensive and central to his interpretation of worldliness in general. That interpretation has to do with his retrieval and elaboration of the ancient and classical Greek construal of being as productive activity (*Herstellen*), particularly Aristotle's account of ἐπιστήμη ποιητική (*epistēmē poiētikē*, knowing how to create or poetic know-how).[119] The way in which that retrieval informs Heidegger's concept of the transcendence is a touchstone in Becker's amending paratranscendence.

What troubles Becker most about Heidegger's concept of the transcendence of Dasein is that existence is super-categorical (*überkategorial*), insofar as categories are concepts that relate to things (*Dingen*). It is precisely the extermination of things in passing beyond them connoted in Heidegger's term *Übersteigendheit* (surpassing) that Becker seeks to displace with the term *Unentstiegenheit* (paratranscendence); and in order to give his distinction of *Unentstiegenheit* grounding in the history of thought, he prefaces it by recounting the conceptual genealogy of transcendence. Like Heidegger, he traces the provenance of the concept to Plato's ἐπέκαινα (*epékeina*), noting its Latinization by the Scholastics as *transcendens* and *transcendentale*. *Transcendens* was used by the early scholastics, Erigena, Abelard, and Anselm, to mean *trans omne ens* (that which surpasses things); Suárez subsequently uses *transcendentalis* as a synonym.[120] Remarking on Kant's liberal use of these two terms and rendering them in German respectively as *transzendent* and *transzendental* to mean two different things, Becker does not think this bifurcation originates with Kant, however, but rather that it was already "dormant in Plato's usage or at any rate was somehow induced in it."[121] Becker concurs with Heidegger that, in Plato's doctrine, the good as an ἰδέα (*idéa*) is an apprehended aspect of εἶδος (*eidos*, essence) and so remains in the place beyond heaven. But he sees here a paradox, if not a contradiction that Plato "can only briefly indicate and formally avoid by introducing the concept of ἕν [*hén*, among], but not really overcome, which is the expression of a tension that may be inherent in the idea of transcendence."[122]

That same tension carries over into Aristotle's discussion in *Metaphysics* of the πρώτη φιλοσοφία (*protí philosophia*), "first philosophy," which Andronicus collected under the rubric τὰ μετὰ φυσικὰ βιβλία (*tà metà phusikà biblía*), "the books after [the books on] physics." This tension, however, has more to do with the Scholastics' misinterpretation of Andronicus's title of the collection as "the science of what is beyond the physical," *metaphysica*, than what Aristotle says in the referenced work. Accordingly, Becker seizes on Aristotle's saying in book 11 (Kappa), apropos there being a science of being qua being (ἐπιστήμη τοῦ ὄντος ᾗ ὄν καί, *epistēme tou óntos ēi hón kai*) dealing with substance (οὐσία, *ousía*) that exists separately from physical things and is immovable (ἀκίνητος, *akínetos*): "If there is an entity of this kind in the world, it surely must be the Divine [τὸ θεῖον, *tó theíon*] and this must be the first and most fundamental principle."[123] Being adept at summarizing elliptical paraphrase, he presents this as Aristotle's answering a question he poses late in book 11: "The question might be raised whether or not the science of being qua being [τοῦ ὄντος ᾗ ὄν, *toú óntos ēi ón*] should be regarded as universal [καθόλου, *kathólou*]."[124] Aristotle raises this question immediately after having delineated the three kinds of speculative science (θεωρητικῶν ἐπιστημῶν, *theoretikōn epistemōn*): physics, mathematics, and theology—the latter being one of his alternative designations for the science of being qua being, which is the highest of the three because it deals with the most important side of existence. The use of the term καθόλου (*kathólou*), "universal," in these passages is particularly interesting to Becker, leading him to say that "two types of transcendence are intertwined: first, the actual transcendence of being itself over the entity, of ὄν ᾗ ὄν [*ón ēi ón*] over each γένος [*genus*] and εἶδος [*eidos*]. For the ὄν [*ón*] in Aristotle is not . . . a genus. Second, the quasi-transcendence of the first being, of the divine, over all the other grades he has graduated from."[125]

Not only does Kant's bifurcation of transcendent and transcendental stem from this tension expressed in Aristotle's thinking, but Becker's own concept of *Unentstiegenheit* reiterates it as a dialect; thus, "improving-on" Heidegger's interpretation of Plato's ἐπέκεινα (*epékeina*) as "transcendence" and countering the extermination entailed in his concept of transcendence as *Überstieg* (surpassing). In the dialectic tension connoted with *Unentstiegenheit*, what emerges from existent things remains, to a certain extent, connected to them without completely or absolutely rising above. Disputing the subsuming of nature to world in Heidegger's existential analytic, whereby it too belongs to Dasein and is surpassed along with the world, Becker argues that nature is never *totally* surpassed by Dasein, but remains a primordial constitutive element, connecting it and the world to the earth. A key element in his argument is the identification of mathematics and ontology, or, in Aristotle's terms, mathematics and the science of being qua being. This is an old fundamental point of difference between Becker and Heidegger going back to *Mathematische Existenz*, where the principal concern is exploring the being-sense (*Seinssinns*) of mathematical phenomena, and then the applicability of pure mathematics in the natural sciences, most notably physics. That exploration, Becker takes care to point out, is not merely logical, which would be in the vein of Dedekind and Cantor; but it gives particular emphasis to "ontological investigations. "The term 'ontological' is not meant . . . in the sense of a being that is constituted by phenomenological investigation. It is precisely the constitutive questioning itself, and moreover, in a certain sense, a particularly concrete form of constitutive questions."[126] In other words, some sixty-one-years before Badiou's *L'être et l'événement* (Being and Event), Becker proposes not only that mathematics is performatively ontological but it is philosophy qua phenomenology that can exposit and investigate this ontology.

HISTORICITY

One of Heidegger's crucial propositions is that existentially projected Being-toward-death is the characteristic of the authentic (*eigentlichen*) self-understanding of Dasein because it "*reveals to Dasein its lostness in the they-self [das Man-selbst], and brings it to face the possibility to be itself, primarily unsupported by the careful solicitude [die besorgende Fürsorge], but to be itself in passionate, anxious freedom toward death, which is free of the illusions of the they [das Man], factical, and certain of itself.*"[127] Such anticipation toward death "absolutely individualizes Dasein and lets it become certain of the wholeness of its potentiality-of-being."[128] That individuation is the "subject-character" of Dasein discovered in the existential analytic by asking *who* is the entity for which understanding being-in-the-world is its way of being? It is in the course of addressing this question that the analytic demarcates and then explores the relationship between authentic Dasein, *they* as an existentiale of Dasein, and the inauthentic *they-self* that is determined and dominated by the *they*. Becker points out that "the phenomenon, *they*, has a very specific sociological meaning within Tönnies's recently introduced concept of 'social' [*gesellschaftliche*] structure itself: which is preceded, in terms of organic developmental history, by the societal form of 'community' [*Gemeinschaft*] (cohabitation [*Lebensgemeinschaft*], blood, tribal-community [*Stammesgemeinschaft*], etc.)."[129] Becker characterizes these as the "more primitive 'we' phenomena," which he holds "are in contrast to both the 'I' and the 'they.'" The temporality characterizing the primitive *we* "is almost natural-temporality [*Naturzeitlichkeit*]," which is why he refers to them as *das naturhafte Sein der Naturvölker*, "the natural being of primitive peoples."[130]

In posing this primitive *we*, Becker addresses the inadequacy in the fundamental ontological account of human Dasein, which has everything to do with what is connoted in the existential analytic by *Geschichte*, "history." He gets at this by attending to what Heidegger says about death as just one of the ends that formally enclose the totality of Dasein; the other end is the beginning, birth (*Geburt*). "Only the being that is 'between' birth and death," Heidegger says, "presents the totality in question.... The 'between [*Zwischen*]' related to birth and death lies *in the Being* of Dasein."[131] Neither birth (*Geburt*) or death (*Tod*) refers here to merely biological events, whereby one is something past in the sense of no longer present-to-hand and the other something still outstanding and so not yet present-to-hand. Birth and death are *with* Dasein as its ends. They, as well as their between, *are-in-time*, meaning, "they *are* within the horizon of Dasein's temporal constitution."¹³² Factical Dasein exists as being born already dying in the sense of being-toward-death (*Seins zum Tode*).¹³³ In the somewhat restless existential movement, Dasein is *stretched along stretching-itself along* (*erstreckten Sicherstreckens*), existing as anticipatory-running-forward (*Vorlaufen*) from birth to death.¹³⁴ This is what Heidegger calls *historizing-occurrence* (*Geschehen*), the structure of which relates the existential-temporal conditions of its possibility, instantiating Dasein's primordial temporality (*ursprünglichen Zeitlichkeit*), what he terms its *historicity* (*Geschichtlichkeit*; a term coined by Hegel in passing, to denote the formal path of *Geist* coming to self-sufficiency in the world).¹³⁵ Heidegger's use of *Geschichtlichkeit* is not anchored in the spirit, however, and is expressly appropriated (*Aneignung*) from the sense elaborated by Graf Yorck in his correspondence with Dilthey as a technical term designating a defining characteristic in the ontology of human existence.¹³⁶ In Yorck's thinking, *Geschichtlichkeit* identifies human beings as unique, concrete entities, giving it a decidedly more materialist connotation than Hegel's initial usage.

Heidegger's usage of *Geschichte* denotes what happens, the "actual realization" of work. He uses *Historie* and its adjectival cognates, in the main, to reference historiology "as the systematic study, science, of what has happened [der Wissenschaft von der Geschichte gesucht werden]."¹³⁷ Recalling that *Historie* is a German borrowing from the Latin *historia*, which is borrowed in turn from the Greek ἱστορίκός (*historikós*), a declanation from ἱστορία (*historía*), meaning inquiry of one who has witnessed, we can arguably render this as "the story that is told." Heidegger reserves the adjective, *geschichtlich* (historical), and its cognates, on the other hand, for what we might term "the story that has happened." When he says, then, that Dasein *is historical* (*ist geschichtlich*), this does not mean that it is a story told—although he is clear that Dasein *is* in speaking, which we shall get to momentarily. Nor is it historical, in the sense of *geschichtlich*, because it "stands in history [*in der Geschichte steht*]."¹³⁸ Dasein has history, is historical because it is *constituted* by historicity. It "is temporal in the very basis of its Being [*im Grunde seines Seins*]," occurring *there* (*Da*), thrown (*Geworfen*), as Heidegger puts it, within a preexisting world.¹³⁹

The pertinence of saying, "Dasein *has* history because it is constituted by historicity" to our own interrogation of paraontological discourse is made clearer by considering the first three of the six different ways Heidegger delineates of speaking about history (*Geschichte*).¹⁴⁰ In the first instance, when one says, "'My friend studies history,' or as the beautiful expression puts it, 'He majors in history [*macht in Geschichte*],'" what is meant is the systematic study, the science of history (*Geschichtswissenschaft*).¹⁴¹ In the second, when someone is working on a philosophical problem and is given the advice "'orient yourself somewhat in the history,'" what is meant is the transmitted "actual realizations of the processing of the problem," which is effectively a description of a field of facts.[142] The third way of speaking is in the privative: "One speaks of 'history-less peoples [*geschichtslosen*]' tribes and peoples," which means, Heidegger says, "they have no tradition [*sie haben keine Tradition*]."[143] Subsequent analyses and addenda further elaborate in detail the connotations of each way of speaking. The science of history, while indeed concerned with "factical life experience," is a goal-directed acquisition of knowledge, aimed at making the historical past available to oneself. "That is to say, a nexus of tasks for theoretical knowing, from which tasks this knowing is determinative of particular methods."[144] History as that which has occurred as an objective field of facts can be known without requiring the nexus of theoretical knowledge. But it is the third way of speaking of history as *Tradition* that proves most crucial to Heidegger's analysis of *Geschichte* and *geschichtlich*, of history and the historical. It is customary, he reminds us, "to also call history-less [*Geschichts-lose*] tribes and people 'barbaric,'" which we can take as synonymous with "primitive."[145] Elsewhere in the existential analytic of *Being and Time*, Heidegger turns toward the life of primitive people as a distinctive kind of Dasein with its own specific everydayness and non-everyday existence, the interpretation of which "has positive methodological significance" in discovering the difficulties of securing a "natural concept of world."[146] In other words, Heidegger adduces the primitive as a useful heuristic for describing the ontological foundations of Dasein, and does so with the qualification that his "knowledge [*Kenntnis*] about primitive peoples has been provided exclusively by ethnology."[147] Thereby, he is admitting that the heuristic is merely empirical, and hence already circumscribed and determined "by certain preliminary concepts and interpretations of human being in general," with which ethnology operates, "beginning with its initial 'recording' [*Aufnahme*] of material, its sifting-examination [*Sichtung*] and its findings."[148]

Arguably, this is in reference to the fieldwork-driven collecting and analysis of such ethnologists as Adolf Bastian, who postulated that the scientific psychological analysis of cross-cultural data makes accessible the underlying psychic unity of humankind, which is indicative of a single common beginning but not, *pace* Comte and Spencer, a unilinear civilizational-cultural development.[149] Bastian's ethnology entailed an acute interest and investment in those non-European peoples regarded as "primitive" because they exhibit "a peoples' chemistry of thought [*Völkerchemie der Gedanken*] that leads us to primary mental [*geistige*] elements."[150] And it is, indeed, the Hegelian sense of *Geistes* that is at play here. For Bastian, studying prehistorical (*vorgeschichtlichen*) psychology provides a point of departure in understanding the relationship between humankind and the natural world. The primitive exhibits the primordial human activity of constituting the world in and by means of signification, uncontaminated with "theorization." The investment is to study them as the instantiation of what "we" were before differentiation in dispersal and civilizational development, in order to rediscover our commonality in a universal mind. Such investment is consonant with, if not identical to, the already elaborated-on primitivism of the American Transcendentalist William Francis Allen, and the French avant-garde ethnologist Marcel Griaule. Indeed, Bastian had a similar investment in the Negro, minus their philia.[151] Heidegger's specifically referring to Bastian is further confirmed by his explicitly invoking Bastian's use of scientific psychology to analyze the collected cross-cultural data and deduce the general psychic unity of humankind and cultural evolution: "It has not been agreed upon whether the commonplace psychology or even the scientific psychology and sociology the ethnologist brings to bear can provide any scientific guarantee of adequate access to, or interpretation and transmission of the phenomena under investigation."[152] His methodological caveat notwithstanding, Heidegger concurs with the tenets of primitivism, postulating that the reason interpretation of the primitive is a useful heuristic in discovering the difficulties of securing a natural concept of world is because "primitive Dasein often speaks to us more directly from a primordial absorption in 'phenomena' (taken in a pre-phenomenological [*vorphänomenologischen*] sense). What may seem, from our perspective, an awkward and crude conceptualization can be positively conducive to a genuine illumination of the ontological structures of phenomena."[153]

The heuristic usefulness, then, of primitive peoples is their nontheoretical, prephenomenological, and concomitantly, preontological, as well as prehistorical, knowing of the surrounding world. They are a prime exhibit of the nonepistemic careful-dealing with the world Heidegger calls *Umsicht* (circumspection). Bearing this in mind, let us refocus our attention on his analysis of speaking about history in terms of history-less primitives. To say that such people are without history (*ohne Geschichte*) does not mean, with respect to their Dasein, they are without memory of the past. Of course, primitives remember a past "in which things happened to their antecedents [*Früheren*] in ways perhaps similar to what occurs with those subsequent to one's [*Späteren*] living now."[154] We could even say, along these lines, that the primitive tribe has a history, "meaning the relationship of objectively coming to or not coming to the-concrete-thing [*gegenständlichen*]. The primitive tribe, as an actual entity is subject to development: that which today has such and such tribal population, decades before had another chief, etc."[155] Put another way, the primitive tribe's understanding of its past is *existentiell* in having to do with the ontic facts of existence; it is a preontological understanding of the choices made and avoided. The primitive tribe has no history in the sense that "they do not feel [*fühlen*] as the later-ones or prior-ones. The past is not a character for them, in which they factically live and that somehow permeates the content of their life-experience [*Lebenserfahrung*]; they do not cultivate and nourish [*pflegen*] the past."[156] In that same vein, living each day according to what the day may bring, history-less tribes "have no future, no tasks. Conversely, what they have done and lived does not interest them either. They are even indifferent to the achievement of the present, which to them is a free-standing self-evident result that is 'over.'"[157] Elucidating in addendum giving "the Zulu Negro [*Zulukaffern*]" as an illustration of history-less primitives, he states: "The primitive tribe Dasein is such that the past, what has happened prior, is available to it and it makes use of that availability, learning from the latest hunt for instance. Nevertheless, the tribe does not 'have' *its* past."[158] Heidegger gives "to have" (*Haben*) a very precise meaning here: "It is a *preserving* [*Bewahren*], in one's own becoming Dasein itself, of what has become *as* something which has become of this one's own becoming (to become having-along-with [*Mithaben*] and constantly having-anew [*Neuhaben*])." Having, in this sense, is preserving of one's own Dasein "*in one's achievements*. . . . The rhythm of one's own Dasein *is* in the preserving; at the same time, it *is* with such a preserving and belongs to it."[159]

Having, thus, "belongs to the innermost Dasein itself . . . as preserving and cultivating [*Pflegen*] one's own past and being there [*da sein*] with this preserving itself."[160] This Dasein-immanent (*daseinsimmanenten*) relationship of having is "culture" (*Kultur*), which Heidegger uses here synonymously with *Tradition*, stipulating that "it is from this being there with the preserving and cultivating of the past that the term history [*Geschichte*] gets its precise meaning."[161] More to the point, having history entails "relating to the past as *one's own*; 'preserving' more than remembering, recalling, or thinking of it; one's *own past plays into* one's own Dasein."[162] The historicity of Dasein's being-in-the-world means that understanding its temporality is prerequisite to understanding the historical world—a world that *is* because of Dasein's temporality, the primary phenomenon of which is the future (*Zukunft*).[163] This is about *Sorge*, "care" not in the sense of careful invested-dealing with useful things, but rather Dasein's attending to its being-toward-death with apprehensive concern for the future. As thrown into the world, Dasein exists authentically with resoluteness (*Entschlossenheit*), which is a distinctive mode of its self-interpreting disclosedness (*Erschlossenheit*) that allows for "the time-play-space [*Zeit-Spiel-Raumes*] of existence."[164] This resoluteness, with which Dasein is delivered back to itself (*zurück*), discloses current factical possibilities of authentically being-in-the-world; and it does so "*in terms of the heritage* [*Erbe*] that very resoluteness, as thrown, *takes over*."[165] Being "resolutely thrown" entails transformative repetition, a retrieving (*Wiederholung*) of a possibility of existence that has-been-there (*dagewesenen*). "Repetition," in this sense, "is explicitly handing down [*Überlieferung*]; that is to say, going back [*Rückgang*] into the possibilities of the Dasein that has-been-there."[166] On this, Heidegger is rather emphatic: "*Only a being that is essentially futural* [*zukünftig*] *in its being so that it is free for its death—that is to say, only a being that, as futural, is equiprimordially in the process of* **having-been** [*gewesend*]—*can, by handing down to itself the inherited possibility, take over its own throwness and be* **in the moment** [*augenblicklich*] *for 'its time.' Only authentic temporality* [*eigentliche Zeitlichkeit*], *which is at the same time finite, makes something like fate* [*Schicksal*], *i.e., authentic historicity* [*eigentliche Geschichtlichkeit*], *possible.*"[167]

In keeping with his flair for connotative play, Heidegger gives the German term *Schicksal* a precise meaning in contrasting relation to the term *Geschick*, which is etymologically related to *Geschichte* through common derivation from the Middle High German *geschicke*, meaning "event" (*Begebenheit*), "order/formation" (*Bildung*), or "pattern" (*Gestalt*). It is also related to the Middle High German *geshicket*, which is the participle of the verb *schicken*, meaning "to arrange [*anordnen*], set in order [*einrichten*]."[168] *Schicksal* has an overlapping etymology, being derived from the verb *schicken*. In idiomatic modern German, *Schicksal* and *Geschick* are synonymous, carrying the same connotation, which translates into English as "fate" or "destiny." Heidegger introduces a sharp differentiation, however, wherein *Geschick* connotes the collective "destiny" of the group or of Dasein as a member of the group, while *Schicksal* connotes the destiny of the resolute individual Dasein, which is its "fate." Dasein *is* its own fate in the sense of existing fatefully in the resoluteness it hands down to itself in anticipatorily running toward death, letting death become powerful in itself. By so becoming free for death, Dasein "understands itself in the superior power [*Übermacht*] of its own finite freedom . . . which 'is' only in its having chosen to make such a choice."[169] Nevertheless, because fateful Dasein is essentially being-in-the-world in being-with-others, its historizing-occurrence is a *historizing-occurrence-with* (*Mitgeshehen*) and is determined as destiny (*Geschick*), which is not *composed* of individual fates. Our individual fates have already been guided in advance in being-with-oneanother (*Miteinandersein*) in the same world and in our resoluteness for definite possibilities. In other words, our fate is determined by our destiny, which Heidegger says, "is the historizing-occurrence of community [*das Geschehen der Gemeinschaft*], of a people."[170] The point is further made: "The fateful destiny of Dasein in and with its '*Generation*' constitutes its complete, authentic happening."[171] He is expressly following Dilthey in using the Latinate *Generation* to denote "the relation of the contemporaneity of individuals," meaning the historicity of a generation, in relation to which each specificity-of-awhileness (*Jeweiligkeit*) of Dasein as mine is expressed.[172] The authentic retrieval of Dasein's fateful destiny is the appropriation of that historicity.

Accordingly, "whatever 'has a history' [*Geschichte hat*] is in the interconnection, the nexus of becoming."[173]

To *have a history* in this way is to simultaneously *make* such a history, to determine a *future* in the present. "What 'history' means here is an event and 'productive nexus [*Wirkungszusammenhäng*],'" Heidegger says, deploying another of Dilthey's terms, this one denoting the efficacy of life and the historical world understood as productivity prior to any causal or teleological analysis.[174] In this sense, the carriers of history, whether individuals, cultures, institutions, or communities, are productive systems capable of producing meaning and realizing purposes. Whatever is given as handed down (*Überlieferte*) is *historical* (*geschichtlich*). The upshot is that "history is the specific historizing-occurrence of existing Dasein happening in time, such that the occurrence, which in being-with-one-another is 'past' [*vergangene*] and, simultaneously, 'handed down' [*überlieferte*], continues to have effect."[175] We can say, then, resoluteness disclosing the current possibilities of being-in-the-world in terms of heritage is the handing down that is *Tradition*—which, of course, is precisely what the primitive does not have.

The primitive's not having history, however, discloses a paramount difficulty confronted especially in the beginning approach of an existential analytic of Dasein. The ontological difference, delineating between ontological problematics and ontical research, entails a desideratum that has long disturbed philosophy, but which it repeatedly fails to fulfill: "*Working-out the idea of a natural conception of the world.*"[176] The "wealth of knowledge about the remotest and manifold cultures forms of human Dasein" made available through ethnological interpretive collecting encourages the delusion that fulfilling the ancient philosophical desideratum is within reach.[177] Here lies the thrust of Heidegger's methodological caveat. Syncretistic comparison and classification of all human Dasein's diverse forms, subjecting the manifold to tabulation, does not guarantee a real understanding of what is being ordered. It was remarked earlier regarding Robert Allen's and John Lomax's proto-ethnological collecting, as well as the properly scientific ethnological work of Marcel Griaule and Michel Leiris, that the principle of collecting and ordering has its own content that is never found *in* the ordering, but is already presupposed *by* the ordering. Heidegger, of course, is not disparaging philosophy's long-held aspiration for a natural conception of the world. What he challenges is the way, in pursuit of that goal, the philosophical tradition has been fundamentally inattentive to the real problem of existence, a problem exacerbated by the presumption that putting together various pictures of the world will yield a genuine knowledge of the world. On the premise that the world itself is something constitutive *for* Dasein, the task of the existential analytic is to gain insight into Dasein's basic structures in order to achieve a proper conception of the world.

The issue presented with the primitive is about the relation between nature and the world, as well as the phenomenon of Dasein for which the world is and that exhibits in it. Having tradition qua having history is a function of Dasein's historicity, which, as we know, is a matter of ontological interpretation. The primitive has not yet achieved an ontological understanding of Being, has not yet properly objectified things in the world as distinguishable from the world. As we shall see momentarily, Heidegger considers this a flaw in signification, and so an interference in understanding Dasein's potentiality-of-being authentic. His remarking that it is customary to call history-less tribes and people "barbaric" takes us back again to Aristotle's asserting the capacity for talking ὀρθός λόγος (*orthós lógos*), *right principle-discourse*, is what articulates the distinction between civilized *man* (*andros*) and the other forms of *anthrōpos*, the quasi-human not fully out of nature and animality nor in civilization. For Aristotle, and the tradition of political, as well as ethical philosophy he inaugurated, this is the basis of political discourse. Yet, it is an ontological proposition whereby such well-speaking performs a rupture or break in the continuum of extent entities in the mode of Plato's ἁπλά διήγησις (*haplé diegesis*—which Shorey renders as "pure narration"), differentiating the human way of existence from the non-human.[178] Such narration is the instrumentality of the Supreme Good that both Lacan and Du Bois critique. Heidegger is elaborating on that tradition when he maintains that Dasein *is* in speaking. And this speaking is an articulation of temporality in the world, as is expressly set out in the first three of the eight fundamental structural characteristics of Dasein's own temporality enumerated in his 1924 Marburg Lecture, "Der Begriff der Zeit" (The Concept of Time). The first fundamental is that Dasein is the entity that is characterized as being-in-the-world (*In-der-Welt-sein*) in the sense of dealing and tarrying (*umgehen*) with, actively performing in while contemplating it. Second, along with this being-in-the-world, Dasein is being-with-one-another [*Mit-einander-sein*], that is to say, "having there [*dahaben*] the same world with others, encountering one-another, being with-one-another [*miteinander sein*] in the manner of being-for-one-another [*Für-einander-seins*]." It is the third characteristic, which draws from this being with-one-another in the world as a distinctive determination-of-being, that expressly concerns speaking and warrants full quotation:

> The fundamental way of Dasein's world, having it there with-one-another, is speaking [*Sprechen*]. Fully regarded, speaking is: one *gives* expression to oneself [*sich aussprechendes*] *with* another *about* something. Humanity's being-in-the-world plays itself out [*spielt sich ab*] predominantly in speaking. Aristotle already knew this. *Dasein's self-interpretation* [*Selbstauslegung*] is given in how it speaks in its world about the way of dealing with its

world. It says how Dasein specifically understands itself, as what it takes. In speaking-with-one-another [*Miteinandersprechen*], in the spreading around of talk [*herumspricht*], therein lies each specific self-interpretation of the present; it dwells [*sich aufhält*] in this conversation.[179]

Speaking, that is to say, discourse in itself, is temporal and how being-in-the-world "plays itself out" in the historizing-occurrence, the temporalizing of Dasein. This is what is meant in saying Dasein's historicity is the historicity of the world, that Dasein being-in-the-world is what is *primarily* historical. On that score, even Nature is historical—although, Heidegger tells us, it is so insofar as we speak of it as place, as a countryside landscape, an area of settlement and exploitation, a battlefield, or place of worship. It is not historical, however, when we speak of "natural history" (*Naturgeschichte*).[180] Because the transcendence of the world is temporally founded, what is historical is always already "objectively" there without being apprehended historiographically (*historisch*). So too with regard to "natural" calendar-time (*Zeitrechnung*), the marking of recurrence in earthly happenings under the same sky—the rotation of the earth in its orbit around the sun, attended by constantly returning cycles of biological, climatic, and geological processes. These may be experienced publicly by the artifice of ready-to-hand time pieces—from primitive sundials reckoning the sun's repeating progress across the sky to mechanical clocks that, while patterned on the cycle of day and night, reckon purely formulaic intervals, just for the sake of marking the pace of our passage. Yet all of that is grounded in Dasein's temporality, in its anticipatory-running-forward toward death, its future. Giving significance to the recurrences of nature, thereby caring (*Sorge*) about it, is what articulates "world-time" (*Weltzeit*), which is such "not because it is *present-at-hand* as an entity within-the-world, which it can never be, but because it belongs to the world [*zur Welt*]" as an expression of Dasein's existential-Being.[181] Insofar as all time is essentially Dasein, there is no nature-time or *natural* time except that it also belongs to the world. Indeed, it is grounded in the temporalizing temporality (*Zeitigung der Zeitlichkeit*) of Dasein; primordially, there is *only* world-time. The clock is the quotidian illustration of this as the material expression of an arithmetic that, while fundamentally related to nature, instructs us in new possibilities for a kind of time-measurement (*Zeitmessung*) relatively independent of the day and any explicit observation of the sky. Nature, understood ontologically and categorically in this way, is a limiting case of the existence of possible inner-worldly entities that Dasein can discover only in a definite mode of its own being-in-the-world.[182]

So, it is by way of the existential analytic of Dasein's being-in-the-world that something like the world and worldliness (*Weltlichkeit*) come into view. As we noted earlier, understanding the transcendence of Dasein is inextricably bound to the ontological investigation of the world, which, in turn, belongs to the existential analytic of Dasein itself as being-in-the-world in everydayness. And the point of departure for the analytic of the worldliness of Dasein is the *pragmata*, the ready-to-hand useful things (*Zeug*) encountered in our everyday careful invested-dealings in the nearby surrounding world. For our purposes, with respect to the relationship between nature, worldliness, and the primitive, we need not rehearse the full analysis of *Zeug*, just highlight some of the key characteristics that enable it to bring the world into view.

In accordance with Heidegger's reviving the Middle High German meaning, "a thing you 'pull to you' to do something," *Zeug* is essentially "something '*in-order-to* [*etwas um-zu*],'" in the sense of an *instrumentality*. Strictly speaking, there is no such thing as *an* instrument. A fundamental of the existence of a thing's instrumentality is its always belonging to a totality of useful-things (*Zeugganzes*), the context in which it can be what it is: ink to pen to paper to desk, and hammer to nail to board. When we pull something into use in-order-to, we pull its context along with it. There are various ways of in-order-to, such as serviceability, helpfulness, usability, and handiness, which constitute a totality of useful-stuff (*Zeugganzheit*).[183] Structurally, each and every in-order-to entails a referral (*Verweisung*) of something to something else that is exhibited in the instrument's readiness-to-hand (*Zuhandenheit*). The exhibition of readiness-to-hand is not grasped theoretically, but by a circumspection (*Umsicht*) that is all the more careful (*Besorgen*) for the immediacy of its dealings with things in use. *Zeug*, then, is not present-at-hand (*Vorhandenes*), an objectively occurring thing, but a referral to the activity of using things and all that entails—hence, "useful things" or "instruments."

Take note, with Heidegger's instruments, we have wandered back again into Aristotle's terrain, this time revisiting the precincts of τέχνη ποιητική (*technē poiētikē*). What he calls *Umsicht*, circumspection, can be equated with *technē* as *know-how-in-a-certain way*. And as with *technē*, the work (*Werk*), both in the sense of the thing produced (*Herzustellende*) and the activity, the *praxis*, of being at work (*das in Arbeit befindliche*), is always a using of something for something. Work, thus, bears the referential totality (*Verweisungsganzheit*) in which the instrument is encountered as useful thing, the *what for* (*Wozu*)—for instance, the shoe being produced for wearing in-order-to walk about, and the clock for telling time in-order-to set the rhythm of living. The work also refers to the material *of-which* (*Woraus*) it is produced: the work of producing shoes depends on leather, thread, and nails, which in turn are produced from hides and metal. The hides are taken from animals that are present-at-hand because, whether found in the wild or bred, they produce themselves. This referential totality also entails that entity *for-sake-of which* (*Worumwillen*) the what-for in-order-to is. The point is that the structure of the existence of what is ready-to-hand as instrument is determined by references (*Verweisungen*), and the working referential totality of useful things phenomenologically exhibits the surrounding-environment-of-nature (*Umweltnatur*), making nature accessible in the realm of useful things. This is not to suggest that the worldliness of the world is constituted or even consists of these things; rather, in their referentiality, they shed light on the presupposition of the world.

That presupposition is particularly lit up when three conditions obtain whereby the constitutive reference of the in-order-to gets disrupted. One such disturbance is when instruments become *conspicuous* (*Auffallen*) by being somehow no longer immediately useful and so un-ready-to-hand (*Unzuhandenes*). For instance, a pen is unusable when it has run out of ink; it now becomes, in circumscriptive comprehension, "an instrument-thing [*Zeugding*]," something present-at-hand in its being-ready-to-hand.[184] And that conspicuousness as something there without immediate use, having once been a useful thing, sharply illuminates just how much its utility is contingent on an order of referentiality articulated in relation to a presumed world. Another disturbance occurs when something that has been ready-to-hand gets mislaid. Because the instrument always belongs to a totality of useful things in relation to which it can be instrumental, when something becomes un-ready-to-hand because it is simply missing, then what is presently ready-to-hand becomes *obtrusive* (*Aufdringlichkeit*). For instance, when chalk is mislaid from the classroom blackboard, we become aware the board is an instrument-thing in the same sense as with the useless pen. The third disturbance is the un-readiness-to-hand of what was never useful—unlike the useless pen or missing chalk—being instead that which stands in the way of our careful dealings with useful things because it presents itself *within* the referential totality of instruments without belonging there. The disturbance stems from its not being what Heidegger calls relevant-together with (*Bewandtnis mit*) the ready-to-hand useful things in (*bei*) their instrumentality.[185] We might also say it lacks *involvement* within the totality. We are careful in the encounter with such an entity, by not letting it be as discovered, but by working on it to bring it into the totality or, failing that, set it aside or destroy it. This work brings to circumspection the initial *obstinacy* (*Aufsässigkeit*) of that which is ready-to-hand. Circumspection pays attention to the fact that it is pulling things to it as relevant-together in-order-to *on some grounds*; and that is referentiality. Each of the mentioned instances of un-readiness-to-hand precipitates a break in referentiality by drawing attention to the characteristic of presence-at-hand in what is ready-to-hand. This does not mean that readiness-to-hand is revealed to be ultimately grounded in presence-at-hand. Instruments are still not merely things found in the road, as it were. The structure of the existence of what is ready-to-hand as instrument is determined by the constitutive reference of the in-order-to (*Um-zu*) to a what-for (*Dazu*). In our average careful everyday dealings, the reference themselves are there, unobserved. But in a disruption of reference, the referentiality becomes explicit for circumspection—in the annoyance at the damaged or mislaid instrument, or the thing in the way of work.

This brings us to the crux of the matter in Heidegger's analysis of how readiness-to-hand as instrument illuminates the world and its worldliness. The ontical circumspect noticing of the reference to the particular what-for brings it, along with the whole context of the work, into view as "that wherein care (*Besorgen*) always already dwells." The context of useful thing (*Zeugzusammenhang*) is, thus, lit up; and not as something never seen before, but as a referential totality constantly sighted beforehand *in circumspection*, wherewith the world announces itself. It turns out that referential totality is constitutive for worldliness after all, not as the sum product of useful things, but as the activity of referentiality, the relational character of which Heidegger calls "signifying" (*bedeuten*). "In its familiarity with these relations, Dasein 'signifies [*bedeutet*]' to itself, primordially giving itself to understand its existence and potentiality-of-being with respect to being-in-the-world. The for-sake-of-which signifies an in-order-to that signifies a what-for that signifies a what-in [*Wobei*] of letting-something-be-relevant [*Bewandenlassen*], as well as the what-with [*Womit*] of relevance."[186] These relations are interlocked among themselves as a primordial totality of relational signification (*Bedeutsamkeit*), constituting the structure of the world in which Dasein as such always already is. The activity of signification is fundamental to worldliness, to discovering entities that are ready-to-hand in the world.

No wonder Heidegger says, "Signs [*Zeichen*] themselves, in the first instance, are *useful*-things [*Zeug*], the specific instrumental character [*Zeugcharakter*] of which consists of indicating [*Zeigen*]."[187] Indicating is a kind of referring, taken here in a pronouncedly formal sense to mean relate (*Beziehen*), whereby "being-a-sign-for something is formalized to a universal kind of relation"; so that "the sign-structure yields an ontological guideline for characterizing any entity whatsoever."[188] By Heidegger's analysis, "signs are not things that stand in an indicating relationship to another thing," *pace* Peirce, "but rather they are *instruments that explicitly bring a totality of useful things to circumspection so that the worldly character of what is ready-to-hand makes itself known at the same time*."[189] More succinctly put, "Signs always indicate 'wherein' one lives, what sort of relevance [*Bewandtnis*] there is."[190] Signs let what is ready-to-hand be encountered; more precisely, they let its context become accessible in such a way that our careful dealings with existence take on a sustainable orientation; and they do so by "taking over the 'work' of letting things at hand become conspicuous."[191] It is signs that become conspicuous, thereby preserving the inconspicuousness of the other instruments ready-to-hand. The activity of signification creates the circumspectly oriented accessibility of a totality of useful things (*Zeugganzen*) and the surrounding environment (*Umwelt*) in general.

It should be rather clear at this juncture that Heidegger's analysis of signification, *Bedeutsamkeit*, as constituting the world and its worldliness is what we have been referring to consistently throughout this work as *semiosis*, although it is not aligned with what is meant by *para-semiosis*. The sign's thingliness does not present a problematic to *para-semiosis* as it does to Heidegger's analysis of signification. We still need to extend our interrogation of *Bedeutsamkeit* (significance), however, before we can fully grasp what is at stake in the difference between it and *para-semiosis*.

PRIMITIVE THINGLINESS

Pushing ahead, it is of some significance to the interrogation that, in order to illustrate the preeminent role played by the activity of signification, of signs as instruments in everyday care for understanding the world, Heidegger turns once again to the primitive as heuristic, citing their "extensive use of such 'signs' as fetishes and magical charms [*auber*]." Or rather, he notes the temptation—again precipitated by the ethnological data—to turn to the primitive way of using fetishes and magical charms for geomancy and divination as indicative of an a-theoretical establishment of signs. That temptation is preempted, however, once it becomes clear, on closer examination, that interpreting fetishism and magic under the ontological guideline of the idea of signs is extremely insufficient for comprehending the kind of being-ready-to-hand (*Zuhandenseins*) of entities encountered in the primitive world. If we adhere to the idea of signs discovered in the phenomenological analysis of fundamental ontology, what can be said of the fetish is that it coincides with what it indicates. In fact, the fetish can represent what it indicates not only in the sense of replacing it, but in such a way that the fetish itself always *is* what is indicated. This remarkable coincidence is what excludes the fetish from being a true sign insofar as there has been no objectification of the fetish as an indicating-thing (*Zeigding*); that is, it has not yet been freed from what it indicates, and so has no referentiality, but rather is still completely absorbed in its existence so that a sign as such cannot be at all detached. "This means, however," Heidegger concludes, "that [primitive] signs are not at all discovered as instruments [*Zeug*], that, in the end what is ready-to-hand in-the-world does not have the kind of existence of instruments." He then says rather perfunctorily: "Perhaps this ontological guideline (readiness-to-hand and instrument) cannot provide orientation for an interpretation of the primitive world, let alone the ontology of thingliness [*Dinglichkeit*]."[192]

This is quite a statement in the immediate context of an ontological analysis of signification as the structure of the world and of signs as instrumentalities, in which the fetish is an illustration, provided by ethnology, of how signs indicate the sort of relevance of useful things wherein Dasein lives. We can take Heidegger to be saying here that, as far as the ontological analysis of signification is concerned, the fetish is conspicuous. Nor is it the case that the objectification of signs—which would detach the fetish from the existence of that being indicated—is missing, in the sense of having been mislaid. Were such the case, it would suggest the primitive is a degenerate Dasein. On the contrary for Heidegger, the primitive's heuristic value is precisely that it is a primordial rudimentary Dasein with preontological circumspective comprehension of the world. Objectification is simply not yet there within the primitive referential totality. In other words, the fetish is a methodological instrument in the ontological analysis that is relevant-together with—and I do mean *Bewandtnis mit*—ethnology. Recalling our previous discussion of the fetish with respect to Kant, Hegel, and Leiris, it is recognizably a sign in the referential totality of the theoretical human sciences, including philosophy, as well as ethnology—except that its conspicuousness as a sign, rather than preserving the inconspicuousness of philosophical and ethnological signification, which is the referential totality of ontological understanding, foregrounds their obtrusiveness. To be more precise and careful, ethnology records the primitive fetish in use as ontically relevant; that is to say, it records and reports the primitive's "factical careful letting something ready-to-hand *be* such and such *as* it is in the moment and *so that* it be such."¹⁹³ It then collects the fetish as an objective sign of that use, giving it relevance within the ontological referential totality of *Geisteswissenschaft*—and here let us render this as "the science of *Man*" rather than the conventional "human sciences." What the ontological interpretation cannot grasp, however, is the relevance of the fetish *for* the primitive. It cannot encounter it *as* the primitive does *in* the primitive's own terms. The primitive clearly lets the fetish be relevant ontically, which means that the primitive signifies, as do all modes of Dasein, and so the fetish must be construed as a sign entailing a dynamic semiosis beside the ontical. This, of course, becomes the focus of the symbolic anthropology where the primitive signification presents as something to be worked on in-order-to bring it into relevance within the *anthropological*—and emphasis here is on the Kantian sense of the term—account of man. Heidegger's statement aims to remark how that working-on foregrounds the obtrusiveness of the instruments of fundamental ontological analysis, as well as ethnology.

The ontological analysis encounters in the dynamic semiosis of the primitive something that cannot be read according to its interpretive guidelines of readiness-to-hand. But not only that, the conspicuousness of the "primitive," as a sign, exposes that there is something missing among the instruments of ontological analysis. Now, in Heidegger's formulation, this is something useful that has been mislaid—a misplacement that occurs with Plato's and Aristotle's inauguration of the philosophical project—exposing the obtrusiveness of the ontological analysis in addressing the very question of ontological thingliness. The problem exposed with the primitive fetish is one of ontological relevance, the presumptive "freeing of *everything* ready-to-hand as a thing ready-to hand, whether it is relevant in the ontic sense or whether it is such an entity that is precisely not relevant ontically."[194] Any authentic ontology of Dasein must also account for the primitive. This relates to Heidegger's disputing the relevance of mythical signification, specifically as exposited by Ernst Cassirer in his *Philosophy of Symbolic Form*, to Dasein's ontological analysis. Heidegger critiques Cassirer's account for failing to see that the primitive sign lacks referentiality precisely because it disregards the fundamental ontological question. He says, in what is meant to be a dismissal of philosophical anthropology *tout court*: "The essential interpretation of myth as a possibility of human Dasein remains random and directionless as long as it cannot be based on a radical ontology of Dasein in the light of the problem of being in general."[195] From the phenomenological perspective of the existential analytic, the primitive fetish is merely "a clumsy and crude conceptualization [*Begrifflichkeit*] of being-in-the-world whereby the sign has not yet been freed from what it indicates, but which can be of use positively for a genuine elaboration of the ontological structures of phenomena."[196] Heidegger's dismissal of philosophical anthropology notwithstanding, the primitive fetish, however clumsy and crude, is still a conceptualization of being-in-the-world. As such, it involves a present-at-hand circumspection, the opacity of which poses a serious problem of comprehension for the fundamental ontology. Accordingly, the existential analytical encounter with the primitive as a mode of Dasein compels an adjustment in the analytic so that it can account for the primitive Dasein's prehistorical (*vorgeschichtlichen*), preontological (*vorontologische*) circumspective understanding of existence, as well as the authentic historicity of advanced Dasein, if any viable account of the worldliness of the world is to be achieved. And as we already know, that adjustment, the thing that Heidegger asserted distinguished his project from Hegel's, is to reduce Dasein to temporality.[197]

Having tradition qua having history in heritage is a function of Dasein's authentic historicity. Primitives, having no tradition, no history in heritage, have no authentic Dasein, and so no reflective grasp of the ontological difference. In Heideggerian terms, the Dasein of the primitive tribe is preontological, but not in the sense referred to earlier, whereby their Dasein is a preconceptual understanding of Being, lacking interpretive orientation. Primitives are instantiations of a mode of being, the historizing-occurrence of which is ontologically incomprehensible. Remember that, in Heidegger's analysis, "history" (*Geschichte*) signifies the transformations and destinies (*Geschicke*) of human collectives (*Verbanden*) in time, which is distinguished from nature as *Geist* and culture. To the extent that, in the course of the fundamental ontological existential analysis, the issue with the primitive is about the relation between nature and the world, it turns out to be truly about particular limitations of *Geist* and culture. As a sign-instrument in the existential analysis of fundamental ontology, the primitive is not merely conspicuous, it is opaque. And it is not a passive opacity; that is to say, it is not merely a function of the limit of the ontological analytic in the way Heidegger casts it. Rather, the opacity is an effect of the primitive semiosis at work with the fetish. That semiosis presents to the ontological analytic as a sign indicating something is happening, is occurring, which the analytic can only glimpse at by way of the fetish but cannot grasp or comprehend into its ambit. We can say that the fetish-semiotics, *in its workings*, defies ontological analysis. This is not to suggest that it offers no ontological resistance, which seems to be how Heidegger construes its conspicuousness, as an ontic phenomenon that cannot be comprehended ontologically. Nor is it to suggest that fetish-semiosis resists ontological analysis. Rather, it is to say that it simply defies, or better put, "flies far away from" ontology.

We cannot lose sight of the fact it is primitive thinking as semiosis (*Bedeutsamkeit*) that is opaque to the ontological analytic. We can say, then, with respect to Heidegger's expressed heuristic, the primitive Zulu Negro, that the Negro "flies away"; and whatever articulation of cognizance and interiority happening in that flying is ontologically incomprehensible. Ethnographic data notwithstanding, there is little to nothing even fundamental ontology can say about the *Zulukaffern* that is meaningful beyond signing a limiting case (*Grenzfall*). *Negro* is the index of that limit the existential analytic simply cannot get beyond. This is the problematic limit to Heidegger's fundamental ontology Becker redresses with the paraontological analysis of the primitive *we*.

Keep in mind Becker's alignment of primitive mantic semiosis with mathematics is fundamental to his paraontological investigation. Along those lines, in the course of considering Cantor's theory of transfinite numbers, he notes that it prompts the ontological question, "What mode of temporality [*Zeitlichkeit*] is suited to these 'infinities' as specific phenomena?"[198] The question arises because Cantor's transfinite numbers indicate a temporality not in accord with either Aristotelian indefinite potentiality or the Euclidean definition of number as a plurality of units. It is a temporality "according to which no measurable (in the ordinary classical sense of counting) function can be exercised."[199] Becker calls this *historische Zeitlichkeit* (historical temporality), contrasting it with what he refers to as *nicht-historischen Zeitlichkeit* (nonhistorical temporality), but more often as *naturhafte Zeit* (natural time). When bifurcating temporality thusly, he claims that *historical* temporality equates with what Heidegger calls authentic temporality (*eigentlichen Zeitlichkeit*). In this usage, however, he disregards the distinction Heidegger makes between *Geschichte* and *Historische*. As we have already noted, when Heidegger uses the phrase *Naturzeit* or *naturhafte Zeit*, it is to assert there is no such time, and not that it is *nonhistorical*. On the contrary, "Even nature is historical."[200] The closest he comes to Becker's *nicht-historischen* is the cognate, *unhistorischen*, by which he means "nonhistoriological," as in without the science of historiology. Heidegger does, however, use two formulations meaning nonhistorical in Becker's sense: *nicht geschichtlich*, and *ungeschichtlich*. The first is used when he critiques Yorck's calling ontic entities nonhistorical [*nicht geschichtliche*] as a residual effect of the traditional philosophical ontology.[201] The second is used in reference to the absence of historiology in primitive cultures: "Nonhistoriological [*Unhistorische*] eras are not, as such, nonhistorical [*ungeschichtlich*]."[202] Nevertheless, disregarding Heidegger's usage is consonant with Becker's contending that the existential analytic loses sight of the ongoing role nature's original process (*Original-Vorganges*) plays in Dasein's being-in-the World by subsuming the eventfulness of that process to Dasein's temporalizing. Pressing on Heidegger's analysis, whereby there is no nature-time except insofar as it is grounded in the temporalizing temporality of Dasein, Becker expands the meaning of *nature* to include not only all existent inorganic as well as organic entities, "but also expressly the naturalistic existence [*naturhafte Sein*] of primitive peoples [*Naturvölker*], children (the 'naïve') and those humans driven by *instinctual life* [*Trieblebens*]." He further stipulates that "*primitive psyche*, therefore, is also part of nature. All these phenomena are characterized by their 'nonhistorical' temporality, and not in the sense of some empty form in which they are situated, but rather it is what makes (constitutes) them ontically."[203]

Extending the connotation of *nature* to include human psyche, or at least particular instantiations of human psyche, implies they are *essentially* constituted as natural in the very same sense Heidegger's Dasein is *existentially* constituted as historical. By equating historical temporality with authentic temporality, and the nonhistorical nature-time with the "time of Dasein in its everydayness [*Alltäglichkeit*]," Becker is taking issue with Heidegger's analysis of Dasein's "I am" in relation to *das Man* (the they).[204] Heidegger elaborates the nature of that relationship as the fifth fundamental structural characteristics of Dasein's temporality in the same passage we considered earlier from his "Der Begriff der Zeit" (The Concept of Time) lecture:

> Insofar as Dasein is an entity that I am and is simultaneously determined as being-with-one-another [*Mit-einander-Sein*], then for the most part and on average, I am not my Dasein by myself, but rather am so with the others as well [*mit den Anderen ebenso*]. No one is himself in everydayness. What someone is, and how someone is, is nobody [*ist niemand*]: no one, yet

everyone with-one-another [*miteinander*]. Everyone is not themselves. This Nobody [*Niemand*], by whom we ourselves are in lived in *everydayness* is "the *they*" ["*das Man*"]. They say, they hear, they are in favor of it, they care about [*besorgt*] it. The possibility of my Dasein lies in the obduracy [*Hartnäckigkeit*] of this dominion [*Herrschaft*] of this they [*dieses Man*], and out of this levelling the "I am" is possible.²⁰⁵

Becker is correct to understand this to mean that "the 'they,' of everydayness is what authentic time does not have; that is to say, this 'they' is representative of the non-historical life of Dasein."²⁰⁶ We know from *Being and Time* that the being of Dasein is stretched along between, that Dasein is in every case what it can be between birth and death, and in the way in which it is its possibility. While inauthenticity (*Uneigentlichkeit*) and authenticity (*Eigentlichkeit*) are two vectors of possibility, *being-possible* (*Möglichsein*) is an existentiale of Dasein, pertaining to Dasein's potential-for-being (*Seinkönnen*) toward itself, for the sake of itself. "Mineness [*Jemeinigkeit*] belongs to any extent Dasein as the precondition that makes authenticity and inauthenticity possible. Dasein exists in one or the other of these modes, or it is modally undifferentiated [*Indifferenz*]."²⁰⁷

Yet, if the self-expression of "I am" is meaningful *only* in all this careful talking with-one-another about the world that constitutes the world, two questions present themselves. The first is: How does Dasein understand itself as a self at all? The second is: *Who* is it that Dasein is in its everydayness? The question of *how* is best addressed in relation to *who*. The question of *who* relates to the totality of relational signification or referentiality, which constitutes the worldliness of the world in which Dasein always already is in its everydayness. The *who* is all about referentiality, which is to say Dasein's being in referential relation toward entities encountered within-the-world, including entities that are neither ready-to-hand useful things (*Zeug*) nor present-at-hand objective things (*Dingen*), but rather Dasein-like others that "*are also there with it.*"²⁰⁸ While the assertion that it is "I myself" who in each case Dasein is, is ontically obvious, it is not clear that its mere ontical content prompts an ontological interpretation, or even if it does proper justice to the stock of phenomena belonging to everyday Dasein. It could be that the "'who' of everyday Dasein just is not the 'I myself.'"²⁰⁹ In the context of an existential analytic of factical Dasein, the question, "who I am," is reevaluated as referencing "a noncommittal *formal indicator*"; which means that its givenness is not indubitable but structurally contingent, so that an isolated *I* is not initially, nor is it ever given. Yet, even if the *they* are already there with *I* in being-in-the-world, and if this is ascertained phenomenally, that still is not obviously given. Heidegger's task becomes, then, "to make the nature of this Dasein-with [*Mitdaseins*] in nearest everydayness phenomenally visible, and to interpret it in an ontologically appropriate way."[210] A requisite to the pursuit of this task is recognizing that the world of Dasein is always one that *I* shares with others. It is a *with*-world (*Mitwelt*), such that, "being-in [*In-Sein*] is being-with [*Mitsein*] others. Even the innerworldly being-in-itself [*Ansichsein*] is being-there-with [*Mitdasein*]."[211] We keep encountering this *being-with* in nearly every stage of the existential analytic because it is an essential characteristic of Dasein, primordial with its being; in Heidegger's terms, it is an *existentiale*. In this respect, *with* is used existentially and not categorically, meaning the Dasein-with of others is encountered in terms of what is ready-to-hand as being-there-also (*Auch-da-sein*) *in working referentiality*, and not as one of the present-at-hand human-things (*Menschendinge*).[212] Even when no others are ontically present-at-hand or perceived, Dasein is being-with in the world because being-with is not based on the occurrence together of several subjects. In other words, *I* and the *others* are being-with-one-another (*Miteinandersein*) in the referential totality of signification constituting the everyday surrounding world (*Umwelt*) of Dasein. All said and done, "the others are encountered in the everyday world as what they are; and they *are* what they do."[213] The question remains, however, for us as well as Becker: Who is *they*?

THE THEY OF PRIMITIVE WE

By Heidegger's account, in everyday being-with-one-another, Dasein is in subjection (*Botmäßigkeit*) to others; its everyday possibilities-of-being (*Seinsmöglichkeiten*) are at the discretion of others, not any specific or definite others, but any other whatsoever. These others are those *who* are there immediately in everyday being-with-one-another, those *who* one belongs to in everyday existence, enhancing their power by constantly caring about whether or how one differs from them. Heidegger calls such caring *Abständigkeit* (distantiality), which inclines one to minimize the distance between oneself and the others by subtle coercion or cooption. Such coercion or cooption is most powerful when one is being constantly shaped by it unconsciously, which is what Heidegger means when he says: "The only decisive thing about the others is their inconspicuous domination [*übernommene Herrschaft*], which Dasein as being-with has already taken on unawares."[214] That dominion gets obscured by calling those who are there immediately in everyday being-with-one-another the *others*. But by *others*, "We do not mean everyone else but me—those over against whom 'I' stands out. They are rather those from whom, for the most part, one does not distinguish oneself—those among whom one is also."[215] Insofar as the others are indefinite, are not these ones or those ones, not anyone, we refer to them "in the neuter as the *they* [*Man*]."[216] *They* is averageness, mediocracy (*Durchschnittlichkeit*), which is related to Aristotle's μέσον (*méson*), "mean"; it is the normal proper way of acting, *comme il faut*. By this measure, *they* prescribes what may and may not be ventured. Whatever is primordial and archaic becomes glossed as something that is well known, whereas, that which is exceptional, emerging in struggle with the norm, is something to be manipulated and its verve dissipated. *They* is there in a nebulous constancy. It is the *nobody* (*Niemand*) that is everybody that is answerable for everything— "they do this, they say that"—to which Dasein has already consigned itself in being-among-one-another (*Untereinandersein*).[217] *They*, not *I myself*, is the *who* of Dasein; it is there along-side (*bei*) Dasein in the everydayness of its environing world, and not as something present-at-hand, but rather as an existentiale belonging to Dasein's positive primordial constitution. The particular Dasein, the *I*, is dispersed into the *they* in its everydayness, meaning "the self of everyday Dasein is the *they-self* [*Man-selbst*]," which is the personification of *they*.[218]

Regarding person, Heidegger refines Husserl's and Scheler's phenomenological interpretation of personal-being (*Personsein*), but especially Scheler's. What is worked through from Scheler is the differentiation of the transcendental subject of reason, the *I* that acts according to certain laws of logic. Person, in contrast, is the immediately experienced unity (*Einheit*) of living-through (*Erlebens*) all possible acts (*Akten*). Existentially, such acts are experienced only in the performance (*Vollzug*) of the act itself; and it is in the course of action that they are given in reflection.[219] As Scheler says: "Person is given as a performer [*Vollzieher*] of intentional acts bound together by the unity of meaning. . . . Acts are performed [*vollzogen*], person is the act-performer [*Aktvollzieher*]."[220] In a manner informing Heidegger's distinction between the *I myself* of Dasein and the *they-self*, Scheler differentiates between the *individual-person* (*Einzelperson*), and the collective or *group-person* (*Gesamtperson*). The *group-person* is neither a composition of individuals or the resulting synthesis of the interaction between individuals; it is not a construction at all, but rather is a performance of lived reality constituted in the referential totality of living-with-one-another (*Miteinandererleben*). Since that totality is constituted in the living-with-one-another of persons, and each of these persons, as such, "constitutes the concrete act-center [*konkrete Aktzentrum*] of living-through this living-with-one-another, their 'consciousness-of' [*Bewußtsein-von*] is always included in the consciousness-of a total finite person as an action, and by no means a transcendent to it."[221] Along these lines, *they* personified, *they-self*, is an expression of Dasein's referentiality within a totality-of-significations (*Bedeutungsganze*).[222] Dasein's being familiar with itself as *they-self* means *they* prescribe the way of being-in-the-world, and the way of interpreting being-in-the-world. "*They* articulates the referential context of signification, which *they-self* personifies,"[223] in other words, the symbolic order.

Heidegger goes along with Scheler's postulate that the differentiation of consciousness and its dispersal into *they* is not a bodily determination any more than it is transcendental, so he pays little heed to the bodiliness, let alone the fleshliness of Dasein. In fact, he argues neutrality toward the body is requisite for a phenomenology aiming at an existential analytic of Dasein transcending and so disclosing the essentialities of existence in its everydayness. In a very real sense, fundamental ontology requires conscientiously turning the gaze away from the body so as to avoid getting embroiled in the contestation of Cartesian dualism and empiricist determinism. Rather than attempting a resolution, as did Kant with his transcendental critique, Heidegger's tactic is to simply pass over the problematic of the body altogether. There is the well-probed statement in *Being and Time*, a relative clause really that is all the more vexing because of its cavalier tones, where, in the course of investigating the orientation characterizing Dasein's spatiality, out of which arise the fixed directions of right and left, expressed through the instruments of signs, Heidegger says: "Dasein's spatialization in its 'bodiliness' [*Leiblichkeit*], which entails a problematic of its own not to be treated here, is also marked out in accordance with these directions."[224]

Bodiliness aside, when Heidegger says *they* "has various possibilities of concretion as a characteristic of Dasein [and] the extent to which its dominance becomes compelling and explicitly expressed can change historically,"[225] he is marking not only what we might call the cultural specificity of *they*, but also that there is a continuum of possibilities. And given the distinction he makes between the *they-self* and the authentic self of Dasein—the self that, differentiating itself from the *they*, takes itself in hand—this is a developmental continuum. What needs underscoring here is that the *they-self* is *divisible* in its being dispersed into the *they*, whereas the particular Dasein that, taking hold of itself, frees itself from absolute subservience to *they*, is *indivisible*; it is called to consciousness of its singularity. We shall have occasion momentarily to revisit this question of divisible versus indivisible person and explore is significance with respect to *poiēsis in black* as *para-semiosis*. As far as Heidegger's existential analytic is concerned, there is a continuum of historical possibilities, along which the points where Dasein is least subservient to *they* are the points of authentic and so advanced Dasein; and the points where *they* is most dominate are those of the more primitive and so inauthentic Dasein. In each instance, *they* is implicated in the process of the formation of Dasein as an individual self-relating entity, the individuation occurring with *being* as stretched between birth and death, whereby *I* differentiates itself from an undifferentiated mass of extent entities and so is authentically. In the case of authentic Dasein, that differentiation is being-toward-death: "*Authentic Being-toward-death—that is to say, the finitude of temporality—is the concealed* [*verborgene*] *basis* [*Grund*] *of Da-*

sein's historicity."[226] Death, we are told, is Dasein's ownmost possibility; and in being toward this possibility, Dasein discloses its own ownmost potentiality-for-being (*Seinkönnen*), whereby its very existence is the issue. But, when Heidegger then says that in this being-toward-death, Dasein is "wrenched away from the 'they,'" manifesting the distinctive possibility of its own self, he means that it is wrenched from absolute subservience to the *they*. And this wrenching is something Dasein does itself by heeding the call (*Ruf*) of consciousness to its self. The call passes over (*übergeht*) the *they* of the *they-self*, appealing only to the self. In passing over the *they*, the call diminishes its significance, thereby depriving the self of this refuge of accommodation, bringing it to itself. The *self* is summoned (*angerufen*) to itself as unrelated (*unbezügliche*) to *they*. Not in the sense that it is forced inward on itself, closing itself off from the external world. "The tendency of the call is not such as to put the summoned self on trial; rather it calls Dasein forth ('ahead of itself') into its ownmost possibilities, as a summons to its ownmost *potentiality*-for-being-its-self."[227] They may be passed over and diminished by the call of consciousness, but it does not disappear altogether. Granted, Dasein, in resolute anticipation toward-death, can be authentically itself only if it makes this possible of its own accord, projecting itself upon its ownmost potentiality-for-being rather than upon the possibility of the *they-self*. The more nonrelationally (*unbezüglicher*) Dasein hears the call of consciousness—that is, the less it is distorted by "what is fitting and accepted"—the more authentic is the understanding of its ownmost *potentiality*-for-being. Again, through this process, the particular Dasein becomes singularly indivisible to itself. Yet, paradoxically, because *they* is a positive existentiale of Dasein's constitution, it has a share in conditioning the possibility of any existence whatsoever. It is interpolated in the call.

This interpolation of *they* in the process of Dasein's individuation is what Becker seeks to emphasize in his paraontology, bearing in mind it is an aspect of what Heidegger refers to as Dasein's heritage (*Erbe*), which circumscribes as well as preconditions the potentiality-for-being. In Becker's assessment, however, Heidegger overstates the extent of authentic Dasein's nonrelationality in order to underscore the indivisibility of the authentic Dasein that is free for death; and over emphasizing the specific-awhileness of my Dasein and its being-in-the-future (*Zukünftigsein*) precludes any genuine second coming (*Wiederkunft*), in the theological sense of *parousia*, the Second Advent of Christ.[228] What distinguishes nature-time from historical time is precisely "the existence of the possibility of the return of the same [*Wiederkehr des Gleichen*], the self-recurring [*Sich-Wiederholens*] same event."[229] *Wiederholung*, "repetition," in Heidegger's analytic means that things always come pointedly to my Dasein in its distinctive awhileness; they may be handed down as possibilities but can never recur in the exact same way, because then they would unequivocally lose their distinctiveness. Strictly speaking, then, the category of the same is precluded in historical time, in which there is "only the identical [*Nämliches*] . . . in the strict sense."²³⁰

This distinction between the identical (*Nämliches*) and the same (*Gleiches*) is central to Becker's bifurcation of temporality and subsequently his paraontological investigation of the primitive. He draws it on etymological grounds, citing as his authoritative source Hermann Ammann's *Die menschliche Rede* (Human Speech), according to which the nominative neuter *Nämliches* is a declination of the adjective *nämlich* that—like its English-language cognate, *namely*—derives from the substantive, *Name*, connoting distinct individual designation.²³¹ *Gleiches*, on the other hand, is a nominalization of the adjective *gleich* (from the Old German *galeiks* = having an identically matching [*übereinstimmenden*] body [*Leib*], "having the same texture"), connoting *equality*, which Becker emphasizes by expressly correlating it with the Greek ὁμοειδές (*homoeidés*), which is usually translated into German as *Geleichartigkeit*, a feminine substantive meaning similarity, uniformity, analogy, and homogeneity. "The relationship of 'identity' [*Nämlichkeit*] . . . in its full meaning applies only to humans," Ammann further reports; so that "the ultimate meaning of the identity in objects, as in animals, is *always related* to humans, in the role that 'this' object has played in my life. . . . The unity of the object, that which allows its identification, *ultimately rests* [*ruht*] *in the unity of the self that knows itself as identical*."²³² Supported thus by Ammann, Becker states: "This holds true (with the consciously endowed human being). The primitive (early human [*frühmenschliche*] thinking) does not yet know the identity of the person."²³³ The parentheses sign a qualification with distinction. Identity is not true with every type of human, just with the type that is self-conscious of its personhood. To the extent that personhood is a characteristic of Dasein being-in-the-world, then the distinction of types of human being is made along lines of temporality. Construing these etymological determinations of *Nämliches* and *Gleiches* as quasi-ontological, Becker sees reflected in them a contrast between the anticipatory-running-forward futural temporality, identity, and the cyclical temporality of the return of the same. This contrast, in turn, reflects "the same basic contradiction between the historical and the non-historical temporalities," which is recognized as being "between '*Geist*' and 'nature.'"²³⁴ He is expressly thinking of Hegel when he claims the historical as the "temporality of the mind [*Zeitlichkeit des Geistes*]" and is tracking a connection between the *Phänomenologie des Geistes* and Heidegger's project in *Sein und Zeit*.²³⁵ Insofar as historical time is worldly, then the hermeneutic analysis of Dasein's historicity is an analysis of spirituality (*Geistigkeit*). Moreover, what Heidegger refers to as the rhythm (*Rhythmus*) of nature-time is not such because it *belongs* to the world; nor is it *merely* that limiting case of the existence of possible entities within-the-world. The appearance of natural time does not occur exclusively as within-the-world, but is felt as a cosmic primal phenomenon, chiefly in the directly perceived rhythm where natural temporality is unveiled in its proper nature.

The underlying claim being made is that Heidegger's analysis of nature belonging to the temporality of Dasein, to the historical world of Dasein, leaves us in the dark about nature's own essence (*Eigenwesen*) and the role that it continues to play in human being. And Becker means Heidegger's historical world of Dasein leaves out the Earth. In asserting the primitive does not yet know the identity of the person, however, he is claiming there is a nonhistorical temporality of human existence, which, not being an expression of Heidegger's sense of Dasein's *historicity*, is earthly. More pointedly, the existential analysis of Dasein alone cannot adequately account for the fullness of human temporality. Doing that requires an improvement (*überbieten*) on Heidegger's investigation, the aim of which is to augment his analysis of human existence as futural possibility with natural necessity. And this precisely is at play in the distinction between the temporality of anticipatory-running-forward (*Vorlaufen*) of Heidegger's Dasein and the return of the same (*Wiederkunft*) of nature-time, as well as the contrast between *Nämlichkeit* and *Gleichheit*. In both cases, time is a manner of *principium individuationis*, individuation. As already noted, nature-time allows for the recurrence of exactly the same (ὁμοειδές, *omoeidés*) "at different periods."[236] Even though *exact* equality is never realized, it is, Becker claims, ideally possible; that is to say, "One can think exactly the same recurrence. A natural process can be directly characterized in terms of time as a timeline, which means that a precise recurrence is essentially possible."[237] Approaching this producing of a purely periodic process as a question of memory, in light of then recent psychological and ethnological research by Rudolph Jaensch and Lucien Lévy-Bruhl, Becker claims that "primitive, natural temporal form appears as the pictorial [*bildhafte*] repetition of a past situation and situation-chain [*Situationskette*] (which, like a film, can repeatedly 'roll on')."[238] What matters most is the eidetic image, which can account for "the tremendous memory of primitives (literal recitation of long epics, recognition of all the details of a long, confusing path, etc.) in terms of a 'rewinding' [*Wiederabrollen*] of the original process."[239] The schematic form of this eidetic memory, which Becker likens to the Platonic doctrine of ἀνάμνησις (*Anamnesis*, remembrance), "is itself natural-temporal, and individuates by isolating quite identifiable, no longer distinguishable objects."[240]

The continued prevalence of natural temporality among so-called primitive people is adduced to mark its ontical perpetuation in humans. "Naturam expellas furca, tamen usque recurret," Becker says, quoting Horace: "You may drive out nature with a pitchfork, yet she still will hurry back." Indeed, the structure of historical time itself proves to be a twofold: a uniform formal schema, the time-character of which itself actually accords with nature-chronology; and a completely unschematized creation, which is at the same time a perpetual dying. The question this poses to Heidegger's explication of human existence as time is: Where does the formal come to share in historical temporality? Heidegger's answer is, as Becker paraphrases it: "In the self-conscious anticipatory-running-forward to its own past that lets Dasein be totally beside itself [*bei sich selbst stehen*] in the midst of the noise of everyday life."[241] If that is so, then schematic, natural moment does not play any role in the temporality of the individual, which is precisely what Becker contests. It may be true that every single historical individual dies only once as an individual; but that individual also knows itself as a link in the chain of generations, which is drawn up as a formal scheme for any number of succeeding generations. "It is precisely here that the natural element in the 'chain of procreations' [*Kette der Zeugungen*] plays a part. The name (*generatio*) itself indicates this," Becker says, adding: "The natural moment in the temporality of the historical development of a group of people is thus due to the natural part of this group itself, which always has something of the Heideggerian 'they' to it."[242] Because the individual is interpolated with *they*, the schematic moment is never strictly a referring to the reiteration of awhileness; it is not a kind of formal display in the Heideggerian sense, but is rather a juxtaposition or interdependence, the very phenomenon of the "chain" (*Kette*), in the Dedekindian sense. When considering the lives of several individuals in Heidegger's way, we may discern a formal-schematic analogy in their relation to death and time; but this analogy never leads to a juxtaposition that somehow eliminates the futurity, the obsession with the temporality of the individual. What we arrive at is the understanding that in death all are equal; "Through this equality [*Gleichheit*], the historical time 'individuates' [*individuiert*] the individual, isolating him, making impossible his comparison to others with regard to the 'what' of his qualitative peculiarities: his rank, or value, etc."[243] The common destiny of dying does not alleviate the individual's demise as a historical being. In the existential analytic, that ending "does not signify Dasein's being-at-an-end (*Zu-Ende-sein*), but rather being-toward-the-end (*Sein zum Ende*) of this entity."[244] Dasein does not discover itself fulfilled at the end, which would raise a whole series of investigations about whether still another existence is possible "after death," or whether Dasein "lives on" or "outlasts" itself and is "immortal." Bodily demise may be an ontical certainty—a phenomenon of life in general, "whatever is begotten, born, and dies," to which Dasein considered as a biological and physiological entity belongs—but dying is an ontological way of being whereby Dasein is *toward* its death. "As soon as a man comes to life he is straightway old enough to die [*sterben*]."[245] The existential interpretation of death is the foundation for any investigation of death that is biographical or historiological, ethnological or psychological.

In this case, what is meant, Becker asks, by human existence [*Dasein*]? The question aims to cast doubt on the prioritizing of death over birth in Heidegger's existential analytic of Dasein's process of individuation. Being-born is also a possibility for Dasein, that in the process of self-understanding, Dasein is being-toward-birth as well as toward-death. This concept of *being-bornness* (*Geborenwerden*) is expressly "the metaphysical counterpart to Heidegger's guiding fundamental-ontological concept of existential 'throwness-in-the-world' [*Geworfenheit*]," a concept Becker reads to mean that "existing man is powerless on his own grounds, having neither skill [*Können*] or knowledge [*Wissen*]."[246] In contrast, *Geborenwerden* means not being created out of nothing, which Becker calls "paratranscendence realized," emphasizing that "paratranscendence is above all the natural (the given in nature), wherever it appears."[247] Tracing the German *Natur* back etymologically to the Latin *natura*, which stems from *natus*, as well as the archaic *gnatus*, "to be born, arisen," which he construes as stemming from the Greek γένος (*genos*) and γένεσις (*genesis*), Becker says: "Birth is a primordial concept, derived from the myth of origin, the *Theogony*."[248] The natural man knows intuitively about birth and origin as a primordial phenomenon, which like all primordial phenomena, can ultimately be grasped *only* intuitively. Birth, Becker maintains, determines the existence of the unbroken man (*ungebrochenen Menschen*), which is how he references the primitive. More precisely, birth determines the mode of existence (*Existenzweise*) of man, as long as he is unbroken. The paraontological investigation, thus, discovers "where basic experiences, such as belonging to a certain nationality, a certain race and the native landscape have their place."

Having postulated nationality, race, and natal geography as universally basic human experience, he continues:

> What becomes apparent in these basic experiences is the ancient maternal powers of the blood and the earth [*des Blutes und der Erde*], which have always been mythically related. This is the earth as Sophocles characterizes it in a choral part of his *Antigone* . . . "Earth, the highest of the gods, the everlasting, inexhaustible." This is also the blood, that apparent material force, which, in truth, is the strongest mass-shaping and formative force, "beating out" the types of man, the fundamental forms of what is possible for man to became in reality. Blood and the race combined, are . . . always . . . realized in organic procreation, always determining the γένος [*génos*], the origin, the εἶδος [*eidos*], the appearance. From here the unbroken man gains his existence [*sein Dasein*].[249]

Natural unbroken man derives his power from blood and soil straightforwardly, and not at all in the manner of the existential paradox determined by thrownness-in-the-world. To equate human being with thrownness-in-the-world as transcendence, Becker maintains, is a falsification of the concept of the natural human, which paraontology rectifies by regaining knowledge of the grounding of being prior to thrownness. Human beings are not thrown into the world projecting the nothingness of death, but rather are born into the world projected in blood and soil. In the paraontological investigation, space (*Raum*), the specific space on earth where biological birth occurs, not time is of paramount significance in the essential character of authentic human existence.

Becker extrapolates his blood and soil argument for birth over thrownness from the philosophical anthropology of Ludwig Ferdinand Clauss, another of Husserl's students. Clauss, who, like Heidegger and Becker, allied himself with National Socialist ideology, applied phenomenology to anthropology in the study of what he called race psychology (*Rassenseele*).[250] Repudiating the narrowly physiologically based race theories of other Nazi ideologues, such as Hans F. K. Günther and Eugen Fischer, he uses Scheler's phenomenological investigations of empathy in service of a rather Kantian anthropology, according to which geography, climate, and terrain determine psychology and lead to distinct racial characteristics: a people's collective psychology and world-view (*Weltanschauung*), their *Geist*, is constituted in the interaction with its own particular landscape.[251] In the taxonomy of Clauss's geo-determined psychological theory of race, there are desert peoples and forest peoples, people living in open expanses, for whom space is infinite, such as the Nordic, and peoples who live in more restricted horizons. While not reducing racial characteristics to the body, Clauss maintained that the psychical racial form is essentially in accord with the bodily form as a matter of style, which is determined by the ancestral physical environment. A single-minded, pure-minded psyche needs a body of the same lines in order to be able to express itself according to its style. In Clauss's terms, this is "a psycho-somatic configuration [*seelisch = leibliche Gesamtgestalt*], which is, in this sense, a 'consummate' and pure style."[252] Accordingly, the openness of Nordic landscape determines the essence of Nordic psyche, which is to move through space unhindered, to penetrate and dominate the world. In deploying Clauss's anthropological race psychology, Becker presses the point on the two problematics stymying existential analytic: the body and the primitive semiosis, both of which Heidegger passes over in order to secure the integrity of the analytic. The problematic of the body is passed over as not being a concern for fundamental ontology, but rather for the metaphysics of Dasein, which takes up the question of what man is, the investigation of which Heidegger called in passing *Metontologie* ("metontology").[253]

As has already been noted, the problematic of primitive semiosis presents as an opacity fundamental ontology cannot penetrate. It is not possible for the ethnologist to enter into the primitive self without interpreting it according to their own system of referentiality, which fails to extend beyond the ethnocentric grasp—the primitive *they-self* and *I myself* becoming simply the *other-self* for the ethnologist. Heidegger was somewhat emphatic about the opacity of the primitive, specifically the Negro thinking, even for, or particularly for, the ethnologist. In his analysis of the structure of lived-experience (*Erlebnisstruktur*), he argues that the meaningfulness of the experience of things is environmental (*Umweltliche*); that is to say, it is determined by the totality of referentiality handed as heritage, the world toward which Dasein transcends. To that point, he gives in evidence the unscientific (not: uncultured) *Senegalneger* (Senegalese Negro), who, when suddenly transplanted here, encountering a lectern for the first time, "sees it not as a mere something [*bloßes Etwas*] that is there, but something 'about which he knows nothing' [*mit dem er nichts anzufangen weiß*]."[254] His heuristic turns on the distinction between being unscientific (*nichtwissenschaftliche*) and uncultured (*kulturlose*). The Senegalese is cultured, is the subject of an environing-world, the determining characteristic of which is fetishistic magic and not mathematical science. In contrast, Becker maintains that mathematics and the natural sciences arise from the archaic arts of divination (μαντική, *mantikē*) and magic, postulating a developmental continuum from primitive divination to mathematics. So that when he says the mathematician and naturalist are closer to nonhistorical, natural time, he is remarking a resonance between primitive semiosis and mathematics, between magical signs and mathematical signs, thereby suggesting it is indeed possible to understand primitive signification. The primitive exhibits, in his magical signs, the fundamental natural process whereby world and earth are codetermined, and the psyche is embodied.

With respect to embodiment, Becker, à la Clauss, understands that the substance of man is *Geist* as the synthesis of soul and body, that the soul of a people, which determines the character and quality of their intelligence, is delimited by the body through which it is manifest. Becker has some truck with Heidegger in this, as can be discerned in remarks Heidegger made when distinguishing between Dasein and Cassirer's concept of *Aktionsraum* (space-for-action). Expressly stating that what he calls Dasein is not codetermined essentially by *Geist*, he then says: "Rather, what matters is the original unity and the immanent structure of the relatedness [*Bezogenheit*] of a human being who is, so to speak, bound in a body. And with that boundedness in the body, [Dasein] is in a particular bond with entities, in the midst of which it finds itself."[255] Dasein's finding itself bonded with entities is not that of *Geist* looking down, but is that of being thrown in the midst of entities as free, carrying out an incursion, a break-in—*Einbruch* Heidegger calls it—into existence that is always historical (*geschichtlich*) and as such accidental, so that the highest form of existence for Dasein can only be traced back to very few and rare moments of the duration between life and death. Heidegger's description here of Dasein turns on its head the mythical tale in Plato's *Timaeus*, according to which, in forming the cosmos as intelligence (νους, *nous*), soul (ψυχή, *psyche*), and body (σῶμα, *sóma*), the Demiurge creates soul as the essential vehicle for intelligence *before* the body. Pressing the point, however, Becker adheres to a raciological taxonomy of the flesh (blood) that delimits person to the body. Not only does body come before soul, but it determines the coherence and singularity of soul. What's more, in emphasizing the determinative bodily delimitation of psyche, paraontology also adheres to Clauss's conception of person as the expression of a racial type (*Rassentypus*), a geo-environmentally determined style (*Stiltypus*) of human being thus disputing Heidegger's subordination of nature to historicity with its resultant disarticulation of world from earth. Accordingly, Becker disputes whether we can call the natural way of living Dasein in the terminologically fixed sense of Heidegger's existential analysis. In his own gesture at Nietzschean philological play, he retrieves the Middle High German term *wesen*, meaning "to exist essentially," and proposes the coinage *Da-wesen* (*there-essentially*) in lieu of *Dasein*, or as he writes it, *Da-sein*.[256] The paramount question becomes, then, not about the facticity of human existence, but the essence of human existence; more precisely, it is about human "*essencing essence* [*wesendes Wesen*]."[257] With this shift, Heidegger's claim to the fundamental understanding of ontology is adjusted. Becker glosses the ontological difference discovered by the existential analytic as "nothing more than the transcendence of being beyond entities," which he takes to be the fundamental principle of ontological heterogeneity of psyche and body, expressed formulaically as: "*Being* [*Das Sein*] *surpasses* [*übertrifft*] *existent entities*."[258] *Da-wesen* connotes the opposite of heterogeneity. The fundamental principle of existing essentially is "paraontological equivocity [*paraontologische Gleichung*]," expressed formulaically as: "*Essence* [*Das Wesen*] *is identical with entities* [*dem Wesenden*]."[259] Furthering the contrast with Heidegger's concept of the ontological difference, Becker calls the nondifferentiation of essence and entities *paraontologische Indifferenz* (paraontological indifference), maintaining that "natural-essence [*Naturwesen*] is only paraontologically and no longer ontologically determinable."[260]

We come, then, to the critical point in recounting Becker's originary elaboration of paraontology as a corollary improvement on Heidegger's fundamental ontology. It is all about embodiment. More exactly, it is about racialized embodiment. Indeed "Transzendenz und Paratranszendenz" can be read as the first of Becker's two published efforts to make Heidegger's existential analytic be more robustly and expressly raciological. The second of these is his 1938 essay, "Nordische Metaphysik" (Nordic Metaphysics), where he explicitly charges Heidegger's analytic with being unable to account for *das Volk*—read, "race"—and the state; then citing the Nazi philosopher Hans Heyse's work, *Idee und Existenz*, he goes so far as to assert the superiority of pure Nordic metaphysics over classical Greek. The magical origins of mathematics notwithstanding, Becker adopts Clauss's theory of person as the geo-environmentally determined expression of a racial type (*Rassentypus*) to postulate that philosophy and scientific discovery are distinctive to the Nordic psyche and impossible for the primitive. And he is rather explicit about it, proclaiming that "the true unspoilt Nordic researcher will never acknowledge that the magic-believing world-view of a Congo Negro in its kind could be as good as the results of his arduous observation of nature and conscientiously and scrupulously thought-through conclusions. Rather, he knows that he alone sees nature as it is.... The technology grounded on the Nordic natural science has conquered the world, not the magical art of primitive people."[261] The distinction Becker makes, between the primitive and the Nordic *I* of authentic Dasein, in the course of paraontological improvement, engages the way in which Heidegger's adduces descriptive ethnological accounts of the primitive in the existential analytic. While Heidegger may have been more daunted than Becker by the opacity of primitive semiosis, and considerably more cautious about the pitfall of ethnocentrism in taxonomizing it according to the Western philosophical evaluation, both draw from the same Kantian and Hegelian construal of the fetish as magical-thinking, with a limited capacity to truly know the world. All of which is to say, regarding whatever native semiosis the Negro has, both dismiss it either as utterly incomprehensible or, to the extent it is comprehensible, as an archaic and inferior mode of knowing and talking about the world. In this respect, the paraontological is inextricably bound to the ontological. And that project flounders before the fluid plasticity of the flesh, needing to fix it in a homeostasis of body taxonomics, in which different bodily types express different modalities of knowledge, arranged in a hierarchical line of civilization. Paraontology is all about the body because it is still invested in somehow adjusting the ontological project. And the ontological project is about the body because it cannot think with the flesh. All of this is fundamentally about precluding thinking disorder, and is manifestly so in Becker's alignment of mantic and mathematical knowledge. Mathematics arises *from* the *mantikē*, but, under the guidance of philosophy, beginning with Plato, it becomes a proper *epistēmē*, a proper science. In that vein, the paraontological concern for the body's priority over the soul still postulates that it is the spirit, the *Geist*, driving civilization.

This brings to mind a story about body and soul told by the ethnologist Maurice Leenhardt in his 1947 book, *Do Kamo*.[262] Reporting on an exchange he had with a venerable Canaque sculptor, Boesoou, with whom he had become quite familiar during his time as a missionary in New Caledonia, Leenhardt tells of wanting to "measure the progress made in Canaque thinking" as a result of his "long years of instructing them."²⁶³ With this intent, he made a presumptuous suggestion: "All said and done, it is the notion of spirit that we [Christians] have added to your thinking." To which Boesoou retorted: "The spirit? Bah! You did not bring the spirit. We already knew the existence of the spirit. We were already proceeding according to the spirit. But what you did bring us was the body."²⁶⁴ True to ethnological form, Leenhardt must explain "the significance implied in the response." The soul Boesoou refers to is not the Cartesian qua Christian *esprit* but the Caledonian *ko*, to which "corresponds the mythical and magical ancestral influx." Leenhardt rather blithely disregards the rhetorical force of Boesoou's contradictory retort, "Bah!" as well as the irony of his subsequent "But [*Mais*]," construing the entire response as acknowledging receipt of the firmly delimited personhood precluded (*empêchait*) by the diffusion of the Canaque sociomythical domain. In Leenhardt's deft exegesis, Boesoou's response is evidence of what the Canaque had done with the Christian knowledge he imparted to them, creating a new syncretic understanding of human existence, combining the circumspection of *ko* with the epistemology of Cartesianism:

> Boesoou, in a word, defined a new contour: the body. The body had a part in all the mythical participation. His psychic impulses were the result of supernatural, totemic or other influences; he had no proper existence, nor a specific name to designate him; he was only a support. But, from now on [with the body] the constituency of the physical being ends and makes possible its objectification. The idea of a human body becomes clearer. It is a discovery that immediately leads to discrimination between the body and the mythical world.²⁶⁵

This story of Leenhardt's is recounted here not merely because it is illustrative of paraontology's alignment with colonialist ethnography, but because of how it precipitated another ethnological reading that contests his understanding of Boesoou's response, and corollarily the paraontological, opening the way to a more careful understanding of what is meant by *poiēsis in black* as *para-semiosis*.

In Para-Semiosis, Divisible Person Us Be

Some twenty-six years after the publication of *Do Kamo*, Roger Bastide writes the essay "Le principe d'individuation" (The Principle of Individuation), in which he rehearses and critiques Leenhardt's exegesis of Boesoou's response as being along the lines of a Scholastic, specifically Thomist, reformulation of Aristotle's notion of matter as the primary principle of individuation (*principium individuationis*).²⁶⁶ Bastide reads in Boesoou's response something other than an affirmation of the Canaque having assumed the Western concept of bodily delimited personhood. Not only is it a contradicting retort to the claims of Christian epistemic largess, but it is affirming Canaque semiosis. "Indeed," Bastide remarks, "the Melanesian does not conceive of himself except as a node of participations; he was outside more than inside himself, in his totem, his lineage, in nature and the social. The Christians would teach him to sunder [*couper*] these alterities in order to discover his identity—and that identity is marked by the frontiers of his body, which is isolated from other bodies."²⁶⁷ Bastide gives this reading as one of two illustrations—the second is the cult of Jamaa in the Congo—of how the problem of individuation enters into primitive Melanesian and African societies touched by the Christianity of the West, engendering what he terms *mutation*. Renowned for his ethnological studies of syncretic Afro-Brazilian and Afro-Caribbean religions, Bastide specialized in such mutation. In "Le principe d'individuation," however, having presented the two illustrations of mutation, he passes over their investigation in order to consider the understanding of the existence of individual person in the most traditional, as in untouched by the Christianity of the West, African societies. His declared orientation in this investigation is philosophical, by which he means to consider patterns of thinking abstracted out of certain practices of sign-reading, specifically geomancy and divination, and speculations about general practices of initiation and lineage. The agenda is to interrogate the inventory of ethnological data resulting from a vast investigation of the person in Africa in order to arrive at a general African theory of person. Although Bastide does not pursue the sort of rigorous existential analytic Heidegger undertakes in his own interrogation of ethnological data, there is a certain affinity. Both investigate the ethnological inventory in service of the philosophical project of extrapolating a form of human existence and the attendant ways of representing the world—that is to say, in Heideggerian terms, investigating a mode of Dasein. The immediate question of Heidegger's investigation is the historicity of Dasein; for Bastide, it is the principle of individuation. Because what emerges from the ethnological inventory is the plurality of the constituent elements of the person, "the principle of individuation is posed for most African ethnic groups in the following way: What constitutes the unity of this plurality?"²⁶⁸

Bastide begins addressing this question by pointing out that many of these constituent elements have existence independent of the human body; they are heterogeneous to the flesh, dynamically engaging it in the constitution of bodily function. He further pronounces that the autonomy of these various principles is beyond dispute in African thought. This presents an aporia for the Western philosophical ontological tradition, according to which the individual person is "defined by his intrinsic unity, he is *indivisum in se* [indivisible]," whereas the person conceived by Africans, Bastide tells us, "is divisible."[269] Working from the Western assumption that the unity of the individual necessarily presupposes the indivisible human person, Bastide is prompted by the contrasting plurality of the African person to ask: "Is this the unity of an aggregate, a node of participations, or a structure?"[270] Having posed the question, he points out that the various constituents of the person do not appear at the first stroke, at the moment of birth; they often put themselves in place one after the other. The idea of the person is as a continuous progressive creation analogous to and correspondent with the continual creation of the cosmos. Even so,

> the fact remains, a certain unity of the person emerges, or more exactly: it is postulated by the life cycle of the individual. But is this postulated unity a thought unity? For the African, it cannot be said that the principle of unity is the body, since there are many bodily souls [*âmes corporelles*], and even if there was a bodily unity, the body could not impart that unity to the soul because there are many spiritual souls [*âmes spirituelles*]: vital force, shadow, double. It is known that African thought is a thought by mystical correspondences and not, like ours, by logical "interlocking [*emboîtements*]." We do not encounter with them, as we do with the Scholastics, who started from the existence of the three souls, a vegetative soul, a sensitive soul, an intellectual soul, the solution of the interlocking: they are one in the other as the triangle is in the tetragon and the tetragon in the pentagon. We can only discover a solution in correspondence. That is to say, we must seek the key [*la clef*] of the individual reality in the set of relationships, which bind man to the various constitutive principles of Cosmos, and to all social relations (including, well heard, those he sustains with the Dead). The old ethnology, more preoccupied with differentiating ourselves from the primitives and looking for what distinguishes us from them, did not take an interest in discovering this "key." It dwelt on the idea of plurality of souls, wanting to see only one unit of aggregation. Contemporary ethnology, from the works of Griaule, finds the key to a structural unity in the order of the symbolic.[271]

It is not so much the key to a solution Bastide finds. By his own account, there is no problem among the Africans needing solution. The pluralism of souls does not prevent the unity of the person as an individual. The individual is a formal unit in a dynamic network of successive states of equilibration, imbalance, and re-equilibration between forces that extend beyond while being within it. The person, precisely in the awareness of self, is a composite nodal instantiation of all this articulation. Bastide adduces as supporting evidence two ethnological reports: the descriptive analysis of the Dogon concept of *kikínu*, provided by Marcel Griaule's daughter, Geneviève Calame-Griaule, in her *Ethnologie et langage: La parole chez les Dogon*; and the Franciscan priest Placide Fran Tempels's description of the generic Bantu, a euphemism for Negro, concept of *muntu*.[272] Of these two, Bastide finds Calame-Griaule's to be the most methodologically viable, in its combining Bronisław Malinowski's theory of the relevance of social context to linguistic study with the methodology of structuralist linguistics. He cites at length her account of the eight *kikínu*, organizing principles that have independent existence apart from humans and a relationship of correspondence to personal psyche. *Kikínu* are divided into two groups of four, the *gòdu kikínu* (corporal *kikínu*) and the *ɔgɔ kikínu* (sexual *kikínu*). Both groups further divide into two sets of fraternal twins, one of intellect and one of animality. On the one hand are the twins *sáy ána* (male intelligent) and *sáy yà* (female intelligent). On the other, are the twins *bòmɔnɛ ána* (male animal) and *bòmɔnɛ yà* (female animal). In the *gòdu kikínu* group, *sáy ána* is associated with perspicacity (*yìru*), abstraction (*ásubu*), and will (*dì: ɲɛ*), and *sáy yà* with joy, love, affection, and pleasant feelings; *bòmɔnɛ ána*, also called in Dogon *kíne bánu* (red heart), is associated with violence, and *bòmɔnɛ yà* also called *kíne gɛnu* (black heart) with spite, jealousy, hatred, and dread. In the *ɔgɔ kikínu* group, *sáy ána* is associated with virility (*ilí: ɛdu*), *sáy yà* with libido (*dá:ru ɛdu*), while *bòmɔnɛ ána*, is associated with impotence (*ilí: mɔɲu*) and *bòmɔnɛ yà* with anaphrodisia and menses.[273] Bastide's interest in Calame-Griaule's description has to do with the way in which the plurality of these *kikínu* as dynamic principles are "moving from places outside the individual, where they stand in reserve, to organs in the body where they stay, so that the personal psychic life is defined by itineraries." His use of Tempels's work is more circumspect. Like Leenhardt, Father Tempels was a missionary first of all. His preoccupation in preparing *La Philosophie bantoue* with thematizing pertinent African procedures was aimed at developing appropriate methods for successfully proselytizing Africans, which is immanently verified by his initiating the Jamaa movement after finishing the book. Bastide's invocation of that movement as an illustration of vexed syncretism, which he then puts aside, indicates his own ambivalence about Tempels's constructed object of a Bantu vitalist conception of the world, which, following Bastide, has been critiqued as more ethnological description than philosophical elaboration.[274] Nevertheless, alongside Calame-Griaule's description of the person among the Dogon, Bastide finds sufficient ethnological evidence of a ubiquitous African formalism in Tempels's writing to claim that "various African populations may have different systems—unless the expressions of these systems in Western language are different, which we would be inclined to think personally. But the definition of the unity of the person is always given in terms of formal or structural unity, whether in 'routes' or paths, whether in 'tensions' and 'nodes.'"²⁷⁵

What is more significant for us here is the appositive remark concerning translation into Western languages of these systems. The problem requiring solution is a problem chiefly for "Western language," or more precisely for ethnographic discourse in its effort to comprehend the thinking of these so-called primitives—and even Bastide calls them such. That problem clearly belongs to what he considers "the old ethnology," the ethnology of Bastian with which Heidegger was conversant. But even the more "contemporary ethnology," like that practiced by Calame-Griaule, remained plagued by this problem; something about which she had expressed concern, noting that in previous publications devoted to the Dogon ideas of personality, the notion of *kikínu* is regarded from a mythical angle, and so it is translated as "*âmes* [soul]."²⁷⁶ Because her work, in contrast, seeks to "determine what is the psychological reality" concomitant with the Dogon word, she eschews the term *âmes* altogether, except when quoting others' use of it, proffering instead a brief philological explanation that *kikínu* "is formed by root reduplication, a feature even more apparent in Tòmbo where the word takes the form *kíndu kíndu*."²⁷⁷ Elaborating further that "the Dogon associate this word with *kínu*, 'nose, breath, life,' because the principles move about as a wind and enter the individual as he breathes," she adds in a footnote: "Other plays on words are: *kè:ne*, to 'organize' (because the *kikínu* organize the person), *kíne*, 'liver,' and *kiní*, 'shadow,' which serves as a carrier to some *kikínu*."²⁷⁸ Calame-Griaule seeks some relief from the problem of translation by glossing *kikínu* as "pôles d'identification" (identification poles); Bastide followed suit.²⁷⁹ Nevertheless, her philological grappling makes clear the persistence of the problem for Western languages—and it should be obvious here that we are talking about *la langue* in Ferdinand de Saussure's sense of the abstract systematic rules and conventions of a semiotic system—of comprehending and adequately representing a radically heterogeneous semiosis articulating an equally distinct understanding of human being-in-world.

With this grappling, we touch again on Heidegger's recognition of the primitive's opacity as a heuristic sign, an instrument for the ontological analysis, and in a way that goes to the crux of Becker's paraontological improvement: the relation between *I myself* and *they* of Dasein. It is particularly germane to our considerations that, in Heidegger's existential analytic, "the *they*, with which the question of the *who* of everyday Dasein is answered, is the *nobody*, to whom every Dasein has already surrendered itself in Being-among-one-another."²⁸⁰ Here we must pause and reconsider the way we have attended to Heidegger's existential analytic of Dasein, which is as an entity. In this we have been adhering closely to his own terminology regarding the transcendence of Dasein, according to which Dasein surpasses existence itself—which is to say, "every entity that can be or become unconcealed [*unverborgen*] to Dasein, therefore *also and precisely* the very entity as which it [Dasein] 'itself' exists. *In* surpassing [*Im Überstiegt*], Dasein first of all comes to such an entity as it is, regarding its 'self.' Transcendence constitutes selfhood."[281] We repeat ourselves here, but with the repetition take note that this is a process of formation. In that process, as Becker shows us, birth and death function not just as the existential being-toward, but as actual birth and demise. In light of Becker's refinements, Dasein is not an entity transitioning from an inauthentic to an authentic state; to quote him again in this respect: "We do not believe that one can call the natural way of living in that terminologically fixed sense of existential analysis, '*Dasein*.'"[282] It is instead the very process of individuation, the emergence of that entity having the capability-of-being (*Seinkönnen*) self-consciously individual, of understanding its own differentiated selfhood, which, ontologically speaking is an incursion, a break-in that tears open a rent in the continuum of entities. In that tear, the human stands out against that which exists and is not human, facilitating the formation of an individual having the potentiality for self-understanding and interpretation. Nor is paraontology less tearing in its emphasizing the indivisible person's boundedness in the geo-environmentally determined body.

Should we give credence to Bastide's exposition of the African concept of person, however, taking seriously Calame-Griaule's descriptive analysis of *kikínu*, there is no tear; the question is not the *who*, but the *what* of Dasein. Put differently, the question is not *who* is human put *what* is human being and *how*. And if this question is not amenable to the fundamental ontology, neither is it amenable to ontic metaphysics, to metontology. We need some other way of thinking that is eventful and dynamic. We find ourselves back again with Du Bois. But more to the point at this moment, the problem of the *who* Heidegger analyzes as inauthentic Dasein and associates with the primitive mode of being, which Becker then takes up as the true essence of human existence, is not at all a concern for the African semiosis considered by Bastide et al. In the dynamically fluid relation of correspondence between the multiplicious plurality of forces—it is perhaps more adequate to think of entities mathematically—subject to chance as well as contingency; what human being is is a possible nodal articulation, a point expressed in the fluidity of events of happening occurrence. "If we understand properly," Bastide says, "in each and every person, there is, for example, the pole of identification with the Father [the progenitive Ancestor], which constitutes the identification apart from otherness (the chain of generation in the lineage)."[283] This would mean that Heidegger is correct: the primitive does not *have Geschichte*, for to do so would mean having achieved a position of indivisibility. The primitive, the Negro, the

African, is eventful, but not in the sense of being *historizing-occurrence*, precisely because the person is not born as an integral individual running ahead to death, but rather is perpetually being generated in the open-ended dynamics of semiosis, which entails but does not end with death. And there is no annihilation of the person because there is no annihilation of generation.

Indubitably, the Dogon *they-self* is an existential and primordial phenomenon, articulating the referential context of Dasein's significance. It is, in Heidegger's terms, "dispersed [*zerstreut*] into the *they*. Adjusted in accordance with Bastide's reflections on the Dogon, the individual is divisible into the *they-self*, which is neither a leveling (*Einebnung*) nor an averaging (*Durchschnittlichkeit*) that disburdens the individual of the particularity of its existence. Nor is the person characterized by Heideggerian distantiality (*Abständigkeit*). But here, Bastide too stumbles back into ontology. More to the point, he takes us straight back to Lacan, and expressly so. In his effort to explain how the Dogon unity of person can be the basis of the principle of individuation and not the principle itself, since it is a structure or form that the dialectical game of principles or different elements assumes, Bastide draws a heuristic comparison between the divisible African person and how "Lacan distinguishes the symbolic order, which gives the law of formal composition of any subjective structure, the Father or the Big Other, . . . and the imaginary, which forms a combination of differentiated signifiers, distinguishing one individual from another."[284] Characterizing his account thus far of the formal structure of the African person to have remained in the symbolic order, he seeks to define what distinguishes one individual from another by turning to Lacan's account of the imaginary order. "But, of course, this order of the imaginary can be deployed only in the order of the symbolic," Bastide says, situating the principle of reincarnation of an ancestor in the symbolic.[285] The point is to construe the ancestor as analogous to *Man* the signifier in Lacan's register of the symbolic, that to which the I, the ego, is most intimately bound. In Lacanian psychoanalysis, the ego is not a purely logical function meant to orient ontological thinking, such as Kant's transcendental ego. It is, in a way that is still rather Kantian, an articulation of intersubjective structure, taking the modality of experience. That is why Lacan treats the ego as an object, rather than some postulated transcendental point from which perception is ultimately possible. The ego is fully an effect of the dynamic interaction between the imaginary and symbolic orders; it marks the convergence of the enunciation of the symbolic that enunciates. Arguably, this is why Bastide sees Lacan's psychoanalysis as a heuristic of African conceptions of person.

There is always the slippery slope of obfuscation in the effort to make the African person understandable within the terms of an anthropology that, in its quest for the equivocity of signification, is still inextricably bound to the ontological project. So, what cannot be comprehended ontologically must still be interpreted in ontological terms. Yet, as Lévy-Bruhl came to understand after committing decades to the effort, the opacity of primitive semiosis drives the ethnologist, in despair, back to positivistic recording and calculation. In setting aside philosophy's account of person with regard to the African, Bastide finds that something still must be said. He finds that saying with Lacan, who in refusing to renounce his fraternity with Heidegger's saying "truth, ἀλήθεια = *Verborgenheit* [concealment]," repurposes Becker's *Paraontologie* as *par-être* in the service of repeating, from practice, ontology as indisputable.[286] Lacan's *par-être* is no way out, however, his valiant effort notwithstanding. At the end of the day, psychoanalysis remains invested in discovering the indivisible subject. The signifier *Man* cannot cover the totality of subjective experience because there is always something of the subjective experience that escapes capture by the letter, a remainder that cannot be symbolized, which Lacan designates as *le réel* (*the real*). Dedicated as it is, for the most part, to the question of the *mathème*, the challenge posed to Lacanian psychoanalysis is how to make the transition from linguistic equivocity to the formula, to the formalization that is both the limit and the negation. This point is reached when Lacan asks how one passes in the cure from the impotence of the imaginary to the impossibility of *the real*. Or, as Badiou poses it: "What is the gap in the equivocal language that brings to the surface the void of univocity?"[287] What is of interest to Badiou—indeed, by his own account, the only thing that interests him—is Lacan's claim of anti-philosophy. Like all others making such claims, from Gorgias and Pascal to Rousseau, Nietzsche, and Wittgenstein, Lacan addresses to philosophy a singular new object—*the Real*—that it has overlooked or suppressed examination of, which in itself challenges and displaces philosophy's established pretensions. The exhibition of that object inevitably inscribes anti-philosophy in a singular declension *of* philosophy. In Lacan's case, the declension is knowledge of truth—More precisely, the conceptual triplet, *vérité-savoir-réel*, "truth-knowledge-*the real*," which Badiou places at the frontier of the two discourses of psychoanalysis and philosophy.[288] What distinguishes the two discourses is how they operate this triplet. The philosophical operation proposes, under the name "wisdom" (*sophia*), in love, the axiom: "There is one meaning of truth [*sens de la vérité*] because there is one truth of what is real [*vérité du réel*]."[289] Philosophy, thus, segments the triplet into pairings: *truth of the real* and *knowledge of the real*, and *knowledge of truth*. Contrary to this, Lacan argues, "There is no meaning of truth because there is no truth of *the Real*."[290] As such, *the Real* is definable as the absence of meaning—in other words, as the empty set or void. The possibility of the *mathème* as transmissible formula lies here in the proposition that every function of *the Real* in knowledge bears affirmatively on absence, on zero.

We can fairly say that the *mathème* is a hieroglyph, not of the flesh but of the body, or rather of the constituting event whereby the body exists in a meaningful way as that which is valued as nothing more than energy in-reserve. This is not to suggest that the encounter with the sentient flesh is what Lacan designates as *the Real*—whether in the early period of his register theory where *the Real* refers to material existence, becoming a pure undifferentiated plenum during the "return to Freud" period in the 1950s, or the forever unattainable Supreme Good, the fixed vanishing point of all desiring, that which Lacan calls "*das Ding* (*la Chose* [the thing])" in the 1970s when he turns to set theory. It is at the point of untranslatability that the irreducible living flesh is traced as such. To speak of this as a moment of transgressive play (*jouissance*) or resistance, as Lacan does, is to uncritically concede hegemony—absolute universal dominion over the imaginary—to one given symbolic order. This tendency, or rather, this desire, is what inclines him toward mathematical formulation, which is supposed, but really presumed, to be apathetic and so supremely transparent. For Lacan, the *mathème* is precisely this formal space in which one can project and transmit the subjective experience of the cure; the latter is therefore a relation to a rational, scientific matrix that can be transmitted without remainder. Whatever the modality of symbolization, however, whether mathematics, logic, or topology, it can only trace the fundamental impasse of symbolization and the subjective experience of *the Real*. This point is in keeping with Lacan's own earlier argument, contra logical positivism, "that there is no metalanguage, that no language can tell the truth about truth, since truth is founded on what it speaks [*ce qu'elle parle*], and that it has no other means [than speaking] to do this."[291]

For Lacan, as a matter of history, the capacity to recognize the activity of *the Real* occurs with the dissolution of the project of eudaimonic civilization, which began when the apophantic discourse of *arithmetization* disassociates in a certain way from the *enérgeia* of *poiēsis*—a protracted process commencing with Galileo's *Il Saggiatore* and achieving definitive form from Descartes onward. We cannot help but to discern here a faint echo of Du Bois's account of the genealogy of modernity in "The Renaissance of Ethics," where his feminizing *bona* surreptitiously undermines the virtuous right principle discourse of civilization. The point is not that Lacan was *in fact* echoing Du Bois or even influenced by his thinking; rather it is that Du Bois expressly forecasts the Lacanian project when he calls for a "science of mind" on which to base a proper "science of ethics." Or more broadly, he forecasts the work of psychoanalysis that would come in the wake of James's "'new' psychology." This matter of genealogical priority is important to our marking how *para-semiosis* is distinguished from Lacan's *par-être*, as well as Becker's *Paraontologie*, on which it draws.

There are two distinct lines flowing from Du Bois's thought. One, which reads double consciousness and the question of the color line as ontological problematics, carries us to paraontological discourse. The other extrapolates from the Du Boisian sense of *Negro* as indicial of a dynamic thinking-in-action that is at once incomprehensible to the philosophical discourse of ontology and dubious of it. Although, it should be noted, given that from its inception, *Negro* is among the indices of a perennial crisis of ontology—which can be described as the despotic violence of the incursion into existence fundamental to the definition of free *Man*, ἀνδρὸς εὖ (*andros eū*)—any Negro movement *historically* cannot but be in relation to ontology; all the more so in ignorance. To state what we all know but persist in refusing to take fully into account, there cannot be *Man* without the barbarian qua slave—and not just in the sense of a conceptual dialectic, but in the sense that it is the instrumentalization of the slave *enérgeia* that creates for the master the material situation in which *theoría*, deliberative contemplation and *phrónesis*, is possible.

Once again, we should pause and note that while this is true of the decree *Negro* in distinctive ways, it is distinctive to *Negro* only insofar as it is distinctively constitutive of the historical philosophical ontological project Heidegger set out to redeem in all its discursive modalities. There are comparable indices. For instance, the *indios* Bartolomé de las Casas has reference to in his *Memorial de remedios para las Indios* and *Historia de las Indias*, in distinction from *negros*. While the index, *Indian* (*los indios*), connotes for Casas the indigenous inhabitants of the New World islands and Tiera Firme, who, while being barbarous and lacking any knowledge of Christ, possess salvageable human souls; that is to say, in their bodily existence as savages, they are totally expendable and subject to legitimate extinction, but their souls can be saved.[292] The imperial Spanish *Requerimiento* of 1513 follows the principles of the Doctrine of Discovery, the basis and justification for which was established by three papal bulls, beginning with the *Dum Diversas* issued by Pope Nicholas V in 1452, authorizing the Portuguese king, Alfonso V, to conquer the land of the Saracens and pagans in Africa.[293] Nicholas V reinforced and extended the Portuguese crown's authority to conquer and enslave Saracens, pagans, and infidels to the newly discovered lands on the West African coast with his 1455 bull, *Romanus Pontifex*. That authority was extended to all Catholic sovereigns, most notably Ferdinand and Isabella, and its territorial scope was expanded to include any new lands they may discover by Pope Alexander VI's 1493 bull, *Inter Caetera*, along with its supplemental *Dudum siquidem*, which divided the non-Christian world beyond Europe between Portugal and Spain, limiting the Portuguese *ius patronatus* in the New World in favor of Spain. Following this line of reasoning, the *Requerimiento* addresses the indigenous population of the Americas as souls to be brought back to Christ—even though they had never had any prior direct knowledge—in accordance with the Augustinian principle of "Lex tua scripta est in cordibus hominum [The law is written in the hearts of men]," as elaborated by Aquinas: "Sed lex scripta in cordibus hominum est lex naturalis. Ergo lex naturalis deleri non potest [But the law written on the human heart is the natural law. Therefore, the natural law cannot be erased]."²⁹⁴ By implication, the indigenous population of the Americas, like the African subjects of the *Dum Diversas*, possess valued souls that are to be "gained for Christ" (*Christo lucrifent*), in the language of the *Romanus Pontifex*. The *Requerimiento*, as well the papal bulls on which it rests, distinguishes between types of human being on the basis of confessional faith, eschewing the Aristotelian categorical distinction of biological capacity for reason. The determining premise is the universal divine imperative, *cordibus hominum*, to become human *qua* Christian, whether by willful or forced confession, thus legitimating the exercise of violence in the constitution of the beloved community. In contrast, the index *Negro*, as has already been noted in some detail, connotes the embodiment of capital—animate sentient instrumentalities of production. In contradistinction to the *Requerimiento*, the 1662 Virginia law of *Partus sequitur ventrem* and the Code Noir, with their respective juridical definition of the black body as chattel property, revisit Aristotle's biological grounds for the condition of hereditary slavery. The violence done to the flesh in constituting the black body is not even titularly salvific; the irrelevance of the black soul is underscored in Article 2 of the Code, stipulating that all blacks are to be baptized and instructed in the Roman Catholic faith. The expressed aim and effect of this violence is nothing more or less than the constitution of the black body valued only in its pure embodiment as capital energy, an embodiment that is a simulacrum of, or as Kant would say, derived from *Man*.

Taking full account of this distinction means leaving aside ontology altogether, along with its *meta* and *para*.

Looking once more at Du Bois's exchange with Barton in this regard, *Negro* refers to fantasy in the order of Barthes's *le mythe petit-bourgeois du Nègre*, or in more Lacanian terms, to the knowledge attending the dynamics of the imaginary and symbolic orders. Du Bois concedes this, noting the logic of the signifier: "Names are only conventional signs for identifying things. Things are the reality that counts." He further notes that this reality is of the symbolic, and in its conventionality, indicates its own limits. Whether *Negro* or *Cheiropolidi*, the sign formalizes the impasse between what is symbolized and what is unsymbolizable. *Negro* denotes the experience of that impasse as the point at which the real subject of experience—in contrast to the subject of science—is encountered in its irreducible incomprehensibility, connoting in Du Boisian terms the paradox of law and chance. Perhaps the most profound thing about *Negro* is that throughout its historical usage in our modernity, each and every enunciation continually expresses paradox, continually brings to the fore the necessity of formal symbolization along with that which can never be fully symbolized in form. The gist of Du Bois's response to Barton's charge that *Negro* is a white man's term is: Yes, indeed, the Negro is a white man's fable; more exactly, it is a fable about an imaginary type of being that is enunciated in the symbolic order of capitalist modernity. In the conjoining of the symbolic and imaginary, it is an element in the constitution of the world reality that has been imposed on humanity at large.

In contrast to Lacan's real subject which resists symbolization, however, *Negro* not fully symbolized is an articulation in free-play between the symbolic and imaginary—which is to say, because it was never fully symbolized, it is not transgressive, just an altogether other game. Every expression of *Negro* is an invocation of the inexpressible real, which does not exist just beyond the limit of the symbolic but is in the overlapping confluence of symbolic orders. The fundamental impasse Lacan seeks in order to discover *the real* point of the subject is resonant with what Du Bois seeks to describe in his analogy of the asymptotes of the hyperbola. As we saw with Dedekind, and even Frege, this is indeed an *impasse* and not a limit, which engenders the infinite progression of signification, of counting-for—no matter if the beginning number is 0 or 1, what is traced at the number-site (*Zahlenreihe*) is multiplicity of multiplicities. Du Boisian hyperbolic (asymptotic) thinking, however, does not transvalue truth and knowledge as effects of semiosis set against the inassimilable real accessed through the purely subjective play of transgression. Asymptotic truth and knowledge are certainly effects of semiotic dynamics; they are articulations of semiosis in common—saying something, if you will. But this saying-in-common, while clearly the articulations of assemblage and relation of multiplicities, the *existence* of which is given in the dynamics of semiosis, is not forgotten behind the said. There is nothing said that goes without saying.

US AIN'T PARAONTOLOGICAL

Staying attuned to resonances, the Buzzard Lope, with its conceivable syncretism of Christian semiosis and those of what Allen, Herskovits, and Parrish labeled "Africanism," enacts the same process of divisibility Bastide discerned in the nodal eventfulness of supposedly African semiosis. Indeed, this may very well be where *Negro* and *African* share the same connotation: the dynamically fluid relationality of human being. Explaining this is requisite to explaining the relationship between *para-semiosis*, *poiēsis*, and *blackness*—that is to say, elaborating further what I mean to connote by these three designations.

Chinua Achebe once remarked that "Africa is not only a geographical expression; it is also a metaphysical landscape—it is in fact a view of the world, of the whole cosmos perceived from a particular situation."²⁹⁵ Valentine Mudimbe presented just fifteen years ago some remarks of his own that, while not expressly directed at Achebe's, complicates them in a way imminently pertinent to the distinction I'm drawing here between paraontology and *para-semiosis*. Mudimbe's remarks touch directly on the question, "What is African thinking and how do we encounter it?" which haunts our engagement with Bastide on the divisible person. But also, in its total disregard of the Negro in relation to the African, it prompts the question of blackness as bound up with the distinction between paraontology and *para-semiosis*—and let us be clear about this now, that distinction has to do with whether thinking-in-action is critical and auto-critical semiosis is philosophical; the claim being made throughout this work is that it is altogether doing something else. In the course of reflecting on the motivation behind changing the title of the *Bulletin of the Society of African Philosophy in North America*, to the *Bulletin of the Society for African Philosophy in North America*, Mudimbe expresses

> a general suspicion concerning the concept of African Philosophy, the question of a supposed confusion of philosophy understood as *Weltanschauung* and, on the other hand, philosophy defined as a critical, auto-critical, explicit reflection bearing on language and human experience. Such hesitation was signified in the privilege that the Society chose to give the preposition "for" as a way of naming its own task. In effect, to the implications of the genitive with its slippery issue of origin in the expression "Society of African Philosophy," in which the adjective "African" might seem to represent an intrinsic and essential difference, in sum the singularity of a nature, we chose the detour expressed by the preposition "for," as indicative of a project, its objective, the practice of philosophy by students of African descent, or by individuals conceiving their identities, in any case their perceptual, or their real behavior, as marked by an African geography, be it mythical, in any case simply representational. Such an epistemological prudence was to allow us, among other things, an elegant and critical handling of two metaphors: on the one hand, Heidegger's affirmation that philosophy is Greek; on the other hand, the pertinence of a common sense saying, no one speaks from nowhere; and, in practical terms, this meant a postulate, that any *parole* is always, in its difference, qualified by a locus, a time, the consciousness and indeed the unconsciousness of the speaker.
>
> In such an orientation, we were expressing a right and a duty, and also simultaneously, the fact of a *Bindung* and an *Entbindung*, bond and unbinding, linking the African speaking subject to a self and to a locality, at the same time positing the subject as inextricably mingling with an alterity, with someone else, an *alter*, thus very precisely as unstable, insofar as such a

subject cannot negate its own expansion, its existence outside itself, in the alter in whom it can bind to itself. It followed that it was only reasonable for us African students of philosophy, to be attentive to Martin Heidegger's challenge, his pronouncement on philosophy as being essentially Greek. How could one avoid the Greek initiative, and the already long history of philosophical practices, while acknowledging the obvious around us, testimonies of intellectual investments witnessing its African experience.[296]

The lengthy passage is presented here so as to fully display the flow of Mudimbe's thinking, which turns on three salient points. First the aspirational preposition "for" already concedes the hegemonic force of philosophy as a privileged modality of critical, auto-critical reflection on language and human experience. Declaring the project is to do philosophy presumes it is worth doing in its own right; and that is to accept the fundamental terms of the ontological project from its earliest moment of incursion: *We have broken-in to existence in order to understand existence best of all, and so define who is human.* It follows from this that to take up the project as Africans not only adheres to the anthropological taxonomy—a taxonomy that Mudimbe works hard to deconstruct elsewhere—but concedes to the project of acculturation, the expanding imposition of the master discourse. Indeed, Mudimbe's essay is a moving personal account of missiology and acolyte induction into the philosophy of *Anthrōpos*: "say a scholastic education, a socio-cultural context, and indeed the spiritual and ethical (in-)securities of identification (*mimesis*) with, and resemblance (*homiosis*) to models; in sum, an intellectual history, its detours, and the vertigo of its internal logic."[297] Heidegger's challenge is accepted on Heidegger's terms, and the issue of the African is not quite adequately addressed. Obvious, yet unavoidable questions pose themselves here. What does it mean to be marked by an African geography? Does it mean to be marked *in* the discourse of Rome? Or is it the discourse of racialized capitalist modernity? Cartography constitutes the world, in precisely Heidegger's sense of a totality of referentiality. It is a matter of relevance for whom?[298] For philosophy, of course; the *necessity* of the original Greek incursion, that is Heidegger's challenge. There is a crucial line in Mudimbe's reflection, where, in reference to the African orientation to philosophy, he expresses a right and duty to link the African speaking subject to a self and locality while at the same time positing itself as inextricably mingling with others. The positing aims to engage a subject that is "unstable, insofar as it cannot negate its own expansion, its existence outside itself, in the *alter* in whom it can bind to itself." With an eye toward Bastide's depiction of the African person, we can rephrase this as "a subject that is divisible insofar as it instantiates the pluralities existing outside itself that bind the subject to them, and so to itself, in constant and continual signification."

If we can listen to Bastide with any credulity, however, that divisible subject is an ancient testimony of intellectual investment, which he finds at work in scattered places across the globe, such as Brazil. Herskovits, Hurston, and Lomax also see signs of it throughout the Caribbean and southern coast of the United States, which is to say everywhere they cared to looked.

The quandary Mudimbe shares with us is not about bringing philosophy to Africa—Heidegger's challenge is a shibboleth of little consequence. The quandary is not even how to Africanize philosophy. Rather it is, once African testimonies of intellectual investments witnessing its African experience encounters philosophy, philosophy stalls and loses its verve. Recall, Heidegger himself announced this in his inability to think with the *Zulukaffern* and *Senegalneger* semiosis. For him, *Negro* denotes that incomprehension. There is, indisputably, existence there, and it is equally indisputably human existence precisely in his sense of world constituting signification. It is just that ontology, that is to say, philosophy, cannot speak to it or even of it in any comprehensible way. It can only look on dumbfounded. So much for the universal necessity of the incursion.

This brings us to the third point. To say that "any *parole* is always, in its difference, qualified by a locus, a time, which determines the consciousness and unconsciousness of the speaker," is merely to point out that speaking is a performative action of positionality in some order of referentiality within a totality of signification: I say something to you with the presumption that what I say is of relevance to us both. That relevance constitutes what we have in common. Along these lines, Mudimbe's ambition is to make Africa a position from which speaking is received as relevant to the already long history of philosophical practices initiated by the Greeks, as the story goes. Leaving aside for the moment the problematical limitations of Mudimbe's expressly focusing the project only on Franco-Germanic philosophy, Africa is not merely a philosophical invention. It may have started out that way as that space, both phenomenal and conceptual, outside epistemic grasp, except as the extreme beyond where thinking is severely curtailed. But with its embodiment in actuality—that is to say, with the invention of *Negro* as sub- or quasi-human property—there emerges a plethora of potentialities of possible being, of actual ways of being, for which *Africa* designates an orientation in flight, as in the parable of flying Africans told by folks across the Georgia Sea Islands.[299] This African orientation is asymptotic, the positing of a point from which one knows to have arrived only at arrival in slavery—the "new African" must be broken in a process euphemistically called "seasoning"—and then as an orientation in flight from enslavement. *Africa* is a symbol of being nowhere yet constantly on the move there, in an order of signification, a *Negro* discourse, that has no relevance (in the Heideggerian sense of *Bewandtnis*) to philosophy except as dismissible mythical tales, folklore. Let me suggest, however, that this discourse is a far more generative *alter* to whom the so-called African might speak in pursuit of critical and auto-critical reflection on language and human experience. In it, *Africa* signs that which has no *proper* historical field other than the historicity of the expression constituting the world of referentiality. In this sense, *Africa* is an indicial sign of the perpetual activity of translation and transvaluation constituting the world and worldliness of modernity. To paraphrase Achebe, Africa is not a geographical expression; it is a generative symbol in a careful semiosis of the world, of the whole cosmos perceived from a particular situation of nowhere. Displacing "metaphysical landscape" with "careful semiosis" presses on the philosophical implications of Achebe's saying. The "nowhere" qualifying the particular takes us back to the specificity of situation Chandler speaks of, with which we began our interrogation of the paraontological, working our way through it in an unsettling movement so as to leave it behind us, never to return, except as occasional tourists. That situation and movement is the nowhere from which we ask with Moten, now no longer paraontologically: What is blackness as an aspect of a life in common?

PARA-SEMIOSIS, BEING-IN-FLIGHT-WITH-ONE-ANOTHER

A careful response is: being-*in-flight*-with-one-another apart from, which is what is meant by *para-semiosis*. This in-flight apart from is not a matter of running away. Again, it is the *un-stealable life* that is in-flight without fixing an alternative telos or mythology. Nor is it a running beneath or before ontology as with Becker's paraontology, or in its wake as with Heidegger's metontology, or above it as with Badiou's metaontology. The *para-semiosis* of being-with-one-another in-flight means leaving-off ontology altogether, *without much more thought*. The hyphenated *para-*, the "beside," does not merely denote parallel movement alongside of ontology. It is a dynamic constitutive *besidedness*; that is, *being-in-besidedness*, not as a bijective function; not being *as* the break-in, but *in* the break, à la Moten. *Para-semiosis* denotes the dynamic of differentiation operating in multiple multiplicities of semiosis that converge without synthesis. This is what is referred to in the Blues, but also in numerous instantiations of "Africanisms" across the New World, as *being-at-the-crossroads*, the figure of which is called varyingly "the Devil," "the Black Man," "Exu," "Eshu," and "Legua," but more widely "Legba," or "Papa Legba." Legba is the figure of discursive mastery, that which removes obstacles and provides possibilities. The relationship between these possibilities is dynamic in the sense that the only "determinate" is the continual activity of creating referentiality, *poiēsis*.

Considering this activity in terms of the *para-*, we may also refer to it as *para-poiēsis*, because it is dynamically constituting the world in which individuals are meaningfully representative as positionalities, locative designations; as such, these can be designated *para-mime*, whereby *mime*—the etymon of which is μῖμος (*mímos*), from which *mimesis* derives—connotes both performer and performance in action. Idiomatically in English, we mean by *mime* the performer and performance of a silent exclusively bodily mimicry. We recall here the ancient Greek meaning of μῖμος and the derived Latin *mīmus* as the farcical depiction of scenes from ordinary everyday life by mimicking the accents and vernacular of the common people and foreigners, keeping in mind Plato's concern about what sort of mimics, μιμητικους (*mimetikos*), the guardians should be. Plato's concern, of course, was with virtuous pedagogy; and so, the goal of mimicry is to secure the integrity of the individual, to assimilate virtuous character thereby becoming an individuated free man, standing apart in service of the absolute good. The *para-mime* performs something else. Think of the solo dancer in the Buzzard Lope described earlier. To repeat the description, this is the performance of persona *occasioned* by ancestral forces sustained formally in the stylistic conventions of that performance, much as the Greco-Roman was occasioned by everyday life. Indeed, the ancestral forces are in the action of the everyday ordinary. The person as *para-mime* is an event of interstitial growth that can also be called *para-individuation*, to speak in somewhat more familiar terms of individuation. Except, bear in mind the interstitial is not at all akin to the Heideggerian differentiation that aims at the indivisible integral human being. The *para-mime* is divisible by *para-semiosis*. Were we to furthermore speak in familiar terms, proffering a suppositional conjugation analogous to Lacan's *par-être*—keeping in mind we are dealing with a term of dynamic action, of modality and not quantified existence—then it would be along the lines of: I *para-semiosis*, you *para-semiosis*, they *para-semiosis*, we *para-semiosis*, et cetera. As with Juba and the Buzzard Lope, this is an intra-semiosis, involving multiple centers of play—what is called *stylistic virtuosity*. In some sense, this is again what Herskovits and Hurston, but also Lucy McKim, Richard Allen, and Alan Lomax were referring to by *African*, whether consciously or not. There are good grounds, however, for understanding Hurston and Herskovits to have been very much aware that *African*, as well as *Negro*, connote such *para-semiosis*; and in referring to Negro Africanism, they mark the provenance of such a way of being. In that respect, we can say the *para-semiosis* of being-with-one-another in-flight exhibited with Juba and the Buzzard Lope is an enactment of *poiēsis in black*, in the sense of a *poiēsis* enacted with the sentient flesh embodied as *Negro*—not in all so embodied, but definitely *with* such embodiment of flesh. This distinction made, having elaborated what *para-semiosis* and *para-poiēsis* connote, it is possible to define blackness in relation to them: blackness is a poetical, as in *poiēsis*, expression of *para-semiosis*, which is a dynamic constitution of the world as a fluidity of multiple enactments of referentiality whereby being human is enunciated in the flow.

Du Bois's concept of intellect-in-action stemmed from his contemplation of how and why *Negro* indexes the material historical possibilities of humanity's eventfully thinking the world, *poiēsis* in the sense of the *historizing-occurrence*, as in temporalizing constitution, of the world. Accordingly, we have paraphrased it "thinking-in-action," elaborating therewith the concept of *poiēsis in black*. But, let us give pause for a moment to that paraphrasis and pay some attention to a passage from Du Bois's Philosophy IV Notebook, which, although overlooked in our earlier interrogation of that work, expresses the keynote at play here. "If will is invoked for an orderly universe, should we not invoke one for a disorderly universe," Du Bois inquires, and then responds, "I say order for order, chaos for chaos as cause, Anaxagoras supposes a νους [*nous*] super induced on chaos—but you must explain chaos, and that as an effect must logically have as well an intending will. The whole theistic argument of intending thought (Paley's watch) is founded on the suppositions of a coexistent chaotic power—it is really a polytheistic argument."[300] Taking this into account, the thinking-in-action concomitant with the advent of *Negro* as an embodiment of sentient flesh as property—that is to say, *poiēsis in black*—is actually a thinking-in-disorder.

John Jones is a primary figure of this thinking-in-disorder; and his story, "Of the Coming of John," is a principal investigation into the relationship between *para-semiosis* and the processes of individuation predicated on the Western philosophical ontological tradition. As stated a few lines ago, this is a relationship in crisis. The moment in which the ontological project, by means of its derived juridico-legislative discourse of polity, decrees *Negro* indexes that project's failure at achieving a necessary universal account of existence qua existence, and hence a universal definition of the human. Saying *Negro* is indicial of a perennial crisis of ontology is not to say that *poiēsis in black*, although emergent in that crisis, is circumscribed by ontology. Rather, it is *in dynamis*, in active flight, moving according to un-ontological *para-semiosis*. Per our investigation of the semiology of the flesh, although a certain cutting in lines of flight, a tearing that disrupts, occurs in the crisis, the multiplicious movements are from and of elsewhere. Those movements are unquestionably inflected by the crisis, such inflection being the embodiment of *Negro*. Still, being *in* the crisis, inflected in some ways by it, is not the same as being *of* the crisis. This is the situation Chandler describes as setting in motion "a form of supra-inhabitation of thought . . . in the midst of . . . the particularities of existence [which] solicits the development of a paraontological discourse."[301] He and I are clearly moving in the same shout, carried along in the flow of the same lineage of screams to the same rhythms, each proffering a solo dance in the center. Yet, there is a distinction between the inflection we give the *para* in our respective choreographies, with him stepping in relation to an ontological course that I am not at all concerned with. Then again, given the great lengths I have just taken in elaborating how and why *para-semiosis* and *poiēsis in black* have nothing to do with ontology, para or otherwise, perhaps it is better to say that with which I am *no longer* concerned.

That distinction is made all the more pertinent by the fact that the occasion for Chandler's calling on paraontological discourse is his reading of Du Bois's "The Present Outlook for the Dark Races of Mankind," a text that stands in important relationship to "Jefferson Davis as a Representative of Civilization." It too was a speech, delivered nine years after the Harvard commencement to the Third Annual Meeting of the American Negro Academy on December 27, 1899, and was published the following year in the *A. M. E. Review*.[302] This was the second time Du Bois addressed the academy; the first was "The Conservation of Races," delivered at its founding meeting in 1897. When we consider these three texts together, reading them sequentially in the order of their composition and presentation, we see how Du Bois used them to develop his thinking about a specific concept while at the same time putting that thinking into public play. The specific concept under consideration across these three addresses is civilization, and concordantly, as we've been expositing in our reading of "Jefferson Davis," the human.

As Chandler observes, Du Bois crafted the 1899 address into a form simultaneously combining scholarly treatise and oratory, or sermon, the rhetorical register of which is admonishment. He starts by admonishing the gathered preeminent national Negro leadership to recognize that what they took to be a parochial national issue must be properly considered as a global problematic, in the course of which he makes his first public declamation "that the color line belts the world and the social problem of the twentieth century is to be the relation of the civilized world to the dark races of mankind." The admonishment flows seamlessly into scholarly treatise, which Du Bois acknowledges is a "hasty and inadequate survey . . . of the race problem in space," recounting the geographical expansion over time of the conquering imperial European capitalist civilization as the history, in the Hegelian-Marxist sense, of the current geopolitical world order, for which the color line is a synecdoche. After casting the social problem of the twentieth century in terms of the relation of the civilized world to the dark races of mankind and surveying the various forms of the racialized hierarchical social orders founded in conquest from Africa and Asia to South America, Du Bois focuses on the race question in North America, now situated in the global context. Understandably, this is a more detailed account. After all, this is the space from which he speaks as a member of a disparaged race at a moment when the prevalent public attitude toward the Negro was severely negative. It is here, in this conceptualization of the historicity of the current moment in relation to the American Negro question, where Chandler discerns a paraontological discourse, one in which, as he says, "Du Bois is led to speak of the general rhythms of history, to pose a conceptualization or metaphorization of history in general, with regard to the human engagement with what he calls 'social problems.'"[303] Remarking on the significance of the generally negative attitude toward the Negro, Du Bois characterizes it as "the critical rebound that follows every period of moral exhalation," adding that it is not "to be unsparingly condemned." He then goes on to describe it in terms of a general cycle of societal development in which are found "great waves of sympathy seizing mankind at times and succeeded by cold criticism and doubt." The phase of reaction is further differentiated into two possibilities: one "chokes and postpones reform or even kills it"; the other "leads to more rational and practical measures than mere moral enthusiasms could possibly offer." There does indeed appear to be putting into play a "dialectic of 'sympathy' and 'criticism,' of generosity and reaction." Such a reading is reinforced by Du Bois's illustrative account of the development in society's attitude toward poverty, whereby the cycle begins with "stern unbending morality" condemning the poor (thesis), followed by "the century of sympathy" toward them (antithesis), succeeded by a period of critical analysis employing statistics and sociology in assessing the conditions of poverty (synthesis). Significantly, the synthesis, or "reconciliation" as he terms it, entails both "the ideals of human betterment" (a synonym of sympathy) and critical rational inquiry, meaning quantitative measurement and analysis, what he refers to as "science." So, the terms of the dialectic have shifted to *idealism*—"the still persistent thrust for a broader and deeper humanity"—and *criticism*—"the still powerful doubt as to what the Negro can and will do"—the synthesis being *scientific analysis*—"a disposition to study the Negro problem honestly, and to inaugurate measures of social reform in the light of the scientific study."[304]

An abstraction occurs here, however, whereby anti-black racism is recognized as an instantiation of the general human tendency to constitute society through the delineation and hatred of the other. This has a double effect. On the one hand, it undermines or at least weakens the force of the metaphysics behind racism: the proposition that there is in nature such a thing as the Negro. On the other, it construes the Negro as a phenomenon of sociopolitical significance. While the bloody consequences of the invention of *Negro* as an instrumentality for violently forcing sentient flesh to embody fungible property is a principal concern, its denoting skin color and a physiognomic variety is rendered accidental, a trivial fact, to the general tendency. Du Bois goes so far as to equate anti-black racism with the sectarian hatred of the Reformation and Counterreformation, as well as the sixteenth-century Spaniard's attitude toward Englishmen, and Frenchmen's toward Italians with that of twentieth-century Englishmen toward Hottentots, and Americans toward Filipinos. Again, this is a dialectic, so there is a counter tendency working concomitantly with the primary tendency of bloody differentiation in a progressive teleological movement toward an order of universal recognition. A corollary to the construal and abstraction of racism instantiating a general human tendency to base community on violent differentiation is that of the processes of capitalist expansion instantiating an equally general tendency toward rational order. In this way, while "the whole problem of the color line is peculiarly the child of the nineteenth and twentieth centuries," it is recognizable in its global expansion as a function of the general rhythms of history.[305] These are remarkably European rhythms set to an Enlightenment melody, culminating in a Kantian cosmopolitan peace. Perhaps such orientation is understandable, if not forgivable, given the depth of Du Bois's commitment in 1899 to the Negro Academy agenda, which was to achieve racial uplift through reason and full enfranchisement within the American project.

Bear in mind, the admonition to recognize the local situation as an aspect of a global problem was enunciated within the precincts of the political capital of the emerging American empire. It is not a trivial matter that "The Present Outlook for the Dark Races of Mankind" is delivered in the second year of McKinley's first term as president a little over a mile away from the White House at the Lincoln Memorial Church, where the academy was situated. Du Bois's analysis of capitalist imperial global expansion is expressly in regard to what he calls "the new imperial policy" of the United States that was being implemented by McKinley's administration in the acquisition by military conquest of the overseas colonies of Puerto Rico, Guam, and the Philippines, as well as the annexation of the independent Republic of Hawaii, and military occupation of putatively independent Cuba. In other words, Du Bois was speaking at the dawn of what will come to be regarded as the American phase of capitalist expansion, which Henry Luce christened at its mid-twentieth century apex, "the American century." Recognizing the Negro question in relation to "the whole problem of the color line" worldwide leads to an analysis of the constitution of a capitalist-driven global social order. Du Bois in 1899 is already discerning and critiquing the emergence of a worldwide imperialism of the market, an American economy of force he describes in *Dusk of Dawn* as an "evil and hindrance blocking the way of life . . . whose current [raciological] form depended on the long history of relations and contact between thought and idea."[306] In all its iterations, *Negro* is emblematic of capitalist modernity's historical formations. It is an articulation across the transformations in the configuration of capital from the mercantile accumulation of principality, to the European-centered national market system of imperialist colonialism, to the U.S.-centered imperialist international financial system that emerged during the period framed by the end of Reconstruction in 1868 and the 1918 Treaty of Versailles. Yet, this assessment of the emergent worldwide capitalist order is done *from* the American perspective, subsuming the worldwide color line to the "greater Negro question." It is worth quoting Du Bois at length to remove any doubt that when he refers to the color line as a belt round the world he means the subsumption of the dark races in general under the designation, *Negro*:

> The expansion of nations to-day is leading to countless repetitions of that which we have in America to-say—the inclusion of nations within nations—of groups of undeveloped peoples brought into contact with advanced races under the same government, language and culture. The lower races will in nearly every case be dark races. German Negroes, Portuguese Negroes, Spanish Negroes, English East Indians, Russian Chinese, American Filipinos—such are the groups which following the example of the American Negroes will in the 20th century strive, not by war and rapine but by the mightier weapons of peace and culture to gain a place and a name in the civilized world.

Arguably, this is an elaboration with broad historical exempla of the Strong Man/Submissive Man dialectic set out in his 1890 Harvard speech. In the 1899 Negro Academy address, however, submission is aligned with universal suffrage and civilizational advance. When Du Bois charges his fellow academicians to "quit ourselves like men," and not simply to follow but to lead civilization, he is calling them to challenge the strong man paradigm of civilization. He warns them to be wary of the ideals of the rabble who insist being victorious in this world requires them "to wade through war to peace, through murder to love, and through death to life"; and using language foreshadowing that used by John Jones in his welcome home speech to the gathered congregations at Altamaha, he admonishes: "Moral mastery over the minds of men—the ability, through work and purity of purpose—these things and these things alone will ensure victory to any group of men if the 20th century fulfill its promise."[307] After calling them to work and morality as the only viable means to overcome strong man brutality and achieve civilization, he concludes with a statement of necessity: "And finally, we need in large measure the spirit of sacrifice."[308]

This is a rather freighted term in Du Bois's vocabulary. He first publicly uses it in his 1890 Harvard address, emphasizing that the submission of strength in community is "not in mere aimless sacrifice." Even though the extent of the load is not readily apparent there, it is at the heart of the doctrine of submission. His use of it here in the 1899 Negro Academy address sets the heft: "I do not mean anything maudlin or sentimental," Du Bois declaims. "I mean clear calculating decision on the part of Negro men and women that they are going to give up something of their personal wealth, their own advancement and ambition, to aid in the ultimate emancipation of the nine millions of their fellows in this land, and the countless millions the world over. Without this we cannot co-operate, we cannot secure the greatest good of all, we cannot triumph over our foes." Du Bois then enigmatically ends by quoting Emerson's poem, "Sacrifice":

> THOUGH love repine, and reason chafe,
> There came a voice without reply,—
> "'T is man's perdition to be safe,
> When for the truth he ought to die."

There is a pronouncedly ambiguous relation between Du Bois's definition of sacrifice and Emerson's quatrain. While his saying sacrifice is nonsentimental or maudlin gibes with the first clause in line one of Emerson's quatrain, dismissing love's dissatisfaction, his emphasis on clear calculating decision is at odds with the dismissal of reason's objection. The perdition of safety being taken as a metaphor for personal wealth is commensurate with Emersonian transcendentalism. But what about death as truth? Du Bois's call is not to give up life for some transcendent aim but to surrender personal gain for the greater good of collective freedom. The contradictory tension between Du Bois's definition and the Emerson quatrain he quotes compels us to ask: What precisely does he mean by sacrifice?

LOVE AIN'T SACRIFICIAL

When describing the liberatory life-enhancing effect of the *studia humanitatis* curriculum in "Of the Wings of Atlanta," the fifth chapter of *The Souls of Black Folk*, Du Bois gives as motto a line taken from Goethe's *Faust*: "Entbehren sollst du; sollst Entbehren!" He will have frequent recourse to this motto in subsequent writings, generally presented untranslated in the original German. An example of such is the July 1914 *Crisis* editorial where, commemorating the recently deceased Samuel Henry Bishop, Du Bois quotes the phrase in German without translation, characterizing it as the tenet of "a peculiar self-Forgetful idealism" that Bishop often cited and lived by.[309] Where he does translate the phrase, it is as: "Thou shalt forego; shalt do without!" For instance, in chapter 13 of his autobiography, where he quotes the full passage from "Of the Wing of Atlanta" in which he first deploys the Faust line, he displaces the original German with his translation; and in the last chapter of the same book where he offers both the German and his English-language translation, claiming, "This is a call for sacrifice."[310] Du Bois's translation reflects his reading against the irony of Faust's expression, uttered in refutation of the Christian doctrine of sacrificing this world for the next as he prepares to sign the contract with

Mephistopheles. To put it in its original context, the line is from Studierzimmer 2; it is part of Faust's response to Mephistopheles's entering the room and remarking on the nobility of his attire:

> *In jedem Kleide werd ich wohl die Pein*
> *Des engen Erdenlebens fühlen.*
> *Ich bin zu alt, um nur zu spielen,*
> *Zu jung, um ohne Wunsch zu sein.*
> *Was kann die Welt mir wohl gewähren?*
> *Was kann die Welt mir wohl gewähren?*
> *Entbehren sollst du! sollst entbehren!*
> *Das ist der ewige Gesang,*
> *Der jedem an die Ohren klingt,*
> *Den, unser ganzes Leben lang,*
> *Uns heiser jede Stunde singt.*[311]

G. M. Priest, in his 1808 translation, calls the scene "Faust's study 2," and renders it

> *I'll feel, whatever my attire,*
> *The pain of life, earth's narrow way*
> *I am too old to be content with play,*
> *Too young to be without desire.*
> *What can the world afford me now?*
> *What can the world afford me now?*
> *Thou shalt renounce! Renounce shalt thou!*
> *That is the never-ending song*
> *Which in the ears of all is ringing,*
> *Which always, through our whole life long,*
> *Hour after hour is hoarsely singing.*[312]

Exercising a bit more poetic license, Charles T. Brooks gave the same lines as

> *In every dress I well may feel the sore*
> *Of this low earth-life's melancholy.*
> *I am too old to live for folly,*
> *Too young, to wish for nothing more.*
> *Am I content with all creation?*
> *Renounce! renounce! Renunciation—*
> *Such is the everlasting song*
> *That in the ears of all men rings,*
> *Which every hour, our whole life long,*
> *With brazen accents hoarsely sings.*[313]

While not taking quite such license, Du Bois's paraphrase—"Thou shalt forego; shalt do without!"—is itself somewhat against the grain, presenting, as Wilson Jeremiah Moses has noted, the fundamental, and one might add Augustinian, paradox that self-fulfillment comes from self-denial.[314] Du Bois referred to this varyingly as "the Gospel of Sacrifice," "the spirit of sacrifice," and "renunciation," the latter being a distillation of the Faust-derived motto. In each instance, however, he is always careful to emphatically mark its nontheological and nonmetaphysical denotation. That is to say, what he did *not* mean by sacrifice is surrender of oneself, of life to a redemptive aspect in aspiration of salvation: it does not mean martyrdom. Even as renunciation, the most elaborate explication of which is provided in his 1906 essay "Saint Francis Assisi," it is certainly not renunciation of this world. Two years earlier, in his undelivered commencement address to the 1904 class of the renowned Washington, DC, M Street High School, entitled "The Joy of Living," he had written: "To give up the joy of the world to no purpose is a sinful thing."[315] And on that assessment, doing so in the expectation of eternal happiness in the afterlife is to no real purpose. What sacrifice as renunciation means for Du Bois is unselfishness in direct contradiction to the dominant doctrine of society at large, derived from Locke's concept of property enshrined in the Constitution, according to which the foundations of civilization is personal gain and the protection of such. Sacrifice is not the *absolute* renunciation of personal gain, however. "It is not always thus necessary." On the contrary, personal gain is secured only through sacrifice, which means, Du Bois says, "a plain practical facing of this fact that in order that there shall be the largest sum of *you* in the world it is often necessary for you to give up some of *your* personal pleasures. . . . Most of the sacrifices in life are little things in themselves—they entail but small discomfort to you and yet they make thousands happier and healthier and better."[316]

There is, accordingly, one rule of life: "not simply my Joy but the Joy of the world." Again, this emphatically means the material phenomenal world.

> It is simply reasonable that living as I do in a world of men, I should seek the highest joy of that world. I should try and make the earth a beautiful place for them and for me. I should try to keep their bodies and my body in the fullness of health and strength that we may enjoy the world about us and within. They and I ought to think the thoughts of other men and know the knowledge of the world. We ought to view and enjoy the beauty of picture and song and about all and through all we should let like souls seek like, to think and dream of the way of Life.[317]

Sacrifice in this sense, although not as extreme as Rousseau's theory of total alienation to the community as requisite for a viable just society, is in the same vein as what Aristotle called distributive justice. It is one of three great constants in Du Bois's radical program to secure Negro worldliness—the freedom to love and aspire in this world now and in its future. Addressing the matter in relation to humanist learning as the highest human aspiration, he states: "In the higher life . . . there are three things: Work, and Love and Sacrifice—these three—but the greatest of these is Sacrifice.³¹⁸ Once again, Du Bois is paraphrasing 1 Corinthians 13.13. Only here, he elides Pauline "charity" with Du Boisian "sacrifice." What connects charity and sacrifice is desire, which is love at its most primitive level, appetite. This is the message of John Jones's homecoming speech when he calls on the combined black Protestant congregations of Altamaha to join the world of the twentieth century, where broader ideas of human brotherhood and destiny supersede religious affiliation, and then speaks of the need for "charity and popular education, and particularly of the spread of wealth and work."

The circuit I am proposing, from John's invocation of charity to the equating of it with sacrifice and desire is all the more legitimate and open since it flows toward a word that can properly be considered *the* synonym of the term "charity" as he deploys it there. The word, of course, is ἀγάπη (*agapē*), which, as we have already noted is Paul's, and is central to Royce's ethical project, as well as that of Peirce, on whose thinking Royce so relies. It is also a term overlaid with theological significance in the long history of Bible translation, beginning with the Septuagint, where, as has already been noted apropos Nietzsche's critique of the Pauline doctrine of love, it is first deployed to translate the Hebrew Torahic "אהבה [*ahava*]" as a selfless love in contradistinction to Plato's sense of ἔρως (*eros*) as the acquisitive desire that begins with the physical body but aspires to the truly Good and Beautiful beyond appearances. Paul's deploying the Hellenized Leviticus term served his effort to displace law and duty—the formal order of *halakha*, the actual practices of which were to sustain, or save, the world—with faith, hope, and love. The Greek Canonical Gospels follow Paul's usage of *agapē* in I Corinthians 13:13 in particular, where it, along with faith and hope, displaces law and duty, expressed as: "And now faith, hope, and love [*agapē*] abide, these three; and the greatest of these is love [*agapē*]." The *Vetus Latina* renders *agapē* as *caritas* in the same passage from I Corinthians: "Nunc autem manent fides, spes, caritas, tria hæc: major autem horum est caritas," although elsewhere, say in John, it is given as *dīligō*, meaning something like esteem, suggesting an abstract or non-corporal love. Jerome's Latin Vulgate repeats this, giving *caritas* in I Corinthians. Tyndale, relying on his philological understanding of the Septuagint and the Hebrew Bible, as well as being encouraged by Erasmus, who thought the Vulgate translation did not match known pre-Christian usage, uniformly renders *agapē* as "love" throughout his translation of the Bible.³¹⁹ His eschewal of the Vulgate's *caritas* for love as the most precise English rendering of *agapē* was one of the three instances of mistranslated words Thomas More offered as evidence that Tyndale's English Bible was corrupting the Gospels to the "devilish" heresy of Luther.[320] This dispute over the proper translation of Jerome's *caritas* into English between these two key figures of the English Reformation and Counterreformation goes to the heart of the question of whether Du Bois's concept of sacrifice is charity.

Even though More gives his argument a philological cast in dispute with Tyndale's own philological grounds for his translation,[321] the principal force of his indictment against Tyndale's "love" is theological: "It seemeth that he laboureth of purpose to minish the reverent mind that men bear to charity, and therefore he changeth that name of holy virtuous affection, into the bare name of love common to the virtuous love that man beareth to God, and to the lewed love between flecke & his make [a worthless fellow and his paramour]."[322] Differentiating between Holy virtuous love and lewd love follows the distinction Jerome makes in the Vulgate between *caritas* (selfless love of God) and *cupiditas* (mundane earthly love), which Augustine explicates as a principle of theology. Bringing the Greek philosophical tradition's understanding of desire (ὄρεξις, *orexis*), most particularly Plotinus's, to bear on Pauline *agapē*, Augustine postulates that love is nothing else than to crave something for its own sake. Love is desire (*appetitus*), and every desire is bound to a definite object that sparks it, toward which it moves or seeks to attain. Augustine's theology is arguably anthropology in disguise, and pronouncedly so in his disquisitions on love, where the assertion that all humans always desire something outside themselves is supported by the premise that each and every individual human is not self-sufficient. The existential necessity of human sociality leads to the logical conclusion that to be human is to desire: "For what person is there who does anything at all except by love?"[323] Desire articulates a tripartite economy of the desiring subject, the object of desire, and the desire.[324] "What, then, is love [*amor*]," Augustine asks, "except a kind of life which binds or seeks to bind some two things together, namely, the lover [*amantem*], and that which is loved [*amatur*]?"[325] To be human is not only to desire, but the specific character or quality of one's humanity is determined by the nature of the object of desire. Hence the admonition, "Love! But be careful what you love! Love of God [*Amor Dei*] and love of neighbor [*amor proximi*] is called *caritas*; love of the world and love of the age of humanity is called *cupiditas*. Let *cupiditas* be tethered, *caritas* stirred up!"[326] Tyndale's retort is that both *agapē* and *caritas* in their archaic pre-Christian usages signified other than "godly love," and that *agapē* in particular "is common unto all loves."[327] The implied argument being that the fine distinctions of types of love is a construction of church theology and not the Scriptures themselves. Furthermore, the use of "charity" to mean the special sense of godly love denoted by *caritas* "is no known English."[328] Here, he is on solid philological grounds; "charity" comes into English as a

Christian term, with a very church-bound connotation. And that is at the crux of his effacing it from his English translation of Scriptures as well as More's outrage at the effacement.

Back of the philological dispute between these two English scholars of Greek, fueled by differences in their theories of translation, was the more urgent ecclesiological one. Charity is foundational to the institution of the church (Ephesians 5:25–30), as Tyndale well knew, which is why More points out that his refusal to use it even in passages such as I Corinthians 13 where a distinct kind of *good* love is being made indicates more than merely a matter of scholarly philological interpretation. Tyndale's not recognizing important distinctions between types of love stems from his disregarding the Vulgate for the Septuagint and the 1522 edition of Erasmus's Greek New Testament, *Novum Testamentum omne*. In tandem with his translating ὁμολογήσῃς (*homologēsēs*) as "knowledge" rather than "confession" and μετάνοια (*metánoia*) as "repentance" rather than "penance," foregoing the *Vulgate confitearis* and *pœnitentiæ* respectively, the effacing of charity undermines the Scriptural basis for the sacrament of penance (confession)—which Tyndale, taking a page from Erasmus's *Colloquies*, considers "clean against the scripture, . . . and a foul stinking sacrifice unto the filthy idol Priapus."³²⁹ His refusal of *caritas* is, thus, an aspect of the Protestant assault on the church's dispensation of indulgences as instrumentalities of salvation, the primary instance of which was of the church's long tradition of offering indulgences for good works of charity in penance. At issue is the nature of grace. Charitable giving done as penance in *gratia gratum faciens* with the aspiration of achieving consummating grace (*gratia consummans*) benefits the individual giver whom it heals and sanctifies. The nature of the charitable act was very much at hand for More in his criticism of Tyndale's uniformly translating *agapē* as love, because of how it disarticulates charity in almsgiving from penance on the basis of the Protestant proposition that sanctification is achieved through faith alone, *sola fide*. Charitable giving is not done in hope of being rewarded by grace (in penance), but rather it is done as a fruit of grace having already been given freely with the acceptance of Christ's sacrifice, which makes it, for Tyndale, like baptism and the Eucharist, a sign of acceptance of Christ's sacrifice and obedience to God. Such almsgiving in charity, with love, does not benefit the giver, who is already sanctified, which is *why* he gives charity; it benefits the recipient. The gift is given in selfless love, with the principal beneficiary being the recipient whose alleviation from poverty has communal effect, which is the true performance of loving the neighbor. Effacing charity from Scripture is so entangled with denigrating the sacraments it not only erodes centuries of church tradition manifesting and elucidating the truth of Godly love (*caritas*), but also the legitimacy of the visible church as the body of Christ. "For this is much to be marked," More writes, "that Tyndale cannot bear the fleshliness of *our* spiritualty because the fleshliness of *their* church is spiritual! . . . Tyndale would we should ween that this eight hundred years and more, Christ hath had no church in the world at all."[330]

By invoking charity expressly in the name of a human brotherhood and destiny and claiming it issues from contemporary earthly knowledge rather than from hope and faith in a divine future, John Jones gives it a very worldly aspect. He binds love, the milk of kindness, to the drives, appetites, and aspirations of humanity rather than the Passion of Christ, foreclosing on the theology of love that reads in Christ's suffering the supreme act of charity. This, combined with his remarking on the edifying force of charity in terms of capitalist industrialization and philanthropy, reversing the rhetorical thrust of I Corinthians 13, challenges the very foundation of the beloved community: the certainty that the answer to the question "What is the relevance of the neighbor and oneself?" is "In loving fellowship with God." This fellowship is precisely what the black congregants gathered at the Baptist church in Altamaha "held sacred." And they held it so over and against the profane, decadent irresponsibility of the life-world of neo-slavery in the reconstructed republic where slavery's legacy of blurring the differentiation between thing and person was still in force. The republic's life-world was decadent because it was disrupted at its innermost core, its Constitution, according to which realizing its foundational Lockean principle of natural moral personhood required its simultaneous negation. Constitutionally, the slave was a laboring thing without the *full* moral standing of a person. The only moral aspect attributable to the slave was culpability for crime.[331] Property adumbrating personhood notwithstanding, although forced to work like "hogs or horses," unlike them the slave was held responsible for specific acts of moral turpitude. In the face of that political-economic system, the black church offered hope in loving fellowship with God.

Granting this, we know full well that the black congregations of Altamaha holding on to church fellowship was not at all based on the Augustinian theological grounds over which Tyndale and More struggled. Du Bois rather clearly mapped the grounds on which they stood in "Of the Faith of the Fathers" when, referring to what was known as "Shouting," he says:

> The mad abandon of physical fervor—stamping, shrieking, and shouting, the rushing to and fro and wild waving of arms, the weeping and laughing, the vision and the trance. All this is nothing new in the world, but old as religion, as Delphi and Endor. And so firm a hold did it have on the Negro, that many generations firmly believed that without this visible manifestation of the God there could be no true communion with the invisible.[332]

He is talking, of course, about ἔκστασις (ecstasy), marking its pre-Christian ritualization in the ancient Greek Dionysian Mysteries, as well as Saul's oracular consultation. In the context of American slavery, however, rather than classical Greek or Hebraic sources, the pre-Christian means African. Shouting, with its enraptured bodily ecstasy, confusing the limits of physical animality, the human, and the divine in a manner often seen as demonic, provided an experience of freedom in release from the decadent responsibility of slavery. As such, the ecstatic rapture pronounces an estrangement from the life-world of responsibility, opening up to an alternative world of irresponsibility. There is no equivalence between the two worlds, but rather there are two possible lives, only one of which is the true life of the human. In the energy of Shouting, the enslaved human finds his true self. The superimposition of Christianity subjects this energy to the supreme good, the *summum bonum* of God's self-forgetting love, vesting the demonic ecstasy with responsibility in fellowship with God, in the inscrutable relation to the absolute highest being in whose hands each soul is internally. It is now the divine gift of pentecostal moments when "the Spirit pours out upon all flesh,"[333] such as the deacon facilitated with the rude eloquence of his retort to John's admonitions, using his words not only in rebuttal of John, but also to break from the profane life of slavery, transcending the phenomenal reality of existing with and among things bestowing on it a meaning that would otherwise be unknown. If the life of a slave is constantly threatened by loss—losing family and friends to the auction-block, losing whatever limited freedom of movement the master permits, losing even one's very life; in short, losing all to the desires of the master—the true life is that ecstatic moment of rapture where the happiness of having is eternal and not at all subject to fear of loss. Freedom from this fear is what the black church gave the slave. More than freedom from the fear of pain and death, faith in fellowship with God freed the slave from the psychological trauma of the unrelenting violent terror of ordinary life—"yeah though I walk through the valley of death, I shall fear no evil"—by providing a lifeline—"My soul followeth hard after thee: thy right hand upholdeth me"—whereby the path to salvation and the eternal happiness of dwelling with the Lord is assured.[334] This situation does not change with slavery's abolition in law. The social transformation inaugurated by that abolition consisted in the rather dramatic shift of the burden of labor from a *thing* owned as property to some other *disowned thing*, the Negro, who had a greater personal culpability disproportionate to personal rights, which amounted to the criminalization of black life itself as an instrumentality of coercively binding the Negro to "involuntary servitude."[335] So the church still functioned as the preserve of person in the enduring aspiration of an existence free from fear, an existence that is beyond the terrible material world of man. It still offered hope in loving fellowship with God.

John Jones challenges all of this to the core when he demands the actualization of *caritas* now, which means he holds to a conception of humanity that differs from the Pauline/Augustinian anthropology. According to Jones's anthropology, humanity is inherently capable of empathetic love without needing to discover its basis in a greater transcendent power. There is no need for salvation through divine charity manifest in absolute sacrifice of the self, because humanity's natural state is not that of sin, of the fallen. What humanity must rid itself of is the foundational violence of the social order, which is to say, it must rid itself of the putative necessity of the rite of blood sacrifice as the requisite for securing the social order. On the verge of meeting his violent death at the hands of a white lynch mob for daring to threaten that order, John does not say: "Therefore doth my Father love me, because I lay down my life."[336] The love John Jones professes and enacts does not call for violence in proof of its force. His murder is not a death for salvation. We have already considered how his utterance of the *Lohengrin* bride-song line "Freudig geführt, ziehet dahin [Joyfully led, enter this place]" at precisely that moment is a renunciation of the ethos of sacrifice on his part. Singing that line, at precisely that moment forecloses on John's being taken up into a narrative of redemptive self-sacrifice. There is no Passion there, no scene of prolonged torture and violent death, in which the fleshly suffering of the victim expunges the flesh of its frailties and flaws redeeming it.

"Of the Coming of John" does not entail the sort of Christian typology found in the dozen or so short stories Du Bois wrote between 1900 and 1935, in which a black, Christ-like figure is hung for preaching a gospel of social justice and equality. These stories have recently attracted the attention of Du Bois readers such as Jonathon Kahn, who, acutely attentive to Du Bois's use of religious figures and phrasings as indicating a proto-black liberation theology, discerns in them "a religious disposition that is synonymous with social criticism of this-worldly conditions and concerns."[337] Characterizing the stories as typological lynching parables, modeled on the Passion of Christ, he regards them as constituting one half of what he calls "Du Bois's sacrificial discourse." The other half consists of Du Bois's explicit references in essays and talks to the "Gospel of Sacrifice" as a prescription of civic ethics. Given the complex association of sacrifice with Christianity, and Christianity with the horror of lynching, Kahn is compelled to ask: "Why Du Bois did not conclude that sacrifice was an American category thoroughly rooted in blood, abuse, and suffering, and thus forever tainted and one that society is better off working to live without?"[338] Why does he use the word *sacrifice* to denote a nonmetaphysical black virtue of social transformation?

Addressing this question, Kahn invokes Ralph Ellison's description of lynching as "the ritual sacrifice that was dedicated to the ideal of white supremacy," which he takes to imply "that lynchings are embedded in an economy of religious practice."[339] Having called on Ellison, he immediately turns to René Girard's theoretical work on ritual sacrifice and the scapegoat, claiming that it "uncannily describes American lynching and confirms what Ellison and black America writ large intuitively knew long ago: African Americans were being subjected to a system of human sacrifice by a white Christian America."[340] This turn to Girard's theory of sacrifice is central to Kahn's account of what Du Bois is doing with sacrifice and the way he reads the lynching parables in relation to "Of the Coming of John." Among the stories he pays particular close attention to is the two-page "The Son of God," which Du Bois published in the December 1933 issue of *Crisis*.[341]

This story opens with a scene of domestic violence—"Joe struck her hard, right in the face," reported from the perpetrator Joe's perspective. Mary, his wife, has just told him she is having a baby who was not his, and the only reply she will give to his demanding to know the father is: "He is the Son of God!" Joe eventually accepts as his own the child born of Mary whom she names Joshua. At twelve, Joshua is already decisively disputing church doctrine with the Methodist preacher in Sunday school, and telling the church elders "what was what." He chooses to become a carpenter after completing his schooling. But rather than carpentry, he dedicates his time to what he calls "his father's business." On hearing this, Joe replies, "It ain't no business of mine," and begins complaining to Mary that Joshua is "hanging around a lot of Communists and talking on street corners and saying things about property that white folks ain't going to stand for." Mary only replies: "He is the Son of God." At one point, Joshua is reported to have raised his friend Laz Simmons, whom a white mob has beaten and left for dead, simply by saying "Laz, get up." At hearing this story, Mary goes to prayer meeting where she shouts: "He is the Resurrection and the Life. He that believeth in Him, though he were dead, yet shall live!" Joshua keeps running with Outcast and tramps, holding his own meetings on street corners, saying things like: "Poor people are better than rich people because they work for what they wear and eat. There won't be any rich people in heaven." And: "Don't work all the time. Sit down and rest and sing sometimes. Everything's all right. Give God time." Eventually, he leaves home on a long journey with a "Hail Mary!" Over the years, Joe and Mary hear rumors of Joshua's doings, and when he reaches his early thirties, they receive news he has been lynched by a white mob on numerous charges: "Worshipping a new God." "Living with white women!" "Getting up a revolution." At hearing of his death, Mary, sitting in a black dress of mourning in her parlor, "where an oil lamp in the window lit the rigid halo of her hair and threw across the yard the black shadow of a noosed and hanging rope," reflects on Joshua's life, saying: "His name shall be called Wonderful, Councillor [sic], the Mighty God, the Ever-Lasting Father, and the Prince of Peace.... Behold the Sign of Salvation—a noosed rope." Joe, crushed and also mourning, "saw the shadow of the Noose across the world and heard Mary's voice looming in the night: 'He is the son of God!'"[342]

Clearly, this story is typological in a way "Of the Coming of John" simply is not. Nevertheless, Kahn situates them together, reading "Of the Coming of John" as a parable pivoting on "the triangular confrontation between the secular black protagonist, John; the Southern church of his rural community; and the town's white racist power structure . . . that results in John's being lynched, transforming him into a figure of Christ-like sacrifice."[343] Yet there is no indication whatsoever *in* the "Of the Coming of John" narrative that such transformation occurs. In fact, there is no depiction of the lynching, only John Jones's awareness of the men on horses thundering toward him, led by the judge. Significantly, the lynching event is not depicted in "The Son of God" either; nor, for that matter, in nearly all the so-called lynching parables. Rather, it is referred to, argued for and against, with its mysterious significance remarked in the aftermath by some usually female survivor, in this case the victim's mother. The exception to this is the 1911 story "Jesus Christ in Georgia," which was subsequently published in a slightly revised version in *Darkwater* as "Jesus Christ in Texas."[344] Even then, it is described minimally: "The mob snarled and worked silently. Right to the limb of the red oak. They hoisted the struggling, writhing black man." And, as with the other stories its significance is remarked by a female, this time the white woman for whom the lynching was enacted at her husband's demand, but who knew the victim's innocence, having initially accepted his friendship on faith before seeing his color. No matter, in all the so-called lynching parables, there is nothing redemptive about the lynching; nothing about it that forestalls catastrophe or alleviates a plague or sanctifies the polity or land. The expressions of sanctification by survivors such as Mary are desperate invocations of a transcendent, after-life justice, demanded by the persistence and magnitude of murderous violence. They are expressions not of submission, but rather of resistance: the restoration of the beloved community lost to slavery and racialized oppression on the other side of the River Jordan. In these stories, Du Bois depicts the futility of that resistance: Mary's refrain cannot even console her husband's despair at Joshua's lynching, the closing sentence of the story is "And Joe buried his head in the dirt and sobbed."[345] Rather than symbolizing resolution of societal tensions and salvation, the lynching adumbrating each of these stories indicates a fundamental paradox, if not outright contradiction: How can an act of blood sacrifice, of an individual's murder to appease the collective, be in evidence of love? Insofar as Du Bois's typological depiction of Jesus Christ as a black man highlights the essence of true Christian ethics, what he exposes is not merely the evil of white racism, but the scapegoat mechanism at work in Eucharistic mythology, thereby precluding its mythologization. In all of these stories, those traumatized by the lynching are incapable of explaining, even to themselves, its meaningfulness except as simply an act of bloody cruel murder. This failure of narration on their part means they cannot successfully mitigate its violence with a tale of purpose, a teleological story of ultimate meaning. They have only the unresolved trauma, which is psychosis-inducing. Regarding these lynching parables in relation to Du Bois's Gospel of Sacrifice, the relevant question is not why does he use sacrifice as prescription for civic ethics, but what does he mean by *sacrifice*?

The answer to this is found, once again, in his translation of the Faust line, "Entbehren sollst du; sollst Entbehren," on the basis of which he elaborates the Gospel of Sacrifice. Arguably, that sense of sacrifice is emblemized by John Jones, but not in the way Kahn reads the story. The difference lies in its non-depiction of lynching, which is a possible imminent event regarded disdainfully from John Jones's stream-of-consciousness perspective as an anticipated interruption of his robust engagement with living-in-the-world, a background rhythm "of horses galloping, galloping on" that he knows will terminate the engagement by force, but to which he will not surrender his being. "Then, as the storm burst round him, he rose slowly to his feet and turned his closed eyes toward the sea. And the world whistled in his ear." Jones's possibly imminent lynching is not a sacrifice. It can only be construed as such if the nondepicted killing is the meaning of the story. But we know, in fact, when carefully attending to the narrative, that "Of the Coming of John" is not about death or the redemption of meaningful life in violent death at the hands of the mob.

When Ellison describes lynching as "the ritual sacrifice that was dedicated to the ideal of white supremacy," he is describing the significance of the murder for its perpetrators, its social value form them.[346] Ellison's investment in James Frazer's theoretical work on scapegoating set out in *The Golden Bough* as applicable to lynching is evident throughout his critical writing.[347] In Frazer's theory "scapegoat" or "scapegoating" designates in the abstract any rites involving the symbolic transference of whatever evil afflicts humans to something, whether inanimate objects, animals, or other humans, so that entity becomes the embodiment of the evil and is expelled, which often entails its destruction or killing, as a way of cleansing the community. Frazer elaborates his theory utilizing Robertson Smith's evolutionary decipherment of Leviticus achieved through combining the typology of scriptural high criticism with a mixture of Darwinian evolution and Comtean positivism.[348] He extrapolates from the biblical term "scapegoat"—which is Tyndale's coinage, rendering the sense of the Septuagint χίμαρος ἀποπομπαίου (*chímaros apopompaíou*), itself rendering the contextual meaning of the Hebrew term, עֲזָאזֵל (*'azāzel*)—used in Leviticus 16:8: "And Aaron shall cast a lot on two goats [שְׁנֵי הַשְּׂעִירִם, *shanī has-'irim*]: one lot for the Lord, and the other lot for *'azāzel* [לַעֲזָאזֵל]." The

חַטָּאת קָרבָּן

one for the Lord is to be קָרבָּן חַטָּאת (*qorban khatta'ah*), the expiatory blood sacrifice that draws God near.³⁴⁹ The important thing to note here is that the *'azāzel* is not a *qorban*. It is not a gift to God, which is the fundamental sense of sacrifice in the biblical, Torah, context; it is instead sent far away from the Tabernacle into the wilderness, where it is eventually cast ceremoniously from the heights of mount *'azāzel* to its death on the rocks. In this respect, however much Frazer's theory of scapegoating informed Ellison's description of lynching, it does not apply to what happens with Jones in "Of the Coming of John."

Along these same lines, Girard's *le mécanisme du bouc émissaire*, "the scapegoat mechanism," which he sets against Frazer's conception of "scapegoating," is equally inapplicable—although, it may well reflect Ellison's description of lynching in general, as Kahn claims, which is somewhat ironic given Ellison's reliance on Frazer. Girard disputes the primacy of ritual hypothesis propagated by Frazer along with the other anthropologists of religion and society who were known as the Cambridge Ritualists. He is particularly critical of the governing thesis of *Golden Bough* that all religions and the foundation of human society originate in fertility cults centered on the worship and sacrifice of a sacred king, which Frazer formulates as the dying-and-raising god myth, with ritual blood-sacrifice, particularly scapegoating, being the technology of the mythic cult. Honing in on the fact that this thesis is based on simply turning "straight to Leviticus for a Hebrew rite to head the list of a whole nonexistent category of ritual," Girard dismisses Frazer's interpreting the biblical expression *scapegoat* in only the ritual sense and making a generalization of it. That interpretation dehistoricizes Bnei Yisra'el, and in so doing disregards the fundamental question of whether there exists a connection between religion in general and the type of phenomenon alluded to when we say that an individual or a minority group acts as "scapegoat" for the majority. To rectify this, Girard postulates that first there was an actual murder, driven by what he calls *mimetic desire*, which inaugurates the process of homonization, the passage from animality to humanity, and makes human society possible. The correlation of ritual and myth is consequent to that human killing, narrativizing it in themes such as the agricultural cycle or the dying-and-rising king in order to attribute to it an inevitable necessity. According to the theory of *mimetic desire*, the model of mimicry is the desiring other; and insofar as mimicry of the other's desire—that is to say, desiring the same thing the other first desired—entails distinct propriety, it is pervaded with a desire for the disappearance or death of the model, which is reciprocated by the model. Mimetic desire, thus, precipitates a contagious similarity, which Girard refers to as "une crise d'indifférenciation généralisée [a crisis of generalized undifferentiation]," prompting a state of competition leading to a cycle of reciprocal violence that risks escalating into communal self-destruction. The actual event of primal murder consolidates originary community solidarity by transferring the energy of mimetic rivalry and its attendant reciprocal violence into the communal act of murdering one individual. What Girard describes is the mechanism and not a rite of scapegoat sacrifice, and his concept of mimetic desire is focused primarily on the etiology of desire, with mimicry being a mechanism or instrumentality of desire. His hypothesis that the shift from animality to humanity is facilitated by mimicry is compelling in its stupendous archeological evidence. It is also rather archaic. Plato speaks of μιμητικους (*mimetikos*) in book 3 of the *Republic* where Socrates's concern is with mimicry as a pedagogical means of managing the violence of the guardians needed to preserve the *polis*. This concern with mimicry's pedagogical function has to do with Plato's understanding that mimicry means changing one's psyche, assimilating it to the character of the model; which is why the guardians must not imitate women, slaves, men of low character or conduct, banausic persons, or the voices of animals, except in juvenile play (παιδικός, *paidikos*). The guardians must engage in mimicry of a singular kind, assimilating virtuous, heroic character and thereby becoming individuated free men, standing apart in service of the absolute good as a means of sustaining the well-being of the *polis*, which requires their properly directed violence in defense of the *polis* against those threating it from outside. Reading along with Girard, we can recognize in Plato's distinction between good and bad mimicry the latter's antecedence; primordial mimicry of the other indeed leads to violence, but a violence that threatens communal existence as well as solidarity. The point of Plato's insistence on proper mimicry sanctioned by and in the service of the *polis* is to defuse this primordial mimicry, the incalculable consequence of which is apocalyptic internecine warfare, through a pedagogy that harnesses the violence by transposing mimicry as a self-destructive tendency fundamental to human nature into a properly philosophical virtuous expressive form: *haplé diegesis*.

Arguably Girard's theory of mimicry amends the Platonic account, postulating that prior to the management of mimicry-induced violence through philosophical narrativization, it was defused through the mechanism of scapegoat blood-sacrifice, which "reintroduces difference into a situation where everyone has come to resemble everyone else" in order to rescue society. Because Girard's concept of mimetic desire is focused primarily on the etiology of desire, mimesis functions as little more than the primary mechanism driving the scapegoat mechanism. Each time the community is rescued by the scapegoat mechanism, its tranquility is short lived because the mechanism of mimetic desire is still very much at work, compelling the community to try to re-create stability by immolating a new victim. This engenders the rite of sacrifice, engendering, in turn, the mythology of sacrifice, which works as a countermeasure against mimetic desire by first misconstruing its inherent self-destructive tendency as a social crisis or cultural catastrophe deemed to have been caused by some crime or inequity that then is attributed to a culprit, the scapegoat, who is guilty by association or affiliation and not direct involvement in the crime—he calls this *les signes victimaires* (victim signs).[350] The scapegoat's ritual murder short-circuits the reciprocal violence of the community's mimetic rivalry by transferring its energy into an actualization of the myth's narrative force that repeats the primordial act of violence with which community solidarity was originally constituted. This too is a *semiosis*, albeit pointedly not of the Aristotelian sort, which engenders a specific narrativization of violence as mythology. Indeed, the myth of the scapegoat, having been created to legitimate the rite, drives the repetitive ritual sacrifice. Girard maintains, "This is what happens whenever human communities survive and flourish.... Humanity's first cultural initiative is the imitation of the founding murder, which is one with the invention of *ritual sacrifice*."[351] Mythology does not free humanity from the self-destructive violence precipitated by its inherent tendency of mimicry, however. It merely forestalls the apocalyptic consequences by temporarily defusing the escalation in reciprocal violence, which continues to escalate across time because the scapegoat mechanism, in order to be effective, is predicated on the victim's guilt. Girard characterizes this culpability of the victim in his own murder as the mystification of archaic religions. This aspect of his theory of scapegoat sacrifice does indeed resonate with Ellison's description of lynching, suggesting that the lynching as "the awe-inspiring enactment of the myth of white supremacy" is an archaic religious rite.

Yet, even if it is granted that Girard's account of the scapegoat mechanism fits Ellison's description of lynching, it still does not account for why Judge Henderson's posse descends on John Jones, who has just murdered Henderson's son in order to stop him from raping his sister, Jennie. John's crime is homicide, albeit arguably justifiable homicide, and should the posse lynch him, it would be mob justice. I say, "should the posse lynch him," because, in point of narrative fact, we do not know what happens next, whether they simply apprehend him or string him up on the spot, despite the judge's threat to "lynch every Nigger in the land" in order to keep the Negro subordinate to white men. And truth be told, it does not matter, neither to John nor to the meaning of his story. "Of the Coming of John" is decidedly not a lynching parable. It is a story of living, of John's arriving at a keen sense of his freedom through his own efforts at thought and deed. If it is at all a parable, it is that of how, when left to his own devices, the Negro can and will excel. John is free, and in the very moment he is aware of that freedom and how he always already was so, he feels dutybound to take to his people back home, to, as Jennie remarks, make them all "unhappy" in precisely the way he is.

In straightforward narrative terms, what Jones's encounter with Henderson's posse achieves is the end of the narrative. Whatever violence may ensue, although it might terminate his narrative stream-of-consciousness, it has had absolutely no bearing on his development. Unlike Joshua in "The Son of God," the threat of lynching does not adumbrate John's actions. It is not foretold by a concerned loved one, such as Joshua's father, Joe. Even Judge Henderson's threat, with its attendant admonition to stay subservient, is taken in stride by John as so much predictable prerequisite noise that is to be acknowledged as a precondition for starting the school, only to then be simply disregarded. There is no meaning whatsoever to the immanent violence, except that it is immanent violence. John's signing a line from Wagner's opera when confronting the posse rather than a spiritual preempts any effort to redeem the violence for meaning, any narrative of salvation or scapegoat expurgation, exposing the imminent violence for what it truly is: a Roman circus that legitimates the collective mob's bloodlust by simply exercising the prerogative to kill, to consume flesh in ecstatic terrible sublime pleasure. Recall Lilburn Lewis's pleasure at butchering George alive. This touches on another aspect of Girard's theory of sacrifice that is germane here not merely because it too is inapplicable to "Of the Coming of John," but because it entails precisely the conception of sacrifice Du Bois's gospel sets on its head, freeing his concept of sacrifice from any investment in soteriology.

Let us assume the applicability of the scapegoat mechanism to lynching in general as manifestly an archaic religious rite with its predication on the victim's guilt. When Girard draws a distinction between this and what he calls "the only true religion . . . the one that demystifies archaic religions," he expressly means Christianity.[352] More specifically, he means the Passion, whereby Christ came to take the victim's place, putting himself at the heart of the system to reveal its hidden workings. And here he provides as clear a statement as any of his overall agenda in postulating his theory of mimetic desire: "Mimetic theory does not seek to demonstrate that myth is null, but to shed light on the fundamental discontinuity and continuity between the Passion and archaic religion." By Girard's account, the Passion of Christ is the only way out of the apocalyptic violence of mimetic desire: by first "teaching us that humanity results from sacrifice, is born with religion," and then by revealing the victim's innocence, it "makes positive what was still negative in myths: we now know that victims are never guilty."[353] Girard looks upon this revelation as leading to what he calls "indifférenciation positive [positive undifferentiation], in other words being *identified with others*. This is Christian love."[354] The love Girard has in mind here is not Paul's but that of the *lamb of God* proclaimed in the Gospel of John. Describing the scapegoat mechanism in terms of persecution, from the perspective of the persecutors, even though the expression "scapegoat" is not used in the Gospels, Girard interprets the *lamb of God* as "a perfect substitute." His claim that the Passion is what first reveals the innocence of the victims is not quite right, however. It is the fundamental aspect of the paradigmatic substitutionary sacrifice: Abraham's binding of Isaac, הָעֲקֵידָה (*ha-'Aqedah*). Abraham's unhesitant willingness to offer his only son whom he loved (אָהַבְתָ, *āhabtā*) as a burnt offering, לְעֹלָה (*le'olāh*), at the behest of a God testing his faith had already dispelled the conceit of the victim's guilt. His substitution of the ram at the behest of that same God reinforces the disarticulation of guilt from sacrifice. Even though ritual homicide is no longer required to appease God in order to secure humanity, some blood-sacrifice, זֶבַח (*zevach*), some life must be taken in *qorban*, in approaching God. This is done in duty, מִצְוָה (*mitsvá*): the law requires blood atonement. There is neither empathy nor sentimentality involved; there is no identification between the sacrificial animal and the sacrificing human. After Abraham, sacrifice is devoid of pathos, as well as tragedy; it involves no catharsis, merely the offering of pure-life in appeasement and atonement to the law. Girard's claim that the Passion is what first reveals the innocence of the victims entails a shift in orientation toward the *'Aqedah*, however, which now belongs to the discourse of persecution. Christ's assuming the station of the sacrificial lamb reintroduces the human as sacrificeable, reenacting the circumstances of the *'Aqedah*. Only now it is God who makes the offering of his only son, whom he loves, in demonstration of his unwavering love for humanity. The lamb of God is the good shepherd, who gives his life for all the sheep. The Gospel of John, 10:14–18 reads: "As the Father knoweth me, even so know I the Father: and I lay down my life for the sheep. And other sheep I have, which are not of this fold: them also I must bring, and they shall hear my voice; and there shall be one fold, *and* one shepherd. Therefore doth my Father love me, because I lay down my life, that I might take it again. No man taketh it from me, but I lay it down of myself." Christ's willing sacrificial death in innocence demonstrates Godly love and restores humanity's innocence, freeing it from the duty of blood sacrifice. All that is required, instead, is to merely partake in consumption of the sacrificial flesh and blood. Girard's theory of the scapegoat mechanism and mimetic desire is predicated on the Pauline doctrine of Christian love, which is supposed to be ecumenical and so universal (love your neighbor because we are all the children of God the Father, and he loves each and every one of us).

Taking all of this into account, it is quite clear that whatever happens to John Jones at the end of "Of the Coming of John," it cannot be construed in this Christian mode. To read the scene as his transformation "into a figure of Christ-like sacrifice" is simply wrong. More to the point, to misread it as such means disregarding Du Bois's usage of the Faust line on the basis of which he elaborates the Gospel of Sacrifice. His gospel disarticulates sacrifice from death. Sacrifice denotes a way of living that neither refuses the eventuality of death nor construes it as sanctifying and salvatory. In accordance with Du Bois's gospel, John's sacrifice is not in how he is killed; it is in how he lived *not* in pursuit of fulfillment through acquisition. John neither lives or dies *by* God's charity. He lives and dies as he admonished his people to do *with* charity and education in pursuit of intellectual enrichment as the way to achieving full social justice.

Sacrifice, in Du Bois's gospel, denotes critical enrichment through giving up things—and there is a sense of it being a gift here—some desire toward the *socius*, toward social justice and universal human dignity. A sense of this can be gleaned from the commencement address Du Bois gave to the 1940 graduating class of Wilberforce University, in which, characterizing the significance of the Passion as a civic ethics, he tells them: "Above all, Christianity means unselfishness; the willingness to forego in part one's personal advantage and give up some personal desires for the sake of a larger end which will be for the advantage of a greater number of people. And finally, Love is God and Work is His Prophet."[355] The chiasmus of the last sentence, inverting the gospel of love, brings our attention back, for a moment, to "The Renaissance of Ethics," where so much of Du Bois's critique of Scholasticism focuses on its elaboration of the Augustinian distinction of kinds of love—*caritas* versus *cupiditas*—both of which are fundamentally forms of desire, differentiated by their respective object. Augustine poses the question: "What ought to be loved [Quid amandum sit]?"[356] To which he replies: "To love is indeed nothing else than to desire something for its own sake."[357] Love mediates between its subject and object, binding them together in identity: "What else is desire except a kind of life that binds, or seeks to bind, together some two things, namely the lover and the beloved." So, to love God and receive God's love is to be bound to him; in loving God and being loved by God together we recognize that we are one through his love, constituting the beloved community. Following this reasoning, Du Bois maintains that "if man seeks the Highest Good he will make his life like God's," and this mimicry "should make man perfect, which it does, but not in this world—only in the higher life, which must be eternal, lest the fear of losing it impair the happiness: this life, then, is only relative to the next."[358] The individual lover's longing to be one with the beloved God cannot be fulfilled except in the after-life, making it a longing for death. The beloved community founded on this cannot bring about a viable ethical community on earth, however, precisely because its prerequisite is the establishment of the *universal morality* of Pauline love. Longing for salvation in death does not transform the world. Du Bois's marking Scholasticism's construing worldly knowledge as *bona utila*, the means to subjective "knowledge and love of God," sets the stage for challenging the proposition that *caritas* is the basis for a viably just worldly community of humankind. The Wilberforce address chiasmus troubles this conception, relating love to sacrifice with connotations that depart from Pauline *agapism*, as the basis for a viable community, à la Royce, as well as Nietzsche's neo-paganism.

PARA-SEMIOSIS, POIĒSIS IN BLACK, AND LOVE-IMPROPER

Renouncing the Pauline love that longs for the afterlife looks forward to the end-of-days, Du Bois's "Gospel of Sacrifice" calls us to embrace the very love Nietzsche attributes to aristocratic virtue, the love of living, of fulfillment in community of the living, but *without* the proprietary force Nietzsche gives it. The Du Boisian ethics of submission attending the advent of the Negro as a type of human is predicated on something altogether different from anthropocentric cruelty, or its spiritualization and deification through *ressentiment* and the sacrificial annihilation of self. The sacrifice Du Bois advocates does not stem from a love of that which is mine through force of arm or will, or which I can assimilate to myself in mimicry. It is what we might call, carefully, knowing there is need for considerable elucidation, *love-improper*, love that does not seek to comprehend the other; it does not bring the object of love into grasp, into the fold of its proper self, but encounters it and opens itself up to its incomprehensibility. We may well think of it as the love of *poiēsis in black*.

Yet, insofar as that *poiēsis* is a function of *para-semiosis*, it is a potentiality-of-being that might very well attend multiple, multiplicious embodiments of flesh. While indissolubly associated with *Negro* embodiment, *poiēsis in black* as semiosis is not identical with black people, even though it indisputably belongs with them. In this sense, *para-semiosis* does indeed approximate Glissant's *créolisation*, that is to say, "a mode of forming a complex mix [*l'emmêlement*] that is only exemplified by its processes and certainly not by the 'contents' on which these operate." The resonance is fine, and indeed para-semiotic! *Poiēsis in black*, as a function of *para-semiosis*, iterates the fluid *approximating* dynamic of formal performance that permitted the Bahamian drummer, Nathaniel Rahmings, to orchestrate the Mississippi flutist, Ed Young, along with the Virginia mountain banjoist, Hobart Smith, in musical accompaniment to the Georgia Sea Island Singers' doing the Buzzard Lope in Williamsburg on April 28, 1960. That is to say, Du Bois, Douglass, Windham, Bessie Jones and the Davises, along with Spillers, Chandler, Wilderson, Gooding-Williams, and Moten, to name just a few in a very large ensemble, are, in all the particularities of their respective individual performances, improvising on the same standard. Let us call that standard "Being Artistically Rhythmical in the Interstices of Capitalist Modernity"; this is a too long a song title, however, the gist of which is better expressed by Dizzy Gillespie's "Interlude," more commonly known as "A Night in Tunisia," or maybe better still by Charlie Parker's twelve-bar blues "Barbados," or Hasan Hakmoun's "Marahaba." Such iterative approximating cannot bear the judgment of authenticity, which is why Lomax was skeptical when recording the 1960 Williamsburg performance. Authenticity, of course, is a residual of the philosophical discourse of ontology, where we no longer ought to tarry. Once we have left that line, the more generative question may be broached: What does the *para-semiosis* of *poiēsis in black* have in common with other embodiments of flesh? Can *para-semiosis* be a commonplace whereby a planetary worldliness of vestibularity enables multiplicious possibilities? This, of course, is a question of poetic socialities that, while bearing relation to polity, are neither grounded in or circumscribed by it, nor do they provide material basis for realizing a perfected political order. That is to say, considering the multiplicious possibilities of *para-semiosis* as commonplace entails radically reimagining what is human.

Gifting Blues Love-Improper

In the opening chapter of his novel *Un passager de l'occident*, Nabile Farès recounts a moment early on in his 1970 interview with James Baldwin, conducted for the Tunisian-based journal *Jeune Afrique*, when he reveals to Baldwin that his by-line, Brandy Fax, is a journalistic *nom de plume*. With this revelation, made off the record, Farès is presenting to Baldwin something of himself; in appreciation, Baldwin promises him an exclusive interview, which takes place the following day, over a rather fraternal lunch of chicken and copious amounts of wine and alcohol—a symposium of two. The very first question Farès asks in the interview, conducted in French, is prompted by the gift of the blues he understood to have been given him in Baldwin's 1962 novel, *Another Country*. "Mister Baldwin, why didn't you make a short story out of Easy Rider [*Voyageur insouciant*]?"[1] He was referring to "Book One: Easy Rider, in the novel, which took its subtitle from the chorus of W. C. Handy's song "Yellow Dog Blues," the fourth and fifth lines of which are:

> *All you Easy Riders got a stay away,*
> *So he had to vamp it but the hike ain't far.*

Baldwin paraphrases these as the epigraph to Book One:

> *I told him, easy Riders*
> *Got a stay away,*

So he had to vamp it
But the hike ain't far.

The Handy song—which was one of his first and best-selling blues lyrics, having been recorded by the Joe Smith Orchestra at Victoria Records in 1919, and Bessie Smith at Columbia in 1925 with Joe Smith on trumpet, Charlie Green on trombone, and Coleman Hawkins on tenor sax—was a response to the question posed by an earlier 1913 Shelton Brook's vaudeville composition that had been made popular by Sophie Tucker, "I Wonder Where My Easy Rider's Gone." To glean what is at stake in Handy's response, we must first attend to the call:

VERSE:
Miss Susie Johnson is a crazy as can be
About that easy riding kid they call Jockey Lee
Now, don't you think it's funny, only bets her money
In the race friend Jockey's goin' to be
There was a race down at the track the other day
And Susie got an inside tip right away
She bet a hundred to one that her little Hon
Would bring home all the mon.
When she found out Jockey was not there
Miss Susie cried out in despair

CHORUS:
I wonder where my easy rider's gone today
He never told me he was goin' away
If he was here he'd win the race
If not first, he'd get a place
I never saw that Jockey trailing anyone before

VERSE:
I'm losing my money, that's why I am blue
To win a race, Lee knows just what to do
I'd put all my junk in pawn
To bet on any horse that Jockey's on
Oh! I wonder where my easy rider's gone
Oh! I wonder where my easy rider's gone
He went to put my brand new watch in pawn
I see him comin' round that turn
What a trail that man can burn
He's gonna win because my dough is on the nose
Just watch my Jockey's easy rider stance

He'll hit that home stretch, win it by a mile
I want him to win this spree
And keep a-goin' till he comes to me
Oh! I wonder where my easy rider's gone
Oh! I wonder where my easy rider's gone

The erotic nature of Miss Susie Johnson's longing for Jockey Lee is not merely identified with her capital investment, it subsumes it into a self-centered, one is inclined to say narcissistic, circuit of desire in which Lee's value is in his performance both on the race track and in bed as her "easy rider." Mae West sang Brook's lyric, as the character Lady Lou in the 1933 movie *She Done Him Wrong*, emphasizing the expression of unreserved proprietary female desire in the color of her voice and bodily performance. That longing is what Handy responds to, answering Miss Johnson's query:

VERSE:
E'er since Miss Susan Johnson lost her Jockey, Lee,
There has been much excitement, more to be;
You can hear her moaning night and morn.
"Wonder where my Easy Rider's gone?"
Cablegrams come of sympathy,
Telegrams go of inquiry,
Letters come from down in "Bam",
And ev'ry where that Uncle Sam
Has even a rural delivery.
All day the phone rings, but it's not for me,
At last good tidings fill our hearts with glee,
This message comes from Tennessee:

CHORUS:
Dear Sue, your Easy Rider struck his burg today
On a southboun' rattler sidedoor Pullman car.
Seen him here an' he was on the hog.
(spoken: The smoke was broke, no joke, not a jitney on him.)
Easy Riders got a stay way,
So he had to vamp it but the hike aint far.
He's gone where the Southern cross' the Yellow Dog.

VERSE:
I know the Yellow Dog District like a book,
Indeed I know the route that Rider took;
Ev'ry crosstie, bayou, burg and bog.
Way down where the Southern cross' the Dog,

Money don't zactly grow on trees,
On cotton stalks it grows wid ease;
No racehorse, racetrack no grandstand
Is like Old Beck and Buckshot land,
Down where the Southern cross' the Dog.
Every kitchen there is a cabaret,
Down there the boll wevil works while the darkies glee,
This Yellow Dog Rag the livelong day.

CHORUS:
Dear Sue, your Easy Rider struck his burg today
On a southboun' rattler sidedoor Pullman car.
Seen him here an' he was on the hog.
(spoken: The smoke was broke, no joke, not a jitney on him.)
Easy Riders got a stay way,
So he had to vamp it but the hike aint far.
He's gone where the Southern cross' the Yellow Dog.
He's gone where the Southern cross' the Yellow Dog.

Handy based this response on a blues lyric he heard at the Tutwiler Mississippi railroad depot sometime in 1903, being performed by "a lean, raggedy Negro guitarist . . . singing of going to where the 'Southern cross the Yellow Dog.'" A classic blues railroad motive of the crossroads where creativity is born and the devil has his way, it referred to Moorhead, Mississippi, where the north/southbound Southern Railway met the east/westbound Yazoo and Mississippi Valley Railroad, the latter having been christened the "Yaller Dawg" by black rail workers. Having spent her cash and broke her heart Miss Johnson's easy rider, Jockey Lee, is on the lam. Her inability to find him through all the official mainstream channels, the U.S. post, telegraphy and telephony, marks the limits of the "legal" world. Albert Murray, remarking on Bessie Smith's changing the lines "And ev'ry where that Uncle Sam / Has even a rural delivery" in Handy's first verse to "Everywhere that Uncle Sam / Is the ruler of delivery," points out that Handy's lyric signals the gulf between the, albeit parallel, white and black worlds of American society. From that angle, the lyric is indeed a kind of societal barometer, giving the subjective expression of a social antagonism. Not even Murray sees easy rider as a romantic figure, however. The report of his flight mocks the sentimentality of Miss Johnson's desire, chastening her for confusing exchange, especially erotic exchange, with love. Handy is not criticizing the decadence of capitalist American society and its infatuation with money and things. He's simply explaining to Miss Johnson where her easy rider has gone, how, and why: the man just be keeping on moving. This is an expression of the perpetual movement Murray saw as signature to the blues lyric, and

Ellison as the existential condition connoted by *Negro*. Claude McKay called it "vagabondage"; Fred Moten and Stefano Harney have termed it "undercommon fugitivity." All these are references to a performance of human thinking-in-action that isn't quite so readily subjugated to the political economy and that is not so much a barometer of societal relations, staging a subjective individual rebellion, à la Rimbaud's *Illumination*, or Benjamin's *flâneur*, but rather articulates in the expression the possibilities of something else in the interstices. This is neither Sheldon Wolin's sense of fugitive, based on a despairing hopelessness at the prospects of democratic freedom, nor Derrida's "discernment" of an alternative ontology. The figure of Easy Rider's movement is privative. He ain't none of that. And the movement from privative to fugitive is other than despairing, nor is it hopeful; it's just simply what gets underway in the break between law and chance. This is not a fleeing *from* or *to* experience as the grounds giving meaning to life and self; it is rather fugitivity from the universal history that would fix the fate of the self providentially, putting it in its proper place in the cosmic order of things. Its hyperbolic path is what Du Bois calls the "hypothetically possible," which is akin to the rhythmic attitude of something else Fanon spoke of in the creative dialectic between the rhythms of law and irascible chance Du Bois took society to be. All of which is to say, the blues lyric does not hope for the human universality through unreserved individuation (*Von rückhaltloser Individuation*) Adorno spoke of.[2] The blues lyric articulates a human loving that is improper, the love-improper of *poiēsis in black*.

Baldwin's epigraphic paraphrase signs all of this, and Farès knows it, which is why he persists in pressing the point further, insisting that as a short story "Easy Rider" "would have had the same power as a Jimmy Yancey blues song.... And it would have been as if each word, just like Yancey's piano notes, plugged up the exits of the universe, as if, inexorably, they were leading us back to the coop where we were born [*cette cage où nous sommes nés*].... But maybe now it is impossible to bear this coop. Maybe the language of the blues is too true for what it says to still be bearable."[3] Baldwin is compelled to say in response:

> That's about what is happening. The blues has become a condition. There's love as well. But all that has to change. How to do so? . . . I know I can go on talking for my brothers. But how to say? . . . To who to say? . . . I've not arrived at the answer to these questions . . .
> Maybe it suffices to speak. With all the sincerity in the world.
> If that were sufficient, for the world. That could be enough.[4]

The conversation runs a bit differently in the published *Jeune Afrique* interview, with Farès asking: "Is the blues only an expression of a condition and a rage?" To which Baldwin replies: "There are three elements in the blues: the reflection of a condition, the expression of a rage, and an avowal of love. It's love that gives the blues their ironic and tragic tone. The blues are tragic, but in the manner of the corpses in Harlem. They are tragic because love lets us bear our condition and our rage." This is the gift Farès understands to have received from *Another Country*, and he reciprocates by giving Baldwin an autographed copy of his own novel, *Yahia, pas de chance*, inscribed "A James Baldwin dont la sincérité d'écriture provoque des réconforts"—"To James Baldwin, whose literary sincerity brings comfort."[5] This was Farès debut novel, published by Seuil in 1970. He wrote it between 1957 and 1962, when he was a young fighter in the Armée de Libération Nationale (ALN), the armed wing of the Front de Libération Nationale (FLN) during the Algerian War of Liberation, charged with recording the names of those killed in combat. The experience affected him profoundly, and he came to refer to himself as "le scribe de la mémoire des morts [the scribe of the memory of the dead]."[6] The novel's title, *Yahia, pas de chance* (Yaha, No Luck), is a play on words related to Farès's experience of the war and its aftermath, when those who survived the struggle were unlucky bearers of its horrors. The moment of his giving it to Baldwin is, à la Mauss, a bond by thing, in which Farès's gifting it to Baldwin is presenting something to himself; and Baldwin, by accepting the gift, is receiving something of Farès's soul, which he knows he cannot retain and so must reciprocate, thereby keeping the circuit of reciprocal gift-giving open.[7] That circuit, precipitated by the blues, opens up into a play of *para-semiosis*—Farès's *Un passager de l'occident*, whereby he exhibits his own writing, "covered in an impression of blue" that, while in resonate engagement with *poiēsis in black*, is not derivative of nor identical with it.[8] This resonant conversation without the necessity of identity bespeaks the possibility of a human love-improper that is non-agapeic and so not sacrificial, but also not egocentric.

Although offered in a minor key, this moment of the gift is an iteration of a major theme of *Un passager de l'occident*, one that Farès had already set out at the start with his recollection of how he introduced himself to Baldwin when telephoning to arrange the interview. Speaking to the writer for the very first time and establishing the nature of his French—"Oui. Je parle 'froncé.' J'ai déjà vécu à Paris"[9]—while casting about for some word that might resemble an artist's palette, as he puts it, Farès hears Baldwin say, in English: "Oh, what is your name?" to which Farès replies: "Je m'appelle Brandy Fax." We are back in French, of course, which is where both the interview and the novel will stay.[10] And Farès continues accordingly, "And I spelled out each letter of my lovely name, one after the other." But it is the subsequent clause that strikes the major chord: "comme vous auriez effeuillé les pétales d'une sainte alliance," which I read as something like, "as you would pluck the petals of a holy alliance," picking up the allusion to the counterrevolutionary coalition formed on September 26, 1815, between the three European monarchist state powers, Prussia,

Austria, and Russia, after the victory over Napoleon, which was emphatically opposed to democracy and secularism. The allusion marks Farès's own ironizing of post-independence centralist nationalist state formations in Africa, both pan-Arabist and pan-Africanist. Farès has always been keenly attentive to, and an outspoken critic of, the reductivist violence of these formations and their inevitable tendency to annihilate the variety of human of life and imagination. So he is struck when Baldwin tells him that his decision to move back to Paris "is like a closing of a circle. . . . So, leaving, today, this is very serious for me . . . they've killed all my friends."[11] A great deal is at stake for Farès conceptually, historically, and poetically in Baldwin's saying, "Et ils ont tué tous mes amis [And they have killed all my friends]." Stopping short on Baldwin's lips, the saying is an incantation for Farès:

> [It] moved towards me, stunned me, shook me, filled me with an indescribable pain, as if suddenly I saw again A'moura (that was his name, [*c'était son nom*]) dying before the door of the *gourbi* where we lived, in the forest during that fucking Algerian war. A'moura that was his name [*c'était son nom*], in the 17th battalion of the Algerian army, the number one army in the world, and whom I loved . . . A'moura . . . who was someone who shaved before going to set bungalor booby-traps along the Maurice Line, saying: "that way they cannot say we were Fellaghas." A'moura with shaven face, splattered by a B26. What a crock. And the donkey that continued grazing uncomprehendingly around his face . . . "They have killed all my friends . . ." the only ones I had, and no longer have, all technocrats, spectators decorated with official ranks, travelers on a mission . . . but what the hell are they doing, and why is it so barren . . . "They have killed all my friends . . ."[12]

With this incantation evoking friends killed, Farès sees Rufus Scott, the easy rider (*voyageur insouciant*—and in calling him this, Farès is taking seriously the fact that Rufus is represented not as victim but complicit in his pathology), leaping to his death from the George Washington Bridge, and as he "pitches towards the river crying, 'Why? . . . Why?'"[13]

Let us be clear about what is at stake in all this. Responding to Farès telling him the book leaves the impression that the evolution of American society is completely conditioned by the negation of the black man, Baldwin says: "Rufus's cadaver, that's the black cadaver in the American conscience. All of American society has been built in order to kill—not to deny the black man, or humiliate him, but kill him." This is an expression of the trap of a certain black beauty, exemplified in Rufus Scott's inability to live in *Another Country*. Rufus's insouciance is elemental to his suicide being a murder that is not sacrificial. He is no totem, sacramental or otherwise; nor is he a scapegoat. And to fully appreciate the negation's significance, let us note in passing that the concept of totem as the archaic expression of social cohesion is what E. E. Evans-Pritchard will expound into his theory of totems as a symbolic representation of the group, rejecting Bronislaw Malinowski's functionalist hypothesis that the totem was "good to eat," its sacredness functioning to ensure collective survival through its preservation. Malinowski set out to resolve the problematic William Robertson Smith first noted of the sacrificing of the totem, which he termed "totemic sacrament," characterizing the function of sacrificing the totem as Eucharistic: killing and eating the sacred sustains the community in spirit and body. Claude Lévi-Strauss took up Evan-Pritchard's explanation of totem and used it as the basis for his diverting the theme of anthropology toward the understanding of human cognition.[14] Not reading Rufus as scapegoat makes all this ethnographic primitivist *epistēmē* irrelevant to the lynching of black men in America. His willful disavowal of his sexuality in rebuffing Eric, and his rage as part of the pathology of murder that is American society cannot be addressed in terms of his emasculation at the hands of the white world. His cruelty and abuse of his white lover, Leona, is symptomatic of the patriarchal conceptualization of the origins of society. In insisting Rufus Scott's death is the death of the black man upon which all of American society is built and portraying Scott as a robust participant in that death, Baldwin shows there must be another way out, eschewing the premise of man underlying the proposition of emasculation in slavery and its underlying postulation of normative society. Regarding Rufus, it is abundantly clear how that premise, along with the corollary proposition and postulate, suffers from what Du Bois called the empty abstraction based on the epistemic fallacy of "confounding Things with Thoughts of Things."[15] There can be no redemption of man; but rather there is the expression of other genres of humans, another species, to paraphrase Fanon. There is something fundamentally androgynous about Rufus, and so too about the Negro. Baldwin recognizes that Farès gets it, in a way that few others did.

Farès is obsessed with a line he recalls from *The Fire Next Time* that, for him, enunciates the American problematic: the fundamental, foundational violence of society. The line, as he recalls is: "What the U.S. must do is come to realize that it is a mixed-race [*métisse*] nation."[16] This phrase was, in fact, a "twisting" (*retournement*) of Baldwin's thinking by Albert Memmi in his introduction to the French translation of *The Fire Next Time*, *Le prochaine fois, le feu*. Still, Farès attends to this little Memmi qua Baldwin dictum as "sayings that will never be understood . . . like the Sphinx before Oedipus, the words of an enigma no one, no violence, no rending can ever solve." And it is precisely in the face of such an enigma that extreme violence against oneself and others arises "because the enigma is too strong, the question and its response too eager, especially when the question, the real question, kills us." Farès knows the real, killing question is the *moitié-moitié* (half-this-half-that) nature of the sphinx itself and what it says about man's own androgyn, that what he is or is not, or even is halfway (à moitiè) is open to question. The very thought of the question of his androgyn is so unbearable to man that killing is the only response he has found to whoever poses it as a bodily reality. And yet, Farès realizes,

> It is this very question the existence of the black man [*l'homme noir*] poses to the white man [*l'homme blanc*]. "What the U.S. must do is come to realize that it is a mixed-race [*métisse*] nation." This means the issue is that of the white man's impossibility. As a matter of fact, it is easier for the black man to recognize he is mixed [*métis*], than for the white man to know himself as mixed. And, when Baldwin announces the only solution is a recognition of mixing [*métissage*], it is as if he had put a live grenade into the chest of his best friend, and he is waiting for the grenade to explode after twenty seconds and some sputtering, and his friend continues to smile at him. Something that, in all common sense, seems strictly impossible to believe or accept.[17]

In this moment of realizing that placing exploding grenades into whites is exactly what Baldwin continues to do, Farès first asks why "Easy Rider" wasn't a short story. After explicating the blues as love in response and receiving the gift of *Yahia, pas de chance*, Baldwin asks Farès: "How are things in Algeria?" To which Farès replies: "Fine. . . . Except that, there is a general Government." Seeming to get the joke about military rule, and thereby solidifying Farès's rapport with him, Baldwin then says something Farès finds extremely moving: "Tell me, what is there to do? . . . I don't know at all what to do."[18] At which point, an acquaintance of Baldwin's arrives whom he introduces to Farès without giving his name and whom Farès identifies only as "a very good-looking young man." This young man subsequently interrupts Farès's effort to pursue further with Baldwin the Sphinx-like enigma at play in his remark, "They have killed all my friends." The good-looking young man's interruption, while seemingly banal, is, in fact intrusive. Asking Farès what country is his from and hearing Farès's response, "Algeria," he turns the conversation to himself: "I was born . . . in Bône. Annaba, as you call it." With this turn he intrudes a racialized colonial element into the conversation by not only claiming the French colonial name for the northeastern Algerian seaport city, but also identifying Farès with the Arabic name. At this point Baldwin leaves momentarily to deal with the hotel concierge, and Farès is left alone with the good-looking young man, whose telling him he left Annaba in 1955 and then asking Farès where he was born prompts recollections of unhappiness and miseries: "I was born on a peninsula [*presqu'île*], surrounded by water, in Lesser Kabylia at Collo."

What he then begins to daydream is worth recounting in full:

It is a truth, Lesser Kabylia, a truth of permanent agitation. even the Lesser Kabyles have never wanted power for the very good reason (the only true reason) that it has always been taken from them, and if it has always been taken from then, it is because they (the Lesser Kabyles) have never wanted power. the rest belongs to the invaders of the plains, and they have always been plentiful. us, situated in our peninsula [presqu'île], we always pretty much know what happening elsewhere, in the areas near the major routes. we know, for example, that they give a good deal of money to the learned, or to certain people so that may become learned. we also know that people far from our peninsula, who have power, have a strange mania that back home we only be understood with much stupefaction, that of seizing power for a Swiss bank. . . . this mania astounds us for, used as we are to our peninsula, we don't understand when one of us goes to the city and on returning recounts stories about how those maniacs live, how someone can desire power to such extent. . . . what we can say is, is that Kabylia (Greater and Lesser) suffers from an unfathomable malaise. it's what we call the malaise of the fig tree. there is even a song, a song pronounced almost under ones breath, showing one knows what to say but doesn't want to be heard. such a lovely song of the times! so intimate. . . . so, this song says to us, "our fig tree has always been invaded by mushrooms," and "the arrival of these people of the plains has rotted our orchard," and "if the fig tree no longer speaks, it's because his friend has been stolen. his friend the hedgehog." this stealing the hedgehog is, for us, the inhabitants of the peninsula, a completely narcissistic malaise, like a malaise of the name. because if you say, outside the peninsula, to the Algerian you encounter: "I am Kabyle," what do you suppose he will respond? . . . he will say to you: "that's wrong, you are Algerian before being Kabyle," which, for us, is historically unthinkable. Algeria came along after Kabylia. that's the fact. For Algeria is a recent creation of people's rights to self-determination. and its people have the right to self-determination, we don't understand, we the inhabitants of the peninsula, why these habitants, these people don't determine themselves. I am Kabyle doesn't mean I am not Algerian, but it simply means that, as much as I am Algerian, I am firstly Kabyle. there's nothing to get dramatic about. unless Kabylia is now a cesura in the national conscience, a cesura that does not belong to Kabylia but to the national conscience. because, for us inhabitants of the peninsula, the national conscience preoccupies us far less than the malaise of our fig trees.[19]

In his daydream, Farès is attempting to do more than just stave off the good-looking young man's banality. There is a greater threat, manifest in the young man's saying to Baldwin on his return: "You know, we are from the same country," a remark Farès takes to mean the splendid coasts, immense vistas, richly colored earth—in short, the land devoid of people so that, apparently all the explanations of tearing asunder and displacements, of disasters, and historical struggles in Algeria had been encumbered by a great forgetting, the very forgetting expressed in certain of Albert Camus's works, such as *L'énvers et l'endroit* (Betwixt and Between), *Noces* (Nuptials), or *L'été* (Summer). This is the great explanatory forgetting that only the sort of poetics of Algeria expressed in Kateb Yacine's *Nedjma* can make understandable, "because any real approach to Algeria can only be—ARTISTICALLY SPEAKING, POETICALLY SPEAKING—a discovery of the allegorical reality of Algeria's beauty."[20] That allegory of beauty is a trap (*piège*), a loving dramatization of Algeria, such as the good-looking young man and Camus indulge it, and for which the people of Algeria have always paid dearly and continue to pay as the reconquest of Algeria unfolds on the level of a boasting tourism, "a nostalgia for the beautiful colonial space perpetuated by a stream of advertising: 'This is the spot that inspired Camus, etc.'"[21]

Farès does not stop short there, however, but asks: "If the beauty of Algeria is a trap, why can't Kateb Yacine's *Nedjma* be turned into an advertising campaign?"[22] The question is aimed at provoking reflection on the conflict between aesthetics and politics, between artistically lived and party-dominated life. This is a matter of forms of consciousness. "To put it more plainly," he says, "Camus belongs, like many men and women of Algeria, to those forms we (the inhabitants of the peninsula) call jellyfish consciousness [*la conscience méduse*] (after aquatic beings found along the beaches of Algeria)."[23] Such jellyfish consciousness is yielded by forms of realism. In fact, it is "a constitutive element of the most reactionary artistic ideology there is: the ideology of realism. That is why reactionary politics will always have in its entourage: the valets of realism [*les valets de réalisme*], whose main function is making viewers of television and cinema believe what they are seeing is true; the effect of which is 'a jellyfish consciousness [*conscience méduse*].'"[24] These valets are the instrumentality of a reductive, and in the Algerian case, socialist realism, aimed at convincing the people that verisimilitude of mimetic expressions has to do with there being true copies of what is really happening. "That is why the inhabitants of the peninsula [*presqu'île*] bear witness to passage from an allegorical reality to an allegory that's become reality."[25] The phrase *la presqu'île* (the peninsula), literally, "almost an island," used here and repeated throughout Farès's daydream, is his descriptive designation for Kabylia. It is also a pun on the Arabic name, الجزائر (*al-jazā'ir*), of the modern nation-state called in French *Algérie* and in English Algeria, which is the archaic plural of جزيرة (*jazīra*, "island"), referring to the four islands that were once off the coast of the capital city. The singular also means peninsula, as in جزائر العرب (*jazīra al-'arab*, the Arabian peninsula). Farès's pun, then, is that الجمهورية الجزائرية الديمقراطية الشعبية (*al-jumhūrīya al-jazā'irīya ad-dīmaqrāṭīya aš-š'abīya*, the People's Democratic Republic of

Algeria) consists of many cultural and linguistic peninsulas. Yet, despite all the valets of realism's efforts, the artistic essence and presence of Algeria endures in works that sweep aside those efforts, inclining Farès to proclaim:

> Hence, this OUTLANDISH hope we have: to see artistic expression offer to reality a density that it has never been able to seize.... The reality of this hope being the next departure of the allegorical raft of *The Medusa*, on through eternity! And the task will fall to him, to the symbolist Géricault, to be the founder of a vast movement, going from allegory to reality.... With respect to the reigning political line, only an artistic discovery, or a life ARTISTICALLY LIVED, can yield any meaning, or give evidence of some meaning other than that of political slavishness.[26]

Without rehearsing the significance of Géricault's *The Raft of the Medusa* in the history of artistic modernism or its attendant political controversy, it suffices here to recall T. J. Clark's remarking apropos that specific Géricault painting that politics "is the form par excellence of the contingency that makes modernism what it is," so that "art, at many of its highest moments in the nineteenth and twentieth centuries, took the stuff of politics as its material and did not transmute it.... Modernism turns on the impossibility of transcendence."[27] Farès's evoking Géricault painting the way he does makes emphatically clear he has in mind the scandalous inadequacy of making patriotic sacrifice the foundation of political order when he spells out each letter of his *nom de plume* as you would pluck the petals *d'une sainte alliance*. In witnessing the passage from allegorical reality to an allegory that becomes reality, the move is towards parable. The parabolic entails a conception of humans being-in-common whereby the mind is societal, *is* always in relation with others and things. This has some resonance, I think, with Gilbert Simondon's concept of transindividuation, which may itself have been inspired in part by Algeria, not merely through the mediation of Durkheimian sociology as mediated itself by Ignace Meyerson to form the basis for historical psychology, but also by the direct events of the Fourth Republic.

Be that as it may, Farès all the while remains preoccupied with thinking androgyny—not thinking about androgyny, but thinking in between, in admixture that never resolves being a little bit of this and a little bit of that. He remains preoccupied with the Memmi qua Baldwin dictum, which means for him that the issue is the white man's impossibility. Farès's sense of androgyny is much nearer to what Baldwin actually wrote in *The Fire Next Time* than is Memmi's twist:

> America, of all the Western nations, has been best placed to prove the uselessness and obsolescence of the concept of color. But it has not dared to

accept this opportunity, or even to conceive of it as an opportunity. White Americans have thought of it as their shame, and have envied those more civilized and elegant European nations that were untroubled by the presence of black men on their shores ... What it comes to is that if we, who can scarcely be considered a white nation, persist in thinking of ourselves as one, we condemn ourselves, with the truly white nations, to sterility and decay, whereas if we could accept ourselves *as we are*, we might bring new life to the Western achievements, and transform them.[28]

Attending to Baldwin's claiming American well-suitedness in making color obsolete, brings to mind the English-language term *miscegenation*, which was coined in 1863 by David Goodman Croly and George Wakeman in an anonymously published pamphlet entitled *Progress of Public Opinion and National Policy towards Miscegenation*.[29] Posing as proponents of the Republican Party, they propounded its policy regarding the abolition of slavery to be predicated on understanding "the necessity of the mingling of the [Negro] race with ours as the only means of preserving us from the decay that inevitably follows the highest state of enlightenment and exclusiveness," declaring Republicans to be "the party of miscegenation."[30] This sense of mixing, along with its sociopolitical connotations, is akin to that of the Spanish term *mestizo*, denoting a racial category of the *sistemas de castas* (system of lineages qua races) established in the seventeenth and eighteenth centuries throughout the viceroyalties of New Spain, Peru, and New Granada—which is to say most of the territorial land-mass of the Western Hemisphere, including the Caribbean. The system described hierarchically various types of racial mixtures of the three primary *castas*: *españoles* (whether Iberian-born *peninsulares* or American-born *criollo*), *indios*, and *negros*. The term *castas* itself, which derived from the Latin *castus*, meaning "chaste" or "pure," was a fundamental concept of the *Limpieza de sangre* implemented in post-Reconquista Iberia to identify and purge from the peninsula crypto-Jewish and crypto-Muslim elements. Maintaining the connotation of purity, its application in the Americas was pronouncedly biological, referring to the results of the historical process of racial mixing that attended the New World conquest and colonization called *mestizaje*. While the term *mestizo*, which initially denoted an *españoles* and *indios* mixture, derived from the Late Latin *mixtīcius*, it is eventually deployed across the colonial Spanish imperium, in Hispanic Asia and Oceania, as well as the Americas, as the generic denotation for mixture. The French term *métis* is also a cognate of *mixtīcius* and was initially used in reference to the descendants of French and Amerind mixture in Canada, where it currently designates a distinct ethnicity. Like mestizo, *métis* also became the generic denotation for mixture across the colonial French imperium, which is how Farès uses it when quoting Memmi misquoting Baldwin.

Memmi's persistence in twisting Baldwin's remarks, bearing as heavily as they do on the issue of *métissage*, are tellingly indicative of a conceptual mixture of awe and fear of blackness. For instance, in the same Memmi's preface to *Le prochaine fois*, he misreads Baldwin's passage referring to Bobby Kennedy in a tellingly pronounced way: "A few weeks ago Bob Kennedy, the Attorney General, and brother of the President, declared that it was only some individuals who completely and definitively refused . . . 'No!' Baldwin replied. 'It is not only a few individuals, it is not some adjustments. It is the whole of American society that is sick about American Black.'"[31] Now, here is what Baldwin in fact said:

> White Americans find it as difficult as white people elsewhere do to divest themselves of the notion that they are in possession of some intrinsic value that black people need, or want. And this assumption—which, for example, makes the solution to the Negro problem depend on the speed with which Negroes accept and adopt white standards—is revealed in all kinds of striking ways, from Bobby Kennedy's assurance that a Negro can become President in forty years to the unfortunate tone of warm congratulations with which so many liberals address their Negro equals. It is the Negro, of course, who is presumed to have become equal—an achievement that not only proves the comforting fact that perseverance has no color but also overwhelmingly corroborates the white man's sense of his own value. Alas, this value can scarcely be corroborated in any other way; there is certainly little enough in the white man's public or private life that one should desire to imitate.[32]

A statement like this, made in 1963, when *The Fire Next Time* was published, was about the rejection of integration qua assimilation as a prerequisite for social justice and freedom. What was being rejected was the implied premise: "The Negro must become equal to the white in order to become free." Baldwin challenges that premise by first disarticulating equality from "becoming." The Negro is already equal to the white as a human being. Becoming is then put in the service of becoming human, which is the species-wide challenge of history or world-making (worldly history).

Baldwin had previously broached this question of becoming in relation to artistic life in a speech he gave at the Community Church in Harlem on November 29, 1962, entitled "The Artist's Struggle for Integrity." After a preamble reflecting on the connotative ambiguity of words such as "artist" or "integrity," while accepting they denote "something which is real and which lives behind the words" and that all said and done he is an artist and there is such a thing as integrity, Baldwin turns to the meat of the matter: "It seems to me that the artist's struggle for his integrity is a kind of metaphor, must be considered as a kind of metaphor for the struggle, which is universal and daily, of all human beings on the face of this terrifying global order to get to become human beings."[33] This gets a rephrasing in *The Fire Next Time* along the lines of: How do we as a species of life on Earth achieve a state of being, or a state of grace *on Earth*, or what he calls love in "the tough and universal sense of quest and daring and growth"? That is the ninth and climatic description of love in the book. The gambit of these remarks gives the full sense of how the challenge, then, is to achieve love in common. Memmi does not so much paraphrase all this as reach over it to another event involving Kennedy in order to identify the black American with the colonial oppressed. This involves Memmi's own investment in elaborating a sense of absolute oppression of the psyche, as well as the body under modern capitalist imperial colonialism, which means eliding the question of love so paramountly at play in *The Fire Next Time*.

To reiterate, for Baldwin, the issue at stake in that question is the possibility of becoming-in-common, which cannot be the representation of heroes or sacrificial victims, but rather must be the generative activity of *poiēsis*, that which Farès calls "life ARTISTICALLY LIVED." Recounting his personal story of becoming an artist as a heuristic to the Community Church crowd, Baldwin addresses that issue in terms of the artist's need to grapple with the pain of alienation from family, as well as society at large, resulting from being or wanting to be an artist: "And what is crucial here is that if it hurt you, that is not what's important. Everybody's hurt. What is important, what corrals you, what bullwhips you, what drives you, torments you, is that you must find some way of using this to connect you with everyone else alive. This is all you have to do it with. You must understand that your pain is trivial except insofar as you can use it to connect with other people's pain."[34] Baldwin is talking about the challenge to live life artistically in general, but also specifically the challenge to do so as a young black boy in Harlem in the twentieth century. In recounting his struggle to be an artist, Baldwin draws attention to the way the question with which Du Bois frames *The Souls of Black Folk*—How does it feel to be a problem?—is about how what we may call black being is on-the-line. Black being is being in ruination without any mitigating redemptive metaphysics or theology. It is emergent with the separation of space and time from the everyday practice of living and from each other that occurred in the Guineaman's hold—the architecture of which purposefully aimed at smelting the preexistent formations of the enslaved's socialities, in order to extract from them dynamic human energy, which, liquified, is poured into the capitalist mold of the Negro as exchangeable labor-property, where it resolidifies as such. Black being is being in ruination because the smelting is imperfect. There are elements from before in the fluidity that cannot be expelled or melted away, which have enough residual cohesion to be manifest in the solidified form.

That cohesion in liquefaction is black being; which, neither reducible to the Negro or any longer circumscribed by the preexistent formations, is being on-the-line of animality and humanity, and so, perpetually exhibiting the material processes of hominization without requiring the veneer or conceit of civilization as the legitimation of violent carnage. As we know, Du Bois's addressing the issue of black being is an aspect of his *quaestio* of the color line, which was rapidly becoming *the* worldwide demarcation of humanity under capitalism of a certain abstract sort. So, black being, being-on-the-line, is an index of the general human condition in the twentieth century. It is also, to Baldwin's point, what being an artist—read ποιητής (*poiētḗs*) in Aristotle's sense—is. And in a very real sense, to the extent his talking about life lived artistically bears on the question of Negro being, that is all about mimesis's species-constituting activity. But not at all in the way of René Girard's mimetic theory, according to which mimesis as an instrumentality of homonization is predicated on untethered animalistic desire—and he clearly has in mind Augustine's conception of *cupiditas*. Nor in the way of Roger Caillois's much earlier theory, which, extrapolating from Henry Bates's and Edward Poulton's research on biological mimicry, conceives human mimesis as role playing on a continuum with aposematic mimicry, whereby one species mimics the color and appearance of another dangerously toxic or predatory species.[35] The distinction between the sense of mimesis meant here apropos Baldwin's artistic performance, and that of both Girard and Caillois, is marked by Baldwin when he belittles "the white man's sense of his own value" as *the* exemplary model for human being and says, "There is certainly little enough in the white man's public or private life that one should desire to imitate."

As already noted, this statement is a rejection of assimilationist integration. Moreover, it flies in the face of what has been a tenet of the sociology of power since ibn Khaldūn first postulated the social fact of الاقتداء (*al-iqtidā'*, imitative assimilation), according to which the defeated will always mimic their conquerors in mores, custom, and habit, because it is universal human nature to emulate perfection and to identify the victorious as perfect.[36] While the prolegomena to ibn Khaldūn's multivolume historical work, كتاب العبر (*Kitābu-l-'ibar*, Book of Lessons), is generally regarded as a precursor to modern sociology, it also reflects his engagement with the field of فلسفة المدنيّة (*falsafa al-madanīya*)—whereby the Arabic noun المدنيّة (*al-madanīya*) translates the technical term Aristotle coins for his scientific study of polity, Πολιτικά (*Politicā*), but also the term with which Plato entitled his dialogue on the commonwealth, or republic, Πολιτεία (*Politeia*). Even though this Arabic phrase literally translates into English as something like, "the philosophy of civilization," in keeping with our earlier rendering of Aristotle's ζῆν καλῶς (*zēn kalōs*, good-living) as "civilization," which relates to Plato's καλλίπολις (*Kallipolis*, ideal polity), we render it as "political philosophy." It was first designated as such by al-Fārābī, whose foundational text, المدينة الفاضلة (*Al-madīnat-ul-fāḍila*, The Ideal Polity), informs ibn Khaldūn's own sociology of power.[37] Yet, whereas al-Fārābī's work leaned rather more heavily on Aristotle's *Politics* than Plato's *Republic*, ibn Khaldūn's theory of imitative assimilation is arguably an elaboration on Plato's account of the guardians' proper mimicry of a singular kind—assimilating a singular model, the virtuous man—as crucial to political psychic health. That singular of mimicry and model broaches no androgyny: "If our guardians, released from all other crafts, are to be expert craftsmen of civic liberty [ἐλευθερίας τῆς πόλεως, *eletherías tis póleos*], and pursue nothing that is not conducive to this," Socrates says to Adeimantus in *The Republic*, "then it would be unfitting for them to do or even imitate anything other than virtuous men [ἀνδρείους, *andreíous*]. . . . They should neither do nor mischievously imitate things unbecoming the free man [ἀνελεύθερα *aneleíuthera*], lest they assimilate these. We will not allow our charges, whom we expect to prove good men, being men, to play the parts of women or imitate women. . . . Nor may they imitate slaves, female or male, doing what slaves do."[38] In the healthy ideal republic, free good men imitate free good men only; there can be no confusing of gender, no ἀνδρόγυνος (*andrógynos*), no androgyny. Baldwin's not wanting to imitate the white has everything to do with androgyny. And we must keep in mind that Farès's engagement with androgyny occurs with the gifting blues manifest in the enigmatic style of Baldwin's writing, in which there is a sense of black being as mimesis. Moreover, it warrants reiterating here that this is not at all aligned with Girard's mimetic theory. That theory is inflected with despair over how mimesis unbridled and reinforced by mechanical reproduction results in precisely the contagious sameness of capitalist modernity, a sameness that Antonio Gramsci recognized as the bourgeoisie's autotherapy from having achieved consciousness of its historical agency, that it was creating the world without transcendent divine sanction—what Weber called *Entzauberung* (disenchantment) and Nietzsche "nihilism." Benjamin experienced this as melancholy, Heidegger as loss, and Sartre as existential despair. In contrast to all of that, Baldwin's bluesish mimesis, although flourishing in the grounds of the very same capitalist bourgeois modernity, defies despair and seeks no salvation in regaining *agapē*, or quasi-primitivistically rediscovering enchantment's spectral aura in the mundanely reproduced mimetic object. In other words, the blues gifts a love that is pointedly not melancholic, but rather is a *fascination* whereby the idea of oneself mastering the situation is abandoned.[39] This is not at all akin to the demonic drive that ascending Diotima's ladder achieves fulfillment by transmuting fleshly erotic desire into esoteric love of beauty in itself, αὐτοῦ ἐκείνου καλοῦ μά (*auto ekeínou kaloũ*), as Plato puts it. On the account of that Platonic love, proper mimesis is the representative reproduction of ideally meaningful knowledge of beauty (ἐπιστημῶν κάλλος, *epistēmōn kállos*), which is to say, the comprehensive transcription of the history of the world.⁴⁰ The blues does not seek any such comprehensive transcription. Quite the contrary, to paraphrase Baldwin, "it came into existence as an exceedingly laconic description of black circumstances, and as a way, by describing these circumstances, of overcoming them."⁴¹ This iron necessity of incomprehensibility entails what Adorno called *Mimetische Verhalten*, mimetic comportment characterized by acute a-conceptual awareness of oneself being *in* temporality without univocity. We can, in this respect, once again invoke *Another Country*, where Rufus Scott's father tells him: "*A nigger . . . lives his whole life, lives and dies according to the beat. Shit, he humps to that beat and the baby he throws up in there, well, he jumps to it and comes out nine months later like a goddamn tambourine.*"⁴² That loving someone is to abandon the idea of and desire for mastery is a recurrent theme of the blues standard, from "Easy Rider" to "The Thrill Is Gone." There is no longing for the lost love, merely the coming to terms, as Albert Murray would have it, with the lover's being gone.

Farès well understood the blues gift is an eclectic pronouncedly mixed experimental poetic style and knowledge, full of technique. Plato would have recognized this as mimetic cleverness (σοφίας, *sophías*) of the order of μῆτις (*mêtis*), as in Odysseus's skillful cunning—πολύμητις Ὀδυσσεύς, *polymêtis Odysseus*—the skill Nestor advised his son Antilochus to utilize in the games.⁴³ Another aspect is added to Farès's preoccupation with mixture apropos Baldwin, all the more so when we take into consideration that the French rendering for the Greek *mêtis* is *métis*. The connection is more than merely homophonic, however. After all, the discourse of *métissage*, like that of *mestizaje* and miscegenation, presumes the character, intelligence, and quality of an individual is a determination of flesh; something that is perhaps more expressly stated in the *sistemas de castas* whereby the *mestizo*, the *Pardo* (*españoles*, *indios* and *negros* mixture), and *Zambo* (*indios* and *negros* mixture) possess intelligences distinct from one another resulting from the precise nature of their respective mixtures. Each and every one of these mixtures is inferior to that of the whites who are *los gente de razón* (people of reason), with all the historical connotative freight that phrase conveys, from the right-principle-discourse (ὀρθός λόγος, *orthós lógos*) of Aristotelian civilized man to the *Bildung* of nineteenth-century German *Neuhumanismus* and the *eigentliche Geschichtlichkeit* (authentic historicity) of Heideggerian Dasein. In other words, the intelligence of the *mestizos* and *métis* is on the order of *mêtis*, a cunning of fleshliness that presents a danger to the purity of white *epistēmē*, more precisely to the vital integrity of its ontological anthropology, which, whether thinking along lines of polygenesis or monogenesis, is compelled by the presumed necessity of singular universality. Recall Plato's account of proper mimicry circumscribed and regulated by the pure simple narration (απλῆ διηγήσει, *haplé diegísei*) of philosophy as a way of maintaining political psychic health. Mimicry purified with philosophical discourse is the key to happiness (εὐδαιμονία, *eudaimonia*). In this respect, there is no substantive difference between Plato's καθόλου βέλτιον (*kathólou beltion*), "Universal Good," and Aristotle's καθόλου λόγου (*kathólou lógou*), "universal formulae."

The danger posed by *métis/mêtis* is twofold. The admixture of varieties of nonwhite human being, each of which on its own presents a challenge to ontology, necessitating a refinement in the anthropological taxonomy, concentrates and exacerbates that challenge, thereby increasing the danger of epistemic crisis and collapse. Husserl proclaimed the imminence of this collapse in his *Die Krisis der europäischen Wissenschaften* (Crisis of European Science), although characteristically not attributing it to the proliferation of *métissages*.[44] It was more evident in the crisis of ethnography of the 1970s and the resultant call for a methodological shift from epistemic to practical knowledge on the ethnographer's part. Then again, insofar as any *métis* entails white elements, depending on the proportion, there is an additional possibility of the sort of mimicry Poulton called "episematic"—the functionality of coloration or markings that help individuals of the same species recognize one another—which is called "passing" in the biological-racial discourse of miscegenation. In his long meditation on mimicry, Caillois recognizes such passing to be a mode of sociability that functions according to a universal biological *loi de déguisement pur* ("law of pure disguise").[45] Lacan draws on Caillois's concepts of mimicry and *la psychasthénie légendaire* ("legendary psychasthenia") in his elaboration of the mirror stage as a moment in the symbolic fiction of the subject, on the basis of which Homi Bhabha subsequently extrapolates his notions of mimicry and hybridity as performative acts of social formation in the colonies.[46] This deserves remarking because the question of colonial mimicry is fundamentally analogous to "passing" in that both still imply an ideal model, the emulation of which is required for access to social legitimacy. This is precisely the sort of mimicry Baldwin deprecates.

There are, however, many other ways to think on mimicry that are less favorably inclined to this proposition of imitating a proper model. One that is most proximate to Baldwin's remark is found in Zora Neale Hurston's "Characteristics of Negro Expression," which she starts by asserting:

> The Negro's universal mimicry is not so much a thing in itself as an evidence of something that permeates his entire self. And that thing is drama.
>
> His very words are actions. His interpretation of the English language is in terms of pictures. One act described in terms of another. Hence the rich metaphor and simile.

> The metaphor is of course very primitive. It is easier to illustrate than it is to explain because action came before speech.... Every phase of Negro life is highly dramatized. No matter how joyful or how sad the case there is sufficient poise for drama. Everything is acted out.... So we can say, ... the Negro thinks in hieroglyphics.[47]

Mindful that Hurston's description of Negro mimicry decidedly aligns with Vico's conception of primitive poetic wisdom, our recognizing it as an iteration of the Aristotelian sense of *mimesis* as dynamic process of engaging reality is substantiated not only by her expressly identifying it with drama, but also by what she says subsequently under the heading "Imitation":

> The Negro, the world over, is famous as a mimic. But this in no way damages his standing as an original. Mimicry is an art in itself. If it is not, then all art must fall by the same blow that strikes it down. When sculpture, painting, acting, dancing, literature neither reflect nor suggest anything in nature or human experience we turn away with a dull wonder in our hearts at why the thing was done. Moreover, the contention that the negro imitates from a feeling of inferiority is incorrect. He mimics for the love of it.... Let us say that the art of mimicry is better developed in the Negro than in other racial groups. He does it as the mocking-bird does it, for the love of it, and not because he wishes to be like the one imitated. I saw a group of small Negro boys imitating a cat defecating and the subsequent toilet of the cat. It was very realistic, and they enjoyed it as much as if they had been imitating a coronation ceremony. The dances are full of imitations of various animals. The buzzard lope, walking dog, the pig's hind legs, holding the mule, elephant squat, pigeon's wing, falling off the log, seaboard (imitation of an engine starting), and the like.[48]

Another way of thinking about mimicry that, while far more distant in time from Baldwin's remarks than Hurston's, is remarkably resonant with hers is found in كتاب البيان والتبيين (*Kitāb al-Bayān wa at-tabyīn*, The Book of Eloquence) by the ninth-century Arabic literatus Abū ʿUthman ʿAmr ibn Baḥr al-Kinānī al-Baṣrī, more widely known as al-Jāḥiẓ. This work is one Farès was undoubtedly familiar with, and its thinking about mimicry has considerable bearing on the Algerian play of *para-semiosis* opened up by the gifting blues. In that regard, proclaiming how it is possible to tell a person's ethnicity by accent, al-Jāḥiẓ tells of a locksmith raised among the Arabs in the streets of Kufa who spoke excellent idiomatic Arabic, but whoever listened to him would know by how he articulated his sounds that he was of Nabataean origin. The same would hold true if it were a Khurāsanī speaking.[49] Yet, al-Jāḥiẓ points out, there occasionally occurs an individual possessing extraordinary skills of mimicry, who can impersonate the native accents of Yemini, as well as Khurāsanī, Ahwāzī, Zinjī, Sindī, Habbashī, and more besides, with such precision you'd think he was of those origins. The same mimic simulates stuttering to the point of epitomizing the condition, or blindness so well he captures every facial expression and body movement of every blind person you've ever seen. Al- Jāḥiẓ refers to such an individual as الحاكية (al-ḥākīa); this is an archaic form of what we today would call الحاكي (al-ḥākī), which can be rendered in English as "impersonator" or "mimic." He is talking about the sort of professional mimics who performed the art of impersonation, المُحاكاة (al-muḥākāh), in which they simulated animal sounds and sundry Arabic-ethnic accents at the imperial court and in the salons of the urban elite, as well as at the gates of the city and in the markets. It bears noting that the root verb, حكى (ḥakā), from which both the Arabic term for the impersonator, الحاكي (al-ḥākī), and the performance, المُحاكاة (al-muḥākāh), derive, has a very expansive range of meaning designating the activity of narrating or telling a tale, as well as those of imitating and simulating something. And it means these actions simultaneously idiomatically, across the various vernaculars, giving us the common cognate حكاية (ḥikāya, tale, or narration). In fact, in his telling of the virtuoso mimic, al-Jāḥiẓ states: "The virtuoso mimic [الحاكية, al-ḥākīa] impersonates [يحكي, yaḥki] the enunciations of the inhabitants of Yemen . . . and so that is his story [حكايته, ḥikāyatuh]." These professional mimics' repertoire of mimicking the accents and vernacular of common people and foreigners was not unlike the sort of things found in the μίμος (mímos), mimes, of Sophron and Xenarchus to whom Aristotle refers in his *Poetics*.[50] Also known as μιμίαμβοι (mimíamboi, mimic-iambics), for their metrical rhythm, these are thought to have been the stylistic model for Plato's Socratic dialogues, a supposition encouraged by Aristotle's listing Σωκρατικοὺς λόγους (Sokratikoús lógous) alongside of *mimíamboi* as one kind of μέτροις (métrois, meter). The classicist John Arbuthnot Nairn once surmised that along with farcical depictions of scenes from common people's everyday life, these mimes tended in their earliest forms toward buffoonery (παιγνοται, paigniotai), mimicking animal sounds and sounds of nature. Indeed, the character Metro, in Herodas's mime "The Gossiping Friends" claims to "bark like a dog [κύων ὑλακτέω, kúōn hylaktéo]."[51] By the Byzantine Greco-Roman period the term, μίμος (mímos) designated the buffooning actor, who provided popular entertainment in the market place, as well as at court banquets in the urban centers throughout the Byzantine Empire, including the provinces of Palaestina Salutoris and Arabia Petraea, which means the ancestors of al-Jāḥiẓ's Nabataean were undoubtedly well-acquitted with them.[52] Should we accept Irfan Shahid's philological speculations, those Nabataeans Arabized the Greek μίμος (mímos) as مَيْمِس (maimis). There is no reason to believe that al-Jāḥiẓ had these μίμος (mímos) or مَيْمِس (maimis) in mind when describing what he terms الحاكي (al-ḥākī), a decidedly Arabic term having no Greek etymon. Nevertheless, in the polyvocality of their respective performative styles, both the Hellenic and Arabic professional mimics exhibit precisely the sort of polyrhythm Plato thought detrimental to political psychic health precisely because they are "capable in their cunning [σοφίας, *sophías*] of imitating everything [μιμεῖσθαι πάντα, *mimeísthai pánta*]," expressing their mimicry in a mixed type [κεκραμένον, *kekeraménon*] of speech.⁵³ Plato's injunction is not against heterogeneity but admixture as a threat to the stability of the *kallipolis*.

Al-Jāḥiẓ's attitude toward both mimicry and admixture could not have been any further from this than it was. He tells another tale about another mimic, a مولَى (*mauwlī*). A cognate of المَوالِي (*al-muwālī*), this term is not quite translatable because it indexes a complex set of conventional social relationships that the customary rendering, "client," with its sense of transactional contract, does not adequately capture. The difficulty stems from the fact that the sociopolitical order of the early Islamic imperium under the Umayyad was fundamentally tribal. The term was used initially to denote the elements of the diverse population—Persians, Egyptians, Ethiopians, Greeks, Turkmens, and Kurds—brought under Arab rule who were Muslim and adopted into the ruling Arab tribes as client-affiliates. Having been assimilated into the tribe, the *muwālī* were fully acculturated in their language and sociability. In other words, they were Arabized in every way except blood. By contrast, in the patrilineal tribal Arab society, الهُجَناء (*al-hujanā'*, hybrid), offspring of Arab fathers and non-Arab, usually slave-concubine, mothers, *were* Arab by blood. In some respect, these were akin to the French *gens de couleur libres*, referring to the *métis* of white fathers and black slave mothers, who were regarded as *créoles*, both in the archaic sense of French born in the colonies and *métissage*. On the report of his sororal nephew, the polymath grammarian, poet, and historian Yamūt ibn al-Muzarra' al-'Abdī, al-Jāḥiẓ was himself a هجين (*hajīn*) of mixed Ethiopian and Arab descent and a مولَى (*mauwlī*) of Banu Kināna.⁵⁴ As will be clear momentarily, the question of *métissage* is central to al-Jāḥiẓ's thinking about mimicry and more. Anyhow, there was a *muwālī* of the Ziyād named Abū Dabūba az-Zinjī who would stand at al-Karkh gate in Baghdād near the muleskinner's corral and bray with such effect that every donkey, however old, sick, lame, tired, or broken down, would bray with him in a way that not none of them would have if any of their kind really had brayed. He had managed to combine all aspects of a jackass braying into one bray, which he also did with dog barks, thereby confirming the ancients' postulate that mankind can be regarded as a microcosm of the world.⁵⁵

The significance of dog barking, النُّباح (*an-nubāḥ*) is central to al-Jāḥiẓ's thinking about mimicry and human identity. We have, for instance, another anecdote, this time in كتاب الحيَّوان (*Kitāb al-ḥayawān*, The Book of Living), where he relates Abū al-Ḥassan recounting Abū Maryam telling the story of a man, a merchant, in Medina who had so much debt he had to hide in his house from his creditors. One of them who came to his place, and after some cajoling was allowed in, said to him: "What would you do for me if I could show you a ruse that will get you out of the mess you're now in and free you from all your creditors?" To which he replied: "I'd pay you what I owe you and whatever else you wanted from my possessions." Having gotten his oath on that, the creditor told him: "Before prayer tomorrow, have your servant sweep your door, wash your patio, and put your shop in tip-top order, setting up a comfortable place for you to recline out front. After this, you sit down and wait for people to pass, and each time someone says hello to you, bark in his face. Make sure you bark indiscriminately at *everyone* who talks to you, even your relatives and servants, or creditors, or anyone else, until your behavior comes to the attention of the magistrate, in which case bark at him too, and continue to do so no matter who addresses you. Once the prefect has made certain that you are not faking, no doubt he will declare you mentally incompetent and exonerate you of all your responsibilities." Our debtor did as instructed, and when some of his neighbors greeted him in passing the next morning, he barked in their faces, and when others passed by, he did the same until his creditors got wind of his behavior and came round to see for themselves. Of course, he barked at them when they greeted him and continued at it, which so vexed them they seized him and took him before the magistrate, where he continued to bark in response to the latter's interrogation. This prompted them to take him before the judge at whom he barked as well. The judge sentenced him to a few days in jail under close observation, during which time he persisted in only barking, at which point the judge ordered his release from jail to house arrest under strict observation. When he continued to bark even then, the judge determined that he was mentally incompetent and exonerated him of all responsibilities whatsoever. At the end of all this, the creditor who had instructed the indebted merchant in the ruse came to him demanding his due payment, and when he spoke to him, the merchant only barked. To which the creditor said: "Hold on friend, you bark at me too, and I'm the one who taught you the ruse!" To which our man replied with more barking, thereby freeing himself from all his creditors without paying a cent.[56]

Certainly a farcical tale, or, as al-Jāḥiẓ would say, المَزاح جِدّ, (*al-mazāḥ jidd*), "a serious joke," the mimicry is so good not even the inventor of the fraud can tell if it is real or not. Its ruse is predicated on the assumption that the capacity of deliberative reason is the basis for social responsibility as virtue, that animals, specifically dogs, lack this capacity, and that consistent demonstrated performance as a dog—mimicry—is symptomatic of a cognitive disfunction, specifically a pathology of *phantasia aesthetis*, or sensory imagining, which causes a human animal to behave as a nonhuman animal, and so incapable of being held responsible. The ability to distinguish between fraudulent and virtuous behavior turns on the capacity of deliberative reason to differentiate between particular things—and then again in the abstract—on the basis of what they are essentially, which is determined by what they must do in the world, and then to gather those particulars resembling one another into a collection. In other words, the work of reasoning intelligence is collection and division, both generic classification and speciation. Here in al-Jāḥiẓ's anecdote, the genus is animals, which includes the species *Homo sapiens*, whose determinate activities are language and deliberative reasoning. Yet, if those are the determinates of belonging to the species, then what is an animal that looks like a human being but barks like a dog so incessantly there is good reason to infer the absence of reason? The problematic is enhanced by the fact that this individual behaves in every other way as one would expect a reasonable member of society to behave. He wears clothing, lives in a house, and responds to communicative action from other human beings, albeit by barking, but is responsive nevertheless, just as a dog would be. And there is the rub, because a dog too is responsive to human beings talking at it, so much so that we are inclined to imagine, if not outright construe, that there is a heterospecies communicative transaction occurring, which raises another set of questions about just how far we can rely on a theory of reason-based communicative activity as a determinate of the species. Pursuing these questions takes us back once more to Plato, who was the principal purveyor of that theory and whose formulation of it in *The Republic* deploys the analogy of barking dogs.

Just prior to dismissing serious mimicry of barking dogs as base and beneath the guardians, Plato has Socrates discussing the art of war and remarking that the guardians as its practitioners must be in nature like the well-bred or noble dog (γενναίου σκύλακος, *gennaíou skylakos*) in respect of guarding and watching: "Keen of perception, quick in pursuit of what it apprehends, and fiercely strong in the effort at catching it."[57] The doglike strength in pursuit hinges on an equally doglike bravery that stems from an inherent high-spiritedness, which raises an additional political problem. Given the ferocity of high-spiritedness, there needs to be an equally inherent countering gentle nature to prevent the guardians from savaging one another as well as the rest of the citizenry. The good guardian must possess a disposition that is at once gentle and high-spirited. Once again, the most suitable analogy for this is the noble dog, whose "natural disposition is to be perfectly gentle to those whom it knows, and the opposite with those who are unknown."[58] Once Socrates has gotten Glaucon to acknowledge the noble dog as a suitable model of mimicry for the guardians, he reflects further on how the noble dog becomes enraged at the sight of an unknown person without having suffered any prior injury from him, but will fawn over someone it knows even if it has received no kindness whatsoever from him. He then slips in a provocative remark: "But surely that is an exquisite aspect of its nature and that shows a true lover of wisdom [φιλόσοφον, *philósophon*]."[59] Socrates asks, seemingly ironically, "How can the love of learning [φιλομαθὲς, *philomathés*] be denied a creature whose criterion for distinguishing the friendly and alien is knowledge and ignorance?"[60] On the assumption that love of learning (φιλομαθὲς, *philomathés*) and love of wisdom (φιλόσοφον, *philósophon*) are the same, Plato has Socrates conclude that if the guardian is to possess the right combination of high-spirited fierceness and gentleness, then he must, like the noble dog, be by nature a lover of learning and wisdom. The guardian must be a philosopher as is the noble dog. In this respect, it behooves us to bear in mind what a dog does when confronted with the stranger in its territory: it barks incessantly and fiercely. While mimicking a dog barking cannot be done seriously, being like a dog that barks at the unknown is required of philosophers. T. A. Sinclair once wrote of this philosophical dog argument that it was the sort to which Plato's enemies point when they want to show how silly Plato was. His friends, such as the classist, Warner Jaeger, say quite rightly that we must not take Plato's little jokes seriously; to which Sinclair then asks, "But what is the point of the joke? If this is just another instance of the Socratic habit of homely comparisons, there is no joke and we have to hand the passage back to Plato's foes."[61] Sinclair's fix is to suggest—and it is really no more than a rather tentative suggestion offered to preserve some dignity—that the philosophical dog argument is a parody of the Sophists. He offers no significant textual evidence in support of this. Other, more conservative minds that generally want to take the *Republic* very seriously, like Allan Bloom and Leo Strauss, dismiss the philosophical dog argument outright as not at all serious.

Yet, as al-Jāḥiẓ well knew, disputing about the better attributes of dogs is no trivial matter, and neither are jokes. He expressly makes this point in the introduction to *Kitāb al-ḥayawān*, where, in responding to the book's unnamed addressee who has taken umbrage at the "mixing [مزج, *mazj*] of farcical humor [الهزل, *al-hazl*] with gravitas" characteristic of al-Jāḥiẓ's writings, he says: "You did not grasp any argument I wrote or anything I wanted to exposit seriously through humor, or the rhythm at play in it. You did not get that the joke is serious if it is deployed in serious disputation."[62] Among the farcical accounts al-Jāḥiẓ deploys in seriousness that the addressee deprecates as deleterious to intellectual and social well-being is the debate between two expert Mu'tazila scholars of علم الكلام (*'ilm al-kalām*), al-Jāḥiẓ's teacher, Abū Isḥāq an-Naẓẓām, and a fellow named Ma'bad over the respective merits and detriments of dogs and roosters. The designation علم الكلام (*'ilm al-kalām*) literally translates into English as "science [علم, *'ilm*] of the speaking [الكلام, *al-kalām*]," whereby *kalām* has a connotation resonant with de Saussure's uses of *parole*. The definite article denotes a specific speaking, that of God, كَلِمة الله (*kalima Allah*), revealed as the Qur'an. What the phrase علم الكلام designates in situ is the expert practice, the science of disputation over the meaning, the signification, of the word of God. Because that is the topic and the method is disputation, the customary practice is to render it as "speculative" or "scholastic" theology, drawing an analogy to Medieval Christian Scholastics. That analogy aside, المتكلمون (*al-mutakallimūn*), the practitioners qua speakers of the science of disputation, expressly understood themselves to be engaged in discourse on the very nature of signification in relation to human thinking and being about things. In that respect, such issues as whether the Qur'an is eternal or the correct way in which its words are to be understood were fundamentally disputes about the analysis and interpretation of divine signification in relation to everyday human language and speaking. Hence, the expansive philological range of the science, covering all manner of Arabic expression utilizing diverse, including non-Arab, speculative tools. In the case of the Mu'tazila, this entailed the tools of speculative reasoning translated and adopted from the Greek philosophical tradition. Accordingly, there is warrant for rendering علم الكلام as "semiotics." An-Naẓẓām was one of the most adept and prominent of the Mu'tazila semioticians. A polymath who excelled in poetry, jurisprudence, and history, as well as rationalist analysis of the word, he also adhered to the tenets of تجربة (*tajriba*, empirical experience) as evidence gleaned from direct and reported observation of phenomena. That aspect of his work is very much on display in al-Jāḥiẓ's recounting and elaborating on his dispute with Ma'bad over the respective merits and detriments of dogs and roosters. An-Naẓẓām's intellectual esteem was a motivating factor in the addressee of *Kitāb al-ḥayawān* being scandalized by al-Jāḥiẓ's treating what must have been, like Plato's philosophical dog argument, simply a joke, مَزاح (*mazāḥ*) as the grounds for serious intellectual work. In that vein, the addressee accuses al-Jāḥiẓ of writing books of witty anecdotage and curios, replete with sophistic tricks and deceptions. Having acknowledged the accusation, al-Jāḥiẓ proceeds to list its charges, two of which have bearing on our concern with mimicry and *métissage*. Of these is the charge he has written books preoccupied with the question of Arab purity (الصُّرَحاء, *aṣ-ṣuraḥā'*) and hybridity (الهُجَناء, *al-hujanā'*), as well as the Abbasid imperium's ethnic admixture, glorifying the blacks (السُّودان, *as-sūdān*) and the reds (الحمران, *al-ḥamrān*) and praising the accomplishments of *al-muwālī* and Persians (العجم, *al-'ajam*). He is also charged with a style of writing that is overly eclectic and multifaceted, dominated by encyclopedic pedantry, repetitiveness, and multiplicious verbosity (التكثير, *at-takthīr*) that needlessly overburdens people.[63]

These charges are very much interconnected. *Kitāb al-ḥayawān* presents the dog-rooster debate between an-Naẓẓām, and Ma'bad as its paratext, undertaking a laboriously detailed expositional elaboration of all the issues at play regarding the multiplicious relations of admixture in nature. Composite mixture (المُركَّب, *al-murakkab*) and interstitial diversity (المُتَلاقِحات, *al-mutalāqiḥāt*) of classes of things (الجنس, *al-jins*) that do not readily subsume into any one universal class other than that of the living is a through-line of the book. In fact, the principal investment of *Kitāb al-ḥayawān* is in expositing the perennial dynamics of mixture as the *enérgeia* of the living. When reading *Kitāb al-ḥayawān*, we are immersed in tales of mongrels and mutts. "Continuing our earlier discussion of the mongrel [الخلق المُركَّب, *al-khalq al-murakkab*] and cross–fertilization of different species," al-Jāḥiẓ tells us at one point, "it is postulated that العِسْبار [*al-ʿisabār*] is the offspring of a hyena from a wolf."[64] In the course of his exposition, al-Jāḥiẓ evokes Aristotle, to whom he refers as صاحب المنطق (*ṣāḥib al-manṭiq*, "Master of Logic"), and his assertion in *History of Animals* that "there are in nature a variety of species hybrids among wild animals such as the Seleucid dog generated from the fox copulating with the dog-bitch, and the Indian hound which was generated from the animal the Greeks call طاغريس [*tāghrīs* = τίγριος, tīgiros, tiger] copulating with the dog-bitch."[65] While concurring with Aristotle's theory of hybridization as speciation, al-Jāḥiẓ disputes his postulate that, once engendered, species are morphologically immutable, maintaining on the contrary that all zoological life, including human, is fundamentally transmutational (المِسْخ, *al-miskh*) with a variety of environmental factors, such as profound degenerative change in atmosphere, water, and soil, precipitating change in the natural morphology of animal life over time.[66] The principal problem al-Jāḥiẓ has with Aristotle's postulate of immutability is that his illustrations of imaginary as well as existing creatures lack any empirical verification. As already noted, al-Jāḥiẓ puts great stock in تجربة (*tajriba*), which he uses as a specialized term of knowledge denoting experimental empirical knowledge, or اختبار (*ikhtibār*). He also makes use of its more colloquial connotation as "practical experience" in the general sense of how one lives life cunningly. In both the specialized and more general sense, a formal corollary of تجربة (*tajriba*) is إبداع (*ibdāʿ*), commonly translated as "innovation," but more aptly rendered as "creativity" or *poiēsis*, in the sense of fundamental transformative activity, the activity of giving coherent expression in transmutational forms. In this sense, we can say تجربة (*tajriba*) is about poetic transformation, which is by definition experimental form. The principal record of such experimental form al-Jāḥiẓ consults is pre-Islamic Arabic poetry and Bedouin proverbs on the basis of their ekphrastic *enérgeia*, the capacity of their material expression to evoke the eventfulness of experience. In its composition *Kitāb al-ḥayawān* entails a style of narration that al-Jāḥiẓ calls "حكاية" (*ḥikāya*), by which he means verbatim quotation of diverse contesting views to the point of impersonating them. In other words, compositionally, *Kitāb al-ḥayawān* is a performance of mimicry throughout, which al-Jāḥiẓ deploys in his effort to achieve ekphrastic *enérgeia* in an emergent, "modern" Arabic prose. "This is a book in which the *desiderata* [رغبة, *raġba*] of every community is treated equally," he says, "both the Arab and non-Arab [العَجَم, *al-ʿajam*] are assimilated [تتشابه, *tutašābuh*] in it; that is because whereas what is Arabic [عَرَبيًّا, *ʿarabīyan*] is Arab [أعرابيًا, *aʿrābīyan*], Islam is inclusive of all [جماعيًا, *jamāʿīyan*]. It has taken from philosophy, and combined oral knowledge, as well as verifiable empirical knowledge [علْم التجرِبة, *ʿilm at-tajriba*] in engagement with the knowledge of the Qurʾan and Sunna. It engages sensual affect and natural instincts."[67]

What al-Jāḥiẓ means by "assimilate" (تشابه, *tašābuh*) here is mimicking the postulations and tenets of every community on its own terms. In other words, he espouses their positions as though one of them. We might arguably characterize this, albeit anachronistically, as *immanente Kritik* (immanent critique) to use Karl Rosenkranz's designation for Hegel's "following up on what Kant refrained from doing."[68] On the matter of expository style, Aristotle's apophantic discourse (λόγος ἀποφαντικός, *lógos apophantikós*) aims at superimposing order on the chaos of perception (αἴσθησις, *aesthesis*) by filtering conceptualizations through the discipline of formulaic statement (ὀρθός λόγος, *orthós lógos*). The classical philosophical discourse predicates the eventual universal form that subsumes all particularity to its style of definition and taxonomy, construing contradiction as illegitimate (fallacious), and accounting for paradox as a tentative limit of reason; the oxymoron is an exotic rarity. We already know that even when Aristotle says "art imitates nature," he means it mimics the formal efficacy of nature. By contrast, al-Jāḥiẓ's narrative style in *Kitāb al-ḥayawān* of assimilating (تشابه, *tašābuh*), in mixture aims at representing the dynamic interaction between perception and conceptualization in order to exhibit the pivotal and essential role the spontaneity of imagination plays in what and how humans are in the world. As he says concerning Arabic poetic expression: "Everything with the Arab is spontaneous [بديهة, *badīha*] and extemporaneously improvised [ارتجال, *irtijāl*]. Rather than arriving at meaning through ponderous abstract thought and book-study, the Arab transforms [يصرف, *yusraf*] his imaginings [وهم, *wahm*] directly into discourse or into metered declamation [رجز, *rajaz*]."[69] This is expression in situ: "in every instance, the Arab transforms his imaginings into a general direction, into whatever purpose he intends, achieving the full meaning in the expression and articulation of the words in practice."[70] The key term here is وهم (*wahm*), which al-Jāḥiẓ uses not in the more commonplace sense of "doubtful, mistaken, or delusional thought," but rather in the philosophical sense al-Kindī gives it in his translation of Aristotle's *De Anima* as the Arabic rendering of *phantasia*. Al-Jāḥiẓ's usage also carries the additional Stoic use of *phantasia* to denote the images engendered as we imagine things and the concepts by which we think discursively of them. He, thus, goes one step further than al-Kindī by suggesting the poetic image is a material manifestation of imagination as the faculty essential to thinking *in the world*. Accordingly, the poetic image is an affective transformative and generative act of expression, giving shape to the actualities of living while at the same time being transformed by them.

Rather than a universal form that subsumes all particularity to its style of definition and taxonomy, al-Jāḥiẓ's formal mimicry predicates a specific, fundamentally localized pure form—the space of Arabic purity, بلاد الأعراب الخلص (*bilād al-aʿrāb al-khalaṣ*), situated in the desert beyond the management of civilization and remaining asymptotic—which expands spatially through engagement with a perpetual variety of heterogenous styles, engendering a new form, that of the المولّدون (*al-muwalladūn*, the mixed impure Arab), in which infinite admixture abounds as constitutive. This is the Arabic of the العرب المستعرب (*al-ʾarab al-mustaʿarib*, "Arabicizing Arabs") who inhabit الأمصار (*al-amṣār*, big cities) and القروى (*al-qarawī*, villages). Its open-ended literary style, called الادب (*al-adab*), of which al-Jāḥiẓ is the recognized master, was emerging among the rather diverse urban elite under the early Abbasid imperial regime. Jāḥiẓian Arabic, with its expressly asymptotic العرب (*al-ʾarab*), assimilates everything it encounters and transmutes it in the process; it is perpetually transmutational in mimicry and admixture. Whereas the Greek philosophical discourse gives us the harmonics of synthesis, *al-mustaʿarib* literary Arabic presents the harmonic dissonance of nonsynthesizing mixture, mixture of heterogenous forms without their assimilation into a resolving hybrid. It is also noteworthy that al-Jāḥiẓ's description of Arab spontaneous improvisation aligns with Hurston's of Negro artful mimicry—which is to say, the characteristics of her Negro in mimicry seem very much like those of his Arab.

Regarded together, it becomes clear how both Hurston's account of mimicry in Negro expressive style and al-Jāḥiẓ's compositional form of mimicry as حكاية (*ḥikāya*) in his recounting instances of multiplicious transmutation undermine the conceit of purity. They turn on difference, or, more precisely, differentiation. In the performance of mimicry, the mimic assimilates what he is not. In so doing, he marks his distinction from the model he strives to be like, and, *pace* Plato, "being like" is not an identity but a masquerade. Mimicry shows off the motivationality of signifying practices: "that a sign signifies only in being an object that stands for another to some mind," as Charles Sanders Peirce put it, expounding his tripartite theory of the basic sign structure as entailing a sign or signifier, an object or signified, and an interpretant, which is the understanding we have of the sign/object relation.[71] In other words, the meaning of a sign, such as a bark, is manifest in the interpretation it generates in sign users. In the case of the Abu Maryam anecdote al-Jāḥiẓ recounts about the debtor who consistently barked like a dog, the sign users are somehow readily identifiable as human, and so social subjects within the same species. In that of Abū Dabūba al-Zinjī, whose braying convinced every jackass he was one of theirs, they are heterospecies. The concern here is with mimicry both as a species activity and a conceptualization and performance of speciation. There is another take on the Abu Maryam anecdote about the debtor, however. Perhaps he no longer speaks his own language, having lost himself in mimicking a barking dog. The interpretant as some understanding of the relation between sign and object gives a translation of the sign, and as such is a further sign in an infinite process of semiosis, or representations. In this respect, al-Jāḥiẓ's assimilation (تشابه, *tašābuh*) of heterogeneity is a performance of admixture that transmutes into a dynamic perennially open *semiosis* akin to what we have been attending to in our elaboration of *para-semiosis*. Jāḥiẓian mimicry, with all that it entails concerning *métissages*, suggests a rudimentary theory of the semiotics of resemblance. Relating this theory to Farès's engagement with the Baldwin's writing and the blues as *poiēsis in black*, in which he sees a reflection of his writing as a revolutionary Amazigh of Algeria, we can recognize the resonance of *para-semiosis* across the heterogeneous practices of being-in-common artistically called Negro and Berber, Black and Kabyle, respectively.

Going along these lines, as far as Farès is concerned, entails pondering the existential semiotics of Algerianness, about which he thought a great deal, arguing for a radically para-semiotic revolutionary Algeria, where saying, "*I am Kabyle doesn't mean I am not Algerian, but it simply means that, as much as I am Algerian, I am firstly Kabyle.*" Farès's *métisse* Algeria is not only the confluence of polyglossia, but also that of polycosmos, including autochthonous, chiefly Amazigh, polytheisms along with the Abrahamic monotheisms of Judaism, Christianity, and Islam. In that respect, Farès severely critiqued the nation-statist project of universally enforced Arabicization (التعريب, *at-ta'arīb*) with its attendant premise that precolonial Algeria was Arabo-Muslim as a mode of imperial colonization. On the way to Orense with his Spanish lover, Conchita, soon after his encounter with Baldwin in Paris, he muses: "It would never dawn on anyone to deny that Algeria was a very lofty place of paganism before becoming the crossroads of the edifying discourses of Christianity and Islam. . . . Algeria's true patria is its old history, and the oldest history of Algeria—AESTHETICALLY SPEAKING—is paganism."[72] The point is to rework this old paganism into a belief in life without barriers as the new path of Algerian artistic consciousness in the conviction that the confluence of revolutionary and pagan expressions would intensify the political fervor of the postcolonial moment. Such confluence would vanquish the bureaucratic technocracy of the valets of realism. The aspiration is that this reworked "pagan thought will activate the revolutionary critique of an essentially statist ideology. Thus will appear, in the authenticity of its future, an Algerian history liberated from all the conquests it has known. . . . This total history of Algeria will be different from the other history (conquest—depersonalization) in that it will not be a therapy for small brains, but a social dialectic."[73] The Revolution must be, by definition, an open-ended process of *para-semiosis*. Its political aims must be to foster and facilitate the aesthetics of *métissages* without barriers, that is to say, without a synthesizing telos or unitary adumbration. Farès took the richness of the Amazigh cosmos-poetics and folktales, particularly those of Kabylia, as the fount for revolutionary aesthetics, which he represented in French, unlike his fellow Amazigh, Kateb Yacine, who from 1970 until he death in 1989 wrote plays in Algerian Arabic and Tamazight. At issue in their difference of idiomatic expression is the tension between commemorative and innovative functions of language: Can particular linguistic practices invoke iteration of very particular historical understandings concordant with actual life practices, while at the same time facilitating emergent expressions?

Again, regarding all this in relation to Jāḥiẓian mimicry, there is every reason to expect in the postcolonial Algerian context a comparable, compatible Arabic-expressed *para-semiosis*. And indeed, there has been, one of the most prominent proponents of which was Farès's fellow writer and Amazigh, aṭ-Ṭāhir Waṭṭār. Considered by many as the father of modern Algerian Arabic literature, Waṭṭār shares Farès's aversion to the valets of realism, as well as the commitment to an Algerian life artistically lived in a *métissage* conceived in expressly Jāḥiẓian terms. Concordant with that commitment, he founded الجمعية الثقافية الجاحظية (*al-jamāʿiya ath-thaqāfiya al-Jāḥiẓīya*, the Jāḥiẓian Cultural Association) in 1989, which, in a manner rather akin to the Modernists' conception of *mestizaje*, aimed at the assimilation of the diverse Algerian practices of living and thinking into a presumptively plastic Algerian Arabic literary form. Waṭṭār's energy was focused on achieving a formally transformative Arabic in keeping with his "fundamental commitment to the principle of the dialectic of form and content," predicated on his conception of "the innovation [ابتداع, *ibtidā*] of form that embodies what is purported, embodies the content, like a language that is in harmony with the atmosphere."[74] This does not amount to the idealization of form entailed in Hegel's dialectical conception of the integral *Geist* expressing itself in some ideal, such as Greek art or the bourgeois novel. Rather, Waṭṭār uses dialectic of form and content "in the sense of making room for content to be formed, and for form's being transformed by that content while at the same time being liberated from its matrix."[75] There can be no "consecration [تقديس, *taqdīs*] of form" in the creation of innovative revolutionary Algerian Arabic literature.[76] By that same token, however, he was invested in (التعريب, *at-taʿarīb*) as the way to foster a revolutionary postcolonial Algerian Arabo-Amazigh-Islamic identity and fervently opposed to regarding Francophone Algerian writing as national literature. The plurality of admixture he sought in articulating a revolutionary Algerian aesthetics was circumscribed and comprehended in Arabic. It was to be woven not exclusively but principally from the threads of various "native" Arabic-language forms, such as امثال (*amthāl*, parables), especially Sufi parables, مُوَشَّحات (*muwaššaḥāt*, a post-classical poetic form), مَقامات (*muqāmāt*, rhymed prose), as well as حِكايات (*ḥikāyāt*, narrative takes) and modern Arabic novels. The resulting Arabic presents a harmonic dissonance of nonsynthesizing admixture. Along those lines, Waṭṭār's formal artistic struggle was not so much to Arabicize Algeria in accordance with a postulated originary oriental Arab authenticity, اصالة (*aṣāla*), as it was to make Arabic Algerian in a way that, his opposition to Francophonie notwithstanding, accords with Farès's conception of the Revolution as open-ended *métissages*. The question is whether Waṭṭār, by construing the statist project of Arabicization as Jāḥiẓian admixture, can proceed without its theological ideologic qua ethno-imperial underpinning. Can there be an Arabic *para-semiosis* without a pure Arab grounding originality? If the Arabic of Algeria comes *out of* the admixture of Arabicized Algerian polyglossia and polycosmos, then how does it relate to the Arabic of its neighbors, assuming, in the Jāḥiẓian mode, that they too are places of confluence. The challenge becomes to conceive a creolizing Arabic lingua franca not aimed at restoring an authentic originary عروبة (*'urūba*, Arabism). Waṭṭār once described such authenticity as "stalled in the epoch of ibn al-Muqaffaʿ," which is to say the second half of the eighth century, "by those who are gathered under the banner of the Arab Renaissance [النهضة] who are pillagers of modernity in their rush to classicism."[77] This is an outright rejection of Hegelian *translatio*, the tale told of the transmission of knowledge from the primordial east (the Arabian peninsula) to the west (the Maghreb). The struggle to achieve a formally transformative, revolutionary Algerian Arabic form is not so much a question of to whom or what language does poetic expression originally belong; rather it's a question of the nature of the *who* articulated *with* and *by* the expression. In other words, what are the poetic possibilities of Algerian Arabic?

This question is at the heart of one of Waṭṭār's earliest and most controversial short stories, "الزنجية والضابط" ("az-Zinjīya wa aḍ-ḍābṭ," The Negress and the Officer), which was originally published in 1973 in the Lebanese literary journal الآداب (*al-Ādāb*), just two years after Farès's *Un passager de l'occident*.[78] Although there is no evocation of Baldwin or the blues in Waṭṭār's story, the way in which the Negress of the title is depicted resonates with the way Farès reads Rufus Scott and the blues. This has to do with her being emblematic of both Arabic formal innovation and the Algerian people. Formally, "az-Zinjīya wa aḍ-ḍābṭ" is a parable presented as the story of a voyage north across the Algerian Sahara, in a car with four occupants besides the driver: a journalist, a party hack, a military officer, and a Negress who is the representative of a local cooperative council. These four are not really characters as much as personages, symbolic representations. It is obvious what the hack and military officer symbolize—the National Liberation Front, the ruling political party generally referred to by its French acronym, FLN, and the ALN, the Army of National Liberation, respectively. The journalist symbolizes the intelligentsia, and the Negress the people. Gender is important here. In the same passage about Algerian paganism cited earlier, Farès says, regarding the Revolution's language: "The term 'brother' should be banished from revolutionary language, because of course (at least this how it is understood) the word 'brother' has a patriarchal and not a revolutionary heritage. And, what gives weight (in the sense of fatness) to patriarchy in Algeria, is this Islamic idea that 'only the Father exists' and that 'we, daily workers of patriarchal history, we all are brothers.' It is not surprising, then, that the only matters appearing in Algerian literature are 'tribal,' fraternal.'"[79] The implication is that the Islamizing Arabs tribes—particularly the Banu Hilāl, Banu Sulaym confederation—were themselves a colonizing force that subjugated the Amazigh matrilineal transmission of value to their patrilineal tribal order. So, it is of no small moment that the people in Waṭṭār's story are symbolized by a Negress and that she is autochthonous, of the land, the earth, which must be circumscribed in patria in order to become invested with meaning. This gendering of land and power has some bearing on the seating arrangement in the car, with the party hack initially siting up front beside the driver, and the other three in the rear: the journalist on the left, the officer in the middle, and the Negress on the right. For much of the trip the officer flirts with the Negress and surreptitiously fondles her, taking advantage of the car's tossing on the road. The party hack overlooks the officer's indiscretion in the name of some solidarity. After all, the party needs the military to secure the nation from all dangers, domestic as well as foreign. The journalist tries to stop the officer's inappropriate behavior by launching into conversation that draws attention to the Negress's person and intelligence and soon ferrets out that she is a poet with a sublime recitation voice, making the officer feel both slightly guilty and wanting to possess her all the more. He is attracted to the potency of her poetry—its siren-like affect—as well as her sexuality, but equally repulsed by her physicality, her blackness. The Negress is not passive and reflects on the connection between the officer's unwelcome advances and the order of state power in which foreign white women are to be married, but the likes of her merely fucked and possessed for their beauty and artistry. After a break in the trip, she insists on a rearrangement in the seating. The reason she gives for this is that she wants to recite her poetry to the journalist, to which the officer protests: "Recite to us all!" The Negress prevails so she is to the left of the journalist who now sits between her and the officer. Remarking on this arrangement, the journalist says: "This is the proper place for the intellectual in the Third World: boxed in between the poetic people [الشعب الشاعر, *aš-ša'ab aš-šā'ir*] and the governing army."[80] The Negress then recites one of her poems in a decidedly Algerian Arabic dialect, which is not set off but runs in the texts, giving the impression of the seamlessly fluidity of her recitation:

عندما يدلهم الظلام. وعندما لا يبقى هناك مجال للرؤية. ويستيقظ الشياطين والخفافيش، واللصوص من كل نوع. اطفئ بدوري الشمعات في الداخل واتعرى لأرقص وارقص. ارقص في الظلمة، بدون موسيقى، إلا ما يصطخب في اعماقي، أرقص للشياطين. للخفافيش. للصوص وقطاع الطرق. أرقص للملائكة أيضاً، وكل من يرقص مثلى. حتى أسقط مغمياً على. وعندما افتح عيني. أجد النور يعم كل شيء. بيد ان السواد طال. وها انني ارقص عارية منذ أزمان. دنو أن أسقط مغمياً على

As soon as night descends. As soon as vision dims. And the demons and bats and thieves of every kind awake. I put out the candles in the house and strip naked to dance, and I dance. I dance in the dark without music to the sound of my inner rage, I dance for the demons. For the bats. For the thieves and highwaymen. I dance for the angels too, and for all who dance like me. Until, in ecstasy, I faint. And when I open my eyes. I find light shining on everything. However vast the long black darkness. And here I dance naked forever. Without fainting.[81]

With this, she expresses her resistance, and for a spell interrupts the order of things, prompting the journalist to shout and the officer to mutter "beautiful . . . wonderful." But the interruption is only momentary; the beauty and wonder must be interpolated back into the order as the only antinomy recognizable and permitted as such. "This is an eloquently fluent [مسيلمة, *maslīma*] recitation, a praise-song [تسابيح, *tasābīḥ*] of Rābi'a al-'Adwīya," the party hack declaims, identifying the Negress with the eighth-century black Iraqi slave who was famous for her Sufi poems expressing arduous love, العشق (*al-'išiq*) for God.[82] She emphatically resists this re-interpolation back into the order of sacrifice. Yet, it is reinforced by the journalist who, on asking her the title of her ode, disregards her emphatic refusal to give titles to any of her poems and insists on naming it صمت الثورة (*Samat ath-thaura*, Silence of the Revolution).[83] To which the Negress, taking his face in her hands as though he were a wayward obstinate child, says, condescendingly: "I protest." The officer and party hack together recognize the journalist's insistence, the Negress's refusal of a name, and her flirtation with him as acts of blatant public opposition to their governance and so threats to public security. It is the journalist, however, whom they recognize as the greater threat in accord with their gendered understanding of things. The party hack goes so far as to remark, to the officer's chagrin, that, under cover of freedom of the press, the journalist has written effective articles about all their activities as well as women's rights, rights with which the officer will familiarize himself later that night, suggesting the Negress's sexual availability.

The struggle, then, is between them and the journalist intellectual over the significance of the Negress and her poetry. And in the midst of their cacophonous chatter filled with inappropriate innuendo and laughter, she recites another poem:

النزيف الكبير. ذاكم الذي لا موضع لنبعه، لا ولا لمصبه. أعذب نزيف. لأنه أصل كل الفصول. الشتاء والصيف. الربيع والخريف. وأنا في أعماقي نبع نزيف. تاه الغائصون في إدراكه، وتاه الظامئون في الاهتداء الى مصبه، أو حتى الى مجراه. انه مخصص لفارس همام، يخرج من أمواج المحيطات أو ينزل من زوابع رميلية فوق الركام، يشق بسيفه اللحم والعظام. ويصل شرابين قلبه بنبع النزيف.. ويرتوى في كل الفصول. في الربيع والخريف. في الشتاء والصيف.

> The great fluidity. The source from whence it springs you do not know, nor its estuary. I find the fluidity sweet. Because it is the source of all seasons. Winter, summer, spring, and fall. In my deepest depths fluidity springs. Daughter of those who are immersed in its perception, and daughter of those who thirst at the cross-roads of its course, even as it flows. It is destined for a noble knight who will emerge from the ocean waves, or descend from the whirlwind sands above the rubble. His sword cutting flesh and bone. He comes to drinks from the heart of the fluidity's source. He recounts stories in all seasons. In spring and fall. In winter and summer.[84]

This poem impresses the three men even more, with the officer being particularly struck by the image of the knight, whom he thinks he resembles. The party hack, who has known the Negress longest of all, remarks that he never knew she was such a stunning poet, to which she replies that she does not often recite her poems because "there are not many who can ride the whirlwind cry of my heart." This poem, however, she has given a title, which she whispers to the inquisitive journalist: "Its name is 'Your Son.'"[85]

To repeat, the Negress belongs to the land; and she is such very much in the same way Farès describes Ali Saïd as belonging to the mountain in "The Notebook of Ali Saïd," the story embedded in the seventh section of *Un passager de l'occident*, called "7. La Presqu'île de Cangas" (The Peninsula of Cangas). It is the story about which Farès lies to Conchita in order to console her after having abused her emotionally, telling her: "*I wrote it for you, this first line of a song about the blue bullet,*" adding in an aside not directed at her, "and I wrote (all night) this blue appeal (from Kabylia), of Ali-Saïd's (the lucky one)"[86]—lucky because he was killed in combat on Akbou mountain peak in 1955, the early days of the War for Independence. Just as military developments overtake Ali

Saïd on the mountain as a sacrifice to the struggle for liberation, so too the Negress is depicted as totemic sacrament. It is the dispensation of the Negress, her abuse at the hands of the military and sacrifice for the party, that consecrates the nation as a unity. In this rite, reprobation, guilt over her treatment, is created by the journalist, and not in recognition of, nor even direct engagement with her poetic voice as conceptually constitutive of the public discourse. Any ambivalence about this sacrifice is dispensed with when the party hack assertively allegorizes the Negress's poetry in accordance with the authoritative categories of the Arabist project of national formation, translating it into a sign of that very project. Her poem becomes "as a praise-song of Rābi'a al-'Adwīya," or is properly named, "Silence of the Revolution." Even the intellectual's mediating function serves the project of some sort of amalgamation, a mixing of elements that will enable a future community. This is not a community in love, however; the only love generating solidarity is the passion for the future, expressed in Arabic. Arabic is the totality that can comprehend the mix in the nation-state. That is precisely what Farès is clearly and emphatically against. Love of the future in the nation-state is allegorical in the worst way, stripping the beauty of artistic living—much as the petrol-chemical industry strips the earth—to make it meaningful according to a set order of things. The ending of "az-Zinjīya wa aḍ-ḍābṭ" disturbs all that, however. As the travelers approach the inn where they will spend the night, the officer, persisting in his forwardness toward the Negress, whispers in her ear: "I want you tonight and for as long as you desire." She is doubtful, responding: "You mean as long as we are traveling." But he insists that it is not just for this night but for every night to come, saying he'll send his wife north, thereby exchanging one woman for another in the same way one would change an old well-used currency note for a new crisp one, assuming they have the exact same value. Seeming to finally succumb to his advances, the Negress offers him some enticement: "Leave the door of you room unlocked, and I will come to you at two o'clock." "Why two o'clock?" he asks; and she tells him: "It is the hour of my birth, and I want you at that very moment."[87] Agreeing to her conditions, he waits anxiously until two o'clock, then two-fifteen, and finally at two-thirty, he leaves his room slipping quietly into hers only to find it empty and the bed still made. Looking for her, he sneaks into the party hack's room. Finding him sound asleep and alone, he heads for the journalist's room in a fury, swearing to "kill them both and drink their blood." Yet, when he approaches the door of the room, from under which emanates a warm light, he hears a voice reciting poetry in a sad tone. Pushing the door enough ajar to stick in his head, he is dumbfounded by what he witnesses: "The Negress laying on the bed atop the covers in a white nightgown is reciting poetry with closed-eyes, and the journalist is sitting at her feet on a rug on the floor engrossed in writing."

Unlike the poems she recited earlier in the car, the poetry the Negress recites at the end of the story is not directly represented to us as readers. We have only the officer's experience of her performance, which is akin to Allen's and Parrish's experiences of slave songs: the inadequate transcription of a not fully comprehensible expression. It is also like the mountain where Ali Saïd died in combat and from which he was carried to Akbou village, which "was a response because it was already a place of words where the various questions that one could ask about a way of acting found their meaning."[88] Just like the Negress's great fluidity of unknown origin, no one among the villagers could say how the mountain came into being. Yet, just as the villagers go to the mountain when their lives need some clarity, so too the journalist as well as the officer seek the Negress out, the one wanting her body to somehow appease his insatiable desire, the other her poetic voice as the basis for his own writing. The two poetic recitations of the Negress given to us directly are uttered in an Algerian Arabic full of mixed meaning exemplified by its processes and certainly not by the supposed purity of the contents on which these operate. It is in the mode of العرب المستعرِب (*al-'arab al-musta'arib*), the Arabicizing Arab we spoke of earlier—that is to say, the very Arabic *créolisation* al-Jāḥiẓ seeks to master, and Waṭṭār professes to write. Yet, in writing in this creolized Arabic of admixture, he undermines the nation-statist project of Arabicization he professes to be writing *for*. All said and done, "az-Zinjīya wa aḍ-ḍābṭ" is the blueish of his writings. The tension between its form and thematic content is oxymoronic in the way Murray understood blues' form to be; giving material form in Arabic to the great fluidity that is both the flesh as well as the thinking of the Algerian peoples. To put this in the words of al-Majnūn (the Madman) who is the protagonist of Waṭṭār's 1989 novel, تجربة في العشق (*Tajriba fī-l 'išiq*, Experience in Love): "Thinking, after all, is essentially a superabundance flooding [فيض, *faiḍ*] the brain that gets translated into written letters and words, or into voice in the form of discourse. Yet when it is so translated my insanity is manifested."[89] It should be noted, al-Majnūn's charge that giving material form to thinking in language, whether in writing or speaking, leads to insanity is directed at Arabic—more precisely at the Arabic of him and his fellow Algerians, adumbrated as it is by the imperial languages of Europe as well as the Arabic East.

Once, again Farès's story of Ali Saïd's notebook gives some sense of the stakes here. Having written "*this first line of a song about the blue bullet*," not for Conchita but in the wake of wounding her heart, Farès reflects: "I imagined, with respect to several pages I had written, a set of words that correspond to the state or journey that had guided, until now, my lines. I divined that the lines traced could only testify to a time other than that of an annoyance towards a reality that dispossessed me of a place which, in any way, I had never occupied."[90] Wanting to live out life artistically as an inhabitant of the peninsula, he understands that "the written work, unlike the painted brush stroke, is not matter; it is voice, voice lost in infinity."[91] With this Farès brings us to the ninth section of *Un passager de l'occident* called "9. Légende du monde," which is composed of his reworking of four Amazigh parables reminiscent of "a voyage of thought, (more precisely, this voyage of thought belongs to the oldest Black American music, the blues.) (This voyage could be a thought that glided on the fingernails of a guitarist named Taj Mahal).... I would say that to experience some thought it suffices to paint the letters of the mailbox in BLUE."[92] Even though the poetry the Negress recites at the end of "az-Zinjīya wa aḍ-ḍābṭ" is not directly represented to us, if we attend to it in terms of Farès's blue letters, ever mindful she is the "daughter of those who thirst at the cross-roads" and recall the representation in the car of her earlier poems, we can allow ourselves to imagine how it might flow with its "sad tones" along lines somehow like those in the last quatrains of Bessie Smith's "Young Woman's Blues," which gave Baldwin the title for one of his more celebrated works:

> *I'm a young woman, and ain't done runnin' round*
> *I'm a young woman, and ain't done runnin' round*
> *Some people call me a hobo, some call me a bum*
> *Nobody knows my name, nobody knows what I done*

That which cannot be named cannot be properly possessed, allegorized, or sacrificed. When Baldwin remarks that love gives blues its tragic tones, he clearly means in Murray's sense of oxymoronic form. On this note, we recall the description early on in *Another Country* of the young jazz saxophonist Rufus was jamming with one night, who, dry humping the air, "screamed through the horn '*Do you love me?*' again and again, focusing the attention of his audience on the entirety of a life palpably lived as he hurled his outrage at them with the same contemptuous pagan pride with which he humped the air." Farès understood that *Another Country* is an exhibition of the force of such love. It is the black beauty he saw in Rufus's pitching toward the river from the George Washington Bridge, which brings him to recall the pagan beauty of Algeria. With that recollection, he gives us another Amazigh blues line:

> At this moment, at the apotheosis of my existence (thirty years) I envisage a dazzling apotheosis around the thirty-first year, an apotheosis that would consist in not risking a single glance toward a desperate thirty-second year.
> In other words, I would rejoin the other vertigo of my birth, and not by idleness or suicide, but by pure ambition. So, I drink.
> I drink; and yet I should say I used to drink.
> I should say I used to drink because, ever since I've had this awareness of the impression of blueness, it seems to me (and this impression is as recent

as what I'm able to write here) that everything could still change and on this condition: performing the ensemble of renunciations that will permit me to exist. That would amount, in short, to an instance of a totally artistic life.[93]

Farès's drinking started at twilight (*crépuscule*). That has its own story along with the Earth, "Terre et Crépuscule" (Earth and Twilight), which is the third parable in "La Légende du Monde." In a 1979 *Fountains* interview with Peter Beatson, he explains the origin of that story,

> It dates back to a time in '68–'69 when my friends had gone back to Algeria and when I lived in almost total isolation. From the time I decided to cut myself off, writing was my only recourse, the only way I possessed to try to master fragmentation and disintegration. That passage moves towards a state of pure poetry, a movement in which a desire for poetry and the desire for death meet at the moment of twilight. Twilight is transfiguration of day and night, of the coupling of day and night. Twilight is the moment of half-light, the half-light of everything one might become. It is a gentle time, a time when there are no heroes but in which, perhaps, great poets may appear.[94]

It is a time of drinking and thinking in disorder.

Preface

1 John Smith, *Generall Historie of Virginia*, 126.
2 *Oxford English Dictionary Online*, s.v. "Negro, n. and adj.," March 2020, https://www-oed-com.pitt.idm.oclc.org/view/Entry/125898. Also see Richard Grenville in Hakluyt, *Principall Navigations*, 734.

Introduction

1 Saidiya V. Hartman, *Scenes of Subjection: Terror, Slavery, and Self-Making in Nineteenth-Century America*, 4–5.
2 Hartman, *Scenes of Subjection*, 5.
3 Frederick Douglass, "What to the Slave Is the Fourth of July?," in *The Frederick Douglass Papers, Series 1*, 2:369.
4 John Locke, *An Essay Concerning Human Understanding*, 448.
5 Locke, *Human Understanding*, 448.
6 Mattie Erma Edwards Parker, ed., *The North Carolina Colonial Records*, 1:187–205; John Locke, *The Fundamental Constitution of Carolina*, 175.
7 Hortense Spillers, "Mama's Baby, Papa's Maybe: An American Grammar Book," 206.
8 Maurice Merleau-Ponty, *Le visible et l'invisible*, 119.
9 Fisk University Social Science Institute, *Unwritten History of Slavery: Autobiographical Accounts of Negro Ex-Slaves*, 85.
10 Hartman, *Scenes of Subjection*, 78.
11 Immanuel Kant, *Ueber den Gebrauch teleologischer Principien in der Philosophie*, 174 fn.
12 See Cedric Robinson, *The Terms of Order: Political Science and the Myth of Leadership*.
13 See Alejo Carpentier, Prólogo a *El reino de este mundo*. The prologue was originally republished as the essay "Lo real maravilloso de América" in *El Nacional*, April 8, 1948. It was subsequently republished with significant modification and additional material under that title in Alejo Carpentier, *Tientos y diferencias* (Montevideo: Arca, 1967), 96–112. Carpentier gave another version of it in a paper entitled "Lo barroco y lo real maravilloso," which he presented on May 22, 1975, to the Razón de Ser Conference at Ateneo de Caracas, in Venezuela.
14 Carpentier, Prólogo a *El reino de este mundo*, 1.
15 Carpentier, Prólogo a *El reino de este mundo*, 2.
16 Carpentier, Prólogo a *El reino de este mundo*, 2.
17 Carpentier, Prólogo a *El reino de este mundo*, 2.
18 Carpentier, Prólogo a *El reino de este mundo*, 3.
19 See Alejo Carpentier, *¡Ecué-Yamba-O: Historia afro-cubana!* (Madrid: Editorial España, 1933). Carpentier began this novel in 1927, while he was imprisoned for having signed a democratic anti-imperialist manifesto against the Gerardo Machado y Morales regime; it was completed and published in 1933. The novel's title is the Lucumí expression used by the society's members, *los ñáñigos*, in their ritual dance; the

protagonist's name, Menegildo Cué, is an allusion to the *Abakuá* drum, *Ekué*. This same drum also appears Carpentier's poems "Liturgia" and "Juego santo" (Alejo Carpentier, *Obras completas*, 1:211–213, 1:218–220). Guadalupe Silva has recently argued that the negrophilia (*negrismo*) informing Carpentier's concept of *lo real maravilloso* has its roots in *¡Ecué-Yamba-O: Historia afro-cubana!* See Guadalupe Silva, "Alejo Carpentier del negrismo a lo real maravilloso (Alejo Carpentier: From Negrophilia to the Marvelous Real)," *Anclajes* 19.1 (2015): 53–70.

20 Juan Marinello, "Una novela cubana," in *Literatura hispanoamericana: Hombres-meditaciones* (México: Ediciones de la Universidad de México, 1937), 171.

21 See Denise Ferreira da Silva, "Hacking the Subject," 19.

22 "Une grammaire est ce qui permet aux membres d'une communauté de juger correctement, c'est-à-dire de lier correctement à des discontinuités survenant dans le monde (corps, objets, matériaux, gestes, paroles) des descriptions et d'éprouver vis-à-vis de certaines de ces descriptions un sentiment d'évidence." Cyril Lemieux, *Le devoir et la grâce*. This is the second of his 189 propositions.

23 Frantz Fanon, "Ici la voix de l'Algérie," in *Sociologies d'une révolution (L'an V de la Révolution algérienne)* (Paris: Maspero, 1968 [1959]), 73.

24 Albert Murray, "In Response to Being Awarded a Citation for Distinguished Literary Achievement by an Alabamian (2003)," in *Albert Murray and the Aesthetic Imagination of a Nation*, 13.

25 Albert Murray, "A Conversation with Albert Murray," in *Albert Murray and the Aesthetic Imagination of a Nation*, 130–131.

26 Ibn Sīnā, *Kitāb aš-Šifā*, 4:54.

27 Frantz Fanon, *Peau noire masques blancs*, 177.

28 Fanon, *Peau noire*, 6.

29 Claude McKay, *Banjo: A Story without a Plot*, 137.

30 Ralph Ellison, *Invisible Man* (1994), 433.

31 James Baldwin, *Another Country*, 4; emphasis in the original.

32 See Ignace Meyerson, *Écrits, 1920–1983: Pour une psychologies historique*; and Gilbert Simondon, *Deux leçons sur l'animal et l'homme* (Paris: Ellipses, 2004).

33 Fanon, *Peau noire*, 88–89.

34 Fanon, *Peau noire*, 88.

35 Michel Foucault, "The Ethics of the Concern for Self as a Practice of Freedom: An Interview with Michel Foucault," in *Ethics: Subjectivity and Truth: Essential Works of Michel Foucault, 1954–1984*, vol. 1, ed. Paul Rabinow, trans. Robert J. Hurley (London: Penguin, 1997), 283.

On *Lohengrin*'s Swan

1 Barton to Du Bois, South Bend, Indiana, March 1928, in W. E. B. Du Bois, *Writings*, 1220–1222. The original handwritten letter from Barton is catalogued in the W. E. B. Du Bois Papers at the University of Massachusetts Amherst Library. The date on it is January 26, 1928. See Barton, Roland A., Letter from Roland A. Barton to W. E. B. Du Bois, January 26, 1928, W. E. B. Du Bois Papers (MS 312). Du

Bois wrote a letter back to Barton, dated February 1, 1928, in which he informed him: "I am answering your letter in the March *Crisis*"; Letter from W. E. B. Du Bois to Roland A. Barton, February 1, 1928, W. E. B. Du Bois Papers (MS 312).

2 Du Bois to Roland Barton, in *Writings*, 1220.
3 Du Bois to Roland Barton, 1221.
4 "'Negro' with a Capital 'N,'" editorial, *New York Times*, March 7, 1930.
5 Du Bois, *The Ordeal of Mansart*, 315–316.
6 An entry in Du Bois's private notebooks regarding this last point outlines a plan to disprove the Cartesian privileging of ratiocination over feelings in the institution of human intelligence.
7 Although the scholarly controversy cannot be disregarded when reading "Of the Coming of John," it is not my aim to rehearse its details. I point out, nonetheless, that among those whose work has helped establish the importance of Du Bois's style are: Stanley Brodwin, "The Veil Transcended: Form and Meaning in W. E. B. Du Bois's 'The Souls of Black Folk'"; Arnold Rampersad, *The Art & Imagination of W. E. B. Du Bois*; and Stepto, *From behind the Veil*. Russell Berman was one of the first to focus attention on Lohengrin in "Du Bois and Wagner: Race, Nation and Culture between the United States and Germany." Shamoon Zamir notes how his experimental short story "A Vacation Unique," suggests a struggle of narrative form around the issue of how to represent the black self; see Shamoon Zamir, *Dark Voices*, 107. Sieglinde Lemke has offered an insightful reading of the story in her essay, "Of the Coming of John." Equally invaluable is the third chapter of Pricilla Wald's *Constituting Americans: Cultural Anxiety and Narrative Form*, "The Strange Meaning of Being Black: *The Souls of Black Folk* and the Narrative of History." Also see Robert Gooding-Williams *In the Shadow of Du Bois: Afro-Modern Political Thought in America*, the third chapter of which, "Du Bois's Counter-Sublime," provides an extensive reading of the story with some consideration given to the Lohengrin. In an unpublished paper delivered in 2003 at the Northeast Modern Language Association Conference entitled "Why the Music 'Put [Him] All A-Tune': Wagner's *Lohengrin* and the Politics of Cultural Segregation in Du Bois's 'Of the Coming of John,'" Erica Williams makes a compelling case for reading Du Bois's use of Lohengrin in "Of the Coming of John" as the basis for elaborating a universalist aesthetics.
8 Du Bois, *The Souls of Black Folk*, in *Writings*, 521.
9 Du Bois, *Souls*, 522.
10 Du Bois, *Souls*, 523.
11 Du Bois, *Souls*, 487
12 Du Bois, *Souls*, 390. For Rampersad's gloss, see Arnold Rampersad, "Slavery and the Literary Imagination: Du Bois's *The Souls of Black Folk*," 113. Gooding-Williams puts Rampersad's term to considerable work in his reading of the relationship between "Of the Coming of John" and "Of Alexander Crummell."
13 Du Bois, *Souls*, 487
14 Du Bois, *Souls*, 489.
15 Du Bois, "The Negro as He Really Is," 848–866.
16 Du Bois, *Souls*, 525.

17 Du Bois, *Souls*, 525.
18 Du Bois, *Souls*, 524.
19 Du Bois, *Souls*, 364.
20 Du Bois, *Souls*, 364–365.
21 Some illustrative examples of this consensus are Elliott M. Rudwick, *W. E. B. Du Bois, Propagandist of the Negro Protest*; Dickson D. Bruce Jr., "W. E. B. Du Bois and the Idea of Double Consciousness"; Willard B. Gatewood Jr., *Aristocrats of Color*; Adolph Reed, *W. E. B. Du Bois and American Political Thought*; Keith E. Byerman, *Seizing the Word*; Eric Sundquist, *To Wake the Nations*; Sandra Adell, *Double-Consciousness/Double Bind*; Paul Gilroy, *The Black Atlantic*; Paul Macombe, *The Soul-Less Souls of Black Folk*; Shamoon Zamir, *Dark Voices*; Hazel V. Carby, "Souls of Black Men"; Mitchell Aboulafia, *Transcendence: On Self-Determination and Cosmopolitanism*; Roger A. Salerno, *Beyond the Enlightenment*; Winfried Siemerling, *The New North American Studies*; Ross Posnock, *Color & Culture*; Keri E. Iyall Smith, "Hybrid Identities: Theoretical Examinations"; as well as Gooding-Williams, *In the Shadow of Du Bois*. See also Itabari Njeri, "Sushi and Grits: Ethnic Identity and Conflict in a Newly Multicultural America," Alton B. Pollard III, "Last Great Battle of the West: W. E. B. Du Bois and the Struggle for African America's Soul," Molefi Kete Asante, "Racism, Consciousness, and Afrocentricity," and Eric Lincoln, "Du Boisian Dubiety and the American Dilemma: Two Levels of Lure and Loathing," all of which are in *Lure and Loathing: Essays on Race, Identity, and the Ambivalence of Assimilation*, edited by Gerald Early.
22 One of the first to suggest this lineage was Claire Rosenfield, "The Conscious and Unconscious Use of the Double"; Dickson Bruce subsequently gives a more elaborate account in "W. E. B. Du Bois and the Idea of Double Consciousness."
23 Du Bois to Herbert Aptheker, 10 January 1956, *The Correspondence of W. E. B. Du Bois*, 3:395.
24 James, *The Principles of Psychology*, 1:358. See also Azam, *Hypnotisme*.
25 Daryl Scott, *Contempt and Pity*, 2–5.
26 John Moffatt Mecklin, *Democracy and Race Friction*.
27 Mecklin, *Democracy and Race Friction*, 153.
28 Robert Ezra Park, "Negro Race Consciousness as Reflected in Race Literature," 510.
29 Park's use of the term "amalgamation" aimed at casting the idea of racial admixture in a more positive light than that of the then more widespread term "miscegenation," which denoted degenerative racial contamination. It is not at all a triviality that the latter term had been coined by David Goodman Croly in the 1863 pamphlet he co-authored anonymously with George Wakeman, *Miscegenation: The Theory of the Blending of the Races, Applied to the American White Man and Negro*, as a political hoax in which, purporting to represent the views of progressive Republicans, he declared: "The miscegenetic or mixed races are much superior, mentally, physically, and morally to those pure or unmixed.... All that is needed to make us the finest race on earth is to engraft upon our stock the negro element" (8, 11). The goal of the hoax was to inflame the public, whose majority

ideology was ardently anti-black racism, against the Republican party for promoting a policy of racial amalgamation: "It is idle to maintain that this present war is not a war for the negro.... It is a war, if you please, of amalgamation ... a war looking, as its final fruit, to the blending of the white and black" (18). The exposure of the hoax meant the failure of its political aims; but it did succeed in replacing "amalgamation" with "miscegenation" in the popular imagination and to the identification of the mulatto as a danger to the integrity of American civilization.

30 Robert Ezra Park, "Human Migration and the Marginal Man," 893.
31 Robert E. Park, "Mentality of Racial Hybrids," *American Journal of Sociology* 36, no. 4 (January 1931): 540.
32 Ernest Allen has presented a careful conceptual critique of the genealogy of Du Bois's double consciousness and its possible meaning or significance in his overall work, as well as a historicizing critique of the general consensus about the phrase's meaning. Tracing the latter back to Mecklin and Park, he challenges the current assumption of the facticity of Du Bois's figure, including in the work of Gerald Early, Adolph Reed, and Eric Sundquist. See Ernest Allen, "Du Boisian Double Consciousness: The Unsustainable Argument." Rutledge Dennis has also given us an account of the long history of misreadings of Du Bois's phrase, focusing careful attention on the persistence of misconstrual in the work of Denise Heinze, Hazel Carby, and Paul Gilroy. Rutledge also adds to that a comparative analysis of Du Bois's empirical sociological work, challenging the assumption that his "double consciousness" merely describes an existing social psychology, or even if Du Bois thought it did. See Rutledge Dennis, "W. E. B. Du Bois's Concept of Double Consciousness."
33 James, *Principles*, 1:280.
34 James, *Principles*, 1:281.
35 James, *Principles*, 1:283.
36 William James, "Does 'Consciousness' Exist?," in *Essays in Radical Empiricism*, 3–4.
37 James, "Does 'Consciousness' Exist?," 5.
38 James, "Does 'Consciousness' Exist?," 6.
39 James, "Does 'Consciousness' Exist?," 6.
40 James, "Does 'Consciousness' Exist?," 4.
41 William James, "The Experience of Activity," in *Essays in Radical Empiricism*, 170n.
42 James, "The Experience of Activity," 170n.
43 James, "The Experience of Activity," 170n.
44 William James, "Reflect Action and Theism," in *The Will to Believe and Other Essays in Popular Philosophy*, 112–113.
45 Although its speculative conceptual foundations are generally attributed to Descartes's account of automatic physiological reaction, set out in his 1633 *Treatise of Man*, then more fully elaborated in *Discourse on Method*, and then even more so in *The Passions of the Soul*, the doctrine of reflex action proper is Marshall Hall's, who, expanding on the previous work of Willis and Legallois, and very likely

Prochaska, demonstrated the phenomenon in 1837. Cf. René Descartes, *L'homme et un traitté de la formation du foetus*. Also see Marshall Hall, "On the Functions of the Medulla Oblongata and Medulla Spinalis," 635–665.

46 James, "Reflect Action and Theism," 114.
47 James, "Reflect Action and Theism," 113.
48 James, "Reflect Action and Theism," 114.
49 See Hans Linschoten, *On the Way toward a Phenomenological Psychology: The Psychology of William James*, 242.
50 Linschoten, *On the Way toward a Phenomenological Psychology*, 242.
51 It was Weber's student Joseph Schumpeter who coined the phrase *methodologischer Individualismus*, referring to Weber's conception of sociology's methodological foundations, in his 1908 work *Das Wesen und der Hauptinhalt der theoretischen Nationalökonomie*. He subsequently translated the phrase into English as "methodological individualism" in his 1909 *Quarterly Journal of Economics* paper, "On the Concept of Social Value" (Schumpeter, *Das Wesen*, 213–232). Weber himself subsequently elaborated on his conception in the first chapter of *Wirtschaft und Gesellschaft* (*Economy and Society*), entitled "Methodische Grundlagen" (Methodological Foundations), 6–7.
52 Paul Schilder, "The Somato-Psyche in Psychiatry and Social Psychology." He elaborates this into a full psychoanalytic theory of the body-image's fundamental role in the formation of self-consciousness in *The Image and Appearance of the Human Body*.
53 For a consideration of the continued importance of this issue in contemporary cognitive science, see Shaun Gallagher's work. Of particular relevance is his essay "The Body in Social Context."
54 Du Bois, "The Renaissance of Ethics."
55 The concept of the extended mind was introduced by Andy Clark and David Chalmers in 1998, who postulated that the cycle of activity running from brain through body and world and back again is what constitutes cognition. The mind, in this account, is not restricted to the biological organism but extends into that organism's environment. Even though it aimed at moving beyond the Cartesian idea of cognition as something happening in a private mental space, which still is the predominant presupposition in cognitive science, the Clark-Chalmers concept of extended mind is predicated on what they termed the "parity principle." According to that principle, "If, as we confront some task, a part of the world functions as a process which, *were it done in the head*, we would have no hesitation in recognizing as part of the cognitive process, then that part of the world *is* . . . part of the cognitive process." Andy Clark and David Chalmers, "The Extended Mind," *Analysis* 58, no. 1 (January 1998): 7–19. For a thorough account of the connection between pre-reflective self-consciousness, embodiment, and sociality, see Shaun Gallagher and Dan Zahavi, "Phenomenological Approaches to Self-Consciousness," *The Stanford Encyclopedia of Philosophy* (Summer 2019 edition), ed. Edward N. Zalta, https://plato.stanford.edu/archives/sum2019/entries/self-consciousness-phenomenological/.

56 This is not casual, although it is admittedly an opportunistic paraphrase of a passage from Tyndall's 1868 essay, "Scientific Materialism." The paraphrased passage stands out because Tyndall, whose 1874 presidential address to British Association for the Advancement of Science at Belfast famously proclaimed the ascendant authority of scientific knowledge and method over all other modes, emphatically marks the inability of physical science to have knowledge of the facts of consciousness, saying: "The passage from the physics of the brain to the corresponding facts of consciousness is inconceivable as a result of mechanics. Granted that a definite thought, and a definite molecular action in the brain, occur simultaneously; we do not possess the intellectual organ, nor apparently any rudiment of the organ which would enable us to pass, by a process of reasoning, from one to the other. They appear together, but we do not know why" (Tyndall, "Scientific Materialism," 86–87).

57 Du Bois, *Souls*, 514.

58 Du Bois, *Souls*, 365.

59 Du Bois, "Strivings of the Negro People," 195. Ernest Allen also makes good use of a comparative reading of these two texts, drawing a different conclusion about what double consciousness denotes. See Allen, "Du Boisian Double Consciousness," 217–253.

60 From a certain perspective, that of raciological differentiation, it is possible to see in these passages Park's reason for describing the Negro's motivating desire as "amalgamation."

61 Du Bois, "Strivings," 195.

62 Rousseau, *Du contrat social*, 8. Rousseau spells this out at length in Book 1.

63 "Ce qu'il y de singulier dans cette aliénation, c'est que, loin qu'en acceptant les biens des particuliers, la communauté les en dépouille, elle ne fait que leur en assurer la légitime possession, changer l'usurpation en un véritable droit et la jouissance en propriété. A lors, les possesseurs 'tant considérés comme dépositaires de bien publie, leurs droits étant respectés de tous les membres de l'État et maintenus de toutes ses forces contre l'étranger, par une cession avantageuse au public et plus encore à eux mêmes, ils ont, pour ainsi dire, acquis tout ce qu'ils ont donné" (Rousseau, *Du contrat social*, 14).

64 "L'homme est né libre, et partout il est dans les fers" (Rousseau, *Du contrat social*, 1).

65 Precisely because of the role property rights played in facilitating the Constitution's tacit protection of slavery, it is noteworthy that, without referencing Locke's participation in drafting the clause on Negro slavery in the Fundamental Constitutions of the Carolinas, or his concept of slavery as a function of war in the *Two Treatises on Government*, Rousseau directly challenges the notion that humans can become alienated from their liberty as property. Taking up the topic, Rousseau considers Grotius's argument: "If an individual, says Grotius, can alienate his liberty and make himself the slave of a master, why could not a whole people do the same and make itself subject to a king?" Understanding "alienation" to mean "give" or "sell,'" Rousseau responds: "To say that a man gives himself gratuitously, is to say something absurd and inconceivable; such an act

is illegitimate and null, if only because he who does it is out of his mind. To say the same of a whole people is to suppose a people of madmen; and madness creates no right. Even if each man could alienate himself, he could not alienate his children: they are born men and free; their liberty belongs to them, and no one but they has the right to dispose of it." ["Dire qu'un home se donne gratuitement, c'est dire une chose absurde et inconceivable; un tel acte est illégitime et nul, par cela seul que celui qui le fait n'est pas dans son bon sens. Dire la même chose de tout un people, c'est supposer un people de fous: la folie ne fait pas droit. Quand chacun pourrait s'aliéner lui-même, il ne peut aliéner ses enfants; ils naissent homes et libres; leur liberté leur appartient, nul n'a droit d'en disposer qu'eux"] (Rousseau, *Du contrat social*, 5).

66 C. L. R. James, "Individuality 1776–1876," in *American Civilization*, 41. To underscore the scope of James's assessment that America provided "the *ideal* conditions for bourgeois *individualism*," it is worth quoting the statement verbatim in context:

> The history of America as a nation falls within certain well-defined periods: 1776–1831; 1831–1876; 1876–1914; 1914 to the present day. The first period begins with one of the great events in international political history. It is the Declaration of Independence, the expulsion of the British, the organization of a new state on lines hitherto unknown in the history of the world.
>
> America at the time presents a spectacle of economic and social equality unknown in history. No one is very rich, no one is very poor. Opportunity is open to all. Thus, in actual living conditions America is unique. The social conditions embody the *ideal* conditions for bourgeois *individualism*. All individuals start level, the race is to the energetic and the thrifty, the bold. Ideologically, however, the European past hangs over the country. Jefferson is the product of Locke. The great pamphleteer of the revolution is a European, Tom Paine, the embodiment of the revolutionary consciousness of Europe (40–41).

67 C. L. R. James, "Individuality," 41.
68 C. L. R. James, "Individuality," 41.
69 U.S. Constitution, Twenty-Second Amendment, sects. 1 and 2.
70 This is the gist of Mary Law Chaffee's understanding of the significance of the "Of Our Spiritual Strivings" passage, when she invokes it at the end of her 1956 *Journal of Negro History* essay on Du Bois, concluding: "This duality of Negro life has its white counterpart. Whites in America find themselves faced with the paradox of the high democratic ideals of the American Creed and their actual discriminatory practices toward their Negro fellow-citizen." See Mary Law Chaffee, "William E. B. Dubois's Concept of the Racial Problem in the United States," 258.
71 Richard Wright, introduction to *Black Metropolis*, xviii. Besides his literary output, Wright was actively involved in the establishment of the Lafargue Clinic in Harlem, about which he wrote in the 1946 essay, "Psychiatry Come to Harlem," where he emphasized the centrality of psychological sociology to his profile as literary artist and cultural critic.
72 Wright, *Black Metropolis*, xxx.
73 Du Bois, "The Renaissance of Ethics," 44.
74 Du Bois, "Sociology Hesitant," 38.

75 Wright, "Psychiatry Comes to Harlem," 51.
76 W. E. B. Du Bois, "The Conservation of Races," in *Writings*, 817.
77 See Weber, *Wirtschat und Gesellschaft*, 194–215. Weber is reformulating Ferdinand Tönnies's analytical category of *Gemeinschaft* (communal society), which is contrasted to *Gesellschaft* (associational society). *Gemeinschaft* is a cooperative formation organized around personal ties and interactions that are affectively determined by a sense of *Wesenwille* (natural will) expressed in terms of moral obligation to others. Such social relations are prevalent in preindustrial agricultural societies. *Gesellschaft*, which consists of indirect impersonal interactions determined by *Kürwille* (rational will), prevails in modern capitalist cosmopolitan societies governed by bureaucratic state institutions and large-scale industrial corporations. See Tönnies, *Gemeinschaft und Gesellschaft*. Cf. Ferdinand Tönnies, *Community and Civil Society*, ed. Jose Harris, trans. Jose Harris and Margaret Hollis (Cambridge: Cambridge University Press, 2001). Weber reformulates this latter type of sociality as *Vergesellschftung* (formation of association, or incorporation). Using the gerund underscores the dynamic aspect of both social formations.
78 Dunbar, *Lyrics of Lowly Life*.
79 Du Bois, *Souls*, 524–525.
80 Du Bois, *Souls*, 365.
81 Du Bois, "Review of *The Souls of Black Folk* by W. E. B. Du Bois," 1152.
82 Du Bois, "Review," 1152.
83 Dilthey, "Die Einbildungskraft des Dichters: Bausteine für eine Poetik," 6:103–241; henceforth cited as "Poetik." Cf. Wilhelm Dilthey, "Imagination of the Poet: Elements for a Poetics," in *Poetry and Experience*, trans. Louis Agosta and Rudolf Makkreel, vol. 5 of *Wilhelm Dilthey Selected Works*, ed. Rudolf Makkreel and Frithjof Rodi (Princeton, NJ: Princeton University Press, 1985), 29–173.
84 Dilthey, "Poetik," 6:233.
85 See Rudolf Makkreel's *Dilthey, Philosopher of the Human Studies* for an insightful and detailed reading of Dilthey's philosophical project and the centrality of the question of poetics to it.
86 Wilhelm Dilthey, "Die drei Epochen der modernen Ästhetik und ihre heutige Aufgabe," in *Wilhelm Diltheys Gesammelte Schriften*, 6:242–287.
87 Maurice Lee, "Du Bois the Novelist: White Influence, Black Spirit, and *The Quest of the Silver Fleece*," 389.
88 See Lukács, *Die Theorie des Romans*, 6–7. Cf. Georg Lukács, Preface, *Theory of the Novel*, 12–13.
89 Du Bois, *Souls*, 526.
90 E. T. A. Hoffmann, *Sämtliche Werke*, bd. 6, 417.
91 Du Bois, *Souls*, 525.
92 Poe, "The Man of the Crowd," 388–399.
93 Poe, "The Man of the Crowd," 392.
94 Poe, "The Man of the Crowd," 396.
95 Springinklee was a prolific and well-regarded student of Dürer's, most of whose bookwork, as Alfred Pollard reported, was done for Anton Koberger, who published some of it at Nuremberg, while some was sent to the Lyon printers Clein,

Sacon, and Marion, who were in Koberger's employment (Alfred William Pollard, *Fine Books*, 183). A border of his design bearing the arms of Bilibaldus Pirckheimer is found in several works that Pirckheimer edited (1513–1517). Fifty of the woodcuts in Grunninger's 1500 edition of *Hortulus Animae* are by Springinklee, as are those in the 1516 edition printed by J. Clein for Koberger at Lyon. Erhard Schön was the chief illustrator in the 1517 edition, which included only a few of Springinklee's woodcuts. Springinklee produced a new set of cuts for the subsequent 1518 edition, and Schön's work was less used. The *Hortulus Animae* was as popular in Germany as the illustrated *Horae* in France and England.

96 See Stephen Rachman, "'Es läßt sich nicht schreiben' Plagiarism and 'The Man of the Crowd.'"

97 Printed in the *American Whig Review* in 1845.

98 This can be rendered in English as "this great misfortune, to not be able to be alone," but *de ne pouvoir être seul* can also be rendered as "to be able only to be." Both senses seem to be at play in the convalescent's relation to the old man.

99 Baudelaire, "Le peintre de la vie moderne."

100 "C'est en flânant dans Paris que Balzac a fait tant de précieuses trouvailles, entendu tant de mots, déterré tant de types"; Victor Fournel, *Ce qu'on voit dans les rues de Paris* (Paris: E. Dentu, Libraire-Editeur, 1867), 268.

101 Fournel, *Ce qu'on voit dans les rues de Paris*, 268.

102 Baudelaire, "Le peintre de la vie moderne," 64.

103 Baudelaire, "Le peintre de la vie moderne," 64.

104 Baudelaire, "Le peintre de la vie moderne," 64.

105 Baudelaire, "Le peintre de la vie moderne," 65.

106 Balzac, *Physiologie du mariage*.

107 Walter Benjamin, "Paris, Capital of the Nineteenth Century: Exposé (of 1939)," 21–22.

108 Benjamin, "Paris, Capital of the Nineteenth Century," 22.

109 Benjamin, "Paris, Capital of the Nineteenth Century," 21. Adorno, in his February 1, 1939, letter to Benjamin, still thought that his handling of Phantasmagoria in the 1939 Exposé, as in his earlier 1935 version, "risk[ed] subjectifying the phantasmagoria." See Adorno to Benjamin, [New York], February 1, 1939, in Adorno, *Briefwechsel*, 394. Margaret Cohen's "Walter Benjamin's Phantasmagoria," *New German Critique* 48 (Autumn 1989): 87–107, remains a significant discussion of this, as does Susan Buck-Morss's "Redeeming Mass Culture for the Revolution," *New German Critique* 29 (Spring–Summer 1983): 213.

110 Walter Benjamin, "Exchange with Theodor W. Adorno on the 'Flâneur' Section of 'The Paris of the Second Empire in Baudelaire,'" in *Walter Benjamin: Selected Writings*, 4:22.

111 Charles Brockden Brown, *Edgar Huntly; or Memoirs of a Sleep Walker*, ed. Sydney J. Krause (Kent: Kent State University Press, 1984), 3.

112 Lukács provides a thorough and philosophically critical account of Goethe's concept of archetype as "the perceptible unity of concrete universality within a phenomenon itself; a phenomenon conceived abstractly with all accidental qualities eliminated but never losing its basic particularity. In the language of the

idealistic dialectic of the time: the conceptual prototype of the particularity in the phenomenon" (Lukács, "The Writer and the Critic," 217–218).

113 Brown, *Edgar Huntly*, 3.

114 The entire passage, which Benjamin quotes almost in full in "Paris of the Second Empire," reads:

> Ainsi, la poésie de terreur que les stratagèmes des tribus ennemies en guerre répandent au sein des forêts de l'Amérique, et dont a tant profité Cooper, s'attachait aux plus petits détails de la vie parisienne. Les passants, les boutiques, les fiacres, une personne debout à une croisée, tout offrait aux Hommes-Numéros à qui la défense de la vie du vieux Peyrade était confiée, l'intérêt énorme que présentent dans les romans de Cooper un tronc d'arbre, une habitation de castors, un rocher, la peau d'un bison, un canot immobile, un feuillage à fleur d'eau. [Thus, the poetry of terror that the stratagems of the warring enemy tribes spread within the forests of America, and of which Cooper had benefited so much, attached itself to the smallest details of Parisian life. The passers-by, the shops, the cabs, a person standing at a crossroads, all offered to the Number-men to whom the defense of the life of old Peyrade was entrusted, the enormous interest that presents in the novels of Cooper a tree trunk, a beaver house, a rock, the skin of a bison, a motionless canoe, foliage at the water's edge.] (Honoré de Balzac, *Splendeurs et misères des courtisanes*, 175)

115 See Dana Brand, *The Spectator and the City in Nineteenth Century America*, 79–105.

116 "Glorifier le culte des images (ma grande, mon unique, ma primitive passion)" (Charles Baudelaire, "Mon cœur mis à nu," 90).

117 As already remarked in an earlier note, Shamoon Zamir makes reference to Du Bois's experimental short story "A Vacation Unique," as suggesting a struggle of narrative form around the issue of how to represent the black self. The story itself can be found in the Fisk University Library's Du Bois Archive in Folder 10 of Box 53, which is marked "Short Stories" and includes a number of other unfinished short story manuscripts. "A Vacation Unique" is an undated twenty-three-page handwritten manuscript, and has a surreal conceit along the lines of Schuyler's *Black No More*, reversing the transformation by offering whites the opportunity to experience being a Negro. It begins with an advertisement: "Vacations of all styles and degrees of thinkableness done to order: We are sure we can suit the most exacting temperaments. Send for Circular. The Sears-Adams Co. (Limited) 130 Beacon Street, Boston"; and it contains fragmentary dialogues such as: "Have you heard of the fourth dimension, fool? Has your imagination reveled in its infinite possibilities? Now would you like to spend a summer in that portion of space?"

118 Stepto, *From behind the Veil*, 56.
119 Stepto, *From behind the Veil*, 64, 66.
120 Stepto, *From behind the Veil*, 66.
121 Stepto, *From behind the Veil*, ix, x, 53.
122 Stepto, *From behind the Veil*, 62.
123 Du Bois, "The Negro as He Really Is," 848–866.

124 On the four Safari books, see Dugmore, *Camera Adventures in the African Wild*, *The Wonderland of Big Game*, *The Vast Sudan*, and *Through the Sudan*.

125 Dugmore, *The Vast Sudan*, 62, 64. The analogy is an allusion to an event during Dugmore's first African safari in 1908, which he recounts in his autobiography, when he photographed a rhino charging directly at him no more than sixteen yards away. See Arthur Radclyffe Dugmore, *The Autobiography of a Wanderer* (London: Hurst and Blackett, 1930).

126 The Norton Critical Edition of *The Souls of Black Folk*, edited by Henry Louis Gates Jr. and Terri Hume Oliver, mistakenly identifies Dugmore, who was an American citizen born in Dublin in 1870, as a German photographer. It reprints eighteen of the photos he took for "The Negro as He Really Is," omitting one of the three photos occurring on page 854 with the caption "Parson and part of his flock." See W. E. B. Du Bois, *The Souls of Black Folk: Authoritative Text, Contexts, Criticism*, 195. Regarding Dugmore's national origin, see Dugmore, *The Autobiography of a Wanderer*, and Thomas Lowell, *Rolling Stone: The Life and Adventure of Arthur Radclyffe Dugmore*.

127 Stepto, *From behind the Veil*, 60.

128 Stepto, *From behind the Veil*, 60.

129 See Wlad Godzich, foreword to Paul de Man's *The Resistance to Theory* (Minneapolis: University of Minnesota Press, 1985), xiv.

130 The association between ethnographic gaze, surveillance, colonialism, and the technological developments of capitalist modernity is a commonplace and need not be elaborated or rehearsed here. See, for instance, James Clifford and George Marcus, eds., *Writing Culture: The Poetics and Politics of Ethnography* (Berkeley: University of California Press, 1986); Douglas Harper, "Framing Photographic Ethnography"; and Michael Ball and Greg Smith, "Technologies of Realism? Ethnographic Uses of Photography and Film." A book that takes up photography's function in establishing the ethnographic perspective with particular focus on the so-called Middle East, a history that Dugmore's *The Vast Sudan* played no small part in, is Ali Behdad and Luke Gartlan, *Photography's Orientalism: New Essays on Colonial Representation*.

131 Stepto, *From behind the Veil*, 61.

132 See Erdélyi, *Asymptotic Expansions*, 72.

133 Poincaré, "Sur les intégrales irrégulières," 296–297.

134 The problem is named after the English mathematician George Green, who first postulated it in 1828. See Green, *Essay on the Application of Mathematical Analysis*.

135 Although Carl Friedrich Gauss would take up the problem of Green's functions, it was his student, Dirichlet, who arrived at a solution, hence the problem's being named "The Dirichlet Problem." Dirichlet demonstrated how continuity and discontinuity relate to integrability of function, deriving this from Fourier's theorem that it is not required for any function to be representable analytically by a simple formula. In his 1837 paper, "Über Die Darstellung ganz willkürlicher Funktionen durch Sinus- und Cosinus reihen," he gave a broad definition of function, which Boyer paraphrases as: "If a variable y is so related to a variable x that whenever a numerical value is assigned to x, there is a rule according

to which a unique value of *y* is determined, the *y* is said to be a function of the independent variable *x*." Boyer further notes that this "comes close to the modern view of a correspondence between two sets of numbers, but the concepts of 'set' and 'real number' had not at that time been established" (Boyer, *History of Mathematics*, 510). See also Dirichlet, "Über Die Darstellung ganz willkürlicher Funktionen durch Sinus- und Cosinus reihen," 133–160.

136 Riemann demonstrated in his 1854 *Habilitationsvortrag* (Habilitation lecture), "Über die Hypothesen, welche der Geometrie zu Grunde liegen" (On the Hypotheses which Lie at the Foundations of Geometry), that the fundamental ingredients for geometry are a space of points in the sense of class (*Mannigfaltigkeit*). It was in his *Habilitationsschrift*, "Über die Darstellbarkeit einer Function durch eine trigonometrische Reihe," that he defined the Riemann integral. Dedekind, who had been Riemann's classmate and friend at the University of Berlin, published Riemann's *Habilitationsvortrag*, along with his *Habilitationsschrift*, in 1868, two years after Riemann's early death in 1866. See Riemann, "Über die Darstellbarkeit einer Function durch eine trigonometrische Reihe," and "Über die Hypothesen, welche der Geometrie zu Grunde liegen."

137 Increasingly concerned about the lack of a truly scientific justification of arithmetic, Dedekind undertook to find a solution to the tensions within differential and integral calculus. The fundamental issue was that although the differential calculus is concerned with constant magnitudes, there was no arithmetical explanation of that continuity; even the strictest representations of differential calculus did not base their validity on continuity, but rather appealed to geometrical or geometry-induced ideas, or to propositions that were not proved purely arithmetically. Convinced that such propositions could be sufficient foundation for infinitesimal analysis once their true origin in the elements of arithmetic was discovered, thereby obtaining a real definition of continuity, he focused on discovering an arithmetical definition of continuity. His first step was to construct real numbers by partitioning a totally ordered set of rational numbers into two non-empty parts A_1 and A_2, such that all members of A_1 are less than those of A_2 and such that A_1 has no greater member. Dedekind called these partitions of the system of rational numbers *Schnitte* (cuts). If A_1 has a largest number or A_2 a smallest number, then the cut defines a rational number. If, on the other hand, A_1 has no largest number and A_2 no smallest, then the cut defines an irrational number. As Dedekind explains: "Every time we have a cut (A_1, A_2) that is not produced by a rational number, we create [*erschaffen*] a new, irrational number α, . . . there corresponds, therefore, to every definite cut a definite rational or irrational number, and we regard two numbers as *different* or *unequal* if and only if they correspond to substantially different cuts." The complete totally order field of real numbers, which includes all the rationals and all the irrationals is thus constructed corresponding to the cuts engendered by them. Although Dedekind first made this breakthrough on November 24, 1858, and communicated the findings to his friend, Heinrich Durège, in a letter dated November 30, 1858, and then presented them to the Braunschweig Scientific Association on January 11, 1864, he did not publish the work until 1872 in what was to be one of his most influential papers in the foundations

of mathematics, *Stetigkeiten und irrationale Zahlen* (Continuity and irrational numbers).

138 Georg Cantor, "Ueber eine Eigenschaft des Inbegriffes aller reellen algebraischen Zahlen," *Journal für die reine und angewandte Mathematik*, 258–262. Ernst Zermelo, whose proof of the well-ordering theorem—every set can be well ordered—(also known as Zermelo's theorem) was crucial to developing the continuum hypothesis. He also initiated the axiomatization of set theory, which was improved by Adolf Fraenkel, and proclaimed that set theory was historically "created by Cantor and Dedekind." See Ernst Zermelo, "Untersuchungen über die Grundlagen der Mengenlehre," 261–281. See José Ferreirós, "The Early Development of Set Theory," *Stanford Encyclopedia of Philosophy* (Fall 2016 edition), ed. Edward N. Zalta, https://plato.stanford.edu/archives/fa112016/entries/settheory-early/.

139 Du Bois, "Sociology Hesitant," 38. Further indication that Du Bois was mindful of the developments taking place in the foundations of mathematics is found in his library.

140 Paulsen, *Geschichte des gelehrten Unterrichts*, 523. See in particular in that volume, Zweites Buch und Zweiter Abschnitt, "Das allmähliche Aufsteigen des neuen Humanismus im Zeitalter der Aufklärung. 1740–1805," 419–512; the second chapter of which, "Die Universität Göttingen und die neuhumanistische Philologie und Gymnasiapädagogik," gives an account of how Göttingen became the epicenter of *Neuhumanismus*, as well as research in higher arithmetic. A thorough English-language study of the same period is found in Bas van Bommel, *Classical Humanism and the Challenge of Modernity*.

141 Wolf described the pedagogical program of *Neuhumanismus* as "*Studia humanitatis,* encompassing everything that contributes to the purely human formation [*rein menschliche Bildung*] of all cognitive [*Geistes*] and emotional forces [*Gemütskräfte*] into a beautiful harmony of inner and outer man" (Wolf, *Darstellung der Alterthumswissenschaft*, 45).

142 See Gauss, *Disquisitiones Arithmeticae*. For a well-documented account of how *Neuhumanismus* was connected with the arithmetization of analysis, see Bernd Bekemeier, *Martin Ohm (1792–1872): Universitätsmathematik und Schulmathematik in der neuhumanistischen Bildungsreform*, and "Die Arithmetisierung der Mathematik." Also see Jahnke, *Mathematik und Bildung in der Humboldtschen Reform*; Gert Schubring, *Die Entstehung des Mathematiklehreberufs im 19 Jarhundert*; Lewis Pyenson, *Neohumanism and the Persistence of Pure Mathematics in Wilhelmian Germany*; and José Ferreirós, "'Ο Θεὸς Ἀριτματίζει," 250–252.

143 Du Bois, "Sociology Hesitant," 38.

144 Comte, *Cours de philosophie positive*, 114. With the exception of the first and second lessons, which present the objectives and plan of the *Cours de philosophie positive* respectively, the entirety of volume 1—chapters 3–18—is on the science of mathematics.

145 Comte, *Écrits de jeunesse (1816–1828)*, 308.

146 Du Bois, "Sociology Hesitant," 38–39. Du Bois quotes the following passage from *Cours de philosophie positive*, in evidence of Comte's hesitation:

Now in the inorganic sciences, the elements are much better known to us than the Whole which they constitute; so that in that case we must proceed from the simple to the compound. But the reverse method is necessary in the study of Man and of Society: Man and Society as a whole being better known to us, and more accessible subjects of study than the parts which constitute them.

The original French is a bit more detailed and reads:

Or, il existe nécessairement, sous ce point de vue, une différence fondamentale, qui ne saurait être éludée, entre l'ensemble de la philosophie inorganique et celui de la philosophie organique. Car, dans la première, où la solidarité, suivant nos explications précédentes, est très peu prononcée, et doit affecter faiblement l'étude du sujet, il s'agit d'explorer un système dont les élémens [*sic*] sont presque toujours bien plus connus que l'ensemble, et même d'ordinaire seuls directement appréciables, ce qui exige, en effet, qu'on y procède habituellement du cas le moins composé au plus composé. Mais, dans la seconde, au contraire, dont l'homme ou la société constitue l'objet principal, la marche opposée devient, le plus souvent, la seule vraiment rationnelle, par une autre suite nécessaire du même principe logique, puisque l'ensemble du sujet est certainement alors beaucoup mieux connu et plus immédiatement abordable que les diverses parties qu'on y distinguera ultérieurement [Now, from this point of view, there is necessarily a fundamental, unavoidable difference between in the whole of inorganic philosophy and that of organic philosophy. For, in the first, where solidarity, according to our preceding explanations, is barely pronounced, and must hardly effect the subject of study, it is a question of exploring a system whose elements are almost always better known than the whole, and even ordinarily alone directly observable; which requires, in fact, that one usually proceed from the least to the most compound case. But, in the second, on the contrary, where man or society constitute the principal object, the opposite course becomes the only truly rational one in most cases by another necessary consequence of the same logical principle, since the whole of the subject is certainly much better known and more immediately accessible than the diverse parts which will be distinguished subsequently]. (Comte, *Cours de philosophie positive*, 4:358)

Du Bois is quoting from Harriet Martineau's 1853 translation, *The Positive Philosophy of Auguste Comte*, vol. 2:82. Martineau severely abridged the *Cours de philosophie positive*, using the previously cited Bachelier edition and reducing its six volumes of published lectures down to two. Her argument for doing so, presented in her preface, was that Comte's work, in its original form of lectures spread over the course of years, "does no justice to its importance, even in France; and much less in England." She found particularly "wearisome, especially towards the end of his work," Comte's style of constantly recapitulating key concepts. While that practice might have strength in the series of lectures spread over twenty years, it becomes weakness when those instructions are presented as a whole. Martineau's decision to divest the *Cours* of this redundancy in the English-language translation resulted in considerable telescoping of material, with large segments elided. There is no such elision in the case of the passage Du Bois cites, however. Still, the sentences immediately preceding it warrant recording, in both the French and Martineau's English translation, to underscore the contextual basis for Du Bois's charge of hesitation:

> Pour mieux apprécier cet important caractère d'ensemble propre à la méthode sociologique, il faut regarder scientifiquement une telle condition comme n'appartenant pas d'une manière exclusive à la physique sociale, où elle atteint seulement sa plus entière prépondérance, mais comme étant, à un degré quelconque, nécessairement commune à toutes les diverses parties de l'étude générale des corps vivants, qui se distingue ainsi profondément, sous l'aspect purement logique, de toute la philosophie inorganique. Un aphorisme essentiellement empirique, converti mal à propos, par les métaphysiciens modernes, en dogme logique absolu et indéfini, prescrit, en tout sujet possible, de procéder constamment du simple au composé: mais il n'y en a pas, au fond, d'autre raison solide, si ce n'est qu'une telle marche convient, en effet, à la nature des sciences inorganiques, qui, par leur développement plus simple et plus rapide, et par leur perfection supérieure, devaient inévitablement servir jusqu'ici de type essentiel aux préceptes de la logique universelle. Toutefois, on ne saurait, en réalité, concevoir, à cet égard, de nécessité logique vraiment commune à toutes les spéculations possibles que cette évidente obligation d'aller toujours du connu à l'inconnu, à laquelle, certes, il serait difficile de se soustraire, et qui, par elle-même, n'impose directement aucune préférence constante. Mais il est clair que cette règle spontanée prescrit aussi bien de procéder du composé au simple que du simple au composé, suivant que, d'après la nature du sujet, l'un est mieux connu et plus immédiatement accessible que l'autre. (*Cours*, 357–358)
>
> Before we go onto the subject of social dynamics, I will just remark that the prominent interconnection we have been considering prescribes a procedure in organic studies different from that which suits inorganic. The metaphysicians announce as an aphorism that we should always, in every kind of study, proceed from the simple to the compound: whereas, it appears most rational to suppose that we should follow that or the reverse method as best may suit our subject. There can be no absolute merit in the method enjoined, apart from its suitableness. The rule should rather be (and there probably was a time when the two rules were one) that we must proceed from the more known to the less. (Comte, *Positive Philosophy*, 467–468)

Comte's point is twofold here: first, that the proper object of positivist science is the complexity of systems (dynamic interconnectivity), which are subject to natural laws, admitting of scientific calculation (*la prévision scientifique*); and second, that society is such a system. The distinction he makes between what he terms the Statical and Dynamical conditions of society is heuristic and necessary for exploratory purposes and must not be stretched beyond that use. It is, in other words, not a distinction between two classes of facts, but between two aspects of theory, corresponding to the double conception of order and progress, where order consists (in a positive sense) in a permanent harmony among the conditions of social existence, and progress consists in social development of change. Accordingly, the ideas of order and progress, which are in perpetual conflict in existing society, occasioning infinite disturbance, are reconciled in social physics and made necessary to each other, becoming as truly inseparable as the ideas of organization and life in the individual being. The scientific principle of Comte's social physics is that there must always be a spontaneous harmony between the whole and the parts of the social system, the elements of which must inevitably be, sooner or later, combined in a mode entirely conformable to their nature. This consolidated whole must be always connected, by its nature, with the corresponding state of the integral development of humanity, considered in all its aspects, of intellectual, moral, and physical activity. The fundamental unit of study is the whole. See Comte, *Cours de philosophie positive*, 4:257.

147 Comte, *Cours de philosophie positive*, 4:257, 6:726.
148 Du Bois, "Sociology Hesitant," 38–39. See also Comte, *Cours de philosophie positive*, 4:257, 6:726.
149 Du Bois, "Sociology Hesitant," 38–39.
150 Du Bois, "Sociology Hesitant," 38–39.
151 Herbert Spencer, *First Principles*, 143.
152 Du Bois, "Sociology Hesitant," 39.
153 Du Bois, "Sociology Hesitant," 39. Cf. Herbert Spencer, *Descriptive Sociology, or Group of Sociological Facts*.
154 Du Bois, "Sociology Hesitant," 39. Charging Spencer with verbal jugglery in this respect, Du Bois quotes the following passage from volume one of *The Principles of Sociology* in evidence: "We consistently regard a society as an entity, because, though formed of discrete units, a certain concreteness in the aggregate of them is implied by the general persistence of the arrangements among them throughout the area occupied." Cf. Herbert Spencer, *The Principles of Sociology*, 1:466. This truncated quotation is taken from Part II, "The Inductions of Sociology," Chapter 1, "What Is Society?" in which Spencer sets out to determine whether or not to regard society as an entity, and if so what kind. More precisely, it is from the last paragraph of the first section, §212, of the chapter. In the next chapter, "A Society Is an Organism," Spencer draws a heuristic analogy between biology and sociology to determine that society is an organic entity in its operations. That analogy is in accordance with Spencer's epistemology, which posits: "By reality we mean persistence in consciousness: a persistence that is either unconditional, as our consciousness of space, or that is conditional, as the consciousness of a body while grasping it. The real, as we conceive it, is distinguished solely by the test of persistence; for by this test we separate it from what we call the unreal" (Spencer, *First Principles*, 160). It is because societies exhibit "the general persistence of the arrangements among them throughout the area occupied" that they are real or concrete." With the charge of "verbal jugglery," in effect accusing Spencer of sophistry disguised as logical argument, Du Bois draws attention to the fact that the crux of the problem with Spencer's social methodology is his epistemology, which, dispensing with the problematic of apperception, conceives of individual consciousness as the epiphenomena of physical, biological forces, and so is knowable as an element in the aggregate.
155 Du Bois, "Sociology Hesitant," 41.

156 Du Bois, "Sociology Hesitant," 41, 40. Du Bois is alluding here to two pioneering giants of analytical sociology—the first being Franklin Giddings, who, influenced by Comte's positivism and Spencer, was at the forefront in transforming sociology in the United States from a field of philosophy into a research science grounded in statistical and analytic analysis. Thinking it a mistake to describe society in biological terms, maintaining instead that sociology is a psychological science with principles admitting of logical organization, Giddings postulated that *consciousness of kind* is the original and elementary subjective fact in society, defining it as: "a state of consciousness in which any being, whether low or high in the scale of life, recognizes another conscious being as of like kind with itself" (Franklin Giddings, *The Principles of Sociology*, 17–18). The second is Gabriel Tarde, who also thought sociology was psychological science, but postulated *imitation* as the fundamental psychological interaction between individuals responsible for social organization; see Gabriel Tarde, *Les lois de l'imitation, étude sociologique*, 158–212.

157 Du Bois, "Sociology Hesitant," 41.

158 Galileo Galilei, "The Assayer," in *The Controversy of the Comets of 1618*, trans. and ed. Stillman Drake and C. D. O'Malley (Philadelphia: University of Pennsylvania Press, 1960 [1623]).

159 Du Bois, "Sociology Hesitant," 42.

160 Du Bois, "Sociology Hesitant," 41.

161 Du Bois, "Sociology Hesitant," 41.

162 Du Bois, "Sociology Hesitant," 42.

163 Du Bois, "Sociology Hesitant," 42.

164 Du Bois, "Sociology Hesitant," 43.

165 For Mill's definition of moral science, see John Stuart Mill, *A System of Logic, Ratiocinative and Inductive*, 2:537.

166 See Dedekind, "Was sind und was sollen die Zahlen?," in *Gesammelte Mathematische Werke*, 3:336. Citations to works in this *Gesammelte* henceforth will include volume and page number followed by section and paragraph number where applicable. See also Cantor, *Grundlegen einer allgemeinen Mannigfaltigkeitslehre*.

167 Du Bois, *Souls*, 368.

168 Dedekind, "Über die Einführung neuer Funktionen in der Mathematik," in *Gesammelte Mathematische Werke*, 3:428–429.

169 Du Bois, "Sociology Hesitant," 43.

170 Du Bois, "Sociology Hesitant," 43.

171 Du Bois, "Sociology Hesitant," 43.

172 See Du Bois's critique of statistical sociology in *Souls of Black Folk* (368), quoted earlier.

173 Weber, "Leopold Kronecker," 19.

174 Dedekind, "Was sind und was sollen die Zahlen?," 3:335.

175 Dedekind, "Was sind und was sollen die Zahlen?," 3:334–335.

176 Dedekind, "Was sind und was sollen die Zahlen?," 3:334.

177 Dedekind, "Was sind und was sollen die Zahlen?," 3:334.

178 The motto appears on the title page of "Was sind und was sollen die Zahlen?"

179 Jacobi gives his paraphrase of Schiller under the title "Archimedes und der Jüngling," in a letter he wrote to Alexander von Humboldt, which Kronecker

cites in his "Ueber den Zahlbegriff," quoting Jacobi's entire poem, then characterizing it as an intellectual parody (*geistvollen Parodie*) of Schiller's poem, with which "Jacobi describes the position of the concept of numbers [*Zahlbegriff*] in the whole of mathematics as genuinely poetic [*echt poetisch*], but also quite similar to what Gauss meant in his statement: 'Mathematics is the queen of sciences and arithmetic the queen of mathematics.'" In a footnote to this remark, Kronecker cites the Sartorius von Waltershausen biography, *Gauss zum Gedâchtniss*, as the source for the statement, equating it with Gauss's motto, "ὁ θεὸς ἀριθμητίζει [God continually arithmetizes]." Kronecker remarks in the same footnote that attribution of the assertion "ὁ θεὸς ἀριθμητίζει" to Gauss is based on a letter in Gustav Lejeune Dirichlet's estate from Gauss to Humboldt, which has been authenticated by Humboldt. See Kronecker, "Ueber den Zahlbegriff," 338; also see Wolfgang Sartorius von Waltershausen, *Gauss zum Gedâchtniss* (Leipzig: S. Hirzel, 1856), 79, 97. In his essay "Über Aufgabe und Methode des mathematischen Unterrichts an den Universitäten [On the Task and Method of Mathematical Instruction in the University]," Klein erroneously attributes the Gaussian paraphrasis to Jacobi: "Plato said: 'ἀεὶ ὁ θεὸς γεωμέτρε.' Jacobi changed this to 'ἀεὶ ὁ θεὸς ἀριθμητίζει.' Then Kronecker came and created the memorable expression: 'God invented the natural numbers; all else is the work of man'" (136).

180 Ferreirós, "'Ο Θεὸζ' Αριθμηίίξει,'" ed. 236. Cf. Hilbert, "Die Theorie der algebraischen Zahlkörper," 177; reprinted in David Hilbert, *Gesammelte Abhandlungen*, 1:65.

181 Frege, *Die Grundlagen der Arithmetik*; citations henceforth will include page number followed by section number. This work has been translated into English by J. L. Austin and published as Gottlob Frege, *The Foundations of Arithmetic: A Logico-Mathematical Enquiry into the Concept of Number*.

182 As Dedekind states in the preface to the second edition of "Was sind und was sollen die Zahlen?":

> About a year after the publication of my memoir I became acquainted with G. Frege's *Grundlagen der Arithmetik*, which had already appeared in the year 1884. However different the view adopted in that work about the nature of number [*Wesen der Zahl*] may be from mine, it also contains, particularly from §79 on, points of very close contact with my paper, especially with my definition (44). The agreement, to be sure, is not easily recognized because of the deviation in mode of expression; but the positiveness [*Bestimmtheit*] with which the author speaks of the logical inference from n to $n+1$ ... shows plainly that here he stands upon the same ground with me (xi–xii). (Dedekind, "Was sind und was sollen die Zahlen?," 3:342)

Given his greater recognition as a mathematician, contemporaries such as Charles Sanders Peirce, Ernst Schröder, and David Hilbert, as well as Giuseppe Peano, regarded Dedekind as the principal proponent of logicism. As can be gleaned from the current debate between Ferreirós and Hourya Benis-Sinaceur, Dedekind's centrality in the development of logicism is controversial. See José Ferreirós, "On Dedekind's Logicism"; and José Ferreirós, *Labyrinth of Thought: A History of Set Theory and Its Role in Modern Mathe-

matics. Cf. Hourya Benis-Sinaceur, "Is Dedekind a Logicist? Why Does Such a Question Arise," 1–57.
183 In §14 of *Die Grundlagen der Arithmetik*, contrasting geometry and arithmetic, Frege states: "Is not the basis [*Grund*] of arithmetic deeper than that of all empirical knowledge, deeper than of geometry? The arithmetic truths dominate all that is enumerable. This is the most comprehensive; for not only does the actual, not just the intuitable belong to it, but everything conceivable. So, should not the laws of numbers be in the most intimate connection with those of thought?" (Frege, *Grundlagen der Arithmetik*, 20: §14).
184 Frege, "Der Gedanke. Eine logische Untersuchung," 69. Emphasizing the point in a footnote attached to this passage, Frege states: "One sees a thing, one has an idea, one apprehends or thinks a thought. When one apprehends or thinks a thought one does not create it, but only enters into a certain relation, which is different from seeing a thing or having an idea, to what already existed beforehand."
185 Frege, "Der Gedanke. Eine logische Untersuchung," 69.
186 Frege, *Grundlagen der Arithmetik*, 40: §50. Cf. Ernst Schröder, *Lehrbuch der Arithmetik und Algebra für Lehrer und Studirend*e (Leipzig: B.G. Teubner, 1873), 6: §6.
187 Frege, *Grundlagen der Arithmetik*, 39: §46.
188 Frege, *Grundlagen der Arithmetik*, 43: §57.
189 Frege, *Grundlagen der Arithmetik*, 43: §57.
190 Frege, *Grundlagen der Arithmetik*, 49: §68. In his translation, Austin renders *gleichzahlig* as "equal," adding in a footnote that it is to be understood literally as "identinumerate" or "tautarithmic" (*Foundations of Arithmetic*, 79). He renders the cognate term *gleich*, "identical," as in Frege's definition: "The proposition *a* is parallel to line *b* is to mean 'the direction of line *a* is identical [*ist gleich*] with the direction of line *b*'"; and: "Whether we use 'the same [*dasselbe*],' as Leibniz does, or 'identical [*gleich*]' is not of any importance" (*Foundations of Arithmetic*, 76).
191 See Frege, *Begriffsschrift, eine der arithmetischen nachgebildete Formelsprache des reinen Denken*s. This work has been published in English as Gottlob Frege, *Conceptual Notation and Related Articles*, trans. and ed. Terrell Ward Bynum (Oxford: Oxford University Press, 1972). See also Gottlob Frege, "The Concept of Number," in *Philosophy of Mathematics: Selected Readings*, 2nd ed., trans. Michael Mahoney, ed. Paul Benacerraf and Hilary Putnam (Cambridge: Cambridge University Press, 1983), 139.
192 Leibniz, *Scientia Generalis*, in *Die Philosophischen Schriften*, 7:228.
193 Frege, *Begriffsschrift*, 53: §74.
194 Having discovered the paradox sometime in the late spring or early summer of 1901, Russell presented it to Frege in a letter dated June 16, 1902. Commending Frege's work for containing "discussions, distinctions and definitions that one seeks in vain in the works of other logicians," especially regarding functions, Russell continues:

> There is one point where I have encountered a difficulty. You state (p. 17) that a function too, can act as the indeterminate element. This I formerly believed,

but now this view seems doubtful to me because of the following contradiction. Let w be the predicate; to be a predicate that cannot be predicated of itself. Can w be predicated of itself? From each answer its opposite follows. Therefore, we must conclude that w is not a predicate. Likewise, there is no class (as a totality) of the classes which, each taken as a totality, do not belong to themselves. From this I conclude that under certain circumstances a definable collection [*Menge*] does not form a totality. (Quoted in Jean van Heijenoort, *From Frege to Gödel*, 124–125)

195 Dedekind holds that *anything* can play the role of number, on the condition, with regard to the set of natural numbers, it belongs to a class that has the characteristic of a "simple infinite" set, and, with regard to the set of real numbers, a totally, densely ordered field with the Dedekind cut property. See Dedekind's correspondence with Rudolph Lipschitz dated October 6, 1876, in which he resists identifying the real numbers with his cuts. Richard Dedekind, "Brief an Lipschitz 1," in *Gesammelte Mathematische Werke*, 3:468–474. See also his correspondence with Heinrich Weber where, in response to Weber's proposing to construct and identify the natural numbers as cardinal numbers, Dedekind states: "I should advise not to take the class itself (the system of mutually similar systems) as the number (*Anzahl* [cardinal number]), but rather something new (corresponding to this class), something the mind creates" (Dedekind, "Brief an Weber," 488–490).

196 Frege writes in his preface to volume 1 of *Grundgesetze der Arithmetik*: "Mr. Dedekind is also of the opinion that the theory of numbers is a part of logic; but his work scarcely contributes to confirming this, because the expressions used by him, 'System' and 'a thing belongs to a thing,' are not common in logic and are not derived from recognized logic. I am not saying this as a reproach; For his method may have been the most suitable for him; I only say it, to put my intention in the brighter light by contrast" (1:viii). The entire work has recently been published in English as Gottlob Frege, *Basic Laws of Arithmetic: Derived Using Concept-Scrip*, 2 vols., trans. and ed. Philip A. Ebert, Marcus Rossberg, and Crispin Wright (Oxford: Oxford University Press, 2013).

197 Dedekind, "Was sind und was sollen die Zahlen?," 3:344, §1.1.

198 Dedekind, "Was sind und was sollen die Zahlen?," 3:344–345, §1.2. The signs $S = T$ do not only denote a logically necessary property of equality; they also express an assumption about membership, which Dedekind then presents in a definition: "A system A is said to be *part* [*Teil*] of a system S when every element of A is also an element of S." Dedekind denotes this as "the sign $A \ni S$," corresponding to the more current $A \subseteq S$ denoting A is a subset of S, which he also states as "S is the whole of A," meaning "among the elements of S are found all the elements of A. Since further every element S of a system S by (2) can be itself considered a system, we can therefore employ the notation $s \ni S$" (Dedekind, "Was sind und was sollen die Zahlen?," 3:345, §1.3).

199 Dedekind, "Was sind und was sollen die Zahlen?," 3:360, §6.73.

200 Dedekind, "Was sind und was sollen die Zahlen?," 3:348, §2.21.

201 Dedekind, "Was sind und was sollen die Zahlen?," 3:348, §2.21.

202 "Definition: K is called a chain [*Kette*] when $K' \ni K$. We expressly note that the name does not in itself belong to the part K of the system S, but is given only with respect to the particular mapping $\varnothing$; with reference to another mapping of the system S into itself, K can very well not be a chain" (Dedekind, "Was sind und was sollen die Zahlen?," 3:353, §4:37). In other words, given a mapping $\varnothing: S \to S$, a subset K of S is a chain (*Kette*) if $\varnothing(K') \ni K$. This can be illustrated by the chain of distinct elements: $a, a', a'', a''', \ldots$ After a series of theorems and proof regarding parts of a chain, we get the following: "Definition: If A is any part of S, we will denote by A_o the intersection of all chains (e.g. S) of which A is part; this intersection A_o exists (17) because A is itself a common part of all these chains. Since further by (43) A_o is a chain, we will call A_o the *chain of the system A*, or briefly the chain of A. This definition is also strictly related to the fundamental determinate mapping $\varnothing$ of the system S into itself" (Dedekind, "Was sind und was sollen die Zahlen?," 3:353, §4.44). Accordingly, any sub-collection of a system S is itself a system, and so a *thing*.

203 Dedekind, "Was sind und was sollen die Zahlen?," 3:356, §5.64.

204 Dedekind, "Was sind und was sollen die Zahlen?," 3:356, §5.6.

205 Dedekind, "Was sind und was sollen die Zahlen?," 3:359, §6.71.

206 See William Ewald's prefatory remarks to his revision of Beman's translation of "Was sind und was sollen die Zahlen?" in *From Kant to Hilbert: A Source Book in the Foundations of Mathematics*, 2:789. According to both Hellman and Shapiro, Dedekind is the forbearer of the (informal) mathematical structuralism of Bourbaki, and the subsequent main varieties of formalized mathematical structuralism, which are delineated as: (1) *set-theoretic* structuralism, deploying model theory in which fixed ontology of pure sets is presupposed, in a so-called Platonist perspective, to describe mathematical structures and their interrelations; (2) *ante rem* structuralism as developed by Shapiro, which conceives of structures as sui generis universals comprising "places" as objects in their own right, standing in the relations implicitly defined by the second-order Peano-Dedekind axioms and exemplified by any *system* of objects forming a model—Shapiro uses Dedekind's term *system* to denote *in re* structures, the places of which are occupied by objects from a given background ontology, because the places are filled by something else, the *ante rem* structure is a Platonic universal, an abstract pattern answering to that which all progressions hare in common; (3) *modal* structuralism as developed by Hellman, which avoids literal quantification over structures or places, appealing instead to the second-order modal logical possibility of a domain wherein suitable relations fulfill implicit defining conditions given by typical axiom systems. On modal structuralism, see Geoffrey Hellman's *Mathematics without Numbers*; the invocation of Dedekind as progenitor, citing "Was sind und was sollen die Zahlen?," occurs on vii. On *ante rem* structuralism, see Stewart Shapiro's *Philosophy of Mathematics*, where Dedekind is claimed as a "direct forerunner of *ante rem* structuralism," and that "his development of the notion of continuity and the real numbers, in 'Stetigkeit und irrationale Zahlen,' [and] his presentation of the natural numbers via the notion of Dedekind infinity, in ["Was sind und was sollen die Zahlen?"], and some of his correspondence con-

stitute a structuralist manifesto" (14). Hellman provides a comparative critical analysis of the current main varieties of mathematical structuralism, excluding category theoretic structuralism, in his essay, "Three Varieties of Mathematical Structuralism." Erich Reck, who identifies one other current version of mathematical structuralism as *methodological*, while discerning aspects of Dedekind's work that may very well lend themselves to *set-theoretic, modal, ante rem*, as well as *methodological* structuralism, argues that Dedekind was primarily a "logical structuralist." He arrives at this based on a reevaluation of Dedekind's notions of abstraction and free creation, gleaned from passages in the unpublished third draft of "Was sind und was sollen die Zahlen?" found in his *Nachlaß*, in conjunction with Dedekind's correspondence with Rudolph Lipschitz and Heinrich Weber. See Erich Reck, "Dedekind's Structuralism: An Interpretation and Partial Defense," 369–419. Reck interprets Dedekind's statement, "I understand by *thing* [*Ding*] every object of our thinking," in non-psychologistic terms, construing his notion of thought "in a (Fregean) non-subjective sense" (411). Reviewing the same material, José Ferreirós also places Dedekind among the logical structuralist. See Ferreirós, "On Dedekind's Logicism."

207 Dedekind, "Was sind und was sollen die Zahlen?," 3:367, §5.66. This proof leads, of course, to Russell's paradox, also known as the "Russell antinomy," the discovery of which brought Dedekind himself to view it as fundamentally problematic. Russell discovered his antinomy independently in 1901 while he was working on his *Principles of Mathematics*. It is often referred to as the "Russell-Zermelo paradox" because, although he did not publish it, Zermelo had made the same discovery a year before Russell, sharing it with Hilbert, Husserl, and other members of the University of Göttingen. Taking Dedekind's $\phi(s)$ to denote the naïve or unrestricted Comprehension Axiom—that for any formula $\phi(x)$ containing x as a free variable, there will exist the set $\{x: \phi(x)\}$, the members of which are exactly those objects that satisfy $\phi(x)$, whereby if the formula $\phi(x)$ stands for "x is prime," then $\{x: \phi(x)\}$ will be the set of prime numbers. If $\phi(x)$ stands for "$\sim (x = x)$," then $\{x: \phi(x)\}$ will be the empty set—assuming this axiom gets Russell's contradiction and paradox: if $\phi(x)$ stands for $x \in x$ and $R = \{x: \sim \phi(x)\}$, then R is the set the members of which are not member of themselves. If R is a member of itself, then it must satisfy the condition of not being a member of itself, and so it is not. If it is not, then it must not satisfy the condition of not being a member of itself, and so it must be a member of itself. Either R is a member of itself or it is not. Hence the contradiction. See Andre David Irvine and Henry Deutsch, "Russell's Paradox," *The Stanford Encyclopedia of Philosophy*, ed. Edward N. Zalta (2016), https://plato.stanford.edu/archives/win2016/entries/russell-paradox/. The immediate case of Russell's discovery was Cantor's power set theorem, which worked from Dedekind's simple infinites. Commenting on what he considers the lack of clarity in Dedekind's definition of natural numbers, Russell remarks: "Dedekind does not show us what it is that all progressions have in common, nor give any reason for supposing it to be the ordinal numbers, except that all progressions obey the same laws as ordinals do, which would prove equally that *any* assigned progression is what all progressions have in common.... What Dedekind presents to us is not the numbers, but any pro-

gression: what he says is true of all progressions alike, and his demonstrations nowhere—not even where he comes to cardinals—involve any property distinguishing numbers from other progressions" (Bertrand Russell, *The Principles of Mathematics*, 249). The thrust of Russell's critique is that even assuming the principle of abstraction, progression stands in relation to some things.

208 Reck notes that Dedekind's procedure of using a thought, then a thought of that thought, and so on in his construction of systems is similar to the specification of the finite Zermelo ordinals in set theory, in which we use a set, then the set including that set, and so on, to construct an infinite sequence, the Zermelo-Fraenkel axiom of infinity ("Dedekind's Structuralism," 411).

209 For a critical account of the problematic aspect of Heidegger's paraphrasis, see Jean-Luc Marion's essay "Generosity and Phenomenology: Remarks on Michael Henry's Interpretation of Cartesian Cogito."

210 This, in part, is why Badiou describes Dedekind's set-theoretical approach to number, along with that of Cantor, Zermelo, von Neuman, and Gödel, "platonising" (*Le nombre et les nombres*, 18, 1.3).

211 Dedekind presents this conviction in the prefatory section of "Stetigkeit und irrationale Zahlen" (see *Gesammelte Mathematische Werke*, 3:315–317). He reiterates it in "Über die Begründung der Idealtheorie" when discussing Gauss's remark in article 76 of *Disquisitiones Arithmeticae* concerning Waring's difficulty in discovering the proof for Wilson's theorem because no adequate notation can be imagined: "Such truths should be extracted from notions rather than notations." Referencing this to his earlier argument in "Stetigkeit und irrationale Zahlen" regarding Riemann's functions, Dedekind reiterates that mathematical theorems should be "established in a purely arithmetic manner," the ultimate origin of which are concepts expressing the "characteristic inner properties [*innerliche charakteristische Eigenschaften*]" of the objects, "from which the external form of representation [*die äußerlichen Darstellungs-Formen*] necessarily arise" (see *Gesammelte Mathematische Werke*, 2:55).

212 Edmund Husserl, "Besprechung von E. Schröder's Vorlesungen über die Algebra der Logik (Exakte Logik)," 8. This was originally published in *Göttingsche gelehrte Anzeigen* 153 (1891): 243–278.

213 This is an example of set builder notation specifying the domain of a set defined via predicates of its elements. The domain is specified on the left of the colon separator, which denotes the relation "such that," "for which," or "with the property that." The rule is specified to the right. The ∈ denotes set membership (n is an element of the set of natural numbers, $\mathbb{N}$), and the ∧ denotes logical conjunction ("if and only if"). The ∃ is the sign of existential quantification, denoting "there exists."

214 Dedekind, "Was sind und was sollen die Zahlen?," 3:335. Cf. Michael Dummett, *Frege: Philosophy of Mathematics*, 49–50.

215 Paul Benacerraf. "What Numbers Can Be," 52.

216 Dedekind, "Stetigkeit und irrationale Zahlen," 3:317.

217 Badiou, *Le nombre et les nombres*, 60: 4.29.

218 Cantor, *Gesammelte Abhandlungen mathematischen*, 378.

219 Cantor, *Gesammelte Abhandlungen*, 205.

220 Writing to Dedekind on July 28, 1899, Cantor further elaborates the definition of system delineating two types:

> If we start from the concept of a certain multiplicity (a system, an aggregate) of things, I have found it necessary to distinguish two different varieties of multiplicities (I mean certain multiplicities). A multiplicity can be such that the assumption of a "cohesion" of all its elements leads to a contradiction, so that it is impossible to conceive of the multiplicity as a unity, as "one completed thing." Such multiplicities I call absolute infinite or inconsistent multiplicity.... If, on the other hand, the totality of elements of a multiplicity can be thought of as cohering without contradiction, so that their combination into one thing is possible, I call a consistent multiplicity or a "set [*Menge*]" (this is expressed in French and Italian by the terms *ensemble* and *insieme*). (*Gesammelte Abhandlungen*, 443)

221 Cantor, *Gesammelte Abhandlungen*, 378.

222 In a subsequent letter to Dedekind, dated August 28, 1899, Cantor states, concerning the question of the well-ordered cardinals he denotes as $\aleph_0, \aleph_1,..., \aleph_{\omega 0},... \aleph_{\omega 1},...$, which are sets by the previously given definition:

> Would it not be conceivable that even these multitudes were "inconsistent," and that the contradiction ... had not yet been made perceptible? My answer to this is that this question is also to be extended to finite multiplicities, and that an exact expectation leads to the [following] conclusion: even for finite multiplicities, a "proof" of its "consistency" cannot be derived.... The fact of "consistency" of finite multiplicity is a simple, unprovable truth, it is "the axiom of arithmetic" (in the old sense of the word). Likewise, the "consistency" of the multiplicities to which I assign the aleph [$\aleph$] as cardinal numbers is "the axiom of extended transfinite arithmetic." (*Gesammelte Abhandlungen*, 447–448)

223 Cantor, *Gesammelte Abhandlungen*, 405.

224 Plato's designation for such technical thinking is διάνοια (*dianoia*, mind): "διάνοιαν δέ καλεῖν μοι δοκεῖς τήν τῶν γεωμετρικῶν τε καί τήν τῶν τοιούτων ἕξιν ἀλλ οὐ νοῦν, ὡς μεταξύ τι δόξης τε καί νοῦ τήν διάνοιαν οὖσαν [*Dianoian dé kaleîn moi dokeîs tén tōn geometrikōn te kai tén tōn toioutōn hékin áll hē noun es metaxe ti doxes te kai noũ dianoian ousan*.] [And I think you call the mental habit of geometers and their like mind or understanding and not reason because you regard understanding as something intermediate between opinion and reason]." Plato, *The Republic*, bk. 6, 511d2 [116/117] (citation here and henceforth gives book number and Bekker line citation; the bracketed numbers indicate the Loeb edition page numbers, with the Greek text reference to the left of the slash and the English translation the right).

225 Poincaré uses as an example his own work on Fuchsian functions when describing the role of chance in the process of mathematical invention. See Poincaré, *Science et Méthode*, 53–62.

226 Hegel, *Phänomenologie des Geistes*. Cf. Georg Wilhelm Friedrich Hegel, *The Phenomenology of Spirit*, ed. and trans. Terry Pinkard and Michael Baur (Cambridge: Cambridge University Press, 2018).

227 Hegel, *Vorlesungen über die Philosophie der Kunst*, 40.

228 See Salvo Žižiek, "The Fear of Four Words: A Modest Plea for the Hegelian Reading of Christianity," in Slavoj Žižiek and John Milbank, *The Monstrosity of Christ: Paradox or Dialectic?*, ed. Creston Davis (Cambridge, MA: MIT Press, 2009), 26. For a reading of Žižiek's position on necessity and contingency, comparing it with that of Gorgio Agamben, see Lorenzo Chiesa's essay "Hyperstructuralism's Necessity of Contingency."

229 Peirce, "Evolutionary Love," 315, 290.

230 Du Bois, "The Renaissance of Ethics."

231 Fanon, *Peau noire masques blancs*, 88.

232 See Ellison, *Invisible Man*.

233 Baudelaire, "Le peintre de la vie moderne," 119.

234 W. E. B. Du Bois, "Criteria of Negro Art," in *Writings*, 993.

235 Clark, *Farewell to an Idea*, 17–18.

236 Clark, *Farewell to an Idea*, 21.

237 Clark, *Farewell to an Idea*, 21.

238 Riegl, *Spätrömische Kunstindustrie*, 401. Cf. Alois Riegl, *Late Roman Art Industry*, trans. Rolf Winkes (Rome: Giorgio Bretschneider Editore, 1985), 231.

239 Erwin Panofsky, "Der Begriff des Kunstwollens," *Zeitschrift für Ästhetik und allgemeine Kunstwissenschaft* 14 (1920): 330.

240 Kracauer, "Die Reise und der Tanz," 293. Cf. Sigfried Kracauer, "Travel and Dance," in *The Mass Ornament: Weimar Essays*, trans. and ed. Thomas Y. Levin (Cambridge, MA: Harvard University Press, 1995), 70.

241 Kracauer, "Die Reise und der Tanz," 292.

242 Kracauer, "Die Reise und der Tanz," 291.

243 Kracauer, "Die Reise und der Tanz," 292.

244 Kracauer, "Die Reise und der Tanz," 292.

245 Kracauer, "Die Reise und der Tanz," 293–294.

246 Kracauer, "Die Reise und der Tanz," 293.

247 See Hessel, *Spazieren in Berlin*. Cf. Franz Hessel, *Walking in Berlin: A Flaneur in the Capital*, trans. Amanda DeMarco (Cambridge, MA: MIT Press, 2017).

248 For an insightful account of the importance of Kracauer's thought to the development of popular culture criticism, see Michael Jennings, "Walter Benjamin, Siegfried Kracauer, and Weimar Criticism."

249 See Michael Löwry, "Naphta or Settembrini?—Lukács and Romantic Anticapitalism."

250 Benjamin, "Paris, Capitale du XIXeme siècle Exposé (of 1939)," *Das Passagen-Werk*, in *Walter Benjamin Gesammelte Schriften*, 5.1:58. Cf. Walter Benjamin, "Paris, the Capital of the Nineteenth Century: Exposé (of 1939)," *The Arcades Project*, trans. Howard Eiland and Kevin McLaughlin (Cambridge, MA: Harvard University Press, 1999), 26.

251 Benjamin to Adorno, Paris, February 23, 1939, in Adorno, *Briefwechsel*, 404. Cf. Benjamin to Adorno from February 23, 1939, "Exchange with Adorno on 'the Flâneur,'" in *Walter Benjamin: Selected Writings*, 4:208.

252 Walter Benjamin, "A Child's View of Color," in *Walter Benjamin: Selected Writings*, 1:51.

253 Benjamin, "A Child's View of Color," 51.

254 Theodor W. Adorno, "Charakteristik Walter Benjamins," in *Prismen*, 242. Cf. Theodor W. Adorno, "A Portrait of Walter Benjamin," in *Prisms*, trans. Samuel and Shierry Weber (Cambridge, MA: MIT Press, 1983), 233.

255 Heidegger, "Einblick in das was ist," 36–37. Cf. Martin Heidegger, "Insight into That Which Is," *Bremen and Freiburg Lectures: Insight into That Which Is and Basic Principles of Thinking*, trans. Andrew J. Mitchell (Bloomington: Indiana University Press, 2012), 23.

256 Heidegger, "Einblick," 37.

257 Adorno to Benjamin, [New York], February 1, 1939, in Adorno, *Briefwechsel*, 394.

258 Benjamin to Adorno, Paris, February 23, 1939, in Adorno, *Briefwechsel*, 403.

259 Benjamin to Adorno, Paris, February 23, 1939, in Adorno, *Briefwechsel*, 404.

260 Walter Benjamin, "Exposés, Paris, die Hauptstadt des XIX. Jahrhunderts," in *Gesammelte Schriften*, 5:47. Cf. Benjamin, "Paris, Capital of the Nineteenth Century," 4–5.

261 Benjamin, "Exposés, Paris," 47.

262 Baudelaire, "Le peintre de la vie moderne," 65.

263 Bloch, "Logikum/Zur Ontologie des Noch-Nicht-Seins," 219.

264 Adorno, *Kierkegaard. Konstruktion des Ästhetischen*, in *Gesammelte Schriften* 2:56. Cf. Theodore Adorno, *Kierkegaard: Construction of the Aesthetic*, trans. Robert Hullot-Kentor (Minneapolis: University of Minnesota Press, 1989), 37.

265 Adorno, "Charakteristik Walter Benjamins," 242.

266 Adorno to Benjamin, Hornberg, August 2–4, 1935, in Adorno, *Briefwechsel*, 139. Cf. *Walter Benjamin: Selected Writings*, 3:54.

267 Benjamin adopts this reformulation in *Konvolut 4,3*, referencing a letter from Adorno dated June 5, 1939, believed to be lost. See Benjamin, "Traumstadt, Zukunftsträume, anthropologischer Nihilismus, Jung," in *Gesammelte Schriften*, 5:501. Cf. "Dream City and Dream House, Dreams of the Future, Anthropological Nihilism, Jung," in *The Arcades Project*, 397. Although this letter is believed to be lost, Adorno uses the formulation in his letter to Benjamin of August 2–4 that same year. See Adorno, *Briefwechsel*, 141. Cf. *Walter Benjamin: Selected Writings*, 3:54.

268 See Ergio Sevilla, "Critical Theory and Rationality," *boundary 2* 24, no. 1 (1997): 59–77.

269 Heidegger, "Einblick," 70.

270 Vico, *La Scienza nuova*, 97–253. Cf. Giambattista Vico, *The New Science of Giambattista Vico*, 109–297.

271 Walter Benjamin, "Central Park," in *Walter Benjamin: Selected Writings*, 4:186.

272 See Walter Benjamin, "Critique of Violence," in *Walter Benjamin: Selected Writings*, 1:242.

273 Du Bois, *Souls*, 502.

274 Du Bois, *Souls*, 500.

275 I Corinthians 13:4–13 (Authorized [King James] Version).

276 Du Bois, *Souls*, 529–530.

277 It is noteworthy that the premises of John Jones's speech, specifically the anthropology of new men who are wholly engendered in human interaction, antici-

pates some of the key presuppositions of black liberation theology as elaborated by Dwight N. Hopkins, James Cones's leading disciple. Whereas Hopkins's argument for a Christian theological anthropology, the aim of which is to study the being of God in the world in light of the existential black experience of oppression, presumes that fully understanding the human person still requires understanding the human in relation to God, John's proposition is that fully understanding humanity no longer requires God. See Dwight N. Hopkins, *Being Human: Rave, Culture, and Religion*, 162–163. Du Bois consistently critiqued Christianity as a socio-anthropological institution, the ideologies of which are inconsonant with the dictates of modernity. He acknowledged the fact that, as a social institution, "the Negro church antedated by many decades the monogamic Negro home," regarding it "as peculiarly the expression of the inner ethical life of [the Negro] people" (*Souls*, 499). He thought it was precisely this fact, however, that contributed significantly to the normalization of fatalistic tendencies of submission and resignation among the Negro masses, presenting blockages to effective social formation and sustainable community. This critique notwithstanding, Du Bois recognized the historical affective force of religion in social formation and more specifically, the centrality of the ethical problem of good and evil to the historical process of individuation. For instance, he writes in "Of the Faith of the Fathers," describing a revival meeting and a ring shout: "Those who have not thus witnessed the frenzy of a Negro revival in the untouched backwoods of the South can but dimly realize the religious feeling of the slave; as described, such scenes appear grotesque and funny, but as seen they are awful" (*Souls*, 494). Schematically, this is an antithesis, contrasting "grotesque and funny" with "awful," where the latter suggests commanding, profound respect, or reverential fear—as in Shakespeare's: "An awefull Princely Scepter" (*Henry VI*, pt. 2, act 5, scene 1, line 100)—or solemnly impressive, sublimely majestic—as in Maurice's, "How awful to feel himself there . . . an atom amidst the infinity of nature!" (Frederick Denison Maurice, *Prophets and Kings of the Old Testament*, 39). Cornel West has a contrary reading of this passage, taking "awful" to signify "both dread and fear, anxiety and disgust." In his view, Du Bois suffered from an "inability to immerse himself in black everyday life, [which] precluded his access to the distinctive black tragicomic sense and black encounter with the absurd. He certainly saw, analyzed, and empathized with black sadness, sorrow, and suffering. But he didn't feel it in his bones deeply enough, nor was he intellectually open enough to position himself alongside the sorrowful, suffering, yet striving ordinary black folk. . . . In short, he was reluctant to learn fundamental lessons about life—and about himself—from them. . . . Du Bois's intriguing description [of the revival] reminds one of an anthropologist visiting some strange and exotic people whose rituals suggest not only the sublime but also the satanic" ("Black Strivings in a Twilight Civilization," 57–58, 60). West's reading suggests that because of, as he puts it, "Du Bois's Enlightenment worldview—his first foundation," he could not achieve affective communion with the everyday black folk. Yet, in the very pages on which we encounter the passage in question, Du Bois offers a poignant account of the affective force of the Negro church, starting with its music, which "still remains the most original and beautiful expression of human life and longing yet born on American soil," and extending to an account of the profundity of the Negro religion as the "expression of... higher life" informed, he speculates, by the "African... attitude toward the World and good and evil" (Du Bois, *Souls*, 494, 495). While he is critical of the degenerative tendencies in the institution, he takes these to be indicative of the general degeneracy of Christianity in the environment of capitalist modernity. Rather than being incapable of identifying with black people, Du Bois is challenging the presumption that one can only be in community on the basis of faith. It is possible to be in community with "the gaunt-cheeked brown woman" who "suddenly leaped straight into the air and shrieked like a lost soul," without believing, as she does, that salvation is only through a relationship with God. The task is to achieve a community that includes the Beloved Community of God but is not defined or based on it.

278 For examples of this interpretation, see Stanley Brodwin, "The Veil Transcended: Form and Meaning in W. E. B. Du Bois' 'The Souls of Black Folk'"; Rampersad, *The Art & Imagination of W. E. B. Du Bois*; and Stepto, *From behind the Veil*.

279 Gooding-Williams adduces "Of the Coming of John," together with "Of Alexander Crummell," in evidence of Du Bois's using the concept of double consciousness to diagnose the failure of black political leadership to solve the Negro problem; see Gooding-Williams, *In the Shadow of Du Bois*, 97. This rests on the premise that Du Bois is presenting in *The Souls of Black Folks* a theory of politics as leadership in the mode of rule or governance, while also maintaining that because legitimate black politics is by definition the struggle against social exclusion, it should be an expression of the spiritual identity of the black folk—what Gooding-Williams calls the politics of "expressive self-realization." Getting to this premise necessitates reading the first chapter, "Of Our Spiritual Strivings," as an exposition of the subjectively felt, lived experience of the Negro problem as the lived experience of a false and alienated consciousness. In this analysis of Du Bois's theory of effective political leadership, the successful leader embodies "a synthetic self that has rid itself of the contemptuous, falsifying picture of Negro life that double consciousness expresses." According to Gooding-Williams, bad, ineffective leadership either promotes the pathology of double consciousness, exemplified in "Of Mr. Booker T. Washington and Others," or fails to achieve the truer synthetic Negro self, exemplified in "Of Alexander Crummell" (*In the Shadow of Du Bois*, 88).

280 Alexander Crummell, "The Need of New Ideas and New Aims for a New Era," in *Civilization and Black Progress*, 123.

281 Crummell, "The Need of New Ideas," 123–124.

282 Alexander Crummell, "Civilization, the Primal Need of the Race," in *Civilization and Black Progress*, 195–199.

283 Crummell, "Civilization," 4.

284 Crummell, "The Need of New Ideas," 132–133.

285 Crummell, "Civilization, the Primal Need of the Race," 3–4.

286 Du Bois, *Souls*, 502.

287 Du Bois, *Souls*, 502.

288 Du Bois, *Souls*, 503.

289 Du Bois, *Souls*, 503.

290 Du Bois, *Souls*, 503.
291 Du Bois, *Souls*, 504.
292 Du Bois, "The Talented Tenth," in *Writings*, 842–861.
293 Du Bois, *Souls*, 365.
294 Richard Wagner, *Lohengrin*, trans. Natalia Macfarren, 197.
295 See *Wagner's Opera Lohengrin*, Oliver Ditson Company's Standard Edition of Opera Librettos, 22; and *The Authentic Librettos of the Wagner Operas*, 81.
296 Richard Wagner, *Lohengrin*, trans. Stewart Robb, 15.
297 Richard Wagner, *Bridal Chorus from Lohengrin*, trans. John Rutter, 15.
298 *Dwight's Journal of Music* 17, no. 7 (May 12, 1860), 52.
299 W. E. B. Du Bois, "Opera and the Negro Problem," *Pittsburgh Courier*, October 31, 1936, 130.
300 Du Bois, "Opera and the Negro Problem," 130.
301 In her short essay "Of the Coming of John," Lemke marshals sufficient evidence to counter Berman's claims that Du Bois was making some sort of error, either acoustical or in confusing Schiller's "Ode to Joy," which is incorporated into Beethoven's Ninth, with the libretto of *Lohengrin*. She can make short change of this claim because its grounds are extremely weak, disregarding both Du Bois's fluency in German and his intense familiarity with Wagner's corpus. The same unfounded presumption of Du Bois's ignorance is at work in the current theory that his making the inadvertent error stems from the circulation of parlor libretti that were often plagued by misprints. This speculation, too, must conveniently overlook well-documented biographical information about Du Bois's familiarity with Wagner's operas.
302 Gooding-Williams has presented the most explicit analysis of the Schopenhauer connection published thus far. See Robert Gooding-Williams, *In the Shadow of Du Bois*, 123–124. In an earlier engagement with the story of John Jones, I wrongly held there was something Schopenhauerian about how John Jones's double consciousness appears to entail an unhappiness that renounces the intelligibility of human reality. Even then, however, I cautioned that a careful consideration of what is meant by double consciousness be undertaken before grappling with this complicated question of renunciation. See Ronald A. T. Judy, "The New Black Aesthetic and W. E. B. Du Bois, or Hephaestus, Limping," in "W. E. B. Du Bois: Of Cultural and Racial Identity," special issue, *Massachusetts Review* 35, no. 2 (1994): 255, 277n23.
303 Baudelaire, "Le peintre de la vie moderne," 75.
304 This is what Jack Kerkering proposes in his essay, "'Of Me and of Mine': The Music of Racial Identity in Whitman and Lanier, Dvořák and Du Bois."
305 See Colin Dayan, *The Law Is a White Dog*, especially chapter 2, "Civil Death," 41–64.

Sentient Flesh

1 Tom Windham interview, 210.
2 John Avery Lomax, *Adventures of a Ballad Hunter*, 112.

3 John Avery Lomax, quoted in the 1933 annual report of the chief of the Division of Music, Carl Engel, in *Archive of American Folk Song Annual Report, 1928–1939*, 24.
4 John Avery Lomax, "Self-Pity in Negro Folk-Songs," 141.
5 Lomax, "Self-Pity," 141.
6 Lomax, "Self-Pity," 141.
7 Douglass, *Narrative*, 23.
8 Douglass, *Narrative*, 23–24.
9 Douglass, *Narrative*, 24.
10 Douglass, *Narrative*, 24.
11 Douglass, *Narrative*, 24. The closing quotation, which is from William Cowper's antislavery poem, "The Timepiece," is the second epigraph to Chapter 1 of Lydia Maria Child's *An Appeal in Favor of that Class of Americans Called Africans*. Whether Douglass is quoting Cowper directly or the Child epigraph, he slightly modifies the line, which reads in the original:

> *There is no flesh in man's obdurate heart,*
> *It does not feel for man. The natural bond*
> *Of brotherhood is severed as the flax*
> *That falls asunder at the touch of fire.*
> *He finds his fellow guilty of a skin*
> *Not coloured like his own, and having power*
> *To enforce the wrong, for such a worthy cause*
> *Dooms and devotes him as his lawful prey.*

See William Cowper, "The Timepiece," in *The Task* (London: Cassell & Company, 1899), 2.8.
12 Douglass, *My Bondage and My Freedom*, 184.
13 Douglass, *My Bondage and My Freedom*, 184.
14 Douglass, *My Bondage and My Freedom*, 185.
15 Douglass, *My Bondage and My Freedom*, 185.
16 See Edward L. Pierce, *The Negroes at Port Royal*. Under the Port Royal Relief Committee of Philadelphia auspices, Laura Towne founded the Penn School, the first and largest of such schools for the freedmen, which continued to operate as such until 1948, when it closed, only to reopen in 1951 as the Penn Community Services Center. This effort at education in conjunction with developing institutions of free labor among the freedmen became known as the Port Royal Experiment.
17 McKim, "Songs of the Port Royal 'Contrabands.'" 254–55.
18 McKim, "Songs of the Port Royal 'Contrabands,'" 255. It should be noted that Frances Anne Kemble's oft-cited account of slave singing, although recorded in her journal in 1838, twenty-four years earlier than McKim's *Dwight's Journal* letter and seven years before Douglass's *Narrative*, was not published until 1863 due to the terms of her divorce from Pierce Mease Butler, owner of extensive plantations on the Georgia Sea Islands, including Hampton Point Plantation on St. Simons Island, as well as a plantation in the Altamaha River delta. Kemble's remarks anticipate some aspects of McKim's analysis. She writes, for

instance: "I believe I have mentioned to you before the peculiar characteristics of this veritable negro minstrelsy—how they all sing in unison, having never, it appears, attempted or hear any thing like part-singing. Their voices seem oftener tenor than any other quality, and the tune and time they keep something quite wonderful; such truth of intonation and accent would make almost any music agreeable" (*Journal of Residence*, 127). Although Kemble thought enough of the musicality of the slaves sounds to write what is the most cited passage from her *Journal*, she perceives the improvisation but does not fully grasp the musical significance of its formal originality, thinking only a Western-trained musician could bring it out to value: "The high voices all in unison, and the admirable time and true accent with which their responses are made, always make me wish that some great musical composer could hear these semi-savage performances. With a very little skillful adaptation and instrumentation, I think one or two barbaric chants and choruses might be evoked from them that would make the fortune of an opera" (218). And so, we get George Gershwin. Identifying the original, indigenous musical significance of the slaves' singing would fall to Douglass, and its elaboration through analysis, albeit by translation in received musical notation, was McKim's contribution.

19 McKim, "Songs of the Port Royal 'Contrabands,'" 255.
20 McKim, "Songs of the Port Royal 'Contrabands,'" 255.
21 McKim, "Songs of the Port Royal 'Contrabands,'" 255.
22 *Gideonites* was the collective name given derisively by contemptuous white Union soldiers to the group of fifty-three (forty-one men and twelve women) plantation superintendents, teachers and missionaries, sponsored by the Boston New England Freedmen's Aid Society under the auspices of its Education Commission, the first article of whose constitution states: "The object of the Educational Commission shall be the industrial, social, intellectual, moral, and religious improvement of persons released from slavery in the course of the war for the Union." The Commission had been formed on February 4, 1862, at the home of Rev. Jacob Manning, in collaboration with Rev. Edward Hale, Edward Atkinson, and Governor John Andrew, in response to a letter Pierce sent Manning the month before. See Edward L. Pierce to Rev. Jacob Manning from Port Royal, January 19, 1862, Edward Atkinson Manuscripts, Massachusetts Historical Society. Allen was not a member of the original group of fifty-three Gideonites who had arrived at St. Helena Island in March 1862, but in his service as a teacher he was under the direct employment of one: Edward Philbrick, who, although dispatched by the Educational Commission, took advantage of the 1862 Confiscation Act and acquired eleven plantations amounting to ten thousand acres, at the Treasury tax sale of March 1863. He did this to secure the social experiment of transforming slaves into freedmen from Northern cotton investors, and sold the land to its black workers in 1865.
23 Spaulding, "Under the Palmetto."
24 Allen, *Slave Songs*, ii.
25 Higginson, "Negro Spirituals."
26 Higginson, "Negro Spirituals," 685.
27 Higginson, "Negro Spirituals," 685.

28 William Francis Allen [Marcel, pseud.], "The Negro Dialect," 744.
29 Allen, *Slave Songs*, iii.
30 Leiris, *L'Afrique fantôme*.
31 Le Musée d'Ethnographie du Trocadéro, *Instructions sommaire pour les collecteurs d'objets ethnographiques*, 6.
32 Lomax, "Self-Pity," 141.
33 Higginson, Allen, and Lomax all characterize the Negro as childlike, with Higginson going so far as to describe in detail how his men are "the world's perpetual children," having "absolutely no vices . . . worth mentioning." (*Army Life*, 18, 29)
34 Eugene C. Homes, Assistant Editor for Negro Affairs to the Editor, *The Spokesman*, San Francisco, April 10, 1938, Negro Studies File, Record Group 69, National Archives; Sterling A. Brown, interview by Norman Yetman, July 20, 1965, quoted in Norman Yetman, "The Background of the Slave Narrative Collection," 546.
35 "Supplementary Instructions #9-E to the American Guide Manual," Introduction, Works Progress Administration, *Slave Narratives*.
36 George Cronyn correspondence, April 14, 1937, Introduction, WPA, *Slave Narratives*, xvi.
37 Allen, *Slave Songs*, iv.
38 Allen, *Slave Songs*, iv.
39 Allen, *Slave Songs*, iv.
40 Allen, *Slave Songs*, xxiv.
41 Allen, *Slave Songs*, vi–vii.
42 Allen, *Slave Songs*, vi–vii.
43 Allen, *Slave Songs*, vi–vii.
44 Allen, *Slave Songs*, ix.
45 Allen, *Slave Songs*, ix.
46 Allen, *Slave Songs*, vii.
47 Allen, *Slave Songs*, vii.
48 Allen, *Slave Songs*, x.
49 Allen, *Slave Songs*, x.
50 Higginson, "Negro Spirituals," 693.
51 Higginson, "Negro Spirituals," 693.
52 Higginson, *Army Life*. The material first published in the *Atlantic Monthly* "Negro Spirituals" article was subsequently incorporated with the same title as chapter 9 of this book.
53 Higginson, *Army Life*, 222.
54 Higginson, *The Sympathy of Religions*, 19.
55 Allen, *Slave Songs*, xix.
56 Lomax, "Self-Pity," 141.
57 Lomax, "Self-Pity," 141.
58 Lomax, "Self-Pity," 141.
59 Lomax, "Self-Pity," 141.
60 Lomax, "Self-Pity," 141.
61 Lomax, "Self-Pity," 141.
62 Lomax, "Self-Pity," 142.

63 Lomax, "Self-Pity," 142.
64 George Cronyn, correspondence, dated May 3, 1937, in Introduction, WPA, *Slave Narratives*, xxvi.
65 Douglass, "What to the Slave Is the Fourth of July?," in *The Frederick Douglass Papers*, 2:369.
66 Locke, *Human Understanding*, 335.
67 Locke, *Human Understanding*, 448.
68 Arguably disputing Locke's argument legitimating slavery through war, even if only implicitly so in contradistinction, Rousseau's subsequent theory of natural freedom—the theory Du Bois maintained the Negro adhered to most radically—dismisses as insane the proposition that an individual can be alienated from their liberty as property.
69 The historian David Armitage has provided a powerful recent intervention in the continued controversy over the relationship between the Carolina Constitution and Locke's political philosophy as indicative of the constitutive relationship between liberalism and colonialism. See David Armitage, "John Locke, Carolina, and the Two Treatises of Government," and "John Locke: Theorist of Empire?"
70 Locke, *Second Treatise*, §54, 36.
71 Douglass, *Narrative*, 46.
72 Enacted September 1671 as "ACT IV. *An act providing how negroes belonging to orphans of intestates shall be disposed of*," the law stipulates:

> WHEREAS in the former act concerning the estates of persons dying intestate, it is provided that sheep, horses, and cattle should be delivered in kind to the orphant, when they came of age, according to the several ages the said cattle were of when the guardian took them into his possession, to which some have desired that negroes may be added; this assembly considering the difficulty of procureing negroes in kind as alsoe the value and hazard of their lives have doubted whither any sufficient men would be found who would engage themselves to deliver negroes of equal ages if the specificall negroes should dye, or become by age or accident unserviceable; *Be it therefore enacted and ordayned by this grand assembly and the authority thereof* that the consideration of this be referred to the county courts who are hereby authorized and impowred either to cause such negroes to be duly apprized, sold at an outcry, or preserved in kind, as they then find it most expedient for preservation, improvement or advancement of the estate and interest of such orphants. (Hening, *Statutes*, 2:288)

73 Douglass, "Reception Speech," *My Bondage and My Freedom*, 403.
74 Douglass, "Farewell Speech to the British People," in *The Frederick Douglass Papers*, 2:50.
75 Douglass, "Slavery and the Slave Power: An Address Delivered in Rochester, New York, on 1 December 1850," in *The Frederick Douglass Papers*, 2:254.
76 Douglass, "What to the Slave Is the Fourth of July?," in *The Frederick Douglass Papers*, 2:374.
77 Douglass, *My Bondage and My Freedom*, 237.
78 Douglass, *Selected Speeches and Writings*, 347, 348–349.
79 Douglass, *Narrative*, 71.

80 Aquinas, *Quaestiones Disputatae de Veritate*, 22.3:828.
81 Garrison, Preface, in Douglass, *Narrative of the Life of Frederick Douglass*, 8.
82 Douglass, "Reception Speech," 421.
83 Douglass, *Narrative*, 71.
84 Douglass, *My Bondage*, 311.
85 Child, *An Appeal*, 26–27.
86 Child, *An Appeal*, 27. The date Rankin gives would make Lewis's slaughter of George coincide with the first in the series of the New Madrid earthquakes that struck western Kentucky.
87 Child, *An Appeal*, 99.
88 See Walsh, *Notices of Brazil*, 16. Charles Faulkner's speech is quoted in Child, *An Appeal*, 81. One of the most engaging analyses of the trope of cannibalism in the archive of U.S. slavery, relating it to homoeroticism and the formation of a certain type of black American masculinity, is Vincent Woodard's posthumously published work, *The Delectable Negro*.
89 Coleridge, *A Dissertation on the Science of Method*, 56–57.
90 Coleridge, "Lecture on the Slave-Trade," in *Samuel Taylor Coleridge, Lectures 1795*, 231–251; Coleridge, "On the Slave Trade," in *The Collected Works of Samuel Taylor Coleridge*, 2:130–140. Neil Roberts points out in his *Freedom as Marronage* the degree to which Douglass was taken with Coleridge's work while he was in England has been overlooked by most Douglass scholarship. See Neil Roberts, *Freedom as Marronage*, 63–71. John Wright seeks to correct this oversight in his Introduction to the 2003 Givens Collection edition of *My Bondage My Freedom*, by attending to the literary milieu in which Douglass starts to read Coleridge. See John Wright, Introduction, *The Givens Collection: My Bondage My Freedom*. As Roberts correctly remarks, however, even Wright's effort falls short by not discovering the specific work of Coleridge's that informs Douglass's political thinking in *Bondage*. In fact, there is a pattern of mis-attributing the Coleridge epigraph to the "Lectures of the Slave-Trade." Roberts rectifies this gap in scholarship substantively. Timothy Morton's 1988 essay, "Blood Sugar," remains one of the most probative analyses of this topos in Coleridge's work. See Timothy Morton, "Blood Sugar," in *Romanticism and Colonialism*, 87–106. Morton incorporates this essay, with minor changes, as chapter 4 of his book *The Poetics of Spice*.
91 Douglass, "The Nature of Slavery," in *My Bondage and My Freedom*, 420.
92 Hartman, *Scenes of Subjection*, 4–5.
93 Spillers, "Mama's Baby, Papa's Maybe," 206. In a footnote to another essay in *Black, White, and in Color*, "'An Order of Constancy': Notes on Brooks and the Feminine," Spillers identifies this essay along with "Notes on an Alternative Model—Neither/Nor," as the two studies that examine "these historical/terministic issues with an eye to locating African-American women's community in relationship to questions of feminist investigation," anticipating "a longer work that examines the rift between 'the body' and 'the flesh' as means of social and cultural production" (487fn33).
94 Barthes, "Le mythe aujourd'hui," in *Mythologies*, 179–223; cf. Roland Barthes, "Myth Today," in *Mythologies*, 215–274.
95 Barthes, "Le mythe aujourd'hui," 190.

96 Spillers, *Black, White, and in Color*, 206.
97 Barthes, *Le degré zero*. See also Annette Laver's and Colin Smith's translation of this work, *Writing Degree Zero* (New York: Hill and Wang, 1968).
98 Barthes, *Le degré zero*, 39.
99 Spillers, "Mama's Baby, Papa's Maybe," 206.
100 Barthes, "Le mythe aujourd'hui," 198.
101 Barthes, "Le mythe aujourd'hui," 199.
102 Aristotle, *Poetics*, 1451b5.
103 Barthes, "Le mythe aujourd'hui," 181.
104 A well-noted flaw of the structuralist analysis Barthes deploys is precisely this very process of naturalization through mathematical abstraction, which he ironically remarks in his explanation of how mathematics succumbs to myth; see "Myth Today," 133.
105 Barthes, "Le mythe aujourd'hui," 209.
106 The hermeneutics identified by its adherents as "Afro-Pessimism" reads Spillers as being pessimistic in this manner. See Wilderson, *Incognegro*.
107 Spillers, "Mama's Baby, Papa's Maybe," 206.
108 The designation is Sylvia Wynter's in reference to the conception of "Man" as an abstraction predicated on the bio-economic taxonomy of life emergent with the mechanical philosophy of the seventeenth and eighteenth centuries. It is the lynchpin of the present organization of disciplines of knowledge according to which the human is only an onto/phylogenetic organic entity. Wynter also refers to this matrix as the "ethno-biological," "ethno-disciplines," or "system of ethno-knowledge" ("Unsettling the Coloniality of Being," 317, 318, 295).
109 Spillers, "Mama's Baby, Papa's Maybe," 207.
110 Spillers, "Mama's Baby, Papa's Maybe," 207.
111 See Cyril Harris, *Dictionary of Architecture and Construction*.
112 Shaler, "The Negro Problem," 706.
113 Barthes, "Le mythe aujourd'hui," 189.
114 Barthes, "Le mythe aujourd'hui," 189.
115 Barthes, "Le mythe aujourd'hui," 191.
116 Barthes, "Le mythe aujourd'hui," 190.
117 "Tous les Esclaves qui seront dans nos Isles seront baptisez & instruits dans la Religion Catholique, Apostolique & Romaine. Enjoignons aux Habitans qui achèteront des Negres nouvellement arrivez s'en avertis les Gouverneur & Intendant desdites Isles dans huitaine an plus tard, à peine d'amende arbitraire, lesquels donneront les ordres nécessaires pour les faire instruire & baptiser dans le tems convenable" (France, *Code Noir*, art. 2).
118 For an analysis of the immutability of this link, see Frieda Ekotto, *Race and Sex across the French Atlantic*, 51–52.
119 The preamble of the 1616 Act reads:

> Whereas heretofore many good laws and ordinances have been made for governing, regulating and ordering Negroes, Slaves on this Isle, and sundry punishments appointed to many of their misdemeanours, crimes, and offences which yet did not have the effect desired, and might have been reasonably expected

had the Master of Families and other inhabitants of this Isle been so careful of their obedience and compliance with the said Laws as they ought to have been, And these former Laws being in many clauses imperfect and not fully comprehended of the true constitution of the Government in relation of their Slaves, an heathenish, brutish and an uncertain dangerous pride of people who if surely in any thing we may extend the legislative power given us of laws for the benefit and good of this plantation, not being contradictory to the Laws of England, there being in all the body of that law no track to guide us where to walk nor any rule set us how to govern such Slaves. Yet we well know by the right rule of reason and order, we are not to leave them to the arbitrary, cruel, and outrageous wills of every evil disposed person, but so far to protect them as we do many other goods and chattels, and also somewhat further as having created men though without knowledge of God in the world, we have therefore upon mature and serious consideration of the premises thought good to renew and revive whatsoever we have found necessary and useful in the former laws of this Isle concerning the ordering and governing of Negroes and to add thereunto such further laws and ordinances as at this time we think absolute needful for the public safety and may prove to the future behoveful to the peace and utility of this Isle by this Act repealing and dissolving all other former laws made concerning said Negroes.

See "An Act for the Better Ordering and Governing of Negroes," *Barbados 1661* (Public Record Office, Kew, United Kingdom, CO 30/2/16–26), 25–28, 32–33; quoted in Stanley Engerman, Seymour Drescher, and Robert Paquette, eds., *Slavery*, 105–113. The 1661 law was enacted by the first post-Restoration House of Assembly of Barbados, under the speakership of Sir Thomas Modyford, who, on becoming governor of Jamaica in 1664, brought with him seven hundred planters and their slaves, along with the slave code on Barbados, introducing slavery wholesale to that island.

120 The Virginia law was enacted December 1662 in reaction to Elizabeth Key's successful lawsuit for her freedom (also known as a freedom-suit). Key, who was born in 1630 in Warwick County, Virginia, to a Negro slave mother and Thomas Key, white planter and a member of the House of Burgesses, filed her suit in 1655 against the estate of Colonel John Mottram, who had just died, the executors of which classified Elizabeth and her infant son, John, as Negroes and property. She based her suit on the claim that under English common law, both she and her son were free English persons because their fathers were so. Elizabeth's father, Thomas Key, was compelled by the courts to take responsibility for his daughter in accordance with common law, under which children, including those born out of wedlock, followed the social status of the father, who was obligated under law to support the child including arranging an apprenticeship through which the child would acquire a viable life-trade. Having acknowledged Elizabeth as his daughter and expressly taking responsibility for her welfare as such, he had her baptized in the Church of England, and prior to his death in 1636 put the then six-year-old girl in the indenture of Humphrey Higginson for a period of nine years, with the expressed expectation that Higginson would serve as her

guardian until she was fifteen and secure her life as a free English woman. Higginson instead transferred her indenture to Mottram when she was ten. During her indenture to Mottram, Elizabeth had a son, John, sired by a young English lawyer named William Grinstead, who was also indentured to Mottram. Of the three counts on which Keys won her case the most significant was that, based on English common law, her social status was that of her father. The Key's case incited the Virginia General Assembly to enact a series of three laws, all in 1662, regulating the fruit of sexual activity between masters and servants: "ACT VI. *Women servants gott with child by their masters after their time expired to be sold by the Churchwardens for two yeares for the good of the parish*; ACT VIII. *Men servants getting any bastard child to make satisfaction to the parish after their service ended*; and ACT XII. *Negro womens children to serve according to the condition of the mother.*" The remarkable thing about ACT XII is that in order to prevent anything like the Key's case from being legally possible, the Assembly stepped outside of common law and utilized Roman law governing domestic chattel, what the *Code Noir* calls *meuble*:

> WHEREAS some doubts have arrisen whether children got by any Englishman upon a negro woman should be slave or ffree, *Be it therefore enacted and declared by this present grand assembly,* that all children borne in this country shalbe held bond or free only according to the condition of the mother, *And* that if any christian shall committ ffornication with a negro man or woman, hee or shee soe offending shall pay double the ffines imposed by the former act. (Hening, *Statutes*, 1:170)

121 Enacted October 1705 as "CHAP. XXIII. *An act declaring the Negro, Mulatto, and Indian slaves within this dominion to real estate*," the law stipulates:

> I. FOR the better settling and preservation of estates within this dominion,
> II. *Be it enacted, by the governor, council and burgesses of this present general assembly, and it is hereby enacted by the authority of the same,* That from and after the passing of this act, all negro, mulatto, and Indian slaves, in all courts of judicature, and other places, within this dominion, shall be held, taken, and adjudged, to be real estate (and not chattels;) and shall descend unto the heirs and widows of persons departing this life, according to the manner and custom of land of inheritance, held in fee simple.
> III. *Provided always,* That nothing in this act contained, shall be taken to extend to any merchant or factor, bringing any slaves into this dominion, or having any consignments thereof, unto them, for sale: but that such slaves, whilst they remain unsold, in the possession of such merchant, or factor, or of their executors, administrators, or assigns, shall, to all intents and purposes, be taken, held, and adjudged, to be personal estate, in the same condition they should have been in, if this act had never been made. (Hening, *Statutes*, 2:333)

122 Barthes, "Le mythe aujourd'hui," 190.
123 These are, in fact, precisely the questions Tom Tyler asks of Barthes's "quia ego nominor leo" in illustration of the long philosophical and critical theory tradition of deploying animals as ciphers and indices. Even though Tyler marks this

in distinction of the more attended to example of the saluting Negro, the problematic of making something a cipher and index in order to undue stereotype pertains in both examples. See Tom Tyler, "*Quia Ego Nominor Leo*: Barthes, Stereotypes, and Aesop's Animals," 47.

124 See Victor Hugo, *Notre-Dame de Paris*, 145. See also Gaius Julius Phaedrus, "Fabula V. Vacca, Capella, Ovis, et Leo," in *The More Familiar Fables of Phædrus*, 4.
125 Barthes, "Le mythe aujourd'hui," 190.
126 Tyler, "*Quia Ego Nominor Leo*."
127 Barthes, "Le mythe aujourd'hui," 197.
128 Roland Barthes, "Bichon chez les Nègres," in *Mythologies*, 60–63.
129 Barthes, "Bichon chez les Nègres," 62.
130 Barthes, "Bichon chez les Nègres," 62.
131 This imperial imprimatur was made official on March 31, 1931, when the French Parliament unanimously passed a law granting the Mission Dakar-Djibouti official status for purposes of funding.
132 Barthes, *La Chambre claire*, 73–80.
133 Leiris, *L'Afrique fantôme*, 182.
134 Leiris, "Alberto Giacometti," 209.
135 Leiris, "Alberto Giacometti," 209.
136 Aristotle, *Physics*, 2.2.194a16.
137 Plato, *Symposium*, 205c.
138 Aristotle, *Nicomachean Ethics*, 6.4.1140a6.
139 For a fuller account of this sense of *enérgeia*, see Joe Sachs, "Aristotle: Motion and Its Place in Nature," *Internet Encyclopedia of Philosophy*. In his account of the translation of Aristotle's sense of *enérgeia*, Sachs raises concerns about following the Latin translation leading to "actuality" as the English-language rendering because of that word's prominent meaning in English. He writes: "The root of *enérgeia* [ἐνέργεια] is *ergonó* [ἔργονου], deed, work, or *actó* from which comes the adjective *energon* [ἐνεργον], used in ordinary speech to mean active, busy, or at work. *Energeia* is formed by the addition of a noun ending to the adjective *energon*; we might construct the word, 'is-at-work-ness,' from Anglo-Saxon roots to translate *enérgeia* into English, or use the more euphonious periphrastic expression, being-at-work."
140 Aristotle, *Metaphysics*, 9.5.1048b18–20.
141 Aristotle, *Metaphysics*, 9.5.1048b35.
142 Aristotle, *Poetics*, 1448a1.
143 Aristotle, *Politics*, 3.1325b20–30.
144 Aristotle, *Metaphysics*, 9.4.1048b34.
145 Aristotle, *Physics*, 2.2.194a22.
146 Aristotle, *Physics*, 2.2194a23.
147 Aristotle, *Physics*, 2.2.194a27.
148 Aristotle, *Physics*, 2.3.194b24–35.
149 Aristotle, *Physics*, 2.3.194b24–35.
150 Aristotle, *Physics*, 2.8.191a17.
151 Aristotle, *Physics*, 2.2.195a35–37.
152 Take note how Aristotle's *enérgeia* foreshadows Dedekind's *Abstraktion*.

153 Aristotle, *Physics*, 2.2.194b23–26.
154 See Heidegger, "Die Frage nach der Technik," 9–11.
155 Heidegger, "Die Frage nach der Technik," 10.
156 Aristotle, *Poetics*, 1451b5.
157 Leiris, "Alberto Giacometti," 209.
158 Immanuel Kant, *Beobachtungen über das Gefühl des Schönen und Erhabenen* [Observations on the Feeling of the Beautiful and Sublime], in *Kants Gesammelte Schriften*, 2:253.
159 Leiris, "Alberto Giacometti," 210.
160 Sally Price and Jean Jamin, "A Conversation with Michel Leiris," 158.
161 Leiris, "Alberto Giacometti," 209. The reference is to Lew Leslie's *Blackbirds* revue, which performed in 1929 at the Moulin Rouge, close to Montmartre in the eighteenth arrondissement, suggesting that the "*négresse*" was its star, Adelaide Hall.
162 Jacqueline Delange and Michel Leiris, *L'Afrique noire*, 30.
163 Guillaume Apollinaire, *Zone*, 7–15. *Zone*, which Martin Sorrell thought to be "*the* great poem of early Modernism," is the first poem in the collection *Alcools*, although it is chronologically the last of the collection to be written.
164 Delange and Leiris, *L'Afrique noire*, 30.
165 Leiris, *L'Afrique fantôme*, 98.
166 Leiris, *L'Afrique fantôme*, 98–99.
167 Leiris, *L'Afrique fantôme*, 443.
168 Leiris, *L'Afrique fantôme*, 104.
169 Leiris, *L'Afrique fantôme*, 140.
170 Leiris, *L'Afrique fantôme*, 100.
171 Lomax, *Adventures of a Ballad Hunter*, 11–12.
172 Lomax, *Adventures of a Ballad Hunter*, 11–12.
173 Barthes, "Bichon chez les Nègres," 63.
174 Barthes, "Le mythe aujourd'hui," 191.
175 Bearing in mind the etymology of *actualitas*, which is attuned to the Aristotelian conception of *enérgeia*, along with the more familiar and common English-language connotation of "actuality" as what a thing is, using this term in regard to the Negro as a mythic signifier of modernity highlights the fact that for modern racialized capitalist slavery, "Negro" signifies quasi-human "is-at-work-ness."
176 Spillers, "Mama's Baby, Papa's Maybe," 206.
177 See Daniel Birnbaum and Anders Olsson, "An Interview with Jacques Derrida on the Limits of Digestion," *e-flux Journal* 2 (January 2009), under "Derrida on transubstantiation," http://www.e-flux.com/journal/an-interview-with-jacques-derrida-on-the-limits-of-digestion/.
178 On Hegel's usage of *aufheben* and *Aufhebung* see Hans Küng, *Menschwerdung Gottes*, 470. See also Errol E. Harris, *An Interpretation of the Logic of Hegel*, 30–33.
179 Enacted September 1667 as ACT III. *An act declaring that baptisme of slaves doth not exempt them from bondage*, the Virginia law states:

> WHEREAS some doubts have risen whether children that are slaves by birth, and by the charity and piety of their owners made pertakers of the blessed sacrament of baptisme, should by vertue of their baptisme be made ffree; *It is enacted*

and declared by this grand assembly, and the authority thereof, that the conferring of baptisme doth not alter the condition of the person as to his bondage or ffreedome; that diverse masters, ffreed from this doubt, may more carefully endeavour the propagation of christianity by permitting children, though slaves, or those of greater growth if capable to be admitted to that sacrament. (Hening, *Statutes*, 2:260)

In December 1682, the same assembly passed ACT I. *An act to repeale a former law makeing Indians and others ffree*, which stipulates:

WHEREAS by the 12 act of assembly held att James Citty the 3d day of October, Anno Domini 1670, entituled an act declareing who shall be slaves, *it is enacted* that all servants not being christians, being imported into this country by shipping shall be slaves, but what shall come by land shall serve if boyes and girles untill thirty yeares of age, if men or women, twelve yeares and noe longer; and for as much as many negroes, moores, mollatoes and others borne of and in heathenish, idollatrous, pagan and mahometan parentage and country have heretofore, and hereafter may be purchased, procured, or otherwise obteigned as slaves of, from or out of such their heathenish country by some well disposed christian, who after such their obteining and purchaseing such negroe, moor, or molatto as their slave out of a pious zeale, have wrought the conversion of such slave to the christian faith, which by the laws of this country doth not manumitt them or make them free, and afterwards such their conversion, it hath and may often happen that such master or owner of such slave being by some reason inforced to bring or send such slave into this country to sell or dispose of for his necessity or advantage, he the said master or owner of such servant which notwithstanding his conversion is really his slave, or his factor or agent must be constrained either to carry back or export again the said slave to some other place where they may sell him for a slave, or else depart from their just right and tytle to such slave and sell him here for noe longer time then the English or other christians are to serve, to the great losse and damage of such master or owner, and to the great discouragement of bringing in such slaves for the future, and to noe advantage at all to the planter or buyer; and whereas alsoe those Indians that are taken in warre or otherwise by our neighbouring Indians, confederates or tributaries to his majestie, and this his plantation of Virginia are slaves to the said neighbouring Indians that soe take them, and by them are likewise sold to his majesties subjects here as slaves, *Bee it therefore enacted by the governour councell and burgesses of this general assembly, and it is enacted by the authority aforesaid,* that all the said recited act of the third of October 1670 be, and is hereby repealed and made utterly voyd to all intents and purposes whatsoever. *And be it further enacted by the authority aforesaid* that all servants except Turkes and Moores, whilest in amity with his majesty which from and after publication of this act shall be brought or imported into this country, either by sea or land, whether Negroes, Moors, Mollattoes or Indians, who and whose parentage and native country are not christian at the time of their first purchase of such servant by some christian, although afterwards, and before such their importation and bringing into this country, they shall be converted to the christian faith; and all Indians which shall hereafter be sold by our neighbouring Indians, or any other trafiqueing with us as for slaves are hereby adjudged, deemed and taken, and shall be adjudged, deemed and taken to be slaves to all intents. (Hening, *Statutes*, 2:491)

180 Barthes, *La Chambre claire*, 51. Cf. Roland Barthes, *Camera Lucida*, 28.
181 Barthes, *La Chambre claire*, 73.
182 Barthes, *La Chambre claire*, 73.
183 Barthes, *La Chambre claire*, 93.
184 Barthes, *La Chambre claire*, 115.
185 Husserl, *Natur und Geist*, 139–140.
186 Husserl, *Ideen zu einer reinen Phänomenologie und phänomenologischen Philosophie II*, 185.
187 Husserl, *Ideen II*, 185.
188 See Gerd Brand, *Welt, Ich, und Zeit*, 19.
189 Cottingham argues that Descartes made no distinction between *mens* (mind) and *anima* (soul), using the latter in the scholastic sense as the Latin translation of Aristotle's φυχή (*psyche*). See John Cottingham, "Cartesian Dualism: Theology, Metaphysics, and Science," 236. Descartes asserts in the *Meditationes*, with the existence of the body still in doubt:

> But what about the attributes I assign to the soul [*anima*]? Nutrition or movement? Since now I do not have a body, these are mere fabrications. Sense-perception? This does not occur without a body, and besides, when asleep I have appeared to perceive through the senses many things that I afterwards realized I did not perceive through the senses at all. Thinking [*Cogitare*]? At last I have discovered it: thought; this alone is inseparable from me ... I am, then, in the strict sense, only a thing that thinks; that is, I am a mind, or soul, or intellect, or reason; words the meaning of which I have been ignorant of until now. (Rene Descartes, "Meditatio Secunda, De natura mentis humanae: Quod ipsa notior quam corpus," 21)

190 Husserl, *Ideen II*, 173.
191 Husserl, *Ideen zu einer reinen Phänomenologie und phänomenologischen Philosophie I*.
192 Husserl, *Ideen I*, 130.
193 Husserl, *Ideen II*, 174.
194 Husserl, *Natur und Geist*, 186.
195 Husserl, *Ideen II*, 195.
196 Husserl, *Ideen II*, 189.
197 Husserl, *Ideen II*, 189.
198 See Brand, *Welt, Ich, und Zeit*, 17.
199 Husserl, *Ideen II*, 190.
200 Husserl, *Ideen II*, 190.
201 Husserl, *Ideen II*, 190.
202 Husserl, *Ideen II*, 191.
203 Husserl, *Ideen II*, 191.
204 Husserl, *Ideen I*, 146.

205 In the opening paragraph of *L'assassinat de l'expérience par la peinture, Monory*, under the rubric "L'EXPERTISE," Lyotard writes:

> Experience is a modern figure. To begin with, it needs a subject, the instance of an "I" who speaks in the first person. It needs a type of temporal arrangement, Augustine's *Confessions XI* (a modern work if ever the was one), where the view of the past, present, and future is always taken from the point of an elusive actual consciousness. With these two axioms, one can already engender the essential form of experience: I am no longer what I am, and I am not yet what I am. Life signifies the death of what one is, and this death certifies that life has a meaning, that one is not a stone. A third axiom gives to experience its full scope: the world is not an entity external to the subject, it is the common name of the objects in which the subject alienates itself (is lost, dying to itself) in order to achieve itself, to live. Thus, the figure of experience is Christian, as we can see, like everything modern. It governs by far the idea of salvation, therefore of progress, of revolution, it suffices to give Jesus different names. (Lyotard, *L'assassinat de l'expérience par la peinture, Monory*, 8)

206 Husserl, *Ideen II*, 190–200.
207 Kant, *Kritik der reinen Vernunft*, A 346/B4 404 (374); all references incorporate the first edition of 1781, noted as "A," and the second edition of 1787, noted as "B"; henceforth citation includes edition page notation, then the Meiner page number in parenthesis. For those wishing to consult a full English-language translation of the text, see Immanuel Kant, *Critique of Pure Reason*, 414; henceforth page citation to this edition appears in brackets, following original.
208 Kant, *Kritik*, A 671/B 699 (626), [606].
209 Merleau-Ponty, *Le visible et l'invisible*, 119.
210 The question relates Barthes "quia ego nominor leo" to a remark made by Wittgenstein in a manuscript he left unfinished at his death in 1951, *Philosophische Untersuchungen*: "Wenn ein Löwe sprechen könnte, wir könnten ihn nicht verstehen." Elizabeth Anscombe, who translated and published the German manuscript in English in 1953, renders the remark as: "If a lion could talk, we could not understand him" (Ludwig Wittgenstein, *Philosophical Investigations*, 190). P. M. S. Hacker and Joachim Schulte give a more interpretive translation of Wittgenstein's remark that, "If a lion could talk, we wouldn't be able to understand" (Wittgenstein, *Philosophical Investigations*, 223). A thoughtful engagement with the controversy in philosophical circles over the Wittgenstein remark has been provided by Constantine Sandis, "Understanding the Lion for Real," 138–161.
211 Egypt, Masuoka, and Johnson, *Unwritten History of Slavery*, 85.
212 Hartman, *Scenes of Subjection*, 78.

Sentient Flesh Dancing

1 Douglass, *My Bondage and My Freedom*, 288.
2 A distinction needs to be made between Pattin' Juba and the Juba dance—the one being the stylized beating on the body for musical rhythm, and the other the

ring dance performed widely throughout the North American South as well as the Caribbean. Pattin' Juba was performed in a circular dance formation customarily with variations on the basic rhythm, in the form of syncopation and shifting accented notes; these dance movements were not exclusively linked to the song Juba and were used for a variety of song. A form of the Juba dance was a principle feature of American minstrelsy in a complicated mocking and admiration of slave aesthetic forms known as "jigs." In that context, the word *Juba* became identified with one of the first black minstrel performers, William Henry Lane, who from the early 1840s was known as "Master Juba," or "Boz Juba." A reporter for the Manchester Examiner, after having seen Lane perform on one of his tours of England, wrote: "Surely he cannot be flesh and blood, but some special substance, or how could he turn and twine, and twist, and twirl, and hop, and jump, and kick and throw his feet with such velocity that one think they are playing hide-and seek with a flash of lightning!" (*Manchester Examiner*, October 17, 1848). Scholarship on Juba and other slave vernacular dances is extensive. Among some of the most significant work is Thomas, *No Man Can Hinder Me*; Fine, *Soulstepping*; Knowles, *Tap Roots*; Constance Valis Hill, *Tap Dancing America*; Malone, *Steppin' on the Blues*; Beverly J. Robinson, "Africanisms and the Study of Folklore"; Jones and Lomax Hawes, *Step It Down*; and Parrish, *Slave Songs*.

3 Douglass's rendition is abbreviated:

> *We raise de wheat*
> *Dey gib us de corn;*
> *We bake de bread,*
> *Dey gib us de cruss;*
> *We sif de mea,*
> *Dey gib us de huss;*
> *We peal de meat,*
> *Dey gic us de skin,*
> *And dat's de way*
> *Dey takes us in.*
> *We skim de pot,*
> *Dey gib us the liquor,*
> *And say dat's good enough for nigger.*
> *Walk over! Walkover!*
> *Tom butter de fat;*
> *Poor nigger you can't get over dat;*
> *Walk over!*

Jones and Lomax Hawe give a fuller version with parenthetical commentary provided by Jones:

> *Juba dis and Juba dat,*
>> (That means a little of this and a little of that.)
>
> *And Juba killed da yellow cat,*
>> (That means mixed-up food might kill the white folk.
>> And they didn't care if it did, I don't suppose.)

And get over double trouble, Juba

>(Someday they meant they would get over double trouble . . .)

You sift-a the meal, you give me the husk,
You cook-a bread, you give me the crust,
You Fry the meat, you give me the skin,
And that's where my mama's trouble begin.

>(You see, so that's what it mean—mother would always be talking to them about she wish she could give them some of the good hot cornbread or hot pies or hot what-not. But she couldn't. She had to wait and give that old stuff that was left over. And then they began to sing it and play it . . .)

And then you Juba,
You just Juba.
Juba up, Juba down,

>(That mean everywhere,)

Juba all around the town.

>(All around the whole country.)

Juba for ma, Juba for pa,
Juba for your brother-in-law

>(See, that meant everybody had Juba. And they made a play out of it. So that's where this song came from; they would get all this kind of thing off their brains and minds . . .)

Jones and Lomax Hawe also provide this version in full with choreography instructions, as well as instructions for the pattin' rhythms. See Jones and Lomax Hawes, *Step It Down*, 36–40. Jones, the "native informant," describes Juba as "one of the oldest plays I think I can remember our grandfather telling us about, because he was brought up in Virginia." She then provides an etymology, the significance of which Lomax emphasizes by italicizing it: "*He used to tell us about how they used to eat ends of food; that's what 'juba' means. They said 'jibba' when they meant 'giblets'; we know that's ends of food. They had to eat leftovers*" (37). Relying on the ethnography of Herskovits, as did Lydia Parrish, Lomax Hawes rather condescendingly corrects Jones's "native" etymology on the grounds that slaves in the United States had long forgotten "the original African meaning," which is supposed to be "a variation of one of the West African day, which were used also for girls' given names" (37).

4 Bibb, *Narrative of the Life*, 23.
5 Bibb, *Narrative*, 23.
6 Douglass, *My Bondage and My Freedom*, 291.
7 Hartman, *Scenes of Subjection*, 70.
8 Hence the 1668 effort in Barbados, as well as that of the Virginia General Assembly in 1705, to define the Negro slave as real estate. In defense of the subse-

quent practice of entailing slaves without annexing them to the land, the Virginia attorney general, Sir John Randolph, argued in 1768 that the 1705 act "cannot give them the immobility and permanence of lands; but it can, and does give them, the adventitious or legal properties which belong to lands"; see *Blackwell v. Wilkinson, 1768*, in Thomas Jefferson, *Reports of Cases Determined in the General Court of Virginia from 1730–1740 and 1768–1772*, 13–85.

9 Parrish, *Slave Songs*.
10 Cornelia Bailey of Sapelo Island, who was celebrated as the Geechee griot, says: "Now the Buzzard Lope is what everyone on Sapelo called a shout, and Geechee and Gullah on some of the other islands called a ring dance shout. By 'shout' I don't mean a loud or unruly shout from your mouth. It's more like a celebration, and organized celebration, done in a circle, to the beat of a stick, a broomstick" (Bailey, *God, Dr. Buzzard and the Bolito Man*, 173).
11 See Turner, *Africanisms*, 202. Under the rubric "Africanism in the Gullah Dialect," Turner gives the following entry:

| ʃʊʈ "a religious ring dance in which the participants continue to perform until they become exhausted" | CF. Ar. *ʃaut* "to move around the Kaaba (the small stone building at Mecca which is the chief object of the pilgrimage of Mohammedans) until exhausted"; *ʃauwata* "to run until exhausted" |

In keeping with his IPA phonetic transcription of the Gullah terms, Turner transcribes the voiceless postalveolar fricative pronounced *sh* as in the English word *shame*, as ʃ, writing *ʃʊʈ* for the Gullah word. Still following IPA transcription guidelines, he transliterates the Arabic voiceless postalveolar fricative, ش, also pronounced *sh*, and so renders شَوْطَ as *ʃaut*, giving the root verb, شَوَّطَ, as *ʃauwata*. When we modify Turner's transliteration of the Arabic according to the ALA-LC or EALL standards, his *ʃaut* and *ʃauwata* become *shauṭ* or *šauṭ* (شَوْطَ) and *shawwaṭa* or *šawwaṭa* (شَوَّطَ) respectively. Parrish cites Turner in chapter 3 of *Slave Songs*, "Afro-American Shout Songs," as follows: "But Dr. L. D. Turner has discovered that the Arabic word *Saut* (pronounced like our word 'shout'), in use among the Mohammedans of West Africa, meant to run and walk around the Kaaba" (Parrish, *Slave Songs*, 54). She disregards Turner's usage of the IPA in transcription, displacing "ʃ" with "S," and so erroneously attributes to him the transliteration *Saut*. Because Parrish's book is a primary source for ethnomusicologists, as well as cultural historians and ethnologists whose work focuses on the ring shout as an African survival, her misquotation has been repeated numerous times and led to considerable confusion regarding Turner's etymology. Some, with minimal training in linguistics and even greater unfamiliarity with Arabic phonology, philology, and Islamic science, have accepted Parrish's misreporting of Turner's *ʃaut* as *Saut* and dispute the soundness of his etymology. For instance, Sterling Stuckey, who maintains that Turner's "work on Afro-America culture is of primary importance," and thinks his etymology the most interesting explanation for the origin of the Gullah name *shout* because it associates the counterclockwise ring shout with the counterclockwise circumambulation of the

Kaaba, quotes Parrish verbatim in presenting that etymology: "Dr. L. D. Turner has discovered that the Arabic word *Saut* (pronounced like our word 'shout'), in use among the Mohammedans of West Africa, meant to run and walk around the Kaaba" (Stuckey, *Slave Culture*, 16). Yet, upon presenting Parrish's erroneous transliteration to the Africanist John Hunwick, who specialized in Arabic literature of Africa, Stuckey is given "reason to question the view that *saut* refers to 'shout'" because of Hunwick's informing him that *saut* transliterates the Arabic word for "voice" or "sound" (Stuckey, *Slave Culture*, 16). Such a transliteration, however, would be in violation of all twelve accepted systems of European language transliteration of Arabic, from BGN/PCGN and ALA-LC to EALL and ISO. The Arabic word translated to mean "voice" or "sound" is صَوْت (*ṣaut*). Again, adhering to the ALA-LC, the initial consonant of this word, the voiceless dento-alveolar, ص, is transliterated as *ṣ*. Correctly transliterated, the Arabic word for voice reads *ṣaut*, in contrast to Parrish's *saut*, the initial consonant of which, "s," transliterates the Arabic voiceless sibilant, س. It is conceivable that Hunwick, on Stuckey's informing him that the Arabic term in question was reportedly in common use among West African Muslim Arabic speakers, allowed for the تَحْرِيف (*taḥrīf*, "distortion") common among such speakers of displacing the voiceless dento-alveolar ص (*ṣ*) with the voiceless sibilant س (*s*), as well as the voiceless dento-alveolar emphatic ط, transliterated as *ṭ*, with the voiced aspirated, ت, transliterated as *t*; so that what would be transcribed in written in Arabic as صَوْت (*ṣaut*) gets pronounced as *saut*—it should be noted that Turner, who studied Arabic at Yale in 1938, adjusts for this in his IPA transcription of both the Gullah and Arabic. In light of Hunwick's familiarity with West African pronunciations of Arabic, it is understandable why he would inform Stuckey that the Arabic word being transliterated was صَوْت (*ṣaut*), meaning "voice" or "sound," which is why "Tuner's tantalizing view" is called into question (Stuckey, *Slave Culture*, 16). Yet, even if we allow for all of that, there is no clear phonological path from شَوْط (*shauṭ*; *šauṭ*) to صَوْت (*ṣaut*), The only reason we are there, however, is Parrish's misrepresentation of Turner's etymon. Others who have been led astray by Parrish's error, compounded by their own unfamiliarity with Arabic, include the ethnomusicologist Johann Buis, who seeks to connect the mistaken *saut* to "shout" by relying on Henry Farmer's *A History of Arabian Music to the Thirteenth Century* (London: Luzac and Company, 1929), in which reference is made to Abu Faraj al-Isfahani's discussion of صَوْت (*ṣaut*) as verse set to music, and then proposes, based on the ethnological reportage of Jean Jenkins and Poul Olsen in their book, *Music and Musical Instruments in the World of Islam* (London: World of Islam Festival Publishing Company, 1976), that the Bahrainian musical genre "designation ... *saut* [sic] parallels the *genre* designation of the ring shout," finding sufficient enough similarity between the rhythmic accompaniment to the Bahrainian music and the rhythmic pattern central to the ring shout to warrant concluding "them to be related"; see Johann Buis, "Historical Essay, the Ring Shout: Revisiting the Islamic and African Issues of a Christian 'Holy Dance,'" 161–164. Parrish's misleading so many researchers notwithstanding, it is indisputable that the etymon Turner gives is شَوْط (*shauṭ*; *šauṭ*), and that, as far as its meaning is concerned, he is on firm ground, except for the claim of movement to exhaustion. Whereas the root verb, (*šawwaṭa*), means to run a course, to race, it does not stipulate to exhaustion. In that suit, the verbal noun, شَوْط (*shauṭ*; *šauṭ*), is indeed used in the discourse of Islamic jurisprudence (الفقه, *al-fiqh*) to describe a single counterclockwise circumambulation of the Kaaba at Hajj, seven of which constitute the ritual rite, الطواف (*aṭ- ṭawāf*), lending support to Turner's etymology. We know, of course, from such examples as Ben Ali on Sapelo, but also Umar bin Said, and Kebe, that there were scholars of *al-fiqh* among the enslaved African Muslims, and it is conceivable that they may have been the source for designating the slave-ritual circumambulation by this term. On the jurisprudential usage of شَوْط (*shauṭ*; *šauṭ*), see Muḥammad ʿAbdur-Raḥmān ʿAbdul-Manʿa, "*šauṭ*," *fī Muʿajm al-muṣṭalaḥāt wa al-alfāẓ al-fiqihiya* (al-Iskandariya: Maktaba al-Iskandariya, 2010).

12 Parrish wrote regularly to Herskovits between 1936 and 1942, before publishing *Slave Songs of the Georgia Sea Islands*. See Northwestern University Archives, Melville J. Herskovits Papers, Series 35/6, Box 18, Folder 2, Parrish, Lydia 1936–1942. She augmented Herskovits's theory of African survivals with a sentimental personally redemptive Negrophilia that, like John Avery Lomax's, stemmed from childhood memories of Negro singing, from an effort to reclaim the sense of rich humanity that signing freed her to feel. For Lomax, that humanizing sound was identified with one idealized individual, Nat Blythe, whom he was always searching for in his phonographic expeditions among Negroes. In Parrish's case, the inspiration to collect came from recalling the singing of the Negro inhabitants in the Salem, New Jersey, Quaker community where she was raised, and wanting to somehow reclaim the way it had liberated her from the liturgical constraints and affective rigidity of the Society of Friends to which she belonged. The consistent exuberance, whether in kitchen or fields, of "the Negro's music filled a real need" (Parrish, *Slave Songs*, xxv). Parrish's recollections of all that came to her when she first heard "slave songs" being sung on the Georgia coast in 1909, where she had begun spending winters to escape the emotional alienation and sexual infidelity of her husband, the renowned commercial artist Maxfield Parrish. In 1905, fifteen-year-old Susan Lewin, who was initially hired as the children's nanny, became Parrish's principle model, at which point he moved out of the main house to live in his studio cottage with Lewin. Except for a brief interlude of a few months when Lewin stayed at Harlakenden House, the mansion of the American novelist Winston Churchill until it burned down in October 1923, she and Parrish continued to live together until 1960. She was the model for much of his subsequent work, among which is included *Princess Parizade and the Singing Tree* (1906), *Garden of Allah* (1917), and rather ironically given Lydia's Negrophilia, *Primitive Man* (1920). The difficulty of this marital situation was a chief factor in her deciding to winter on the Georgia coast and sea islands until her death in 1953. So, Negro singing once again filled an affective personal need. Justifying her claim to knowing Negro song, Parrish says: "As we all know, opportunity rarely knocks more than once, and this time I took steps to insure that the songs should not escape me. Herein, I believe rests my right to know something about them" (Parrish, *Slave Songs*, xxvi). This claim to a proprietary personal

right to Negro songs has everything to do with her experience of what they do *for her*, and nothing whatsoever with what they do as and in performance for their creators—with respect to whom, Parrish's general attitude was one of maternalistic preservation and dispensation. "The Negroes frankly say that it was a good thing I arrived on St. Simon's when I did," she declares, "and I know that if I had been there years earlier I could have saved many priceless songs which are now lost" (Parrish, *Slave Songs*, xxvi).

13 Parrish, *Slave Songs*, 108.
14 Parrish, *Slave Songs*, 108.
15 Parrish, *Slave Songs*, 108.
16 Parrish, *Slave Songs*, 108.
17 Parrish, *Slave Songs*, 108.
18 Parrish, *Slave Songs*, 111.
19 Parrish, *Slave Songs*, 111.
20 Parrish, *Slave Songs*, 111.
21 Parrish, *Slave Songs*, 111.
22 Herskovits, *Rebel Destiny*, 330.
23 This remark was reportedly made to Bess Lomax Hawes, John Avery's Lomax's daughter, at some point during the production of her 1964 film, *Georgia Sea Island Singers*, in which she filmed Bessie Jones and the Georgia Sea Island Singers performing the Buzzard Lope. It may very well in fact be something she got from one of the interviews her brother, Alan Lomax, recorded with the singer, which are cited in the film credits as a source.
24 Herskovits, *Rebel Destiny*, 37.
25 Parrish, *Slave Songs*, 10.
26 See Henri Labouret and Paul Rivet, *Le royaume d'Arda et son évangélisation*, 18, cited in Herskovits, *Dahomey*, 105.
27 In conversation with Fleming Brown in 1963, Smith repeatedly insisted that his playing merely replicated John Greer's, and when Fleming asked where Greer learned it, Smith replied "without ado, that a Black man named Henry Hays from the Laurel Fork community taught him. Moreover, Greer 'played just like him.'" See Stephen Wade, "Hobart Smith *In Sacred Trust*," in booklet accompanying *The 1963 Fleming Brown Tapes: Hobart Smith "In Sacred Trust*," recorded October 2–17, 1963, Smithsonian Folkways, 2005, compact disc.
28 Parrish, *Slave Songs*, 243.
29 Samuel A. Floyd, "Ring Shout! Literary Studies, Historical Studies, and Black Music Inquiry," 277.
30 Stuckey, *Slave Culture*, 16.
31 They are neither the first to think this way, nor the last. There is, to mention a few of the renowned antecedents, Albert Murray's conception of style, Ralph Ellison's conception of the Blues, as well as that of Amiri Baraka (née, Leroi Jones); or Roger Abraham's study of *tropism*, and Claudia Mitchell-Kernan's analysis of signifying.
32 Glissant, *Poétique de la relation*, 103.
33 Moten, *In the Break*, 7.
34 Moten, *In the Break*, 22.

35 Parrish, *Slave Songs*, 20.
36 Parrish, *Slave Songs*, 20.
37 Parrish, *Slave Songs*, 22.
38 Parrish, *Slave Songs*, 21.
39 Jones, *For the Ancestors*, 46.
40 Jones, *For the Ancestors*, 47.
41 Bailey, *God, Dr. Buzzard and the Bolito Man*, 178–186.
42 Bailey, *God, Dr. Buzzard and the Bolito Man*, 182–183.
43 Bailey, *God, Dr. Buzzard and the Bolito Man*, 182–183.
44 See Detienne and Vernant, *Les ruses del'intelligence*. This work still remains one of the most probative studies of μῆτις (*mêtis*).
45 On μῆτις (*mêtis*) as somatic intelligence, see Debra Hawhee, *Bodily Arts: Rhetoric and Athletics in Ancient Greece* (Austin: University of Texas Press, 2005).
46 By Aquinas's explanation, the corporeal substances of bread and wine are transubstantiated, becoming the body and blood of Christ, so that the accidental elementals—bread and wine's giving sustenance to accidental bodies—no longer have any corporeal substance to which they can inhere, except for the corporeal substance of quantity—mass and extension—which is how the Eucharist elementals can nourish the body of the recipient, can act upon and be acted upon by other bodies, can be metabolized, with the host becoming corrupted and the blood turn into vinegar. See Thomas Aquinas, *Summa Theologica*, part III, question 77.
47 Karl Marx, "Die trinitarische Formel," in *Das Kapital*, 3:824. Cf. Karl Marx, *Capital: A Critique of Political Economy*, vol. 3, trans. David Fernbach, 954.
48 Karl Marx, "Der Fetischcharakter der Ware und sein Geheimnis," in *Das Kapital*, 1:97. See also Karl Marx, *Capital: A Critique of Political Economy*, vol. 1, trans. Ben Fowkes, 176.
49 As William Pietz, from whom I take this formulation, points out, philosophy's dismissal of the fetish, which we already noted in regard to Kant's calling it trifling (*Läppische*), includes Marx's commodity-fetish. See William Pietz, "The Problem of the Fetish, I."
50 See *Medical Dictionary for the Health Professions and Nursing*, s.v. "apposition" and "appositional growth," retrieved January 6, 2017, http://medical-dictionary.thefreedictionary.com/appositional+growth.
51 See Christopher G. Morris, ed., "Apposition," in *Academic Press Dictionary of Science and Technology*, 141.
52 Murray, "A Conversation with Albert Murray," in Baker, *Albert Murray*, 130.
53 Murray, "In Response to Being Awarded a Citation for Distinguished Literary Achievement by an Alabamian," in Baker, *Albert Murray*, 13.
54 What I have called here *heterologous fleshly sentient capacity*, I have referred to elsewhere as *an indeterminate subjectivity*, which Frank Wilderson has paraphrased as "an interdiction against subjectivity," drawing an analogy to Marx's remark about the "speaking implement" (Wilderson, *Red, White & Black*, 56). Cf. Ronald A. T. Judy, *(Dis)forming the American Canon: African-Arabic Slave Narratives and the Vernacular* (Minneapolis: University of Minnesota Press, 1993), 176.
55 Karl Marx, "Die Produktion des absoluten Mehrwerts," in *Das Kapital*, 1:210–211fn17. See also Marx, *Capital*, 1:303–304fn17.

56 See Varro, *Rerum rusticarum*, 1.17.1, 224.
57 Marx, *Das Kapital*, 1:211fn17; Marx, *Capital*, 1:303–304.
58 James Ford III, "From Being to Unrest, from Objectivity to Motion: The Slave in Marx's *Capital*," 22–30.
59 Moten, *In the Break*, 6.
60 Moten, *In the Break*, 6.
61 Rather than sentient flesh being converted through the efficacy of law, predicated on the metaphysics of modernity, into fungible human bodies, Wilderson reads Spillers's essay "Mama's Baby, Papa's Maybe" to be maintaining that slavery "'advances' from a word which describes a condition that anyone can be subjected to, to a word which reconfigures the African body into Black flesh" (*Red, White & Black*, 18). Consequently, it is precisely the capacity of semiosis to achieve any significant intervention that he disputes, postulating that "emancipation through some form of discursive or symbolic intervention [such as pattin' Juba or Buzzard dance] is wanting in the face of a subject position that is not a subject position.... In other words, the Black has *sentient* capacity but no *relational* capacity" (*Red, White & Black*, 56). Granted, the position from which the Negro slave executes his or her art, circumscribed as it is by the teleology of racialized capitalist slavery, is not the subject position purported in bourgeoisie individuation, or even that which is recognizable as its proletarian counterpoint. Those, however, are not the only possibilities, not even conceivably, of individuation and subjective conscious. This is a principal point I have sought to exposit in my reading of Du Bois's "Of the Coming of John" in the 1st Set. It is also the point here, in my account of contesting semiosis. In other words, the heterologous fleshly sentient capacity persistently energized in semiosis *is* a relational capacity. It is the fundamental capacity of sociality.
62 Giorgio Agamben, *Homo Sacer*, 109.
63 See 1 Kings 19:18: "I have reserved to myself seven thousand men, who have not bowed the knee to the image of Baal"; Isaiah 10:22: "Though the number of the Israelites be like the sand by the sea, only the remnant will be saved"; and Romans 11:5: "In the same way then, there has also come to be at the present time a remnant according to God's gracious choice."

Poiēsis in Black

1 W. E. B. Du Bois to Roland Barton, March 1928, in *W. E. B. Du Bois: Writings*, 1221.
2 Du Bois to Barton, 1221.
3 Du Bois to Barton, 1221.
4 Du Bois, *Souls*, 359.
5 W. E. B. Du Bois, "The Conservation of Races," in *W. E. B. Du Bois: Writings*, 820.
6 Du Bois, "The Conservation of Races," 820.
7 Du Bois, "Pan-Africa and New Racial Philosophy," 247.
8 Du Bois to Barton, 1221.
9 Du Bois to Barton, 1221.

10 Du Bois to Barton, 1221.
11 See Peirce, "Some Consequences of Four Incapacities," 147.
12 On the distinction between the factitious thinkable (*pensabili fattizi*) and the necessary universal thinkable (*pensabili universali necessari*), see Bernardino Varisco, *I massimi problemi*, 318–319.
13 See, for instance, Peirce, "A Large Number of Repetition," 145–147.
14 Laertius, *Lives of Eminent Philosophers*, 2:658.
15 Laertius, *Lives*, 2:658.
16 Du Bois, "Sociology Hesitant," 42.
17 Du Bois to Aptheker, *Correspondence*, 395.
18 For a full list of the published paper topics from 1896 to 1914, see W. E. B. Du Bois, "My Evolving Program for Negro Freedom," in *What the Negro Wants*, 45–53. See also Elliott M. Rudwick, "W. E. B. Du Bois and the Atlanta University Studies on the Negro."
19 Du Bois, "My Evolving Program for Negro Freedom," 49.
20 Schmoller was a prominent late nineteenth-century German economist and the chief proponent of the "younger historical school of economics," a designation he coined in response to Carl Menger's 1883 book, *Untersuchungen über die Methode der Socialwissenschaften und der politischen Oekonomie insbesondere* (*Social Sciences with Special Reference to Economics*), which attacked the inductive method of economics being promoted in the work of Wilhelm Georg Friedrich Roscher and Bruno Hildebrand, "the older historical school." Menger was the leading proponent in Germany of the neoclassical economic methodology of philosophical logic, working from axiomatic first principles deduced from universals, which Schmoller characterized derisively as the rather provincial "Austrian school of economics." The younger historical school was ardent in its utilization of inductive analysis of cultural tendencies as key elements of economic analysis. Menger's retort in his 1844 pamphlet, *Die Irrthümer des Historismus in der deutschen Nationalökonomie* [The Errors of Historicism in German Economics], inaugurated a ferocious intellectual dispute that came to be known as the *Methodenstreit* (methodological dispute), which was fundamentally about the capacity of any science to satisfactorily explain the dynamics of human action. The *Methodenstreit* dispute was the academic front in the political struggle between monarchism, advocated by Menger, and welfare-statism, advocated by Schmoller, who was a leading *Sozialpolitiker* (social policy advocate). It reached its crescendo while Du Bois was a student in Berlin.
21 Du Bois, "My Evolving Program for Negro Freedom," 127.
22 Du Bois to Aptheker, *Correspondence*, 395.
23 Du Bois, "The Renaissance of Ethics," 1.
24 Du Bois, "The Renaissance of Ethics," 36.
25 Du Bois, "The Renaissance of Ethics," 30.
26 Du Bois, "The Renaissance of Ethics," 30–35.
27 Martineau, *A Study of Religion*, 1: xii, 1, 3, 15–21.
28 Martineau, *A Study of Religion*, 1:137.
29 Martineau, *A Study of Religion*, 1:x.

30 Du Bois, *Philosophy IV Notebook*. The University of Massachusetts Amherst library dates the note book as circa 1889, as suggested by the heading on its first page, which states, "2nd Half-Year."
31 Du Bois to Aptheker, *Correspondence*, 394. Reverend Erastus Milo Cravath was a field secretary with the American Missionary Association, an abolitionist organization active in establishing field schools in contraband camps throughout the south during the war. Postbellum, the AMA established eleven Negro colleges and universities, the Fisk Free Colored School in Nashville, Tennessee, being one. Others included Atlanta University, Hampton Institute, Tougaloo College, and Howard University. Having founded Fisk with Reverend Edward Parmelee Smith and John Ogden in 1866, after its incorporation as Fisk University in August 1867, Cravath served as its president from 1875 until 1900.
32 Du Bois, "The Renaissance of Ethics," 52.
33 Du Bois, "The Renaissance of Ethics," 27.
34 Peirce, "The Pragmatic Maxim," in *Collected Papers*, 5:317. Peirce gave many formulations of this maxim, this being perhaps the simplest. Its most frequently cited formulation is the first one he gave in 1878 in *Popular Science Monthly*: "Consider what effects, that might conceivably have practical bearings, we conceive the object of our conception to have. Then, our conception of these effects is the whole of our conception of the object" (*Collected Papers*, 5: 258).
35 Peirce, *Collected Papers*, 5: 414.
36 Charles Sanders Peirce, "What Pragmatism Is," in *Collected Papers*, 5:289.
37 Du Bois, "The Renaissance of Ethics," 1.
38 Du Bois, "The Renaissance of Ethics," 2, 4–5.
39 Du Bois, "The Renaissance of Ethics," 5.
40 Thomas Aquinas, *Summa Theologica*, part I, question 10, answer 3 (251).
41 Du Bois, "The Renaissance of Ethics," 10–13.
42 Du Bois, "The Renaissance of Ethics," 15–16.
43 Du Bois, "The Renaissance of Ethics," 17, 25.
44 Du Bois, "The Renaissance of Ethics," 7.
45 Du Bois, "The Renaissance of Ethics," 6.
46 Bacon, *Advancement of Learning*, 8:512.
47 Jean Marie Frédéric LaPorte pointed out the teleological aspect of Meditation Six in his *Le rationalisme de Descartes*. Some thirty-one years later, Peter Machamer noted what he calls a global teleology throughout Descartes's work, in his "Causality and Explanation in Descartes's Natural Philosophy." More recently, Alison Simmons has provided a compelling, albeit contested, reading of Meditation Six in "Sensible Ends: Latent Teleology in Descartes's Account of Sensation."
48 Du Bois, "The Renaissance of Ethics," 15.
49 Du Bois, "The Renaissance of Ethics," 26–27.
50 Du Bois, "The Renaissance of Ethics," 26–27.
51 Du Bois, "The Renaissance of Ethics," 26–27.
52 Du Bois, "The Renaissance of Ethics," 26–27.
53 Du Bois, "The Renaissance of Ethics," 26–27.
54 Du Bois, "The Renaissance of Ethics," 26–27.

55 Royce, *The Problem of Christianity*, 14. Martineau's *A Study of Religion* was one of the few books he took with him on his sabbatical voyage to Australia.
56 Du Bois, "My Evolving Program," 75.
57 Du Bois, *Philosophy IV Notebook*, 7.
58 James, "Royce's *Religious Aspect of Philosophy*," 840.
59 James, "Royce's *Religious Aspect of Philosophy*," 841.
60 James, "Royce's *Religious Aspect of Philosophy*," 842.
61 See Ralph Waldo Emerson, "Essay IX. The Over-Soul," in *Emerson: Essays and Lectures*, 383–400.
62 James, "Royce's *Religious Aspect of Philosophy*," 842.
63 James, "Royce's *Religious Aspect of Philosophy*," 842.
64 James, "Royce's *Religious Aspect of Philosophy*," 842.
65 James, "Royce's *Religious Aspect of Philosophy*," 842.
66 Martineau, *A Study of Religion*, 202.
67 Martineau, *A Study of Religion*, 202.
68 Martineau, *A Study of Religion*, 203.
69 Royce, *The Religious Aspect of Philosophy*, 140–41.
70 Martineau, *A Study of Religion*, 204–05.
71 Royce, *The Religious Aspect of Philosophy*, 133.
72 Royce, *The Religious Aspect of Philosophy*, 133.
73 Royce, *The Religious Aspect of Philosophy*, 134.
74 Royce, *The Religious Aspect of Philosophy*, 134.
75 Royce, *The Religious Aspect of Philosophy*, 134.
76 Royce, *The Religious Aspect of Philosophy*, 134.
77 Royce, *The Religious Aspect of Philosophy*, 134.
78 Royce, *The Religious Aspect of Philosophy*, 136.
79 Royce, *The Religious Aspect of Philosophy*, 137.
80 Royce, *The Religious Aspect of Philosophy*, 138.
81 Royce, *The Religious Aspect of Philosophy*, 139.
82 Royce, *The Religious Aspect of Philosophy*, 140–41.
83 Martineau, *A Study of Religion*, 205.
84 Martineau, *A Study of Religion*, 206.
85 Martineau, *A Study of Religion*, 206.
86 Royce, *The Religious Aspect of Philosophy*, 189. Royce, meaning to quote from line 400, where The Earth speaks on humanity, gives the following:

> *One undivided soul of many a soul*
> *Whose nature is its own divine control,*
> *Where all things flow to all, as rivers to the sea.*

The line in Shelley's play reads:

> *Man one harmonious soul of many a soul*
> *Whose nature is its own divine control,*
> *Where all things flow to all, as rivers to the sea.*

Percy Bysshe Shelley, *Prometheus Unbound*, in *The Complete Poetical Works of Percy Bysshe Shelley*, 4:259.

87 Martineau, *A Study of Religion*, 212.
88 Martineau, *A Study of Religion*, 212. The quotation, which Martineau cites, is from page 377 in Royce, *The Religious Aspect of Philosophy*.
89 Royce, *The Religious Aspect of Philosophy*, 377; Martineau, *A Study of Religion*, 213.
90 Martineau, *A Study of Religion*, 213.
91 Royce, *The Religious Aspect of Philosophy*, 422.
92 Du Bois, *Philosophy IV Notebook*, 9.
93 Royce, *The Religious Aspect of Philosophy*, 422.
94 Du Bois, *Philosophy IV Notebook*, 9.
95 Martineau, *A Study of Religion*, 213.
96 Royce, *The Religious Aspect of Philosophy*, 476.
97 Du Bois, "Lesson III," *Philosophy IV Notebook*, 4.
98 Du Bois, "Lesson V," *Philosophy IV Notebook*, 5.
99 Du Bois, "Lesson V," *Philosophy IV Notebook*, 5. See Alois Riehl, *Der Philosophische Kritizismus und seine Bedeutung für die positive Wissenschaft* (Leipzig: Engelmann Verlag, 1876).
100 "The Will to Interpret" is the title of Lecture XII in *The Problem of Christianity*, in which Royce draws heavily from Peirce's semiotics, particularly his 1868 essays, "Questions Concerning Some Faculties Claimed for Man" and "Some Consequences of Four Incapacities," to formulate out of the Pauline gospel of divine love, a theory of community as an activity of teleological semiosis (167–291).
101 Du Bois, "The Renaissance of Ethics," 39.
102 Quintilian, *Institutio Oratoria*, 356, 357.
103 Cicero, "Pro Roscio Amernio," 146.
104 Friedrich Nietzsche, *Genealogy of Morals*, in *The Works of Friedrich Nietzsche*, 478.
105 Homer, *Iliad*, 13.237–239.
106 Homer, *Iliad*, 1.131.
107 Homer, *Iliad*, 14.113.
108 Homer, *Iliad*, 24.384.
109 Plato, *Meno*, 71e.
110 Plato, *The Republic*, 5.455d9.
111 Plato, "Ὅροι [Horoi] (Définitions)," 164. This is a critical edition of the extant Greek text brought out in the *Omnia Platonis Opera*, complied by Aldus Manutius in 1513, with a French translation. The entry for εὐδιμονία (*eudaimonia*) is rendered as "Bonheur: bien compose de tous les biens; ressources pleinement suffisantes pour bien vivre; perfection dans la vertu; pour un être vivant, avoir ce qu'il lui faut pour se suffire [Happiness: the good composed of all good; sufficient resources to live well; perfection in virtue; for a living being to have that which suffices]." The attached footnote states: "Ces diverses notions très probablement empruntées à la sagesse populaire, ont été adoptées par les écoles socratique et platonicienne, puis synthétisées par Aristote" [These diverse notions, most likely taken from conventional wisdom, were adopted by the Socratic and Platonic schools, and further systematized by Aristotle]. It is not inconsequential to our considerations here that Gauthier and Jolif have demonstrated that Plato's *eudaimonia* connotes an activity. See Aristoteles, *L'ethique a Nicomaque*, commentaire Gauthier and Jolif, 2:66.

112 Plato, *The Republic*, 6.508e.
113 Aristotle, *Nicomachean Ethics* 1.5.1096a, 1096b13.
114 Aristotle, *Nicomachean Ethics*, 1.1.1094a1.
115 Aristotle, *Nicomachean Ethics*, 1.8.1097b10.
116 Aristotle, *Nicomachean Ethics*, 1.7.1097b10.
117 Aristotle, *Nicomachean Ethics*, 1.7.1098b2.
118 Aristotle, *Politics*, 1.2.1254a29–31.
119 Aristotle, *Politics*, 1.2.1254b4–10.
120 Aristotle, *Nicomachean Ethics*, 1.7.1098a1.
121 Aristotle, *Nicomachean Ethics*, 1.13.1102b1.
122 Aristotle, *Nicomachean Ethics*, 1.13.1102b1.
123 Aristotle, *Nicomachean Ethics*, 1.13.1103a1.
124 Aristotle, *Nicomachean Ethics*, 1.13.1103a19.
125 Aristotle, *Nicomachean Ethics*, 1.7.1098a15.
126 Aristotle, *Nicomachean Ethics*, 1.7.1098a15.
127 Aristotle, *Nicomachean Ethics*, 1.1.1094a23, 1.1.1095a21.
128 Aristotle, *Nicomachean Ethics*, 1.1.1095a21.
129 Aristotle, *Nicomachean Ethics*, 1.3.fn. a.
130 Aristotle, *Nicomachean Ethics*, 1.3.1095a8.
131 Aristotle, *Nicomachean Ethics*, 1.5.1095b1–6.
132 Aristotle, *Nicomachean Ethics*, 1.5.1095b1–6.
133 Aristotle, *Nicomachean Ethics*, 1.13.1103a5–6.
134 Aristotle, *Nicomachean Ethics*, 1.13.1103a7–10.
135 Aristotle, *Nicomachean Ethics*, 2.1.1103a15.
136 Aristotle, *Nicomachean Ethics*, 2.1.1103a30.
137 Aristotle, *Nicomachean Ethics*, 2.1.1103b25.
138 Aristotle, *Nicomachean Ethics*, 2.1.1103b30.
139 Aristotle, *Politics*, 1.1.1252a1–5.
140 Aristotle, *Nicomachean Ethics*, 2.1.1103b6.
141 Aristotle, *Nicomachean Ethics*, 4.1.1138b5.
142 Aristotle, *Nicomachean Ethics*, 2.1.1103b30.
143 Aristotle, *Nicomachean Ethics*, 2.1.1103b30.
144 Aristotle, *Nicomachean Ethics*, 2.1.1104a4–5.
145 Aristotle, *Nicomachean Ethics*, 6.1.1138b5.
146 Aristotle, *Nicomachean Ethics*, 6.3.1139b4.
147 Aristotle, *Nicomachean Ethics*, 6.7.
148 Aristotle, *Nicomachean Ethics*, 6.3.1140a1–2.
149 Aristotle, *Nicomachean Ethics*, 6.4.1140a24–25.
150 Aristotle, *Nicomachean Ethics*, 6.8.1142a30.
151 Aristotle, *Nicomachean Ethics*, 6.5.1140b30.
152 Aristotle, *Nicomachean Ethics*, 6.7.1144a6.
153 Aristotle, *Politics*, 4.5.1293b1–5.
154 Aristotle, *Politics*, 4.6.1294a10.
155 Aristotle, *Politics*, 4.5.1293b15–16.
156 Aristotle, *Politics*, 1.2.1260a20–29.
157 Aristotle, *Politics*, 1.5.1259b21–29.

158 Aristotle, *Politics*, 1.2.1254a14–18, 1256b29–30.
159 Aristotle, *Politics*, 1.1.1252b9.
160 Aristotle, *Politics*, 1.5.1259b1.
161 Aristotle, *Nicomachean Ethics*, 2.6.1106a25.
162 Aristotle, *Nicomachean Ethics*, 2.6.1106b30.
163 Aristotle, *Nicomachean Ethics*, 2.9.1109a20–25.
164 "ἔφη δὲ τὸν σοφὸν ἀπαθῆ μὲν μὴ εἶναι μετριοπαθῆ δε [*Ephē de ton sophon apathē men má einai metriopathē de*] [He said too that the wise man was not exempt from all passions, but indulged them in moderation]" (Laertius, *Lives*, 478/479).
165 Aristotle, *Nicomachean Ethics*, 2.2.1104a7.
166 Aristotle, *Nicomachean Ethics*, 2.2.1104a7.
167 Aristotle, *Politics*, 3.2.1277a1, 1277b8.
168 Bruce A. Kimball, "'This Pitiable Rejection of a Great Opportunity,'" 5–20.
169 Kimball, "'This Pitiable Rejection,'" 14.
170 W. E. B. Du Bois, "Jefferson Davis as a Representative of Civilization," in *W. E. B. Du Bois: Writings*, 811.
171 Du Bois, "Jefferson Davis," 811.
172 Du Bois "Jefferson Davis," 811–812.
173 Du Bois "Jefferson Davis," 812.
174 Du Bois "Jefferson Davis," 812.
175 Du Bois "Jefferson Davis," 812.
176 Du Bois "Jefferson Davis," 812.
177 Du Bois "Jefferson Davis," 812.
178 W. E. B. Du Bois, "Of Booker T. Washington and Others," in *The Souls of Black Folk*, 396. The Stono Rebellion, also known as Cato's Rebellion, began on Sunday, September 9, 1739, at a bridge over the Stono River, southwest of Charles Town (now Charleston), South Carolina. It began with twenty enslaved Africans, most of whom were Kikongo speakers from the Kingdom of Kongo, located in the Angola region, led by a man identified in the official colony record as the "Angolan 'captain,' Jemmy," but who was known among his compatriots and descendants as Cato. When measured by the proportion of whites killed to that of blacks—thirty blacks and twenty-five whites—it was the bloodiest slave revolt in the English colonies. In its aftermath, South Carolina passed the Negro Act of 1740, severely restricting the ratio of blacks to whites on plantations, limiting the assembly of blacks, and abolishing drumming, which was construed as ancillary to weapons. For more historical detail, see Peter H. Wood, *Black Majority*, and Mark Smith, ed., *Stono*.
179 Du Bois, "Jefferson Davis," 813.
180 Du Bois, "Jefferson Davis," 813.
181 Du Bois, "Jefferson Davis," 813.
182 Du Bois, "Jefferson Davis," 812.
183 Du Bois, "Jefferson Davis," 812.
184 Du Bois, "Jefferson Davis," 813.
185 Du Bois, "Jefferson Davis," 813.

186 Zamir, *Dark Voices*, 64. Zamir provides an extensive analysis of the Hegelianism in Du Bois's writings from 1888 to 1903, within which he reads Du Bois's 1888 Fisk University commencement speech, as well as the 1890 Harvard commencement speech. Joel Williamson was an earlier proponent of Du Bois's Hegelianism. See Joel Williamson, "W.E.B. DuBois as a Hegelian," in *What Was Freedom's Price?*, ed. David G. Sansing (Jackson: University Press of Mississippi, 1978), 41. Russell Berman, in the already cited essay "Du Bois and Wagner," declares the Harvard commencement address to be "Hegelian through and through" (123–124). Robert Gooding-Williams also situates Du Bois within a Hegelian line of thought. See Robert Gooding-Williams, "Philosophy of History and Social Critique in *The Souls of Black Folk*"; also see his "Evading Narrative Myth, Evading Prophetic Pragmatism: Cornel West's 'The American Evasion of Philosophy.'" Along these lines, also see Winfried Siemerling, "W. E. B. Du Bois, Hegel, and the Staging of Alterity." Perhaps one of the more extensive readings of Du Bois as Hegelian is Stephanie Shaw's book *W. E. B. Du Bois and "The Souls of Black Folk"* (Chapel Hill: University of North Carolina Press, 2013).

187 See Berman, "Du Bois and Wagner," 123. Regarding the translation of the *Herrschaft und Knechtschaft* dialectic, Kojève was the first in the French reception of Hegel to render it as "Maître et Esclave [Master and Slave]"; and in so doing, he went against the grain of both French and Anglophone reception of Hegel's work. See Alexandre Kojève, *Introduction à la Lecture de Hegel*. The first French translation of Hegel's *Phänomenologie des Geistes*, Augusto Véra's seriously flawed *Philosophie de l'esprit de Hegel*, rendered "Herrschaft und Knechtschaft" as "domination et servitude," That is also how Kojève's comparably influential contemporary, Jean Hyppolite, gives it in his 1941 translation, and *La phénoménologie de l'esprit*. By comparison, the first English-language translation of the *Phänomenologie des Geistes* by James Black Baille, *The Phenomenology of Mind*, which antedates Kojève's interpretation by twenty-three years, renders "Herrschaft und Knechtschaft" as "Lordship and Bondage." A. V. Miller follows suit in his 1977 translation, *Phenomenology of Spirit*. Terry Pinkard, in his recent translation of the *Phänomenologie*, however, renders it as "Mastery and Servitude," and Michael Inwood, revising Miller's translation, gives it as "mastery and bondage." Kojève, of course, gave the first of his annual lectures on the *Phenomenology* in 1933, and continued to do so through to 1939, and it was not until 1947 that they were gathered and published in a volume edited by Raymond Queneau. This was forty-three years after Du Bois gave his Harvard commencement address, and so has no bearing on how he might have possibly construed the dialectic. So too for the Baille translation, which appeared in 1910. Again, Du Bois read Hegel in German, and so to the extent he was concerned with the *Herrschaft und Knechtschaft* dialectic, it was in Hegel's terms.

188 See Robert Sullivan, *Justice and the Social Context of Early Middle High German Literature*, 74–75.

189 See Andrew Cole, *The Birth of Theory*, 69.

190 Hegel, *Grundlinien der Philosophie des Rechts*, 19. The English is from Georg Wilhelm Friedrich Hegel, *Philosophy of Right*, trans. S. W. Dyde, 3. In the original German, the passage cited here reads: "So z.B. wäre für das römische Recht

keine Definition vom Menschen möglich, denn der Sklave ließe sich darunter nicht subsumieren, in seinem Stand ist jener Begriff vielmehr verletzt."

191 Theodor Mommsen and L. Paul Krueger eds., "Liber primus, *Institutiones*," in *Corpus Iuris Civilis*, 2.

192 The full passage under consideration runs: "The alleged justification of slavery [*Sklaverei*] (in all its more detailed justifications by physical violence [*physische Gewalt*], capture in war, rescue and preservation of life, nutrition, education, well-being, personal consent, etc.), as well as the justification of domination [*Herrenschaft*] as a mere domination [*bloßer Herrenschaft*] above all, and in all the historical views on the law of slavery and domination [*das Recht der Sklaverei und der Herrenschaft*], rests on the grounds of taking man as an existent natural being (including arbitrariness), which is not appropriate to his concept" (Hegel, *Philosophie des Rechts*, 62). For some reason, Dyde elides the reference to *Herrenschaft* altogether in his translation, using only the term, "slavery" (Hegel, *Philosophy of Right*, 62). T. M. Knox also elides the reference to *Herrenschaft*, rendering Hegel's clause "die Berechtigung einer Herrschaft als bloßer Herrenschaft überhaupt" as "the justification of a slave-ownership as simple lordship in general" (Hegel, *Philosophy of Right*, trans. T. M. Knox, 48).

193 Hegel, *Philosophie des Rechts*, 62.

194 Du Bois, "Jefferson Davis," 812. Hegel makes a distinction between empirical sciences such as anatomy, which he characterizes as *Aggregate von Kenntnissen* (aggregate of information), and *Wissenschaft*, connoting science as the pure fluidity of thinking, which is what Hegel claims of the *Phänomenologie* as *Wissenschaft der Erfahrung des Bewußtseins*, "the Science of the Experience of Consciousness" (*Phänomenologie*, 36).

195 On October 13, 1806, the day Napoleon's forces occupied Jena, Hegel, having just completed the preface, in which he states that the system of science he is presenting is "analogous to ultrarevolutionary discourse and action [*ultarevolutionäre Reden und Handeln*]," wrote to Friedrich Immanuel Niethammer: "I saw the Emperor—this world-soul—riding out of the city on reconnaissance. It is indeed a wonderful sensation to see such an individual, who, concentrated here at a single point, astride a horse, reaches out over the world and masters it" (Georg Wilhelm Friedrich Hegel, *Briefe von und an Hegel*, 67–68; for the English translation, see *Hegel: The Letters*, trans. Clark Butler and Christine Seiler, 114). Regarding the identification of Hegel's system with one singular mind as the universal mind of human history, Hegel argues, of course, that the history of mind can only be told retrospectively, at its end, its *télos*, the epoch of which is the extended progress of bourgeoisie formation. Napoleon exemplifies, in a manner very much like Jefferson Davis, the Strong Man thesis of history. As Marx remarked: "The Germans have *thought* in politics what others nations have *done*. Germany has been their *theoretical conscience*" (Karl Marx, "A Contribution to the Critique of Hegel's *Philosophy of Right*: Introduction," in *Early Writings*, 250).

196 Du Bois, "Jefferson Davis," 813.

197 Edward Gibbon, *The History of the Decline and Fall of the Roman Empire*, 1:72.

198 Gibbon, *History of the Decline*, 2:261.

199 Friedrich Nietzsche, *Zur Genealogie der Moral*, in *Nietzsche-Werke: Kritische Gesamtausgabe*, Abt. 6, Bd. 2:323, §11.

200 Kathleen Marie Higgins has provided the most probative exploration of the resonances between Du Bois and Nietzsche so far, with specific regard to double consciousness, in which she reads primarily, but not exclusively, Nietzsche's *Ecce Homo* to gain "considerable insight of use to those concerned with African Americans' societal position." See Kathleen Marie Higgins's essay, "Double Consciousness and Second Sight," in *Critical Affinities*. Higgins's emphasizing Du Bois's uses of double consciousness "to illuminate concrete situations in the experience of African Americans" inclines her to lose sight of the fact that he deploys it as a figure, and then *only once* in first chapter of *The Souls of Black Folk*, and never subsequently elaborates it into a theory. Disregarding the figurality, or literariness, of "double consciousness" tends toward a positivistic and, paradoxically, abstract handling of "the experience of African Americans" along the lines of *the* African American experience. Concordantly, her construing Nietzsche's "speculations about psychological perspectives of the oppressed and of oppressors" in *On the Genealogy of Morals* as being abstracted from actual circumstance strips Nietzsche's texts of their clear references to the historiography of Gibbon as well as Lange, and his engagement with the social expression attending the political and juridical shift of tenth-century Europe. Like Hegel, he is tracking the emergence of the European in the establishment of the feudal Holy Roman Empire of the Germans. Nietzsche also famously extrapolates his theory of slave morality out of the particulars of Rome's Christianization. Nietzsche's theory of psychology types is no less grounded in historical circumstance than Du Bois's "double consciousness"; and Du Bois's "double consciousness" is no less an abstraction than Nietzsche's "slave-morality." Nevertheless, establishing the distinction between Du Bois and Nietzsche of concreteness and abstraction propels a reading of the force of Du Bois's figure for "the white reader" through an analysis of Nietzsche's technique. All said and done, Higgins maps Nietzsche onto Du Bois rather than exploring Du Bois's engagement with Nietzschean thought. That engagement is readily discernable, however, in his deployment of terms and conceptualizations utilized by both William James and Josiah Royce in their respective readings of Nietzsche. There is also the strong resonance between Du Bois and Nietzsche directly in the use of "Teutonic" under consideration here.

201 Du Bois, "Lecture Amen," *Philosophy IV Notebook*, 26–28.

202 Nietzsche, *Götzen-Dämmerung*, in *Nietzsche-Werke: Kritische Gesamtausgabe*, Abt. 6, Bd. 3:98, §6.

203 Nietzsche, *Jenseits von Gut und Böse*, in *Nietzsche-Werke: Kritische Gesamtausgabe*, Abt. 6, Bd. 2:21, §13 (211).

204 Du Bois, "The Renaissance of Ethics," 41.

205 Nietzsche, *Morgenröthe*, in *Nietzsche-Werke: Kritische Gesamtausgabe*, Abt. 5, 1:119, 115. Cf. Friedrich Nietzsche, *Daybreak, Thoughts on the Prejudices of Morality*, trans. R. J. Hollingdale (Cambridge: Cambridge University Press, 1997), 2:119, 76.

206 Nietzsche, *Jenseits von Gut und Böse*, Abt. 6, Bd. 2:61, §187.

207 Friedrich Nietzsche, Vorrede zur zweiten Ausgabe von *Die fröhliche Wissenschaft*, in *Nietzsche-Werke: Kritische Gesamtausgabe*, Abt. 52:3, §2. See also Friedrich Nietzsche, preface for the second edition of *The Gay Science*, trans. Walter Kaufmann, 34, §2.

208 Nietzsche, *Ecce Homo*, in *Nietzsche-Werke: Kritische Gesamtausgabe*, Abt. 6, Bd. 3:367, §5. The English edition is Friedrich Nietzsche, *Ecce Homo*, 94; henceforth parenthetical page citation for translation follows citation of original.

209 Nietzsche, *Zur Genealogie der Moral*, Abt. 6, Bd. 2:323, §11. Cf. Friedrich Nietzsche, *A Genealogy of Morals*, trans. William A. Hausemann, in *The Works of Friedrich Nietzsche*, 31; henceforth parenthetical page citation for translation follows citation of original.

210 Cf. Friedrich Nietzsche, "Human, All-Too-Human," in *Basic Writings of Nietzsche*, trans. Walter Kaufmann, 147.

211 Nietzsche, *Götzen-Dämmerung*, Abt. 6, Bd. 3:67, §10.

212 Nietzsche, *Der Antichrist*, in *Werke*, Abt. 6, Bd. 3:243, §58. See also Friedrich Nietzsche, *The Antichrist*, in *The Portable Nietzsche*, ed. and trans. Walter Kaufmann (New York: Penguin, 1954), 573; henceforth parenthetical page citation for translation appears in parentheses following the original.

213 For a philological analysis of this key coinage of Nietzsche's, see Duncan Large, "A Note on the Term '*Umwerthung*,'" *Journal of Nietzsche Studies*. In footnote 3, Large cites main texts in the philosophical analyses of the different senses of the phrase in Nietzsche's writings, alluding to its putative provenance in Diogenes Laertius. These include: Jörg Salaquarda, "*Umwertung aller Werte*," *Archiv für Begriffsgeschichte* 22 (1978): 154–74; Thomas H. Brobjer, *Nietzsche's Ethics of Character: A Study of Nietzsche's Ethics and Its Place in the History of Moral Thinking* (Uppsala: Uppsala University Department of History of Science and Ideas, 1995), 295–314; Thomas H. Brobjer, "On the Revaluation of Values," *Nietzsche-Studien* 25 (1996): 342–48; Andreas Urs Sommer, *Friedrich Nietzsches "Der Antichrist": Ein philosophisch-historischer Kommentar* (Basel: Schwabe, 2000), 153–159; Andreas Urs Sommer, "*Umwerthung der Werthe*," in *Nietzsche-Handbuch: Leben–Werk–Wirkung*, ed. Henning Ottmann (Stuttgart: Metzler, 2000), 345–346; Winfried Schröder, "*Umwertung aller Werte*," in *Historisches Wörterbuch der Philosophie*, vol. 11, ed. Joachim Ritter, Karlfried Gründer, and Gottfried Gabriel (Darmstadt: Wissenschaftliche Buchgesellschaft, 2001), 106–107; Kathleen Marie Higgins, "Rebaptizing Our Evil: On the Revaluation of All Values," in *A Companion to Nietzsche*, ed. Keith Ansell-Pearson (Malden, MA: Blackwell, 2006), 404–418.

214 Nietzsche, *Der Antichrist*, Abt. 6, Bd. 3:186, §21 (588).

215 The Septuagint passage is: καὶ οὐκ ἐκδικᾶταί σου ἡ χείρ καὶ οὐ μηνιεῖς τοῖς υἱοῖς τοῦ λαοῦ σου καὶ ἀγαπήσεις τὸν πλησίον σου ὡς σεαυτόν ἐγώ εἰμι κύριος

לֹא־תִקֹּם וְלֹא־תִטֹּר אֶת־בְּנֵי עַמֶּךָ וְאָהַבְתָּ לְרֵעֲךָ כָּמוֹךָ אֲנִי יְהוָה׃

The King James Version renders it: "Thou shalt not avenge, nor bear any grudge against the children of thy people, but thou shalt love thy neighbour as thyself: I *am* the LORD."

216 See Plato, *Symposium*, 209a 1–3.

217 On the distinction between *agapē* and *eros*, see Anders Nygren, *Agape and Eros*.
218 Nietzsche, *Ecce Homo*, 94, §5 (94).
219 Nietzsche states in *Jenseits von Gut und Böse*:

> The Jews have brought off that miraculous feat of an inversion of valuations [*Umkehrung der Werthe*], thanks to which life on earth has acquired a novel and dangerous attraction for a couple of millennia: their prophets fused "rich," "godless," "wicked" [*böse*], "violent," and "sensual" into one, and were the first to use the word "world" ["*Welt*"] as an opprobrium. (Abt. 6, Bd. 2:195 [298])

220 Nietzsche, *Zur Genealogie*, Abt. 6, Bd. 2:323, §11.
221 Nietzsche, *Der Antichrist*, Abt. 6, Bd. 3:187, §22 (589).
222 Nietzsche, *Der Antichrist*, Abt. 6, Bd. 3:187, §22 (589).
223 Nietzsche, *Der Antichrist*, Abt. 6, Bd. 3:187, §22 (589).
224 Nietzsche, *Der Antichrist*, Abt. 6, Bd. 3:200, §31 (603).
225 Nietzsche, *Der Antichrist*, Abt. 6, Bd. 3:197, §29 (600).
226 Friedrich Nietzsche, "Homer's Wettkampf," *Fünf Vorreden zu fünf ungeschriebenen Büchern*, in *Nietzsche-Werke: Kritische Gesamtausgabe*, Abt. 3, Bd. 2:249.
227 Du Bois, "Jefferson Davis," 813; Nietzsche, "Homer's Wettkampf," Abt. 3, Bd. 2:249.
228 Nietzsche, "Homer's Wettkampf," Abt. 3, Bd. 2:291.
229 Nietzsche, "Homer's Wettkampf," Abt. 3, Bd. 2:249.
230 Nietzsche, *Jenseits von Gut und Böse*, Abt. 6, Bd. 2:166, §229 (349).
231 Friedrich Nietzsche, *Die Geburt der Tragödie*, in *Nietzsche-Werke: Kritische Gesamtausgabe*, Abt. 3, Bd. 1:5, §2. Cf. Friedrich Nietzsche, *The Birth of Tragedy*, in *Basic Writings of Nietzsche*, trans. Walter, 39, 72; henceforth parenthetical page citation of translation follows that of the original."
232 Nietzsche, *Die Geburt der Tragödie*, Abt. 3, Bd. 1:1, §1 (37). Regarding "the veil of *Māyā*," Nietzsche is referring to Schopenhauer's allusion to the Vedic figure for illusion and magic in his *Welt als Wille und Vorstellung* (*The World as Will and Representation*). Schopenhauer uses it to connote the conceptual power or principle that conceals the true nature of reality: "Rather, the view of the uncultured individual is clouded by, as the Indians say, the veil of *Māyā*: instead of the thing-in-itself, what is revealed is only the phenomenon in time and space, in the *principium individuationis*, and in the remaining forms of the principle of sufficient reason. And in this form of his limited knowledge [*Erkenntniß*], he does not see the essence of things [*Wesen der Dinge*], which is one, but its phenomena as separated, detached, innumerable, acutely differentiated, indeed in opposition" (Schopenhauer, *Welt als Wille und Vorstellung* 1:4, §63). Cf. Schopenhauer, *The World as Will and Representation*, trans. E. F. Payne and J. Kemp, 1:352.
233 Nietzsche, *Die Geburt der Tragödie*, Abt.3, Bd. 1:1, §1 (35–36). Nietzsche quotes the first two clauses of Schopenhauer's statement as: "Wie auf dem tobenden Meere, das, nach allen Seiten unbegränzt, heulend Wellenberge erhebt und senkt, auf einem Kahn ein Schiffer sitzt, dem schwachen Fahrzeug vertrauend; so sitzt, mitten in einer Welt von Qualen, ruhig der einzelne Mensch, gestützt und

vertrauend auf das *principium individuationis*." Kaufmann's translation of this has been given in the main body of the text here. The passage from Schopenhauer warrants being quoted in full in light of its centrality to Nietzsche's concept of the Apollonian:

> Just as in a stormy sea that, boundlessly, raises and falls on all sides in howling mountains of water, a sailor sits in a boat trusting his frail vessel; so in the midst of a world full of agony, the individual sits calmly supported and trusting in the *principium individuationis*, or the way the individual recognizes things as phenomena. The boundless world, full of suffering everywhere, in an infinite past and future, is alien to him, indeed, is to him but a tale [*ein Märchen*] to him: his ephemeral person, his extensionless [*ausdehnungslose*] present, his momentary satisfaction, this alone has reality for him. (*Welt als Wille und Vorstellung*, 1:4, §63; *The World as Will and Representation*, 352–53)

234 Nietzsche, *Die Geburt der Tragödie*, Abt. 3, Bd. 1:6, §4 (46).
235 Nietzsche, *Die Geburt der Tragödie*, Abt. 3, Bd. 1:6, §4 (46).
236 *Nietzsche, Zur Genealogie*, II: 5 (500).
237 *Nietzsche, Zur Genealogie*, II: 6 (503–504).
238 *Nietzsche, Zur Genealogie*, II: 6 (503–504). Indeed, this is his only reference to the Negro, repeating its gist once more in *Nachgelassene Fragmente Sommer-Herbst 1882*, in *Nietzsche-Werke: Kritische Gesamtausgabe*, NF-1882, 3[1].
239 Du Bois, "Jefferson Davis," 812.
240 See Cedric Robinson, *The Terms of Order*, 196. The Tonga word Robinson is concerned with, *mukowa*, has two parallel connotations: a group of matrilineally related kin, and more inclusively, a clan of matrilineal descent. The context for his concern is anarchy, and exploring the possibility that the Tonga conceptualization and practice can provide material for a viable theory of anarchy.
241 Du Bois is being ironic. The German phrase "Ich Dein" (I serve) was adopted by the Black Prince, Edward Prince of Wales, as his motto, along with the crest of ostrich feathers after the battle of Crécy in 1346, from John of Luxembourg, King of Bohemia, who was killed in the battle. See Elizabeth Knowles, "Ich Dien," *The Oxford Dictionary of Phrase and Fable* (Oxford: Oxford University Press, 2006).
242 Du Bois, "Jefferson Davis," 813.
243 See Michel Foucault, "Il faut défendre la société," *Cours au Collège de France (1975–1976)*, 83.
244 Du Bois, "Jefferson Davis," 813.
245 See Hannah Arendt, *The Origins of Totalitarianism* (New York: Harcourt Brace Jovanovich, 1951); *The Human Condition* (Chicago: University of Chicago Press, 1958); and *Between Past and Future* (New York: Viking, 1961).
246 Du Bois, "Jefferson Davis," 813.
247 Du Bois, "Jefferson Davis," 813.
248 Du Bois, "Jefferson Davis," 813.

249 Wilson Jeremiah Moses, "Du Bois's *Dark Princess* and the Heroic Uncle Tom," in *Black Messiahs and Uncle Toms*, 142–143.
250 Du Bois, "On the Faith of the Fathers," *Souls of Black Folk*, 500.

Para-Semiosis

1 Nahum Chandler, "The Problem of the Centuries: A Contemporary Elaboration of 'The Present Outlook for the Dark Races of Mankind,' circa the 27th of December 1899" (unpublished manuscript, February 2006), 40.
2 Chandler, "The Problem of the Centuries," 40fn30.
3 Chandler, "The Problem of the Centuries," 41.
4 See Hortense Spillers, "The Crisis of the Negro Intellectual: A Post-Date."
5 Chandler, "The Problem of the Centuries," 40.
6 Chandler, "The Problem of the Centuries," 41.
7 Chandler, "The Problem of the Centuries," 41.
8 Fred Moten, "Blackness and Nothingness (Mysticism in the Flesh)," 741–742.
9 Chandler, "The Problem of the Centuries," 40.
10 Lacan, "L'amour et le signifiant," in *Le séminaire de Jacques Lacan*, 20:44.
11 Lorenzo Chiesa, "Towards a New Philosophical-Psychoanalytic Materialism and Realism," 9.
12 Lacan, "L'amour et le signifiant," 44.
13 Jacques Lacan, "La fonction de l'écrit," in *Le séminaire de Jacques Lacan*, 20:33.
14 Jacques Lacan, *Le séminaire de Jacques Lacan*, 17:178, 70–71.
15 Lacan, "La fonction de l'écrit," 33.
16 Lacan, "La fonction de l'écrit," 33.
17 Lacan, "L'amour et le signifiant," 44.
18 Lacan, "L'amour et le signifiant," 44.
19 Lacan, "L'amour et le signifiant," 44.
20 Lacan, "L'amour et le signifiant," 45–46.
21 Lacan, "La fonction de l'écrit," 28.
22 Dedekind, "Was sind und was sollen die Zahlen?," 3:344, §1.1–2.
23 Lacan, "L'amour et le signifiant," 47.
24 Lacan, "L'amour et le signifiant," 44.
25 See John Milbank, "The Double Glory, or Paradox versus Dialectics: On Not Quite Agreeing with Slavoj Žižek," in *The Monstrosity of Christ Paradox or Dialectic?*, ed. Creston Davis (Cambridge, MA: MIT Press, 2009), 118.
26 Jacques Lacan, *Le séminaire de Jacques Lacan*, 7:16.
27 Lacan, "L'amour et le signifiant," 44.
28 See Jacques Alain Miller, "La suture (éléments de la logique du signifiant)," 39.
29 Miller, "La suture," 44. Recall from our previous discussion of Frege's *Grundlagen der Arithmetik* that number is identical (*gleichzahlig*) to concept, which is of the non-spatio-temporal third realm; it is an extension (*Umfang*) of the concept, which is what determines is objective existence (*Gegenstand*). Accordingly, with respect to the number 0, its meaning comes from its difference to the thing in the objective third realm it stands in for—the concept of the thing not identical

to itself. As the extension of this concept, o marks the nothing there, it stands in for a void; and it is in that sense Miller states o is written "merely in order to figure a blank, to render visible the lack. From the zero lack [*zéro acani*] to the zero number [*zéro nombre*], the non-conceptualizable is conceptualized" (44).

30 Jacques Lacan, "L'étourdit." The essay title is a Lacanianism derived from the substantive of the adjective *étourdi*, meaning dazed, bewildered, or stupefied. Jack Stone points out in the notes to his English-language translation that Lacan's additional "t" allows the title to be read as *Le tour dit*: "The said turn." Alain Badiou critically engages Lacan's investment in formula in his "Formules de l'Étourdit," in *Il n'y a pas de rapport sexuel: Deux leçons sur L'étourdit de Lacan*, 101–136.
31 Lacan, "L'étourdit," 47.
32 Lacan, "L'étourdit," 5.
33 Lacan, "L'étourdit," 5.
34 Lacan, "L'étourdit," 6.
35 Lacan, "L'étourdit," 6.
36 Lacan, "L'étourdit," 6.
37 Heidegger, *Sein und Zeit*, §34, 62. Our principal concern here is Oskar Becker's engagement with Heidegger's work in his elaboration of "paraontology," and his references are to this volume of the *Jahrbuch*. The translations are mine throughout, although I have paid close attention to the translation by John Macquarrie and Edward Robinson, which has become authoritative in English-language Heidegger scholarship, as well as the subsequent one by Joan Stambaugh, both of which are based on the 1953 seventh edition of *Sein und Zeit*. See Martin Heidegger, *Being and Time*, trans. John Macquarrie and Edward Robinson; Martin Heidegger, *Being and Time*, trans. Joan Stambaugh.
38 Heidegger, *Einführung in die Metaphysik*, 46.
39 Heidegger, *Sein und Zeit*, §7, 33.
40 Heidegger, *Sein und Zeit*, §44, 219.
41 Lacan, "L'étourdit," 7.
42 Heidegger, *Sein und Zeit*, §44, 220.
43 Heidegger, *Sein und Zeit*, §44, 219–220.
44 Heidegger, *Sein und Zeit*, §44, 219–220. While the study of entities is traceable from Parmenides's Pre-Socratic poem (ca. fifth century B.C.E.; see fragment II), and subsequently given systematic coherence with Aristotle, and even though the designation "ontology" has a Greek etymology, the earliest extant record of the term, Latinized as *ontologia*, is in Jacob Lorhard's eight-volume 1606 work, the full title of which is *Ogdoas Scholastica, Continens Diagraphen Typicam Artium: Grammatices (Latinae, Graecae), Logices, Rhetorices, Astronomices, Ethices, Physices, Metaphysices, Seu Ontologiae*. Rudolf Göckel then gives it in Greek characters, οντολογία, in his 1613 *Lexicon Philosophicum Quo Tanquam Clave Philosophiae Fores Aperiuntur*. Thereafter, *ontologia* is in relatively regular circulation well before Johannes Clauberg, whom Heidegger credits with its coinage, uses it in his 1647 *Elementa Philosophiae Seu Ontosophia. Scientia Prima, De Iis Quae Deo Creaturisque Suo Modo Communiter Attribuuntur, Distincta Partibus Quatuo*. Perhaps Heidegger's attribution is due to the frequency with which

Clauberg uses the term in his subsequent work: *Ontosophia Nova, Quae Vulgo Metaphysica, Theologiae, Iurisprudentiae Et Philologiae, Praesertim Germanicae Studiosis Accomodata. Accessit Logica Contracta, Et Quae Ex Ea Demonstratur Orthographia Germanica* (1660); and *Metaphysica De Ente, Quae Rectius Ontosophia* (1664). In fact, the term Clauberg coined as equivalent with *ontologia* was *Ontosophia*. *Ontologia* was well established as a philosophical term of art by the time Christian Wolf wrote his *Philosophia prima sive ontologia methodo scientifica pertractata qua omnis cognitionis humanae principia continentur* (First Philosophy or Ontology) in 1730. The first occurrence of the Latin term *ontologia* in a German-language work is in a 1675 novel attributed to the poet Christian Weise writing under the pseudonym Catharinum Civilem: "Denn durch die PHILOSOPHIE wird allhier nicht eine DISPUTATION aus der ONTOLOGIA verstanden sondern die rechte PHILOSOPHIA PRACTICA, welche sich in dem Lichte der Natur und in denen Menschlichen Verrichtungen umbsiehet und dannen hero einen festen Grund der unverfälschten Klugheit gestellet hat. [Because PHILOSOPHY is not understood here as a DISPUTATION from ONTOLOGIA but as the right PHILOSOPHIA PRACTICA, which itself encompasses the light of nature and human activities, and so [our] hero has shared a firm ground of genuine prudence]" (Christian Weise, *Die drey Klügsten Leute in der gantzen Welt*, in *Sämtliche Werke*, 18:112).

45 Heidegger, *Sein und Zeit*, §44, 219–220. Emphasis in the original.
46 Heidegger, "Vom Wesen des Grundes," 123. The essay was written in 1928, and was first published in 1929 in *Jahrbuch für Philosophie und Phänomenologische Forschung* as part of the Festschrift Heidegger edited commemorating Husserl on his seventieth birthday. See Martin Heidegger, "Vom Wesen des Grundes," Ergänzungsband zum *Jahrbuch für Philosophie und Phänomenologische Forschung* (Halle: Niemeyer, 1929), 71–100. It saw four subsequent editions. The second was in 1931, and the third was published in 1949 by Vittorio Klostermann, with a preface written by Heidegger. The fourth edition, which Klostermann also published, appeared in 1955. It then appeared in the anthology of Heidegger essays published by Klostermann in 1967 as *Wegmarken*. This became the ninth volume of the *Gesamtausgabe* published by Klostermann in 1976, which is the edition cited herein. Heidegger says in the third edition preface that "Vom Wesen des Grundes," was written expressly to investigate *ontological difference*. He wrote at the same time the lecture, "Was ist Metaphysik?" ("What Is Metaphysics?"), to consider the problem of nothingness (*das Nicht*).
47 Heidegger, "Vom Wesen des Grundes," 132.
48 Heidegger, *Sein und Zeit*, §4, 14.
49 Heidegger, *Sein und Zeit*, §6, 22.
50 Regarding the traditional ontological term *existentia*, Suárez writes under the heading, *Conditiones necessariae ut forma causet* (Necessary Conditions of Formal Causation): "Actualis existentia.—Quoad secundum, de conditionibus necessariis ad haec causalitatem exercendam, tres videntur posse conditiones assignari. Prima est actualis existentia ipsius formae, de qua diversimode sentiendum est iuxta diversas sententias de existentia creaturae et distinctione eius ab essentia." [The actual existentia: Regarding the conditions necessary for such a

causality in practice, three conditions appear to be assigned. The first is the actual existence [*existentia*] of a form itself, of which, according to different statements about the existence of a creature to be thought of in different ways, and its distinction from the essence of life] (Francisco Suárez, *Disputationes Metaphysicae*, in *Opera omina*, vol. 25, disputatio 15: 6.3). In part 2, §6, of the introduction to *Being and Time*, "The Task of Destroying the History of Ontology," Heidegger cites this work of Suárez's as a chief place along the path through which "Geek ontology travelled to the 'metaphysics' and transcendental philosophy of modern times" (*Sein und Zeit*, §6, 22).

51 Heidegger, *Sein und Zeit*, §9, 41–42.
52 Heidegger, *Sein und Zeit*, §4, 12–13, 9.
53 Heidegger, *Sein und Zeit*, §44, 220.
54 Heidegger, *Sein und Zeit*, §44, 226.
55 Becker's intellectual relationship and friendship with Heidegger dates back to 1919, when they were both Husserl's students at the University of Freiburg. They each served as his assistant—Heidegger from 1919 to 1923, at which point he went to teach at Marburg, and Becker succeeding him from 1923 to 1924. It was Husserl's expectation that the two of them would continue his phenomenological research, with Heidegger doing so in the human sciences and Becker in the natural sciences. In that vein, they edited together the *Jahrbuch für Philosophie und Phänomenologische Forschung* from 1923 to 1930. The extent of their closeness and intellectual comradery was evidenced when, upon his returning to Freiburg to succeed Husserl in 1928, Heidegger recommended Becker be his successor at Marburg. When Becker did not get the post, Heidegger secured his promotion to Außerordentlicher Professor (associate professor) at Freiburg, which Becker held until being elected as professor ordinarius of the history of mathematics at Bonn in 1931.

Emmanuel Faye erroneously identifies Becker as "one of the main students of Heidegger in the early 1920" in his book *Heidegger, l'introduction du nazisme dans la philosophie*, a work full of flaws and misconstruing (see Emmanuel Faye, *Heidegger, l'introduction du nazisme dans la philosophie*, 14, 262). Interestingly enough, Giorgio Agamben follows suit, in *L'Uso dei corpi*, mistakenly identifying Becker as "uno fra i più dotati tra I primi allievi di Heidegger [one of the most gifted of Heidegger's first students]" (*L'Uso dei corpi*, §14, 244). Dermont Moran appears to repeat this error in his otherwise careful essay, "Dasein as Transcendence in Heidegger and the Critique of Husserl," in *Heidegger in the Twenty-First Century*, ed. Tziovanis Georgakis and Paul Ennis (Dordrecht: Springer, 2015), stating: "It is noteworthy too in this context that Eugen Fink (1905–1975) and Oskar Becker (1889–1964), two of Heidegger's most original and capable students also take up the problem of 'transcendence' in their writings in the thirties and make it a central theme" (32). It is a matter of indisputable record that both Fink and Becker were Husserl's students and Heidegger's contemporaries (Becker and Heidegger were the same age), all three having served as Husserl's assistants. Admittedly, Fink and Becker were significantly influenced by Heidegger's thinking in their work, but as colleagues—perhaps even admiring colleagues, as Marvin Farber described Becker—not students. Becker does, however, refer to himself in his correspondence to Erich Rothacker dated September 9, 1963, as "probably the only student [*der einzige Schüler*] of Heidegger's to strive for principled independence [*prinzipieller Selbständigkeit*]" (quoted in Wolfram Hogrebe, "Von der Hinfälligkeit des Wahren und der Abenteuerlichkeit des Denkers. Eine Studie zur Philosophie Oskar Beckers," 21). *Schüler* here, however, means scholar or one who studies, and not student in the sense of pupil. In Moran's case, unlike that of Faye and Agamben, the error is in all likelihood simply typographical, given that in the original publication of his essay, the same line reads in accordance with the record: "It is noteworthy too in this context that two of Husserl's best students, Eugen Fink (1905–75) and Oskar Becker (1889–1964), take up the problem of 'transcendence' in their writings in the 1930s" (Dermont Moran, "Dasein as Transcendence in Heidegger and the Critique of Husserl," *International Journal of Philosophical Studies* 22, no. 4 [2014]: 499).

56 Husserl, *Ideen I*, §74, 139–140.
57 Becker, *Mathematische Existenz*, 439–768.
58 Husserl, *Ideen I*, §7, 17; §19, 36.
59 Becker, "Transzendenz und Paratranszendenz." Regarding Becker's improvement (*Überbietung*) on Heidegger's hermeneutic phenomenology, Gadamer remarks in a footnote near the end of Section 1 in the first part of *Wahrheit und Methode* (*Truth and Method*), "Die Frage Nacht der Wahrheit der Kunst" (Retrieval of the Question of Artistic Truth): "The brilliant ideas of Oskar Becker on 'paraontology' seem to me to regard the 'hermeneutical phenomenology' of Heidegger too much as a substantive thesis and too little as a methodology. In terms of content, the improvement [*Überbietung*] of this paraontology, which Oskar Becker himself attempts in consistent careful reflection on the problematic, comes back exactly to the point that Heidegger had fixed methodically" (Gadamer, *Wahrheit und Methode*, 1:102n188).
60 Heidegger, "Vom Wesen des Grundes," 124. The Aristotle quotation is from *Metaphysics*, 1013a17.
61 Heidegger, "Vom Wesen des Grundes," 124.
62 Heidegger, "Vom Wesen des Grundes," 124.
63 Heidegger, "Vom Wesen des Grundes," 124.
64 Scotus, *Joannis Duns Scoti*, 12:514.
65 Heidegger, "Vom Wesen des Grundes," 130.
66 Heidegger, "Vom Wesen des Grundes," 132.
67 Heidegger, "Vom Wesen des Grundes," 132.
68 Heidegger, "Vom Wesen des Grundes," 134.
69 Heidegger, "Vom Wesen des Grundes," 135.
70 Heidegger, "Vom Wesen des Grundes," 135.
71 Heidegger, "Vom Wesen des Grundes," 137.
72 Heidegger, "Vom Wesen des Grundes," 137.
73 Plato, *Republic*, 6.509b.
74 Heidegger, "Vom Wesen des Grundes," 160.
75 Heidegger, "Vom Wesen des Grundes," 160.
76 Heidegger, "Vom Wesen des Grundes," 160fn a.
77 Heidegger, "Vom Wesen des Grundes," 161.

78 Plato, *Republic*, 6.508e.
79 Plato, *Phaedrus*, 247c.
80 Heidegger, "Vom Wesen des Grundes," 139. For a probative account of the development of Heidegger's concept of Transcendence, see Moran, "Dasein as Transcendence."
81 Heidegger, "Vom Wesen des Grundes," 139.
82 Heidegger, "Vom Wesen des Grundes," 143.
83 Heidegger, "Vom Wesen des Grundes," 143. We see this connotation, for instance, in I Corinthians 1:21: The world by wisdom knew not God (οὐκ ἔγνω ὁ κόσμος διὰ τῆς σοφίας τὸν Θεόν, *ouk égon o kósmos diá tís sopías tón Theón*), which is reiterated in I Corinthians 3:22 and 6:2, as well as Galatians 6:14. The central meaning of this anthropological concept of world, expressed throughout the Gospels, but most profusely in that of John, is the world in opposition to the divine.
84 For instance, Augustine says in *Enarratio in Psalmum XCI*, 10 and 14, "*Ergo inimici Dei omnes amatores mundi* [All lovers of the world, therefore are enemies of God]"; and "*O miseri homines amatores mundi* [O wretched men, who are lovers of the world]!" See Augustine, *Enarrationes in Psalmos*, in *Hipponensis Episcopi Opera Omnia*, 1411, 1413.
85 Gottfried Wilhelm Leibniz, *Die Philosophischen Schriften*, 3:573. In his consideration of theodicy and the question of Omni benevolence, Leibniz construes God as an optimizer of the collection of compossibles leading to his oft-cited proposition that insofar as God choose this world to exist, it is "the best of all possible worlds" (*le meilleur des mondes possibles*).
86 Christian Wolff, *Philosophia Rationalis sive Logica*, §29, 13.
87 Wolff, *Philosophia Rationalis sive Logica*, §57, 29; §58, 30; §59, 30.
88 Christian Wolff, *Vernünftige Gedanken von Gott, der Welt und der Seele des Menschen, auch allen Dingen*, §544, 331–332.
89 Alexander Gottlieb Baumgarten, *Metaphysica*, §354, 110.
90 Kant, *Kritik der reinen Vernunft*, A 334 f./B 391; here and below, citations give the first edition of 1781 as "A" and the second edition of 1787 as "B," these are followed by parenthetical page number, then edition and line notation. See also Immanuel Kant, *Critique of Pure Reason*, in *Cambridge Edition of the Works of Immanuel Kant*, 405–406; henceforth page citation to this edition appears in brackets, following original.
91 Kant, *Kritik*, A 419 ff., B 446 ff. (447) [466].
92 Heidegger, "Vom Wesen des Grundes," 151.
93 Kant, *Kritik der reinen Vernunft*, A 572, B 600 ff. (552) [553].
94 Heidegger, "Vom Wesen des Grundes," 152.
95 Heidegger, "Vom Wesen des Grundes," 152.
96 Heidegger, "Vom Wesen des Grundes," 161.
97 Heidegger, *Kant und das Problem der Metaphysik*. This book was first published in 1929 by Friedrich Cohen of Bonn, which had been under Vittorio Klostermann's direction since 1928. Due to financial difficulties, remainder stock of that edition appeared in 1934 with Gerhard Schulte-Bulmke of Frankfurt am Main. A second edition was published by Vittorio Klostermann Publish-

ers in 1951, which has been the publisher of the *Kant Book*, as Heidegger called it, ever since, issuing a third edition in 1965 and a fourth in 1973. The fourth edition was expanded to include six appendices, among which are Heidegger's "Aufzeichnungen zum Kantbuch" (Summary Record of the Kant Book) and the second chapter, "Das mythische Denken" (Mythical Thinking) from volume 2 of Ernst Cassirer's book *Philosophie symbolischen Formen* (Philosophy of Symbolic Form), along with the disputation that ensued between Heidegger and Cassirer at the Davos *Hochschule* in March 1929 when they delivered in tandem a series of lectures on Kant. This edition became volume 3 of *Gesamtausgabe*. For those wishing to consult a full English-language translation of the text, see Martin Heidegger, *Kant and the Problem of Metaphysics*, trans. Richard Taft (Bloomington: Indiana University Press, 1973).

98 See Heidegger, *Kant*, 21–25, where Heidegger takes up a critical engagement with the "First book of the Transcendental Dialectic, First Section: On Ideas in General." Regarding that engagement, it is useful to recall that what is at stake for Kant in the distinction between *Anschauung* (intuition) and *Erkenntnis* (cognition or knowledge) is the status of space and time as precognitive representations of relations (*Verhältnisse*) preceding any act of thinking, which is how he defines intuition, stipulating further that "since it does not represent anything except insofar as something is posited in the mind, it can be nothing but the way in which the mind is affected by its own activity [*eigene Tätigkeit*]—namely, this positing of its representation [*Setzen ihrer Vorstellung*], thus the way it is affected through itself, i.e., an inner sense [*innere Sinn*] of its form" (Kant, *Kritik der reinen Vernunft*, A 49, B 67 (89) [189]).

99 Kant, *Kritik der reinen Vernunft*, A 19, B 33 (63) [155]. See Heidegger, *Kant*, 21.

100 Heidegger, *Kant*, 22.

101 Heidegger, *Kant*, 14.

102 Kant, *Kritik der reinen Vernunft*, A 319–320, B 376–377 (354) [398].

103 Heidegger, *Kant*, 22.

104 Kant, *Welches sind die wirklichen Fortschritte*, in *Kants Gesammelte Schriften*, 20:325. Cf. Immanuel Kant, *What Real Progress Has Metaphysics Made in Germany since the Time of Leibniz and Wolff?*, 406.

105 Heidegger, *Kant*, 23.

106 Kant, *Welches sind die wirklichen Fortschritte*, 20:324–325.

107 Heidegger, *Kant*, 25.

108 Kant, *Anthropologie in pragmatischer Hinsicht*, in *Kants Gesammelte Schriften*, 7:119.

109 Kant, *Anthropologie*, 7:119.

110 Kant, *Anthropologie*, 7:120.

111 Kant, *Anthropologie*, 7:120.

112 Kant, *Anthropologie*, 7:120.

113 Heidegger, "Vom Wesen des Grundes," 153, 154.

114 Heidegger, "Vom Wesen des Grundes," 156.

115 Heidegger, "Vom Wesen des Grundes," 157.

116 Heidegger, "Vom Wesen des Grundes," 159.

117 Heidegger, "Vom Wesen des Grundes," 158.

118 *Zeug* is a modern German idiomatic expression that translates idiomatically into English as "stuff" and has a similar connotative range, from "gear or movable property" to "crap." It derives etymologically from the Teutonic verbal root *tuh* (tug), which it shares with the verb *ziehen*, meaning "to tug or pull" (see Friedrich Kluge, "Zeug, ziehen," in *Etymologisches Wörterbuch der deutschen Sprache*, 435). In its Middle High German usage, *Zeug* could be rendered as "thing you 'pull to you' to do something" (Kluge, *Etymologisches Wörterbuch*)—in other words, "useful thing," which is how Stambaugh gives it in her translation, clearly paying attention to how Heidegger expressly deploys *Zeug* to destruct traditional ontology's tendency to "interpret the existence of the world as *res extensa* [existing things]" thereby persisting in "missing the pre-phenomenal basis of worldliness" (Heidegger, *Sein und Zeit*, §14, 67; §15, 68). While Macquarrie and Robinson note that Heidegger's use of *Zeug* as a collective noun is analogous to "gear," as well as "paraphernalia," they opt for "equipment," arguing it is a more general term connoting implement, instrument, or tools. The problem with "equipment" is its own etymological baggage, carrying it back to the verb, "equip" from the French *équiper*, probably derived from the Norse *skipa*, meaning "to man a vessel, or fit it up." Even in its wider sense of anything used in equipping, it is not on par with the generality of *stuff*, which can connote everything useful, from equipment, stores, stock, et cetera, to furnishings, appurtenances, and apparatus, as well as unusable things. This is not a trivial fact, given that Heidegger uses *Zeug* in the sense of that which we encounter in our most immediate careful dealings with existence, the ready-to-hand (*Zuhandenes*) stuff in the surrounding environment (*im Umweltlichkeit*) we can work with—what is pulled, along with its context (*Zeugzusammenhang*), to do something (*um-zu*). Haugeland's way of preserving the polyvalence of *Zeug* in English is to render it as "paraphernalia"; there can, thus, be useful and unusable paraphernalia. See John Haugeland, *Dasein Disclosed* (Cambridge, MA: Harvard University Press, 2013). This seems rather pronouncedly un-idiomatic, or as Macquarrie and Robinson put it, "elaborate." My preference would be to stick with "useful stuff" because it is in keeping with Heidegger's elaboration of *Zeug* as referencing stuff we can work with around us, along with its context. Doing so would convey the colloquial aspect of Heidegger's use of such terms as *Schreibzeug*, "writing-stuff," *Nähzeug*, "sewing-stuff," and *schuhzeug*, "shoe-stuff," or his asserting that "*Zeichen sind aber zunächst selbst Zeuge* [Signs are, in the first instance, themselves stuff]." This, however, would cloud the Middle High German sense of *Zeug* as "*pulling **something** to you to use*" that Heidegger's usage so sharply revives at play in such modern terms as *Werkzeug* (tool) as in Marx's afore discussed characterization of the slave as *sprachbegabtes Werkzeug*, "a speaking tool." "Speaking work-stuff" just would not do; neither would saying "stuff-character" for *Zeugcharakter*. Hence, I have chosen to take up Stambaugh's "useful thing." It will prove efficacious at times to render *Zeug* as "instruments," such as when addressing Heidegger's analysis of signs (*Zeichen*) as being, in the first instance, instruments (*Zeug*).

119 Martin Heidegger, *Aristoteles, Metaphysik IX 1–3*, 33:136–37. The passage of Aristotle's Heidegger refers to is from *Metaphysics*, bk. 9, 1065b1–15.

120 Becker, "Transzendenz und Paratranszendenz," 97. On the early scholastics' usage of *transcendens*, see Armandus de Bellovisu (Armand of Bellevue), *Declaratione diffifilium terminorum*, 4. See also Suárez, *Disputationes*, Disputatio IV. Jan Aertsen has written extensively about the history of the concept in Western history of thought in *Medieval Philosophy and the Transcendentals: The Case of Thomas Aquinas* and *Medieval Philosophy as Transcendental Thought: from Philip the Chancellor (ca. 1225) to Francisco Suarez* (Leiden: Brill, 2012).

121 Becker, "Transzendenz und Paratranszendenz," 97.

122 Becker, "Transzendenz und Paratranszendenz," 97.

123 Aristotle, *Metaphysics*, 1064a30; quoted in Becker, "Transzendenz und Paratranszendenz," 98, as: "das Göttliche, erster und hauptsächlicher Ursprung von allem, sei die verehrungswürdigste und erste Wesenheit [the Divine, first and main origin of everything, is the most venerable and first entity]."

124 Aristotle, *Metaphysics*, 1064b7; Becker, "Transzendenz und Paratranszendenz," 98.

125 Becker, "Transzendenz und Paratranszendenz," 98.

126 Becker, *Mathematische Existenz*, 441.

127 Heidegger, *Sein und Zeit*, §53, 266; emphasis in the original.

128 Heidegger, *Sein und Zeit*, §53, 266.

129 Becker, *Mathematische Existenz*, 663fn2.

130 Becker, *Mathematische Existenz*, 663fn2.

131 Heidegger, *Sein und Zeit*, §72, 374–375.

132 Heidegger, *Sein und Zeit*, §72, 374–375.

133 Heidegger, *Sein und Zeit*, §72, 374.

134 Macquarrie and Robinson translate *Vorlaufen* as "anticipation," even though it would more literally translate as running-ahead (*vor-laufen*); Stambaugh follows suit. But, as Macquarrie and Robinson point out in a footnote, "anticipation" carries the connotation of "waiting for" death or "dwelling upon it" or "actualizing" it before it normally comes. Heidegger's remarks indicate that *Vorlaufen* is not this sort of anticipation. On the other hand, "running-ahead" conveys the sense of "rushing headlong into it," as in the idiomatic English-language phrase "getting ahead of oneself," meaning "to focus excessively on one's plans or on prospective future events without paying adequate attention to the present, to act prematurely" (*OED*). Neither terms alone adequately convey Heidegger's sense of Dasein's as "moving forward towards death in anticipation of it." That, however, is a rather convoluted phrasing. I propose instead "anticipatory-running-forward," as somewhat less so, but also as a way of conveying the Heideggerian sense of forward momentum toward that which is certain while also indeterminate in its particular occurrence.

135 Hegel introduced the term *Geschichtlihkeit* in his *Vorlesungen über die Geschichte der Philosophie* (Lectures on the History of Philosophy), using it only twice. See Hegel, *Vorlesungen über die Geschichte der Philosophie*. The first occurrence is in regard to historical character of Greek thought as philosophy, where he speaks of the Greek "at-homeness [*Heimlichkeit*] in their whole existence, the soil and origin of themselves, not merely existing in it, but possessing and making use of it.... It is in this veritable at-homeness, or, more accurately, in this spirit [*Geiste*]

of at-homeness, this spirit of being-at-home-with-themselves [*Beisichselbstseins*] in their physical, civil, legal, moral and political existence; it is in this character of the free, beautiful historicity [*Geschichtlichkeit*], that they are what they are.... Here also lies the germ of thinking freedom; and so, the necessity that philosophy arose with them" (119).

The second occurrence has to do with the way this Greek philosophy is repurposed by the early Christian Church to give expression to "the Idea of Spirit itself" (*Idee des Geistes selbst*) in the person of Christ as an actual present man (*Christus sei ein wirklicher, dieser' Mensch gewesen*): "These two elements have essentially interwoven in this Christian doctrine: the idea itself and then the form, represented as connected by a single individual existing in space and time. For the church fathers, this story was based on the idea as universal; thus, with them, the true idea of the Spirit [*Geistes*] was in the determinate form of historicity [*bestimmten Form der Geschichtlichkeit*]" (704). Both occurrences have to do with the overarching question in Hegel's system: How does *Geist* come into the world? In this vein, *Geschichtlichkeit*, historicity, has a definitive metaphysical dimension.

136 Graf Yorck to Dilthey, Klein-Öls, June 4, 1895, in *Briefwechsel zwischen Wilhelm Dilthey und dem Grafen Yorck v. Wartenburg* [Correspondence between Wilhelm Dilthey and Count Yorck von Wartenburg], ed. Erich Rothacker (Halle [Saale]: Max Niemeyer, 1923).

137 Heidegger, *Sein und Zeit*, §72, 375; see also §73, 378–382, as well as Martin Heidegger, *Phänomenologie der Anschauung und des Ausdrucks*, 59:43ff.

138 Heidegger, *Sein und Zeit*, §72, 376.

139 Heidegger, *Sein und Zeit*, §72, 376.

140 Heidegger, *Phänomenologie*. He takes up the six means of *Geschichte* in part 1, "Die sechs Bedeutungen von Geschichte und erste Hebung der ihnen gelegenen Vorzeichnungen" (On the Destruction of the A Priori Problem), in sections 6, "Die sechs Bedeutungen von Geschichte und erste Hebung der ihnen gelegenen Vorzeichnungen" (The Six Meanings of History and the First Raising of Their Preliminary Sketches), and 7, "Der rechte Verfolg der Vorzeichnungen: Explikation der Sinnzusammenhänge" (The Right Pursuit of the Preliminary Sketches: Explication of the Meaning-Contexts). Cf. Martin Heidegger, *Phenomenology of Intuition and Expression*, trans. Tracy Colony (London: Continuum International, 2010).

141 Heidegger, *Phänomenologie*, §6, 43.

142 Heidegger, *Phänomenologie*, §6, 43.

143 Heidegger, *Phänomenologie*, §6, 43.

144 Heidegger, *Phänomenologie*, §7, ad I., 49.

145 Heidegger, *Phänomenologie*, §7, ad III., 51.

146 Heidegger, *Sein und Zeit*, §11, 51.

147 Heidegger, *Sein und Zeit*, §11, 51.

148 Heidegger, *Sein und Zeit*, §11, 51.

149 Bastian along with Rudolph Virchow founded the Berlin Society for Anthropology, Ethnology, and Prehistory in 1869 and edited the influential *Zeitschrift für Ethnologie* (Journal of Ethnology) along with Robert Hartmann. During his pres-

idency of the Berlin Geographical Society (1871–1873), he was instrumental in the 1873 founding of German Society for Exploring Equatorial Africa (often just called the "African Society"). Bastian subsequently founded the Berlin Museum für Völkerkunde (Museum of Ethnology) in 1886. Inspired by his mentor, Alexander von Humboldt, he drew on advances in numerous fields of natural science (*Naturwissenschaften*)—to wit, plant physiology, ecology, cellular biology—as well as psychophysics and the human sciences (*Geisteswissenschaften*) to formulate a universal "science of mankind" based on empirically collected evidence from concrete social life in all its ethnic diversity. Accordingly, he pioneered the methodology of psychological analysis of empirically collected cross-cultural data. See Bastian, *Der Mensch in der Geschichte*. Bastian's refusal of unilinear evolution notwithstanding, Edward Burnett Tylor would claim to build his elaboration of unilinear evolutionism based on Bastian's theory of psychic unity. What he took mostly from Bastian was his methodology of analysis, particularly his method of cross-cultural comparative analysis to reconstruct folk ideas and elementary ideas. Bastian's concept of psychic unity prepared the way for Carl Jung's conception of the "collective unconscious," as well as Karl Kerenyi's depth psychology. He also influenced diverse schools of cultural anthropology and ethnology, from the comparative social anthropology of James Frazer to the diffusionism of Fritz Graebner, Bernard Ankermann, and Franz Boas; from the functionalism of Bronisław Malinowski and Alfred Radcliffe-Brown, to the structuralism of Claude Lévi-Strauss, and to the work of Paul Radin.

150 Bastian, *Der Völkergedanke*, 75, 60.
151 See Bastian, *Zur Mythologie und Psychologie*, *Wie das Volk denkt*, and *Der Völkergedanke*.
152 Heidegger, *Sein und Zeit*, §11, 51.
153 Heidegger, *Sein und Zeit*, §11, 51.
154 Heidegger, *Phänomenologie*, §6, 46.
155 Heidegger, *Phänomenologie*, §7, 52.
156 Heidegger, *Phänomenologie*, §7, 52.
157 Heidegger, *Phänomenologie*, §7, 52.
158 Heidegger, *Phänomenologie*, §7, 53.
159 Heidegger, *Phänomenologie*, §7, 53.
160 Heidegger, *Phänomenologie*, §7, 53.
161 Heidegger, *Phänomenologie*, §7, 53.
162 Heidegger, *Phänomenologie*, §7, 54.
163 Heidegger, *Sein und Zeit*, §65, 329.
164 Martin Heidegger, *Beiträge zur Philosophie*, 87–88.
165 Heidegger, *Sein und Zeit*, §74, 384.
166 Heidegger, *Sein und Zeit*, §74, 385.
167 Heidegger, *Sein und Zeit*, §74, 385; emphasis in the original German.
168 Kluge, *Etymologisches Wörterbuch der deutschen Sprache*, svv. "Geschick," 142, "schicken," 337.
169 Heidegger, *Sein und Zeit*, §74, 384.
170 Heidegger, *Sein und Zeit*, §74, 384.

171 Heidegger, *Sein und Zeit*, §74, 385.
172 Heidegger footnotes his use of the term *Generation*, citing Wilhelm Dilthey's *Über das Studium der Geschichte der Wissenschaften vom Menschen*, 5:36–41.
173 Heidegger, *Sein und Zeit*, §73, 379.
174 Heidegger, *Sein und Zeit*, §73, 379. See Dilthey, *Aufbau der geschichtlichen Welt*, 84–85. Cf. Wilhelm Dilthey, *The Formation of the Historical World in the Human Sciences*.
175 Heidegger, *Sein und Zeit*, §73, 379.
176 Heidegger, *Sein und Zeit*, §11, 52.
177 Heidegger, *Sein und Zeit*, §11, 52.
178 Plato, *The Republic*, III, 392d.
179 Martin Heidegger, *Der Begriff der Zeit*, 112–113.
180 Heidegger, *Der Begriff der Zeit*, 112–113.
181 Heidegger, *Sein und Zeit*, §80, 414.
182 Heidegger, *Sein und Zeit*, §14, 65.
183 Heidegger, *Sein und Zeit*, §15, 68.
184 Heidegger, *Sein und Zeit*, §15, 73.
185 As Heidegger says in regard to the temporality of circumspective careful dealing with entities about which we care (*besorgten*): "We are compelled to understand what is consistently dealt with [*des Umgangs*] in this way by reflection on the distinctive character of the ready-to-hand, its *relevance* [*Bewandtnis*]. . . . The relational character of relevance, its 'with . . . in,' indicates that *an* instrument [*ein Zeug*], *a* useful thing is ontologically impossible. Certainly, a single ready-to-hand useful thing can be missing while another is "missing." But what is manifest here is the affiliation [*Zugehörgkeit*] of the directly ready-to-hand *to* another" (Heidegger, *Sein und Zeit*, §69, 353).
186 Heidegger, *Sein und Zeit*, §18, 87.
187 Heidegger, *Sein und Zeit*, §17, 77.
188 Heidegger, *Sein und Zeit*, §17, 77.
189 Heidegger, *Sein und Zeit*, §17, 80.
190 Heidegger, *Sein und Zeit*, §17, 80.
191 Heidegger, *Sein und Zeit*, §17, 80.
192 Heidegger, *Sein und Zeit*, §17, 82.
193 Heidegger, *Sein und Zeit*, §18, 85.
194 Heidegger, *Sein und Zeit*, §18, 85.
195 Heidegger, "Ernst Cassirer: *Philosophie symbolischen Formen*. 2. Teil: Das mythische Denken," in *Kant*, 265.
196 Heidegger, *Sein und Zeit*, §11, 51.
197 As Heidegger says: "Hegel attempts to determine the connection between 'time' and 'spirit' so as to make intelligible why the spirit, as history [*als Geschichte*], 'falls into time.' In its *results*, the foregoing interpretation of the temporality of Dasein and world-time's belonging to it seems to agree with Hegel. But . . . our analysis of time differs in principle from Hegel's at the outset, and . . . is expressly orientated in exactly the opposite direction of his in that it aims at fundamental ontology" (*Sein und Zeit* §78, 405). Contra Hegel's as-

sertion that being is the essence of time, Heidegger's analysis maintains being is time.
198 Becker, *Mathematische Existenz*, 660.
199 Becker, *Mathematische Existenz*, 660.
200 Heidegger, *Sein und Zeit*, §75, 388.
201 Heidegger, *Sein und Zeit*, §77, 403.
202 Heidegger, *Sein und Zeit*, §76, 396.
203 Becker, *Mathematische Existenz*, 663fn3.
204 Becker, *Mathematische Existenz*, 663.
205 Heidegger, *Der Begriff der Zeit*, 113.
206 Becker, *Mathematische Existenz*, 663fn4.
207 Heidegger, *Sein und Zeit*, §12, 53.
208 Heidegger, *Sein und Zeit*, §26, 118.
209 Heidegger, *Sein und Zeit*, §25, 115.
210 Heidegger, *Sein und Zeit*, §25, 116.
211 Heidegger, *Sein und Zeit*, §26, 118.
212 Heidegger, *Sein und Zeit*, §26, 120.
213 Heidegger, *Sein und Zeit*, §27, 126.
214 Heidegger, *Sein und Zeit*, §27, 126
215 Heidegger, *Sein und Zeit*, §26, 118.
216 Heidegger, *Sein und Zeit*, §26, 118.
217 Heidegger, *Sein und Zeit*, §27, 127.
218 Heidegger, *Sein und Zeit*, §27, 129.
219 See Max Scheler, *Der Formalismus in der Ethik und die materiale Wertethik*, 2:246.
220 Scheler, *Der Formalismus*, 355.
221 Scheler, *Der Formalismus*, 402.
222 Heidegger, *Sein und Zeit*, §34, 161.
223 Heidegger, *Sein und Zeit*, §27, 129.
224 Heidegger, *Sein und Zeit*, §23, 108.
225 Heidegger, *Sein und Zeit*, §27, 129.
226 Heidegger, *Sein und Zeit*, §74, 386; emphasis in the original.
227 Heidegger, *Sein und Zeit*, §56, 273.
228 Becker, *Mathematische Existenz*, 662.
229 Becker, *Mathematische Existenz*, 664.
230 Becker, *Mathematische Existenz*, 664.
231 Hermann Ammann, "Nämlich," *Die menschliche Rede. Sprachphilosphische Untersuchungen* 1:71; quoted in Becker, *Mathematische Existenz*, 664fn1.
232 Ammann, "Nämlich." According to Ammann, forms of life are expressed through speech acts, in which social character determines the nature of propositions. See Matías Leandro Saidel, "Form(s)-of-Life: Agamben's Reading of Wittgenstein and the Potential Uses of a Notion," *Trans/Form/Ação* 37, no. 1 (2014): 166–167.
233 Becker, *Mathematische Existenz*, 664fn1.
234 Becker, *Mathematische Existenz*, 664fn1.
235 Becker, *Mathematische Existenz*, 668fn1.
236 Becker, *Mathematische Existenz*, 664.

237 Becker, *Mathematische Existenz*, 665.
238 Becker, *Mathematische Existenz*, 666.
239 Becker, *Mathematische Existenz*, 666fn1.
240 Becker, *Mathematische Existenz*, 666fn1.
241 Becker, *Mathematische Existenz*, 673.
242 Becker, *Mathematische Existenz*, 673.
243 Becker, *Mathematische Existenz*, 673.
244 Heidegger, *Sein und Zeit*, §48, 245.
245 Heidegger, *Sein und Zeit*, §48, 245.
246 Heidegger, *Sein und Zeit*, §48, 245.
247 Becker, "Transzendenz und Paratranszendenz," 102.
248 Becker, "Transzendenz und Paratranszendenz," 101.
249 Becker, "Transzendenz und Paratranszendenz," 102.
250 Becker was an ardent National Socialist (Nazi), as is evidenced in his correspondence with Otto Neugebauer of December 3, 1938, demanding the removal of Otto Toeplitz from the editorship of *Quellen und Studien zur Geschichte der Mathematik* because of his Jewish descent (O. Becker to Neugebauer, December 3, 1938, Courant Institute Papers, file O. Neugebauer). He also participated along with Heidegger, who was a founding member, in the Kulturpolitische Arbeitsgemeinschaft Deutscher Hochschullehrer KADH (Political-Cultural Community of German University Professors), which was organized in May 1933 to regroup those professors and rectors who were committed to a National Socialist renewal of the German university system.
251 See Scheler, *Wesen und Formen der Sympathie*. This is the second edition of the work Scheler published in 1913 under the title *Zur Phänomenologie und Theorie der Sympathiegefühle* (Halle: Max Niemeyer, 1913).
252 Clauss, *Rasse und Seele*, 28.
253 Heidegger, *Metaphysische Anfangsgründe der Logik im Gesamtausgabe*, 26: 157.
254 Heidegger, *Bestimmung der Philosophie*, §14, 72.
255 Heidegger, *Kant*, 290.
256 Becker, "Transzendenz und Paratranszendenz," 102.
257 Becker, "Transzendenz und Paratranszendenz," 103.
258 Becker, "Transzendenz und Paratranszendenz," 103.
259 Becker, "Transzendenz und Paratranszendenz," 103.
260 Becker, "Transzendenz und Paratranszendenz," 103.
261 Oskar Becker, "Nordische Metaphysik," 82.
262 See Maurice Leenhardt, *Do Kamo. La personne et le mythe dans le monde mélanésie*.
263 Leenhardt, *Do Kamo*, 263.
264 Leenhardt, *Do Kamo*, 263.
265 Leenhardt, *Do Kamo*, 263.
266 See Bastide, "Le principe d'individuation," 33–43. On *principium individuationis*, see Thomas Aquinas, *Summa Theologica*, p.1: q.3, a.2, r.3 (33); p. 3: q.6, a.1, r.2 (4651).
267 Bastide, "Le principe d'individuation," 33.
268 Bastide, "Le principe d'individuation," 38.
269 Bastide, "Le principe d'individuation," 39.
270 Bastide, "Le principe d'individuation," 39.

271 Bastide, "Le principe d'individuation," 40.
272 See Calame-Griaule, *Ethnologie et langage*; and Tempels, *La Philosophie bantoue*.
273 Calame-Griaule, *Ethnologie et langage*, 35–37.
274 See Hountondji, *African Philosophy*, 34. Also see Mudimbe, *The Invention of Africa* and "An African Practice of Philosophy."
275 Bastide, "Le principe d'individuation," 41.
276 Calame-Griaule, *Ethnologie et langage*, 35.
277 Calame-Griaule, *Ethnologie et langage*, 36.
278 Calame-Griaule, *Ethnologie et langage*, 36fn2.
279 Calame-Griaule, *Ethnologie et langage*, 38. See also Bastide, "Le principe d'individuation," 41.
280 Heidegger, *Sein und Zeit*, §27, 128.
281 Heidegger, "Vom Wesen des Grundes," 138.
282 Becker, "Transzendenz und Paratranszendenz," 102.
283 Bastide, "Le principe d'individuation," 42.
284 Bastide, "Le principe d'individuation," 41.
285 Bastide, "Le principe d'individuation," 42.
286 Lacan, "L'étourdit," 5.
287 Badiou, "Formules de l'Étourdit," 115.
288 Badiou, "Formules de l'Étourdit," 113.
289 Badiou, "Formules de l'Étourdit," 115.
290 Badiou, "Formules de l'Étourdit," 115.
291 Lacan, "La science et la vérité," 18.
292 See de las Casas, *Historia de Las Indias*.
293 See Brásio, *Monumenta missionaria africana*, 1:270.
294 Aquinas, *Summa Theologica*, p. 2: q.94, a.6:3.
295 Achebe, *Hopes and Impediments*, 92–93.
296 Mudimbe, "An African Practice of Philosophy," 21–22.
297 Mudimbe, "An African Practice of Philosophy," 23.
298 See J. B. Harley, "Deconstructing the Map," *Cartographica* 26, no. 2 (1989): 1–20, and "Cartography, Ethics, and Social Theory," *Cartographica* 27, no. 2 (1989): 1–23; Jeffrey Stone, "Imperialism, Colonialism and Cartography," *Transactions of the Institute of British Geographers*, n.s. 13 (1988): 57; and J. T. Bassett, "Cartography and Empire Building in the Nineteenth-Century West Africa," *Geographical Review* 84, no. 3 (1994): 316.
299 These have been well documented beginning with the WPA project's *Drums and Shadows Among the Georgia Costal Negroes*. See also Endy Walters, "'One Dese Mornings, Bright and Fair, Take My Wings and Cleave De Air': The Legend of the Flying Africans and Diasporic Consciousness," *MELUS* 22, no. 4 (1997): 3–28; Abrahams, *Deep Down in the Jungle* and *Afro-American Folktales*; Hamilton, *The People Could Fly*. For studies of the transmission and elaboration of the parable in Black American poetry and fiction see Bell, *The Folk Roots of Contemporary Afro-American Poetry*; Bontemps and Hughes, *The Poetry of the Negro 1746–1970*; Hayden, "O Daedalus Fly Away Home"; Dance, *Shuckin' and Jivin'*; Morrison, "Rootedness."
300 Du Bois, *Philosophy IV Notebook*, 7.

301 Chandler, "The Problem of the Centuries," 41.
302 W. E. B. Du Bois, "The Present Outlook for the Dark Races of Mankind," in *W. E. B. Du Bois: The Problem of the Color Line at the Turn of the Twentieth Century: The Essential Essays*.
303 Nahum Chandler, "'Beyond This Narrow Now': Or, Delimitations—Of the Thought of W. E. B. Du Bois" (unpublished manuscript, 2019), 225.
304 Du Bois, "The Present Outlook," 116–117.
305 Du Bois, "The Present Outlook," 120.
306 Du Bois, *Dusk of Dawn*, in *Du Bois: Writings*, 557.
307 Du Bois, "The Present Outlook," 122, 123.
308 Du Bois, "The Present Outlook," 124.
309 W. E. B. Du Bois, "Samuel Henry Bishop," *The Crisis* 8, no. 3 (1914): 127.
310 Du Bois, *Autobiography*, 213, 404.
311 Goethe, *Faust*.
312 Johann Wolfgang Von Goethe, *Faust: Parts One and Two*, trans. George Madison Priest.
313 Johann Wolfgang Von Goethe, *Faust: A Tragedy*, trans. Charles T. Brooks.
314 See Moses, *Creative Conflict in African American Thought*. Felipe Smith interprets Du Bois's modifying the Faustian line to be mandated by the general society's perception of the Negro as a creature of unbridled desire. See Felipe Smith, "W. E. B. Du Bois and the Progress of the Black Soul."
315 Du Bois, "The Joy of Living," in *Writings by W. E. B. Du Bois in Periodicals Edited by Others*, 220. As David Levering Lewis notes, the piece was composed for the 1904 class commencement at the renowned Washington, DC, M Street High School, now known as Dunbar High School. Its first print publication was in the February 1965 issue of *Political Affairs* with an explanatory introduction by Aptheker. See Lewis, *W. E. B. Du Bois*, 309. Du Bois never delivered the 1904 commencement speech, "Saint Francis Assisi," which appeared in the *Voice of the Negro*, and was also a commencement address, in this case to the 1906 graduating class of the same high school. Du Bois proclaims his purpose in repeating the themes of that earlier undelivered speech at the close of the 1906 commencement address: "Two years ago it was to have been my pleasure to greet others of your schoolmates on such a day as this. I cannot tell you how much sorrow my misfortune in not being here then, has caused me since; it cannot be atoned for in words but its hurt is helped by the pleasure of greeting you tonight and greeting them through you." Du Bois, "Saint Francis Assisi," in *Writings by W. E. B. Du Bois in Periodicals Edited by Others*, 388.
316 Du Bois, "The Joy of Living," 220.
317 Du Bois, "The Joy of Living," 220.
318 Du Bois, "The Joy of Living," 219.
319 See Tyndale, *The First New Testament Printed in English*. Tyndale was a prominent figure of the English Protestant Reformation. He was a theologian and biblical scholar, who was fluent in French, German, Italian, and Spanish, as well as classical and biblical Greek and Latin. His translation of the Scriptures—both the New and Old Testaments—was the first of the English-language Bibles of the Protestant Reformation. It was also the first English-language Bible

to draw directly from Hebrew and Greek texts and to use "Jehovah" as God's name. He began the translation in 1525, after leaving England for Wittenberg, completing the New Testament by 1526, which was printed by Peter Schöffer in Worms, and afterward in Antwerp. In the wake of the illicit circulation of this translation in England, it was condemned by Bishop Tunstall, who had copies publically burned. Tyndale himself was subsequently condemned as a heretic by Cardinal Wolsey in 1529. He completed his translation of the Old Testament in 1530, then thoroughly revised his New testament translation, which included a second forward opposing the unauthorized changes George Joye had made. Tyndale was seized by the imperial authorities of the Holy Roman Empire in 1535, charged with heresy for his translations in 1536, and publically strangled and burned at the stake in October that year. Subsequent to his death, four English translation of the Bible were authorized by Henry VIII, each of which, including Henry's official Great Bible, was based on Tyndale's translations.

320 A fervent Catholic, More was ardently opposed to the Protestant Reformation, particularly Martin Luther's and Tyndale's theology. As Lord High Chancellor of England under Henry VIII, he played a central role in the prosecution of Reformers as heretics and worked for Tyndale's apprehension. In that same capacity, he refused to acknowledge Henry as Supreme Head of the Church of England and the annulment of his marriage to Catherine of Aragon. As a result, he was convicted of treason and beheaded on July 6 1535—the same year Tyndale was seized by the imperial authorities, and a year and a quarter before his execution. Besides his religious polemics, the *Reponsio ad Lutherum*, against Martin Luthern, and *A Dialogue Concerning Heresies*, to which Tyndale responded with *An Answer unto Sir Thomas More's Dialogue*, More is best known for his literary work, *Utopia*. He was beatified by Pope Leo XIII in 1886, and canonized by Pius XI in 1935.

321 "But now, whereas 'charity' signifieth in Englishmen's ears, not every common love, but a good virtuous and well-ordered love, he that will studiously flee from the name of good love, and always speak of 'love' and always leave out good, I would surely say that he meaneth naught" (More, *A Dialogue Concerning Heresies*, 288).

322 More, *Dialogue*, 289.

323 Augustine, *Enarrationes in Psalmos*, Enarrat. Ps. XXXI. ii. 5. The translation is from T. A. Noble, *Holy Trinity: Holy People: The Theology of Christian Perfecting*, Didsbury Lectures (Eugene, OR: Cascade Books, 2013), 60.

324 Aurelius Augustine, *De Trinitate*, in *Sancti Aurelii Augustini Hipponensis Episcopi Opera Omnia*, vol 8., bk. 8.10.14. The sentence reads in the original: "Ecce tria sunt, amans et quod amatur et amor." The translation is from Stephen McKenna, *Fathers of the Church: Saint Augustine, the Trinity* (Washington, DC: Catholic University of America Press, 1963), 266.

325 Augustine, *De Trinitate*, 8.10.

326 Augustine, *Enarrationes in Psalmos*, 38.228.

327 Tyndale, *An Answer*, 21.

328 Tyndale, *An Answer*, 20.

329 Tyndale, *An Answer*, 22. Priapus was a minor rustic god of fertility, the protector of both fauna and flora, as well as male genitalia. Accordingly, he is symbolized with an oversized permanent erection, which contributed to his popularity in later Roman erotic art and literature. With regard to Christ, Erasmus states in *The Religious Treat*: "I have made him Keeper, not only of my Garden, but of all my Possessions, and of both Body and Mind, instead of filthy Priapus" (Erasmus, *Colloquies*, 1:169).

330 Thomas More, *The Confutation of Tyndale's Answer*, 136. More was retorting Tyndale's assertion in the Preface to *Answer* that the Church's falling into error on faith and good works began with Pope Stephen II anointing Charlemagne's father, Pepin III, signifying the alliance between the Church of Rome with the Franks, which was crucial to the papal claims to Italian territories. Cf. Tyndale, *An Answer*, 9.

331 This decadence is on full display in Article 1, section 9, clause 1, of the 1787 Constitution, known as the "Three-Fifths Compromise." Nowhere is this more plainly stated than in *Federalist 54*, where Madison, writing under the pseudonym Plubius, offers a fraught apologia for the compromise, which warrants full quotation:

> In being compelled to labor, not for himself, but for a master; in being vendible by one master to another master; and in being subject at all times to be restrained in his liberty and chastised in his body, by the capricious will of another, the slave may appear to be degraded from the human rank, and classed with those irrational animals which fall under the legal denomination of property. In being protected, on the other hand, in his life and in his limbs, against the violence of all others, even the master of his labor and his liberty; and in being punishable himself for all violence committed against others, the slave is no less evidently regarded by the law as a member of the society, not as a part of the irrational creation; as a moral person, not as a mere article of property. The federal Constitution, therefore, decides with great propriety on the case of our slaves, when it views them in the mixed character of persons and of property. This is in fact their true character. It is the character bestowed on them by the laws under which they live; and it will not be denied, that these are the proper criterion; because it is only under the pretext that the laws have transformed the negroes into subjects of property, that a place is disputed them in the computation of numbers; and it is admitted, that if the laws were to restore the rights which have been taken away, the negroes could no longer be refused an equal share of representation with the other inhabitants.... Could it be reasonably expected, that the Southern States would concur in a system, which considered their slaves in some degree as men, when burdens were to be imposed [calculating tax liability], but refused to consider them in the same light, when advantages were to be conferred? Might not some surprise also be expressed, that those who reproach the Southern States with the barbarous policy of considering as property a part of their human brethren, should themselves contend, that the government to which all the States are to be parties, ought to consider this unfortunate race more completely in the unnatural light

of property, than the very laws of which they complain? It may be replied, perhaps, that slaves are not included in the estimate of representatives in any of the States possessing them. They neither vote themselves nor increase the votes of their masters. Upon what principle, then, ought they to be taken into the federal estimate of representation? In rejecting them altogether, the Constitution would, in this respect, have followed the very laws which have been appealed to as the proper guide. This objection is repelled by a single observation. It is fundamental principle of the proposed Constitution, that as the aggregate number of representatives allotted to the several States is to be determined by a federal rule, founded on the aggregate number of inhabitants, so the right of choosing this allotted number in each State is to be exercised by such part of the inhabitants as the State itself may designate. The qualifications on which the right of suffrage depend are not, perhaps, the same in any two States.... Government is instituted no less for protection of the property, than of the persons, of individuals. The one as well as the other, therefore, may be considered as represented by those who are charged with the government. (James Madison [Publius], "No. 54: The Apportionment of Members Among the States," from the *New York Packet*, February 12, 1788, in *The Federalist Papers* [New York: Signet, 2003])

332 Du Bois, *Souls*, 494.
333 Acts 2:17.
334 Psalm 23:4, Psalm 63:8.
335 The Thirteenth Amendment to the Constitution abolishing slavery reads: "Neither slavery nor involuntary servitude, except as a punishment for crime whereof the party shall have been duly convicted, shall exist within the United States, or any place subject to their jurisdiction."
336 John 10:17.
337 Jonathon S. Kahn, *Divine Discontent*, 8. Kahn purports to be following Manning Marable's interpretation of Du Bois's engagement with the language of the black church as a key aspect of his black radicalism as laid out in his 1985 *Southern Quarterly* essay, where Marable writes: "Du Bois was simultaneously an agnostic and an Anglican, a staunch critic of religious dogma and a passionate convert to the black version of Christianity" (Manning Marable, "The Black Faith of W. E. B. Du Bois," 15). Kahn misconstrues Marable's assessment of Du Bois's relationship to religion, however, quoting just the closing phrase of the sentence. This accords with his real aim, which is not to align with Marable's reading of Du Bois, but rather to align with Edward Blum, who "turns Du Bois into a Christian" in his *W. E. B. Du Bois: American Prophet*, which Kahn deems "a more resounding and abounding version of Marable's claim" (Kahn, *Divine Discontent*, 9). Blum places Du Bois in Gayraud Wilmore's narrative of radical black Christianity, expressly casting him as a "proto-black liberation theologian." See Edward J. Blum, *W. E. B. Du Bois: American Prophet*, passim. Kahn's misconstrual in support of Blum notwithstanding, Marable does attend closely to texts from Du Bois's writings, elaborating how, in the course of losing his religion, beginning at Fisk, Du Bois comes to recognize the *social* institution of the black

church as entailing elements of a radical political project that is appositional to both Christian theology and ecclesiology.

338. Kahn, *Divine Discontent*, 8.
339. Kahn, *Divine Discontent*, 108. The passage Kahn cites is from Ellison's introduction to *Invisible Man: Thirtieth-Anniversary Edition*, 2.
340. Kahn, *Divine Discontent*, 108.
341. W. E. B. Du Bois, "The Son of God," *The Crisis* 40, no. 12 (1933): 276–277.
342. Du Bois, "The Son of God," 277.
343. Kahn, *Divine Discontent*, 50.
344. W. E. B. Du Bois, *Darkwater: Voices from within the Veil*, 123–133.
345. Du Bois, "The Son of God," 277.
346. Ellison's description of lynching as sacrifice is found in the introduction to *Invisible Man: Thirtieth-Anniversary Edition*.
347. See Frazer, *The Scape Goat*. Regarding Ellison's allusions to Frazer, besides the Introduction to the 1982 *Invisible Man: Thirtieth-Anniversary Edition*, see Ralph Ellison, "The Seer and the Seen," in *The Collected Essays of Ralph Ellison*, 92–93. See also in that same volume the following essays: "On Bird, Bird-Watching and Jazz," 264; "Address to the Harvard College Alumni, Class 1949," 428; "The Little Man at Cehaw Station: The American Artist and His Audience," 595; "An Extravagance of Laughter," 644–646; and "Perspective on Literature," 782.
348. Smith, *Lectures on the Religion of the Semites*.
349. On Tyndale's coinage of "scapegoat" from עֲזָאזֵל (*'azāzel*), see Tyndale, *The First New Testament*. On the exegesis of עֲזָאזֵל (*'azāzel*) and קָרְבָּן חַטָּאת (*qorban khatta'ah*), see Ibn Ezra, *Vayikra, Devarim*, 16:8; and Moses Maimonides, *Dalalat-ul-Hairīn*, 678.
350. Girard, *Le bouc émissaire*, 418.
351. Girard, *Le sacrifice*, 30.
352. Girard, *Achever Clausewitz*, xv.
353. Girard, *Achever Clausewitz*, xv.
354. Girard, *Achever Clausewitz*, 231.
355. Du Bois, "The Future of Wilberforce University," 565.
356. "Quid enim de quoquam homine etiam male operatur, nisi amor?" (Augustine, *De Diversis Quaestionibus*, 60).
357. Augustine, *De Diversis Quaestionibus*, 60.
358. Du Bois, "Renaissance of Ethics," 10–11.

Coda

1. Nabile Farès, *Un passager de l'occident*, 22. The novel has been published in English as *A Passenger from the West*, trans. Peter Thompson (New Orleans: Uno Press, 2010).
2. Adorno, "Rede über Lyrik und Gesellschaft," in *Gesammelte Schriften*, 11:65.
3. Farès, *Passager*, 24.
4. Farès, *Passager*, 25.
5. Farès, *Passager*, 25.

6   See Cherki and Douville, "Nabile Farès," 192.
7   On the gift, see Marcel Mauss, *Essai sur le don* (Paris: Presses Universitaires de France, 1950).
8   Farès, *Passager*, 139.
9   Farès, *Passager*, 17.
10 Farès, *Passager*, 17.
11 Farès, *Passager*, 29.
12 Farès, *Passager*, 30.
13 Farès, *Passager*, 30.
14 On the totem, see Evans-Pritchard, *Nuer Religion*; Malinowski, *The Sexual Lives of Savages*; Radcliffe-Brown, *Structure and Function in Primitive Society*; Smith, *Lectures on the Religion of the Semites*; and Lévi-Strauss, *Le totémisme aujourd'hui*.
15 Du Bois, "Sociology Hesitant," 38–39.
16 Farès, *Passager*, 12.
17 Farès, *Passager*, 21.
18 Farès, *Passager*, 24–25.
19 Farès, *Passager*, 31–32.
20 Farès, *Passager*, 35.
21 Farès, *Passager*, 35.
22 Farès, *Passager*, 35.
23 Farès, *Passager*, 36.
24 Farès, *Passager*, 36–37.
25 Farès, *Passager*, 37.
26 Farès, *Passager*, 35.
27 Clark, *Farewell to an Idea*, 21–22. For an account of the political scandal depicted in Géricault's painting, see Jonathan Miles, *The Wreck of the Medusa: The Most Famous Sea Disaster of the Nineteenth Century* (New York: Atlantic Monthly Press, 2007).
28 James Baldwin, "Down at the Cross: Letter from a Region in My Mind," in *James Baldwin: Collected Essays*, 339.
29 Originally published in 1863, the pamphlet was republished as chapter 16 in David Goodman Croly, *Miscegenation*, 60–69.
30 Croly, *Miscegenation*, 63.
31 Albert Memmi, préface to Baldwin, *La Prochaine fois le feu*, 13.
32 Baldwin, *The Fire Next Time*, 340–341.
33 James Baldwin, "The Artist's Struggle for Integrity," November 29, 1962, Community Church, New York City, WBAI radio broadcast, reel to reel tape CD copy, 1:32, Pacifica Radio Archive, BB3641; subsequently published in a slightly abbreviated form under the same title in *Freedomways* (Winter 1963), 380–387; reprinted in *Seeds of Liberation*, ed. Paul Goodman (New York: George Braziller, 1964); and reprinted more recently in *The Cross of Redemption*, 41–47.
34 Baldwin, "The Artist's Struggle for Integrity," 42.
35 See Bates, "Contributions to an Insect Fauna of the Amazon Valley: Lepidoptera: Heliconidae," and Poulton, *The Colours of Animals*. Poulton first introduces the concept of aposematic mimicry in this work (340). Also see Caillois, "Mimétisme

et la psychasthénie légendaire," 63. A longer version of this essay is in Caillois, *Le mythe et l'homme*. This has been translated by into English John Shepley as "Mimicry and Legendary Psychasthenia," in *October* 31 (Winter 1984): 16–32.

36 See 'Abdur-Raḥman Ibn Khaldūn, *Tārīkh Ibn Khaldūn, al-musammā Kitābu-l-'ibari*, 156.
37 See Abu Naṣr Muḥammad al-Fārābī, *Ārā' 'ahl al-madīnat-il-fāḍila*.
38 Plato, *Republic*, 3.395c–d.
39 This is Andrew Benjamin's sense of fascination as a modality of what he terms "intimate distance," by which he means abandoning oneself to the situation without mastery. See Andrew Benjamin, "Spacing as an Art," in *Territorial Investigations*, 17–18. Fumi Okiji provides an insightful application of this concept of fascination to jazz, which I think applies to the blues as well. See Fumi Okiji, *Jazz as Critique: Adorno and Black Expression Revisited*, 73.
40 See Plato, *Symposium*, 211c.
41 James Baldwin, "Of the Sorrow Songs: The Cross of Redemption," in *The Cross of Redemption*, 149.
42 James Baldwin, *Another Country*, 4; emphasis in the original.
43 Homer, *Iliad*, 1.1.310, 2.23.755.
44 See Edmund Husserl, *Die Krisis der europäischen Wissenschaften und die transzendentale Phänomenologie*.
45 Caillois, *Méduse et Cie*, 99.
46 Homi Bhabha, *The Location of Culture* (London: Routledge, 1994); Croly, *Miscegenation*, 63.
47 Hurston, "Characteristics of Negro Expression," 830.
48 Hurston, "Characteristics of Negro Expression," 838.
49 Al-Jāḥiẓ, *Kitāb al-Bayān wa at-tabiiyn*, 29.
50 Aristotle, *Poetics*, 1447b.
51 John Arbuthnot Nairn, Introduction, in Herodas, *The Mimes of Herodas*, 71.
52 See Alexander Kazhdan, "Mime (μίμος)," in *Oxford Dictionary of Byzantium*, ed. Alexander Kazhdan (Oxford: Oxford University Press, 1991), 2:1375.
53 Plato, *Republic*, 3.397d.
54 Ibrāhīm Ṣālaḥ, "Akhbār ibn al-Muzarra'," 677–684.
55 Plato, *Republic*, 3.397d.
56 Al-Jāḥiẓ, *Kitāb al-ḥayawān*, 2:171.
57 Plato, *Republic*, 2.375a.
58 Plato, *Republic*, 2.375e.
59 Plato, *Republic*, 2.376b.
60 Plato, *Republic*, 2.376b.
61 Sinclair, "Plato's Philosophical Dog."
62 Al-Jāḥiẓ, *Kitāb al-ḥayawān*, 1:37.
63 Al-Jāḥiẓ, *Kitāb al-ḥayawān*, 1:4–5.
64 Al-Jāḥiẓ, *Kitāb al-ḥayawān*, 1:181.
65 Al-Jāḥiẓ, *Kitāb al-ḥayawān*, 1:184. For the passage al-Jāḥiẓ paraphrases, see Aristotle, *History of Animals*, 8.28.607a.
66 Al-Jāḥiẓ, *Kitāb al-ḥayawān*, 4:70–71.
67 Al-Jāḥiẓ, *Kitāb al-ḥayawān*, 1:11.

68 Karl Rosenkranz, *Geschichte der Kant'schen Philosophie*, in *Kant's Sämmtliche Werke*, 12:161.
69 Al-Jāḥiẓ, *Kitāb al-Bayān wa at-tabiiyn*, 280.
70 Al-Jāḥiẓ, *Kitāb al-Bayān wa at-tabiiyn*, 280.
71 Charles Sanders Peirce, "On the Nature of Signs," in *Writings of Charles S. Peirce*, 66.
72 Farès, *Passager*, 74.
73 Farès, *Passager*, 74–75.
74 Aṭ-Ṭāhir Waṭṭār, *Tajriba fi-1 'išiq*, 7.
75 Waṭṭār, *Tajriba fi-1 'išiq*, 8.
76 Waṭṭār, *Tajriba fi-1 'išiq*, 7.
77 Waṭṭār, *Tajriba fi-1 'išiq*, 7.
78 Aṭ-Ṭāhir Waṭṭār, "az-Zinjīya wa aḍ-ḍābṭ."
79 Farès, *Passager*, 75–76.
80 Waṭṭār, "az-Zinjīya wa aḍ-ḍābṭ," 44.
81 Waṭṭār, "az-Zinjīya wa aḍ-ḍābṭ," 54.
82 Waṭṭār, "az-Zinjīya wa aḍ-ḍābṭ," 54.
83 Waṭṭār, "az-Zinjīya wa aḍ-ḍābṭ," 55.
84 Waṭṭār, "az-Zinjīya wa aḍ-ḍābṭ," 56.
85 Waṭṭār, "az-Zinjīya wa aḍ-ḍābṭ," 57.
86 Farès, *Passager*, 75.
87 Waṭṭār, "az-Zinjīya wa aḍ-ḍābṭ," 54.
88 Farès, *Passager*, 106–107.
89 Waṭṭār, *Tajriba fi-1 'išiq*, 26–27.
90 Farès, *Passager*, 110.
91 Farès, *Passager*, 135.
92 Farès, *Passager*, 139.
93 Farès, *Passager*, 142–143.
94 Beatson, "Giving a Name to Exile."

'Abdu al-Man'a, Muḥammad 'Abdu ar-Raḥman. "'Ṣauṭ.'" In *Mu'ajam al-muṣṭalaḥāt wa al-alfāẓ al-fiqhiya*, 125. Al-Iskandariya: Maktaba al-Iskandariya, 2010.

Aboulafia, Mitchell. *Transcendence: On Self-Determination and Cosmopolitanism.* Stanford, CA: Stanford University Press, 2010.

Abrahams, Roger. *Deep Down in the Jungle: Negro Narrative Folklore from the Streets of Philadelphia*. Natboro, PA: Folklore Associates, 1964.

Abrahams, Roger. *Afro-American Folktales: Stories from Black Traditions in the New World*. New York: Pantheon, 1985.

Achebe, Chinua. *Hopes and Impediments*. New York: Penguin, 1990.

Adell, Sandra. *Double-Consciousness/Double Bind: Theoretical Issues in Twentieth-Century Black Literature*. Urbana: University of Illinois Press, 1994.

Adorno, Theodor. *Theodor W. Adorno Gesammelte Schriften*. Herausgegeben von Rolf Tiedemann unter Mitwirkung von Gretel Adorno, Susan Buck-Morss, und Klaus Schultz. 20 Bde. Frankfurt am Main: Suhrkamp, 1970–1997.

Adorno, Theodor. *Briefe und Briefwechsel*. Herausgegeben von Henri Lonitz. Bd. 1, *Theodor W. Adorno, Walter Benjamin Briefwechsel 1928–1940*. Frankfurt am Main: Suhrkamp, 1994.

Adorno, Theodor W. *Prismen. Kulturkririk und Gesellschaft*. Berlin: Suhrkamp Verlag, 1955.

Aertsen, Jan. *Medieval Philosophy and the Transcendentals: The Case of Thomas Aquinas*. Leiden: Brill, 1996.

Aertsen, Jan. *Medieval Philosophy as Transcendental Thought: from Philip the Chancellor (ca. 1225) to Francisco Suarez*. Leiden: Brill, 2012.

Agamben, Giorgio. *Homo Sacer: Sovereign Power and Bare Life*. Translated by Daniel Heller-Roazen. Palo Alto, CA: Stanford University Press, 1998.

Agamben, Giorgio. *L'Uso dei corpi*. Venezia: Neri Pozza Editore, 2014.

Al-Fārābī, Abu Naṣr Muḥammad. *Ārā' ahl al-madīnat-il-fāḍila wa muḍādātihā*. Taḥqīq Ṭāhā al-Daūqī Ḥubayshī. Al-Qāhira: al-Maktabah al-Azharīyah lil-Turāth, 2002.

Al-Jāḥiẓ. *Kitāb al-ḥayawān*. Taḥqīq 'Abdu as-Salām Muḥmmad Hārūn. 7 mujaladāt. Al-Qāhira: Muṣṭafa al-bābī al-Khānjī, 1965.

Al-Jāḥiẓ. *Kitāb al-Bayān wa at-tabiiyn*. Taḥqīq 'Abdu as-Salām Muḥmmad Hārūn. Al-Qāhira: Maktaba al-Khānjī, 1998.

Allen, Ernest. "Du Boisian Double Consciousness: The Unsustainable Argument." *Massachusetts Review* 43, no. 2 (2002): 217–253.

Allen, William Francis [Marcel, pseud.]. "The Negro Dialect." *The Nation* 1, no. 24 (1865): 744–745.

Allen, William Francis. *Slave Songs of the United States*. New York: A Simpson, 1867.

Ammann, Hermann. *Die menschliche Rede: Sprachphilosophische Untersuchungen*. 2. Teil. Lahr: Moritz Schauenburg, 1925.

Apollinaire, Guillaume. *Zone*. In *Alcools*. Paris: Éditions Gallimard, 1913.

Aquinas, Thomas. *Quaestiones Disputatae de Veritate*. Leonine edition. Vol. 22 (3 vols.). Edited by A. Dondaine. Rome: San Tommaso, 1972–1976.

Aquinas, Thomas. *Summa Theologica*. Translated by Fathers of the English Dominican Province. Westminster, MD: Christian Classics, 1981.

Arendt, Hannah. *The Origins of Totalitarianism*. New York: Harcourt Brace Jovanovich, 1951.
Arendt, Hannah. *The Human Condition*. Chicago: University of Chicago Press, 1958.
Arendt, Hannah. *Between Past and Future*. New York: Viking, 1961.
Aristoteles. *L'ethique a Nicomaque*. Introductio, traduction, et commentaire par René-Antoine Gauthier et Jean-Yves Jolif. 2 ts. Louvain: Publications Universitaires de Louvain, 1959.
Aristotle. *Physics*. Translated by Philip H. Wicksteed and Francis M Cornford. 2 vols. Cambridge, MA: Loeb Classical Library, Harvard University Press, 1929.
Aristotle. *Metaphysics*. 2 vols. Translated by Hugh Tredennick. Cambridge, MA: Loeb Classical Library, Harvard University Press, 1933.
Aristotle. *Nicomachean Ethics*. Translated by H. Rackham. Cambridge, MA: Loeb Classical Library, Harvard University Press, 1934.
Aristotle. *Politics*. Translated by H. Rackham. Cambridge, MA: Loeb Classical Library, Harvard University Press, 1944.
Aristotle. *History of Animals*. Translated by A. J. Peck. Cambridge, MA: Loeb Classical Library, Harvard University Press, 1965.
Aristotle. *Poetics*. Translated by Stephen Halliwell. Cambridge, MA: Loeb Classical Library, Harvard University Press, 1995.
Armitage, David. "John Locke, Carolina, and the Two Treatises of Government." *Political Theory* 32, no. 5 (2004): 602–627.
Armitage, David. "John Locke: Theorist of Empire?" In *Empire and Modern Political Thought*, edited by Sankar Muthu. Cambridge: Cambridge University Press, 2012.
Augustine, Aurelius. *Sancti Aurelii Augustini Hipponensis Episcopi Opera Omnia*. 11 vols. Accurante Jacques-Paul Migne. Parisiis: Venit apud Editorem, 1861.
Augustine, Aurelius. *De Diversis Quaestionibus*. Eugene, OR: Cascade Books, 2013.
Azam, Étienne Eugène. *Hypnotisme, double conscience et altérations de la personnalité*. Paris: Baillière, 1881.
Bacon, Francis. *Advancement of Learning*. Vol. 8 of *The Works of Francis Bacon*, edited by James Spedding, Robert Leslie Ellis, and Douglas Denon Heath. Boston: Houghton Mifflin, 1900.
Badiou, Alain. *Le nombre et les nombres*. Paris: Éditions de Seuil, 1990.
Badiou, Alain, and Barbara Cassin. *Il n'y a pas rapport sexuel: deux leçons sur "L'étourdit" de Lacan*. Paris: Ouvertures Fayard, 2010.
Bailey, Cornelia, with Christena Bledsoe. *God, Dr. Buzzard and the Bolito Man: A Saltwater Geechee Talks about Life on Sapelo Island*. New York: Doubleday, 2000.
Baldwin, James. *La Prochaine fois le feu*. Translated by Michel Sciama. Paris: Gallimard, 1963. Originally published as *The Fire Next Time*. New York: Dial Press, 1963.
Baldwin, James. *Another Country*. New York: Vintage International, 1993.
Baldwin, James. *James Baldwin: Collected Essays*. New York: Library of America, 1998.
Baldwin, James. *The Cross of Redemption: Uncollected Writings*, edited by Randall Kenan. New York: Vintage, 2010.
Ball, Michael, and Greg Smith. "Technologies of Realism? Ethnographic Uses of Photography and Film." In *Handbook of Ethnography*, edited by Paul Atkinson,

Amanda Coffey, Sara Delamont, John Lofland, and Lyn Lofland. London: Sage Press, 2013.

Balzac, Honoré. *Physiologie du mariage ou méditations de philosophie éclectique surle bonheur et le malheur conjugal*. Paris: Charpentier, 1830.

Balzac, Honoré. *Splendeurs et misères des courtisanes*. Paris: L. De Potter, 1845.

Barthes, Roland. *Le degré zero de l'écriture*. Paris: Édition du Seuil, 1953.

Barthes, Roland. *Mythologies*. Paris: Édition du Seuil, 1957.

Barthes, Roland. *Writing Degree Zero*. Translated by Annette Laver and Colin Smith. New York: Hill and Wang, 1968.

Barthes, Roland. *La Chambre claire: Note sur la photographie*. Paris: Cahiers du Cinema, Gallimard, Seuil, 1980.

Barthes, Roland. *Camera Lucida: Reflections on Photography*. Translated by Richard Howard. New York: Hill and Wang, 1981.

Barthes, Roland. *Mythologies*. Translated by Richard Howard and Annette Lavers. New York: Hill and Wang, 2012.

Bastian, Adolf. *Der Mensch in der Geschichte: Zur Begründung einer Psychologischen Weltanschauung*. Leipzig: O. Wigand, 1860.

Bastian, Adolf. *Der Völkergedanke im Aufbau einer Wissenschaft vom Menschen und seine Begründung auf ethnologische Sammlungen*. Berlin: F. Dümmlers, 1881.

Bastian, Adolf. *Wie das Volk denkt. Ein Beitrag zur Beantwortung scoialer Fragen auf Grundlage ethnischer Elementargendanken in der Lehre vom Menschen*. Berlin: Emil Felber, 1892.

Bastian, Adolf. *Zur Mythologie und Psychologie der Nigritier in Guinea (Einschließlich des Colonial-Gebietes Togo) mit Bezugnahme auf Socialistische Elementargedanken*. Berlin: Hoefer & Vohsen, 1894.

Bastide, Roger. "Le principe d'individuation (contribution à une philosophie Africains)." Dans *La notion de personne en Afrique Noire: Colloque International du Centre National de la Recherche Scientifique*, édité par Germaine Dieterien. Paris: Éditions du Centre National de la Recherche Scientifique, 1973.

Bates, Henry Walter. "Contributions to an Insect Fauna of the Amazon Valley: Lepidoptera: Heliconidae." *Transaction of the Linnean Society of London*, o.s. 23, no. 3 (1862): 495–566.

Baudelaire, Charles. "Le peintre de la vie moderne." Dans *Œuvres complètes de Charles Baudelaire*, édité par Théophile Gautier, 4:51–111. Paris: Claman Lévy, 1885.

Baudelaire, Charles. "Mon cœur mis à nu." In *Journaux intimes*. Paris: Éditions G. Crés, 1920 [1887].

Baumgarten, Alexander Gottlieb. *Metaphysica*. Halle: Halle im Magdeburgischen, 1739.

Beatson, Peter. "Giving a Name to Exile: Interview with Nabile Farès." *Fountains* 3 (1979): n.p.

Becker, Oskar. "Transzendenz und Paratranszendenz." In *Travaux du IXe congrès international de philosophie*, édité par Raymond Bayer, 97–104. Paris: Herman, 1937.

Becker, Oskar. "Nordische Metaphysik." *Rasse. Monatsschrift der Nordischen Bewegung* 5 (1938): 81–92.

Becker, Oskar. *Mathematische Existenz. Untersuchungen zur Logik und Ontologie mathematischer Phänomene, Jahrbuch für Philosophie und Phänomenologische Forschung*, Bd. 8. Tübingen: Niemeyer, 1973 [1927].

Behdad, Ali, and Luke Gartlan, eds. *Photography's Orientalism: New Essays on Colonial Representation*. Los Angeles: Getty Research Institute, 2013.

Bekemeier, Bernd. "Die Arithmetisierung der Mathematik—Ein grundlagentheoretisches Programm der Mathematik im 19. Jahrhundert." *Wissenschaft und Bildung im frühen 19. Jahrhundert II, IDM Materialien und Studien 27*, no. 30 (1982): 1–96.

Bekemeier, Bernd. *Martin Ohm (1792–1872): Universitätsmathematik und Schulmathematik in der neuhumanistischen Bildungsreform*. Göttingen: Vandenhoeck & Ruprecht, 1987.

Bell, Bernard. *The Folk Roots of Contemporary Afro-American Poetry*. Detroit: Broadside Press, 1974.

Bellovisu, Armandus de [Armand of Bellevue]. *Declaratione diffifilium terminorum tam theologiae quam philosophiae ac logicae*. Basel: Michael Wenssler, 1491.

Benacerraf, Paul. "What Numbers Can Be." *Philosophical Review* 74, no. 1 (1965): 47–73.

Benis-Sinaceur, Hourya. "Is Dedekind a Logicist? Why Does Such a Question Arise." In *Functions and Generality of Logic: Reflections on Dedekind's Logicisms*, edited by Hourya Benis-Sinaceur, Marco Panza, and Gabriel Sandu, 1–57. Heidelberg: Springer, 2015.

Benjamin, Andrew. "Spacing as an Art." In *Territorial Investigations*, edited by Annette W. Balkema and Henk Slager. Lier en Boog, Series of Art and Art Theory, vol. 14. Amsterdam: Editions Rodopi, 1999.

Benjamin, Walter. *Das Passagen-Werk*. In *Walter Benjamin Gesammelte Schriften*, Bd. 5.1, herausgegeben von Rolf Tiedemann. Frankfurt am Main: Suhrkamp, 1991.

Benjamin, Walter. *Walter Benjamin: Selected Writings*. Edited by Howard Jennings, Michael W. Jennings, Marcus Bulllock, Howard Eiland, and Gary Smith. Translated by Rodney Livingston, Edmund Jephcott, and Howard Eiland. 4 vols. Cambridge, MA: Harvard University Press, 1996–2003.

Benjamin, Walter. "Paris, Capital of the Nineteenth Century: Exposé (of 1939)." In *The Arcades Project*, translated by Howard Eiland and Kevin McLaughlin. Cambridge, MA: Harvard University Press, 1999.

Berman, Russell. "Du Bois and Wagner: Race, Nation and Culture between the United States and Germany." *German Quarterly* 70, no. 2 (1997): 123–135.

Bertram, Ernst. *Versuch einer Mythologie*. Berlin: Bei Georg Bondi, 1920.

Bhabha, Homi. *The Location of Culture*. London: Routledge, 1994.

Bibb, Henry. *Narrative of the Life and Adventures of Henry Bibb, an American Slave, Written by Himself*. New York: Henry Bibb; Macdonald & Lee, Printers, 1849.

Bloch, Ernst. "Logikum/Zur Ontologie des Noch-Nicht-Seins." Im *Werkausgabe*, Bd. 13, Tübinger Einleitung in die Philosophie. Frankfurt am Main: Suhrkamp, 1985.

Blum, Edward J. *W. E. B. Du Bois: American Prophet*. Philadelphia: University of Pennsylvania Press, 2007.

Bommel, Bas van. *Classical Humanism and the Challenge of Modernity: Debates on Classical Education in 19th-Century Germany*. Berlin: De Gruyter, 2015.

Bontemps, Arna, and Langston Hughes, eds. *The Poetry of the Negro 1746–1970*. Garden City, NY: Doubleday, 1970.

Boyer, Carl. *History of Mathematics*. New York: John Wiley & Son, 1989.

Brand, Dana. *The Spectator and the City in Nineteenth-Century America*. Cambridge: Cambridge University Press, 1991.

Brand, Gerd. *Welt, Ich, und Zeit: Nach unveröffentlichten Manuskripten Edmund Husserls*. Hague: Martinus Nijhoff, 1955.

Brásio, António. *Monumenta missionaria africana: Africa ocidental*. Vol. 1, *1342–1499*. Lisboa: Agência Geral do Ultramar Divisão de Publicações e Biblioteca, 1958.

Brewer, John Mason. *Dog Ghost, and Other Texas Negro Folk Tales*. Austin: University of Texas Press, 1958.

Brodwin, Stanley. "The Veil Transcended: Form and Meaning in W. E. B. Du Bois's 'The Souls of Black Folk.'" *Journal of Black Studies* 2, no. 3 (1972): 303–321.

Brown, Charles Brockden. "Advertisement" to *Wieland: Or the Transformation: An American Tale (1798)*. In *Charles Brockden Brown: Three Gothic Novels: Wieland, Arthur Mervyn, Edgar Huntly*, edited by Sydney J. Krause. New York: Library of America, 1998.

Bruce, Dickson D., Jr. "W. E. B. Du Bois and the Idea of Double Consciousness." *American Literature* 64, no. 2 (1992): 299–309.

Bryant, Jerry. *"Born in a Might Bad Land": The Violent Man in African American Folklore and Fiction*. Bloomington: Indiana University Press, 2003.

Buis, Johann. "Historical Essay, the Ring Shout: Revisiting the Islamic and African Issues of a Christian 'Holy Dance.'" In *Shout Because You're Free: The African American Ring Shout Tradition*, edited by Art Rosenbaum and Margo Newmark Rosenbaum. Athens: University of Georgia Press, 2013.

Byerman, Keith E. *Seizing the Word: History, Art, and Self in the Work of W. E. B. Du Bois*. Athens: University of Georgia Press, 1994.

Caillois, Roger. "Mimétisme et la psychasthénie légendaire." *Minotaure* 7 (1935): 4–10.

Caillois, Roger. *Le mythe et l'homme*. Paris: Gallimard, 1938.

Caillois, Roger. *Méduse et Cie*. Paris: Gallimard, 1960.

Calame-Griaule, Geneviève. *Ethnologie et langage. La parole chez les Dogon*. Paris: Éditions Gallimard, 1965.

Cantor, Georg. "Ueber eine Eigenschaft des Inbegriffes aller reellen algebraischen Zahlen." *Journal für die reine und angewandte Mathematik*, no. 77 (1874): 258–262.

Cantor, Georg. *Grundlagen einer allgemeinen Mannigfaltigkeitslehre. Ein mathematisch-philosophischer Versuch in der Lehre des Unendlichen*. Leipzig: Teubner, 1883.

Cantor, Georg. *Gesammelte Abhandlungen mathematischen und philosophischen Inhalts*. Herausgegeben von Ernst Zermelo. Berlin: Julius Springer, 1932.

Carby, Hazel V. "Souls of Black Men." In *Next to the Color Line: Gender, Sexuality, and W. E. B. Du Bois*, edited by Susan Gillman and Alys Eve Weinbaum. Minneapolis: University of Minnesota Press, 2007.

Carmer, Carl. *Stars Fell on Alabama*. New York: Farrar & Rinehart, 1934.

Carpentier, Alejo. *¡Ecué-Yamba-O: historia afro-cubana!* Madrid: Editorial España, 1933.
Carpentier, Alejo. "Lo real maravilloso de América." *El Nacional*, April 8, 1948.
Carpentier, Alejo. *El reino de este mundo*. México: Ediapsa, 1949.
Carpentier, Alejo. "De lo real maravilloso americano." In *Tientos y diferencias*. México: Universidad Autónoma de México, 1964.
Carpentier, Alejo. *Obras completas*. Vol. 1, *Écue-Yamba-ó y otros escritos afrocubanos*. México: Siglio XXI, 1983.
Chaffee, Mary Law. "William E. B. Dubois's Concept of the Racial Problem in the United States: The Early Negro Educational Movement." *Journal of Negro History* 41, no. 3 (1956): 241–258.
Chandler, Nahum Dimitri. "The Problem of the Centuries: A Contemporary Elaboration of 'The Present Outlook for the Dark Races of Mankind,' circa the 27th of December 1899." Unpublished manuscript, 2006.
Chandler, Nahum Dimitri. *X—The Problem of the Negro as a Problem for Thought*. New York: Fordham University Press, 2014.
Chandler, Nahum Dimitri. "'Beyond This Narrow Now': Or, Delimitations—Of the Thought of W. E. B. Du Bois." Unpublished manuscript, 2019.
Cherki, Alice, and Olivier Douville. "Nabile Farès." *Psychologie Clinique* 2, no. 44 (2017): 192–204.
Chiesa, Lorenzo. "Hyperstructuralism's Necessity of Contingency: On Jean-Claude Milner." *S: Journal of the Jan Van Eyck Circle for Lacanian Ideology Critique* 3 (2010): 159–177.
Chiesa, Lorenzo. "Towards a New Philosophical-Psychoanalytic Materialism and Realism." In *Lacanian Philosophy: The New Generation*, edited by Lorenzo Chiesa. Melbourne: re.press, 2014.
Child, Lydia Maria. *An Appeal in Favor of that Class of Americans Called Africans*. New York: John S. Taylor, 1836.
Cicero, Marcus Tullis. "Pro Roscio Amernio." In *Cicero Orations*, translated by J. H. Freese. Cambridge, MA: Loeb Classical Library, Harvard University Press, 1930.
Clark, T. J. *Farewell to an Idea: Episodes from a History of Modernism*. New Haven, CT: Yale University Press, 1999.
Clauss, Ludwig Ferdinand. *Rasse und Seele. Eine Einführung in den Sinn der leiblichen Gestalt*. Berlin: Büchergilde Gutenberg, 1938 [1926].
Clifford, James, and George Marcus, eds. *Writing Culture: The Poetics and Politics of Ethnography*. Berkeley: University of California Press, 1986.
Cole, Andrew. *The Birth of Theory*. Chicago: University of Chicago Press, 2014.
Coleridge, Samuel Taylor. *A Dissertation on the Science of Method; or The Laws and Regulative Principles of Education*. London: Charles Griffin and Company, 1859 [1818].
Coleridge, Samuel Taylor. *The Collected Works of Samuel Taylor Coleridge*. Vol. 1, *Lectures 1795 on Politics and Religion*. Edited by Lewis Mann and Peter Patton. Princeton, NJ: Princeton University Press, 1971.
Coleridge, Samuel Taylor. *The Collected Works of Samuel Taylor Coleridge*. Vol. 2, *The Watchman*. Edited by Lewis Patton. Princeton, NJ: Princeton University Press, 1971.

Comte, Auguste. *Cours de philosophie positive, Tome Premier, Les préliminaires généraux et la philosophie mathématique*. 6 vols. Paris: Bachelier, 1830.

Comte, Auguste. *The Positive Philosophy of Auguste Comte*. Translated and edited by Harriet Martineau. 2 vols. London: John Chapman, 1853.

Comte, Auguste. *Écrits de jeunesse (1816–1828)*. Edited by Paulo Arnaud and Pierre Carneiro. Paris: Mouton, 1970.

Cottingham, John. "Cartesian Dualism: Theology, Metaphysics, and Science." In *The Cambridge Companion to Descartes*, edited by John Cottingham. Cambridge: Cambridge University Press, 1992.

Cowper, William. *The Task*. London: Cassell & Company, 1899.

Croly, David Goodman. *Miscegenation: The Theory of the Blending of the Races, Applied to the American White Man and Negro*. London: Trübner & Co., 1964.

Crummell, Alexander. "Civilization, the Primal Need of the Race." American Negro Academy Occasional Papers, no. 2. American Negro Academy, Washington, DC, 1897.

Crummell, Alexander. *Civilization and Black Progress: Selected Writings of Alexander Crummell on the South*. Edited by J. R. Oldfield. Charlottesville: University of Virginia Press, 1995.

Dance, Daryl Cumber. *Shuckin' and Jivin': Folklore from Contemporary Black Americans*. Bloomington: Indiana University Press, 1978.

Da Silva, Denise Ferreira. "Hacking the Subject: Black Feminism and Refusal beyond the Limits of Critique." *philoSOPHIA* 8, no. 1 (2018): 19–41.

Dayan, Colin. *The Law Is a White Dog: How Legal Rituals Make and Unmake Persons*. Princeton, NJ: Princeton University Press, 2013.

Dedekind, Richard. *Gesammelte Mathematische Werke*. Herausgegeben von Richard Fricke, Emmy Noether, and Oeystein Ore. 3 Bde. Braunschweig: Vieweg & Son, 1932.

Delange, Jacqueline, and Michel Leiris. *L'Afrique noire: La création plastique*. Collection l'Univers des Formes. Paris: Éditions Gallimard, 1967.

de las Casas, Fray Bartolomé. *Historia de Las Indias*. Edited by José Sancho Rayon. Madrid: Miguel Ginesta, 1875 [1561].

Dennis, Rutledge. "W. E. B. Du Bois's Concept of Double Consciousness." In *Race and Ethnicity: Comparative and Theoretical Approaches*, edited by John Stone and Rutledge M. Dennis. London: Wiley-Blackwell, 2002.

Descartes, René. "Meditatio Secunda, De natura mentis humanae: Quod ipsa notior quam corpus." In *Meditationes de Prima Philosophia*. Paris: Michael Soli, 1641.

Descartes, René. *L'Homme et un traitté de la formation du foetus; avec les remarques de Louis de La Forge, docteur en médecine, demeurant à la Fleche, sur le traitté de l'homme de René Descartes & sur les figures par luy inventées*. Paris: Charles Angot, 1990 [1664].

Detienne, Marcel, and Jean-Pierre Vernant. *Les ruses del'intelligence. La mètis des Grecs*. Paris: Flammarion, 1974.

Dilthey, Wilhelm. *Aufbau der geschichtlichen Welt in den Gesiteswissenschften*. Berlin: Königlich Preussischen Akademie der Wissenschaften, 1910.

Dilthey, Wilhelm. *Wilhelm Diltheys Gesammelte Schriften*. Herausgegeben von Georg Misch. 26 Bde. Leipzig: B. G. Teubner, 1924 [1892].

Dilthey, Wilhelm. *The Formation of the Historical World in the Human Sciences*. Translated by Rudolf A. Makkreel and Frithjof Rodi. Princeton, NJ: Princeton University Press, 2002.

Dirichlet, Peter Gustav Lejeune. "Über Die Darstellung ganz willkürlicher Funktionen durch Sinus- und Cosinus reihen." Im *G. Lejeune Dirichlet's Werke*, herausgegeben von Leopold Kronecker. Bd. 1. Berlin: Georg Reimer, 1889.

Dorson, Richard M. *Negro Tales from Pine Bluff and Calvin*. Bloomington: Indiana University Press, 1958.

Douglass, Frederick. "What to the Slave Is the Fourth of July?" In *The Frederick Douglass Papers, Series 1: Speeches, Debates, and Interviews*, vol. 2, *1847–54*, edited by John Blassingame. New Haven, CT: Yale University Press, 1982 [1852].

Douglass, Frederick. *My Bondage and My Freedom*. New York: Library of America, 1994 [1855].

Douglass, Frederick. *Narrative of the Life of Frederick Douglass, An American Slave, Written by Himself*. New York: Library of America, 1994 [1845].

Douglass, Frederick. *Frederick Douglass: Selected Speeches and Writings*. Edited by Philip Foner. Chicago: Lawrence Hill Books, 1999.

Douglass, Frederick. *My Bondage and My Freedom*. Givens Collection edition. Edited by John Wright. New York: Washington Square Press, 2003 [1855].

Drake, St. Clair, and Horace Cayton. *Black Metropolis: A Study of Negro Life in a Northern City*. Chicago: University of Chicago Press, 1945.

Du Bois, W. E. B. *Philosophy IV Notebook*. Special Collections and University Archives. University of Massachusetts Amherst Libraries, 1889.

Du Bois, W. E. B. "The Renaissance of Ethics." W. E. B. Du Bois Collection, Box 3, Folder 57. Beinecke Rare Book and Manuscript Library, Yale University, 1889.

Du Bois, W. E. B. "Strivings of the Negro People." *Atlantic Monthly* 80, no. 478 (1897): 194–198.

Du Bois, W. E. B. "The Present Outlook for the Dark Races of Mankind." *A. M. E. Review*, October 1900, 95–110.

Du Bois, W. E. B. "The Negro as He Really Is." *World's Work* 2, no. 2 (1901): 848–866.

Du Bois, W. E. B. "Review of *The Souls of Black Folk* by W. E. B. Du Bois." *The Independent* 57, no. 2920 (1904): 1152.

Du Bois, W. E. B. *Darkwater: Voices from within the Veil*. New York: Harcourt, Brace and Howe, 1920.

Du Bois, W. E. B. "Pan-Africa and New Racial Philosophy." *The Crisis* 40, no. 11 (1933): 247, 262.

Du Bois, W. E. B. "The Son of God." *The Crisis* 40, no. 12 (1933): 276–277.

Du Bois, W. E. B. "Opera and the Negro Problem." *Pittsburgh Courier*, October 31, 1936. Reprinted in *Newspaper Columns by W. E. B. Du Bois*, edited by Herbert Aptheker. White Plains, NY: Kraus-Thomson Organization, 1986.

Du Bois, W. E. B. "The Future of Wilberforce University." *Journal of Negro Education* 9, no. 4 (1940): 553–570.

Du Bois, W. E. B. "My Evolving Program for Negro Freedom." In *What the Negro Wants*, edited by Rayford W. Logan. Chapel Hill: University of North Carolina Press, 1944.

Du Bois, W. E. B. *The Ordeal of Mansart*. Vol. 1 of *The Black Flame Trilogy*. New York: Mainstream Publishers, 1957.

Du Bois, W. E. B. *The Autobiography of W. E. B. Du Bois: A Soliloquy on Viewing My Life from the Last Decade of Its First Century*. New York: International Publishers, 1968.

Du Bois, W. E. B. *Writings by W. E. B. Du Bois in Periodicals Edited by Others*. Edited by Herbert Aptheker. 4 vols. Millwood, NY: Kraus-Thomson, 1982.

Du Bois, W. E. B. *Dusk of Dawn*. In *W. E. B. Du Bois: Writings*, edited by Nathan Huggins. New York: Library of America, 1986.

Du Bois, W. E. B. *W. E. B. Du Bois: Writings*. Edited by Nathan Huggins. New York: Library of America, 1986.

Du Bois, W. E. B. *The Correspondence of W E. B. Du Bois*. 3 vols. Amherst: University of Massachusetts Press, 1987.

Du Bois, W. E. B. *The Souls of Black Folk: Authoritative Text, Contexts, Criticism*. Edited by Henry Louis Gates Jr. and Terri Hume Oliver. Norton Critical Edition. New York: W. W. Norton, 1999.

Du Bois, W. E. B. "Sociology Hesitant." In "Sociology Hesitant: W. E. B. Du Bois's Dynamic Thinking," edited by Ronald A. T. Judy. Special issue, *boundary 2* 27, no. 3 (2000): 37–44.

Du Bois, W. E. B. "The Present Outlook for the Dark Races of Mankind." In *W. E. B. Du Bois: The Problem of the Color Line at the Turn of the Twentieth Century: The Essential Essays*, edited by Nahum Chandler. New York: Fordham University Press, 2014.

Dugmore, Arthur Radclyffe. *Camera Adventures in the African Wild*. New York: Double Day, Page & Co., 1910.

Dugmore, Arthur Radclyffe. *The Vast Sudan*. New York: Frederick A. Stokes, 1924.

Dugmore, Arthur Radclyffe. *The Wonderland of Big Game, Being an Account of Two Trips through Tanganyika and Kenya*. London: Arrowsmith, 1925.

Dugmore, Arthur Radclyffe. *The Autobiography of a Wanderer*. London: Hurst & Blackett, 1930.

Dugmore, Arthur Radclyffe. *Through the Sudan*. London: Pitman, 1938.

Dummett, Michael. *Frege: Philosophy of Mathematics*. Cambridge, MA: Harvard University, 1991.

Dunbar, Paul Laurence. *Lyrics of Lowly Life*. New York: Dodd, Mead and Company, 1896.

Early, Gerald. *Lure and Loathing: Essays on Race, Identity, and the Ambivalence of Assimilation*. New York: Penguin, 1993.

Egypt, Ophelia Settle, J. Masuoka, and Charles S. Johnson, eds. *Unwritten History of Slavery: Autobiographical Accounts of Negro Ex-Slaves*. Nashville, TN: Fisk University Social Science Institute, 1945.

Ekotto, Frieda. *Race and Sex across the French Atlantic: The Color of Black in Literary, Philosophical, and Theater Discourse*. New York: Rowman & Littlefield, 2011.

Ellison, Ralph. *Invisible Man: Thirtieth-Anniversary Edition*. New York: Random House, 1982.

Ellison, Ralph. *Invisible Man*. New York: Modern Library, 1994.

Ellison, Ralph. *The Collected Essays of Ralph Ellison: Revised and Updated.* Edited by John Callahan. New York: Modern Library, 1995.

Emerson, Ralph Waldo. "Essay IX. The Over-Soul." In *Emerson: Essays and Lectures,* edited by Joel Porte. New York: Library of America, 1983 [1841].

Engerman, Stanley, Seymour Drescher, and Robert Paquette, eds. *Slavery.* Oxford: Oxford University Press, 2001.

Erasmus. *The Colloquies of Erasmus.* Edited by Rev. E. Johnson. Translated by N. Bailey. 2 vols. London: F. Hildyard and T. Hammond, 1731.

Erdélyi, Arthur. *Asymptotic Expansions.* New York: Dover, 1956.

Evans-Pritchard, E. E. *Nuer Religion.* Oxford: Clarendon Press, 1956.

Ewald, William. *From Kant to Hilbert: A Source Book in the Foundations of Mathematics.* 2 vols. Oxford: Clarendon Press, 1996.

Fanon, Frantz. *Peau noire masques blancs.* Paris: Éditions du Seuil, 1952.

Fanon, Frantz. *Sociologies d'une revolution (L'an V de la Révolution algérienne).* Paris: Maspero, 1959.

Farès, Nabile. *Un passager de l'occident.* Paris: Éditions du Seuil, 1971.

Faye, Emmanuel. *Heidegger, l'introduction du nazisme dans la philosophie: autour des séminaires inédits de 1933–1935.* Paris: Albin Michel, 2005.

Ferreirós, José. "'Ο Οεὸς Αριτματίζει': The Rise of Pure Mathematics as Arithmetic with Gauss." In *The Shaping of Arithmetic after C. F. Gauss's Disquisitiones Arithmeticae,* edited by Catherine Goldstein, Norbert Schappacher, and Joachim Schwermer, 235–268. Berlin: Springer, 2007.

Ferreirós, José. *Labyrinth of Thought: A History of Set Theory and Its Role in Modern Mathematics.* 2nd ed. Basel: Birkhäuser, 2010.

Ferreirós, José. "On Dedekind's Logicism." In *Analytic Philosophy and the Foundations of Mathematics,* edited by Andrew Arana and Carlos Alvarez, 1–25. London: Palgrave Macmillan, 2011.

Fine, Elizabeth Calvert. *Soulstepping: African American Step Shows.* Urbana: University of Illinois Press, 2003.

Floyd, Samuel A. "Ring Shout! Literary Studies, Historical Studies, and Black Music Inquiry." *Black Music Research Journal* 11, no. 2 (1991): 265–287.

Ford, James, III. "From Being to Unrest, from Objectivity to Motion: The Slave in Marx's *Capital.*" *Rethinking Marxism* 23, no. 1 (2011): 22–30.

Foucault, Michel. "Il faut défendre la société." In *Cours au Collège de France (1975–1976),* édité par Mauro Bertani et Alessandro Fontana. Paris: Hautes Études Gallimard/Seuil, 1997.

Fournel, Victor. *Ce qu'on voit dans les rues de Paris.* Paris: E. Dentu, Libraire-Editeur, 1867.

France. *Le Code Noir ou Edit du Roy servant de reglement pour le gouvernement & l'administration de justice & la police des isles françoises de l'Amérique, & pour la discipline & le commerce des negres & esclaves dans l'edit pays: Donné à Versailles au mois de mars 1685. Avec l'Edit du mois d'aoust 1685. Portant établissement d'un conseil souverain & de quatre sieges royaux dans la coste de l'isle de S. Domingue.* A Paris, au Palais: Chez Claude Girard, dans la Grand'Salle, vis-à-vis la Grande'Chambre: au nom de Jesus, 1735 [1685].

Frazer, James G. *The Scape Goat*. Vol. 9 of *The Golden Bough: A Study in Magic and Religion*. London: Macmillan, 1913.

Frege, Gottlob. *Begriffsschrift, eine der arithmetischen nachgebildete Formelsprache des reinen Denkens*. Halle: Louis Nebert, 1879.

Frege, Gottlob. *Die Grundlagen der Arithmetik. Eine logisch mathematische Untersuchung über den Begriff der Zahlen*. Breslau: W. Koebner, 1884.

Frege, Gottlob. *Grundgesetze der Arithmetik: Begriffsschriftlich abgeleitet*. 2 Bde. Jena: Herman Poble, 1893.

Frege, Gottlob. "Der Gedanke. Eine logische Untersuchung." *Beiträge zur Philosophie des deutschen Idealismus* 1, no. 2 (1918–1919): 58–77.

Frege, Gottlob. *The Foundations of Arithmetic: A Logico-Mathematical Enquiry into the Concept of Number*. Translated by J. L. Austin. Evanston, IL: Northwestern University Press, 1980.

Gadamer, Hans-Georg. *Wahrheit und Methode: Grundzüge einer philosophischen Hermeneutik*. Im *Hans-Georg Gadamer, Gesammelte Werke*, Bd. 1. Tübingen: J. C. B. Mohr, 1990 [1962].

Gallagher, Shaun. "The Body in Social Context: Some Qualifications on the Warmth and Intimacy of Bodily Self Consciousness." *Grazer Philosophische Studien* 84 (2012): 91–121.

Gatewood, Willard B., Jr. *Aristocrats of Color: The Black Elite, 1880–1920*. Bloomington: Indiana University Press, 1990.

Gauss, Carl Friedrich. *Disquisitiones Arithmeticae*. Leipzig: Gerh. Fleischer, 1801.

Georgia Writer's Project (WPA). *Drums and Shadows: Survival Studies among the Georgia Coastal Negroes*. Athens: University of Georgia Press, 1940.

Gibbon, Edward. *The History of the Decline and Fall of the Roman Empire*. Edited by John Bury. 12 vols. New York: Fred De Fau & Company, 1906 [1779].

Giddings, Franklin. *The Principles of Sociology: An Analysis of the Phenomena of Association and of Social Organization*. New York: Macmillan, 1896.

Gilroy, Paul. *The Black Atlantic: Modernity and Double Consciousness*. Cambridge, MA: Harvard University Press, 1993.

Girard, René. *Le bouc émissaire*. Paris: Grasset, 1982.

Girard, René. *Le sacrifice*. Paris: Bibliotèque nationale de France, 2003.

Girard, René. *Achever Clausewitz*. Paris: Flammarion, 2011.

Glissant, Édouard. *Poétique de la relation*. Paris: Éditions Gallimard, 1990.

Gooding-Williams, Robert. "Philosophy of History and Social Critique in *The Souls of Black Folk*." *Sur les Sciences Sociales* 26 (March 1987): 99–114.

Gooding-Williams, Robert. "Evading Narrative Myth, Evading Prophetic Pragmatism: Cornel West's 'The American Evasion of Philosophy.'" *Massachusetts Review* 32, no. 4 (1991): 517–542.

Gooding-Williams, Robert. *In the Shadow of Du Bois: Afro-Modern Political Thought in America*. Cambridge, MA: Harvard University Press, 2009.

Goethe, Johann Wolfgang. *Faust: A Tragedy*. Translated by Charles T. Brooks. Boston: Ticknor and Fields, 1856.

Goethe, Johann Wolfgang. *Faust: eine Tragödie*. Stuttgart: J. G. Cotta, 1867.

Goethe, Johann Wolfgang. *Faust: Parts One and Two*. Translated by George Madison Priest. New York: Covici, Fiede, 1932.

Goethe, Johann Wolfgang. *Zahme Xenien*. Im *Johann Wolfgang Goethe: Poetische Werke*, herausgegeben von Siegfried Seidel, Bd. 2, *Berliner Ausgebe*. Berlin: Aufbau, 1960.

Green, George. *Essay on the Application of Mathematical Analysis to the Theories of Electricity and Magnetism*. Nottingham: T. Wheelhouse, 1828.

Hakluyt, Richard. *The Principall Navigations, Voiages and Discoveries of the English Nation, Made by Seas or Over Land, to the Most Remote and Farthest Distant Quarters of the Earth at any Time within the Compasse of These 1500 years*. London: G. Bishop and R. Newberie, deputies to C. Barker, 1589.

Hall, Marshall. "On the Functions of the Medulla Oblongata and Medulla Spinalis, and on the Excito-Motory System of Nerves." In *Philosophical Transactions, Royal Society of London*. London: Royal Society, 1833.

Hamilton, Virginia. *The People Could Fly: American Black Folktales*. New York: Alfred Knopf, 1985.

Harper, Douglas. "Framing Photographic Ethnography." *Ethnography* 4, no. 2 (2003): 241–266.

Harris, Cyril. *Dictionary of Architecture and Construction*. New York: McGraw-Hill, 1993.

Harris, Errol E. *An Interpretation of the Logic of Hegel*. Lanham, MD: University Press of America, 1983.

Hartman, Saidiya V. *Scenes of Subjection: Terror, Slavery, and Self-Making in Nineteenth-Century America*. New York: Oxford University Press, 1997.

Haugeland, John. *Dasein Disclosed*. Cambridge, MA: Harvard University Press, 2013.

Hawhee, Debra. *Bodily Arts: Rhetoric and Athletics in Ancient Greece*. Austin: University of Texas Press, 2005.

Hayden, Robert. "O Daedalus Fly Away Home." In *The Poetry of Black America: Anthology of the 20th Century*, edited by Arnold Adoff. New York: Harper & Row, 1973.

Hegel, Georg Wilhelm Friedrich. *Vorlesungen über die Philosophie der Kunst*. Herausgegeben von Heinrich Gustav Hotho. Berlin: Duncker & Humblot, 1842.

Hegel, Georg Wilhelm Friedrich. *Philosophie de l'esprit de Hegel*. Traduit par Augusto Véra. 2 tomes. Paris: Germer Baillière, Libraire Éditeur, 1869.

Hegel, Georg Wilhelm Friedrich. *Briefe von und an Hegel*. Bd. 1. Herausgegeben von Karl Hegel. Leipzig: Duncker & Humblot, 1887.

Hegel, Georg Wilhelm Friedrich. *Philosophy of Right*. Translated by S. W. Dyde. London: George Bell and Sons, 1896.

Hegel, Georg Wilhelm Friedrich. *Phänomenologie des Geistes*. Edited by George Lasson. Leipzig: Dürr'shen Buchhandlung, 1907.

Hegel, Georg Wilhelm Friedrich. *The Phenomenology of Mind*. 2 vols. Translated by James Black Baille. London: Swan Sonnenschein & Co., 1910.

Hegel, Georg Wilhelm Friedrich. *La phénoménologie de l'esprit*. Traduit par Jean Hyppolite. Tome 1. Paris: Aubier, Éditions Montaigne, 1941.

Hegel, Georg Wilhelm Friedrich. *Philosophy of Right*. Translated by T. M. Knox. Oxford: Oxford University Press, 1967.

Hegel, Georg Wilhelm Friedrich. *Phenomenology of Spirit*. Translated by A. V. Miller. Oxford: Oxford University Press, 1977.

Hegel, Georg Wilhelm Friedrich. *Hegel: The Letters*. Translated by Clark Butler and Christine Seiler. Bloomington: Indiana University Press, 1984.

Hegel, Georg Wilhelm Friedrich. *Phenomenology of Mind*. Translated by Michael Inwood. Oxford: Clarendon Press, 2007.

Hegel, Georg Wilhelm Friedrich. *Grundlinien der Philosophie des Rechts*. Im *Georg Wilhelm Friedrich Hegel Gesammelte Werke*, herausgegeben von Klaus Grotsch und Elisabeth Weisser-Lohmann, Bd. 14. Hamburg: Felix Meiner, 2009.

Hegel, Georg Wilhelm Friedrich. *Phenomenology of Spirit*. Translated and edited by Terry Pinkard and Michael Baur. Cambridge: Cambridge University Press, 2018.

Heidegger, Martin. *Sein und Zeit*. Vol. 8 of *Jahrbuch für Philosophie und Phänomenologische Forschung*. Halle: Niemeyer, 1927.

Heidegger, Martin. *Being and Time*. Translated by John Macquarrie and Edward Robinson. New York: Harper & Row, 1962.

Heidegger, Martin. "Vom Wesen des Grundes." Im *Gesamtausgabe*, herausgegeben von Friedrich-Wilhelm von Herrmann, Bd. 9 *Wegmarken*, herausgegeben von Friedrich-Wilhelm von Herrmann. Frankfurt am Main: Vittorio Klostermann, 1976.

Heidegger, Martin. *Metaphysische Anfangsgründe der Logik im Ausgang von Leibniz*. *Gesamtausgabe*, herausgegeben von Friedrich-Wilhelm von Herrmann, Bd. 26, herausgegeben von K. Held. Frankfurt am Main: V. Klostermann, 1978.

Heidegger, Martin. *Aristoteles, Metaphysik IX 1–3: Von Wesen und Wirklichkeit der Kraft*. *Gesamtausgabe*, herausgegeben von Friedrich-Wilhelm von Herrmann, Bd. 33, herausgegeben von H. Hüni. Frankfurt am Main: Klostermann, 1981.

Heidegger, Martin. *Zur Bestimmung der Philosophie*. *Gesamtausgabe*, herausgegeben von Friedrich-Wilhelm von Herrmann, Bd. 56, herausgegeben von B. Heimbücel. Frankfurt: V. Klostermann, 1987.

Heidegger, Martin. *Beiträge zur Philosophie (Vom Ereignis) (1936–1938)*. *Gesamtausgabe*, herausgegeben von Friedrich-Wilhelm von Herrmann, Bd. 65, herausgegeben von Friedrich-Wilhelm von Herrmann. Frankfurt am Main: Vittorio Klostermann, 1989.

Heidegger, Martin. *Kant und das Problem der Metaphysik*. *Gesamtausgabe*, herausgegeben von Friedrich-Wilhelm von Herrmann, Bd. 3, herausgegeben von Friedrich-Wilhelm von Herrmann. Frankfurt am Main: Vittorio Klostermann, 1991.

Heidegger, Martin. *Phänomenologie der Anschauung und des Ausdrucks: Theorie der philosophischen Begriffsbildung*. Im *Gesamtausgabe*, herausgegeben von Friedrich-Wilhelm von Herrmann, Bd. 59, herausgegeben von Claudius Stube. Frankfurt am Main: Vittorio Klostermann, 1993.

Heidegger, Martin. "Einblick in das was ist." Im *Gesamtausgabe*, herausgegeben von Friedrich-Wilhelm von Herrmann, Bd. 79, *Bremer und Freiburger Vorträge*, herausgegeben von Petra Jaeger. Frankfurt am Main: Vittorio Klostermann, 1994.

Heidegger, Martin. "Die Frage nach der Technik." Im *Gesamtausgabe*, herausgegeben von Friedrich-Wilhelm von Herrmann, Bd. 7, *Vorträge und Aufsätze*, herausgegeben von Brigitte Schillbach. Frankfurt am Main: Vittorio Klostermann, 2000.

Heidegger, Martin. *Einführung in die Metaphysik. Gesamtausgabe*, herausgegeben von Friedrich-Wilhelm von Herrmann, Bd. 40, herausgegeben von Petra Jeager. Frankfurt am Main: Vittorio Klostermann, 2000.

Heidegger, Martin. *Der Begriff der Zeit (Vortrag 1924). Gesamtausgabe*, herausgegeben von Friedrich-Wilhelm von Herrmann, Bd. 64, herausgegeben von Friedrich-Wilhelm von Herrmann. Frankfurt am Main: Vittorio Klostermann, 2004.

Heidegger, Martin. *Being and Time*. Translated by Joan Stambaugh. Revised and edited by Dennis Schmidt. Albany: State University of New York Press, 2010.

Heidegger, Martin. *Phenomenology of Intuition and Expression*. Translated by Tracy Colony. London: Continuum International, 2010.

Heijenoort, Jean van. *From Frege to Gödel: A Source Book in Mathematical Logic, 1879–1931*. Cambridge, MA: Harvard University Press, 1967.

Hellman, Geoffrey. *Mathematics without Numbers: Towards a Modal-Structural Interpretation*. Oxford: Clarendon Press, 1989.

Hellman, Geoffrey. "Three Varieties of Mathematical Structuralism." *Philosophia Mathematica* 9, no. 3 (2001): 184–211.

Hening, William Waller, ed. *The Statutes at Large; Being a Collection of all the Laws of Virginia from the First Session of the Legislature in the Year 1619*. 2 vols. New York: R. & W. & G. Bartow, 1823.

Herodas. *The Mimes of Herodas*. Edited by John Arbuthnot Nairn. Oxford: Clarendon Press, 1904.

Herskovits, Melville. *Rebel Destiny: Among the Bush Negroes of Dutch Guiana*. New York: Whittlesey House, McGraw Hill, 1934.

Herskovits, Melville. *Dahomey: An Ancient West African Kingdom*. 2 vols. New York: J. J. Augustin, 1938.

Hessel, Franz. *Spazieren in Berlin. Ein Lehrbuch der Kunst in Berlin spazieren zu gehn ganz nah dem Zauber der Stadt von dem sie selbst kaum weiß*. Berlin: Taschenbuch, 2012 [1926].

Higgins, Kathleen Marie. "Double Consciousness and Second Sight." In *Critical Affinities: Nietzsche and African American Thought*, edited by Jacqueline Scott and A. Todd Franklin. Albany: State University of New York Press, 2006.

Higginson, Thomas Wentworth. "Negro Spirituals." *Atlantic Monthly* 19, no. 116 (1867): 685–694.

Higginson, Thomas Wentworth. *Army Life in a Black Regiment*. Boston: Fields Osgood & Co., 1869.

Higginson, Thomas Wentworth. *The Sympathy of Religions: An Address Delivered at Horticultural Hall, Boston, February 6, 1870*. Boston: Reprinted from the *Radical*, 1871.

Hilbert, David. "Die Theorie der algebraischen Zahlkörper." *Jahresbericht der Deutschen Mathematiker-Vereinigung* 4 (1897): 175–546.

Hilbert, David. *Gesammelte Abhandlungen*. 3 Bd. Berlin: Springer, 1932.

Hill, Constance Valis. *Tap Dancing America: A Cultural History*. New York: Oxford University Press, 2010.

Hoffmann, E. T. A. *Sämtliche Werke*. Herausgegeben von Hartmut Steinecke und Wulf Segebrecht, unter Mitarbeit von Gerhard Allroggen und Ursula Segebrecht. Bd. 6. Frankfurt am Main: Deitscher Klassikerverlag, 2004.

Hogrebe, Wolfram. "Von der Hinfälligkeit des Wahren und der Abenteuerlichkeit des Denkers. Eine Studie zur Philosophie Oskar Beckers." Im *Kultur—Mensch—Technik. Studien zur Philosophie Oskar Beckers*, herausgegeben von Carl Friedrich Getmann und Jochen Sattler. München: Wilhelm Fink, 2014.

Homer. *Iliad*. Edited by A. T. Wyatt. Translated by William F. Murray. Cambridge, MA: Loeb Classical Library, Harvard University Press, 1999.

Hopkins, Dwight N. *Being Human: Race, Culture, and Religion*. Minneapolis: Fortress Press, 2005.

Hountondji, Paulin J. *African Philosophy: Myth and Reality*. Edited by Abiola Irele. Translated by Henri Evans and Jonathan Rée. 2nd ed. Bloomington: Indiana University Press, 1996.

Hugo, Victor. *Notre-Dame de Paris 1482*. Paris: Librairie Ollendorff, 1904 [1831].

Hurston, Zora Neale. "Characteristics of Negro Expression." In *Zora Neale Hurston: Folklore, Memoirs and Other Writings*, edited by Cheryl Wall. New York: Library of America, 1995.

Husserl, Edmund. *Ideen zu einer reinen Phänomenologie und phänomenologischen Philosophie I: Allgemeine Einfuhrung in die reine Phänomenologie. Husserliana: Gesemmelte Werke*. Herausgegeben von Walter Biemel. Bd. 3. Den Haag: Martinus Nijhoff, 1950.

Husserl, Edmund. *Ideen zu einer reinen Phänomenologie und phänomenologischen Philosophie II: Phänomenologische Untersuchungen zur Konstitution. Husserliana: Gesemmelte Werke*. Herausgegeben von Marly Biemel. Bd. 4. Den Haag: Martinus Nijhoff, 1952.

Husserl, Edmund. "Besprechung von E. Schröder's Vorlesungen über die Algebra der Logik (Exakte Logik)." Im *Husserliana: Gesemmelte Werke*, herausgegeben von Bernhard Rang, Bd. 22, *Aufsätze und Rezensionen*. Den Haag: Nijhoff, 1979 [1891].

Husserl, Edmund. *Die Krisis der europäischen Wissenschaften und die transzendentale Phänomenologie: Eine Einleitung in die phänomenologische Philosophie*. Herausgegeben von Elizabeth Ströker. Berlin: Felix Meiner, 1996 [1936].

Husserl, Edmund. *Natur und Geist, Vorlesungen Sommersemester 1919. Husserliana: Gesammelte Werke, Materialen*, Bd. 4, herausgegeben von Herman L. van Breda, Michael Weiler, und Samuel Ijsseling. Dordrecht: Kluwer Academic Publishers, 2002.

Ibn Ezra, Abraham. *The Commentary of Abraham Ibn Ezra on the Pentateuch*. Edited and translated by Jay F. Shachter. 3 vols. Hoboken, NJ: Ktav Pub & Distributors, 1986 [1155].

Ibn Ezra, Abraham. *Vayikra, Devarim*. In *The Commentary of Abraham Ibn Ezra on the Pentateuch*, vol. 3, *Leviticus*, translated and edited by Jay F. Shachter. Hoboken, NJ: Ktav Pub & Distributors, 1986.

Ibn Khaldūn, ʿAbdur-Raḥmān. *Tārīkh Ibn Khaldūn, al-musammā Kitābu-l-ʿibari wa dīwani-l-mubtadaʾ wa-l-khabar fī ayāmi-l'arab wa-l-ʿajam wa-l-barbar, wa man ʿāṣrahum min dawī as-salṭāni-l-akbar, al-mujalid al-ʿawal*. 8 vols. Beirut: Dar al-kutub al-ʿilmīya, 1971.

Ibn Sīnā. *Kitāb aš-Šifā'*. 8 vols. Taḥqīq Ahmad Fu'ād al-Ahwānī. Al-Qāhira: Našir wizāra at-tarbiya wa ta'alīm, al-idāra al-'āma lilthaqāfa, 1958 [1027].

Iyall Smith, Keri E. "Hybrid Identities: Theoretical Examinations." In *Hybrid Identities: Theoretical and Empirical Examinations*, edited by Keri E. Iyall Smith and Patricia Leavy. Leiden: Brill, 2008.

Jahnke, Hans Niels. *Mathematik und Bildung in der Humboldtschen Reform*. Göttingen: Vandenboeck & Ruprecht, 1990.

James, C. L. R. *American Civilization*. Edited by Anna Grimshaw and Hart Keith. London: Blackwell, 1993.

James, William. "Royce's *Religious Aspect of Philosophy*." *Atlantic Monthly* 55 (June 1885): 332.

James, William. "Reflect Action and Theism." In *The Will to Believe and Other Essays in Popular Philosophy*. New York: Longmans, Green and Co., 1919.

James, William. *Essays in Radical Empiricism*. Edited by Ralph Barton Perry. London: Longmans, Green and Co., 1942 [1909].

James, William. *The Principles of Psychology*. 3 vols. Cambridge, MA: Harvard University Press, 1981.

Jefferson, Thomas. *Reports of Cases Determined in the General Court of Virginia from 1730–1740 and 1768–1772*. Charlottesville: F. Carr and Company, 1829.

Jennings, Michael. "Walter Benjamin, Siegfried Kracauer, and Weimar Criticism." In *Weimar Thought*, edited by Peter E. Gordon and John P. McCormick. Princeton, NJ: Princeton University Press, 2013.

Jones, Bessie. *For the Ancestors: Autobiographical Memories*. Edited by John Stewart. Urbana: University of Illinois Press, 1983.

Jones, Bessie, and Bess Lomax Hawes. *Step It Down: Games, Plays, Songs & Stories from the Afro-American Heritage*. New York: Harper & Row, 1972.

Kahn, Jonathon S. *Divine Discontent: The Religious Imagination of W. E. B. Du Bois*. Oxford: Oxford University Press, 2009.

Kant, Immanuel. *Kritik der reinen Vernunft*. Herausgegeben von Raymund Schmidt. Hamburg: Felix Meiner, 1956 [1781, 1787].

Kant, Immanuel. *Kants Gesammelte Schriften, Akademie Textausgabe*. Herausgegeben von der Königlich Preußischen Akademie der Wissenschaften. 9 Bde. Berlin: Walter de Gruyter, 1968.

Kant, Immanuel. *Critique of Pure Reason*. In *Cambridge Edition of the Works of Immanuel Kant*, edited and translated by Paul Guyer and Allen Wood. Cambridge: Cambridge University Press, 1998.

Kant, Immanuel. *What Real Progress Has Metaphysics Made in Germany since the Time of Leibniz and Wolff?* In *Cambridge Edition of the Works of Immanuel Kant: Theoretical Philosophy after 1781*, edited by Henry Allison and Peter Heath, translated by Gary Hartfield and Michael Friedman. Cambridge: Cambridge University Press, 2002.

Kazhdan, Alexander, ed. *Oxford Dictionary of Byzantium*. Oxford: Oxford University Press, 1991.

Kemble, Frances Anne. *Journal of Residence on a Georgia Plantation in 1838–39*. New York: Harper & Bro., 1863.

Kerkering, Jack. "'Of Me and of Mine': The Music of Racial Identity in Whitman and Lanier, Dvořák and Du Bois." *American Literature* 73, no. 1 (2001): 147–184.

Kimball, Bruce A. "'This Pitiable Rejection of a Great Opportunity': W. E. B. Du Bois and Clement G. Morgan, and the Harvard University Graduation of 1890." *Journal of African-American History* 94, no. 1 (Winter 2009): 5–20.

Klein, Felix. "Über Aufgabe und Methode des mathematischen Unterrichts an den Universitäten." *Jahresbericht der Deutschen Mathematiker Vereinigung* 7 (1904): 267–346.

Kluge, Friedrich. *Etymologisches Wörterbuch der deutschen Sprache*. Berlin: Gruyter, 2002 [1881].

Knowles, Mark. *Tap Roots: The Early History of Tap Dancing*. Jefferson, NC: McFarland & Co., 2002.

Kojève, Alexandre. *Introduction à la Lecture de Hegel: Leçons sur la Phénoménologie de l'Esprit professées de 1933 à 1939 à l'École des Hautes Études*. Edité par Raymond Queneau. Paris: Gallimard, 1947.

Kracauer, Sigfried. "Die Reise und der Tanz." Im *Siegfried Kracauer Schriften*, herausgegeben von Inka Mülder-Bach, Bd. 5, *Aufsätze 1915–1926*. Frankfurt am Main: Suhrkamp, 1990.

Kronecker, Leopold. "Ueber den Zahlbegriff." *Journal für die reine und angewandte Mathematik* 101 (1887): 337–355.

Krueger, Paul, and Theodor Mommsen, eds. *Institutiones*. Vol. 1 of *Corpus juris civilis*. Berlin: Weidmann, 1870.

Küng, Hans. *Menschwerdung Gottes. Eine Einführung in Hegels theologisches Denken als Prolegomena zu einer künftigen Christologie*. Freiburg in Breisgau: Herder, 1970.

Labouret, Henri, and Paul Rivet. *Le royaume d'Arda et son évangélisation*. Paris: Institut d'Ethnologie, 1929.

Lacan, Jacques. "La science et la vérité." *Cahiers pour l'analyse* 1 (1966): 6–28.

Lacan, Jacques. "L'étourdit." *Scilicet* 4 (1973): 5–52.

Lacan, Jacques. *Le séminaire de Jacques Lacan, Livre VII, L'éthique de la psychanalyse 1959–1960*. Edited by Jacques-Alain Miller. Paris: Éditions du Seuil, 1975.

Lacan, Jacques. *Le séminaire de Jacques Lacan, Livre XX, Encore 1972–1973*. Paris: Éditions du Seuil, 1975.

Lacan, Jacques. *Le séminaire, Livre XVII, L'énvers de la psychanalyse*. Edited by Jacques-Alain Miller. Paris: Seuil, 1991.

Laertius, Diogenes. *Lives of the Eminent Philosophers*. Translated by R. D. Hicks. 2 vols. Cambridge, MA: Loeb Classical Library, Harvard University Press, 1972 [1925].

LaPorte, Jean Marie Frédéric. *Le rationalisme de Descartes*. Paris: Presses université de France, 1945.

Large, Duncan. "A Note on the Term '*Umwerthung*.'" *Journal of Nietzsche Studies* 39 (Spring 2010): 5–11.

Lee, Maurice. "Du Bois the Novelist: White Influence, Black Spirit, and *The Quest of the Silver Fleece*." *African American Review* 33, no. 3 (1999): 389–400.

Leenhardt, Maurice. *Do Kamo. La personne et le mythe dans le monde mélanésien*. Paris: Gallimard, 1971 [1947].

Leibniz, Gottfried Wilhelm. *Die Philosophischen Schriften*. 7 Bde. Herausgegeben von C. J. Gerhardt. Berlin: Weidmannsche Buchhandlung, 1887.

Leiris, Michel. "Alberto Giacometti." *Documents* 1, no. 4 (1929): 209–210.

Leiris, Michel. *L'Afrique fantôme: De Dakar à Djibouti (1931–33)*. Paris: Gallimard, 1988 [1934].

Lemieux, Cyril. *Le devoir et la grâce*. Paris: Economica, 2009.

Lemke, Sieglinde. "Of the Coming of John." In *The Cambridge Companion to W. E. B. Du Bois*, edited by Shamoon Zamir, 37–47. Cambridge: Cambridge University Press, 2008.

Lévi-Strauss, Claude. *Le totémisme aujourd'hui*. Paris: Universitaires de France, 1962.

Lewis, David Levering. *W. E. B. Du Bois: Biography of a Race*. New York: Henry Holt and Company, 1993.

Library of Congress. *Report of the Librarian of Congress*. Annual Report, Division of Music, Library of Congress. Washington, DC: U.S. Government Printing Office, 1933.

Library of Congress. *Archive of American Folk Song Annual Report, 1928–1939*. Washington, DC: Library of Congress Project, Work Projects Administration, 1940.

Linschoten, Hans. *On the Way toward a Phenomenological Psychology: The Psychology of William James*. Pittsburgh: Duquesne University Press, 1968.

Locke, John. *The Fundamental Constitution of Carolina*. Vol. 9 of *The Works of John Locke*. London: Rivington, Egerton, Cuthell, and Arch, 1824.

Locke, John. *Two Treatises of Civil Government*. London: Dent, 1953 [1690].

Locke, John. *An Essay Concerning Human Understanding*. Edited by P. Nidditch. Oxford: Clarendon Press, 1975 [1694].

Lomax, Alan, and John Avery Lomax. *American Ballads and Folk Songs*. New York: Macmillan Publishing Company, 1934.

Lomax, John Avery. "Self-Pity in Negro Folk-Songs." *The Nation* 105, no. 2719 (1917): 141–145.

Lomax, John Avery. *Adventures of a Ballad Hunter*. New York: Macmillan Co., 1947.

Lowell, Thomas. *Rolling Stone: The Life and Adventure of Arthur Radclyffe Dugmore: A Biography*. Garden City: Doubleday, Doran & Company, 1934.

Löwry, Michael. "Naphta or Settembrini?—Lukács and Romantic Anticapitalism." In *George Lukács*, edited by Judith Marcus and Zoltán Tarr. New Brunswick, NJ: Rutgers University Press, 1989.

Lukács, Georg. *Die Theorie des Romans. Ein geschichtsphilosophischer Versuch über die Formen der großen Epik*. Darmstadt und Neuwied: Luchterhand, 1965.

Lukács, Georg. "Georg Simmel." *Theory Culture Society* 8, no. 3 (1991): 145–150.

Lukács, Georg. "The Writer and the Critic." In *Writer and Critic and Other Essays*, edited and translated by Arthur Kahn. London: Merlin Press, 1970.

Lukács, Georg. Preface to *Theory of the Novel: A Historico-Philosophical Essay on the Forms of Great Epic Literature*. Translated by Anna Bostock. Cambridge, MA: MIT Press, 1971.

Lyotard, Jean-François. *L'assassinat de l'expérience par la peinture, Monory*. Paris: Le Castor Astral, 1984.

Machamer, Peter. "Causality and Explanation in Descartes's Natural Philosophy." In *Motion and Time, Space and Matter: Interrelations in the History of Philosophy and Science*, edited by Peter Machamer and Robert G. Turnbull. Columbus: Ohio State University Press, 1976.

Macombe, Paul. *The Soul-Less Souls of Black Folk: A Sociological Reconsideration of Black Consciousness as Du Boisian Double Consciousness*. Lanham, MD: University Press of America, 2009.

Maimonides, Moses. *Dalalat-ul-Hairīn*. Taḥqīq Hüseiyn Atay. Al-Qāhira: Maktabah ath-thiqāfah ad-dīnīyah, 2002 [1974].

Makkreel, Rudolf. *Dilthey, Philosopher of the Human Studies*. Princeton, NJ: Princeton University Press, 1975.

Malinowski, Bronislaw. *The Sexual Lives of Savages*. London: Routledge, 1933.

Malone, Jacqui. *Steppin' on the Blues: The Visible Rhythms of African American Dance*. Urbana: University of Illinois Press, 1996.

Marable, Manning. "The Black Faith of W. E. B. Du Bois: Sociocultural and Political Dimensions of Black Religion." *Southern Quarterly* 23, no. 3 (1985): 15–33.

Marinello, Juan. "Una novela cubana." In *Literatura hispanoamericana: Hombres-meditaciones*. México: Ediciones de la Universidad de México, 1937.

Marion, Jean-Luc. "Generosity and Phenomenology: Remarks on Michael Henry's Interpretation of Cartesian Cogito." In *Essays on the Philosophy and Science of René Descartes*, edited and translated by Stephen Voss, 52–74. Oxford: Oxford University Press, 1993.

Martineau, James. *A Study of Religion, Its Sources and Contents*. 2 vols. Oxford: Clarendon Press, 1888.

Marx, Karl. "A Contribution to the Critique of Hegel's *Philosophy of Right*. Introduction." In *Karl Mark: Early Writings*, translated by Rodney Livingstone and Gregor Benton. New York: Vintage, 1975.

Marx, Karl. *Capital: A Critique of Political Economy*. Vol. 1. Translated by Ben Fowkes. New York: Penguin, 1976.

Marx, Karl. *Capital: A Critique of Political Economy*. Vol. 3. Translated by David Fernbach. New York: Penguin, 1992.

Marx, Karl. *Das Kapital: Kritik der politischen Ökonomie. Karl Marx Frederick Engels: Werke*, herausgegeben von der Rosa-Luxemburg-Stiftung, Bd. 23: *Buch 1: Der Produktionensprozess des Kapitals*. Berlin: Karl Dietz, 2012 [1973].

Marx, Karl. *Das Kapital: Kritik der politischen Ökonomie. Karl Marx Frederick Engels: Werke*, herausgegeben von der Rosa-Luxemburg-Stiftung, Bd. 25: *Buch 3: Der Gesamtprozeß der kapitalistischen Produktion*. Berlin: Karl Dietz, 2012 [1973].

Maurice, John Frederick Denison. *Prophets and Kings of the Old Testament: A Series of Sermons Preached in the Chapel of Lincoln's Inn*. Cambridge: Macmillan, 1853.

Mauss, Marcel. *Essai sur le Don*. Paris: Presses Universitaires de France, 1950.

McKay, Claude. *Banjo: A Story without a Plot*. New York: Harper & Row, 1970 [1929].

McKim, Lucy. "Songs of the Port Royal 'Contrabands.'" *Dwight's Journal of Music* 22, no. 5 (1862): 254–255.

Mecklin, John Moffatt. *Democracy and Race Friction: A Study in Social Ethics*. New York: Macmillan, 1914.

Merleau-Ponty, Maurice. *Le visible et l'invisible*. Paris: Gallimard, 1964.

Meyerson, Ignace. *Écrits, 1920–1983: Pour une psychologies historique*. Paris: Presses Universitaires de France, 1987.

Miles, Jonathan. *The Wreck of the Medusa: The Most Famous Sea Disaster of the Nineteenth Century*. New York: Atlantic Monthly Press, 2007.

Mill, John Stuart. *A System of Logic, Ratiocinative and Inductive: Being a Connected View of the Principles of Evidence and the Methods of Scientific Investigation*. London: John W. Parker, 1843.

Miller, Jacques Alain. "La suture (éléments de la logique du signifiant)." *Cahiers pour l'analyse* 1 (1966): 37–49.

Mommsen, Theodor, and Paul Krueger, eds. "Liber primus" of "Institutiones." In *Corpus Iuris Civilis*. Cambridge Library Collection—Classics. Cambridge: Cambridge University Press, 2014 [1870].

More, Thomas. *The Confutation of Tyndale's Answer, Books 1–4*. Vol. 8 of *The Complete Works of St. Thomas More*, edited by Louis A. Schuster, Richard Marius, and James P. Lusardi. New Haven, CT: Yale University Press, 1973.

More, Thomas. *A Dialogue Concerning Heresies*. Vol. 6 of *The Complete Works of St. Thomas More*, edited by Thomas M. C. Lawler, Germain Marc'hadour, and Richard C. Marius. New Haven, CT: Yale University Press, 1981.

Morris, Christopher G., ed. *Academic Press Dictionary of Science and Technology*. San Diego: Harcourt Brace Jovanovich, 1992.

Morrison, Toni. "Rootedness: The Ancestor as Foundation." In *Black Women Writers (1950–1980): A Critical Evaluation*, edited by Mari Evans, 339–345. New York: Anchor Books, 1984.

Morton, Timothy. "Blood Sugar." In *Romanticism and Colonialism: Writing and Empire 1780–1830*, edited by Tim Fulford and Peter J. Kitson. New York: Cambridge University Press, 1998.

Morton, Timothy. *The Poetics of Spice: Romantic Consumerism and the Exotic*. Cambridge: Cambridge University Press, 2006.

Moses, Wilson Jeremiah. "Du Bois's *Dark Princess* and the Heroic Uncle Tom." In *Black Messiahs and Uncle Toms: Social and Literary Manipulations of a Religious Myth*. University Park: Pennsylvania State University Press, 1993.

Moses, Wilson Jeremiah. *Creative Conflict in African American Thought: Frederick Douglass, Alexander Crummell, Booker T. Washington, W. E. B. Du Bois, and Marcus Garvey*. Cambridge: Cambridge University Press, 2004.

Moten, Fred. *In the Break: The Aesthetics of the Black Radical Tradition*. Minneapolis: University of Minnesota Press, 2003.

Moten, Fred. "Blackness and Nothingness (Mysticism in the Flesh)." *South Atlantic Quarterly* 112, no. 4 (2013): 741–742.

Mudimbe, Valentine Y. *The Invention of Africa: Gnosis, Philosophy, and the Order of Knowledge*. Bloomington: Indiana University Press, 1988.

Mudimbe, Valentine Y. "An African Practice of Philosophy." *Quest: Revue Africaine de Philosophie* 19, nos. 1–2 (2005): 21–36.

Murray, Albert. *Albert Murray and the Aesthetic Imagination of a Nation*. Edited by Barbara Baker. Auburn, AL: Hill Books, 2010.

Le Musée d'Ethnographie du Trocadéro. *Instructions sommaire pour les collecteurs d'objets ethnographiques, en collaboration avec les membres de la mission Dakar-Djibouti.* Paris: l'Institut d'Ethnologie de l'Université de Paris et le Musée d'Ethnographie du Trocadéro, 1931.

Nietzsche, Friedrich. *Genealogy of Morals*. In *The Works of Friedrich Nietzsche*, edited by Alexander Tille, translated by William A. Hausemann. New York: Macmillan, 1897.

Nietzsche, Friedrich. *Nietzsche, Werke: Kritische Gesamtausgabe*. Herausgegeben von Giorgio Colli und Mazzino Motinari. 8 Abt. Berlin: de Gruyter, 1967–.

Nietzsche, Friedrich. *The Gay Science*. Translated by Walter Kaufmann. New York: Vintage Books, 1974.

Nietzsche, Friedrich. *The Birth of Tragedy*. In *Basic Writings of Nietzsche*, translated by Walter Kaufmann. New York: Modern Library Classics, 2000.

Nietzsche, Friedrich. "Human, All-Too-Human." In *Basic Writings of Nietzsche*, translated by Walter Kaufmann. New York: Modern Library Classics, 2000.

Nietzsche, Friedrich. *Ecce Homo: How One Becomes What One Is*. Translated by Thomas Wayne. New York: Algora Publishing, 2004.

Nygren, Anders. *Agape and Eros*. Translated by Philip Watson. Philadelphia: Westminster Press, 1953.

Odum, Howard W., and Guy B. Johnson. *Negro Workaday Songs*. Chapel Hill: University of North Carolina Press, 1926.

Okiji, Fumi. *Jazz as Critique: Adorno and Black Expression Revisited*. Stanford, CA: Stanford University Press, 2018.

Park, Robert Ezra. "Negro Race Consciousness as Reflected in Race Literature." *American Review* 1 (1923): 505–516.

Park, Robert Ezra. "Human Migration and the Marginal Man." *American Journal of Sociology* 33, no. 6 (1928): 881–893.

Parker, Mattie Erma Edwards, ed. *North Carolina Charters and Constitutions, 1578–1698*. Vol. 1 of *The North Carolina Colonial Records*. Raleigh: North Carolina Office of Archives and History, 1963.

Parrish, Lydia. *Slave Songs of the Georgia Sea Islands*. New York: Creative Age Press, 1942.

Paulsen, Friedrich. *Geschichte des gelehrten Unterrichts, Auf den Deutschen Schulen und Universitäten, Vom Ausgang des Mittelalters bis zur Gegenwart 1740–1892*. Leipzig: Veit & Co., 1885.

Peirce, Charles Sanders. "Some Consequences of Four Incapacities." *Journal of Speculative Philosophy* 2, no. 3 (1868): 140–150.

Peirce, Charles Sanders. "Evolutionary Love." In *Scientific Metaphysics*, edited by Charles Hartshorne and Paul Weis. Vol. 6 of *Collected Papers of Charles Sanders Peirce*, Cambridge, MA: Harvard University Press, 1935.

Peirce, Charles Sanders. *Collected Papers of Charles Sanders Peirce*. Vol. 5, *Pragmatism and Pragmaticism and Scientific Metaphysics*. Edited by Charles Hartshorne and Paul Weis. Cambridge, MA: Harvard University Press, 1958.

Peirce, Charles Sanders. "On the Nature of Signs." In *Writings of Charles S. Peirce: A Chronological Edition*, vol. 3, *1872–1878*, edited by Christian J. W. Kloesel. Bloomington: Indiana University Press, 1986.

Peirce, Charles Sanders. "A Large Number of Repetition." In *Writings of Charles S. Peirce: A Chronological Edition*, vol. 4, *1879–1884*, edited by Christian J. W. Kloesel. Bloomington: Indiana University Press, 1989.

Phaedrus, Gaius Julius. *Some of the More Familiar Fables of Phædrus*. Edited by John T. White and D. D. Oxon. London: Longmans, Green, and Company, 1887 [854].

Pierce, Edward L. *The Negroes at Port Royal: Report of E. L. Pierce, Government Agent to the Hon. Salmon P. Chase, Secretary of the Treasury*. Boston: R. E. Wallcut, 1862.

Pietz, William. "The Problem of the Fetish, I." *Anthropology and Aesthetics*, no. 9 (Spring 1985): 5–17.

Plato. *Laches, Protagoras, Meno, Euthydemus*. Translated by W. R. M. Lamb. Cambridge, MA: Loeb Classical Library, Harvard University Press, 1924.

Plato. *Symposium*. Translated by W. R. Lamb. Cambridge, MA: Loeb Classical Library, Harvard University Press, 1925.

Plato. "Οροι [Horoi] (Définitions)." In *Dialogues apocryphes*. Vol. 13 of *Platon: Œuvres completes*. Édité et traduit par Joseph Souilhé. Paris: Société d'édition, Les Belles Lettres, 1930.

Plato. *The Republic*. Translated by Paul Shorey. 2 vols. Cambridge, MA: Loeb Classical Library, Harvard University Press, 1937.

Plato. *Apology. Crito. Phaedo. Phaedrus*. Translated by H. N. Fowler. Cambridge, MA: Loeb Classical Library, Harvard University Press, 1999 [1944].

Poe, Edgar Allen. "The Man of the Crowd." In *Edgar Allen Poe: Poetry and Tales*, by Edgar Allen Poe, 388–399. New York: Library of America, 1984.

Poincaré, Henri. "Sur les intégrales irrégulières des équations linéaires." *Acta Mathematica* 8 (1886): 295–344.

Poincaré, Henri. *Science et Méthode*. Paris: Ernest Flamarion, 1920.

Pollard, Alfred William. *Fine Books*. New York: G. P. Putnam's Sons, 1912.

Posnock, Ross. *Color & Culture: Black Writers and the Making of the Modern Intellectual*. Cambridge, MA: Harvard University Press, 1998.

Poulton, Edward Bagnall. *The Colours of Animals: Their Meaning and Use, Especially Considered in the Case of Insects*. London: Kegan Paul, Trench, Trübner & Co., 1890.

Price, Sally, and Jean Jamin. "A Conversation with Michel Leiris." *Current Anthropology* 29, no. 1 (1988): 157–167.

Pyenson, Lewis. *Neohumanism and the Persistence of Pure Mathematics in Wilhelmian Germany*. Philadelphia: American Philosophical Society, 1983.

Quintilian. *Institutio Oratoria*. Translated by H. E. Butler. Cambridge, MA: Loeb Classical Library, Harvard University Press, 1993.

Rachman, Stephen. "'Es läßt sich nicht schreiben' Plagiarism and 'The Man of the Crowd.'" In *The American Face of Edgar Allan Poe*, edited by Shawn Rosenheim and Stephen Rachman. Baltimore: Johns Hopkins University Press, 1995.

Radcliffe-Brown, Alfred. *Structure and Function in Primitive Society*. London: Cohen & West, 1952.

Rampersad, Arnold. *The Art & Imagination of W. E. B. Du Bois*. Cambridge, MA: Harvard University Press, 1976.

Rampersad, Arnold. "Slavery and the Literary Imagination: Du Bois' *The Souls of Black Folk.*" In *Slavery and the Literary Imagination*, edited by Deborah McDowell and Arnold Rampersad. Baltimore: Johns Hopkins University Press, 1989.

Reck, Erich. "Dedekind's Structuralism: An Interpretation and Partial Defense." *Synthese* 137, no. 3 (2003): 369–419.

Reed, Adolph. *W. E. B. Du Bois and American Political Thought: Fabianism and the Color Line*. Oxford: Oxford University Press, 1999.

Riegl, Alois. *Spätrömische Kunstindustrie*. Darmstadt: Wissenschaftliche Buchgesellschaft, 1987 [1927].

Riemann, Bernhard. "Über die Darstellbarkeit einer Function durch eine trigonometrische Reihe." In *Abhandlungen der Königlichen Gesellschaft der Wissenschaften zu Göttingen*, edited by Richard Dedekind, 13:87–132. Göttingen: Der Dieterischensen Buchhandlung, 1868.

Riemann, Bernhard. "Über die Hypothesen, welche der Geometrie zu Grunde liegen." In *Abhandlungen der Königlichen Gesellschaft der Wissenschaften zu Göttingen*, edited by Richard Dedekind, 13:133–150. Göttingen: Der Dieterischensen Buchhandlung, 1868.

Roberts, Neil. *Freedom as Marronage*. Chicago: University of Chicago Press, 2015.

Robinson, Beverly J. "Africanisms and the Study of Folklore." In *Africanisms in American Culture*, edited by Joseph E. Holloway. Bloomington: Indiana University Press, 1990.

Robinson, Cedric. *The Terms of Order: Political Science and the Myth of Leadership*. Chapel Hill: University of North Carolina Press, 1980.

Rosenfield, Claire. "The Conscious and Unconscious Use of the Double." In *Stories of the Double*, edited by A. J. Guerard. Philadelphia: J. B. Lippincott, 1967.

Rosenkranz, Karl. *Geschichte der Kant'schen Philosophie*. In *Kant's Sämmtliche Werke*, Bd. 12, herausgegeben von Karl Rosenkranz und Friedrich Wilhelm Schubert. Leipzig: L. Voss, 1840

Rousseau, Jean-Jacques. *Discours sur l'origine et les fondements de l'inégalité parmi les hommes*. Dans *Œuvres complètes*, tome 3, édité par Bernard Gagnebin et Marcel Raymond. Paris: Gallimard, 1964.

Rousseau, Jean-Jacques. *Du contrat social, ou principes du droit politique*. Amsterdam: MεταLibri, 2007.

Royce, Josiah. *The Religious Aspect of Philosophy: A Critique of the Bases of Conduct and of Faith*. New York: Houghton Mifflin, 1885.

Royce, Josiah. *The Problem of Christianity: Lectures Delivered at the Lowell Institute in Boston, and at Manchester College, Oxford*. New York: Macmillan, 1913.

Royce, Josiah. "Nietzsche." *Atlantic Monthly* 119, no. 3 (1917): 321–331.

Rudwick, Elliot. "W. E. B. Du Bois and the Atlanta University Studies on the Negro." *Journal of Negro Education* 26, no. 4 (1957): 466–476.

Rudwick, Elliot. *W. E. B. Du Bois, Propagandist of the Negro Protest*. New York: Atheneum, 1968.

Russell, Bertrand. *The Principles of Mathematics*. Cambridge: Cambridge University Press, 1903.

Sachs, Joe. "Aristotle: Motion and Its Place in Nature." *Internet Encyclopedia of Philosophy*. Accessed March 19, 2016. https://www.iep.utm.edu/aris-mot/.

Ṣālaḥ, Ibrāhīm. "Akhbār ibn al-Muzarra'." *Majalla majma' al-luġa al-'arabīya bi Damašq* 54, no. 3 (1979): 677–684.

Salerno, Roger. *Beyond the Enlightenment: Lives and Thoughts of Social Theorists*. Westport, CT: Praeger, 2004.

Sandis, Constantine. "Understanding the Lion for Real." In *Knowledge, Language and Mind: Wittgenstein's Thought in Progress*, edited by Antonio Marques and Nuno Venturinha. Berlin: de Gruyter, 2012.

Scheler, Max. *Der Formalismus in der Ethik und die materiale Wertethik (mit besonderer Berücksichtigung der Ethik Immanuel Kants)*. 2. Teil, Im *Jahrbuch für Philosophie und Phänomenologische Forschung*. Halle: Niemeyer, 1916.

Scheler, Max. *Wesen und Formen der Sympathie*. Bonn: F. Cohen, 1923.

Schilder, Paul. "The Somato-Psyche in Psychiatry and Social Psychology." *Journal of Abnormal and Social Psychology* 29, no. 3 (1934): 314–327.

Schilder, Paul. *The Image and Appearance of the Human Body*. London: Kegan Paul, Trench, Trubner & Co., 1935.

Schopenhauer, Arthur. *Welt als Wille und Vorstellung*. Vol. 1 of *Arthur Schopenhauer sämtliche Werke in sechs Bänden*, edited by Eduard Grisebach. Leipzig: Philipp Reclam, 1909.

Schopenhauer, Arthur. *The World as Will and Representation*. Translated by E. F. Payne and J. Kemp. New York: Dover, 1966 [1958].

Schubring, Gert. *Die Entstehung des Mathematiklehreberufs im 19 Jarhundert. Studien und Materialen zum Prozeß der Professionalisierung in Preußen (1810–1870)*. Weinheim/Basel: Beltz, 1983.

Schumpeter, Joseph. *Das Wesen und der Hauptinhalt der theoretischen Nationalökonomie*. Leipzig: Duncker & Humbolt, 1909.

Schumpeter, Joseph. "On the Concept of Social Value." *Quarterly Journal of Economics* 23, no. 2 (1909): 213–232.

Scott, Daryl. *Contempt and Pity: Social Policy and the Image of the Damaged Black Psyche 1880–1996*. Chapel Hill: University of North Carolina Press, 1997.

Scotus, John Duns. *Joannis Duns Scoti, doctoris subtilis, ordinis minorum opera omnia*. Edited by Lucas Wadding. Vol. 12. Paris: Apud Ludovicum Vivès, 1893.

Shaler, Nathaniel. "The Negro Problem." *Atlantic Monthly* 54 (1884): 696–709.

Shapiro, Stewart. *Philosophy of Mathematics: Structure and Ontology*. New York: Oxford University Press, 1997.

Shaw, Stephanie. *W. E. B. Du Bois and "The Souls of Black Folk."* Chapel Hill: University of North Carolina Press, 2013.

Shelley, Percy Bysshe. *Prometheus Unbound*. In *The Complete Poetical Works of Percy Bysshe Shelley*, edited by Thomas Hutchinson. London: Humphrey Milford, Oxford University Press, 1914.

Siemerling, Winfried. "W. E. B. Du Bois, Hegel, and the Staging of Alterity." *Callaloo* 24, no. 1 (2001): 325–333.

Siemerling, Winfried. *The New North American Studies: Culture, Writing and the Politics of Re/Cognition*. London: Routledge, 2005.

Silva, Guadalupe. "Alejo Carpentier del negrismo a lo real maravilloso." *Anclajes* 19, no. 1 (2015): 53–70.

Simmons, Alison. "Sensible Ends: Latent Teleology in Descartes's Account of Sensation." *Journal of the History of Philosophy* 39, no. 1 (2001): 49–75.

Simondon, Gilbert. *Deux leçons sur l'animal et l'homme*. Paris: Ellipses, 2004.

Sinclair, T. A. "Plato's Philosophical Dog." *Classical Review* 62, no. 2 (1948): 61–62.

Smith, Felipe. "W. E. B. Du Bois and the Progress of the Black Soul." In *American Body Politics: Race, Gender, and Black Literary Renaissance*, 227–233. Athens: University of Georgia Press, 1998.

Smith, John. *The Generall Historie of Virginia, New-England, And the Summer Isles: With the Names of the Adventurers, Planters, And Governours From Their First Beginning, Anô: 1584. to This Present 1624. With the Procedings of Those Severall Colonies And the Accidents That Befell Them In All Their Journyes And Discoveries. Also the Maps And Descriptions of All Those Countryes, Their Commodities, People, Government, Customes, And Religion Yet Knowne. Divided Into Sixe Bookes*. London: printed by I. D. and I. H. for Michael Sparkes, 1624.

Smith, Mark, ed. *Stono: Documenting and Interpreting a Southern Slave Revolt*. Columbia: University of South Carolina Press, 2005.

Smith, William Robertson. *Lectures on the Religion of the Semites: The Fundamental Institutions*. London: Adam and Charles Black, 1889.

Spaulding, Henry G. "Under the Palmetto." *Continental Monthly*, August 1863, 188–203.

Spenser, Herbert. *First Principles*. 3rd ed. London: Williams and Norgate, 1870.

Spenser, Herbert. *Descriptive Sociology, or Group of Sociological Facts*. New York: Appleton and Company, 1873.

Spenser, Herbert. *The Principles of Sociology*. 3 vols. New York: D. Appleton and Company, 1883.

Spillers, Hortense. "The Crisis of the Negro Intellectual: A Post-Date." *boundary 2* 21, no. 3 (1994): 65–116.

Spillers, Hortense. "Mama's Baby, Papa's Maybe: An American Grammar Book." In *Black, White, and in Color*. Chicago: University of Chicago Press, 2003.

Stepto, Robert. *From behind the Veil*. Chicago: University of Chicago Press, 1979.

Stuckey, Sterling. *Slave Culture: Nationalist Theory and the Foundations of Black America*. Oxford: Oxford University Press, 1987.

Suárez, Francisco. *Disputationes metaphysicae*. In *Opera omina*, vol. 25, edited by Andrê Michel and Charles Berton. Paris: Ludovisum Vivès, 1861 [1597].

Sullivan, Robert. *Justice and the Social Context of Early Middle High German Literature*. London: Routledge, 2001.

Sundquist, Eric. *To Wake the Nations: Race in the Making of American Literature*. Cambridge, MA: Belknap Press of Harvard University Press, 1993.

Tarde, Gabriel. *Les lois de l'imitation, étude sociologique*. Paris: Ancienne Librairie Germer Baillière, 1890.

Tempels, R. P. Placide Fran. *La Philosophie bantoue*. Paris: Pesence Africaine, 1959.

Thomas, Velma Maia. *No Man Can Hinder Me: The Journey from Slavery to Emancipation through Song*. New York: Crown, 2001.

Tönnies, Ferdinand. *Gemeinschaft und Gesellschaft. Abhandlung des Communismus und des Socialismus als empirischer Culturformen*. Leipzig: R. Reisland, 1887.

Turner, Lorenzo Dow. *Africanisms in the Gullah Dialect*. Chicago: University of Chicago, 1946.

Tyler, Tom. "*Quia Ego Nominor Leo*: Barthes, Stereotypes, and Aesop's Animals." *Mosaic* 40, no. 1 (2007): 45–59.

Tyndale, William, ed. and trans. *The First New Testament Printed in English*. Worms: Peter Schöffer, 1526.

Tyndale, William. *An Answer to Sir Thomas More's Dialogue*. Edited by Rev. Henry Walter. Cambridge: Cambridge University Press, 1850 [1536].

Tyndall, John. "Scientific Materialism." In Vol. 1 of *Fragments of Science: A Series of Detached Essays, Addresses, and Reviews*, by John Tyndall, 75–90. London: Longmans, Green, 1892.

Varisco, Bernardino. *I massimi problemi di Bernardino Varisco*. Seconda Edizione. Milano: Libreria editrice Milanese, 1914.

Varro, Marcus Terentius. *Rerum rusticarum*. In *Cato and Varro on Agriculture*, translated by William Davis Hooper and Harrison Boyd Ash. Cambridge, MA: Loeb Classical Library, Harvard University Press, 1934.

Vico, Giambattista. *The New Science of Giambattista Vico*. Translated by Thomas Goddard Bergin and Max Harold Fisch. Ithaca, NY: Cornell University Press, 1968.

Vico, Giambattista. *Giambattista Vico, La Scienza nuova, a cura di Paolo Cristofolini e Manuela Sanna*. Roma: Edizioni di Storia e Letteratura, 2013 [1744].

Wagner, Richard. *Lohengrin: A Romantic Opera in Three Acts*. Edited by Berthold Tours. Translated by Natalia Macfarren. London: Novello, Ewer and Co., 1890.

Wagner, Richard. *Wagner's Opera Lohengrin: Containing the German Text, with an English Translation and the Music of the Principal Airs*. Oliver Ditson Company's Standard Edition of Opera Librettos. Boston: Oliver Ditson Company, 1890.

Wagner, Richard. *The Authentic Librettos of the Wagner Operas*. New York: Crown Pub., 1938.

Wagner, Richard. *Lohengrin: Opera in Three Acts: Original Text and English Translation*. Translated by Stewart Robb. G. Schirmer's Collection of Opera Librettos. New York: Schirmer, 1963.

Wagner, Richard. *Bridal Chorus from Lohengrin*. Edited and translated by John Rutter. Oxford Choral Classic Octavos. Oxford: Oxford University, 1997.

Wakeman, George, and David Goodman Croly. *Miscegenation: The Theory of the Blending of the Races, Applied to the American White Man and Negro*. New York: H. Dexter, Hamilton & Co, 1863.

Wald, Pricilla. *Constituting Americans: Cultural Anxiety and Narrative Form*. Durham, NC: Duke University Press, 1995.

Walsh, Robert. *Notices of Brazil in 1828 and 1829*. London: Frederick Westley & A. H. Davis, 1830.

Waṭṭār, aṭ-Ṭāhir. "'az-Zinjīya wa aḍ-ḍābṭ.'" In *aš-Šuhadā' yaʿudūn haḏā al-usbūaʿ: majmūʿa qiṣaṣ*, by aṭ-Ṭāhir Waṭṭār. Algiers: al-muʿsasa al-waṭanīya, 1984.

Waṭṭār, aṭ-Ṭāhir. *Tajriba fi-ṭ ʿišiq*. Nicosia: al-muʿsasa al-waṭanīya, 1984.

Weber, Heinrich. "Leopold Kronecker." *Jahresbericht der Deutschen Mathematiker-Vereinigung* 2 (1893): 5–31.

Weber, Max. *Wirtschaft und Gesellschaft*. Tübinger: J. C. B. Mohr, 1922.

Weise, Christian. *Die drey Klügsten Leute in der gantzen Welt* [Leipzig, J. Fritzsch, 1675]. In *Sämtliche Werke*. Berlin: de Gruyter, 2005.

West, Cornel. "Black Strivings in a Twilight Civilization." In *The Future of the Race*, edited by Henry Louis Gates Jr. and Cornel West. New York: Vintage, 1996.

Wilderson, Frank. *Incognegro, a Memoir of Exile and Apartheid*. Durham, NC: Duke University Press, 2008.

Wilderson, Frank. *Red, White & Black: Cinema and the Structure of U.S. Antagonisms*. Durham, NC: Duke University Press, 2010.

Windham, Tom. Interview by Bernice Bowden. In *Slave Narratives: A Folk History of Slavery in the United States from Interviews with Former Slaves, Volume II: Arkansas Narratives*, edited by Federal Writers' Project of the Works Progress Administration. Washington, DC: Library of Congress, 1937.

Wittgenstein, Ludwig. *Philosophical Investigations*. Translated by G. E. M. Anscombe. Oxford: Blackwell, 2001 [1953].

Wolf, Friedrich August. *Darstellung der Alterthumswissenschaft, nebst einer Auswahl seiner kleinen Schriften: und litterarischen Zugaben zu dessen Vorlesungen über die Alterthumswissenschaft*. Leipzig: August Lehnhold, 1807.

Wolff, Christian. *Philosophia Rationalis sive Logica, methodo scientifica pertractata et ad usum scientiarum atque vitæ aptata. Præmititur Discursus præliminaris de philosophis in genere*. FrancoFurti & Lipsiæ, 1728.

Wolff, Christian. *Vernünftige Gedanken von Gott, der Welt und der Seele des Menschen, auch allen Dingen überhaupt*. Halle: im Magdeburgischen, 1747.

Wood, Peter H. *Black Majority: Negroes in Colonial South Carolina from 1670 through the Stono Rebellion*. New York and London: W. W. Norton, 1974.

Woodard, Vincent. *The Delectable Negro: Human Consumption and Homoeroticism within U.S. Slave Culture*. Edited by Justin A. Joyce and Dwight A. Mcbride. New York: New York University Press, 2014.

Works Progress Administration, Federal Writers' Project, ed. *Slave Narratives: A Folk History of Slavery in the United States from Interviews with Former Slaves*. Washington, DC: U.S. Government Printing Office, 1941.

Wright, Richard. Introduction. In *Black Metropolis: A Study of Negro Life in A Northern City*, by St. Clair Drake and Horace Cayton. Chicago: University of Chicago Press, 1945.

Wright, Richard. "Psychiatry Comes to Harlem." *Free World*, September 1946, 49–52.

Wynter, Sylvia. "Unsettling the Coloniality of Being." *New Centennial Review* 3, no. 3 (2003): 257–337.

Yetman, Norman. "The Background of the Slave Narrative Collection." *American Quarterly* 19, no. 3 (1967): 546–553.

Zamir, Shamoon. *Dark Voices: W. E. B. Du Bois and American Thought, 1888–1903*. Chicago: University of Chicago Press, 1995.

Zermelo, Ernst. "Untersuchungen über die Grundlagen der Mengenlehre." *Mathematische Annalen* 65, no. 2 (1908): 261–281.

Abakuá, 12
Abelard, 271, 344
abolitionists, 8, 155, 157, 158, 211, 249, 511n31
absolute, 108
abstraction, 105; symbolic, 107
abstract mathematics, 92
abstract structures, 105
Accent (television show), 232
Achebe, Chinua, 387–88, 391
A. C. McClurg and Company, 67
actualitas, 192, 193
actualities-in-action, 283
actualities-of-doing, 288
actuality, 192, 193
actuality-in-doing, 290
actuality-of-doing, 288, 293
admixture, 440
Adorno, Theodor, 124–27, 297, 436
Advancement of Learning (Bacon), 269
a-epistemic knowledge, 11
aesthetic theory, 191
Aesthetic Theory (Adorno), 127
African, 5–6, 387–89
Africanism, 387, 391
African philosophy, 390–91
L'Afrique fantôme, 159
Afrocentrism, 197
Afrocubanísimo, 12
Afro-pessimism, 320
Agamben, Giorgio, 249, 525n55
Agapē (ἀγάπη), 165, 308, 400–403, 435, 519, 564
agapism, 282
Agassiz, Louis, 34
agency: authenticity and, 162, 164; conscious, 259; of reading, 62; self-conscious, 149
Age of Discovery, 303
"Ain't It Hard to Be a Nigger, Nigger" (song), 153
Aktionsraum (space-for-action), 373
Alan Lomax Collection, The (recording), 227
A la Recherche du temps perdu (Proust), 87
alétheia (ἀλήθεια), 97, 329–32
Alexander VI (Pope), 385
Alfonso V (King), 385

Algeria, 424, 429–30, 448–51, 457
Algerian War of Liberation, 424
alienation: of capital assets, 210; of double consciousness, 137; from rights, 171; total, 43–44, 400
Allen, Ernest, 33, 463n32
Allen, Richard, 319, 392
Allen, Robert, 352
Allen, William Francis, 157, 159–66, 200, 218, 224, 349; methodology and, 164; transcription and, 162, 163
ALN, 424, 450
amalgamation, 238, 462n29
A. M. E. Review (journal), 394
American Anti-Slavery Society, 173
American Guide Manual (WPA), 151
Americanization, 254
American Missionary Association, 511n31
American Negro Academy, 255, 319, 394, 396, 397
American Slave Code in Theory and Practice Shown by Its Statutes, Judicial Decisions, and Illustrative Facts, The (Goodell), 184
Ammann, Hermann, 368
analytical sociology, 476n156
anarchy, 135, 140
animals: humans as distinct from, 170; psychic being of, 204
animate body, 204
Another Country (Baldwin), 18, 419, 424, 425, 436, 456
Anselm, 344
ante rem structuralism, 480n206
Anthropologie in pragmatischer Hinsicht (Anthropology from a Pragmatic Point of View) (Kant), 341–42
anthropology, Kant on, 341–42
Anthrōpos (ἄνθρωπος), 16, 100, 115, 284, 291–92, 353, 389
anti-black racism, 395
anticapitalism, romantic, 123
anticipation, 530n134
anti-modernism, 159
anti-theism, 280
Apollinaire, Guillaume, 195

Appeal in Favor of that Class of Americans Called Africans, An (Child), 175
appetitive, 286
apposition, 245–46
Aptheker, Herbert, xv, 88, 92, 97, 111, 259, 260, 263, 266
Aquinas, Thomas, 267, 270, 386
al-ʿarab al-mustaʿarib (العرب المستعرب), 447, 455
Arabicization (التعريب, *at-taʿarīb*), 448–49
Arab Renaissance, 450
Arcades Project (Adorno), 124
archetype, 64, 66, 468n112
Archimedes und der Schüler (Schiller), 100
Archive of American Folksong, 152
Arendt, Hannah, 249, 315
areté (ἀρετή), 284–87, 292–93, 307, 313, 316
aristocratic virtue, 293
Aristotle, 292, 307, 312, 313, 322, 523n44; aristocracy and, 290, 293; community and, 218; *enérgeia* and, 192, 193, 218, 259; *hexis* and, 288; individuation and, 377; Lacan critique of, 326, 327, 329, 330; on metaphysics, 344; *mêtis* and, 242; on mimes, 439; mimesis and, 8, 13, 14, 86, 191, 194; Negro and, 337; *poiēsis* and, 14, 127, 182, 243, 289; primitivism and, 337; *right-principle-discourse* and, 353; sentience and, 286; slavery and, 291; on speculative sciences, 345; on study of polity, 434, 435; Supreme Good and, 287; *techne* and, 355; Unity-of-Virtue doctrine and, 290; Universal Good and, 286
arithmetization of analysis, 90–92, 97, 100, 112–15, 324, 384
Armée de Libération Nationale (ALN), 424, 450
Armstrong, Joe, 224
Army Life in a Black Regiment (Higginson, T. W.), 165
Arnold, Mathew, 141
art: black being and, 433; commodity as, 126; knowledge and, 191; Kracauer on, 121–22; nature imitated by, 191; political consciousness and, 126; politics and, 430; as propaganda, 119
articulated flesh, 199
artifacts, 190
artifice, 160, 169, 198
artistic expression, 121
"Artist's Struggle for Integrity, The" (Baldwin), 432
l'art pour l'art, 119
assimilation (تشابه, *tašābuh*), 446, 448
asymptotes, 88, 97, 109
asymptotic expansion, 88
asymptotic series, 88, 89
asymptotic thinking, 86–99
Atlanta Conferences project, 262
"Atlanta University Studies, The" (conferences), 262
Atlantic Monthly, 41–42, 45, 47, 67, 158, 273, 316
Augustine, 267, 269, 307, 402
authenticity, 417; agency and, 162, 164; of self-understanding, 346; of specimens, 164
Authentic Librettos of the Wagner Operas, The, 143
authoritative hermeneutics, 69
automatic physiological reaction, 463n45
autonomous will, 99
autre lecture, 323
axiomatic definitions, 96
axiomatic laws, 92–94
Ayler, Albert, 236
Azam, Étienne Eugène, 34

Bacon, Francis, 177, 204, 207, 267, 269, 270
Badiou, Alain, 108, 345, 383, 391
Bailey, Cornelia, 241–43
Baker, Josephine, 195
Baker, Thomas, 156
Baker, William A., 158
Baldwin, James, xix, 18, 419, 423–28, 430–37, 448, 456
Balibar, Etienne, 17
Balzac, Honoré de, 62, 63, 124
Banjo (McKay), 17
Banu Hilāl–Banu Sulaym confederation, 451

Barbados House of Assembly, 171, 187
barking dogs, 440–42
Barnicle, Mary Elizabeth, 224
Barthes, Roland, xvi, 180–82, 185–89, 196, 198–202, 208, 209, 386
Barton, Roland, 27, 254, 256, 386–87
"Basic Problems of Phenomenology, The" (Heidegger), 331
al-Baṣrī, Abū ʿUthman ʿAmr ibn Baḥr al-Kinānī (al-Jāḥiẓ), 438
Bastian, Adolf, 348, 349
Bastide, Roger, xviii, 376–82, 390
Bates, Henry, 434
Baudelaire, Charles, xv, 63, 120; indecipherability and, 125; on "The Man of the Crowd," 62; modernism and, 118, 125
Beatson, Peter, 457
Becker, Oscar, xvii, 332–34, 345, 525n55; bifurcation of temporality, 368; Dasein and, 373, 374, 381; *Geist* and, 373; nature-time and, 369; Nazis and, 535n250; paraontology and, 374–75, 383; primitive semiosis and, 361, 362, 375; thrownness-in-the-world and, 372; time and, 363, 368, 370; transcendence of Dasein and, 344
becoming-in-common, 433
Bedeutsamkeit, 357–61
"Begriff der Zeit, Der" (The Concept of Time) (Heidegger), 353, 362
behavioralism, 34
Being and Time (Heidegger), 332, 348, 363, 366
being-beside, 327
being-bornness, 371
being-in-common, 317
being-in-flight, 321
being-in-the-world, 342, 350, 353, 354, 360, 368
being-toward-birth, 371
Benacerraf, Paul, 107
Benjamin, Walter, xv, 63–65, 87, 120, 123–26, 128, 435
Bergson, Henri, 87, 111
besidedness, 391
Bestandstücke, 124
Bhabha, Homi, 437

Bibb, Henry, 215, 216
"Bichon chez les Nèfres" (Bichon among the Negroes) (Barthes), 189, 198
Bilali, Sapelo, 222, 223
Binet, Alfred, 33
binomial distributions, 260
biocentric ethnoclass, 183
Bioho, Domingo, 297
Bird Homes (Dugmore), 68
birth, 371
Birth of the Nation (film), 67
Bishop, Samuel Henry, 398
black being, art and, 433
Black Boy (Wright), 48
Black Codes, 117, 302
Black Flame Trilogy (Du Bois), 49, 139, 149
black liberation theology, 485n277
Black Metropolis (Wright), 48
black performance, 249
Block, Ernst, 125
blood-sacrifice, 414
Bloom, Allan, 443
Blues, 247–48, 391, 436; perpetual movement in, 422–23; as *poiēsis in black*, 448
Blythe, Nat, 197, 506n12
Boas, Franz, 152, 224
bodiliness, 366
bodily experience, 38
bodily instrumentality, 290
body, consciousness and, 204
body-image, 38
Bogues, Tony, 15
Bona: utila, 268, 415; *vir* to *mulier*, 283–84, 293, 314, 384
Bonus, 283–84, 293, 307, 314; vir, 283–84, 292, 309–10, 327
Book of Gems, The (Hall, S. C.), 61
Boston New England Freedmen's Aid Society, 490n22
Bourbaki, Nicolas, 324
Bowden, Bernice, 1, 151, 169
Brackett, John Q. A., 295
Bradford, George, 262
Breton, André, 11
bricolage, 52, 54
Bridal Chorus, 143–44
Bridgewater Treatises, 265

Brook, Shelton, 420
Brooks, Charles T., 399
Brown, Charles Brockden, 64, 65
Brown, Henry Box, 155
Brown, James, 236
Brown, John, 158
Brown, Sterling, 161
Bulletin of the Society for African Philosophy in North America, 388
Bumstead, Horace, 262
Butler, Benjamin, 155
Buzzard Lope, xvi, 218–27, 231–45, 249–50, 317–18, 387, 392, 416
"By an' by-e I'm Goin' t' See the King" (Song), 235
Byzantine Empire, 439

Cabrera, Lydia, 12
Caillois, Roger, 434, 437
Calafate, Manoel, 297
Calame-Griaule, Geneviève, xviii, 379–81
calculability problem, 94, 325
calculative faculty, 289
calculus, 471n137
Camus, Albert, 429
Canaque, 376–77
Cantor, Georg, 90, 91, 102, 108, 345
Capital (Marx), 248
capital, *télos* of, 244
capital assets, 6, 7, 210
capitalism: commodity, 123, 129; critiques of, 248–49; international, 139; slavery as process of, 171
capitalist modernity, 19, 396, 435, 470n130
Capuchin monks, 227
cardinal measure, 97
Carolina Constitution, 3, 4, 171, 210, 465n65
Carpentier, Alejo, 11, 12
Cartesian dualism, 94
Cartesian psychology, 203
cartography, 389
Cassirer, Ernst, 121, 360
castas, 431
categorical metaphysics, 306
Catherine of Aragon, 538n320
Cato (slave), 297

Cato the Elder, 283
causality, 265; divine will and, 281; Heidegger on, 194
CBS Television, 232
Chalmers, David, 464n55
Chambre claire, Le (Barthes), 202–3
chance, 86; in human action, 88, 94; law and, 98, 113; sociology as measurement of, 90, 261
Chandler, Nahum, xvii, 319–22, 329, 333, 393–95
"Characteristics of Negro Expression" (Hurston), 437–38
charity, 136–37, 401, 403, 404
Chase, Salmon, 155
Chicago School of Sociology, 35, 47, 48
Chiesa, Lorenzo, 321, 323
Child, Lydia Maria, 8, 175, 211
children, as creatures of nature, 120
Christianity, 282, 303, 307–10
Church of England, 538n320
Ciardi, John, 232–35, 240
Cicero, 284, 292
citizenship, 45, 46
Citizenship Clause, 46
civic ethics, 406, 415
civic liberty, 435
civil freedom, 44
civilization, 120, 179, 292–93, 310, 315–16; *Geist* and, 375
Civil Rights Acts, 47
Civil War (English), 42
Civil War (U.S.), 45, 158
civitas, 327
Clansman, The (Dixon), 67
Clark, Andy, 464n55
Clark, T. J., 119, 430
Clauberg, Johannes, 523n44
Clauss, Ludwig Ferdinand, 372, 374, 375
Cleveland, Francis, 295
Code Noir, 6, 20, 187, 188, 201, 386
cognition, 464n55; consciousness and, 257; Kant and, 341; mimicry and, 277; semiosis and, 9, 251, 257; subject and, 257; as thinking intuition, 340
Colbert, Jean Baptiste, 187
Cole, Andrew, 300

Coleridge, Samuel Taylor, 166, 176, 177, 493n90
colonial imperiality, 199
colonialism, 470n130; imperialist, 254, 396
commodification, 112, 124, 125, 128–29, 321
commodities, as art, 126
commoditization, 253
commodity capitalism, 123, 129
commodity economy, 125
commodity fetish, 123
common association, 15
communal feeling, 307, 312
community, 207, 346; historizing-occurrence of, 351
complaining songs, 153
Comte, Auguste, 91–98, 100, 114, 265, 348, 472n146, 476n156
concepts: objects and, 101; signifiers and, 182; sociopolitical order of racialized capitalist slavery, 185
conceptual schemata, 53
concrete mathematics, 92
concretion, 366
Confederate States of America, 296
Confiscation Act of 1862, 490n22
conscious agency, 259
consciousness: body and, 204; cognition and, 257; double, xv, 33–35, 39, 40, 47–49, 51, 118, 137, 257, 315, 463n32, 518n200; field of, 38; immanence of, 126; intentional objects of personal, 204; interiority and, 118; jellyfish, 429; of kind, 476n156; political, 126; race, 258; self, 37, 38, 40–41, 52, 53; self-understanding and, 121; semiosis and, 257; sociality and, 6, 17–18; socially extended, 18, 40; stream of, 49
"Conservation of the Races, The" (Du Bois), 18, 47, 49, 141, 255
Constitution, U.S., 44, 45; Article IV of, 46; slavery and, 465n65; Three-Fifths Compromise, 539n331
consumption of flesh, 176
Continental Monthly (magazine), 158
contingency, 119
continuum hypothesis, 472n138
Cooper, Anna Julia, 319

Cooper, James Fenimore, 64, 65
I Corinthians 13, 136–37, 401, 403, 404
Corpus juris civilis (Justinian), 4
correct formalization, 327
co-subjectivity, 206
Council of Learned Societies, 152
Counterreformation, 395, 402
Cowboy Songs and Other Frontier Ballads (Lomax, J.), 151
Cravath, Erastus, 266
creole, 236
créoles, 440
créolisation, 236, 246, 455
Crisis (journal), 27, 255, 398, 407
Critique of Practical Reason (Kant), 9
Critique of Pure Reason (Kant), 36, 40, 339, 340
Croly, David Goodman, 431, 462n29
Cronyn, George, 161, 168
Crummell, Alexander, 137–39, 141
cultural continuity, 112
cultural miscegenation, 39
cultural vestibularity, 184
culture: actualization through, 206; Kant on, 218; primitives and, 361; as signification-conferring structures, 218
Curiosities of Literature (D'Israeli), 61

dance, xvi, 215, 216
Dark Princess (Du Bois), 149
Darkwater (journal), 408
Dasein, 331–38, 342, 345; *Aktionsraum* and, 373; authentic self-understanding of, 346; being-toward-death and, 366–67; as being-with, 364; bodiliness of, 366; concretion and, 366; entities and, 343; existence and, 343, 381; fate and, 351; historicity of, 353, 354; historizing-occurrence of, 352; history and, 347–49; individuation of, 367; nature and, 369; personhood and, 368; *potentiality*-for-being and, 367; referentiality of, 365, 382; self and, 363; signs and, 359; *they* and, 364–65, 380; time and, 346–47, 350, 362; transcendence of, 343, 344; worldliness and, 355; world of, 364; world structure and, 357

David, Jacques-Louis, 119
Davis, Jefferson, 168, 294–98, 394
Davis, John, 224, 227, 231
Davis, Peter, 223, 224, 231–36, 239, 240, 243
death, 370–71
Declaration of Independence, 44, 170
Decline and Fall of the Roman Empire, The (Gibbon), 303
Dedekind, Richard, xv, 345, 471n137, 477n182, 479n195, 480n206, 481n207; discontinuous functions and, 90; number theory and, 99–110, 112, 114; objects of thought and, 97, 323–26; on truth and knowledge, 97, 99
Dedekind cuts, 90
Degré zéro de l'écriture, Le (The Degree Zero of Writing) (Barthes), 181, 182
De Jure Personarum, 301
de las Casas, Bartolomé, 385
deliberative excellence, 290
deliberative faculty, 289
Demiurge, 374
democracy, 45
Democracy and Race Friction (Mecklin), 34
democratic freedom, 44
Dennis, Rutledge, 463n32
Derrida, Jacques, 201, 252, 423
Descartes, René, 203, 267, 269, 270, 384
descriptive psychology, 55
Descriptive Sociology (Spencer), 93
desiderata, 446
desire, 179
destiny, 351
desuetude, 119
Determination of the Concept of Race (Kant), 9
determinism, 87
diachrony, 85
dialect, 163
dianoia, 113
Dickey, William, 175
differential calculus, 471n137
"Dilemma of Determinism, The" (James, W.), 304
Dilthey, Wilhelm, xv, 54–56, 84, 87, 95, 120, 347
Diogenes Laertius, 292

Dirichlet, Gustav, 90, 470n135
Dirichlet series, 90
discourse: grammar of, 321, 323; of humanism, 2; logical, 326; paraontology, 322; *right-principle-discourse*, 326
Discourse on the Origin and Foundations of Inequality among Men (Rousseau), 316
dis-emplacement, 142
displacement, 320, 322
D'Israeli, Isaac, 61
Dissertation on the Scientific Method, A (Coleridge), 166, 176, 177
distantiality, 382
distributive justice, 400
Divine love, 309
divisible person, 376–87
Dixon, Tom, 67
Doctrina Christiana, 227
Doctrine of Discovery, 385
doctrine of love, 309
"Doctrine of Sacrifice" (Du Bois), xix
doctrine of submission, 263–318
documentary images, 68
documentation, 14
dog: barking, 439–42; dog-rooster debate, 444; noble, 442–43; philosophical, 443–44
Do Kamo (Leenhardt), 375, 376
domination, 517n192
double consciousness, xv, 33–35, 39, 40, 47–49, 51; alienated, 137; critique of, 463n32; interiority and, 118; Nietzsche and, 518n200; as second sight, 258, 315; semiosis and, 257
double existence, 122, 128
Douglass, Frederick, xvi, 2, 4, 7, 66, 162, 174–78, 210; capitalism critiques and, 248–49; on dances, 215, 216; "Dred Scott Decision" speech, 173; on freedom as natural right, 170–72; London speeches by, 172; natural rights and, 166; personhood and, 178; on rights of person, 171; on slave-singing, 153–56
"Dred Scott Decision" speech (Douglass), 173
Du Bois, W. E. B., xiv–xv, xvii, xix, 25, 30–32, 51, 71–83, 135, 252, 423; on art as

propaganda, 119; Atlanta Conferences and, 262; on attitudes toward Negros, 395–97; authorial narrative control and, 70; autonomous will and, 99; Barton and, 386–87; Baudelaire and, 63; on Bishop, 398; bodily experience and, 38; *bonus-bona* alteration, 283–84, 293; Bridal Chorus and, 143–44; calculability problem and, 325; on change in conception of civilization, 316; civic ethics and, 415; commencement addresses by, 537n315; Comte and, 91–93; conceptions of Negro, 112, 114; Dilthey and, 56; on doctrine of submission, 302, 306; "double consciousness" and, 33–35, 39, 40; on Emancipation, 42, 46; Emerson and, 398; ethical styles and, 87–88; Goethe and, 398–400; Harvard address of 1890, 294–98, 302–4, 310, 313–14, 318, 397; hyperbola asymptotes analogy, 88–91, 97, 109, 111, 259, 260, 263; intellect-in-action and, 17, 18, 393; James, W., and, 39, 264–66; law-chance paradox, 98, 113; Martineau and, 272, 274, 280; on modernity, 384–85; narrative style and, 54; Negro as type and, 139; "Negro" usage by, 27–29, 41–42, 252, 254, 256, 258, 320; Nietzsche and, 304–6, 310–11, 518n200; on northern and southern Negro differences, 140; on novel and psychology, 18, 48, 49; paraontology and, 394; Poe and, 59, 65; positivism and, 93, 97, 98; religion and, 317, 540n337; Rousseau and, 44–45; Royce and, 275, 280, 281; on sacrifice, 414–16; Scholasticism and, 267–69; self-consciousness and, 40–41; on Shouting, 404; on sociology, 261, 262; on sorrow songs, 50, 85; Strong Man/Submissive Man dyad and, 298, 299, 302; Supreme Good and, 353; on Talented Tenth, 141; theistic teleology and, 266, 269, 272; truth and, 96, 259; on "vicious logical circle" of sociology, 93; Wilberforce address, 415–16
Dudum siquidem (Alexander VI), 385
Dugmore, Arthur Radclyffe, 68, 69, 71–83
Dumas, Alexander, 64
Dum Diversas, 386
Dummett, Michael, 107
Dunbar, Paul Laurence, 51
durée, 87
Durège, Heinrich, 471n137
Dusk of Dawn (Du Bois), 396
Dwight's Journal of Music, 143, 156, 157, 166
dynamic confluence, xiii

economics, schools of, 510n20
economy, commodity, 125
¡Ecué-Yamba-O: Historia afro-cubana! (Carpentier), 12
Edgar Huntly (Brown, C. B.), 65
education: liberal arts, 31–32; *neuhumanistischen Bildungsreform*, 115
Educational Commission, 490n22
Edward, Jonathan, 183–84
ego: constitution of world and, 206; things and, 204–5
ego-subject, 206, 250
Egypt, Ophelia Settle, 8, 211
"Einbildungskraft des Dichters, Die" (Dilthey), 55
ekphrasis, 54
élan vital, 111
Éléments de mathématique, 324
Eliot, Charles, 294, 295
Ellison, Ralph, 114, 406, 407, 409, 410, 412, 423
emancipation: Du Bois on, 42, 46; freedom and, 46
emblems, 61
Emblems Divine and Moral (Quarles), 61
emergent intelligence, 96
Emerson, Ralph Waldo, 33, 274, 398
enérgeia (ἐνέργεια), 282, 283, 286, 293, 446
enfranchisement, 46
Engel, Carl, 152
enslaved captive body, 5, 179, 180, 183, 184
enslavement, as capitalist process, 171
entelecheia (ἐντελέχεια), 193, 259
entities, 533n185; Dasein and, 343; study of, 523n44
L'énvers et l'endroit (Betwixt and Between) (Camus), 429

environmental world, 203
episematic mimicry, 437
epistēmē (ἐπιστήμη), 238–40
epistemic collapse, 437
epistemic dualism, 36, 93
Epoché (Husserl), 206, 209
equal concealment (*Verborgenheit*), 332
Equiano, Olaudah, 66
equinumerosity, 326
Erigena, 267, 344
Erlebnis, 54–55, 87
Erlebnis und die Dichtung, Das (*Poetry and Experience*) (Dilthey), 87
error, truth and, 279, 280
Essay Concerning Human Understanding, An (Locke), 3, 170
L'Été (*Summer*) (Camus), 429
ethical doctrines, 276
ethical styles, 88
ethnicity, 183
ethnocentrism, 375
ethnographic gaze, 84, 470n130
ethnographic museums, 190
ethnographic photography, 70
ethnographizing, 198
Ethnologie et langage (Calame-Griaule), 379
ethnology, 380; fetish and, 358, 359
ethnomusicology, 159
"L'étourdi" (The Said Turn) (Lacan), 328
L'etre et l'évenement (*Being and Event*) (Badiou), 345
etymology, 284
eudaimonia (εὐδαιμονία), 192, 287, 288, 290, 292, 326
Evans-Pritchard, E. E., 426
evolutionary love, 282
existence, 331, 381
existentia, 331, 524n50
existential analytic, 374, 375, 381
experience, 501n205; of collectors, 160; inner, 55; lived, 55, 56
experience-lived-in-the-moment, 54
explained supernatural, 64
expressions, experience of, 160
extended mind, 464n55
external referentiality, 217

Fables (Phaedrus), 188
Fairbanks, Wright, 173, 174
fait nègre, le, 209
Fanon, Frantz, 13, 16, 19, 20, 114, 423, 426
al-Fārābī, 435
Farès, Nabile, xix, 419, 423–31, 435, 436, 448–50, 453–57
"Farewell Speech to the British People" (Douglass), 172
fate, 351
Faulkner, Charles, 176
Faust (Goethe), 33, 398, 399
Fax, Brandy, 419
Faye, Emmanuel, 525n55
Federalist 54, 539n331
Federal Reserve, 1, 151
Federal Writers Project, 1, 151, 160; Office of Negro Affairs, 161
Ferreira da Silva, Denise, 13
fetish, 253; ethnology and, 358–59; ontology and, 358, 359
fetishism, 194, 195, 243; liberating, 245; *objet d'art* and, 191
fetishistic semiosis, 334
Fichte, Johann, 127
fiction, 14
field of consciousness, 38
Fifteenth Amendment, 46, 47
final-cause explanation, 269
Fire Next Time, The (Baldwin), 426, 430, 432, 433
Fischer, Eugen, 372
flânerie, 62–64, 120, 122, 123; Baudelaire and, 125
flâneur, xv, 62–65, 124; interiority and, 128; subjectivity and, 126
flesh: *captive body*, 182, 185, 207; as fungible asset, 217; human, xv–xvi, 2, 4–10, 151, 169–71, 174, 176, 178, 199, 208, 210, 250, 251, 293; person, 208; sentience in semiosis, 251
fleshiness, xvi, 178; persona and, 207, 208
fleshly thingness, 210
flesh/person, 208
FLN, 424, 450
Floyd, Samuel, 235, 236
folklore, 160

folksong, 151, 153
folkways, 151
Ford, James, 248, 249
form, 180; signifiers and, 182
formal causality, 194
formulas of sexuation, 328
For the Ancestors (Jones, B.), 240
Foucault, Michel, 21, 183, 315
Fountains (journal), 457
Fourteenth Amendment, 46
Foxe, John, 84
Frazer, James, 409, 410
freedom: citizenship and, 46; entitlement to, 178; forms of, 44; interiority and, 128; Kant and, 209; natural, 43, 492n68; Negro and, 46; political society and, 43, 47; Rousseau theory of, 42; transcendental idea of, 39
free will, 306
Frege, Gottlob, 100–103, 326, 328, 478n194
French Imperialism, 198; semiological order of, 189, 190
"Freudig geführt, ziehet dahin," 143–44, 146–47, 406
Front de Libération Nationale (FLN), 424, 450
Frye, Northrop, 66
fugitive discourse, 248
fulfillment-in-actuality, 293
functions, 90, 104, 470n135
Fundamental Constitution of the Carolinas, 3, 4, 171, 210, 465n65
fundamental ontology, 331
fungible assets, flesh as, 217

Gall, Franz Joseph, 93
Galton, Francis, 34
Garrison, Wendell, 157, 174
Garrison, William Lloyd, 155, 157, 174, 175
Gauss, Carl Friedrich, 91, 100, 260, 470n135
Gautier, Théophile, 119
Geist, 110, 111, 201, 205, 253, 348, 368, 372, 449; Becker and, 373; civilization and, 375; primitives and, 361
Geistesgeschichte, 126
Geisteswissenschaft, 55, 84, 95–96, 126, 359

Geitesgeschichte, 120
Gemeinschaft (communal society), 139, 142, 467n77
Genealogy of Morals (Nietzsche), 307
General Instruction for Collectors of Ethnographic Objects, 159
Georgia Sea Islands, Vols. I and II (recording), 225
Georgia Sea Island Songs (recording), 231, 232
Géricault, Théodore, 430
Geschichte, 348, 351, 531n140
Geschichtlihkeit, 347, 530n135
Gesellschaft (Associational society), 467n77
Giacometti, Alberto, 191, 195
Gibbon, Edward, 303, 304, 306
Giddings, Franklin, 476n156
Gideonites, 157, 490n22
Gillespie, Dizzy, 416
Girard, René, 407, 410–14, 434, 435
Glissant, Édouard, 236, 416
Gluckman, Max, 314
Godkin, Edward Lawrence, 157
Goethe, Johann Wolfgang Von, 33, 64, 66, 398–400
Golden Bough, The (Frazer), 409
"Golden Isles, The" (television segment), 232
golden mean, 292
Gonniosaw, Ukasaw, 66
good: kinds of, 268; paramount, 326, 327; supreme, 287, 292, 353; universal, 286, 437
Goodell, William, 184
"Gossiping Friends, The" (Herodas), 439
Grail *motif*, 130, 131, 133
grammars: collision of, 52; of discourse, 321, 323; *Gemeinschaft* and, 142; of sociality, 32, 50, 258
grammaticality, 13
Gramsci, Antonio, 15, 435
Great Depression, 1, 151
Great House Farm, 153, 154
Green, Charlie, 420
Green's functions, 90
Greer, John, 227

Grenville, Richard, xiv
Griaule, Marcel, 159, 189, 190, 197, 349, 352, 379
Griffith, D. W., 67
Grinstead, William, 495n120
Grotius, 465n65
group-person, 365
Grovenor, Reuben, 222
Grundlagen der Arithmetik, Die (The foundations of mathematics) (Frege), 101
Grunninger, John, 61, 65
Guillén, Nicolás, 12
Gullah, 219, 504n11
Günther, Hans F. K., 372
Guys, Constintin, 63, 120, 125

Habilitationsvortrag (Dedekind), 97
Haiti, 11
al-ḥākīa (الحاكية), 439
Hakluyt, Richard, xiv
Hakmoun, Hasan, 417
Hall, S. C., 61
Handy, W. C., 419–22
"Hangman Johnny" (song), 165
haplé diegesis (ἁπλᾶ διήγησις), 353, 411
harmonics, 447
Harney, Stefano, 15, 423
Hartman, Saidiya, 2, 178, 208, 211, 216, 217, 313
Hawes, Bess Lomax, 247
Hawkins, Coleman, 420
Hays, Henry, 227
Hegel, Georg Wilhelm Friedrich, 55, 196, 274, 302, 305, 347, 517n195, 530n135; *Geist* and, 110–12, 201, 368; idealist teleology of, 299; infinite metabolism concept, 201, 211; Roman law and, 300–301
Heidegger, Martin, xvii, xviii, 20, 244, 329–77, 435, 523n44, 525n55; on art, 121; on being-toward-death, 366–67; *Bestandstücke* and, 124; on causality, 194; Dasein and, 342, 343, 346, 349, 350, 364, 366, 373; distantiality and, 382; on entities, 343; ethnology and, 380; existential analytic, 374, 375; *Geschichte* and, 347, 351; historicity and, 346–48, 352; instruments and, 355, 356; on intuition and thinking, 341; Kant and, 339, 340; metaphysics and, 338–40; nature and, 368–69; ontological difference and, 331; person-being and, 365; *poiēsis* and, 127; primitive semiosis and, 375; primitivism and, 349, 358, 361; readiness-to-hand and, 356, 357; referentiality and, 389; signification and, 358–60; on signs, 357; they-self and, 382; time and, 362, 363, 370; on tradition, 353; transcendence of Dasein and, 343, 344; on truth, 329; on worldliness, 338, 339; *Zeug* usage by, 355, 529n118
Hellenophilia, 91, 197
Henry VIII (King), 538n320
Heraclitus, 288
hereditary slavery, 386
Herodas, 439
heroic ethics, 308
Herskovits, Melville, 219, 223, 226, 231, 237–39, 243, 392, 506n12
Hessel, Franz, 122, 123
heterogeneity, 374
hexis (ἕξις), 191–92, 288, 336–37
Heyne, Christian Gottlob, 91
Heyse, Hans, 375
hieroglyphics: of flesh, 199; *mathème* as, 384; Negro and, 201–2
Higgins, Kathleen Marie, 518n200
Higginson, Humphrey, 495n120
Higginson, Thomas Wentworth, 158, 159, 165, 166, 200
Hilbert, David, 100
Historia de las Indias (de las Casas), 385
historicity, 346–58
historizing-occurrence, 393
history: etymology of, 347; having and making, 352; natural, 354; nature and, 362; primitive and, 352
History of Animals (Aristotle), 445
Hobbes, Thomas, 42, 314, 316
Hoffman, E. T. A., 59, 60
Holy Roman Empire, 303
Homeric Greek, 284–85
Homo sapiens, 2, 4, 115, 171, 218, 442
honor, 287

Hopkins, Dwight N., 485n277
Hortulus Animæ (Grunninger), 61, 62, 65
Hugo, Victor, 188
al-hujanā' (الهُجَناء), 440, 444
human action: calculability problem and, 94; chance in, 88, 94; sociology and measurement of, 88, 92, 94
human condition, 17
human flesh, 5–8
human institutions, 86
humanism, 2, 9
human rights, 199
humans: animals as distinct from, 170; modernity and treating as things, 205
human types, 307
Hume, David, 281
Hunwick, John, 505n11
Hurston, Zora Neale, 224, 329, 392, 437–38, 447
Husserl, Edmund, 37–38, 216–18, 250, 317, 333, 339, 525n55; consciousness and, 203–4, 206; on culture and signification, 218; on epistemic collapse, 437; on humans as natural objects, 205, 207; phenomenology of, 202, 203
hyperbola asymptotes analogy, 88–91, 97, 109, 111, 259, 260, 263
Hypnotisme, double conscience et altérations de la peronnalité (Azam), 34

ibn Khaldūn, 434–35
ibn Rushd (Averroes), 14
ibn Sīnā (Avicenna), 14
iconography, 198; flesh and, 207
idealism, 279–81, 286, 287, 332, 339
Ideen II (Husserl), 203
Idee und Existenz (Heyse), 375
identity, 368
ideographic systems: culture as, 206; of myth, 198
illegibility, 135
'ilm al-kalām (علم الكلام), 443
'ilm at-tajriba (علم التجربة), 446
image-word relationship, 70
imitation, 476n156
immanence of consciousness, 126
imperialism, 255

imperialist colonialism, 254, 396
impersonation, 439
improper-love, xix
indecipherability, 124–25
indeterminate enérgeia, 283
individual-acting-in-collective, 95
individualism, 45; methodological, 95, 464n51; possessive, 43, 44
individualized self, 37
individual-person, 365
individuation, 312, 346, 377; of Dasein, 367
infinite metabolism, 201
infinity, 106, 108
inner experience, 55
Innewerden (reflexive awareness), 55, 87
innovation, 261
instrumentality, 355, 356, 429; bodily, 290
instruments, signs as, 358
integral calculus, 471n137
intellect-in-action, 17, 27, 87, 111, 115, 252, 282, 393; sociology and, 109
intellectual virtue, 288
intelligence, emergent, 96
intentionality, 335
Inter Caetera (Alexander VI), 385
interiority, 116–49; double consciousness and, 118; *flâneur* and, 128; freedom and, 128
international capitalism, 139
internationalism, 116
intersubjectivity, 203, 206, 317
"In that Old Field" (song), 220–21
intuition, 341
involuntary memory, 87
irrational, 286
"I Wonder Where My Easy Rider's Gone" (song), 420

Jacobi, Carl Gustav Jacob, 100
Jacobinism, 44
Jaeger, Warner, 443
Jaensch, Rudolph, 369
al-Jāḥiẓ. *See* al-Baṣrī, Abū 'Uthman 'Amr ibn Baḥr al-Kinānī
James, C. L. R., 45

James, William, 18, 56, 384; chance and, 260; consciousness and, 33–40, 49; determinism and, 304; philosophy course taught by, 264–66, 271–74, 281, 283
Jamestown colony, xiii
Jamin, Jean, 195
Jazz, 195, 247–48
Jefferson, Thomas, 175
"Jefferson Davis as a Representative of Civilization" (Du Bois), xvii, 294, 303, 304, 314, 318, 394
jellyfish consciousness, 429
"Jesus Christ in Georgia" (Du Bois), 408
"Jesus Christ in Texas" (Du Bois), 408
Jeune Afrique (journal), 419, 423
Jim Crow, 26, 53, 148, 302; social constraints of, 133
Johnson, Alexander, 34
Johnson, Isaac, 222, 223
Johnson, Naomi, 222
Jones, Absalom, 319
Jones, Bessie, 224, 232–34, 240, 241, 247
"Joy of Living, The" (Du Bois), 400
Juba, xvi, 245, 250, 317–18; *poiēsis in black* and, 246
Juba beating, 215–17
Juba dance, 501n2
jubilee beating, 215, 216
juridical deracination, 205
juris gentium, 301
Justinian, 4

Kahn, Jonathon, 406, 408, 409, 540n337
Kant, Immanuel, 9–10, 19, 55, 265, 306, 345; anthropology and, 341–42; cognition and, 341; Comte and, 93; on culture as breeding, 218; Dasein and, 342; fetishism and, 194–96; freedom and, 209; Heidegger and, 339, 340; on mathematical concepts, 99; metaphysics and, 338–41; transcendental ego and, 39; Transcendental *I*, 92, 93, 95, 257; transcendental psychology and, 40; on world, 342
Kant und das Problem der Metaphysik (Kant and the Problem of Metaphysics) (Heidegger), 339

Kate Field's Washington (periodical), 296
Kemble, Frances Anne, 489n18
Kennedy, Robert, "Bobby," 432, 433
Key, Elizabeth, 495n120
Key, Thomas, 495n120
kikínu, 379
Kimball, Bruce, 294
Kitāb al-Bayān wa at-tabyīn (كتاب البيان والتبيين, The Book of Eloquence) (al-Jāḥiẓ), 438–48
Kitāb al-ḥayawān (كتاب الحيّوان, The Book of Living) (al-Jāḥiẓ), 440, 443–46
Kitābu-l-'ibar (كتاب العبر, Book of Lessons) (ibn Khaldūn), 434
Kittredge, George Lyman, 151
knowledge: a-epistemic, 11; art and, 191; of objects, 93; orders of, 96; universal, 197
Kono fetish, 197
Kracauer, Sigried, 120–22, 125, 128, 321
Krisis der europäischen Wissenschaften, Die (Crisis of European Science) (Husserl), 437
Kronecker, Leopold, 99
Ku Klux Klan, 167
Kunstwollen, 120–21, 123

labor: property rights and, 44; racialization of, 254; wage, 248
Labouret, Henri, 226–27
Lacan, Jacques, xvii, 201, 250, 321–30, 332–34, 382–84, 387, 392; Supreme Good and, 353
Lachatañeré, Rómulo, 12
lalangue, 323
lamb of God, 413–14
Langer, Susanne, 13
Laplace, Pierre Simon, 260
Last of the Mohicans (Cooper, J. F.), 65
law, 86; chance and, 98, 113; Negro defined in, 301
laws of nature, 39
leadership, political, 487n279
Le Bon, Gustave, 47
"Lecture on Slavery" (Douglass), 172
"Lecture on the Slave Trade" (Coleridge), 177
Lee, Maurice, 56
Leenhardt, Maurice, xviii, 375, 376

legal persons, 206
"Légende du Monde, La" (Farès), 457
Leibniz, Gottfried Wilhelm, 102; universe conceptions of, 338
Leiris, Michel, 159, 190, 191, 194–97, 244, 245
Lemieux, Cyril, 13
Leroi-Gourhan, André, 189
Lesser Kabylia, 427, 428
Letters on Slavery (Rankin), 175
"Let Us Cheer the Weary Traveler" (sorrow song), 84
Lévi-Strauss, Claude, 180, 189, 426
Lévy-Bruhl, Lucien, 195, 369, 383
Lewin, Susan, 506n12
Lewis, Lilburn, 175, 176, 211, 215, 413
liberal arts education, 31–32
liberating fetishism, 245
liberty: assertion of, 208; civic, 435; entitlement to, 178; fraudulent, 216
Library of Congress: Archive of American Folksong, 152; Division of Music, 152; WPA Writers Unit, 151
Limpieza de sangre, 431
Lincoln, Abbey, 236
Lincoln, Abraham, 168
lived experience, 55, 56, 373
Lives of the Martyrs (Foxe), 84
living-with-one-another, 365
Locke, John, 2–3, 127, 170, 171, 210, 465n65; property and, 44, 45
logical discourse, 326
logicism, 100–102, 477n182
Lohengrin (Wagner), xv, 26, 29, 57, 129–33, 147, 148; Bridal Chorus, 143–44
Lomax, Alan, xvi, 5, 224, 227, 231–41, 392, 417
Lomax, John Avery, xv, 5, 152–53, 169, 197, 218, 234, 352, 506n12; questionnaire by, 151, 167, 168; spirituals and, 160, 161, 166–67
"London Reception Speech" (Douglass), 172, 175
Louis XIV (King), 6, 187
love-improper, 416–17
Luce, Henry, 396
Lukács, Georg, 56, 118, 123, 468n112

Luther, Martin, 303, 538n320
Lyotard, Jean-François, 206
lyrics, transcribing, 162

Ma'bad, 443–44
Macfarren, Natalia, 143
Mächtigkeit (cardinal-power), 336, 337
Mackandal, François, 297
Al-madīnat-ul-fāḍila (The Ideal Polity) (al-Fārābī), 435
Madison, James, 539n331
Malê Revolt, 297
Malinowski, Bronislaw, 379, 426
"Man of the Crowd, The" (Poe), xv, 59–62, 120, 124, 125
Mansart (Du Bois), 49
Mantik, 333
mantikē (μαντική), 333, 373, 375
mapping, 104, 107, 108, 325
Marable, Manning, 540n337
Marat à son dernier soupir (painting), 119
Marinello, Juan, 12
Markmann, Charles Lam, 19
Martineau, James, 264, 265, 272, 274–76, 278–80, 282
Marx, Karl, 123, 217, 243, 244, 248, 249
mathematical structuralism, 480n206
Mathematische Existenz (Mathematical Existence) (Becker), 332
mathème, 327, 383–84
matriarchal family structure, 183
Mauss, Marcel, 189
mauwlī (مولي), 440
McDougall, William, 47
McKay, Claude, 17, 423
McKim, James Miller, 155, 157
McKim, Lucy, 155–58, 161, 166, 218, 224, 392; transcription and, 162, 163
McKinley, William, 396
McTell, Blind Willie, 153
meaning, 180; of signifier, 181–82; signifier and theft of, 208
mécanisme du bouc émissaire, le (Girard), 410
mechanical reproduction, 126, 127, 435
Mecklin, John Moffatt, 34
Meditationes de prima philosophia (Descartes), 267

Memmi, Albert, 426, 430–33
Memorial de remedios para las Indios (de las Casas), 385
memory: involuntary, 87; slavery and, 138
menschliche Rede, Die (Human Speech) (Ammann), 368
Merleau-Ponty, Maurice, 37, 209
mesotēs (μεσότης), 291–93, 312, 327
mestizaje, 431
mestizo, 431
meta-discourse, 196
metaontology, 391
metaphysics, 204, 265, 269–71, 338–41; categorical, 306; Nordic, 375; racism and, 395; Scholastic, 338
Metaphysics (Aristotle), 344
Methodenstreit (methodological dispute), 510n20
methodological individualism, 95, 464n51
métis, 431, 436–37, 440
mêtis (μητις), 242, 436–37, 508
métissage, 238, 427, 432, 436–37, 440, 444, 450
metonymic chains, 108
Meyers, Sidney, 227
Meyerson, Ignace, 18, 430
Michelet, Jules, 125, 126, 297
Middle Passage, 237–38
Mill, John Stuart, 95
Miller, Jacques Alain, 326
mimesis, 14, 86, 114, 191, 192, 196, 435, 438
mimetic cleverness, 436
mimetic desire, 410, 411
mimetic practice, 160
mimetic theory, 434, 435
Mimetische Verhalten, 436
mimicry, 219, 242, 282, 411, 434, 436–42, 444, 447, 449; assimilation and, 446; cognition and, 277; episematic, 437; myth and, 412
mind: science of, 113; universal, 283
miscegenation, 238, 431, 462n29
Miscegenation (Croly and Wakeman), 462n29
Mission Dakar-Djibouti, 159, 189
modal structuralism, 480n206
mode of being, primitives and, 360

modern capitalist semiological order, 200
modernism, xv; Baudelaire and, 118, 125; constitutive features of, 119; dehumanizing effects of, 200; "Of the Coming of John" and, 118; politics and, 119
modernity, 267; capitalist, 19, 396, 435, 470n130; constitution of human society in, 207; Du Bois on, 384–85; humans as things and, 205; racialized capitalist, 200; violence and, 8
modern poetry, myth and, 182
Mohican de Paris (Dumas), 64
de Moivre, Abraham, 260
de Moivre-Laplace Theorem, 260
monetary policies, 1, 151
moral freedom, 44
morality: etymology and, 284; natural, 43; Nietzsche theory of types of, 307
moral science, 95
moral theory, Kant and, 9
moral types, 306, 307
Moran, Dermont, 525n55
More, Thomas, 403, 538n320
Morgan, Clement G., 294, 295
Morrison, Henry, 224
Moses, Charlie, 2
Moses, Wilson Jeremiah, 400
Moten, Fred, xvii, 15, 236, 249, 320, 423
motive-will, 4–6, 179
Mottram, John, 495n120
Moynihan, Daniel Patrick, 183
Moynihan Report, 183, 185
Mudimbe, Valentine, 388–90
mulattoes, 254
Mules and Men (Hurston), 224
multiplicity, 108, 483n220
muntu, 379
"Murder in the Rue Morgue, The" (Poe), 64
Murray, Albert, 13–15, 247, 422, 436, 456
musical form, development of, 248
musical notation, 162, 219, 220
Music of Williamsburg (film), 227
al-mutakallimūn (المتكلمون), 444
al-muwālī (الموالي), 440, 444
My Bondage and My Freedom (Douglass), 154, 156, 173, 175, 176
"My Evolving Program" (Du Bois), 272

myth: ideographic system of, 198; mimicry and, 412; modern poetry and, 182; pre-generic, 66; semiology of, 180, 209, 257
mythe petit-bourgeois du Nègre, le (Barthes), 386
mythical signification, 360
Myth of the Negro Past, The (Herskovits), 237
Mythologies (Barthes), 189, 202
"Myth Today" (Barthes), 180, 198

NAACP, 27, 118
Nairn, John Arbuthnot, 439
name-habit, 256
Napoleon, 425
Narrative (Bibb), 215
Narrative of Arthur Gordon Pym, The (Poe), 124
Narrative of the Life of Frederick Douglass (Douglass), 153, 171, 172, 174
National Liberation Front, 424, 450
National Socialists (Nazis), 372, 535n250
Nation Magazine, 157, 296
Native, Son (Wright), 48
natives, 10
natural freedom, 43, 492n68
naturalism, 28, 112, 113
naturalistic psychology, 205
naturalist photography, 70
naturalization, 208
Naturalization Clause, 46
natural law, slavery as violation of, 170
natural morality, 43
natural moral personhood, 404
natural numbers, 99, 105, 107, 479n195
natural philosophy, 267, 269, 270
natural rights theory, 2–4, 166, 178
natural science, 95
nature: art imitating, 191; barbarians as slaves in, 291; children as creatures of, 120; Dasein and, 369; Heidegger and, 368–69; history and, 362; psychic ego-subject of, 204
nature-time, 368, 369
Naturgeschichte (natural history), 354
Naturwissenschaft (natural science), 95
Nazis, 372, 535n250
an-Naẓẓām, Abū Isḥāq, 443–44

Nedjma (Yacine), 429
"Need of New Ideas and New Aims for a New Era, The" (Crummell), 138
Nègre, 209
Negro, xvii, xviii, 5, 20–21; Aristotle and, 337; attitudes toward, 395–97; Barthes and, 198, 199; being-in-flight, 321; as capital asset, 6, 7, 210; commoditization and, 253; conversion to Christianity, 201; criminalization of, 117; culture, 112; duality of, 117; Du Bois conceptions of, 112, 114; Du Bois usage of term, 27, 28, 45, 252, 254, 256, 258, 320; ethnicity, 183; as fantasy, 386–87; freedom and, 46; as fungible property, 127; hieroglyphics and, 201–2; hunts, 176; intellect-in-action and, 252; law defining, 301; mimicry and, 438; movement of, 385; *New York Times* usage of term, 27; Nietzsche and, 313; northern and southern differences, 140; origins of term, xiii–xiv, 252–53; Peirce on, as man, 257–58; personhood of, 178; as phonemicization of ideogram, 201; *poiēsis* and, 9; primitive and, 11; self-consciousness and, 41; semiological functions of term, 185; as semiological system, 207; semiosis and, 256; signification and, 256; slave value and, 117; symbolization of, 387; tariffs on enslaved, 187–88; thinking-in-action and, 385; time, 112; as type, 139; uncalculability of, 325
"Negro as He Really Is, The" (Du Bois), 67, 71–83; photographs accompanying, 68–70; revisions of, 70, 84
"Negro Dialect, The" (Higginson, T. W.), 158
Negro Family, The (Moynihan Report) (Moynihan), 183, 185
negro hunts, 176
Negrophilia, 234
Negro problem: demystification of, 262; question behind, 263; semiological order of, 185, 186
"Negro Race Consciousness as Reflected in Race Literature" (Park), 35
Negro social pathology, 183, 185

"Negro Spirituals" (Higginson, T. W.), 158
Negro Submissive Man, 298
Negro traditional music, musical notation and, 219–20
Nelson, Frank, 67
Neohumanism, 91, 99
neo-Kantianism, 121, 281
Neo-Platonism, 267
neo-slavery, 31, 32, 51, 128, 136, 148, 404
Neue Humanismus, 91, 472n141
neuhumanistischen Bildungsreform (neohumanist education reform), 115
New World slavery, 199
New York Times, "Negro" usage in, 27
Nicholas V (Pope), 385
Nicomachean Ethics (Aristotle), 326
Nietzsche, Friedrich, 304–7, 309–14, 401, 435; Du Bois and, 310–11, 518n200; Negro and, 313
Nightriders, 167
nihilism, 435
Noble, Don, 14, 247
noble morality, 307
Noces (Nuptials) (Camus), 429
"Nordische Metaphysik" (Nordic Metaphysics) (Becker), 375
Normal Distribution, 260
Notebooks (Gramsci), 15
Notices of Brazil in 1828 and 1829 (Walsh), 176
Notker the Stammerer, 299
Notre-Dame de Paris (Hugo), 188
novels, psychology and, 48–49
Novum Organum Scientiarum (Bacon), 177, 204, 267, 270
nullibility, 328
number theory, xv, 479n196; thinking and, 99–116

obia dance, 223
objectification, 359
objective objects, 101–2
objects: concepts and, 101; knowledge of, 93; numbers as, 102–3; of personal consciousness, 204; of thoughts, 106
objet d'art, fetishism and, 191
Ockham, William, 271

"Of Alexander Crummell" (Du Bois), 40, 66
Office of Negro Affairs, 161
"Of Our Spiritual Strivings" (Du Bois), 32, 34, 35, 41, 42, 45–47, 49, 141
"Of the Black Belt" (Du Bois), 31; thinking-in-action and, 99
"Of the Coming of John" (Du Bois), xiv–xv, xix, 25–32, 50–59, 63–67, 85–87, 115, 258, 393, 406–14; Bridal Chorus and, 143–44; interiority and, 116–49; *Lohengrin* passage, 129–33; modernism and, 118; phantasmagoria and, 125; problem of thinking in, 86; thinking of John in, 116
"Of the Dawn of Freedom" (Du Bois), 31
Of the Different Races of Human Beings (Kant), 9
"Of the Faith of the Fathers" (Du Bois), 135, 139, 141, 317, 404
"Of the Passing of the First Born" (Du Bois), 66
"Of the Quest for the Golden Fleece" (Du Bois), 31
"Of the Sons of Master and Man" (Du Bois), 30, 31
"Of the Wings of Atlanta" (Du Bois), 398
Oliver Ditson Company, 143
Olmsted, Frederick Law, 248
"On Ideas in General" (Heidegger), 340
On the Generation of Animals (Aristotle), 193
On the Soul (Aristotle), 193
On the Use of Teleological Principles in Philosophy (Kant), 9, 10
ontological difference, 331, 335
ontological truth, 335
ontology, 114, 325, 330, 523n44; fetish and, 358, 359; fundamental, 331; of thingliness, 333
orators, 283–84
Ordeal of Mansar, The (Du Bois), 28
orders of knowledge, 96
ordinal numbers, 105
Origen, 267, 307
"Origin of the Work of Art" (Heidegger), 121

orthós lógos (ὀρθός λόγος), 288, 292–93, 326–27, 329, 353, 436, 446
Ortiz, Fernando, 12

Page, Walter Hines, 67, 68
Paley, William, 265
"Pan-Africa and New Racial Philosophy" (Du Bois), 255
Pan-Africanism, 116, 255, 425
pan-Africanization, 238
pan-Arabism, 425
Pan-Negroism, 255
Panofsky, Erwin, 121
pantheism, 282
pantheistic monism, 274
paradigm shifts, 261
para-individuation, 392
paraliteracy, 319–21
para-mime, 392
Paramount Good, 326, 327
paraontological discourse, 320
paraontology, xvii, xviii, 321–37, 372, 388; Becker on, 374–75, 383; *para-semiosis* and, 321, 322; *poiēsis in black* and, 320
para-poiēsis, 391
para-semiosis, xiii, xvii–xix, 9, 21, 318, 438, 448; Arabic, 449, 450; being-in-flight-with-one-another and, 391–98; divisible person in, 376–87; para-ontology and, 321, 322, 324, 334, 388; *poiēsis in black* and, 317, 366, 376, 416–17
paratranscendence, 332, 343, 371
par-être, 323–25, 383, 392
Paris-Match (magazine), 185, 189, 196
parity principle, 464n55
Park, Robert Ezra, 35, 48
Parker, Charlie, 417
Parker, Theodore, 158, 159
Parrish, Lydia Austin, xvi, 218–25, 231, 234–37, 504n11, 506n12; Buzzard Lope and, 239, 240
Parrish, Maxfield, 506n12
Partus sequiter ventrem, 301, 386
passager de l'occident, Un (Farès), xix, 419, 424, 450, 456
Patterson, Orlando, 5, 117, 179
pattin' Juba, 215, 245, 249, 317, 501n2

Paulsen, Friedrich, 91
Peabody, Francis G., 294
Peirce, Charles Sanders, xv, 260, 282, 401, 447; on Negro as man, 257–58; pragmatism and, 266; semiotic theory of, 217, 255, 283; synechism and, 112
Penn School, 489n16
Pennsylvania Anti-Slavery Society, 155
Pennsylvania Freeman, 155
perception, 38
performances, 249; transcribing, 162
performative animal mimicry, 242
performative persona, 15
person: defining, 4; divisible, 376–87; ego as, 204; Locke definition of, 3; phenomenology of, 365; racial type and, 374; rights of, 4; things and, 204
persona, xvi, 5, 178, 180; defining, 4; fleshiness and, 207, 208; performative, 15
personal-being, 365
personal ego, 203
personal redemption, 197
personhood, 4; Dasein and, 368; Douglass and, 178; juridical deracination of, 205; natural moral, 404; rights and, 171; self-conscious, 129; as universal property, 171
persons, legal, 206
Phaedrus, Gaius Julius, 188
Phänomenologie des Geistes (Hegel), 111, 299
phantasia, 446
phantasia aesthetis (sensory imagining), 441
phantasmagoria, 123, 125, 126
phenomenology, 202, 299, 335; humans treated as things and, 205; of person, 365; psychology and, 204
Philadelphia Negro, The (Du Bois), 34, 262
Philadelphia Port Royal Relief Committee, 155
Philcox, Richard, 19
philology, 91
philosophie bantoue, La (Tempels), 379
Philosophy of Right (Hegel), 300
Philosophy of Symbolic Form (Cassirer), 360
phonographic recordings, 152
photography, 68–70

phronesis (φρόνησής), 242, 290, 308–9, 311
physical torture, 211
Physics (Aristotle), 191, 192
Physiologie dumariage (Balzac), 63
Pierce, Edward Lillie, 155
Pietz, William, 253
Pioneers (Cooper, J. F.), 65
Pittsburgh Courier (newspaper), 143
Plato, 20, 307, 309, 329, 330, 337, 353, 442–43; arithmetization and, 100; civilization and, 434; mimesis and, 86; on mimicry, 277, 411, 435, 436–37; moral philosophy and, 284–85, 287; on polyrhythm, 440; transcendence and, 336, 344, 345
plurality, 37
Plutarch, 100
Poe, Edgar Allen, xv, 59–64, 119, 120; Benjamin on, 65, 124
poetic expression, 14, 15, 55, 56
poetic imagination, 55
poetic invention, 16
"Poetic Principle, The" (Poe), 119
Poetics (Aristotle), 13, 191, 193, 194, 312, 337, 439
poetic socialities, 15
"Poetik" (Dilthey), 120
poetry, myth and, 182
poiēsis, xiii, 120, 149, 194, 196; becoming-in-common and, 433; Buzzard Lope and, 242–44; as dynamic process of invention, 236, 245; as historizing-occurrence, 182; mimesis and, 16, 86; Negro and, 9, 13; of pattin', 245; thinking as, 127
poiēsis in black, xvi–xvii, xviii, xix, 19, 20, 327, 393, 416–17; blues as, 448; defining, 13; as dynamic process of transformation, 246; imagination and, 245; Marx and, 248, 249; ontology and understanding, 334; paraontology and, 320, 334; *para-semiosis* and, 317, 366, 376
Poincaré, Henry, 88, 89, 109
Poincaré expansion, 88
political action, 87
political consciousness, art and, 126
political economy, of slavery, 2, 169
political hoaxes, 462n29
political leadership, 487n279

political philosophy, 434–35
political society: freedom and, 43, 47; property and, 44
politics: art and, 430; modernism and, 119
Politics (Aristotle), 312, 435
Politics, Law and Ritual in Tribal Society (Gluckman), 314
Polycleitus, 193
polyrhythm, 440
"Poor Rosy, Poor Gal" (song), 156, 158
Port Royal Experiment, 157, 489n16
positivism, 56, 88, 92, 93, 97, 207, 265, 472n146, 476n156; Kracauer critique of, 121
possessions, 43, 44
possessive individualism, 43, 44
postbellum economy, 117
post-Reconstruction South, 31, 302
potentiality-for-being, 367
Potter, Henry C., 295
Poulton, Edward, 434, 437
power, sociology of, 435
power set theorem, 481n207
practices-of-living, 10, 13, 15, 19, 28
practices-of-living-in-common, 10
pragmata, 355
pragmatism, 266
praxis (πρᾶξις), 191–92, 289, 343, 355
pregeneric myths, 66
"Present Outlook for the Dark Races of Mankind, The" (Du Bois), 319, 394, 396
Priapus, 403, 539n329
Price, Sally, 195
Priest, G. M., 399
primitive, 10–11, 196; Becker and semiosis of, 361, 362; as heuristic, 358; history and, 352; mode of being and, 360; opacity of, 380
primitive semiosis: Becker and, 361, 362, 375; Heidegger and, 375
primitive thingliness, 358–64
primitive thinking, as semiosis, 361
primitive we, they of, 364–76
primitivism, 120, 159, 164, 190, 195, 197, 200, 234; Aristotle and, 337; Heidegger and, 349, 358, 361

Principal Navigations, Voyages, Traffiques and Discoveries of the English Nation, The (Hakluyt), xiv
"principe d'individuation, Le" (The Principle of Individuation) (Bastide), 376
Principles of Psychology, The (James, W.), 33–35, 37
Principles of Sociology, The (Spencer), 475n154
Privileges and Immunities Clause, 46
Problem of Christianity, The (Royce), 272, 282
prochaine fois, Le (Memmi), 432
progressivism, 67, 462n29
Progress of Public Opinion and National Policy towards Miscegenation (Croly and Wakeman), 431
Prometheus Unbound (Shelley), 279
propaganda, 119
propertiness, 210
property rights, 43–45, 465n65
proprietorship, 43
Protestant Reformation, 303, 537n319, 538n320
Proust, Marcel, 87
psychic dualism, 34–35
psychic ego-subject, 204
psychoanalysis, 323, 325, 382
psychology, 349; descriptive, 55; Dilthey and, 56; naturalistic, 205; novels and, 48–49; phenomenology and, 204; race, 372; transcendental, 92
"Psychology of Race Prejudice, The" (Thomas), 47
Publius, 539n331
punctum, 202–3
pure cognitive intelligence, 281
pure experience, 36

Quarles, Francis, 61
Quest of the Silver Fleece, The (Du Bois), 56, 149
quiddité, 323
Quintilian, 283

race, Kant on, 9–10
race-consciousness, 258
race prejudice, cultural perspective on, 47–48
race psychology, 372
racial admixture, 462n29
racialization of labor, 254
racialized capitalist modernity, 200
racialized capitalist slavery, 198; sociopolitical order of, 185
racialized slavery, 254
racial type, 374, 375
racism, 67, 395
Rackham, H., 287
Radcliffe, Ann, 64
radical black Christianity, 540n337
radical empiricism, 36, 265
Raft of the Medusa, The (painting), 430
Rahmings, Nathaniel, 227, 239, 416
"Rain fall and wet Becky Martin" (song), 165
Rampersad, Arnold, 31
Ramsey, Emma, 224
Rancière, Jacques, 17
Rankin, John, 175, 176
rational, 286
"Raven, The" (Poe), 61
readiness-to-hand, 355–57
real estate, slavery and, 503n8
realism, 28, 429, 449
reality: human institutions as mimesis of, 86; truth and, 279
real marvilloso ("marvelous real"), 11–12
Rebel Destiny (Herskovits), 223
Reconstruction, 397
Reconstruction Amendments, 45
Redfield, Robert, 48
referentiality, 356, 357, 382, 389; working, 364
referential totality, 355, 356
reflex action theory, 37, 463n45
reflexive awareness, 55, 87
Reformation, 303, 395, 402
regressive semiological systems, 182
reino de este mundo, El (*The Kingdom of This World*) (Carpentier), 12
relationality, 92
relation of motivation, 204
religion: Du Bois and, 540n337; as socio-anthropological institution, 485n277

Religious Aspect of Philosophy, The (Royce), 273, 274, 276, 282
"Renaissance of Ethics, The" (Du Bois), xvii, 18, 39, 48, 49, 263–318, 327, 384, 415
representations, 340; human institutions as, 86
Republic, The (Plato), 277, 285, 336, 411, 435
republicanism, 44
Requerimiento, 385, 386
Rerum rusticarum (Varro), 248
revolts, 297
Révolution surréaliste, La (journal), 11
rhythmic attitude, 16
Rickert, Heinrich, 203
Riegl, Alois, 120–23
Riehl, Alois, 281
Riemann, Bernhard, 90, 471n136, 482n211
Riemann integral, 90, 471n136
Riemann zeta function, 90
right-principle-discourse, 289, 326, 327, 353, 436
rights: humans as things and, 205; personhood and, 171
Rivet, Paul, 227
Roach, Max, 236
Robb, Stewart, 143
Robinson, Cedric, 10, 314
Rogers, James, 158
"Roll Jordan" (song), 158
Roman Church, 307, 308, 386
romantic anticapitalism, 123
Romantics, 33
Romanus Pontifex (Nicholas V), 385, 386
Romulus Augustus, 303
Rosenkranz, Karl, 446
Ross, E. A., 47
Rousseau, Jean-Jacques, 6, 42–43, 46, 316, 400, 465n65
Royce, Josiah, 112, 264, 266, 271–82, 299, 401
Russell, Bertrand, 102, 108, 478n194, 481n207
Russell-Zermelo paradox, 481n207
Rutter, John, 143

Sachs, Joe, 192
sacrifice, 406–7, 411, 414–16
Said, Edward, 16
"Saint Francis Assisi" (Du Bois), 400
Sánchez, Ventura, 297
Santayana, George, 299
Sapienza Poetica ("poetic wisdom") (Vico), 127
scapegoating, 409–10, 412, 413
Scheler, Max, 365–66, 372
Schicksal, 351
Schilder, Paul, 38
Schiller, Friedrich, 100
Schmoller, Gustav, 56, 84, 262
Scholasticism, 207, 264, 265, 267–71, 278, 322, 323, 415, 444; metaphysics of, 338
Scholastic method, 263
Schön, Erhard, 61
Schopenhauer, Arthur, 144, 312, 520n232
Schröder, Ernst, 101
Schumpeter, Joseph, 464n51
science: ethics and, 266, 271; humans treated as things and, 205; of mind, 113; moral, 95; natural, 95; positivist philosophy of, 92–93; teleology and, 264
Science et méthode (Poincaré), 109
"Science of Morals" (Nietzsche), 304, 306
scientific faculty, 289
scientific inquiry, 271
"Scientific Materialism" (Tyndall), 465n56
scientific method, 261
scientific revolution, 98
Scott, Daryl, 34
Scott, Rufus, 425, 450
Scott, Walter, 158
Scotus, John Duns, 334
Sea Island dialect, 162, 219
Second Great Awakening, 316–17
Secret Committee of Six, 158
self, 35–37; Dasein and, 363
self-conscious agency, 149
self-consciousness, 37, 38, 40–41, 52; false, 53
self-conscious personhood, 129
self-education, 91
selfhood, 343
self-knowledge, 91
self-pity, 166–68

"Self-Pity in Negro Folk-Songs" (Lomax, J.), 153, 166
self-preservation, 43
self-understanding, 121
semicolons, 50, 52
semiological order: of French Imperialism, 189, 190; of modern capitalism, 200; of *Negro problem*, 185, 186
semiology, xvi; of myth, 180, 209, 257
semiosis, xv, 8, 217, 283, 448; Becker and primitive, 361, 362; Buzzard Lope and, 243; cognition and, 257; cognition as, 9, 251; double consciousness and, 257; fetishistic, 334; flesh sentient in, 251; of flesh thinking, 179–200; Negro and, 256; primitive thinking as, 361; second sight and, 315; sentient flesh in relation with, 249; signification and, 250; slavery and, 509n61; solos and, 247; tripartite, 110
sensory imagining, 441
set-theoretic structuralism, 480n206
set theory, 323, 472n138
sexual violence, 211
sexuation, 328
Shahid, Irfan, 439
Shaler, Nathaniel, 28, 34, 185
Sharp, Cecil, 152
She Done Him Wrong (film), 421
Shelley, Percy Bysshe, 279
Shout (ring), 157, 219, 227, 234–36, 240–42, 249, 304, 393, 486, 507; as Shouting, 404–5; as شَوْط (šauṭ), 219, 504–6
Sibawayhi, 13
signification, 164, 179, 180; cultures as structures conferring, 218; flesh and, 207; Heidegger on, 358–60; mythical, 360; "Negro" and, 256; role of, 358; semiosis and, 250
signification-conferring structures, 218
signifiers: *flesh/captive body*, 185; meaning of, 181–82; theft of meaning and, 208
signs: Dasein and, 359; Heidegger on, 357; as instruments, 358; representative function of, 258; subject as, 257; victim, 412
Simondon, Gilbert, 18, 430

simple infinite, 108
Sinclair, T. A., 443
sistemas de castas, 431
skepticism, 276, 277
slave codes, 117
slave-morality, 308, 518n200
Slave Narrative project, 160
Slave Narratives (Federal Writers Project), 1, 151
slavery, 517n192; abolition in U.S. of, 45–46, 540n335; commodity value of, 117; Constitution and, 465n65; dehumanizing character of, 154; depersonalizing practices of, 216; Douglass on, 2, 4, 171–72; hereditary, 386; Locke and, 3, 170; Lomax, J., on, 166–67; Marx on, 248; memory and, 138; as natural law violation, 170; New World, 199; political economy of, 2, 169; racialized, 254; racialized capitalist, 185, 198; real estate and, 503n8; semiosis and, 509n61; *télos* of, 245; violence and, 8; wage-labor and, 248
slaves, tariffs on, 187–88
slave singing, 154, 156, 489n18, 506n12
Slave Songs of the Georgia Sea Islands (Parrish, L.), 218
Slave Songs of the United States (McKim, L.), 157, 158, 164, 166, 218
Smith, Bessie, 420, 422, 456
Smith, Hobart, 227, 232
Smith, Joe, 420
Smith, John, xiii, xiv
Smith, Robertson, 409
social contract, 43, 46, 50
Social Contract, The (Rousseau), 42, 44, 316
social death, 5, 179
social disorder, 185
socialist realism, 429
sociality, 5, 207, 249; consciousness and, 6, 17–18; grammar of, 32, 50, 258; natural morality and, 43; poetic, 15
socialization, 39, 167
socially extended consciousness, 18, 40
social psychology, 47, 48
societal function, rate of change of, 90

sociology: analytical, 476n156; calculability problem and, 94; Du Bois on, 261, 262; intellect-in-action and, 109; measurement of chance as work of, 90, 261; origins of, 91, 92; positivist, 92; of power, 435; statistical, 109; "vicious logical circle" of, 93

"Sociology Hesitant" (Du Bois), 49, 91, 99, 114

Socrates, 127, 128, 191, 285, 290, 435, 442–43

Socratic moralism, 307

solos, semiosis and, 247

"Somato-Psyche in Psychiatry and Social Psychology, The" (Schilder), 38

Song of the Contrabands "O Let My People Go," The (Baker, T.), 156

Songs of the Freedmen of Port Royal (McKim, L.), 156

"Son of God, The" (Du Bois), 407–8, 413

sorrow songs, 50, 84, 85

Souls of Black Folk, The (Du Bois), 18, 25–33, 47, 50, 56, 65–67, 70, 111, 116, 149, 398; compositional style of, 54; "double consciousness" and, 33; political leadership and, 487n279; racialization of labor and, 254; Stepto on, 66, 84

Southern Journey (recording set), 225

Southern Literary Messenger, 61

South to a Very Old Place (song), 247

sovereignty, 315

Spaulding, Henry G., 158

speaking implement, 248

specular doubling, 201

Spencer, Herbert, 34, 87, 93–95, 348, 475n154, 476n156

Spillers, Hortense, xvi, 200, 217, 250; on flesh and body, 5, 9–10, 207–8; fleshiness and persona and, 178–85; hieroglyphics of flesh and, 199, 201; iconography and, 198; performative persona and, 15; semiotic transmission and, 203; on torture, 201–2

Spinoza, 282

spirit, 110; time and, 533n197

spirituals: Allen, W. F., and, 160–61, 166; Higginson, T. W., and, 158, 166; Lomax, J., and, 166–67; McKim, L., and, 166

Spiritual Singers Society of Coastal Georgia, 224, 227, 231, 233, 235, 237–39

Springinklee, Hans, 61

Spyglass Tree (song), 247

Standard Edition of Opera Librettos, 143

state of nature, 43

statistical sociology, 109

Stepto, Robert, 66, 67, 84, 85, 111

stimuli, 204–5

Stirling series, 90

Stoicism, 292

stolen life, 249

Stono Rebellion, 297, 515n178

Strauss, Leo, 443

stream of consciousness, 49

"Strivings of the Negro People" (Du Bois), 41, 67, 316

Strong Man, 298, 299, 302, 314, 315, 397

structuralism, 180; mathematical, 480n206

structuralist linguistics, 379

Stuckey, Sterling, 235, 236, 238, 243, 504n11

studium, 202–3

Study of Religion, A (Martineau), 265, 272, 274

stuff, 343–44, 529n118

Suárez, Franscisco, 331, 338, 344

subject: cognition and, 257; as sign, 257

subject-character, 346

subjectivism, 38

subjectivity, 203; *flâneur* and, 126; transcendental, 123

subject/object distinction, 19, 55

subject-object relationships, 336

Submissive Man, 298–302, 306, 310, 311, 315, 316, 397

substitutivity, 102

Sullivan, Robert, 299, 300

Summa Theologica (Aquinas), 270

Supreme Court, U.S., Dred Scott decision by, 173

Supreme Good, 287, 292, 353

Surrealist Manifesto (Breton), 11

surrealist movement, 11

surveillance, 470n130

symbolic abstraction, 107

Symposium (Plato), 309

synechism, 112
System der Wissenchaft (Hegel), 302

tajriba (تجربة), 444–45
Tajriba fi-l 'išiq (Experience in Love) (Waṭṭār), 455
Talented Tenth, 141
Tales of the Grotesque and Arabesque (Poe), 61
tangential lines, thinking as functions along, 90
Tarde, Gabriel, 34, 476n156
tariffs, 187
taxonomizing collectors, 124
taxonomy, 169; Africans and, 389; of human types, 307
technē (τέχνη), 191, 192, 196, 245, 246, 355
technē poiētikē (τέχνη ποιητική), 235, 238–40, 242, 243, 250
teleology, 112, 113, 269, 271; of hierarchical bifurcation, 291; truth and, 264, 279
télos (τέλος), 192–94, 196, 197, 243, 261, 265, 316, 517; of capital, 244; of mind's actualization, 302; of slavery, 245; Supreme Good and, 287
Tempels, Placide Fran, 379
temporality, 346, 368–70
Terms of Order, The (Robinson), 314
"Terre et Crépuscule" (Earth and Twilight) (Farès), 457
Teutonic civilization, 298
Thayer, James B., 295
theistic teleology, 264, 266, 269, 272
theological inquiry, 271
Théorie des ensembles (Set Theory), 324
there-being, 331
they: Dasein and, 364–65, 380; interpolation of, 367; of primitive we, 364–76
they-self, 346, 367, 373, 382
thingification, 207
thingliness: ontology of, 333; primitive, 358–64
thingness, 210
things, 355; ego and, 204–5; modernity and humans treated as, 205; as objects of thought, 96; persons and, 204; symbolic abstraction and, 107; useful, 357

thinking, 38, 341; functions along tangential line and, 90; historical and situational nature of, 126; number theory and, 99–116; in "Of the Coming of John," 116; as *poiēsis*, 127
thinking-in-action, 96, 97, 99, 115, 147
thinking-in-disorder, xiii, 11, 17, 18, 393
thinking-in-time, 87
Thirteenth Amendment, 45, 540n335
Thomas, William Isaac, 47
thoughts: conceptual, 101; numbers as objects of, 102–3; objects of, 106; things as objects of, 96; universal, 273, 274, 279, 281–83
Three-Fifths Compromise, 539n331
"Throw Me Anywhere" (song), 220, 222
thrownness-in-the-world, 372
time, 112, 218; Becker and, 363, 368, 370; Dasein and, 346–47, 350, 362; Heidegger and, 362, 363, 370; spirit and, 533n197
total alienation, 43–44, 400
tourism, 122
Toward Perpetual Peace (Kant), 9
Towne, Laura, 489n16
tradition, 350–53
Train Whistle Guitar (song), 247
transcendence, 335–37, 339, 345; of Dasein, 343, 344
transcendental community, 206
transcendental condition, 55
Transcendental Deduction, 36, 93, 209
Transcendental Dialectic, 339
transcendental ego, 36, 39, 41
transcendental ego-subject, 250
transcendental *I*, 92, 93, 95, 257
transcendental idea, of freedom, 39
transcendental intersubjectivity, 55, 206, 210, 217, 317
Transcendentalism, 159, 274
"Transcendentalist, The" (Emerson), 33
Transcendentalist anti-modernism, 159
Transcendentalist primitivism, 164, 200
Transcendentalists, 33
transcendental psychology, 40, 92
transcendental subjectivity, 123
transcription, 162, 219, 220

transindividuation, 430
translation, 398, 402
transubstantiation, 201, 508n46
"Transzendenz und Paratranszendenz" (Transcendence and Paratranscendence) (Becker), 333, 374
travel, 122, 128
travelogue photography, 70
Treaty of Versailles, 397
Trench, Richard Chenevix, 138
"Trinity Formula" (Marx), 217
Trowbridge, C. T., 158
truth: Du Bois and, 96, 259; error and, 279, 280; ontological, 335; reality and, 279; teleology and, 264, 279; unanimity and, 335
Tucker, Sophie, 420
turkey vultures, 219
Turner, Lorenzo, 219, 504n11
12,000,000 Black Voices (Wright), 48
Two Treatises of Government, The (Locke), 2–3, 170, 465n65
tychism, 112
Tyndale, William, 401–3, 409, 537n319, 538n320
Tyndall, John, 40, 270, 465n56
Types of Ethical Theory (Martineau), 265, 282

"Ueber eine Eigenschaft des Inbegriffes aller reellen algebraischen Zahlen" (On a property of the collection of all real algebraic numbers) (Cantor), 91
Umwelt, 203, 206, 337, 358, 364
unanimity, 335
Uncle Tom's Children (Wright), 48
unconcealment (*Unverborgenheit*), 332
undercommons, 15
Unity-of-Virtue doctrine, 285, 290
Universal Good, 286, 437
universal justice, 199
universal knowledge, 197
universal mind, 283
universal morals, Kant on, 9–10
universal rights, 2
Universal Thought, 273, 274, 279, 281–83
Universal Will, 273, 275, 278, 279

un-stealable life, 249, 391
Unverborgenheit, 330–32
Urphaenomen (Goethe), 64, 66
useful things, 357
use-value, 211

Van der Zee, James, 202
Varro, Marcus Terentius, 248
Verborgenheit, 329–32, 383
Vergemeinschaftung (communitization), 50
vestibularity, xvi, xix, 6, 184, 199–200, 250, 417
vestibule, 184
"Vetters Eckfenster, Des" ("The Cousin's Corner Window") (Hoffman), 59
Vico, Giambattista, 120, 127, 438
victim signs, 412
violence: modernity and, 8; slavery and, 8
vir bonus, 283, 309, 327
Virginia General Assembly, 171, 172, 176, 187–88, 201
Virginia House of Burgesses, 187
virtue, 284–85, 287, 288, 292, 293, 308
virtue ethics, 293
virtus, 283–84, 307, 309, 313
vital capacity, 286
Volkgeister, 111
"Vom Wesen des Grundes" (The Essence of Causes) (Heidegger), 331, 334, 337
von Humboldt, Wilhelm, 91
Vorlaufen, 530n134
voudun cults, 223, 231
vultures, 219

wage-labor, 248
Wagner, Richard, xv, 26, 29, 132, 413
Wakeman, George, 431, 462n29
Walsh, Robert, 176
Ware, Charles P., 157, 158, 218
Washington, Booker T., 168
"Was sind und was sollen die Zahlen?" (Dedekind), 101, 324
Waṭṭār, aṭ-Ṭāhir, xix, 449, 450–55
Weber, Max, 11, 38, 50, 435
"Welches sind die wirklichen Fortschritte" (What Real Progress Has Metaphysics Made in Germany) (Kant), 340

Weld, Theodore Dwight, 8, 211
well-ordering theorem, 472n138
Weltanschauung, 120, 141
Weltgeist, 111
West, Garrison, 173
West, Mae, 421
West African/enslaved captive body, 179, 180
white supremacy, 68
Wieland (Brown, C. B.), 64
Wilderson, Frank, 320
will, 127, 277; causality and divine, 281; Royce on, 273, 275, 278, 279; universal, 273, 275, 278, 279
willful creation, 112
Wilmore, Gayraud, 540n337
Windham, Tom, xv–xvii, 1–9, 151, 169–72, 178–80, 199, 208, 210, 250, 252, 257
Wirth, Louis, 48
wisdom, 383
Wolf, Friedrich August, 91
Wolff, Christian, 338
Wolin, Sheldon, 423
Woodson, Garter Godwin, 118
Works Progress Administration (WPA), xv, 1, 151, 167, 169; Slave Narrative project, 160

world: of Dasein, 364; historicity of, 354; Kant on, 342; terms for, 338, 339
worldliness, 338–46, 354, 355
World's Work (journal), 67
WPA, xv, 1, 151, 160, 167, 169
Wright, Richard, 47, 48
Writing Degree Zero (Barthes), 181
Wundt, Wilhelm, 33
Wynter, Sylvia, 13

Xiorro, Marcos, 297

Yacine, Kateb, 429, 449
Yahia, pas de chance (Fares), 424, 427
Yamūt ibn al-Muzarraʿ al-ʿAbdī, 440
Yancey, Jimmy, 423
"Yellow Dog Blues" (song), 419, 420–22
York, Graf, 347, 362
Young, Ed, 227, 232, 239, 416
"Young Woman's Blues" (song), 456

Zermelo, Ernst, 103, 324, 472n138, 481n207
Zeug, 343–44, 355, 529n118
"az-Zinjīya wa aḍ-ḍābṭ," "الزنجية والضابط" (The Negress and the Officer) (Waṭṭār), 450–55
"Zone" (Apollinaire), 195

www.ingramcontent.com/pod-product-compliance
Lightning Source LLC
Chambersburg PA
CBHW080632230426

43663CB00016B/2837